RUSSIA, 1905–07: REVOLUTION AS A MOMENT OF TRUTH

RUSSIA, 1905 – 07
REVOLUTION AS A MOMENT OF TRUTH

Teodor Shanin

The Roots of Otherness: Russia's Turn of Century

Volume 2

MACMILLAN

First published 1986

Published by
THE MACMILLAN PRESS LIMITED
Houndmills, Basingstoke, Hampshire RG21 2XS
and London
Companies and representatives
throughout the world

Printed and bound in Great Britain by
Anchor Brendon Ltd, Tiptree, Essex

British Library Cataloguing in Publication Data
Shanin, Teodor
Russia, 1905–07: revolution as a moment of truth.
Vol. 2: The roots of otherness: Russia's turn
of century.
1. Soviet Union—History—1904–1914
I. Title
947.08′3   DK262
ISBN 0–333–38252–8 (hardcover)
ISBN 0–333–38253–6 (paperback)

To a Russian friend, who knows . . .

'Master and Margarita', p. 135

It was our childhood
And adolescence
Of our teachers
Boris Pasternak: *1905*

Contents

List of Tables, Figures and Maps

Acknowledgements

As usual, my intellectual debts are too extensive to be fully acknowledged. I shall name only those which are particularly significant and consistent. For their encouragement, advice and comment, I would like to thank Hamza Alavi, Perry Anderson, Philip Corrigan, Boguslav Galeski, Iris Gillespie, Leopold Haimson, Derek Sayer and Israel Shahak. I owe gratitude to a number of Soviet scholars – friends whom I shall not name one by one. My work could not have progressed without effective library back-up for which I owe particular thanks to Jenny Brine of CREES, Birmingham, Agnesa Valentinovna Mushkan of TsGIA, Leningrad, and the librarians of the Wilson Center, Washington. I would also like to thank, for their consistent and effective technical help, Pauline Brooks, Jarmila Hickman, Jamie Sutherland, Linda Stares and Ann Cronley. As to the institutional help, I would like to thank the Wilson Center, Washington, the British ESRC and my own University of Manchester for support and indulgence. I owe particular thanks to the British Academy and especially to Peter Brown and Jenny Lynden of its staff. The same goes for the other type of institutional back-up – the Shula and Aelita team, and all the other of my friends who helped by smiling at me while I scowled.

Preface: The Roots of Otherness

Chronicles are written only by those to whom the present matters.
Goethe

The first Russian attempt at self-understanding in terms of contemporary social theory took the form of a debate between the Slavophiles and the Westerners. Russia was seen as *either* totally unique *or* as a backward section of Europe, a rung behind on a single evolutionary ladder. It was neither. Russia was not unique, nor was it on the threshold of becoming another England. It was not 'feudal' nor was it consequently and simply 'capitalist', or a transitionary mixture of both. At the turn of the nineteenth century Russia became the first country in which a specific social syndrome of what we call today a 'developing society' had materialised; it combined this type of social structure and international setting with a long imperial history, an entrenched state apparatus and a highly sophisticated and politically committed intellectual elite.

The fundamental distinction between human reality and nature at large is the way consciousness, comprehensions and miscomprehensions are woven into it, structuring human action. During the last decades of the nineteenth century the alternatives and strategies of the tsardom's rulers and administrators were laid out in terms of 'catching up with Europe' (or else, deteriorating into 'another China'). Vigorous state intervention along 'German' lines, with Friedrich List as its theoretical forerunner and Bismarck as the symbol of success, produced by the beginning of the twentieth century not another Germany, but a shattering economic and social crisis, a military defeat and, by 1905, a revolution. Consequently this was the time and the place where the relevance of the West European experience for the rest of mankind was first fundamentally challenged. Russia was to produce in actual political deed two major programmes and tests of radical transformation of the type of societies referred to today as 'developing'. Those polarly opposing yet theoretically complementary strategies were symbolised by the names of Stolypin and Lenin, but represented on both sides a spectrum of goals, views, analytical achievements and personalities. Little was added during the three generations to follow to the store of conceptual alternatives then created.

The level of theoretical understanding lagged behind the political strategies. Marx had once remarked on the historical tendency to act out new political drama in costumes borrowed from past generations. The French revolutionaries of 1791 saw themselves in the mould of leaders from the ancient Roman republic. The fact that Russia's political leaders consistently understated the newness of their experience and solutions and bent fact and ideology to present them in West European garb makes it the more instructive. While the government has measured itself by the German imperial successes, the leaders of the Russian dissent related their present and future to the English parliamentarism or to the French revolutions.

The 1905–07 revolution was to Russia a moment of truth. By proceeding in a way unexpected to both supporters and adversaries, this revolution has dramatised a new pattern of social characteristics and promoted unorthodox solutions, political as well as theoretical. A new Russia begins there, with monarchists who learned that only revolutionary social transformation can save their tsardom; and with Marxists who, under the impact of a revolution that failed, looked anew at Russia and at their Marxism. In historically quick succession, both were to gain power for the political exercise of their new understandings. Those who refused to learn have as speedily found themselves 'on the rubbish heap of history', to use a terrible but realistic description of biographies-cum-historiographies.

The growing acceptance of the specificity of the reality, problems and theories of 'developing societies' that has come to the fore since the 1960s, permits the placement of the Russian experience in a new and more realistic, comparative context. This can add to our understanding of Russia/the USSR. It can throw new light on a conceptual transformation – the most significant result of the 1905–07 revolution, decoding Lenin's comment about this 'dress rehearsal' without which 'the victory of the October Revolution in 1917 would have been impossible'. It may also make Russia's history and its contemporary theorising serve the fuller understanding of the 'developing societies' of today. The argument is presented in two separate books.

Russia as a 'Developing Society' looks at Russian society at the turn of the nineteenth century. It attempts to untangle the different yet related themes of the history of Russia on its way towards the revolutionary periods of 1905–07 and 1917–21. Mark Bloch once warned that 'the knowledge of fragments, studied by turns, each for its own sake, will never produce the knowledge of the whole; it will not even produce that of the fragments themselves'. He continued: 'But the work of reintegration can come only after analysis. Better still, it is only the continuation of analysis, its ultimate justification.' This book has chosen as its fundamental 'fragments' the Russian state, peasantry and capitalism, that is, the main power structure, the way of living of the mass of the population, the most challenging economic dynamism in view and their interdependence – a fundamental triangle of social determination. Its initial chapters are set out accordingly. The book then proceeds to consider the peasant economy and the general picture of Russia in flux during the period discussed.

The companion volume, *Russia, 1905–07: Revolution as a Moment of Truth*, is devoted to the Russian revolution of 1905–07. It begins with the revolution's build-up and its two major strands: the struggle in the cities for political freedom and/or socialism and the struggle of the villages for land and for liberty understood from the peasant's perspective. It is followed by an analysis of the interdependence of these struggles and of its main social actors. The last two chapters are devoted to the conceptual revolutions and persistences, relating the revolutionary experience of 1905–07 and its interpretations to the future history of Russia. The Postscript considers some general issues of method and of goals related to the books offered and concerning contemporary history and historical sociology.

*   *   *

The beginnings of the research that went into both books of the two-volume series 'The Roots of Otherness' go back to a study which was eventually published in 1972 as *The Awkward Class*. Further research, debate and experience made me refuse its publishers' kind offer simply to have it reprinted when the stock of its copies ran low. By that time I came to believe that while the essence of the book stood the test of criticism, its form of presentation carried two major weaknesses. It centred on the Russian peasantry and the analytical problems of its differentiation. Looked at from the distance of time it seems clear that one must broaden the focus, that is, to link peasantry more explicitly to general society and to relate the issue of socio-economic differentiation to other fundamental dimensions of analysis. Second, such an analysis must be related more explicitly to historical periodicity. A sequence of books identified by major periods of the history of Russia is therefore to replace the 1972 version of *The Awkward Class*, which will suffer partial dismembering and major readjustment. The research and elements of the text that appeared in the first two chapters of the initial version of *The Awkward Class* have entered parts of *Russia as a 'Developing Society'*, especially in the first and second sections of Chapter 2, and the second sections of Chapters 3 and 5. Even in those places, the reader will find considerable changes resulting from further research. The historical juncture to which this book and its companion volume, *Russia, 1905–07: Revolution as a Moment of Truth*, directly relate was followed by distinctive periods representing the two major political conclusions from the 1905–07 experience, when these have dominated strategies of Russia's effective rulers, and a new revolutionary epoch. The first is the period of 'Stolypin's reforms', 1906–11, that is when the tsar's government had the field to itself after defeating the revolutionary challenge. Its conclusions from the 1905–07 experience were expressed in a concentrated effort immortalised by Stolypin's words about 'putting the wager on the strong'. Next came the revolutions of 1917, a civil war and as a major part of it, the peasant war of 1917–21 expressing the particular livelihood and struggle of the great majority of Russians in the most decisive period of Russia's contemporary history. In the historical sequence, this was followed by the period of Lenin's Russia of NEP, a period to be covered by a new largely revised and partly refocused version of *The Awkward Class*. In addition to the original discussion of the socio-economic differentiation and mobility, the new version of *The Awkward Class* will incorporate a more extensive consideration of Lenin's rural Russia, 1921–8. New introductory chapters replacing the discussion transferred elsewhere will relate this book more directly to the conceptual revolution discussed in *Russia, 1905–07: Revolution as a Moment of Truth*, and update it, considering the changing views concerning the Russian peasantry also as against the civil war of 1917–21 and its aftermath. It will look particularly at Lenin's diverse 'agrarian programmes', formulated as he progressed through the stages of the political experience biographical to him, historical to Russia.

Introduction: *Revolution as a Moment of Truth*

This book forms a sequel to *Russia as a 'Developing Society'*. It argues that new Russia begins in 1905–07 when a failed revolution which proceeded in ways unexpected to its supporters and adversaries offered a dramatic corrective to their understanding of the society in which they lived. Russian history since then has been dominated by the transforming effort of monarchists who learned that only a 'revolution from above' could save their tsardom and by Marxists who, under the impact of a shattering experience of defeat, looked anew at Russia and at their Marxism. Years later and in a different world Boris Pasternak's poem *1905* has thus recalled it for his generation:

> A shadow of guns
> Put to sleep by a strike,
> This night –
> Was our childhood
> And the adolescence of our teachers

The initial section of Chapter 1 of the volume considers the nature of the surprise of the contemporaries who watched the unfolding of the 1905–07 revolution and the world-wide significance of the event. The Chapter then discusses the social forces which came together in 1905–07. Chapters 2 and 3 tell the tale of the revolutionary struggle describing its two main strands: the battle for democratisation as understood by Russia's socialists and liberals as well as the battle for land and liberty understood in a peasant way. Section 2C which links those chapters looks at the particular conflicts and dependencies which shaped the political scene: the power and the weakness of the Russian state, the ethnic problem ('national' to the Russians), the urban class diversities and confrontations, the urban–rural continuum. Chapter 4 returns to this issue to ask the fundamental question about the relations between the urban and rural revolutionary struggles.

Chapters 5 and 6 take up the theme set in Chapter 1 and considered more narrowly in Chapter 4. It is the issue of learning from political experience and more specifically of the way the experience of the 1905–07 revolution reconstructed the cognition of a political generation which dominated the period of 1907–17 and formed the leadership, the marching army and the decisive political chorus in the 1917–21 revolution and its immediate aftermath.

The Postscript presents a different type of lesson and a more personal message. It speaks of sociologically informed history and contemporary historical sociology in relation to the study offered as *The Roots of Otherness*.

1 A Revolution Comes to Boil

It is impossible to live so!
I at any rate cannot and will
not live so. That is why . . .
Lev Tolstoy

It will be best in so far as the Russian revolution [of 1905–07] and our tasks in it are concerned to look at it *neither* as if it was a bourgeois revolution in its usual sense, *nor* a socialist revolution, *but a distinctive process.*

Karl Kautsky

A. THE 'NEITHER . . . NOR . . .' REVOLUTION

Russia began a new century with the revolution of 1905–07. For the rest of the world a new century began with the Russian revolution. To Russia the revolutionary failure of 1905–07 was a dramatic initiation to a period in which the very nature of Russian society was challenged and transformed to a depth never known before. The general significance of that transformation for the world at large – the impact of the eventual establishment of the USSR we know today, is manifest and massive, but there is more to it. The events of Russia were part of a radical wave which in those years swept the world at large: massive strikes, peasant riots, struggles for parliamentary suffrage, armed mutinies, government changes, etc.[1] A long-term view makes this picture more particular in character, delimiting a new type of phenomena. At the non-colonial peripheries of capitalism the Russian revolution of 1905–07 was the first in a series of distinctive revolutionary struggles which offered a fundamental challenge to the Eurocentrism of the nineteenth century's structures of power and patterns of cognition. In quick succession, it was followed by Turkey (1908), Iran (1909), Mexico (1910), and China (1911), to which the somewhat different social confrontations like the 1907 peasant revolt in Moldavia, colonial India's 'period of unrest' (1905–08) and the Indonesian Islamic outburst (1909) can be added.[2] In Russia itself,

1

revolution resumed in 1917, while the revolutions-at-the-periphery have proceeded apace ever since. In some cases the direct impact of the events in Russia could be traced, but not in all.[3] More important were the substantive similarities rooted in the underlying social structures which have later come to be known as the 'developing societies'. That is why the world's first 'developing society' experienced the world's first 'developing societies' revolution – a new category of revolutionary phenomena.

In consequence and in retrospect it is not surprising that the 1905–07 revolution provided the point of fundamental reconceptualisation of the Russian revolutionary context in ways destined to reverberate in other lands and in times yet to come. Political theories relating goals and means to the assumed nature of a society are central to revolutionaries, as well as to the more intelligent of their enemies. Without some – even rudimentary – mental map of the world around us, and images of a distinct and better future, people riot when provoked to the utmost but never make a revolution. Consciousness of transformation and transforming consciousness, even if 'unrealistic,' are a necessary part of the fundamental leap in social structure that can rightly be called revolutionary change.

The particular aspect of cognition central to our concern is that of conceptual models of the contemporary and the ideal society as well as of the roads leading from the first toward the second. In relation to it, political interpretations, evaluations and predictions are made. Such models necessarily reflect the social and political realities in which they are embedded, but also show considerable measures of autonomy with respect to their characteristics, dynamics and impact.[4] What makes this autonomy neither whimsical nor purely accidental is its being firmly rooted in past experience and the process of its interpretation, the social and intellectual history of a specific society. This interpreting is ever comparative and generalising. It is also 'biased' in the sense of reflecting very selective 'fields of vision' of the laymen as well as intellectuals looking at experiences deemed relevant. The consequent concepts and ideas, the prevailing systems and languages of plausibility and of analysis are much more limited and limiting than we are usually ready to grant. That is why the social process of learning, via the readjustment of models and archetypes under the impact of historical experience, is central to social history realistically treated.

At the beginning of the nineteenth century the basic model of revolution for the contemporary Russian *literati* was generally that of the 1848 *Spring of the Nation* in Europe. To remind readers, these events constituted an international wave of urban democratic revolutions triggering off one another, aimed at the royal power and brought down with help of the reactionary countryside and/or soldiers, often either foreign or ethnically divergent. In Germany and Austria, the counter-revolution was more immediate, executed by an army of obedient peasants, often originating from the economically-backward Slav peripheries of those countries. In Hungary, which was short of this counter-revolutionary ingredient, an army of similar ilk was imported from Russia. In Italy and Romania a foreign army put down a national–liberal movement in the towns while the peasant majorities watched unmoved, securing thereby 'their' nation's defeat. In France, once the revolution restored popular suffrage, the peasants promptly used it to vote the revolutionaries out, establishing a monarchist majority in the parliament of the republic. The counter-revolutionary and/or conservative nature of peasants and/or the economically-backward ethnic peripheries were seemingly established beyond doubt. So too were the ambivalence and the conservative tendencies of the bourgeoisie which claimed democracy but feared the demands of its workers, as dramatised in Paris in June 1848. Once the monarchy was abolished and demands for social justice raised by the republican and socialist Left, the Parisian proletariat was smashed into submission by its former bourgeois allies. The French parliamentarians then proceeded to lose power in quick succession to a barbaric General and to a burlesque Emperor supported once again by the peasants – the peculiar Bonapartist 'hieroglyphic' of a conservative rebellion in defence of the myth of a revolutionary past. It was Germany, Austria–Hungary and in particular France which came to act in Russia as the main reference points to the 1848 period and to the revolutionary phenomenon as a whole. Evolution was mostly seen as the natural law of human history. Russia was backward by, say, half a century – the approximate time which had elapsed between the 1848–9 revolutionary wave and the beginning of a new century. Consequently . . .

Three more revolutionary events were utilised, if to a lesser degree, in Russian political thought at the turn of the century. France 1789 to 1793 was often used in the terminology and the rhetoric, such expressions as 'Jacobine' or 'Thermidor' and the melody of the Marseillaise coming easily to the tongues of those politically in opposition.[5] Yet, substantively, it seemed to belong to a different world of the pre-industrial past. To Russian socialists the Parisian

Commune in 1871 was closer in time and relevance. However, it mostly accentuated insights concerning the counter-revolutionary tendencies to the bourgeoisie and the rise in the capacity of the workers for revolutionary action and self-organisation – insights already drawn by Marx and others from the 'days of June' 1848. Finally, the revolutionary populist organisations of the 1870s and 1880s offered indigenous revolutionary experience, which seemed mostly negative in kind. The attempt to organise peasants was a failure. The attempt at individual terror which culminated in the killing of Alexander II neither triggered off a revolutionary wave nor made the tsardom retreat. Indeed, it was followed by a massive reactionary relapse. Those who subsequently came to dominate the Russian dissent of the late 1880s and 1890s rejected those attempts as irrelevant if not directly harmful. Even the early theorists of the Party of Socialist Revolutionaries (the PSR, in common usage the SR) who claimed direct People's Will parentage, were, at the beginning of the twentieth century, of two minds as to the direct usefulness of Russia's past revolutionary experience for the future struggle. Overtly, to the large majority of the Russian dissenters of the end of the nineteenth century the Revolutionary Populists of the 1860s to 1880s belonged with the 1789 French Revolution – something to be revered, but definitely of the past. Only the policemen and the bureaucrats still tended to treat a revival of People's Will terrorist action as the main type of danger to be expected from revolutionaries.[6]

The basic 1848 model (some amendments excepted) played a major role in shaping the strategy and expectations of the 1905–07 revolution.[7] Central to that event and its aftermath became the fact that the actual revolution did not follow this model and the predictions assumed. Nor was it simply a matter of a few anomalous facts which did not quite fit the theories and expectations (and were only to be expected within an immensely complex revolutionary process). It was the very core of the self-evident assumptions and images concerning revolution, as well as the Russian society *in toto*, which was challenged. The revolution proved the nature of the Russian society to be different from that assumed by its various theorists and activists. The revolution itself was new in type. As Karl Kautsky put it, 'It will be best in so far as the Russian Revolution [of 1905–07] and our tasks in it are concerned to look at it *neither* as if it was a bourgeois revolution in its usual sense, *nor* a socialist revolution . . . but a distinctive process'.[8] Typically, even this disjoiner was placed in the nineteenth century historiographic scheme and verbalised in the language of models/stages known and expected.

The lasting heritage of the revolution of 1905–07 were the lessons drawn from it by individuals, factions, parties and classes. The revolutionary context gave immense intensity to such lessons, as if centuries of experience were compressed into a few years. Even while the revolution was at its peak there was an urgent, intense and dramatic attempt to come to grips with its unexpected facts by some of those to whom its understanding was of the most vital concern. This proceeded during the post-revolutionary period. The differing capacity of various individuals and groups to learn from political experience was increasingly manifest. It was those who drew the most radical conclusions from the revolutionary experience who came to rule Russia for most of the period which followed. In that fundamental sense, the new Russia/RSFSR/USSR began with the 1905–07 Revolution.

The Stolypin reform of 1906–11, that is, the major result of what we have termed elsewhere the 'second amendment' of the 'classical' political economy,[9] was rooted in the revolutionary experience of the counter-revolutionaries. It was far from being the brilliant invention of a single mind: many of its components had been suggested or considered earlier or elsewhere. Yet its final integration into a grand design of radical transformation of Russian society in the interest of its rulers, its dramatic appeal and the harshness of the struggle over it, resulted directly from the revolutionary experience of 1905–07. Central to it was the new understanding of the nature of the Russian peasantry which linked the failed revolution 'from below' to a revolution 'from above,' designed to follow it and to prevent its reappearance.

At the other end of the ideological scale, Bolshevism in its full-blooded sense and authenticity was established as the grand revision of the Marxist orthodoxy of the day, rooted in the revolutionary experience of 1905–07. That is not what Lenin said, for he consistently underplayed the newness of his problems and the originality of his solutions (not surprising within the European socialist movement, in which the very word 'revisionism' became synonymous with 'reformism' or 'opportunism'). He also fathered a peculiar historiography in which the divisions between the Russian Marxists commenced more or less when their proponents were born, and ended in the Lenin–Martov debate of 1903. Consequently Bolshevism would have existed essentially unchanged since Lenin first spoke his mind (in the 1890s, or else at the 1903 Congress of the RSDWP). Lenin was right more than he cared to admit in his comment made much later about 'the dress rehearsal of 1905, without which the victory of the October revolution would have been impossible.'[10] It was more than a dress rehearsal; it was an 'open university' – open, that is, to the new social and political context of a 'developing society' as dramatically revealed in the lessons of the revolution which were grasped in depth by relatively few, Lenin being one of them. The massive revision of revolutionary strategies concerning the peasants, the national problem, the bourgeois parties, war, imperialism and state power, the style of leadership and revolutionary *élan*, all derived directly from interpretation of the 1905–07 experience and put a decisive wedge between those who were to be Bolsheviks in 1917 and other socialist groups. Not a genius, but a revolution created Bolshevism, even though there were geniuses on the scene and their significance is not to be denied.

As it happens, not even the most radical reconceptualisations of those times completely grasped the specific and relevant problem of 'developing societies' in its Russian context. First-comers are easy to mistake, and it is immensely difficult to originate and establish new analytical thought. Yet Lenin and Stolypin, aiming at diametrically opposed goals, went further than most in grasping the new insights and turning them into explicit strategies of political action. That is why, while intellectual fashions change often in the 'developing societies' of today, Stolypinite ideas and the writings of Lenin are always there, immensely influential and intuitively accepted by the most significant political actors as 'making good sense'. It goes without saying that they appeal mostly to different and opposing classes and factions, just as they did in Russia. Even that division should not be overstated, however, for a developing society's right-winger will often acclaim or tacitly recognise the realism and the uses of some of Lenin's ideas, for example, his ways of shaping and expressing the structure and interdependence of the state and the ruling party in the context, say, of Mexico. The same will hold true for many on the Left concerning the ideas and indices of the modernisation and capital formation, come what may, by the Stolypinites of today.

To place the 1905–07 revolutionary experience in relation to its conceptual heritage, we shall begin with the development of a revolutionary situation during the first years of the twentieth century. We shall proceed to the tale of the revolution and describe and consider its main trends, particularly the role of the peasant majority in it. We shall then return to the meaning of the 1905–07 revolution in Russia as a fundamental lesson in applied political sociology and to its impact on the later revolutions of the twentieth century in Russia and elsewhere.

B. A REVOLUTIONARY SITUATION: MASSES AS ACTORS

If the 1905–07 revolution was indeed a 'dress rehearsal' for the one to come in 1917, the half-decade which preceded 1905 can be called a pre-rehearsal. The basic elements and trends of a revolutionary situation were becoming increasingly apparent. The essential characteristics of each of them could be seen singly and as if in miniature. The interdependence of these elements and processes was central but their ups, downs and breaks did not necessarily meet in time. The outcome of a revolution is often decided by such meetings and misses.

Let us first say something about the way relevant terms will be used. A *revolution* is seen as a leap in social structure involving fundamental systems of domination, property relations and class division as well as transformation of the state apparatus and removal of its rulers. As to its form it assumes a massive popular intervention, an uprising 'from below' in open confrontation with the 'forces of order' marshalled by the state. These are necessarily linked to deep changes in the collective cognitions of those involved. Politically, it includes situations and periods of what has been described as 'multiple sovereignty' versus the taken-for-granted monopolies of authorities expressed in the state. In revolutions which fail, the immediate results differ, but the long-term social transformation triggered off by such a defeat is often very substantial and should be treated in a similar analytical context. The term *revolution from above* has come to be used to delineate a major leap in social structure introduced without the popular intervention confronting and dislodging the state machinery and its rulers; indeed, those changes are induced and controlled by the rulers themselves. In so far as political action rather than political results is concerned, the term 'revolution' is used in such cases metaphorically.[1]

A *revolutionary situation* represents the combination and interdependence of (i) a major crisis of societal functioning, often brought about by war or severe economic depression; (ii) rapid crystallisation

of social classes and other conflict-groups; (iii) the rise of organisations and ideologies offering an alternative outlook and leadership;
(iv) a crisis of the governing elite, of the dominant class(es) and of the
state apparatus, and (v) a linked 'moral crisis', placing in doubt the
socially accepted structures of authority of ideological hegemony and
of common sense. All this appears within (vi) an international
context which facilitates or at least permits the revolutionary
processes to take place. An actual revolutionary situation is
necessarily related to the historical and societal context. A few of the
general characteristics will appear more strongly, others will be more
relevant for one type of society, still others unique to a set of circumstances. The view adopted, stated and argued here is that, subject to
some conceptual restrictions, the most meaningful analytical framework and comparison in our case is that of Russia as a 'Developing
Society' – a specific type of societal phenomenon.[2]

Of the basic 'elements' of the revolutionary situation in Russia at
the turn of the nineteenth century, the economic and social crises
were the most explicit. A crucial facet of this was the crisis of
agriculture, the branch of production providing the livelihood for
most of the population. This was increasingly recognised since the
famine of 1891 as a lingering and deepening disease of the economy
of central Russia.[3] Rapid industrialisation was the bright hope in the
1890s, but since 1899 Russia had experienced a sharp downturn in
industrial production, employment and wages, as well as the
tightening of credits related to a recession in Western Europe. With a
slight improvement in 1903 (which lasted for one year only) this crisis
continued until 1909. In 1905 and 1906 the situation of the rural
majority was exacerbated by a drop in yields which developed into a
famine in some regions. After a slow increase beforehand, the wages
in rural areas had also been dropping since 1901.

The political crystallisation of the social classes and groups was
another central aspect of the build-up towards the 1905–07 revolution. The consideration of social classes defined in Marx's terms, that
is, groups sharing an economic position and united by a social conflict
within a system of relations or production must be explicated and/or
broadened in scope to serve the Russian scene realistically. To make
such a mode of political analysis work effectively it must incorporate
a few social groups whose nature and interests were transitory and/or
extra-economic in terms of production but which displayed significant
class-like qualities in a revolutionary situation, for example, the
students or the soldiers. Second, it must consider ethnic and regional

modifications in the class processes as well as conditions under which ethnic group solidarity may operate as the decisive mobilising factor – an ethnos 'for itself' – while the class conflicts are suspended or overshadowed thereby.[4] (Class conflict and an ethnic confrontation may also combine with significant results for the political outcome.) Finally, not only class crystallisation but also class decrystallisation must be posed as a problem of relevance.

After the relative political calm of the late 1880s and 1890s, a new major wave of open dissent materialised with three successive peaks reached in the confrontation between the Russian state and three groups within the Russian population: the students, the peasants and the workers. In an uncanny sequence, these major social actors of the revolution-to-come stormed onto the scene, captured major attention and then stepped into a corner, never quite to disappear until the time was ripe to act out the drama in full.

In 1899, a limited academic conflict in the University of Petersburg was turned by police brutality, expulsions and deportations into a general solidarity strike of 30 000 of Russia's students inside and outside the universities. After more arrests and some vague conciliatory moves by the authorities, in the 1900–01 session, 183 students of Kiev University were expelled and drafted into the army 'to teach them a lesson'. Students reacted by street demonstrations in twenty-eight of Russia's cities, and were joined in increasing numbers by non-student sympathisers. These demonstrations were attacked by police and by Cossack cavalry units. At the final stage, the 'apolitical' factions of the students, prominent earlier, were in full retreat, with the students politicised and all Russia aware of 'student troubles'. One of their demands became the full restoration of academic freedoms and university autonomy, suspended in 1884 by the counter-reforms of Alexander III.[5] In 1901, at the climax of the protests, the Minister of Education was shot and killed by an ex-student, twice expelled for 'political unreliability'. The wave of 'student unrest' receded in 1902.

During this period, the limitations and strength of student political action came fully to light. The cycles of confrontation followed academic sessions and stopped during vacations, with every student 'generation' having to learn its lessons of dissent anew. Advantageous was the fact that within the framework of the university a constant venue for legitimate contact existed. Limited demands could easily be articulated in broad political terms and a considerable echo achieved within different strata of the population. The students rapidly became both pet darlings and bogeymen. While the intelligentsia showered them with declarations of support and their demonstrations were joined by top intellectuals and even some groups of industrial workers in St Petersburg, the government devotees increasingly came to identify the enemies of the state as 'students, Jews and anarchists'. Some of the remote villages began to use the word 'student' as synonymous with a political activist or a revolutionary.[6]

In 1902 peasants took their turn. 'Agrarian disturbances' were reported in several provinces, especially in Tambov and Saratov, and also on the Caucasian frontier. However, the main attention was focused on an area bridging the neighbouring provinces of Poltava and Kharkov, in the Central Agricultural Zone of the Ukraine. For three weeks, during March and April, the peasants of the area attacked, systematically robbed and partially burned 105 local manorial estates.[7] The 'disturbances' spread in a wave involving altogether 175 rural communes. Despite the manifest wish of the authorities to find some outside instigators to blame for poisoning the peasant souls, police investigation failed to discover any non-peasant involvement over and above a few leaflets which by then could be found in most localities. The peasants were led by self-selected leaders – mostly the communal elders or else the local literates, with a few ex-servicemen prominent among them. Whole villages, including their wealthiest members, participated. Units of up to 400 carts moved into action at a given signal, with a snowball effect spreading the revolt from village to village. State property, including the otherwise vulnerable liquor shops, was studiously avoided. Indeed, the peasants often repeated a claim that their action was in accordance with the Tsar's will or with a manifesto, rumoured to exist and to be carried by a 'Prince Michael with an entourage of students'.[8]

On recovering their wits, the totally surprised authorities reacted with a massive army operation, including shooting and flogging, which eventually broke the rebellion. The governor of Kharkov, from whose province a magistrate reported that 'flogging was administered to everybody and in any way at all, in accordance to the executors' "whimsy" ', received a commendation and so did a local butcher who, anticipating the exploits of the Black Hundreds of 1905, showed initiative in organising vigilantes to rough up 'troublemakers'.[9] The governor of Poltava, who showed less energy and reportedly flogged fewer people, was fired for incompetence. The personal visit by V. Pleve – his first action after his appointment as Minister of the Interior – stressed the importance which the Crown attached to the case.

The attention given by the officialdom to the 1902 peasant revolt has provided considerable documentation, in which facts were recorded and causes extensively discussed. Land shortage was particularly severe in this area. The economic conditions deteriorated, the population increased along with rents and the price of land, while wages had dropped, as had the peasants' other supplementary incomes. A regional failure of crops in 1902 meant both famine and the destruction of livestock, which undercut the chances of future recovery. It was left to a peasant elder to sum up the background of the revolt: 'It is not the little books which are terrible' ran his answer to a magistrate questioning him about the impact of revolutionary leaflets and propaganda, 'but that there is nothing to eat for us and the beast. There is no plough-land, no grain, no grazing land . . . [within a year] livestock has dropped from 400 to 100 head'.[10] This did not stop the authorities from having 837 peasants sentenced to various terms of imprisonment, with a collective fine of 800 000 roubles levied on the villages to recover the State grant paid to the landlords whose property came to harm.

Third in line were the industrial workers. Since the beginning of the industrial crisis in 1899 defensive strikes had been fought here and there against the falling wages and the growing employers' pressure. Revolutionary circles of socialist intelligentsia and some self-education groups were active among workers. Groups of the more politicised workers not only joined student demonstrations, but also held some of their own on May Day in both 1901 and 1902. There were increasing demands for a shorter working-day and freedom of organisation. In the majority of cases the strikes and demonstrations achieved nothing tangible and police repressions followed. Since 1900 the Russian political police had embarked on a more imaginative effort, initiated by a Colonel Zubatov of the gendarmerie, to steal the thunder of the revolutionaries by organising monarchist workers' unions directed or manipulated by the police.[11]

In November 1902, a strike in Rostov in the South became city-wide with mass meetings in which thousands of workers participated. It was suppressed but in the summer of 1903 a strike-wave rose and spread developing into a series of general strikes in the cities of Southern Russia. More than double the largest annual number of striking enterprises ever recorded was reported by the

Factories Inspectorate in 1903.[12] The strikes began in the oil-producing Baku and rapidly spread throughout the city, with mass pickets stopping work in factory after factory. Within days, transport, telegraph, power stations and shops stopped operating while mass meetings of the strikers followed day after day. The army was called in and the strike brought to an end, but not before some of the oil wells had been set on fire and the strikers had been granted many of their demands. The strikes, mass pickets and meetings spread to Odessa, Tiflis, Batum, Ekaterinodar, Nikolayev, etc. In Odessa it was the very groups of workers who were organised in the police-supervised union and disenchanted with it, which played a major role in strikes and demonstrations.

The economic background of the 1903 strike-wave was in some ways self-explanatory. A period of economic depression seemed to be coming to an end and workers tried to regain their past losses. The 'economic demands' of the strikers for improvement in wages, etc., were this time generally won, and the increasing feeling of class solidarity between the workers of different enterprises and cities, the mass meetings and the wish to listen to political speakers and demands, made for a new atmosphere in the factories of Russia's industrial south. Huge solidarity strikes, protesting against arrests and the oppression of workers elsewhere made the headlines. As usual a wave of repressions followed. The granting of economic demands and the reprisals against the workers' leaders, together with a new industrial downturn and a war with Japan, eventually seemed to work for the authorities. In 1904 strikes in Russia were at their lowest for a decade.

C. A REVOLUTIONARY SITUATION: LEADERS AND 'GREY PEASANT WORKERS'

Since the mid-1890s the Russian police reported increasing signs of the revival of political organisations in Russia.[1] The substance of this process lay in the establishment of relaying points of alternative leadership and of a systematic ideological challenge to the tsardom. The strategy common to all its strands accepted as an initial goal the creation of nation-wide clandestine political organisations due to spread out at some later stage into mass movements. Next to come would be the political transformation of Russia. This strategy provides an ideal sequence to which the actual historical events and periods can be related. After the repetitive attempts, advances and retreats of the 1890s, lasting nation-wide political parties and organisations were established in the first years of the twentieth century. This coincided with the three waves of the spontaneous mass dissent of 1899–1903. The mutual links between the spontaneous and the organised political action had grown at the next stage as the party organisations of Russia developed into mass movements in 1905–06. Their upward momentum was cut short by the defeat of the 1905–07 revolution. What followed was a stage of sharp decline, but the political outline of the party organisations established in 1905–07 never disappeared until the 1930s.

*   *   *

The expression 'a party' and the related political association or images may mislead because of their specifically Russian setting. The core group involved in the initial party-building was that of the Russian intelligentsia, who acted against the background of (i) police restrictions, (ii) the still vivid recollections of the 1880s experience of the People's Will party, and (iii) the conceptual necessity to position oneself in terms of the attitudes toward the West. To specify, any attempts to establish nation-wide organisations were ordinarily barred by the authorities and their initiators persecuted. Even a conference of legally-established local institutions needed official permission, which was often refused. The very concept of a political party was criminal and the only way to proceed with it was clandestinely. We have discussed at length elsewhere the full impact of the past experience of party-building by revolutionary populists, especially the People's Will.[2] Without it the Russian political scene cannot quite be understood. As in the heyday of the nineteenth century revolutionary movements, the root of the Russian dissent and its ideological self-definition was still the response to the West as the economic, political and cultural metropolis and super-model of the contemporary world. The nature of that response was diverse, and it was this diversity which formed the most substantial division defining the three main streams of the Russian political organisations coming into being – Marxist, liberal and populist who described themselves respectively as Social Democrats, Constitutionalists and Social Revolutionaries. They were further divided by fundamental considerations of strategy and by ethnic and regional sub-divisions.

There were some interesting similarities between the otherwise diverse and sharply competitive political organisations of the Russian dissent. They all began as small groups meeting to debate political issues (*kruzhki* – the 'circles') which moved to recruit new members, to produce written materials and to spread the word outside their immediate environment. As the next step, those groups which successfully avoided destruction by arrest or deportation looked for contacts with like-minded groups in order to establish a broader organisation. Further steps inevitably consisted of:

1. The establishment of a newspaper (for security reasons often printed abroad and smuggled into Russia). Such publications operated as a major instrument of unification and ideological guidance, defining an alternative picture of Russia's conditions and future in contrast to the view of its government and the conservative common sense.
2. The establishment of a recognisable leadership able to link the ideological functions of writing or editing with an organisational network and hierarchy of clandestine groups.
3. The formal integration of local groups (which to the revolutionaries also included their exiles in Western Europe) and a party congress adopting a programme, organisational statutes and an elected executive, followed by a tightening of discipline, a hierarchy of authorities and demands for ideological consolidation.

While discussing the political organisations of Russian dissent, we must remember the initially relative nature of these divisions. Different groups of Russian opposition joined hands in confrontations with tsardom. People of different views often joined similar groups, like the 'orthodox' Marxist Social Democrats (SDs) and the 'populist' Social Revolutionaries (SRs) operating jointly in Saratov or revolutionary SDs and the 'legal' Marxists, shortly to join the liberal movement, publishing together the journal *Nachalo*. In the circle *Beseda* of the dissenting *zemstvo*'s activists, there were Slavophiles, Westernisers of radical liberal tendency, as well as some future leaders of Russia's right wing, like Count V. Bobrinskii. On the other hand, as the party organisations began to crystallise, even people with declared similarities of *Weltanschauung* were divided by contradictory strategies which cross-cut doctrinal considerations. The main issues over which such divisions took place were those of:

1. Support for mass spontaneity versus the belief in a necessarily 'strong' party structure, a 'party apparatus', that is, an effective bureaucratic organisation of the activists.

2. The revolutionary versus evolutionary perspective in the confrontation with tsardom (the division between the 'legal' and clandestine work and between 'propaganda' and armed struggle offered, on the Left, further subdivisions along these lines).
3. The issue of political exclusivity, that is, the permissibility of alliances and compromises, such as the discussions as to how far Marxists can ally with bourgeois political movements or permit the petty-bourgeois peasants to join their ranks; whether the revolutionary populists could use legally established institutions to promote their aim, etc.

In party terms it was also the issue of 'cutting edge' (*gran*') inside and outside the party. Reflecting the powerful impact of class analysis on the political thought of contemporary Russia, the goals, strategies and self-descriptions were often couched in terms of the social classes or forces which the particular political movement considered itself to represent. It was the proletariat for the Social Democrats, the labouring class (consisting mostly of workers and peasants) for the Social Revolutionaries and the supra-class unity of all the progressive forces in the Russian nation for the liberal Constitutionalists.

In the 1890s attempts at party building the Russian Marxists had some initial advantages. In the Russian intelligentsia the advanced capitalist industrialisation was broadly interpreted as bearing out their anticipation. The destruction of the People's Will party removed a powerful rival. Marxism offered a language, a claim to science and a new hope of better future. It called for realism (as against the 'populist dreams' of the 1870s) and was understood mainly as the acceptance of social determinism rooted in capitalist industrialisation as necessary-cum-beneficial, that is, PROGRESSIVE. Not only self-confessed Social Democrats but also liberals and populists of the day increasingly used the arguments and terminology of the Second International. Also, the *Emancipation of Labour Group* in Geneva was known nationally and internationally, operating as a broadly recognised leadership and an effective publications-centre outside the reach of the Russian police. Georgii Plekhanov appeared on its behalf as 'the representative of the Russian Social Democrats' at the 1889 Congress of the Second International, to declare that 'Russian socialism will be victorious only as a revolutionary movement of workers or not at all'. The only 'non-fantastic' goal of the socialists was the struggle for constitutional development and democratisation expressing the current pre-bourgeois stage of Russia's development. A variety of local groups defining themselves as SDs used the Emancipation of Labour Group and its publications as a major contact-point and theoretical inspiration. Several of the most widely-read social scientists in Russia, who rejected revolutionary perspective, nevertheless adopted an evolutionist brand of that very view (to be dismissed as 'legal' Marxists by the revolutionaries).[3] They bridged the gap between the Social Democrats and the liberals by sharing ideological 'Westernism' of thought.

In the early 1890s, the activities of all the Russian 'circles' of Marxists – the Social Democrats – were mainly theoretical and educational in nature. In 1894 a debate began about tactics of political action. It attempted first to digest the experience of the SDs in Vilna/Vilnius as presented in A. Kramer's influential leaflet. He called for the combination of the 'propaganda' of the general Marxist world view with 'agitation' for specific economic demands of the workers, aiming to advance their class organisation under the leadership of the SDs. Martov carried it to the clandestine Alliance for the Liberation of the Working Class in St Petersburg, where both he and Lenin began their nationwide careers.[4] On 1 March 1898 in Minsk, a conference of Marxist groups declared the creation of the Russian Social Democratic Workers' Party (RSDWP). The date of the meeting was chosen to indicate the continuity with the People's Will and their aims but, in the words of the party's manifesto, its 'methods would differ in so far as [the party] wants to remain the class movement of the organised working class'.[5] A Central Committee was elected and the *Rabochaya gazeta* (published clandestinely in Russia) declared the party's official mouthpiece.

Within days most of the delegates to this meeting, the new party executive and the paper's editors were arrested by the police. The attempt to establish a party failed and different SD groups proceeded separately for a while. Inside Russia they were increasingly divided between the 'Economists' (supporters of workers' spontaneity which, since 1894, surfaced dramatically in a sequence of strikes) and those who followed Kautsky in treating the socialist movement as a necessary combination of theory-wielding intelligentsia and the proletarian masses.[6] The 'Economists' were sharply attacked by the SD elders, that is, both the Emancipation of Labour Group led by Plekhanov and Axelrod and a 'middle generation' of the newly-exiled activists of whom Lenin and Martov were particularly prominent. The anti-'Economists' combined in a new effort to establish a party. This began in 1900 with the publication abroad of the newspaper

Iskra calling for unification on the basis of 'orthodox' Marxism. It adopted Plekhanov's major strategic assumption that in a country of weak bourgeoisie, fearful of its own working class, the dominant impact of the proletariat and its SD party would be necessary to secure also the forthcoming capitalist revolutionary transformation. The essence of their organisational creed was stated by Lenin in *What is to be Done*. It attacked the 'pre-industrial' methods of organisation (*kustarnichestvo*) and the loosely organised circles. The relation of his image of party cadres to the revolutionary populist tradition was explicit and indeed acknowledged by the book's title, following Chernyshevskii's novel. It called for a disciplined organisation of ideologically trained and totally devoted professional revolutionaries to be the necessary core of a Marxist movement of the working class. Spontaneity was declared to be a major organisational menace.[7] A count-down began towards a party congress due to bring all these developments to completion.

Turning to the second strand of Russia's dissent, the initiation of the constitutionalist political organisation was marked in the 1890s by two separate origins: the reformist nobles in their capacity as the elected officers of *zemstvo* provincial authorities and the so-called liberal professions. The last included university professors, lawyers, writers and those journalists who wrote in Russia's 'serious journals', avidly read by the 'educated public'.[8] What united most of them was Westernism, the belief in 'progress' and the demand for civic freedoms and a parliamentary role coupled with the rejection of violent means. While abroad they defined themselves as liberals and democrats. Many declared that the only difference between themselves and the revolutionaries was one of temperament. Some of them were 'legal' Marxists. A number of *zemstvos*, for example, of Tver', led the movement, passing resolutions which requested new welfare policies as well as some broader constitutionalist demands, from the abolition of legal flogging to 'crowning the edifice founded in 1861' by supplementing the elected *zemstvos* with a nation-wide parliament. When hopes for new policies associated with Nikolai II's ascension to the throne were dashed by his 1895 speech condemning reform as 'mindless dreams', this was followed in 1896 by a conference of nineteen *zemstvo* chairmen who decided to proceed to meet and discuss matters of common interest. They established a standing committee to secure it. The next attempt at such a meeting in 1897 was banned by the government and the standing committee dismantled.

The confrontation between the authorities and the different *zemstvos* grew, as did the government's attempts to restrict the *zemstvos'* legal powers and especially their 'irresponsible use', that is, any extension of *zemstvo* activities to issues of national scope, which the government considered its own preserve. The more active of the *zemstvo* members reacted by a variety of clandestine meetings, of which the most important became those of the discussion group *Beseda*.[9] An increasing number of critical books and essays were by that time being published by the *zemstvo* activists as well as by the liberal writers and journalists of the large cities. The views of liberal lawyers were heard in the courts, and meetings of professional associations ended on an increasingly critical note. The government reacted by further restrictions. In 1900 the budgets of the *zemstvos* were curtailed and the most prestigious association of Russia's social scientists, the Free Society for Economic Analysis, was suspended.

As a result, a growing need was felt for an explicitly constitutionalist focus of unity and organisation. Attempts to secure it led to the establishment in 1902 of a clandestine liberal newspaper, published abroad under the name *Liberation* and edited by the then central figure of Russian legal Marxism, Peter Struve.

In the intellectual atmosphere of the mid-1890s, the clandestine groups which claimed direct continuation of revolutionary populism – the third main strand of Russian dissent – were on the defensive against the predominance of evolutionary Marxism, revolutionary Marxism, liberal progressivism and what seemed like a major success story of Russia's government-induced 'developmentism'. They were often ambivalent as to the heritage they claimed: new conditions and the close relations with the Marxism of the Second International, to which they belonged, strongly influenced their most significant younger theorists, M. Gotz and V. Chernov. All the same, they claimed a separate identity rooted as much in tradition as in the 'cadres' of those who supported the past anti-government struggles, and established groups which grew in influence, especially in some of the provincial towns of Russia, for example, Saratov, Tambov and Minsk. Ideologically, the young populists of those days often selected themselves negatively, that is on a neither/nor basis, as those who embraced the socialist cause confronting tsardom, but rejected constitutionalists (as 'soft' and opportunistic), as well as the SDs (as dogmatic). Membership so defined resulted in their considerable heterogeneity.[10]

The consequent attempts at populist party-building began with the creation of a few inter-city groups, each defining itself as a party and stressing different aspects of the People's Will heritage. For example, the *Workers' Party for Liberation of Russia*, centred in Minsk, stressed terrorist activities as the way to 'agitate by action', the PSR, centred in Saratov and later Moscow, emphasised political action within the urban working class, while a Tambov group promoted particularly peasant organisations. Following up this last experiment (directed by V. Chernov and S. Sletov who were exiled to the Tambov province), an *Agrarian Socialist League* was set up abroad in 1900 to produce printed material in a language specifically aimed at peasant audiences.

A new stage of the Russian dissent – the creation of effective and durable nation-wide parties – began in 1902. The creation of a united party of the revolutionary populists was decided on in this year at a meeting abroad which was attended by its most significant future leaders: G. Gershuni, V. Chernov, the brothers M. and A. Gotz, and E. Azev (who was eventually uncovered as a police spy). They adopted the name of one of the merging components, the Party of Socialist Revolutionaries (PSR), and took over its newspaper, *Revolyutsionnaya rossiya*. (Its publication, begun clandestinely in Russia in 1901 and disrupted by police arrests, was now moved abroad.)[11] A Central Committee was established and rapidly recognised by local organisations in Russia, but heterogeneity persisted. In particular, a major tendency within the PSR doubted the 'ruralism' of the populists of the 1870s. In the words of an important article about the 'practical programme minimum', it was the working class in the larger industrial cities and the learning youth 'who form the basic support of the party' ('while the revolutionary work of the party within peasant masses would be carried out only to the extent to which it is found possible').[12] On the other hand, Chernov proceeded to develop a peasant-directed tendency within the PSR strategy. The Agrarian Socialist League continued for a time with its autonomous existence (in a 'political alliance' with the PSR). A PSR terrorist arm was set up as a distinct organisation under the leadership of Gershuni (*Boevaya organizatsiya* – the BO) and began its activities by an attack on Obolenskii – the governor of Kharkov who excelled in the suppression of the peasants in 1902. In 1903 the PSR initiated a party teachers' union, a number of peasant brotherhoods and some separate workers', military and university students' organisations. All those spread influence and extended the SRs impact but also added to their diversity.

In 1903 a congress of the Russian SDs met in Belgium.[13] It differed considerably from the 1898 attempt but adopted its name for the party (RSDWP) and the consequent numbering of its congresses (hence the 'Second'). It was much larger and more representative.[14] The effective campaign of *Iskra* supporters against the 'Economists' seemed to have ensured its ideological homogeneity. Ideologically, the fire was redirected at them from the earlier attack on populism initiated by Plekhanov in the late 1880s.

Possible diversities among the SDs were narrowed down still further by the strict adherence of all its most significant leaders to the 'orthodox' Marxism of the Second International. To all of them, Marxism was synonymous with science and as precise. The historiography of human evolution was a major part of it. Russia was essentially capitalist and now approaching its bourgeois revolution to be followed in good time by a socialist one. The scientific knowledge was to be brought to the proletariat, and its activities orchestrated by professional revolutionaries. Moreover, in the Russian context 'the party of the proletariat has to take upon itself also the fulfilment of those revolutionary tasks which the bourgeoisie ought to have performed but did not'.[15]

All these assumptions were particularly attractive as they offered a way to reconcile socialism with the laws of industrial progress, and accentuated the general European characteristics of the Russian intelligentsia. They were also fundamentally intolerant. No social or political force could equal the most progressive class and its exclusive party, which grasped the science of society and represented the necessary evolution of humanity. Compared with it, tsardom was backward, the liberals necessarily ambivalent and the SRs reactionary and romantic or even objectively harmful by propagating unscientific views under a socialist facade. The PSR was described at the congress as 'detrimental not only to the political development of proletariat but also to the overall democratic struggle against absolutism . . . in principle no different than . . . liberal representatives of bourgeoisie in general'. The common organisations for example, in Saratov, were to be brought to an abrupt end.[16]

Yet the rigid conceptual pre-definition of RSDWP did not secure its eventual unity. A major split occurred at the Second Congress, which, while proclaiming anew the creation of the party, actually produced three groups of SDs and reinforced the separate nature of a fourth one. The congress divided into a 'majority' led by Lenin, the

Bolsheviks and a 'minority' – the Mensheviks, led by Martov. The Bolsheviks voted for a stricter definition of party membership consistent with harsher discipline of the party toward its leadership. They considered themselves the radical wing of the SD, the Jacobins of Russia's 1791-to-come.

The Mensheviks voted for a contrary view. They were not ready to grant the small Bolshevik majority the palm of true radicalism nor the control of the RSDWP. Both sides searched for doctrinal reasons for the split, but those were still too subtle to form a consistent theoretical structure.[17] Nevertheless, the factional division was harsh and merciless. In the struggle for control over the party executive, the *Iskra* and the local committees, two *de facto* organisations came into being, with separate leading groups, newspapers and networks. Also, a number of activists refused to accept this split and proceeded to attempt a reconciliation, establishing a third force 'in between' which gathered strength as the revolutionary activities intensified in 1905, but never equalled the two main factions in size or in organisation. Finally, the specifically Jewish SD organisation, the Bund, was ready to join the RSDWP only while preserving autonomy and as the exclusive representative of the Jewish proletariat. That ran contrary to the powerful homogenising tendency of the Russian SD and was rejected. As a result, the delegates of the Bund left the congress (accidentally securing thereby the majority of Lenin's group in it). The other SD regional parties of the western ethnic peripheries in the Polish, Lithuanian and Latvian provinces did not even attempt yet to join an 'All-Russian' party organisation.

Finally, the constitutionalists reached the 'next stage' following the 1902 *Consultation Concerning the Needs of Agriculture*, set up by the government and chaired by Witte. The *zemstvos* were excluded from its committees. This gave them new offence and a new reason for meetings and organisations. In May 1902 the *Beseda* group initiated a congress of sixteen *zemstvo* representatives to discuss counteraction. A standing Committee for conferences of the *zemstvo* representatives was again established. This time attempts to suppress the initiative failed and the *zemstvo* conferences became a regular feature. Some of the radical representatives of urban municipalities eventually joined the *zemstvos* in their meetings and demands.[18] They passed increasingly 'political' resolutions, critical of the government.[19] A radical wing of it was set up in 1903 – the organisation of Zemstvo Constitutionalists led by I. Petrunkevich and the brothers Dolgorukov. A contrary tendency, which objected to the West-like parliamentary demands and preferred a national consultative representation – *the Zemskii Sobor* – began to crystallise also, led by the chairman of the Moscow *zemstvo*, D. Shipov.

The 'Liberation' (*Osvobozhdenie*) published abroad was instrumental in working out a distinct political programme of the radical constitutionalists. Its initial editorial statement proclaimed it with admirable clarity. 'The way our publication differs from all of the others is the fact that we would like to unite all groups of Russian society which cannot find other expression to their dismay. Our struggle is neither class-directed nor revolutionary. We would like to express a non-class public opinion and base ourselves on that.'[20] 'Liberation' directed its argument against the tsardom, against Russia's socialists of the RSDWP and the PSR (whose views were, of course, 'class-directed' and revolutionary) but also against the 'sentimental and harmful Slavophile illusions', because, 'like the use of ABC, printing press and electricity' the political changes aimed at were not nation-specific. They were simply a form of a higher culture.[21] Still in 1903, a meeting called in Switzerland by the *zemstvo* supporters of 'Liberation' and a number of urban intellectuals declared the creation of an Alliance of Liberation which was to be a constitutionalist, broader-than-a-party organisation along the ideological lines elaborated by the journal. A clandestine congress took place in St Petersburg in 1904, elected an executive body and decided to begin its activities by a campaign of banquets to celebrate the reforms of the 1860s, using those platforms to call for 'the completion of the structure' then created, that is, the introduction of a parliamentary regime.

*   *   *

To offer a rough guide to Russian political parties in the 1905–07 revolution, it is probably best to put the cart before the horse and to name them as they would have appeared to an observer in 1906.[22] The Party of Popular Liberty, usually referred to as the Constitutional Democrats (KD), was established in late 1905 to act in the forthcoming election. Its initiators were the majority in the Alliance of Liberation and of the Zemstvo Constitutionalists along with some unattached liberals, 'legal' Marxists and 'legal' populists; its leader was P. Milyukov. The conservative minority in the 1902–05 *zemstvo* conferences, led by Shipov, had by that time allied with a few of the merchant dynasties of Moscow, whose most prominent leader was A. Guchkov, to establish the Octobrist Party. A few more liberal parties were set up 'in between' the KDs and the Octobrists but were less continuous and less successful in attracting support. A number of attempts to form a particular constitutionalist party of industrialists and merchants failed.

At the beginning of 1906 a congress of the Party of Social Revolutionaries (PSR) met, voted its programme and formally elected (in fact re-elected) its leadership. This step resulted both in further consolidation and in a dual split. A sizeable right wing refused to accept the revolutionary goals of the party and departed to establish a reformist Popular Socialist Party. A small left faction objected to the stage-by-stage strategy and to the tactics of selective terrorism, defending immediate socialist revolution through the indiscriminate class terror, not unlike Bakunin's dream. They were voted down and left the PSR to establish a separate party of SR Maximalists.

From 1905, under the heavy pressure of its rank and file, the SDs moved in a different direction. The factions of RSDWP negotiated reunification to fight the tsardom. This led to the fourth ('Unificatory') congress in 1906 followed by the fifth congress in 1907, where the main SD organisations of the western peripheries – the Polish, Latvian and Jewish (the Bund) – also joined the common framework of the Russian Social Democratic Workers Party. The factional organisations inside the party, however, remained intact.

By 1906 some political organisation of the extreme Right became increasingly visible, attempting to counter the attack from the Left, both by force and electorally. They were defined by their wish to 'step back' from the constitutional and electoral arrangements decreed in October 1905. Their most effective organisation was the Association of the Russian People (often referred to as the Black Hundreds). 'In between' the Octobrists and the extreme Right, a vague group of 'Nationalists' began to form.

This thumbnail sketch referred to so-called 'All-Russian' party organisation. They were also ethnically Russian in the majority of their members (the Mensheviks faction of RSDWP offered the one exception – most of its members were non-Russians, that is, Georgians, Jews and representatives of some other 'minorities'). Regionally specific and/or ethnically-exclusive political parties were initiated on the western and southern peripheries earlier than in Russia proper. Some of them, particularly in the Polish, Ukrainian, Finnish and Armenian provinces, were 'purely' nationalist, that is, raised demands for autonomy or independence only. The socialists there were divided between those who challenged local nationalism

head-on, objecting to any demands for independence, and those who
believed that the struggle for independence or for cultural autonomy
must merge with the class struggle.

The major political forces operating in Poland exemplify these
dilemmas and their organisational expressions. The Polish SDs, led
by Rosa Luxemburg and Tyshko, objected to any separation of the
Polish provinces from Russia (a step seen as economically regressive,
xenophobic and romantic, that is utopian). The only way to resolve
the plight of the proletariat was a bourgeois and subsequently a
socialist revolution to transform the Russian Empire. A rival Party of
Polish Socialists (PPS) believed in the necessity for a struggle for a
separate Polish entity (they were ambivalent in their choice between
autonomy or total independence). This was due to take place
simultaneously with the struggle for socialism. The National Democracy Party demanded the national unity of all Poles in their struggle
for autonomy within the Russian Empire and was sharply anti-
socialist and anti-Jewish. In the Polish provinces there were also
some extreme nationalists who dreamed about a return to
seventeenth-century Poland (with frontiers 'from one sea to another',
that is, from the Baltic to the Black Sea) and conservatives who called
for compromise with the tsarist authorities, accepting the basic status
quo of the Empire, the *Ugodowcy*.

*   *   *

The political effort of the Russian dissenting intelligentsia was
crowned with a considerable success: the party-building produced on
the eve of the 1905–07 revolution a number of nation-wide and
regional organisations with increasingly consistent ideology, strategy,
leadership and membership. These political organisations differed in
form: the SDs' sharp stress on ideological and organisational
homogeneity (factional, as the party divided), the SRs' tendency to
act as a coalition of ideologically united but partly autonomous
organisations, and the Alliance of Liberation, which did not claim
even ideological unity over and above the broad demand for
constitutional rule and civil rights. Despite many teething problems,
the creation of alternative political leaderships of Russia advanced
dramatically. A reservoir of activists, extensive organisational
networks and expertise, publishing arrangements and actual 'propagandist' literature as well as growing contact outside the circle of
political activists were to play a major role in the events to come.

The social context magnified the impact of the Russian parties of dissent. The strategic anticipation set out already by Chernyshevskii and his followers in the People's Will was now beginning to come true.[23] In a society where most people were poor, parochial and politically dormant, the internal battles were fought between small elites, but the sleep of the plebeian giant was the final arbiter of the Old Order's survival. The nascent political parties still barely scratched the surface, but the Russian masses were now on the move. The growing confrontation between the 'common people' and the 'state' opened before the Russian political activists new perspectives and opportunities.

The contemporary statistics of 'crime against the state' showed the change which occurred during the period preceding the 1905–07 revolution.[24] Between 1884–90 and 1901–03, the annual figures representing 'non-political' crime increased very slowly, but the general number of those charged with crimes against the state increased fivefold (it doubled during the two years 1901–03). Also, while all its social subcategories increased in numbers, the share of those who were university-educated, of noblemen and of liberal professions among those charged dropped by half, or more, their place being filled by culprits with rudimentary education, engaged mostly in manual labour. Reversing the 3:17 urban:rural proportions in the population, two-thirds of those charged with 'crimes against the state' in 1901–02 were city dwellers (this figure was biassed, however, by the fact that Russian legal statistics usually classified rural confrontations as criminal rather than 'political', that is, state crime, but all the same, the high frequency of urban 'political crimes' was clear). The ethnic tilt towards the non-Russians was less directly stated but very strong. It was indicated by the religion of those condemned. Also, the largest cities of the country were ranked with regard to the intensity of the 'crimes against the state', that is, the annual average of those involved per million of population. Of the eight leading cities, six were non-Russian in the majority of their population. The figures were: Kiev (Ukraine) 520; Odessa (Ukraine) 384; Warsaw (Poland) 153; Lodz (Poland) 120; Riga (Latvia) 115; Kharkov (Ukraine) 112; St Petersburg (Russia) 97; Moscow (Russia) 54.

It was the percentage of manual labourers among political criminals which changed most dramatically: by 1901–03 manual labourers formed three-fifths of those charged compared to one-fourth in 1884–90. If defined according to the official 'social estate', the nobility, clergy and rich merchants dropped from 49.1 per cent to 16.4 per cent while the lower urban category (*meshchane*) went up from 27.5 per cent to 43.9 per cent and peasants (often urban residents in actuality) from 19.1 per cent to 37 per cent. Table 1.1 presents the figures by occupation.

TABLE 1.1   *Crime against the state: by occupation*

Occupation	1884–90	1901–03
State and army service	6.2	1.3
Liberal professions, salariat	21.7	17.8
Students	25.4	9.6
	53.3	28.7
Workers in Industry, services and crafts[a]	17.2	50.3
Agriculture[b]	7.4	9.0
	24.6	59.3
Commerce	2.2	4.0
Other or unknown	19.9	8.0

[a] In both periods the majority in this category (in 1901–3 about ⅔) worked in crafts and small enterprises rather than in the large factories.
[b] The figure is understated because most of the rural 'political crime' was defined as criminal rather than as 'crime against the state'.
Source:
E. Tarnovskii, Statisticheskie svedeniya o litsakh obvinyaemykh v prestupleniyakh gosudarstvenuykh, *Zhurnal ministerstva yustitsii* (1906) no. 4.

'Why is it nowadays that more and more political peasants (*politicheskie muzhiki*) are brought in? It used to be gentlemen, students and young ladies, but now it is the grey peasant workers like us (*nash rabochii brat seryi muzhik poshel*)'.[25] This enquiry by an elderly subwarden of the Moscow prison Taganka at the end of the nineteenth century was reported by M. Lyadov, then a prisoner, an RSDWP activist and later its historian. The question has well expressed the changing proportions between the 'political' gentlemen and the plebeians, a fundamental similarity between peasants and workers and an identification of the new rebels as belonging to the social sector from which the prison subwarden himself originated. The observations of the prison warden were shrewd. Prison officers often are.

D. FORCES OF ORDER AND THE FORCE OF ANGER

Notwithstanding romantic tales, revolutions cannot be understood simply by gazing at the revolutionary army. The powers-that-be, their nature and dynamics, their strength, limitations and choices constitute a major element of a revolutionary situation. The rising political tension was acknowledged not only by prison warders but also by the managers of the Russian state. The response was by policies combining suppression with appeasement, that is, a lot of suppression and fairly little appeasement. In 1901 deportations of students were followed by the legalisation of some student meetings under professiorial supervision. In 1902 a *Consultation* was set up under the chairmanship of Witte to advise on new peasant legislation. Following the 'agrarian disturbances' of 1902, the Tsar's manifesto abolished the rural collective responsibility for the payments of dues, while arrears of the peasant debts to the state were cancelled. More religious toleration was also promised at the same time. In 1903, in the wake of the hot summer of strikes, a system of shop stewards ('workers' elders') was officially introduced and the employers' duty to offer a pension to those who suffered work injuries was legislated. Simultaneously, the police penetration of the universities increased, rural guards were established in fifteen of the most troublesome provinces, *zemstvo* leaders and employees were persecuted and exiled and growing numbers of political arrests were made all through Russia, with particular attention given to clandestine party activists and to industrial workers. At 'the top' it meant a constant battle of argument and intrigue along the corridors of the ministerial palaces and at the Tsar's court, as suggestions of reform and repression clashed daily.

In *Russia as a 'Developing Society'* we presented the structure of the Russian state apparatus: the Tsar's closest circle of aides, the hierarchy, the state representation in a province (*guberniya*) and its subdivision (*uezd*), as well as the way the local authorities linked into it. The conflict between the reformist and the suppressive tendencies of the state bureaucrats was fought out at the turn of the century between the Ministry of Finance and the Ministry of the Interior. It climaxed in 1902–03 with a political duel between Witte and Pleve, the respective Ministers. It was the spirit of repression and the Ministry of the Interior which eventually came out on top rather than those who called for greater flexibility of response. Even while the supporters of appeasement had temporarily the tsar's ear, major departments of the Ministry of the Interior and, particularly, the political police and the governors of provinces proceeded to act as states within the state, undercutting or cutting down to size liberal ministerial initiatives and inconvenient laws.

It had been dawning on the more profound among the Russian bureaucrats that the piecemeal approach was insufficient to meet the gravity of the crisis which was building up. Something larger in scale was called for, a *deux ex machina* of some type. It had to be dramatic and come fast; a slow remedy could prove too slow. It was Pleve's turn to dominate Russia's politics as its Minister of the Interior and to produce such a remedy. It came in the form of a plan for a little successful war designed to re-establish social cohesion and order.[1] Japan was chosen as the whipping-boy.

Military prowess was crucial to the Russian state. Most of the country was a fairly recent conquest, and nearly all of it the result of 400 years of never-ending frontier war. The army was the tsar's main concern, guard, darling and legitimation. It was also the main employer and sinecure of the nobles, a major economic enterprise and the final argument in internal political strife. Waves of patriotic fever, triggered off by war, acted as a major mechanism of social consolidation around monarchist and nationalist symbols. For all these reasons, it also invariably took a defeat in war to shake the Russian autocracy to a point leading to a major reform or to its disintegration. Nor was it surprising that Russian dissent produced the toughest-ever group of 'defeatists', that is, of socialists who called for military defeat of their country as the best that could happen to its people. Since the Crimean war, 1853–56, the Russian army was unable singly to fight the Europeans. Colonial wars against the Asian natives could still be carried out successfully and cheaply, as evidenced by the conquest of the rest of the Caucasus in the nineteenth century, the conquest of Samarkand in 1868, of Khiva in 1873 and of Kokand in 1876, etc. The Russian intervention in China in 1900 brought it into direct conflict with Japan. A powerful lobby within the Russian government and the tsar's own family pressed for an aggressive Eastern policy and further conquests. These designs were internationally known, understood and acknowledged: in 1900, the parliament of Japan voted a large military budget declaring its aim to be 'saving the country from becoming another Khiva'.

The war with Japan began in January 1904.[2] To the Russians, it was an extraordinary war of boast, blunder and stupefying disaster. Inside Russia and all through the Western world, the defeat of Japan was considered only a question of time. The Russian standing army was five times that of Japan, its investment in the navy four times as large. Bets and plans were laid for the day of the Russian conquest of Tokyo, finally bringing all of Asia under European sway. The strategic plan prepared by the Russian C.-in-C. ended with 'the conquest of Tokyo and the taking prisoner of the Mikado'. It seemed that the only problem left was the speed with which Russian reinforcements could be transported to the Far East. Yet, all through the war the Russian army failed to win even one battle. They were beaten while still inferior in numbers at Yalu. They were beaten when equal or superior in strength at Lao Yan and Mukden. They even managed to lose when attacking a diminutive Japanese force at Matiey Ling. In every battle, ineffectual generalship, under-trained soldiers, faulty equipment and squandered personal courage of the troops were reported. In December 1904 the main Russian stronghold, Port Arthur, capitulated and its entire garrison was taken prisoner. As a final humiliation, in May 1905 at Tsushima, forty ships of the Russian navy were lost, sunk or captured, without a single ship being lost by the Japanese. Already by the summer of 1904 the fact of defeat was clear, shaking the Russian state to its core. The bankruptcy of tsardom's main justification, its military prowess, rapidly deepened the crisis within and between the Russian bureaucracy and the Russian nobility at the top of the social and political hierarchy of the Russian Empire.

By that time Pleve was dead, killed by a Socialist Revolutionary. His unlikely heir, Mirsky, a liberal within the Ministry of the Interior, attempted appeasement and called for 'a period of public trust', opening the door for petitions and debate. The patriotic addresses of 1903, at the beginning of the war, were now quite forgotten. A campaign of banquets followed, in which progressive landowners, well-moneyed burghers and representatives of the liberal professions called for urgent reforms. They were usually orchestrated by supporters of the Alliance for Liberation. On 6–9 November 1904, an illegal conference of representatives of the local authorities called for a constitution. Another major prop of tsardom, the self-censorship induced by the respectability and law-abiding nature of the middle classes and their loyalty in the face of an 'external enemy', was crumbling.[3] The government and the tsar's court were ambivalent and a beehive of rumours. The tsar himself wavered, a manifesto offering some form of nation-wide elections was drafted in December 1904, then its essential paragraph removed in the last moment before

publication. Dismissals and appointments of generals and ministers
followed in increasingly rapid succession. In December 1904,
Mirsky's influence crumbled, in turn being replaced by that of the
hard-liners.

By the end of 1904, the economic, political and military crisis of
Russian society, the crystallisation of social classes, the building-up of
political alternatives, the confusion, split and loss of nerve within the
ruling elite, all at once, indicated an approaching revolution. Yet the
workers' strikes and the peasant 'disturbances' were at there lowest in
years – the open confrontation was still limited to the upper echelons
of the realm. There, the writing on the wall was clear enough. At the
beginning of December, Prince Constantin, the tsar's uncle, wrote in
his diary: 'It is as if a ditch was breached here, within two to three
months all Russia has become engulfed by the wish for change . . .
Revolution is knocking at the door. Constitution is discussed in a
nearly open way. It's shameful and terrible'.[4]

This was the time for the state leadership to display to the fullest its
ultimate ineptitude and crass brutality. Dismissal of some of its
members led a police-sponsored workers' union to call a strike, which
rapidly escalated into a general strike of the workers of St Petersburg.
Its leader, Gapon, a priest and at least initially a police agent or its
stooge, was swept along by the emotional tide of hundreds of
thousands of poor and destitute and by the feeling of his own
omnipotence within those masses which looked to him for leadership.
He called for a demonstration in which the workers of Petersburg
were to petition their tsar and father against his bad advisers and beg
for improvement of the social and economic conditions for his
people. The spontaneous explosion of workers' demands, dreams
and solidarity swept along all the revolutionary groups which
operated among them and were now completely overtaken by
events.[5] On 9 January, 150 000 workers with their wives and
children, carrying the tsar's portraits and holy icons, went to the
palace to present their petition. They were met by gunfire and cavalry
charges which, by the end of the day, left hundreds of them dead or
wounded.[6] A fortnight after its main fortress at Port Arthur had
fallen to the Japanese, the thrice-defeated Russian army had finally
won a battle, putting down an unarmed demonstration of monarchist
workers on its way to their tsar to beg his mercy.

*   *   *

Social scientists often miss a centre-piece of any revolutionary struggle – the fervour and anger which drives revolutionaries and makes them into what they are. Academic training and bourgeois convention deaden its appreciation. The 'phenomenon' cannot be easily 'operationalised' into factors, tables and figures. Sweeping emotions feel vulgar or untrue to those sophisticated to the point of detachment from real life. Yet, without this factor, any understanding of revolution falls flat. That is why clerks, bankers, generals and social scientists so often fail to see revolutionary upswing even when looking at it directly.[7]

At the very centre of revolution lies an emotional upheaval of moral indignation, revulsion and fury with the powers-that-be, such that one cannot demur or remain silent, whatever the cost. Within its glow, for a while, men surpass themselves, breaking the shackles of intuitive self-preservation, convention, day-to-day convenience and routine. To be sure, it is still a minority which is ready to throw its very life on the scale, yet it must inevitably grow large enough for the scales to begin to move. Different social groups and individuals will respond differently, yet the community of emotions will form a major unifying link of the revolutionary battle-line when the chips are down. It will irresistibly draw the more sensitive and honest members of the ruling class, its youth, its intellectuals and its moralists, and make them turn against their own environment, elders and peers.

It should not come as a surprise, therefore, that it was Lev Tolstoy, Russia's greatest writer, a noble hostile to the revolutionaries, who, in the wake of their suppression in late 1907, voiced most clearly what in those years was in the hearts of many, and without which the tale of the revolution would stay inexplicable. One cannot and should not try to improve on what he said:

I cannot stay silent . . . Today in Kherson on the Strelbitsky field, twelve peasants were hung for 'an attack with intent to rob' on a landed proprietor's estate in the Elisavetgrad district. Twelve of those by whose labour we live, the very men whom we have deprived and are still depriving by every means in our power – from the poison of vodka to the terrible falsehood of a faith we impose on them with all our might, but do not ourselves believe in – twelve of these men strangled by cords by those whom they feed and clothe and house and who have deprived and still continue to deprive them. Twelve husbands, fathers and sons from among those upon whose kindness, industry and simplicity alone rest the whole of Russian life, are seized, imprisoned and shackled. Their hands are tied behind their backs, lest they could seize the ropes by which they are to be hung and they are led to the gallows. Several peasants similar to those about to be hanged, dressed in clean soldier's uniform with good boots on their feet and with guns in their hands accompany the condemned men . . .

This is dreadful, but most dreadful of all is the fact that it is not done impulsively under the sway of feeling that silences reason, as occurs in fights, war and even burglary, but on the contrary it is done at the demand of reason and calculation that silence feeling. That is what makes this deed so particularly dreadful. Dreadful because these acts – committed by men who, from the judge to the hangman, do not wish to do them – prove more vividly than any thing else how pernicious to a human soul is despotism; the power of men over men . . .

While this goes on for years all over Russia, the chief culprits – those by whose orders the things are done, those who could put a stop to them – fully convinced that such deeds are useful and even absolutely necessary, either compose speeches and devise methods to prevent the Finns from living as they want to live and to compel them to live as certain Russian personages wish them to live, or else publish orders to the effect that: 'In Hussar regiments the cuff and collars of men's jackets are to be of the same colour as the latter, while those entitled to wear pelisses are not to have braid round the cuffs over the fur' . . .

Everything now being done in Russia is done in the name of general welfare, in the name of the protection and tranquility of the people of Russia. And if this is so, then it is also done for me who lives in Russia. For me, therefore, exists the destitution of the people deprived of the first and most natural right of man – the right to use the land on which he is born; for me, those half million men torn away from wholesome peasant life and dressed in uniforms and taught to kill; for me the false, so-called priesthood whose chief duty is to pervert and conceal true Christianity; for me, all this transportation of men from place to place; for me, these hundreds of thousands of migratory workmen; for me, these hundreds of thousands of unfortunates dying of typhus and scurvy in fortresses and prisons which are insufficient for such a multitude; for me, the mothers, wives and fathers of the exiled, the prisoners and those who are hanged and suffering; for me, are the spies and the bribery; for me, the internment of these dozens and hundreds of men who have been shot; for me, the horrible work of the hangman goes on . . .

It is impossible to live so! I at any rate cannot and will not live so. That is why I write this and will circulate it by all means in my power, both in Russia and abroad – that one of two things may happen: either that these inhumane deeds may be stopped, or that my connection with them may be snapped and I put in prison, where I may be clearly conscious that these horrors are not committed on my behalf. Or still better (so good that I dare not even dream of such happiness) that they may put on me, as on those twelve or twenty peasants, a shroud and a cap and may push me also off a bench so that by my own weight I may tighten the well-soaped noose around my old throat.[8]

Many thousands of Russians who felt similarly did not have Tolstoy's power of speech in condemnation and the luxuries of a princeling to which to relate horror and shame, but by 1905 they carried the same blazing fury of indignation and revulsion overriding any other concerns. And they were ready to fight.

2 Revolution from Below: Down with Autocracy!

Happy is the nation whose people have not forgotten how to rebel.
Richard Henry Tawney

A. A TALE OF A REVOLUTION: JANUARY 1905 TO APRIL 1906

Most narratives proffer precise dates when revolutions begin. The temptation to keep it so stems from the neatness which such periodisations offer, the usual preference of scholars for unequivocability of time and space. Such dating hides the unevenness of revolutionary developments, that is, a most substantive characteristic of any revolution. That excepted, the date, 9 January 1905, is useful for taking stock of Russia's revolutionary situation.

During the weeks directly following the Bloody Sunday of 9 January, revolutionaries and constitutionalists strained their organisations and propaganda to the utmost, calling for mass protest. The response was considerable. Central to it hundreds of thousands of workers reacted by solidarity strikes protesting against the massacre in St Petersburg. The records, while showing an all-time peak in strike figures, usually neglect regional diversities.[1] The reaction of the workers was geographically uneven: relatively limited in Central Russia, much more substantial at the peripheries. The strike in Moscow was sluggish and petered out fast. Of the Russian provincial cities only the non-industrial Saratov responded by a general strike.[2] In St Petersburg the strike declined after a few days and practically ended by 14 January. On the same day, Warsaw exploded in a general strike, with mass demonstrations under red flags, barricades and confrontations with the army and police, which after a furious week left more than 200 killed and wounded *on both sides*. Strikes

34

and confrontations spread throughout the Polish provinces of Russia and especially to the industrial centre of Lodz, with more killed, wounded and arrested. Within that period there were as many strikers in the Polish provinces (which held less than one-tenth of the population of the Empire) as in the rest of Russia.[3] In the Baltic provinces and in the predominantly Jewish cities of the north-west, the reaction was also very powerful. Political strikes, demonstrations, volleys, cavalry charges and armed responses followed in Riga, Mitava, and Libava, while general strikes took place in Revel, Vilna, Bialystok and scores of smaller places. In the Caucasus, Tiflis witnessed a similar picture of strikes, demonstrations, barricades and armed confrontation which spread all through Georgia. Massive demonstrations under red banners and armed clashes with police were reported in the cities of Finland.

The intelligentsia and the middle classes of Russia sharply stepped up the protest action which had already begun in the summer of 1904. The revolutionaries of 'the educated class' were now on the streets, shoulder-to-shoulder with the demonstrating workers. Since 1904 members of the Alliance of Liberation had been promoting a chain of 'banquets' for the better-off, where constitutional demands were formulated and declared. The Bloody Sunday of 9 January, and further news of defeats from the battlefield, brought this protest to a new pitch. During this period practically every meeting of a professional body, for example, the Pirogov Society of medical doctors or that of the agronomists and rural statisticians, turned into a demonstration of anti-government views and emotions.[4] One after another, they proclaimed constitutional demands and condemned the government for repressions. Members of the Academy of Sciences, writers, lawyers, etc., signed letters of protest. With all universities closed by the authorities 'until further notice', the students were on strike, joining and organising demonstrations all around the country. At the peripheries, ethnically-defined cultural associations which took the initiative in opposing Russification, gained new massive support. Even a major group of Moscow capitalists, in the past a bulwark of traditional loyalism, made their opposition known by protesting publicly against police brutality and demanding legal trade unions free from police interference. The Manufacturers' Association, in a show of defiance, voted to grant financial support to the families of the victims of the Bloody Sunday of 9 January. In February *zemstvo* representatives held another semi-legal conference calling for democratic elections and agrarian reform.

Still in February, while the wave of strikes was beginning to decline, a sharp increase in 'agrarian disturbances' was reported in the rural areas and agricultural strikes began in the Baltic provinces and Poland. Also in February, a PSR terrorist squad killed Prince Sergei, Governor of Moscow, the tsar's uncle and one of the most reactionary members of the ruling elite.

The tsar's first reaction to the revolutionary up-swing was to appoint General F. Trepov as the Governor of St Petersburg on 11 January. (Within a short time he was to become also Vice-Minister of the Interior and for a while the virtual dictator of Russia.) He was curtly told to restore order by all necessary means. The tension of the tsar's court was high. Stern security measures and the fear of terrorists made the tsar a virtual prisoner of his own palace in Tsarskoe Selo. His courtiers and advisers were split, offering contradictory advice, with some of them suggesting reforms and a parliament while the 'hard-liners' called for increased repressions. For a time, Trepov himself wavered between both.[5] In the capital, employers were being pressured by the authorities to give way to the economic demands of the striking workers in order to let off steam. By the middle of February, the defeat at Mukden made it clear that the war with Japan could not be won. On 18 February, the tsar decreed the need to assemble 'the best people of Russia', representative of its population, for consultations on further legislation. The Minister of the Interior, Bulygin, was ordered to work out ways of implementing the new venture. His call for petitions and suggestions on that matter opened a new major channel for public protest and dissent. Not only legal changes, but also major socio-economic reforms were urgently reviewed by the government. In March, the Minister of Agriculture, Ermolov, begged the tsar to take immediate action to increase the land in peasant use before it was too late.[6] At the same time, army units were being dispatched to put down 'agrarian disturbances' and to strengthen the urban garrisons throughout the empire, while arrests of the radicals increased sharply.

During the next half-year, Russia seemed to spark with dissent, opposition, riot and rebellion, which never merged into a general explosion.[7] The forests and grazing land of the nobility were invaded and rural strikes spread. In some parts of the Black-Earth region, estates were 'taken apart' in a way reminiscent of events in Poltava during 1902. A number of spectacular and stubborn strikes were fought in Ivanovo, Nizhnii, Ekaterinoslav, Odessa, Bialystok, Tiflis,

Kovno, etc. However, the national figures for workers on strike never reached even half the numbers of those recorded in January 1905, and the May Day demonstrations were a failure. At the same time the workers' movement had broadened considerably with new occupational groups drawn into self-organisation and strike action; waiters, salesmen, even domestic servants attempted to unionise. A general strike, which led to barricades and street battles, took place once again in Lodz between 5 and 13 June, triggering off solidarity strikes all through Poland. In August, Warsaw saw its fourth political strike since the beginning of the year.

The organisation of the Russian professional middle classes and the trade unions proceeded to grow in strength and in radicalism. New associations were being created by Russia's professional groups. In May, a Union of Unions was set up with its goal the unification of all the middle-class and working-class occupational organisations. The confederation established consisted at first of a rather heterogeneous group of sixteen organisations of journalists and engineers, agronomists and lawyers, railwaymen and bookkeepers, as well as the associations for the equality of Jews, for the emancipation of women, and the *Zemstvo* Constitutionalists faction. Politically, its members and spokesmen represented a variety of views, liberal as well as socialist.[8] They all demanded democratisation and a constitution declaring solidarity with any anti-government struggle. These unions were consistently harassed by the police, and grew increasingly militant with time. A new congress of *zemstvos* met in May and sent a delegation to lecture the tsar about the virtues of an enlightened monarchy and parliamentarianism. Their next congress in July was joined also by the councillors of the municipalities of major cities and adopted a new proposal for a constitution and for democratic freedom aiming to bring Russia in line with its western neighbours. Even the clergy produced demands for reform: the re-establishment of an elective patriarch's office (instead of the church synod being directed by a state official).

For a moment, in late May and June, the threshold of revolution seemed to have been reached. The peasant 'disturbances' reached a climax, while the workers' strikes intensified once again, with more street fighting in the Polish provinces. On 14–15 May a shattering defeat at Tsushima sent the rest of the Russian navy to the bottom of the sea or into captivity. The tsar's most loyal supporters were shocked, the middle classes furious, while the revolutionaries gloated at this new display of official incompetence. The Union of Unions called for demonstrations of protest. The workers' strikes were increasingly political in goals and demands. A peasant meeting, called by the marshal of the nobility of Moscow's *guberniya* to express patriotic support of the government, used the rostrum for a major anti-governmental initiative to organise the Russian peasants. The very edifice of the tsar's power, the army and its loyalty, was now in doubt. Rioting soldiers were reported in the Asian parts of Russia. A conference of Cossack officers, the leaders of the crack force for internal repressions, begged the tsar to offer a constitution to Russia.[9] In June, the Black Sea sailors of the battleship Potemkin rebelled, arrested their officers and brought their ship into Odessa, which was gripped by a city-wide strike. The rest of the navy refused to obey orders to have the ship attacked and sunk.

However, the dissenters and rebels lacked unity, organisation, arms and experience. The State machinery held once more. The army and navy rebellions were contained, with the mutineers court-martialled or on the run. Arrest and punitive expeditions hit hard at the peasants, the workers and the radical intelligentsia. Pogroms against the radicals and the Jews showed signs of mobilisation of the pro-government unofficial terror. Muslim attacks on the Armenians in the Caucasus played a less direct yet similar role, deflecting local anti-government pressure. In August and September the peasant attacks, workers' strikes and political demonstrations were at their lowest point since the beginning of 1905. The government seemed to have weathered the storm once more. On 6 August, the Minister of the Interior published a decree calling a Duma, designed to take care of the constitutionalist demands. The Duma was to act as an advisory body only and to be elected through a system of indirect vote within electoral colleges (*kurii*) consisting of different social estates or property groups. The electoral regulations secured an extensive share of those due to be elected by the Russian peasants – presumed to be monarchist and conservative. On 23 August, a peace agreement was signed with Japan on conditions fairly advantageous to Russia.

The Russian revolutionaries faced the explosions of mass dissent with exasperating feelings of weakness, organisational inadequacy and missed opportunities. The means at their disposal: some thousands of activists, a few illegal publications and printing shops, the thin net of circles of worker and peasant sympathisers and a few caches of small arms, looked pitiful when compared with the tsar's army, bureaucracy and police. To exemplify, the rather optimistic recent estimate of workers–supporters of the RSDWP (all its factions) in St Petersburg of early 1905 was 'nearly 700'.[10] An even greater disparity was evident when the number of organised revolutionaries was compared with the millions of underdogs who were beginning to move into action. Severe ideological tensions, splits and emigration squabbles within the revolutionary camp made things considerably worse.[11]

All this makes the energy with which those groups went into action even more impressive. Braving frontiers and distances, ex-prisoners and emigrés were coming back to join the struggle. New members were rapidly acquired and thrown immediately into action. The budgets of revolutionary organisations increased tenfold, providing resources for printing materials and arms.[12] Russia was showered with millions of leaflets, pamphlets and books calling for an end to autocracy. The three major nation-wide party organisations of revolutionary socialists – Mensheviks, Bolsheviks and the SRs – as well as dozens of regional and ethnic organisations, rapidly acquired consistency of structure, internal discipline, new membership, more sophisticated programmes and tactical experience. Numerous new groups were organised all around the country. The terrorist organisation of the Socialist Revolutionaries (BO PSR) was in action, aiming especially at those leading the army's punitive operations. Inter-party co-ordination committees were being set up in many places to try to overcome divisions which were impediments to action.

Despite all this, and on their own admission, the organised Russian revolutionaries had still barely scratched the surface in so far as the 'deep layers' of Russian people were concerned. Rough estimates spoke of 25 000 revolutionaries in early 1905 for a population of 120 million (excluding the western periphery), a rate of 0.04 per cent within Russia's mature population. At its pre-1917 peak of 1906, the membership of the socialist parties supporting revolutionary struggle in Russia (excluding the Polish provinces) was said to have reached about 190 000, that is, 44 000 SD Bolsheviks, 43 500 SD Mensheviks, 36 500 Jewish Bund and Latvian SD, 60 000 SRs and an assumed 6000 for the smaller groups (SR maximalists, Anarchists, etc.).[13] It would mean a rate slightly above 0.3 per cent or 1:315 of the mature population. The number of available guns and men trained to use them on the side of the revolutionaries could still be counted in hundreds or in dozens. All these figures were many times lower in the countryside.

What made this challenge plausible was the fact that the state apparatus and the ruling classes of Russia were also a drop in the ocean of the Russian population. They were also split, demoralised, for a time bewildered and unsure of the loyalty of the armed forces. They commanded an army which was mostly of peasant stock while a peasant rebellion was growing. Especially in the areas with the highest concentration of revolutionaries, the large industrial cities and the ethnic peripheries, their chances in 1905 did not look at all hopeless.

To proceed with the tale, the next revolutionary wave rose in September 1905. For once, it challenged head-on the general ability of tsardom to master Russia. It commenced with the outburst of opposition to the 'consultative' Duma. The decree published in August produced a united front and a focus for the entire opposition which demanded a proper parliament: the socialists of different brands, most of the liberals, the nationalists at the periphery, the non-party activists. On the last day of August, and nearly accidentally, the government restored the university autonomy which had been abolished in the 1890s, and permitted the universities to reopen. In September the students decided to end their strike but, instead of returning to studies, put the university compounds to revolutionary use. In every university city and especially in St Petersburg and Moscow, the universities were turned into an island of free speech, a permanent mass meeting with thousands of party activists and non-party workers, and 'educated classes' constantly rubbing shoulders, arguing, exchanging literature and organising. Police watched it in bewildered confusion, elderly professors shrugged shoulders but felt bound to tolerate it in view of their own demands for free speech and the manifest lack of any other place where such principles could be exercised. By the end of the month, small underground groups and 'circles' of 'professional revolutionaries' were developing (and partly dissolving) into massive, rapidly growing memberships. New oppositional newspapers were quickly established. New associations and unions came daily into being, by-passing laws and consolidating into new national organisations. The workers' trade unions and militancy were growing rapidly. In the same month, preparing for what by now seemed to be the final battle approaching, a number of covert organisations of army sympathisers were set up by the revolutionary parties. The non-party Officers Union, strongly influenced by the SRs, was the most significant.[14]

At the beginning of October, an unsubstantiated rumour of an arrest of its union's delegates led the newly-created National

Committee of the different categories of railway workers (then in Moscow and under the influence of the SRs) to call a political strike.[15] It brought to a stop all trains, with the exception of those few which carried the Union's delegates to the regional conferences, to discuss the railwaymen's demands. The Union of Unions mobilised support for its largest constituent member – the All-Russian Union of the Railways' Employees. The solidarity strike spread rapidly with other industries, services and professions joining in. By 17 October a national general strike was on. It involved the majority of Russia's industrial workers (about 1.5 million), executive and clerical staff (about 200 000) and most of the country's members of the professions.[16]

It was not only the sheer force of numbers – immense as these were – which shook Russia. For Russia, as well as for the world at large, it was the first general strike in which the great majority of industrial workers, employees and intelligentsia of a multi-ethnic Empire were out in support of common political demands. This time, both the centre of the country and its peripheries were involved. Even the sleepiest of the provincial localities, Russia's 'bear holes', were for the first time drawn into political life.

As a major expression of the strikers' self-organisation, a Council of Factory and Workshop Representatives, that is, a *Soviet*, came into being in the capital.[17] It first met on 12 October in the building of the University of St Petersburg, establishing a working-class parliament in the city. Its 562 delegates represented the city's 147 factories and some fifty workshops. Its executive committee had rapidly grown into an alternative authority within the city and to which, increasingly, workers, political militants and other organisations of dissent looked for leadership and inspiration. Its image struck the imagination of the country as a whole. The Union of Unions was overshadowed by it, but proceeded to operate energetically, focusing the support of radical intelligentsia. Soviets were being set up in other cities: Moscow, Rostov, Odessa, Ivanovo–Voznesensk, etc. (see Map No. 1 on page 72). Militants of the illegal parties surfaced to lead and address massive demonstrations, by now spreading everywhere. News was also coming in about a sharp upturn in 'agrarian disturbances' in the south of Russia. The 'peripheries' of the empire were increasingly reported out of control.

A crescendo of complaints about the insufficiency of army and police units available for the maintenance of 'law and order' rose within the squiredom and the administration. The whole gigantic machinery of autocracy had seemingly come to a halt, with its communication and transportation networks suddenly out of action. Bureaucrats were left without orders, governors and policemen were not told what to do next, army units could not be transported, even the tsar's own day-to-day routine of ruling via ministerial audiences and authorisation of decrees was upset. The order taken for granted was falling apart. Russia could not be run. Panic was growing at the top.

On 12 October, Trepov issued orders to the army 'not to spare ammunition' in the 'suppression of mutiny', but the tsar's advisers were split once more as to what to do. In his report to the tsar Witte summed it up as a straight choice between military dictatorship and constitutional reform. Within days, Prince Nikolai Nikolaievich, the tsar's uncle, commander of the guard regiments and major candidate for the military dictator's job, tearfully begged the tsar to accept conciliatory proposals. On 17 October, an official text of the tsar's manifesto had been published, informing Russia that freedom of speech, assembly, and organisation were granted, while the Duma was upgraded from a consultative to a legislative body. Witte's memorandum, published simultaneously, amplified the aim of the reform as the establishment of a 'legal system' (*Pravovoi stroi*) presented as the new guiding concept (and an implicit antonym to *samoderzhavie*, that is, the autocratic rule by the immediate and unlimited will of the tsar).[18] An amnesty of many of the political prisoners proceeded within days. The democratic constitution of Finland, suspended in 1899, was brought back. A cabinet of ministers was set up (taking the place of the earlier arrangement in which each minister was individually appointed by the tsar and responsible to him only). On 21 October, Trepov resigned. Sergei Witte became the first Prime Minister charged with execution of the reform, while P. Durnovo took over the Ministry of the Interior and the leadership of the repressive apparatus.

The surprise was general, for the changes from above were unexpected or not expected so soon. The organisations which objected to the consultative Duma reacted at once against its amended version. The revolutionary parties, the Soviet of St Petersburg, the Union of Unions, etc., proceeded to demand a 'one-man–one-vote' Constitutional Assembly. By now a split was developing between those who believed that the reform of 17 October should be given a chance and those aiming to destroy the autocracy and to create a republic, or at least to secure effective control of the electorate over 'the executive', then and there. The issue was that of power as opposed to trust in the tsar's constitutional promise. With that in mind, the radicals tried to keep the general strike going, but failed. Most of the strikers celebrated political victory and returned to work. In the meantime, freedom of speech and assembly spread, bypassing the legitimate channels and arrogating civil liberties through the 'self-authorisation' (*yavochnym poryadkom*) of organisations, newspapers and meetings. Russia's political life seemed transformed overnight. This spell of 'blossoming of a hundred flowers' was later to be acclaimed as 'the days of freedom' (*dni svobody*) in the collective memory of Russian intellectual dissent.

The holiday mood came to an end within days, as violence rapidly spread.[19] With the general strike over, the army and the police moved 'to restore order', especially along the railway lines, at the non-Russian peripheries and in rural Russia. Simultaneously, the loyalists of the localities, thousands of small owners and traders, petty officials and impoverished nobles, low-grade policemen, pub patriots and some of the peasants reacted to the scandal of mass disorders, red flags and what seemed like governmental appeasement of mutineers with fury and dismay. Their force lay, to a large degree, with urbanites who did not qualify either as the privileged estate of nobility nor as the rich merchants (the 'White Hundreds' in the medieval Russian usage). This social composition made for their popular nickname – the Black Hundreds. Their gut reaction was often guided or organised by police. Mass pogroms swept Russia, in which thousands of radicals, intellectuals, *zemstvo* activists, socialist workers and students, as well as 'aliens', especially Jews, were hunted down and attacked by crowds carrying the tsar's picture and holy icons, and increasingly armed. Several mass organisations of these forces came into being, and by 1906 the Association of the Russian People became the most prominent. It was promptly accorded the tsar's audience, warmly embraced by many of his officials and granted financial aid from the secret funds of the Ministry of Interior.[20]

On the Left, armed detachments (*druzhiny*) were rapidly being set up, extended and trained in the cities and in some rural areas, both as self-defence against the pogroms and as an armed force prepared to do battle for a republic. On 23 October, the sailors of Kronstadt rebelled, and during the next few months a number of army and navy units attempted mutiny or rejected police duties. These military mutinies were on the whole spontaneous and short-lived. The attempts of the revolutionary parties to direct them failed.[21]

While the Russian cities were increasingly locked in combat over state power, the peasant rebellion spread over half of European Russia. The ambivalence and unease of the authorities was at its highest where Russian peasants were concerned. The October manifesto said nothing of land reform, but on 3 November, a new manifesto by the tsar was rushed through, abolishing the remainder of the 1861 redemption payments and extending the activities of the Peasant Bank aimed at facilitating the peasants' purchase of land. Repressive measures hit the villagers particularly hard, but, at the same time, two of the most influential commanders of the repressive forces within the inner circles of the tsar's advisers – Trepov and Dubasov – declared the need for urgent agrarian reform (and even their own readiness to give up some of their personal landed estates in order to keep the rest).

Most of what happened in Russia was repeated 'with double accentuation' at its western and southern peripheries. We shall discuss the rural struggles there in Chapter 3. The Polish, Latvian, Est, Georgian, Armenian and Jewish urbanites usually outmatched their Russian equivalents in intensity of political confrontation with the government forces. For a while, in late 1905, whole regions of the Baltic provinces and of Georgia were taken over by revolutionaries. The military response was much harsher in the non-Russian areas. Martial law was first declared in the Polish provinces and later spread to most of the provinces in the empire.

Despite the mutinies of some units and lack of sympathy with the 'internal war' by many of its men, the discipline held in most of the Russian armed forces, especially in its cavalry units. This was sufficient for effective repressions to proceed and defined their outcome. Under the martial law, the freshly-granted constitutional provisions were mostly disregarded. Punitive expeditions by army units proceeded all through Russia with numerous executions based on suspicion and often without a trial. They shelled and burned rebellious villages, arrested and executed striking railmen, flogged and fined whole communities. The police concentrated on tracking down and arresting party activists and leaders of the revolutionary movement, workers and intelligentsia, now exposed by the freedom of speech and assembly. Thousands were put on trial, while about 45 000 were exiled by administrative orders during the period October–December. The informal executions of rebels by the

punitive expeditions were matched by the official executions increasingly enacted by the courts for 'crimes against the state'.[22]
Obninskii, a major liberal chronicler of those times, called them, in
retrospect, the period of 'liberty and gallows'.

What was taking place was an open battle over who ruled Russia
and how. At issue was the very existence of autocracy, whatever the
niceties or pretence of the tsar's manifestos, government decrees and
party programmes. The most effective weapon of those who opposed
it was that of the massive political mobilisation of dissent within the
population of the Empire, especially within its plebeian classes, allied
for once with its most outspoken group – the intelligentsia. Vigorous
organisations, newly-established or extended beyond recognition, yet
remarkably effective, created a new political scene. The centuries-old
tsardom found itself face-to-face with an alternative or alternatives,
which took strength from popular support, the mostly spontaneous
self-discipline of the opposition and mass readiness for sacrifices. The
workers' Soviets and unions, the associations of intelligentsia, the
Union of Unions and an All-Russia Peasant Union, ethnic organisations, newspapers, publishing houses and the illegal political parties
provided the structure of the camp of opposition to the autocracy.
The arrogation of authority (*yavochnyi poryadok*) was the main 1905
tactic of the radical opposition, testing as well as defining anew and
extending the frontiers of civil liberty in the face of a retreating
government. In late 1905, industrial workers were its main shock
troops, at least in the large cities of central Russia. Political strike was
their most potent weapon against the government. (See Map 1 on
page 72.)

Against this new world of political opposition stood the Old Order.
To most of the population it had lost, by October 1905, its main
trappings of authority: the common belief in the inevitability of 'what
is', the nationalist appeal, the fear of a uniform as much as the dread
of what 'anarchy' might lead to, the inertia of 'orderly behaviour',
even the tsar's mystique. However, the State machinery for the
management of compulsion stayed largely intact. Also the 'great fear'
of revolution, while making some of the dignitaries look for a
compromise, mobilised at the side of the autocracy (to be exact, at its
politically extreme right wing) a loyalist camp of those who were
usually apathetic.

*   *   *

Witte began his spell as the first constitutional Prime Minister with an attempt to bring the situation under control through a bout of deft political juggling: to broaden the government's political base, to outmanoeuvre the extremists of the opposition, to increase government authority, and to humour the tsar, while keeping him scared enough to leave his Prime Minister to exercise enough of the actual power. Simultaneously, a counter-attack by the army and the police was to bring to an end 'disorders', namely workers' political strikes, peasant jacquery, the breakdown of discipline in some of the army units and the many organisations challenging the state bureaucracy. It became clear within days that Witte was failing in his political solutions and attempts at incorporation – the forces unleashed by the revolution could not be appeased by quick footwork or a clever intrigue. He tried to reach a compromise with the liberals in the process of creating their most powerful party – the Constitutional Democrats (the KDs, who adopted the name of Party of Popular Liberty). The price set by him for a measure of power-sharing in which some of them would join his administration was that of an end to their alliance with the radicals – 'cutting off the Liberationists' revolutionary tail', as he put it. The KDs did not want to, and probably could not, oblige: the radicalisation of the educated middle classes and the struggle in the Russian cities and villages were too powerful to permit such a compromise. Witte's appeal to the workers to moderate their militancy, entitled 'Brothers Workers' (*bratsy rabochie*), drew only the St Petersburg Soviet's humorous response informing the country that the workers of the city do not recognise themselves as having kinship relations with the Minister. The tsar's first minister was deeply mistrusted by the Left as well as by the Right.

This political failure left repression as the only prong of government strategy in the period leading up to the election and the meeting of the country's first parliament. In his later memoirs, Witte blamed the 1905 repressions on Durnovo, the Minister of the Interior, and on the tsar's preference for such policies. Evidence has since shown that Witte was deeply involved in the planning of the repressions, the organisation of punitive expeditions and in the systematic legislative action restraining many of the freedoms granted in the October Manifesto of 1905.[23] The revolutionary situation and lack of response of the KD to his approaches limited his scope of manoeuvre but did not change his goals. These were to keep the essence of autocratic powers in the hands of the state executive (preferably directed by himself).

On the other side, the heterogeneity of the opposition had by now grown and was expressed in the increasing inter-party debate. The SDs, the SRs, the KDs and many of the nationalist movements at the periphery treated the general strike and the October Manifesto as only a preliminary to the 'real liberty', still to be wrenched from the government. What to do next was less clear. The SDs and SRs saw the future as a revolution leading to the establishment of a republic and to massive social reforms. The liberals were increasingly split into those who wanted to make the October Manifesto and the *Duma* work and those who still demanded a one-man–one-vote parliament and social reforms. Even to them the revolutionary forms of struggle were acceptable in October 1905 mainly as a tool to pressure the government into reforms. The nationalist movements at the peripheries were also divided in their tactics between those who took a leaf from the book of Russian Socialists and those who learned from the Russian Liberals (ever aiming to use it for their particular goals, that is, autonomy or independence of the specific regions they represented).

By the beginning of 1906, as the balance of forces shifted against the revolutionaries, the KDs and their equivalents at the 'peripheries' came increasingly to dissociate themselves from the revolutionary Left.[24] Step by step, their position shifted to an absolute commitment to 'legal action' and, by 1907, to the slogan of 'defending the Duma at any cost'.

In November 1905 the results of the confrontation all over Russia seemed still in abeyance. *Ex post facto* it was to be the view of many that November 1905 saw the tsar's government at its weakest. The impact of the socialists was tremendous. Political strikes followed one another to procure the highest monthly figure of strikers in Russia in December 1905. A refusal to pay taxes was called for and an appeal for military disobedience issued in response to the government's repressive action by a coalition of dissenters led by the St Petersburg Soviet. Peasants burned manors; much of Latvia and Georgia refused to obey the 'rightful authorities', as did many urban workers' districts of the Russian and Polish provinces. Siberia was on fire, mutinous troops and rebellious workers blocked for a while the Trans-Siberian railway and took over the city of Irkutsk. Still in the Far East, the garrison of Chita, including its senior officers and the general in charge, called for reforms and spoke against 'the political usage of the army' by the government. In November navy units rebelled in Sevastopol. They were led by Lieutenant Shmidt, who was shortly to enter the list of revolutionary martyrs. Government military action was now often met by force, policemen and soldiers were killed or disarmed. These actions and reactions, however, did not blunt the government offensive. Owners of industry were also now ready to do battle with their workers. They refused the demand for an 8-hour working day and the St Petersburg strike aiming for it was defeated by a massive lock-out.

In late November and early December, the members of the Petersburg Soviet and the General Committee of the Peasant Union were arrested and the impact of these two major 'alternative governments' of the plebeian elected representatives began to decline. New clandestine leaderships were promptly set up but both organisations were eventually destroyed.[25] Only a mute response came from their hard-pressed supporters.

In December and January, civil war was still raging with the government forces gaining the upper hand. The monarchist press referred to the period as that of the 'resurrection of state power' (*vozrozhdene vlasti*). On 7 December one more political general strike was called. It failed in St Petersburg, weakened by arrests, but was powerfully supported in Moscow. On 9 December, the Moscow strike developed into a confrontation with the army and police which led to an armed uprising of the socialist detachments (*druzhiny*) of the SDs and SRs, supported by part of the city's population, especially workers.[26] The courage of the detachments, mostly workers who together with some students and 'professional revolutionaries' fought a house-to-house battle, could not outweigh their small numbers, lack of military skills and shortage of arms. The revolutionaries were caught up in a war for which they were clearly ill-prepared.[27] The attempts to neutralise the army's strength by political appeals failed – no soldiers deserted or disobeyed in the army units crushing the Moscow rebellion. The rebellion lasted until 20 December, by which time it had been put down with the use of the Guards' infantry and artillery. A number of lesser uprisings occurred in other Russian cities in response to the Moscow struggle, and were quashed. On 22 December, the *druzhiny* dispersed themselves in Rostov, the last Russian city where the workers' district witnessed direct control by revolutionaries. During January 1906, government forces reported the quelling of uprisings in the Baltic provinces and the Caucasus, as well as a sharp drop in peasant 'disturbances' in Central Russia. Likewise in January 1906, the punitive expeditions finally overcame dissenting railwaymen and soldiers along the Russian railway lines as well as in the Far Eastern cities of Chita and Vladivostok.

The fight was not over yet, nor did either the governments or revolutionaries believe it to be. The confrontation entered a new stage and took new forms while retaining considerable continuity with the struggle of 1905. In mid-January 1906, Witte reported to the tsar that, while the rebellion in the cities was by now finally crushed, a new wave of peasant unrest was to be expected in the summer.[28] The government was using the respite to reorganise and to improve the grip of the army, police and administration. Incompetent or suspect officers were purged, doubtful army units disbanded, radical newspapers and publications stopped, editors arrested and fined, associations and organisations of the opposition persecuted. There were mass dismissals of 'unreliable' workers in many enterprises as well as of radical employees of the local authorities: engineers, doctors, agronomists, lawyers. Such a dismissal was often coupled with administrative orders of exile. Simultaneously, the state negotiated a major international loan to stabilise the state budget, badly shaken by war and revolution.

The government also proceeded with a major effort to water down the October reforms by further legislation and new restrictive interpretations of the laws already passed. This operation centred on 'secret meetings' of state dignitaries – chaired by the tsar and held in his Summer Palace – to work out new legislation, subsequently decreed by the government or proclaimed by the tsar.[29] On 15 December, 1905, such a meeting decided on the nature of the electoral law. A multi-stage election by social estates and property classes was to take place in which every *Kuria* (that is, a social-and-property related electoral college) was to select its own representatives, the general gatherings of whom were to elect the deputies to the Duma in every *guberniya*. The way the electoral colleges were set up provided for the larger representation of the 'propertied classes'. Women were not given the right to vote and a minimum age of 25 was set for the electors. In February 1906, a new State Council was decreed, to be partly appointed by the tsar and equivalent to the Duma in its powers of legislation. Every law had to be agreed upon by both houses. In April 1906, a new Fundamental Law was promulgated – a type of constitution. It excluded from the realm of authority of the Duma major policy matters (in particular, the control over the army and of foreign affairs). It also reasserted the tsar's power (again described as 'autocratic'), his exclusive right of amnesty, and the fact that the government was to be responsible to him alone. Section 87 of the Fundamental Law stated that in between the parliamentary sessions the government could legislate by decree, subject to the confirmation of such decrees at the next session of the Duma and the State Council. A few days later the first Duma met in its first session.

B. A TALE OF A REVOLUTION: APRIL 1906 TO THE END OF 1907

The Duma met a new government. The consolidation of the conservative forces proceeded apace. Already in January 1906, a meeting of the provincial marshals of nobility called on the government to stand firm by the sanctity of the land–property rights. In May, a Council of United Nobility was set up – a veritable trade union of the squires and a major conservative lobby. The regional governors had been submitting increasingly tough reports and suggestions. The right-wingers were by now on the attack, demanding harsher policies and less appeasing ministers. On their bidding, the reformist Minister of Agriculture, Kutler, who advocated the transfer of some of the manorial land to the peasants, was fired. The relentless pressure proceeded and a few days prior to the first session of the Duma, Witte resigned and his resignation was accepted by the tsar (not before the successful conclusion of Witte's negotiations for a major loan from the French banks to strengthen the government's ailing finances). Witte was never forgiven for his authorship of the October Manifesto, which now seemed to the tsar and his men an unnecessary and dangerous tilt towards the Left. Nor was he forgiven for what seemed an attempt to carve out an independent political base for himself, by a clever balancing of power between the tsar and the Duma. The new government was headed by Goremykin while Stolypin, the young governor of Saratov (a major centre of the agrarian disturbances of 1905 which were quelled with particular energy), became its Minister of the Interior and police supremo.

The elections to the first Duma were boycotted by most of the radical organisations. (In response, on 8 March, 1906, a decree threatening imprisonment for the 'incitement not to vote' was even issued by the government.) Only the KDs decided to participate in elections. With the government attack in full swing, the liberal *Vestnik Evropy* compared the Russian elections with Napoleon III's

1852 victory at the polls – 'with blood in the streets, military repressions and the prisons full'.[1]

The military, political and legal offensive by the authorities and their allies seemed to have secured a docile first Duma. Its powers were curtailed and the multi-stage elections opened to considerable bureaucratic intervention. The electoral boycott failed. The turn-out to vote was massive in the villages and in the cities alike. Even in the most radical of the electoral colleges, that of industrial workers, a majority seemed to have taken part in the elections. While in some major centres of political militancy like St Petersburg or Riga most workers refused to vote, in Moscow 77 per cent of the enterprises voted. As a result of the boycott there were only a few members of the socialist parties in the Duma. The government and its supporters were reassured even further by the fact that half the deputies to the Duma represented peasants, which 'could be seen as valuable ballast securing the ship's stability'. A. Bobrinskii, one of the most reactionary dignitaries of Russia, confidently stated that in the forthcoming Duma 'the waves of rhetoric by the progressive elements will break on the solid mass of peasant conservatism'.[2]

To the shock of the government and the absolute surprise of the opposition, the election produced a Duma with a sharply anti-regime stand and membership. The manifest right-wingers failed to gain any representation at all. The KDs, who demanded a government responsible to the Duma, gained more than one third of the seats. Their success exceeded by far their most optimistic pre-assessments, and was furthered by the fact that their allies at the 'peripheries' also did well. A bloc led by the KDs formed a clear majority in the Duma. In view of the socialist boycott, the KDs saw themselves as the only Duma representatives of the political Left as well as of the centre. They were rapidly upstaged on the Left from an unexpected quarter. A majority of the 'non-party' peasant deputies banded together in a Labour Faction (*Trudoviki*) which adopted political positions to the left of the KDs.

At the first session of the Duma, the ministers were met by a barrage of abuse. The Duma proceeded to demand an instant end to repressions, an amnesty for political prisoners, and land reform. It also demanded a West European type of constitutional law. The government found itself facing a new dimension of political struggle.[3] What made this more serious was the 'chorus' of 'agrarian disturbances', which, as expected, peaked again during the summer of 1906. There was also a new wave of unrest in Poland. Industrial strikes increased in the Russian cities (but in 1906 reached only an estimated 2/5 of the level of 1905).[4] New 'stirrings' were reported from some of the military units.

In early 1906 the high command of the revolutionary parties was openly laying plans and preparing its organisations for a new revolutionary confrontation. Party organisations were being over-hauled. The First Congress of PSRs met in January. The local activists of the different SD factions were joining forces 'from below'.[5] The Fourth Congress of RSDWP met in April 1906 and declared its reunification. Voices were even heard demanding the creation of a united All-Russian Socialist Party bringing together supporters of the RSDWP and the PSR for the decisive battle.[6] Also in April 1906, a congress of KDs met to debate their own parliamentary challenge to the government. There were now, as stated, about 190 000 members in parties of revolutionary socialists, excluding those in the Polish provinces. Their Polish equivalents, the SDPL, Bund and PPS had among them no fewer than 80 000 members. There were in addition 100 000 radical liberals of the KD and at least 50 000 in the parties of the Liberal and nationalist opposition in the ethnic peripheries. From the humble beginning in the early days of 1905, membership in the still illegal (that is, officially non-existent) opposition parties of Russia rose to approximately 400 000.[7] Major parties achieved maximum strength with regard to membership, organisation and press in late 1906 and early 1907. The political attack of Russian dissent was continuing.

At the centre of the confrontation in the first Duma stood the 'agrarian problem', that is, the peasant claim for land, and an attempt by the liberals and those to their left to establish parliamentary control over the government. Three major land-reform projects were debated, the 'Project of 42' proposed by the KDs, the 'Project of 104' drawn up by the Labour Faction and the 'Project of 33' presented separately by its more radical wing.[8] The KDs declared that it was the duty of the government to carry out an equalising land distribution, based on the state lands, and a compulsory but partial takeover of private land, with full compensation to be paid by the state. The Labour Faction demanded the take-over and egalitarian distribution of all private land exceeding labour norms (that is, all but the lands which could be worked by their owner's family labour), while the issue of compensation was left open. The 'Project of 33' was close to the views of the PSRs who accepted the views of the 'Project of 104' but also demanded the immediate abolition of all private ownership of land and its 'socialisation'. Other issues debated included the repressions in Latvia, general amnesty, famine, and – most importantly – the ministers' responsibility to the Duma.

The British parliamentary images of government and opposition facing each other over the mace, in the shadow of the benign wig of the Speaker, differ dramatically from the Russian Duma of 1906. There was no government party in the House. The government, in command of the army and the administration and responsible to the tsar alone, faced a parliament in total opposition. True to this context, in an opening speech reflecting the whole state tradition of 300 years of Romanov rule, Prime Minister Goremykin, stolidly and flatly read out the government's refusal to heed any of the Duma's demands. He promised to proceed to execute the monarch's will and his will alone. Full political amnesty was rejected. The Duma's complaints about political repressions were rejected, as were the requests for land reform. Goremykin and his Minister of Agriculture restated the 'unalienable right of private land property', ruling out any ideas of land redistribution by the state. The only way to improve Russian agriculture and the livelihood of its peasants was to increase the productivity of the land. Mutiny (*kramola*) was to be crushed by the authorities. The sessions of the Duma became an unending confrontation between the Deputies and Ministers, linked to growing factional in-fighting. No actual legislative activity was taking place, none could be expected in the given context. Outside the Duma, repressions and arrests proceeded unabated. On 8 July, the Duma was dispersed by order of the tsar, on Goremykin's advice. New elections were called. A new government was appointed by the tsar with Stolypin as its Prime Minister.

For a moment, everyone seemed to hold his breath, watching the reaction of the country to the dispersal of its first parliament. Army and police units were put on full alert. The majority of the members of the Duma went to Vyborg in Finland, where local autonomy defended them from immediate arrest. There they issued a manifesto calling for a general boycott of the government, a refusal to pay taxes and opposition to the drafting of recruits. A few navy and army units rebelled at once in Kronstadt, Svedeborg and Revel, this time with more direct influence by the revolutionary parties' committees. A number of political strikes took place, but the overall political response in the cities was weak. 'Agrarian disturbances' rose to a new pitch in summer 1906, and the focus of direct confrontation with 'forces of order' clearly shifted to the countryside. (Their relation to the dispersal of the Duma is debatable – we shall return to it in the following chapters.) The tsar and the new government, much reassured, proceeded with repressive legislation, arrests, closures and executions. It was by now aiming to eradicate the remainder of the revolutionaries and to curtail any further opposition from the next Duma. A number of the deputies to the first Duma were imprisoned, others lost their jobs, two were killed by the Black-Hundreds terrorists and a rural priest was made an example by exile to a monastery for 'defiance' after signing the Labourites' land redistribution 'Project of 104'.[9]

The new Prime Minister retained control of the Ministry of the Interior, uniting in one hand the co-ordination of the government, direction of the repression and organisation of the elections of the next Duma. The methods of repression developed by the punitive expeditions at the peripheries were increasingly used in Russia proper. Stolypin and his ministry paid particular attention to the press. While the first Duma sat, ninety-two papers were closed and 141 editors and journalists arrested or exiled. These processes continued. Simultaneously, an increasing number of right-wing papers was being financed from the Ministry of Interior's 'special funds' and a state-supported paper was established to present the government's views.[10]

Once the Duma had been dispersed, the repressions increased. In July, many of the newly-established trade unions were raided and/or banned and their activists arrested. With unemployment growing to 300 000 and the government on the attack, many employers felt safe enough also to set up 'black lists' of union activists barred from any further employment. In August 1906, a new Military Field Court procedure was legislated by decree (that is, on the basis of Section 87 of the Fundamental Law). No trained lawyer was permitted to participate in it and decisions of the court were to be taken within 48 hours and behind closed doors. Under these regulations, army officers were appointed judges. Of the roughly 1100 cases heard before these courts were abolished by the second Duma, 950 ended with the death penalty and 85 more with exile and hard labour in Siberia.[11] By the end of the year, Stolypin was increasingly referred to in anti-monarchist circles as *Veshatel* – 'the hangman' – while the gallows became 'Stolypin's necktie' in common speech.

On the other side of the urban barricade, there was now a rapid increase of terrorist action. Violence was met by violence, with the revolutionaries clearly on the weaker side, yet remarkably effective in reaching many of their targets: General Min, who commanded the government forces in the Moscow uprising, was killed, as was General Alikhanov who had 'pacified' Guria and Admiral Chukhnin who had 'disciplined' the Black Sea navy. Admiral Dubasov – the pacifier of the Chernigov villages and governor of Moscow – was wounded as was General Renenkampf who had 'purged' Siberia. Colonel Zhdanov who had raped a female terrorist whom he investigated was killed together with his mate Abramov, and so on. Stolypin's house in Petersburg was bombed by SR Maximalists (who left the PSR because it was 'too mild'). One of Stolypin's children was maimed, without actual physical harm to the minister himself. The number of soldiers, policemen and officials killed increased during 1906 and 1907.[12]

Terrorist action was but one of the expressions of radicalisation within the camp of the revolutionaries. They reacted to the growing repression by the 'forces of order' and the retreat of the liberals by realignment toward the more militant organisations in their camp. As shown by M. Perrie, during the period 1906–7 the Mensheviks were losing members and supporters to the Bolsheviks, and all the RSWDP lost its activists to the PSR. Simultaneously, some PSR activists deserted, mostly joining the Anarchists and 'wild' clandestine combat groups.[13] Most of the members of the terrror squads were now young workers in industry and the crafts, with the intelligentsia as a substantial second.[14] In the late 1906 election to the second Duma, the SRs defeated the SDs within the workers' electoral colleges of some of the largest factories in St Petersburg. At the Fifth Congress of the RSDWP in 1907 the Mensheviks lost their majority to the Bolsheviks. Interestingly, as part of that process in Georgia, where Mensheviks led an effective and militant anti-government challenge, an opposite realignment took place.[15]

In Stolypin the tsar had found not only an effective chief of repression but also a man with political ambitions and a broad strategy of his own. During the 180 days of the inter-Duma period, the government proceeded not only with repressions but also with broad legislation by decree, attempting to take the wind out of the sails of the future Duma opposition, especially where the peasants were concerned. State lands and some of the tsar's private land (the *udel*) were transferred to the Peasant Bank to be sold to the peasants. The civic rights of the peasants were legally equalised with those of the other 'social estates'. The centre-piece of what was to become known as Stolypin's Agrarian Reform was the Decree of 9

November. It facilitated the privatisation of the peasant communal lands and the creation of homesteads – apart and away from the peasant communes. The new farms were to act as the major units of agricultural progress and as a conservative shield of the monarchy against the revolutionary cravings of the poor within the rural communities. This grand design was well expressed in Stolypin's own words of a later declaration: 'we decided to lay the wager on the sturdy and strong and not on the drunken and weak . . .' aiming at not less than 'to establish for our peasantry a new socio-economic order'.[16] We shall return to the issue in Chapter 6.

While the reform decrees were being enacted, the governors of the provinces were ordered to take a much more active hand in promoting safe, that is, pro-government members for the next Duma. The clergy, especially the rural clergy, were ordered by the Church's Synod to oppose radical and liberal propaganda more actively. Stolypin also tried to induce some of the right-wing liberals to join his government but failed.

The wave of repressions showed results in the further decline of overt political action by the parties of the Left. Simultaneously, the Octobrist Party of right-wing liberals, led now by A. Guchkov, adopted policies closely in line with those of Stolypin, inclusive of support for the punitive expeditions and Military Field Courts. (The party's initial leader, O. Shipov of the Moscow *zemstvo*, resigned from it consequently in disgust.) Yet Stolypin's attempt at establishing a commanding political presence via the electoral process failed. The electorate was by now mostly silenced, but its will to oppose the government remained solid despite the repressions, the monarchist propaganda, the political manipulations and the reforms. The 'electors' chosen in the first round of elections by the particular workers' electoral colleges were leftist to a man. The KD took most of the city electors places and were closely followed in the numbers of electors by self-confessed socialists. Peasant votes for the non-party peasant radicals of the Labour Faction sharply increased and quite a number of self-confessed socialists were also elected by them.[17]

February 1907 witnessed the unlikely scene of the most revolutionary Duma of Russia meeting in a land gripped by vicious reaction with the tsar's government in full autocratic command and secure in its power, yet powerless in the House. True, by now there were in the Duma some devoted monarchists and conservatives, institutionalised and increasingly active. The Octobrist party, though, held only 8 per cent of seats (44 in all) while further to the Right, the Association of the Russian People and a few intermediate groups had taken about 2 per cent (10 seats). The revolutionary socialists, the SDs and SRs (their electoral boycott by now called off) had gained between them 20 per cent of the deputies. There were about 20 per cent in the peasant Labour Faction, 19 per cent KD Liberals and 18 per cent in smaller opposition groups (mostly allied to the KDs); the opposition was once again in a clear majority against the government supporters.[18] Responding to what was to be the last democratic test of the country's mood for a decade, the monarchist press at once demanded the dispersal of the Duma and a change in the electoral laws. In the Duma the few deputies of the extreme Right offered noisy challenge, often bringing the debate to a standstill. Stolypin made some spectacular speeches which met with angry hostility by the parliamentary majority. The inevitable happened, even sooner than in the case of the first Duma. After a few clashes and some remarkable rhetoric, the second Duma was dispersed on July 3, 1907.

Once again, in an increasingly familiar scenario, some of the radical deputies were imprisoned and further repressive measures taken, but this time, together with the dispersal of the second Duma, a new electoral law was unilaterally declared – a governmental *coup d'état* in direct contradiction to the country's Fundamental Law.[19] By the new electoral law, 51 per cent of the Duma's seats went to the representatives of the noble landowners, while the non-Russian peripheries lost most of their representation.[20] The last major base of legal opposition was reduced and brought into line with the actual power relations which prevailed.

The relative size of sections 2A and 2B bears implicit testimony to a view and a bias of evidence as well as of discourse which have been well-established with the historians of Russia. The picture of a larger-than-life 1905 of incredible events is followed by a lingering 1906 and 1907.[21] Many texts indeed refer to it as the 'revolution of 1905'. This is mostly the image of the events looked at *ex post factum* through the eyes of the urbanites in the government's or the liberals' camps. It disregards the life of the revolutionary parties and their firm expectations in 1906 that the Revolution was still on its way 'up'. It forgets the significance of the liberals' own view in 1906 that their government was just around the corner. More importantly, the picture changes sharply when looked at via the experience of the countryside, where 85 per cent of the population lived. We shall devote Chapter 3 to it.

Be this as it may, the second half of 1907 marked the definite end of the revolutionary period. A few navy and army units rebelled in 1907 and a new list of peasant localities joined the fight, but they were rapidly put down. Strikes proceeded and there were even some signs of recovery of the workers' fighting spirit – the political strikes in summer 1907 exceeded those of 1906. However, despite attempts by the revolutionary organisations to keep up the fight, the revolution was by now clearly over. Terrorist attacks continued, but the summer of 1907 saw the last wave of massive political strikes and 'agrarian disturbances'. By the end of the year, a new, purged, conservative and obedient third Duma met to cheer and support the government. In the same days, those leaders of the SDs and SRs who were still alive and free left Russia for a long exile. With the revolutionary cadre and sympathisers dispersed, dead, imprisoned or on the run and the last shots fired by the revolutionary terrorists, with the villages and urban workers' districts sulkily silent, and the prisons full, the government had the field to itself.

C. THE 'INTERNAL ENEMIES OF RUSSIA': REVOLUTION AS A COMPOSITION OF FORCES

In the revolutionary days, Nicholas Sukhotin, a conservative, the Governor-General of Steppe province, an ex-professor at the Military Academy and a future member of the State Council, offered a social analysis of the internal enemies of Russia and of its friends.[1] His views were personal but doubtless articulated the feelings of many within the Russian monarchist establishment of the day. Using the figures of the 1897 census, he first divided the empire's population of 125 million into 76 million 'Russians' (including in his count, Ukrainians and Belorussians) assumed to be loyal, as opposed to 49 million others, distinguished by religion or ethnicity, such as Poles, Jews, Armenians, Muslims, etc., who collectively qualified as Russia's enemies. A similar 3:2 proportion was suggested for the territorial division between Russia *sensus strictu* and its hostile territories, that is, the ethnically non-Russian periphery plus a few 'doubtful' provinces in Russia proper. Next, the internal enemies of Russia in terms of social estate were estimated to consist of 700 000 nobles (mainly non-Russians), 7 million Polish peasants, 8 million Caucasian peasants, 24 million peasants elsewhere, 8 million towns-men, and 12 million unspecified 'others' – 60 million in all, as against 65 million loyal Russians, that is, 1.75 million nobles, 56 million peasants, 4 million townsmen and 3 million others. Finally, Sukhotin estimated that out of the 10 million literates of the realm, 6 million were 'against Russia' while 4 million were 'for it'. The 115 000 university graduates were divided proportionately 2:1 'against' versus 'for' (but 1:4.5 in so far as graduates of the military academies were concerned).

In January 1917, on the eve of the next revolutionary round, Lenin delivered a lecture on the 1905–07 revolution. At its heart lay his own analysis of the forces which had confronted one another in it. On the one hand stood '. . . the tsar . . . the ruling class . . . of big landowners, already bounded by a thousand ties with the big bourgeoisie', helped in the decisive moment by a loan granted by the French bankers. On the other stood the 'revolutionary people of Russia'. Within a few months of the revolution, the 'several hundred revolutionary organisers, several thousand members of local orga-nisations, half a dozen revolutionary papers . . . published mainly abroad . . . grew into many thousands . . . became leaders of between 2 and 2.5 million proletarians . . . Their struggle produced widespread ferment and often revolutionary movement among the peasant masses . . . [which in turn] had its reverberations in the army' (and also promoted the) 'movement of national liberation which flared up among the oppressed people of Russia . . . forcibly russified'. It was, therefore, a 'bourgeois–democratic revolution in its methods of struggle . . . [but] the proletariat was a leading force . . . The strike was the principal means of bringing the masses into motion'.[2]

Such types of analysis are necessarily open to challenge, especially if quantified. All the same, for at least three reasons their significance is doubtless. First, there is no way to understand a revolution without considering the balance of forces within it, abstracting from the individuals and focusing on group conflict. Second, the character of the units of analysis adopted in such consideration will necessarily reflect on the conclusions drawn. Finally, there is no way to understand a revolution without knowing what its participants think about the forces within it, all the more so in that such perceptions often act as self-fulfilling prophecies. Revolution is (also) a matter of cognition.

Both the similarities and differences between Lenin and Sukhotin are therefore significant. To both of them, the revolution represented a composite of different confrontations – indeed, several revolutions in one. These struggles were not equivalent in significance but were structured by the decisive sector of the battle. These were – for

Sukhotin – the Russian autocracy versus the revolutionaries and – for
Lenin – the Russian proletariat fighting its class enemies. Sukhotin
and Lenin saw eye-to-eye in delimiting some of the major forces
arrayed within the revolutionary situation: a government supported
by the Army officers and gentlemen of the Russian nobility against
the anti-government ethnic peripheries and the overwhelmingly
anti-government tendencies in towns. However, while admitting
many peasants to be 'anti-Russia', Sukhotin stressed the large core of
conservative peasant farmers providing, in his view, a major
foundation for the Russian monarchy. He also singled out 'the
educated' as a major revolutionary constituency and left out
altogether industrial workers and railway men (who, it should be
remembered, belonged in terms of 'social estate' mostly to the
peasantry and to a lesser degree to the 'townsmen'). On the other
hand, Lenin, writing a decade later, had nothing to say about the
intelligentsia and considered workers, especially the higher-paid and
skilled metal workers, to be the core of the revolutionary power. A
double-action social trigger mechanism of revolution was assumed by
him: the revolutionaries inducing the industrial proletariat, and the
proletarians inducing the peasants and the ethnic peripheries. In his
lecture, Lenin also left unmentioned the internal divisions within the
social classes, inclusive of the peasantry. Considerable attention was
given by him to the soldiers and NCOs of the army and to their
separateness from the officer corps. Within weeks of Lenin's
deliberations, the revolution and civil war of 1917–21 were to provide
the next major test of them, and to show how shrewd many of these
conclusions were.

Central to every revolution has been its breadth of appeal and
participation, the multiplicity of its dimensions and dynamics of
confrontation, and the complex and contradictory relations between
and within the major forces active in it. The depth of the social gulf
between urban and rural Russia explains why the deepest diversity
and some most significant links within the Russian revolution(s) lay
there. We follow that understanding in the structure of the book.
Before we proceed to the peasantry and its struggle, three other
components of the 1905–07 revolution should be singled out: the
tsarist state, the geo-ethnic periphery and the urban rebellion. In
addition, something must be said about the urban–rural continuum,
concerning both the squiredom and the peasantry.

What follows, therefore, is an analysis of class conflicts but not a
class analysis in its restricted sense, in so far as other dimensions and

types of social conflict and grouping have played a major autonomous role in defining the political context and action. Moreover, social classes carried contradictions within themselves, at times unrelated to class interests in its strict sense, which often proved central to historical processes and should be brought to light. Finally, the composite character of the revolutionary situation explains the significance of combined determinations, when such existed, for example, a Latvian peasant was both a Latvian and a peasant when facing Russian tsardom and the same was true for, say, the Georgian nobles, burghers or proletarians.

*   *   *

The political weakness of tsardom, which surfaced once war and revolution ripped through its fearful façade, reflected the contradictory nature of social forces it relied on, as well as the crisis at the very top, that is, the disarray concerning the tsar, his immediate entourage and the men at the pinnacle of the administrative and the military pyramids.

Nobles were the regime's officially recognised primary social base, the 'empire's first estate', the main owners of private lands, ranks, titles and privileges.[3] Yet, to begin with, many of Russia's nobles were non-Russians and locked in a protracted confrontation over national and corporate rights with tsardom, for example, the nobles of the Polish and Baltic provinces. Even between the ethnically Russian nobles, unity was clearly absent. Reliable conservative monarchism was professed mainly by the middle-sized landowners of the south and at the western frontiers. A considerable number of the local leaders of the nobility, often the best-educated leaders of the *zemstvos*, owners of the largest estates and princes of the realm, such as Princes Dolgorukii, led the Constitutionalist movement. Of the others, those with a 'tradition of service' (and often with less land or with no land at all) identified with the state administration rather than with the landlords, often passing snide remarks at the mercenary tendency of their brethren-by-estate, who feared peasant land-demands most of all. Even the increasingly conservative nobles and landowners of south Russia displayed remarkable helplessness when the peasant revolt struck. While the German barons in the Baltic provinces often armed their servants, created German units of self-defence and faced class enemies gun in hand, their Russian counterparts mostly begged for army escorts and ran for town.[4]

At the other end of the social scale stood the Black Hundreds, devotees of the government.[5] Their shrill monarchism, hooligan excesses, criminal connotations and open involvement in the murder of opposition MPs and in pogroms, made them an effective tool of urban terror, arguably with some potential to check revolutionary propaganda among the peasantry, the workers and the army's lower ranks. But these were supporters whom one could not easily admit into the noble parlour; they were allies of whom some Russian ministers were deeply ashamed. Many of the Black Hundreds were known petty criminals or local drunkards, paid on a *per*-operation basis and directly linked to police agents. The Prime Minister in 1905, Witte, called them simply 'scoundrels', and they paid him back by a barrage of insinuations and, after his retirement, by bombing his private residence. All the same, one should not overstate their marginality to the 'establishment'. We have the evidence of Stolypin's own daughter as to her sympathies with 'these brave men' who used stones and guns to disperse socialist demonstrations in Saratov, while the tsar and princes of the realm declared their patronage of the Association of the Russian People. However, by the very nature of its social recruitment, this group was highly volatile, often uncontrollable and lost impetus once the revolutionary crisis declined. It also added disunity to the monarchists' camp. Lack of an effective political party of the tsar's supporters proved an incessant long-term weakness of the regime.[6] A number of vehemently monarchist preachers and journalists and some mass publications substituted for it, but only up to a point.[7]

Members of the state apparatus, particularly the army and police but also the officialdom and the church, were the third component of tsardom's mass base.[8] On the whole, their ranks stood loyally by the government's side with only a few displaying radical sympathies. More reactionary than the government itself, some of the police chiefs, governors and army officers had even plotted action to save the tsar against his own will and to shield the autocracy from any experiments with parliamentarianism, freedom of speech and the like.[9] These moods or attempts were, however, easily crushed or dissipated.

Armed forces were vital in the revolutionary context. In 1874 national service had been introduced and the whole organisation of the Russian army brought closer to the German and French patterns. Within the social context of Russia, a basic disunity was built into the very structure of the armed forces by virtue of the fact that it consisted mainly of peasant soldiers and NCOs, officered by non-peasants, often nobles in origin. Lenin's lecture quoted above rightly stressed the fact that, for one, the revolutionary acts were initiated by the mass of the soldiers and not only by the officer corps as was the case in the nineteenth century. This was true also for the Russian navy, which developed into a particular focus of political radicalism. The character of the 1905–07 mutinies proved how much the sailor–officer and soldier–officer relations became a frontier of social tension and ambivalence. At the same time, even the monarchist cohesion of the officers' corps was uncertain. A republican Officers Union came into being in 1905; officers of army and navy were court-martialled and executed for supporting revolutionary action (for example, after the naval mutiny at Sevastopol). A massive purge of disloyal and ineffectual officers took place. The privileged Guards' regiment and the Cossacks were kept carefully apart from the field army as the dynasty's final defence – a rampart of absolute loyalty. Yet, even some units of the Guards and the Cossacks rebelled in 1906.[10]

All the same, if a balance sheet were to be drawn up it would run counter to the revolutionaries' hopes and the government's fears. Once in uniform, the great majority of the Russian lower ranks, rather than acting in accordance with their class origin, did as they were ordered. Brutal discipline, internal spies and harsh punishment of mutineers were not the only reasons for this. The networks and hierarchy of army organisation proved effective, the hate some soldiers developed for the rebels, who often did no more than what the soldiers' own families had done in their villages, gave revolutionaries something new to think about. Crucially for the outcome of the revolution, discipline held in the majority of the army and navy units. It was the conclusion drawn by Witte and the tsar's court that the army was reliable after all, which underlay the government offensive in late 1905 and 1906. Trotsky's 'participant observation' that the revolution's main struggle was not against the army but rather for its allegiance and that the revolutionary attack finally broke on the bayonet of the soldier-peasants is central to what happened.[11] The lessons of both the numerous mutinies of the soldiers and sailors as well as the ability of the army's central organisation to contain them were never quite forgotten on the Russian political scene.

Finally, with regard to its potential props, the regime increasingly came to need, yet could not fully rely on, its foreign allies and business partners. A military defeat suffered by Russia at the hands of 'the yellow race', supposedly doomed to colonisation, followed directly by disorders at home, made them all wonder about financing such an ailing relation. England seemed smugly pleased that Russia's Asian policy came to grief. Wilhelm of Prussia sent condolences and advice, but little else. The French bankers – Russia's main sources of foreign financing – were rather slow over the Russian application for a loan. It was granted only in 1906, when the internal war in the towns was at its end.

The uncertainty and the vicissitudes of the regime's top command were the result of the narrowness of and the ambivalence within its socio-political base, but also of its own limitations. Despite the danger, even in the small circle of those closest to the tsar, intrigue followed intrigue while the tsar's own family haggled endlessly over bits of property and privileges.[12] Able and imaginative administrators were few. Most of the government predictions proved dramatically wrong. The reasons why armies were defeated, peasants rioted, workers became revolutionary and intellectuals hostile could not even be considered – to perceive them would be to admit things inadmissible to the tsar and those closest to him. The tsar's personality played a role in this context: his vagueness, his disloyalty to his own lieutenants, his world outlook of a petty squire rather than that of a ruler of a great nation. When Trotsky dismissed it all by a snappy 'the fools got scared of the first gale of a storm' and Witte in his memoirs later concurred,[13] they were right only up to a point. The 'top' was scared – yes! It was foolish – yes! But its fear was not foolish then, for despite the immensity of tsardom, its very nature made the challenge of a few thousand revolutionaries real enough to have it shaken. For a moment it was touch and go.

All this explains also why the gut reaction of the regime was to repress rather than to manoeuvre, and while repressing to do it viciously. The image of a foreign horde, of a Mongol invasion on the rampage, is often repeated by witnesses of repressions in the Russian villages and townships. It was still worse at the non-Russian peripheries. Even to us, after all that has happened since around the globe, the grisly reports of the 'punitive expeditions' have the power to shock and make oppressive reading: names of railway stations whose entire staffs were executed without trial and without exception; Caucasian villages in which, 'to break defiance', every female from infants to women of 70, including nuns, was raped by the

Cossacks while the officers looked on; Russian villages burned; thousands and thousands of peasants flogged and others whose knees were frostbitten by the hours of kneeling in the snow 'to teach them a lesson'; ordinary 'official' executions; executions after court-martial; informal executions nobody bothered to record with exactitude (with *besfamil'nye* – 'no name known' – on many of such graves).[14] Executions and court martials proceeded well after the revolution's defeat.[15] The suicidal, personal terror of 1906–07 by the revolutionaries, aiming particularly at those in charge of pacifications, was increasingly the only response they could muster. It was not enough to make a difference in the outcome. In those days, there was clearly reason enough for those involved to proceed with it to the bitter end.

The tsar's archives, in which the official reports of repression are duly filed, offer an insight into the minds which directed the government camp, and an important rejoinder to Lev Tolstoy's 'I cannot stay silent' already quoted. In a highly centralised regime, the role of the individual at the top was of major importance. In the margins of the 1905–07 reports are comments pencilled in blue in the tsar's own hand.[16] He dismissed a complaint of a police chief at some of the 'excessive' and blatantly illegal acts of a punitive expedition with a curt 'if enough of our officers behaved similarly, we would have no revolution'. He wrote 'splendid fellow' next to another police complaint that, contrary to the regulations, a certain Captain Richter had added hanging to the shooting without trial of those he had arrested in the Baltic provinces, to liven up the procedure. He reacted to a report that the general in charge did not bombard the city of Tukkum in Latvia because it surrendered, because the city fathers begged that it be spared and because his unit was short of shells, with: 'What stupid excuses, he should have destroyed the city'. What all this meant in terms of personal inducement was brought home by a circular from the Prime Minister, Stolypin, in 1906, reminding officers and officials that 'lawful but stern, decisive and brave execution of duty is the best and the only way to distinction and promotion', adding, as if in an afterthought, 'as well as to the sustaining of order in these troubled times'.[17] It was even more direct where the lower ranks were concerned. A soldier-batsman (*den'shchik*) was commended and promoted to corporal for killing on the spot 'a Pole' for 'expressing disrespect towards His Imperial Majesty'.[18] A later comment expressing the conviction that in those days '. . . the more executed, the more your credit with your superiors (*nachal'stvo*)', has summed up well enough a mood and a major causality of those times.[19]

*   *   *

The difference in the intensity of revolutionary action between central Russia and its peripheries was well known and often acknowledged. Sukhotin assigned those areas *in toto* to the 'enemies of Russia'. L. Martov spoke of the 'different rhythm' and the higher levels of mass support for the revolutionaries at the periphery.[20] Lenin remarked that a 'Latvian' intensity of strikes within the main parts of Russia would have defeated the tsardom.[21] In most of those regions, the confrontation with the 'forces of order' had begun earlier, was more militant, more massive and more sweeping in terms of the social groups drawn into it. Also, the role played by the revolutionary organisations there was larger, with less accident and spontaneity involved and with the party committees more in control. Klyuchevsky's remark that in Russia 'the centre lies at the peripheries' is clearly substantiated by our Map 1 on page 72.

One major reason for the extraordinary revolutionary potential of the peripheries was plain enough. The majority of people there were ethnically distinct from the Russians, while, especially since the Polish insurrection of 1830, the Russian state had carried out an increasingly oppressive policy of russification. The exclusive use of the Russian language was imposed in education and official proceedings all throughout the empire. Restrictions were decreed aiming at members of particular ethnic 'minorities' (who usually formed a majority within some of Russia's territories, for example, the Poles or the Armenians). Ethnically Russian officials were sent in to take charge of main aspects of life at the peripheries. A specific type of man – nationalist, xenophobic and crass, whose main claim to office was his Russianness and stolid loyalty, a Colonel Blimp of Russia – was usually appointed or selected himself to rule those lands. Russians referred to them, after a bitter satire by Saltykov – Schedrin, as *Tashkentsy* – the 'men from Tashkent'. The fact that much of the population of the western and southern peripheries was superior to the ethnic Russians in its level of literacy and in economic development added to the mutual resentment. The peripheries were the testing ground for repressive techniques, with an extra dash of cruelty thrown in where 'they' were concerned. Even the famous phrase of Trepov 'not to save ammunition' (in his order of 12

October, 1905) was borrowed directly from the orders of an oppressive viceroy of Poland in the nineteenth century.[22]

One can conclude only too easily that the extra militancy of the periphery was but the natural response to additional oppression. The particular intensity of the workers' or the peasants' revolutionary mood would be a simple addition of class plus nationalist ardour. That is true only in part, for the relations between oppression and the opposition to it are never simple. The heterogeneity of Russia's peripheries offers scope for comparison, with some illuminations to be drawn. The Muslim areas of the Volga and of Asian Russia in 1905–07 were mostly calmer than Russia itself, even though the national oppression there was considerable. Pankratova's study has usefully divided the non-Russian Russia of those times into (i) areas of occupation, that is, where Russia-like states existed before the Russian armies moved in, (ii) equivalents of a colonial empire, presiding over massive colonisation, for example, Siberia, and (iii) areas of colonial rule over dense native populations where no modern nation–states existed before, for example, Central Asia.[23] While some demands for cultural autonomy and the return of tribal lands were voiced in colonial Russia by the pastoral Kazakhs, Buriats, Yakuts, etc. (areas ii and iii of Pankratova), the main revolutionary role in the Asian regions was played, somewhat surprisingly, by the Russian settlers. Especially the railway workers and the local intelligentsia were involved, for example, in Tashkent – in the Uzbekistan of today. In 1905 they were often overshadowed by the mutinies of soldiers of the defeated army who for a short while came to dominate the Siberian cities of Irkutsk, Chita and Vladivostok. However, the main centres of the non-Russian revolution lie elsewhere, in 'occupied' rather than 'colonial' Russia. Even there, the picture was complex, defying blanket explanations.

In the Baltic provinces, Social Democracy was the leading organisation of the opposition. It also became the leading force in the defence of the national rights of the Latvians and Ests against the Russian state and the locally-domineering German barons and patricians.[24] The nineteenth-century russification effort by the officialdom to curtail the ancient privileges of the local German landowners helped to consolidate the ethnic unity of the Latvians and the Ests. Strong workers' unions and SD committees, especially in the industrial harbour city of Riga, led a class-cum-national, anti-German as well as anti-state struggle. Powerful political strikes proceeded in rapid succession. National congresses of teachers, local

artists, etc., demanded cultural autonomy, extending considerably
the anti-autocracy 'popular front'. The villagers of Latvia, peasants as
well as wage-labourers, were also increasingly united in a class as well
as national confrontation over their interests. In many rural districts,
an alternative authority of the revolutionary committees was established for a time, while the tsar's governors and the German nobles
barricaded themselves in cities and castles.

In the Caucasus, the Georgian SDs showed differences as well as
important similarities with their Latvian comrades.[25] There was a
very small proletariat there, but the SD 'circles' came into being and
became powerful at a very early stage. Also, Georgia was the first
region in Russia in which the SD, with much apprehension, came to
lead a national mass movement in which peasants played a major
role, while nobles, tradesmen and craftsmen participated. We shall
return to it below. The impact of the SDs on the other ethnic groups
of the Caucasus was limited mainly to industrial Baku. A powerful
and militant nationalist movement, anti-tsarist but non-socialist,
came to dominate the scene in Armenia. A number of militant
organisations of various ethnic groups professing Islam (described as
'the Tatars') added to the complexity of the ethnic map.

The confrontation between the Armenian and the Islamic nationalists showed to what extent the 'national problem' can act both ways
within a revolutionary crisis. The anti-Armenian pogroms reflected a
peculiar link between Islamic nationalism and the extreme xenophobia of the Russian administration aimed against Armenians and their
powerful Christian church. This enmity facilitated in turn the hold of
the nationalist movement, especially the Dashtusian party, over the
Armenians. Poland offered a different case in point.[26] A major
socialist party already existed there in 1893, and within a short time it
produced the more nationalist PPS, which talked of independence,
and the SDKP, which believed the demands for an independent
Poland to be contrary to true proletarian, that is, progressive
interests. A powerful nationalist undercurrent was strongly felt,
expressed with particular clarity in stubborn insistence on the
universal use of the Polish language, which united most of the Poles
against the authorities but also, up to a point, against their Jewish,
Belorussian and Lithuanian neighbours. In 1904, both the PPS and
the SDKPL took a 'defeatist' stand and rapidly built up large political
followings and impact. At the beginning of the 1905 struggle, in the
demonstrations and strikes the SDKPL and PPS co-operated and
were clearly supported by the majority of the Poles, but at the end of

the year a major split occurred, reflecting also in a split within the PPS. The SDKPL and the PPS (Left) were now attacked with increasing violence by the party of National Democracy, the right wing of the PPS and the militants of the Catholic Church as splinters of national unity fighting for alien revolutionary aims. The SKDP's uncompromising refusal to accept political goals, other than purely proletarian ones, played into the hands of its local enemies. As time went by and the victory of the tsarist authorities became apparent, the SDKPL and its allies also lost ground to the National Democrats. A massive lock-out at the end of 1905 reversed the achievements of the earlier strikes – it was supported by new workers' unions and 'hard guy' gangs created by the nationalists. In the elections to the second Duma, the National Democrats won hands down and hence totally dominated the Polish *Kolo*, that is, the faction of the deputies of the Polish provinces.

In the Russian revolutionary movement, Jews played an outstanding role. They were mainly located in (and legally restricted to) the south and the west of European Russia. Their oppression, both official and unofficial, was particularly harsh. There were few industrial workers and farmers among them, but craftsmen and wage-workers of small enterprises were numerous and most supported the Bund, a Jewish SD party which used Yiddish as its language. By its report to the second congress of the All-Russian RSDW in 1903, the Bund had as many as 30 000 organised workers in its ranks.[27] The Jewish intelligentsia and middle classes were radicalised by the rampant anti-semitism of both official and popular brands and expressed it in the extensive support given to the non-Jewish SDs, SRs and KDs, as well as the particularly Jewish Organisations – the Bund, the Zionists (Left and Right) and the liberal League for the Emancipation of the Jews of Russia. The largely non-industrial provinces of the north-west and the trading cities, like Odessa, were often more revolutionary by the very fact of the large Jewish population there. On the other hand, popular anti-semitism played a role in weakening the socialist movements in Russia and Poland, mobilising respectively loyalist and xenophobic emotions.

One can proceed further with the specification of politically significant ethnic conflicts and struggles, for example the major conflict over the recognition of the very existence of Ukrainians and their language. (To the Russian nationalists they were simply *Malorussy* – the Little Russians. Until 1905 the Ukrainian language was banned from official use and educational establishments as a crude and unseemly brand of Russian, to be best forgotten.) However, the pattern of interdependence between the social and the ethnic conflicts should by now have been made sufficiently clear. To draw it together, one has first to admit the very fact of heterogeneity and the lack of any simple scale of more-and-less, along which this complexity can be ordered. Most of the non-Russian areas fought tsardom with particular vengeance but did so for a mixture of reasons. Class conflict played a major role underlying the militancy of workers in Riga, Warsaw or Lodz but demands for national emancipation were also of importance (unifying as well as divisive). A tie suggested by some of the Russian Marxists between peasant following and nationalist demands – a deductive attempt to claim for the proletariat immunity from such 'archaism', was on the whole left unsubstantiated. At the same time, those socialist revolutionaries of the peripheries who opposed independence in terms of 'progress' as well as expedience (for example, the SDs of Georgia, Latvia and the SDKPL in Poland) found support of that view also far outside the organised working class. In Georgia it was supported mostly by the peasants. In all peripheries it was the intelligentsia which was particularly active in the variety of cultural and linguistic associations organised along ethnic lines.

The success of the revolutionary front-line, small as it often was when compared gun for gun with its foes, was possible as long as it drew massive support from 'the streets' – that is, from people who, while not directly engaged in the struggle, secured the rear of resources, empathy, neutralisation of some government forces, etc. That is where nationalist loyalties took a particularly important place. Mao's image of the strength of the revolutionaries being subject to their capacity to 'swim like a fish' within 'the sea' of broad popular support is very apt here. The significance of 'the whole nation' at the 'periphery' facing the tsardom of the Russians and acting in unison was central in so far as the punch of the revolutionaries was concerned. The tsarist government's increasing awareness of those matters led during 1905 to a variety of compromises aimed at defusing ethno-revolutionary tension: the Finns were given back their autonomy, Poles and Ukrainians permitted to use their language and so on. The partial, transitory and opportunistic nature of these retreats from russification was too blatantly obvious, however, to put at rest the anti-state forces of nationalism in the peripheries.

*   *   *

Marxist class analysis applied manifestly well to the cities of Russia. Workers proved radical and militant. The majority of those who went on strike demonstrated and fought gun in hand in 1905 against the autocracy and those who suffered for it were the industrial and railway workers. Factory workers, more deeply rooted in the urban milieu, more professional and better paid (for example, the metal workers and the printers), went on strike more often, showed more political awareness and, with some important exceptions, massively supported the SDs as their party. (The strike-intensity figures shifted from being highest with the poorly-paid textile workers during the 1895–1904 decade to the supremacy of the elite metal workers during the revolutionary year of 1905.)[28] The new phenomenon of political strikes symbolised new times. Those strikes involved demands reaching far beyond simple wage increases, and nearly half the strikes in 1905–07 were of that type. Membership of trade unions rapidly climbed to 150 000.[29] The readership of *Russkaya gazeta*, the daily sponsored by the Soviet of St Petersburg, reached in December 1905 the figure of 500 000. The establishment of the Soviets was spontaneous to a high degree – a chain of proletarian class parliaments turned into the revolutionary high command by the representatives of factories, workshops and railways. The self-fulfilling prophecy aspect of it all should be kept in mind, the prediction of the proletarian revolutionary spirit made the propaganda effort of the SDs and SRs concentrate on the urban working-class. All the same, the major political model and prediction which worked added considerable substance to the Marxist analysis the world over. (Map 1 gives it a visual expression while at the same time the diverse intensity of the strike action shows its ethnic bias.)[30]

The liberal parties and organisations vacillated, once again as expected by the Marxists, even though they would seemingly have become the most immediate beneficiaries of parliamentary democracy. The approach to political militancy and especially to the armed struggle by the Constitutional Democrats (KDs) resembled the worst of the caricatures drawn of them by the socialists – they were ready to congratulate others who rose in arms (at the first congress of the KDs, October 1905) and quick to condemn such militancy when it failed (at the second conference of the KDs, February 1906). Most of their leaders aimed at a comprise with the tsar and his government. Nevertheless, a simple restatement of Plekhanov's initial view about bourgeois feebleness and the consequent necessity of 'proletarian hegemony', as adopted by the

MAP 1   *Strike intensity and the establishment of Soviets: European Russia 1905*

Soviet historians, is misleading if simply left at that. A formula which links to it, equating militancy with 'progress', was widely used by leaders since the beginnings of the RSDWP: the more industry – the more proletariat – the more revolution. The example of Georgia in 1905–07 challenges it directly. This manifestly rural area, with no major industry at all, topped all revolutionary indices. More generally, simple extrapolation of such anticipations in 1905 would make Pittsburgh, US, and Sheffield, UK, much more revolutionary than St Petersburg, which was clearly not the case. Paul Sweezy suggested, more credibly, that the proletarian revolutionary potential describes a historical arc: it is low at the initial stages of crafts and manufactures, reaches its peak at the early stages of industrialisation, and declines during the subsequent period for reasons which he elaborated.[31] This analysis can provide some sociological content for the major metaphor of the nineteenth century, adopted and promoted by Kautsky, about the focus of proletarian socialist struggle 'moving East': from England or France, to Germany and then to Russia.[32] The revolutionary spirit of the Russian workers was not simply a matter of their position within the political economy, but also of the relational historical context and, one must add, the regional, ethnic and global setting.

Second, the tale of two cities, the bourgeois–liberal one and the proletarian–revolutionary one, hides the fact that no such simple division into workers and capitalists (bound by a common pre-capitalist enemy but facing each other in a conflict defined by an exploitative political economy) can be stipulated. Nor does a possible addition of a declining and therefore inherently reactionary petty bourgeoisie explain satisfactorily the political scene of the Russian cities in 1905–07. Some of Russia's capitalists demanded democratisa-tion, but the ties of the others to the tsarist regime and its system of privileges made them support the autocracy through thick and thin. Numerous attempts at this time to establish political parties of property owners failed.[33] More importantly, the 'orthodox' Marxist class analysis of the opposition made the intelligentsia disappear into the common bag of the bourgeoisie or petty bourgeoisie. When no capitalists could be spotted in the struggle for political power, this social category was redefined into a substitute bourgeoisie. Such procedures consistently mystified the causes of political action. The revolution was not being made simply by students or intellectuals, nor were they in the majority in the 1905–07 firing line, but their part in the revolutionary forces, and later in the prisons, was considerable, significant and not accidental.

A delimitation of the intelligentsia is not sufficient on its own. As with most of the other social groupings, patterns of their diversity was as politically significant as their similarities. One way to clarify it is to look more closely at the short history of the Union of Unions (*Soyuz soyuzov*). The initiative for it came from the Alliance of Liberation which already in November 1904 called for the creation of unions of liberal professions and of workers, to be further consolidated into a super-union of all and sundry.[34] The actual organisation which came into being in May 1905 was even more heterogeneous than had been anticipated: beside the unions of liberal professions, graduate engineers, lawyers, writers and actors, it was joined by 'proper' trade unions of railwaymen, postmen, etc., by white-collar unions like those of pharmacists, teachers and bookkeepers, and by more general emancipatory associations, for example, the feminists or even the national association of the Bashkir. The *Zemstvo* Constitutionalists also participated in it for a time and the Peasant Union representatives joined it later. The unifying credo was the demand for democracy and an agreement according to which no political party would be permitted to join as such, whereas, the individual members of any party which objected to autocracy were welcome.

As stated, the mainstream industrial workers' organisation in the large cities was to find in late 1905 its most spectacular expression in the Soviets. Yet, the Union of Unions left with mainly 'middle class' activists (that is, the non-manual employees and the self-employed), proved one of the most radical organisations of the period. Contrary to firm expectation (rooted in class analysis of the liberals and the socialist alike) it refused to become a major liberal political 'front organisation'. When the issue arose at its third Congress (July 1905), the Union of Union's leadership challenged and out-voted its own chairman, P. Milyukov, and his political allies, who retreated into the formation of the KD party. (Milyukov later complained in his memoirs somewhat amusingly, that the 'Union of Unions followed a Leninist line'.)[35] The consistently radical stand of the Union of Unions, for example, its boycott of the election to the Duma (together with the revolutionary socialists and in conflict with the KDs) and its energetic support of political strikers, cannot be defined simply by the class origins of its members. Nor can the fact that quite a number of initial supporters of the KDs, disappointed with its Right tilt, promptly transferred allegiance to the Union of Unions (and vice versa).

To see the roots of the radicalism of the Union of Unions, one has to consider the specific social context of the intelligentsia within a 'developing society', the ambivalence of its relations with the West and with its own people, its politicisation and its socially constructed burden of shame which, as Marx once said, is a revolutionary sentiment.[36] The image of two cities in one, a revolutionary and a reformist, facing one another while confronting the tsardom, was relevant within limits, and the majority of workers and some capitalists played their respective roles at its diverse wings, but it was the inter-class nature of the revolutionary wave which made it overwhelming in October 1905. This could not have happened without the massive participation of the non-proletarian social strata (and non-socialist public opinion of the non-capitalists who were also non-proletarian).

It has been said by Martov that in December 1905 the revolution 'was suppressed not so much by the use of machine guns as by the split [of the opposition] after the October 17 Manifesto'.[37] The refusal of KD liberals to support the 'illegal' struggle after October 1905 and their dismay at the revolutionary demands and at the proletarian militancy were relevant to the outcome. There was also a class confrontation of Russian workers with their employers. The owners of industry, even those who were ready to support some reforms, had drawn the line at the demand for an 8-hour working day and, by mid-1906, fought wage demands, meeting strikes by lock-outs. However, once again, the KD's membership and leaders were not factory owners and even to represent them as such would not help to explain the retreat of the KDs from their radical 'no enemies on the Left' positions of October 1905 to their 'save the Duma at all costs' views of 1907. Nor can it explain why the retreat of KDs was matched by the radicalisation of the late-day Union of Unions with its fairly similar social constituency. To understand this, one must look at the social roots and intellectual history of Russian liberalism and radicalism – both of which were far removed from the social matrix of the actual capitalism and capitalists of Russia.

As to the proletarian self-organisation, the creation of Soviets was initially treated with suspicion or hostility by many of the SDs, especially the Bolsheviks.[38] It seemed to challenge the party's exclusive nature and smacked of the 'spontaneity' which the *Iskra* group combated so harshly. It was later to be appropriated by the

Soviet historians as the natural organisation of the working class
(with some claims even that it was initiated by the Bolsheviks). The
class-parliament character of the St Petersburg Soviet was in fact
sustained by workers' spontaneous will. Contemporaries have,
however, testified that the Soviet acted not only as the workers'
representation but also very much as a co-ordinating committee of
different socialist tendencies. Indeed, in the areas in which no
multiplicity and relative balance of those parties existed, the
strongest party or a 'federal' committee of socialist parties simply ran
the show without bothering to provide the 'non-party working
masses' with a specific expression of their own, for example, in Riga.
Proletarian 'democracy from below' blossomed only in a specific
multi-party political context, while outside this it tended to slide into
the substitution of the leading socialist party for the proletariat and of
the party committees for the party itself.

The political division within the towns of Russia changed rapidly as
the revolution progressed. Social groups and individuals learned from
the process and reacted to it. From late 1905 onwards political
polarisation was taking place. The described mobilisation of
monarchist extremism, the landowners' lobby and the liberals'
turning to the 'right' were matched in 1906 by the move to the 'left' by
those supporting the socialists – expressed in the Union of Unions, in
the Soviets, and in the increasing preference of the workers and party
activists for leaders and movements representing a more aggressive,
and uncompromising – often armed – stand.

*   *   *

A 'different rhythm' of revolutionary struggle can also be shown in
comparing Russia's towns and its countryside. We shall discuss the
particularity of the peasant dimension presently. What should be
stressed at the outset is a contrary point – that is, the measure of the
interdependence between the major social classes of the Russian
countryside and the urban society. A national pyramid of wealth and
power, with its top in the capitals of the realm, cross-cut the rural–
urban divisions. The socio-geographical mobility of the squires and of
the peasant-workers provided direct contacts and an 'exchange of
personnel'. Something more must be said about the political
dimension of the matter.

The Russian nobles and landowners of middling rank and wealth
were ill-prepared to face the crisis of the 1861 emancipation of serfs,

and the long depression of agricultural prices which followed.[39] Many gave up farming altogether. Others moved out of the capitals into the provinces to supervise their land personally, the more so since the 1896 upturn of the international grain market. They even began to speak of themselves as the 'toiling nobility'. They now resided more often in the provincial town, influencing the local administration and in part blending into it. (The large landowners sons often merged in a similar manner into the tsar's court and the Guards' regiments.) It was the educated elite of provincial squiredom which provided until 1905 the primary base for the nation-wide liberal dissent expressed in the *zemstvos*, for the attempts by the Free Economic Society to promote progressive agriculture and for the increasingly vocal demands for a constitution and social reforms. During 1906 this liberal demeanour of the squiredom's representation changed dramatically. In January, the conference of marshals of the provincial nobility associations (*predvoditeli dvorianstva*) called for unity against Russia's internal enemies and for the uncompromising defence of the manorial land ownership. In April, a meeting of representatives of the nobility summoned by the liberal Prince P. Trubetskoi voted him down as the chairman of the meeting, electing instead the reactionary Count V. Bobrinskii. A Council of United Nobility was then constituted to play the role of a major conservative force in Russia. Liberal nobles were being voted out of their offices in the *zemstvos*, defeated in the electoral colleges of landowners for the Duma election, socially ostracised and even expelled from the regional association of nobility.[40] It seemed as if the politics of the nobility came full circle. In fact, it was the different tendencies within the nobility that clashed and so came to light.

The major composite of the wealth, income and power of the middling provincial nobility was landed property. At the turn of the century, a major part of the Russian squiredom was on the decline, losing its land through debts and sales. Four-fifths of the Russian nobles, according to the reckoning of Prince Trubetskoi, were unable to support their families from their land alone. These squires objected sulkily to Witte's policies of 'milking agriculture' to benefit industrialisation and endlessly begged for scraps of government handouts, sinecures and privileges. It was their refusal to show public initiative which established the liberals' predominance in many *zemstvos*. Now, within one year, the camp of noble liberalism and enlightenment had been engulfed by this 'silent majority' of the squires. During the period 1905–06, this dispirited lot, together with a few effective farmers within the nobility, were shaped by the 'great fear' of peasant rebellion into a 'class for itself'. By 1906, it showed considerable impact, establishing a militant and effective corporate political presence, reactionary in its nature. They were united both by the slogans proclaiming the 'unalienable nature of private landed property', and by the hostile reaction to any peasant demands. They reflected as much the Russian middle nobility's particular failure to penetrate the ranks of capitalism's beneficiaries as its traditional dependence on the state.[41] Witte and Kutler (his reform-minded Minister of Agriculture) were their favourite bogeymen, together with foreign capital, intelligentsia, liberals and Jews. Even the government of Stolypin was being constantly criticised and put under relentless pressure from the reactionary nobles to whom the 'agrarian problem' was no more than 'an invention of revolutionaries and of bureaucratic dreamers who know nothing of the real life in the countryside'.[42] In their view what was needed was simply to re-establish order and to return to the pattern of authority as understood since the olden times.

A manifest, if indirect, dimension of the 1905–07 urban revolution was the rural class-confrontation over land. That was true not only for the squires. On the one hand stood the Russian landowning nobles in the villages and in the towns of Russia, connected with the officialdom's upper ranks and tied by empathy to the tsar and his kin. On the other side stood the peasants, represented in the towns by millions of peasant-workers who kept their land and/or families in the villages. While the cities' struggle deeply influenced the countryside, much of the change in the outlook and politics of the Russian urban-based nobility which occurred during 1905, as well as the views of many workers, had manifestly rural roots. They reflected, on both sides of the urban barricade, the massive attack of the peasants on the nobility's land and rural privileges – a *Jacquery*, an attempt at alternative rule and a forceful political dream which surfaced to haunt, and ultimately destroy, the Russian nobility and the state they treated as their own.

3 Revolution from Below: Land and Liberty!

It is not the little books which are terrible . . .
It is that there is nothing to eat for man and beast.

(Peasant elder questioned about the impact of revolutionary
propaganda on the 1902 'agrarian disturbances' in Poltava.)

Worse than poverty, more bitter than the hunger is the oppression
of the people by their absolute powerlessness.

(Resolution of the assembly of the village Shnyak, Kazan' *guberniya*, 1907.)

A. THE JACQUERY

According to the *Oxford Dictionary*, '*Jacquerie*, also Anglicised -ery'
is the 'revolt of the villains or peasants of northern France, hence,
any rising of Peasantry'. Somewhat humorously for those who look at
it *ex post factum*, the 1901 edition of that major repository of
standard knowledge and common sense proceeds thus to exemplify
the term: 'In Russia . . . the villages scattered here and there in the
midst of great steppe do not afford material even for a successful
Jacquery'. The *Encyclopaedia Britannica* explicated the initial event
as caused by 'the hardship endured by the peasants in the Hundred
Years War and their hatred for the nobles who oppressed them'. The
peasants, it said, 'destroyed numerous chateaux . . . subjected the
whole countryside to fire and sword, committed the most terrible
atrocities'. This was brought to an end when 'an army of Charles the
Bad . . . crushed the rebels . . . and the nobles then took violent
reprisal'.[1] Notice the adverb 'then' and the description of the popular
nickname of the nobles' commander.

Historians of those days speak mostly of the Chronicles' testimony.
Behind the Chronicles stand the chroniclers and their audiences, the
monks and the nobles who wrote and were written for, the owners of
land, power and knowledge who left us the written word. It was they
who derived the word 'Jacquery' from Jacques Bonhome – the vulgar

79

simpleton in the French usage of those times. Theirs was also the *Declinatio Rustico* of the thirteenth century, which told us what the word peasant really meant – its 'six declensions' were 'villain, rustic, devil, robber, brigand and looter; and in the plural, wretches, beggars, liars, rogues, trash and infidels'.[2]

The essence of the term and the image of Jacquery bequeathed to us and taken for granted, is that of riot, a brute sudden outburst when rural underdogs go on the rampage, driven by poverty and hate, to be 'then' bloodily crushed and pacified by the 'forces of order'. The stages of such a process, when the peasant rebellion faces 'unshakeably powerful regimes', were well described by an author talking of the 1902 'agrarian disturbances' in the South of Russia: 'born as from nothing, grown suddenly into a peril, it is extinguished without a trace'.[3] The list of the peasant riots and rebellions all through history and the world over is long. Just as in the case of the initial Jacquery of the fourteenth century, historians will forever argue about such rioters' goals and motives, but would usually agree that the rebellion was surprising, spontaneous, brutal and short-lived, and that the peasants involved were more than usually oppressed or hungry before it happened. Those in sympathy with the underdogs may possibly remember that it was the brutality of the brutalised which exploded, its venom an impeachment of the masters rather than of slaves. Even they would mostly feel uneasy with the fury of mob spontaneity which did not lead to any immediate improvement, for when it was all over there was usually little left but ruins and gallows, soldiers' loot and historians' quarrels.

The long-term impact of such lessons of history taught to and learned by the rulers and the ruled would be less open to view. It is often the victors' fear of those they have vanquished which dominates policies of state and their reassessment in time to come. The long-term results of a crushing defeat can be better than the life of those who bent without a struggle.

The Russian equivalents of the Jacquery were the *bunt, volnitsa* and *pugachevshchina*. Throughout the entire history of enserfment and of serfdom, peasants defied their masters and exploiters by all means imaginable in a never-ending struggle to hand on to an extra sack of grain, an extra hour of leisure, an extra 'ounce' of self-respect. They usually faced the 'unshakeably powerful regimes' with a battery of cunning devices: by hiding, stealing and faking as much as by the Good Soldiers Schweik type of respectful servility with a barb in it. In their day-to-day life during the long periods of relative stability, their stand can be best described by the Puerto Rican peasant saying: *Obezdo pero no cumplo* – 'I obey, but do not comply'. At times they sneakingly revenged themselves through undisclosed murders of nobles and their officials or the 'red rooster', as Russians put it, that is, a barn set on fire by an unknown hand – just enough to make a squire think twice before overstepping some invisible line of the acceptable in the way peasants were milked, ruled and brutalised.[4] At other times, especially when those lines were crudely stamped on and the whole social system shaken by famine, war or pestilence, the social control by fear and manipulation crumbled suddenly and the otherwise hidden fury exploded into *bunt* – an open indeed demonstrative mass disobedience, mob violence, destruction and/or murder, invariably followed by harsh pacification and symbolic shows of repentance. Peshekhonov's comment above described those sequences well. The history of peasants outside Russia shows how much it was part of a general condition of peasanthood and the way peasants as a whole were inserted into the society, at its pit.

At the margins of control by the tsar and the nobles, the *volnitsa* developed – the consequence both of a solidifying autocracy and of its incompleteness. The Cossacks of old – the armed communities of freebooters on the southern frontier and the river-gates to the Orient – were its most colourful, but not its only expression.[5] Enserfment made some of the boldest flee to seek freedom where state power could not reach them: to the wild frontier but also into foreign lands, to the unending forest with its *skity* of religious sects, to brigands' gangs and to other 'social margins'. The very existence of such communities was a permanent rebellion, mostly on the part of peasants and peasant sons, against the powers-that-be. The growth and modernisation of tsardom meant a constant process of penetration, take-over, destruction and incorporation of those islands of social independence.

The Russian peasant wars of the seventeenth and eighteenth centuries invariably involved a fusion of a multiplicity of local peasant *bunts* with the *volnitsa*. Each of them was led by Cossacks, who brought to the conflict military skills and experience. The one led by Pugachev in 1773–5 was the most extensive and 'ideologically' explicit of them.[6] It rested on the claims of a 'false pretender' (Pugachev declared himself to be the murdered Tsar Peter III). Its aim was declared to be the restoration of freedom robbed by the nobles, land for all, and the transformation of the entire Russian peasantry into

Cossacks, that is, the conversion of serfs into free, armed and self-ruled peasant assemblies (*kozachii krug*). It was supported by religious sectarians – the Old Believers, who in the name of the good old days and true Christianity opposed the Church reforms and hierarchy. At its climax, the rebellion also drew in the serf-workers of the factories in the Urals and the Bashkir tribesmen and Chuvash villagers whose lands had been robbed by the state and the Russian nobles. On his march, Pugachev ordered the execution of squires, officials and officers. In an only-to-familiar sequence, the rebellion was eventually crushed and bloodily pacified by the armies of Catherine II, its leaders and many of their followers tortured to death. It was never quite forgotten by those who ruled. The word '*Pugachevshchina*' was passed from generation to generation as a term covering peasant war, plebian brutality and high treason.

It seemed that in Russia the Peasant War led by Pugachev was both the crest and the last of them all. By the end of Catherine II's reign, the peasants were completely enserfed while the state machinery, especially the local authorities and the organisations of nobles, had been overhauled and modernised. Lessons had also been drawn as far as the Cossacks were concerned. Their autonomy was abolished, their organisations brought under tight military control and incorporated within the state machinery via a system of privileges, setting them apart from the peasants as a military caste of the tsar's darlings and henchmen. During the ensuing 125 years the peasant *bunts* proceeded apace, once in a while reaching a crescendo, as during the period 1859–64 and again in 1874 and 1884.[7] These 'agrarian disturbances' were invariably localised now, hopeless and helpless once the army or the police moved in with the usual sequence of executions, flogging and deportations. With the power of the state organisation enhanced and the main reservoir of the 'tactically mobile' and armed *volnitsa* neutralised or turned into a major police reserve, the Russian Jacquery was growing into a faint memory of horror for the squires. Within the peasantry itself it reappeared only in its legends.[8] Some of the anarchists and populists of the 1850s to 1870s tried for a while to bring it back but without avail. Even the localised 'agrarian disturbances' dropped sharply after 1884. The peasants 'suffered in silence' throughout the terrible famine of 1891. The radical intelligentsia increasingly turned to other allies and other tasks. Jacquery seemed a thing of the past for Russia and, increasingly, for the world at large.

With hindsight, we now know that what happened in Russia in

1905–07 commenced a new wave of peasant wars whose specificity is defined by their social and historical situation at the periphery of the global capitalist advance. Erik Wolf has discussed the common characteristics of that wave: Russia 1905–07, Mexico 1910–25, Russia 1917–20, China, Algeria and Vietnam, and suggested that its social roots lie in the economic, demographic and normative crisis of capitalist penetration of the peasant societies and/or de-peasantisation.[9] He has also shown that in the political context of the twentieth century, peasant rebellions have gained both a new lease of life, and a chance to make a considerable impact, even though the final results have never been the establishment of a peasant Utopia. But all that was yet to come. When, in 1902, the stolid quiet of the Russian countryside of Kharkov and Poltava was broken by what looked like the beginning of a more-than-local peasant rebellion, without any external agency taking a manifest hand in it, the surprise sent both state dignitaries and radicals 'back to the drawing-board' to think anew about the peasant revolutionary potential. They were not yet ready to draw conclusions when by 1905 the first peasant revolt of the twentieth century materialised in full.

*　　*　　*

The evidence concerning the 1905–07 peasant revolt is plentiful if uneven. There are several major sources for it. First, there are the results of a massive questionnaire by the Free Economic Society, analysed in 1912 by Prokopovich,[10] whose work has not since been greatly improved upon. Second, there are the reports in the police archives, the studies of which were initiated in the 1920s by Dubrovskii.[11] Third, there are the reports of the press, the peasant petitions and the *nakazy* – the written instructions of peasant assemblies to their elected representatives, which were collected and analysed in a number of publications.[12] The protocols of the congresses of the All-Russian Peasant Union belong to an important category of their own.[13] Additional evidence can also be found in less systematic sources: memoirs, court proceedings, provincial governors' reports to St Petersburg, reports of the different party congresses or committees and so on. Each of the different types of data and analysis employed have their own pitfalls, making their complementary usage essential. New studies, reconsiderations and re-counts of relevant data are still taking place.[14] New evidence can be found in several multi-volume collections compiled by Soviet historians.

To introduce the sequence of events of the Russian Jacquery of 1905–07, it will be best first to lay the foundations by preliminary answers to the questions 'What?', 'When?', 'Where?', 'Who?' and 'Why?'. To begin with the first three of these queries, the so-called 'agrarian disturbances' incorporated a wide range of characteristically peasant acts of defiance, struggle and revolt. A whole new terminology of peasant criminality came into being to encompass it within the records and the law. There were the illicit invasions of the private and state forests to cut timber (*Porubki*) and the invasion of grazing land (*Potravy*). Both had doubtlessly existed as long as landed property itself, but the defiant, massive and often demonstrative 'grab' was new and was rightly treated as rebellion. At the more violent end of the scale stood the mass robbery of stores, warehouses and manors (*Rasborka*), the destruction of estates (*Razgrom*), arson and the murder of squires, of their guards and representatives. Then there were the illegal take-over and ploughing up of non-peasant lands (*zapashka*), the rural strike (illegal, or treated as such), the collective demand for lower rents, and the 'boycott' – when all relations with a local manor were suspended, especially the offer of wage-labour. Finally, there were direct challenges to the state such as the voting out of loyalist peasant elders, the collective refusals to pay taxes, the establishment of alternative local authorities and violent confrontations with the army and police.

Three patterns can be seen at the root of the peasant struggle. Their explication enables us to order and grasp the different dimensions of peasant action, admittedly interdependent yet distinctive. These are the regional divisions, the seasonality and the general course of the peasant struggle during those years. To begin with the region, the map of the 'agrarian disturbances' of the nineteenth century roughly matched that of the 1905–07 Jacquery, suggesting structural reasons for the peasant radicalism in those areas. The most riotous provinces stretched along the so-called Black-Earth Belt of the Ukraine and Russia proper from Chernigov *gubernya* in the west via Orel, Kursk, Voronezh and Tambov, to Saratov and further to Samara, Ufa and Kazan. From Poltava, Kharkov, Ekaterinoslav, Kherson and Tavrida in the south, the area stretched to Penza, Tula and Ryazan in the north, partly outside the central Black-earth zone of better land but much denser rural population. In a number of the *gubernya*s the peasant struggle of 1905–07 was particularly violent, involving massive and spontaneous destruction of the manors. But violence was not all in the rural revolutionary attack. Moving south and south-west from the Chernigov–Saratov axis of peasant violence, peasant strikes increasingly took pride of place while destruction of manors declined or disappeared. The incidence of invasion of grazing land was also higher here and there were more confrontations over rent. The north and north-west of Russia had fewer 'agrarian disturbances' altogether, but a higher share of invasion of forests was reported. Peasant political organisations spread rapidly, as strong in the manor-burning Saratov as in the non-manorial Vyatka province. At the ethnically non-Russian periphery, Georgia led in political boycotts resulting in the establishment of alternative rural govern-ments. Latvia was prominent in strikes of the rural wage labourers and also witnessed boycotts, alternative governments but also in the destruction of manors. Many rural strikes took place in the Polish provinces but peasant activity was lesser in scope (see Map 2 for the rural struggles).

The seasonal rhythm of the 'disturbances' once again resembled the record of the nineteenth century. Peasant defiance and struggle followed the agricultural year, it peaked in summer and nearly disappeared in winter (see Addendum, Table 5, of this volume). During the period 1905–07, October to December of 1905 was the only exception to this, and will be discussed presently. As to the general course of events, a shift in the form of peasant struggle took place. The destruction of manors reached its peak in 1905 and declined thereafter, while 1906 saw the height of strike actions. The overall number of these 'agrarian disturbances' decreased sharply in 1907, which made the upturn in the number of arson cases stand out even more. Also, the huge numbers of events did not necessarily signify national or regional unity. Each peasant locality fought its own battles and even when things 'heated up' the spread of peasant action usually reached only a *volost'* level (i.e., a sub-district of about a dozen villages). Only twice, in the autumn of 1905 and in the summer of 1906, did the mass of local and regional acts of rebellion increase in intensity to form, over large territories, a manifest chain reaction – to use an image from a different world and age.

To proceed to the question 'Who?', this must first be sub-divided into 'By whom?' and 'Against whom?'. There were few cases in which the rich peasants were reported not to have participated in the Jacquery and fewer still where they even banded together to oppose it.[15] Many reports indicated cases where it was the rich who led the peasant attacks and who derived the most benefit from them, for example, a multihorse household could do better in the invasion of

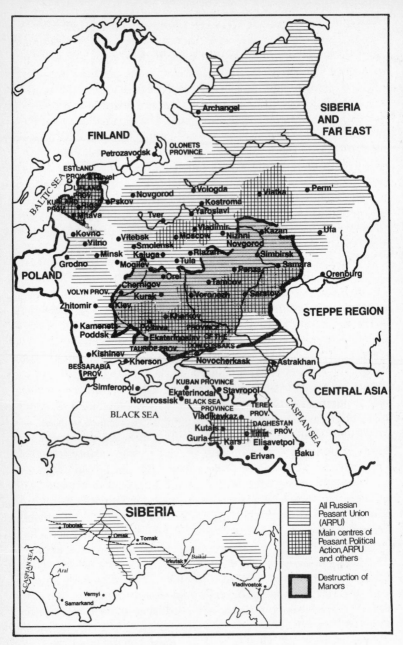

Map 2 *Rural struggles 1905–07.*

Legend (within map):

All Russian Peasant Union (ARPU)

Main centres of Peasant Political Action, ARPU and others

Destruction of Manors

Labels on main map: Archangel, SIBERIA AND FAR EAST, FINLAND, Petrozavodsk, OLONETS PROVINCE, ESTLAND PROV., Revel, LIFLAND PROV., Riga, KURLAND PROV., Mitava, BALTIC SEA, Pskov, Novgorod, Vologda, Viatka, Perm', Kostroma, Yaroslavl, Kovno, Vilno, Vitebsk, Smolensk, Vladimir, Moscow, Nizhni Novgorod, Kazan, Ufa, Minsk, Kaluga, Riazan, Simbirsk, Grodno, Mogilev, Tula, Orel, Penza, Samara, Orenburg, POLAND, VOLYN PROV., Chernigov, Kursk, Tambov, Saratov, Voronezh, STEPPE REGION, Zhitomir, Kiev, Khar'kov, Kamenets Poddsk, POLTAVA PROVINCE, EKATERINOSLAV PROV. OF THE DON COSSAKS, TAURIDE PROV., Kishinev, Kherson, Novocherkask, Astrakhan, BESSARABIA PROV., Simferopol, KUBAN PROVINCE, Ekaterinodar, Stavropol, CENTRAL ASIA, Novorossisk, BLACK SEA PROVINCE, TEREK PROV., CASPIAN SEA, BLACK SEA, Vladikavkaz, DAGHESTAN PROV., Kutais, Guria, Kars, Elisavetpol, Baku, Erivan

Inset map labels: SIBERIA, CASPIAN SEA, Tobolsk, Omsk, Tomsk, Aral, Baikal, Irkutsk, Vernyi, Samarkand, Vladivostok forests, manors or grazing lands. According to all the reports, the rural wage-labourers of Russia (*batraki*) and the poorest of the peasants did not play a prominent or even an active role in the confrontations. Only in the Baltic provinces and Poland were the wage labourers organised and active, but even there only on the large estates – those employed by peasant smallholders of Latvia remained passive.[16] It was the 'middle peasantry' inclusive of its poorer households, that is, smallholders engaged mostly in agriculture on their own holdings but with different amounts of land, equipment and supplementary income available to them, who were the marching army of the Jacquery. They also provided most of its leaders who usually had shown a higher-than-average exposure to the world outside the boundaries of the village through army service, city work, foreign travel or simple literacy, which enabled them to master a newspaper.

The later attempts to single out specifically 'proletarian types of struggle' at times engendered the assumption that a strike is by definition 'proletarian', in other words, synonymous with the struggle of those who lived exclusively, or to a decisive extent, on their wages. In fact, the large majority of rural strikes in Russia 1905–07 were strikes of peasant smallholders, partly or seasonally employed on the neighbouring estates. They were mostly led by their communal assembly (*mir*) which decided on the strike, established its aims, supervised its execution and manned its pickets. The demand to dismiss outside workers (*prishlye*), that is, to secure a 'closed shop' arrangement – a monopoly of the local peasants over the wage-labour of 'their' neighbouring estates – was common. The linkage and interchangeability of demands for higher wages *and* for lower rent in many of those strikes make their peasant nature and goals particularly clear.

The issue of 'Against whom?' was examined with particular care and even quantified by Dubrovskii and by others who have followed up his work. A consensus seems to exist here: to a decisive degree the Jacquery within European Russia was aimed at the squire and his rural holdings. The army, police and state officials came next, attacked mostly as they rushed to the defence of the manors. Rich peasant landowners and/or employers were seldom harmed. Dubrovskii's figures for 1905–07 suggest that 75.4 per cent of the relevant cases were aimed at the squires, 14.5 per cent at the army or police, and 1.4 per cent at the rich peasants, with 8.7 per cent for all the others, such as the clergy.[17] The proportion of the inter-peasant 'anti-*kulak*' attacks actually decreased during the 1905–07 period.

The ethno-geographical periphery differed in the extent of its challenge to the Russian state and its symbols, for example, systematic destruction of the rural offices of the authorities took place in Georgia, Latvia and Poland.[18]

Finally the question 'Why?' can be properly considered only after more has been said about the peasant war and peasant politics. An introductory comment can however help to focus attention here. The permanent and growing crisis of the peasant economy, described in Chapters 3 and 4 of the companion volume *Russia as a 'Developing Society'*, was without doubt, at the root of the explosion. Its major components were the 'vicious circle' of rapidly decreasing land *per capita*, the shortage of income and of investments, the pressure of debts and taxes, the upswing of rents and the lack of alternative or supplementary sources of employment and income. All led to the pauperisation of the peasants. In 1905 the crops failed once more in twenty-five of European Russia's gub., within a region closely corresponding to that of the rebellion. Any crop failure made numerous households, communities and districts cross the very thin line between ordinary poverty and destitution, hunger, and loss of livestock which they could not hope to replace. To make things worse, in more than half the territories hit, the famine of 1905 was repeated in 1906.[19] The report in March 1905 of a colonel of the gendarmerie in Vitebsk *guberniya* was true for many parts of European Russia. It said, 'Not only the stored grain, but also the seeds have by now been eaten with nothing left . . . The bread peasants eat is of such substance as to leave one surprised that they can eat it at all and survive . . .' The report concluded that if no help were offered to counteract the hunger, . . . all that and the lack of supplementary income will lead to terrible results . . . With no bread, no repression can help'.[20] But we must remember that the famine of 1891 did not lead to a peasant revolt but only to apathy and despair. Hunger does not directly translate into revolution.

The few intelligent gendarmes notwithstanding, to the tsar's administrators, nobles and devotees the pet explanation of peasant revolt was enticement or instigation by the non-peasant enemies of the state: anarchists, students, Jews and the like, possibly in the pay of the Japanese. The pro-government press repeated these allegations endlessly. The high plausibility of such causes to the ruling stratum was clear, for it accepted (despite 'the regrettable events') fundamental peasant goodness-cum-conservativism and freed the nobles and bureaucrats from any charges to be answered. Moreover,

the bias of the revolutionaries on that score, was fairly similar to that
of 'the establishment', for it was only too easy to over-estimate one's
own importance in political events of considerable appeal. To be
sure, the so-called 'third element' – the rural intelligentsia employed
by the *zemstvo* provincial authorities, and especially the teachers,
agronomists, doctors and statisticians – had been attempting for
decades to 'raise the peasant consciousness', that is, to educate as
well as to radicalise the peasants. In a few areas the impact of exiles
from the capitals was also felt. Nonetheless, the police search for the
culprits and the post-revolutionary hunt for the non-peasant rural
revolutionaries who *actually* led the peasant revolt in central Russia
produced remarkably scanty results. On the strength of their
evidence, the peasant movement of 1905–07 was, in European
Russia, a spontaneous and/or self-led affair. Only at the periphery
was the situation different. We shall proceed with the issue of 'Who
led whom?' in the 1905–07 peasant revolt and the relevant evidence
after more has been said about peasant struggle and demands.

By 1905 the harsh, meticulous and consistent surveillance of the
state machinery over the Russian countryside weakened. Control by
political manipulation was never a strong point of this officialdom,
the Land Chief and the police officer simply told the peasant what to
do and meted out punishment when the orders and their results
differed. The military defeats, the rumours of 'disorders' elsewhere
and of impending changes had shaken the officials' confidence and
the peasant's inertia of obedience. Soldiers still kept shooting down
mutineers, Cossacks flogged and police arrested. Elements of
stability and order were still in evidence, but stability for what and for
how long? Once the tsar's will could no longer be treated as a force of
nature and the continuity of tsardom could no longer be unquestion-
ably assumed, the whole social world of rural Russia came apart.
Everything seemed possible now. Some of the ex-serfs who had been
lads of 20 in 1861 were still alive and by now only 64. Their memory
carried direct recollections of days when a tsar granted some land and
some liberty to the peasants, if not enough of either. A 'second
freedom', ordered by the tsar's 'golden manifesto', letting the
peasants have the remainder of the noble's land, seemed plausible
now. So, increasingly, was the possibility to take some matters into
peasants hands. That was what they proceeded to do.

* * *

To tell the tale in the order of events, the Russian Jacquery of
1905–07 began in February 1905 in Dimitriev district (*uezd*) of Kursk

province (*guberniya*), at the centre of European Russia.[21] On 14
February, an estate was raided and within days sixteen others were
'taken apart' over a territory of more than 50 square miles. The
records of those events closely resemble one another. A mass of
peasants with hundreds of driven carts congregated at the sign of a
bonfire or when the church bell sounded an emergency (the *nabat*).
They then proceeded to the manorial warehouses, broke locks and
carried away grain and fodder. Usually, nothing else was touched.
The landowners were left unmolested. The peasants at times warned
them as to the exact date when the estate was going to be 'taken
apart' (*razobran*). Only in a few cases did arson take place and one
single policeman was reportedly hurt while attempting to make an
arrest. The grain taken away was often divided between peasant
households in an orderly and communal manner, according to their
size and on the basis of lists prepared in advance for that purpose. In
one of the villages involved, a local blind beggar was provided with a
cart and horses by his village, to secure his share of the 'taken apart'
grain. All the reports stress the sense of righteousness with which the
peasants usually proceeded, which meant that some self-defined
limits were strictly maintained, for example, things considered
personal property were not taken. By April, the 'taking apart' along
fairly similar lines had spread to the neighbouring districts (*uezds*) in
Orel and Chernigov gub., and a few more cases were reported
elsewhere. It was enough for a single newspaper describing the
'agrarian disturbances' in Kursk to reach Biriuch *uezd* in Voronezh
gub., 200 miles distant, for the local peasants to proceed to do
likewise.[22] A number of the rural plants producing vodka and sugar
were also 'taken apart' and then burned. No direct resistance was
offered by the owners and those of them who resided in the
countryside hastily departed to towns.

Other forms of peasant rebellion had by then spread over much
larger areas. Massive invasions of forests had already begun at the
end of 1904 and by April 1905 were recorded in no fewer than
twenty-nine *uezds* all over Russia. Once again, these usually involved
the collective action of many horse-drawn carts and were accompanied by very little violence. When in one place, however, a peasant
was caught in the act by the police and roughed up, his neighbours
stormed and totally destroyed five neighbouring manors, breaking up
furniture, burning down buildings and killing livestock. Elsewhere,
manorial grazing lands were invaded. Rural strikes spread in the
south-west and the Baltic provinces. Throughout the early months of

1905 the peasant action was, to a very considerable degree, a direct and spontaneous response to the hardship and desperate shortage of food, fodder and timber within many of the peasant communities. (One can add that it was a response which proved remarkably orderly and bloodless.)

The government reacted by the usual pacification measures: suppression and appeasement. Punishment expeditions proceeded monotonously to arrest, flog and impose collective fines. Appeasement and educational measures were also tried. Some of the peasant debts to the state were cancelled (5 April) and the governors of the provinces told by a circular of the Minister of the Interior 'to try and propagate order within the villages' (15 April). A new Ministry (*Gosudarstvennoe upravlenie zemledeliya i zemleustroistva* – the GUZZ) and yet another Committee were set up to look into agrarian matters. All that did not bring the disturbances to an end. Their intensity proceeded to grow, reaching a peak in June. The invasion of forests, clashes over rent and cases of arson increased and spread into new areas of the mid-Volga, Ukraine and Belorussia. The invasion of grazing land became massive. The Free Economic Society questionnaire reported rural strikes of exceptional solidarity and orderliness. Peasant communes decided on the demands, and the peasants working on the local estate struck. The servants of the manor, the coachmen and gardeners usually continued to work (often with the commune's explicit permission). The well-to-do peasants usually supported their poorest neighbours by food hand-outs throughout the strike, which improved its chances of success. Some of the peasants began to talk of strike as a method of ridding the area of the squires altogether, reasoning that once wages had risen high enough the state owners would have to go, selling the land to their peasant neighbours.

Outside Russia proper, in Latvia, strikes by rural wage-labourers, for the most part landless, began in February. A general rural strike took place in July and lasted for two weeks. Mobile pickets brought work to a halt at most of the estates. The Ukrainian SDs (the *Spilka*) and the SDs of Georgia were active in their respective rural areas. The revolutionary political parties were more assertive and more effective there. In the ten Polish provinces of 'Visla region' the rural struggle was less pronounced, also it was usually tied to broader national demands, especially to the demand to use Polish as the official language. Beside the clergy and some right-wingers, the PPS operated in the Polish countryside and led the rural strikes (the

SDKPL focused its forces entirely in the towns). All through the empire an increasing number of rural confrontations, strikes and boycott decisions intertwined with demonstrations in which red flags, associated with the socialists of SDs, SRs, PPS, Bund etc., were carried and political declarations made.[23]

Something new was beginning to take shape in Russia proper, in so far as specifically peasant organisation was concerned. In May 1905, a peasant meeting called by the Moscow Marshal of Nobility to support the war effort got out of hand and its participants decided, instead, to condemn officials who 'from the local policemen upwards to the ministers themselves . . . conduct the state-business of Russia wrongly and waste money collected from the poor'.[24] They called for the establishment of an All-Russian Peasant Union whose first (and illegal) Congress of Representatives met consequently on the last day of July 1905, with delegates from 25 *gubernii* present. We shall discuss it in section 3B.

In August 1905, the acts of peasant rebellion and defiance diminished and by September reached their lowest point since February 1905, the date when they had begun. This was sharply reversed in October with the beginning of the railway strike and the national general strike which followed. For a quarter of a century the railway line and railway station had increasingly become the village's main link to the 'big world' beyond the village as well as to the Russian state. It symbolised both of them; massively mechanical, with a machine-like exactitude, unified and uniform, it was a gateway to the cities and the state-capitals for rural workers and for peasant petitioners. Its sudden halt brought about by its workers' own will, was shocking and unbelievable. Peasant crowds gathered at the station gazing and commenting, picking up news, leaflets and newspapers, listening to railwaymen, to their union delegates, and to the local radical intelligentsia.[25] On 17 October, the tsar's manifesto was published, speaking much of freedom and nothing about land – the main thing which mattered. Newspapers, leaflets, soldiers' letters and travellers' stories were full of new and shocking ideas. These were repeated, re-stated, puzzled over, embellished, and mythologised in every village and every peasant gathering. The local officials looked bewildered. The anti-Jewish and anti-intelligentsia pogroms and the police role in these added to the shakiness of the official hold and produced an additional wave of rumours, for example, that 'it will be permitted' to rob Jews and squires for three days, but three days only.

In October 1905, attacks on estates erupted on an unprecedented scale and rapidly turned into a mass destruction of the manor houses in the Black Earth Belt. It began in the Saratov gub., and somewhat later in the Chernigov gub. From these two epicentres it spread like a forest fire in several waves which eventually met, encompassing no less than half of European Russia. The image of a forest fire is real enough, for the descriptions from Saratov speak of a red night-sky illuminated by the blaze of the burning estates, with new points of light appearing one after another and the urban onlookers identifying each by the names of the manor houses of the local nobles. They speak also of lines of horse-drawn carts moving along red horizons: 'a peasant army coming back from its wars'.[26] Once the glow appeared in the sky, one village after another rose, congregating in columns which moved from manor to manor. During the day, the roads were full of noble carriages speeding their owners away to the towns, and of cavalry units riding out on punitive missions. The night belonged to the peasants.

The mass destruction of manors was by that time neither an accident nor an act of mindless vandalism. All over the area of the Jacquery, peasants proclaimed as their aim to 'smoke them out' for good – that is, to remove the squires and to ensure that the lands of the nobility were left to the peasants to hold and to till. The squires and their servants on the premises were still seldom attacked, but the manors were systematically put to the torch. A view from a provincial governor's mansion can both supplement the picture and say something about the feeling of the local dignitaries and nobles who faced the peasant uprising. The daughters of the governor of Saratov, destined soon to go on to a higher estate, M. Bok née Stolypin, recollected it thus: 'The popular riots in the villages increased, peasants burned manors, destroying all that came to hand . . . They almost never stole a thing but burned . . . tore apart, broke . . . From the windows of a railway carriage one could see the steppe lit by enormous bonfires at the burning manor houses'.[27]

By mid-November 1905, the wave of destruction of the manors had receded, partly, it seemed, following the army's harsh response. It rose again, however, and spread into new areas by the end of the month. The invasion of land and forests, strikes and confrontations over rent were massive. The figures given by Prokopovich show that roughly half the *uezds* of European Russia had 'disturbances' in the autumn of 1905, while the destruction of manors was recorded in about a quarter of them. The government reported 2000 manor houses destroyed, estimating the owners' losses as 29 million roubles. Soviet historians have since accounted for nearly 3000 manors destroyed – 15 per cent of the total – and increased the estimate of the resulting losses to more than 40 million roubles.[28] In some of the areas where agrarian disturbances centred, there were hardly any manor houses left standing as 1905 drew to a close.

The government, the thin layer of peasant activists and the radical rural intelligentsia faced a major and spontaneous peasant war on the squires. Political choices had to be made at once, especially on the Left, all the more so since some of the reports about the peasants' revolt made it clear that the peasant attack on the manors had at times been mixed with general attacks on wine-shops, simple robbery and anti-Jewish pogroms. On the burlesque side, stories were being told about a crowd of peasant families working hard to divide equally between them, bit by bit, a manorial piano.

A revolutionary minority now proceeded to try its best to turn the Russian Jacquery into a full-scale revolution. In late October, the PSR organisers in Saratov *guberniya*, where the PSR Peasant Brotherhoods were particularly strong, led an uprising in the *uezd* of Petrovsk.[29] For a while, the area was taken over, the police disarmed and new revolutionary authorities came into being. This act failed to detonate the general peasant war for which they had hoped. The reports of the participants showed the ambivalence, vagueness of plans and lack of military skills and equipment, which meant that on arrival of the regular army units the peasant armed-detachments (*druzhiny*) had no real chance and indeed little stomach to fight. The attempt to spread the uprising to other *gubernyas* failed. A few much smaller affairs, along similar lines, were attempted elsewhere (one by the local SDs) but little became of them.[30]

The view of the mainstream peasant activists was probably best represented at the next congress of the All-Russian Peasant Union which met in the last days of November 1905. The congress condemned government repression, demanded democratic freedoms and amnesty, but focused on the immediate transfer of all land into peasant hands, with a national peasant strike and rural boycott as the ultimate weapons in the struggle for those goals. Its large majority refused to endorse a call for an armed uprising.

The reaction of the government to the peasant revolt of late 1905 followed its usual pattern of heavy repression and largely ineffectual appeasement. On the appeasement side, a government manifesto of 3 November finally abolished the payments still due in lieu of the 1861 emancipation and promised to extend the activities of the Peasant Bank to aid poor peasants in increasing their landholdings. The parallel repressions were vicious – an orgy of brutality and the numbers of its victims standing out particularly in contrast to the relative self-restraint of the peasants when facing squires, soldiers and officials. The explicit order of Durnovo, the Minister of the Interior, was 'not to hold prisoners' but to execute rebels on the spot and to burn down the rebellious villages. To such orders from above a sequence of local initiatives of torture, robbery and rape was added by the forces of order, especially by its Cossack units. Whole villages were kept kneeling in the snow for many hours and flogged without exception to 'teach them a lesson'. On the spot deportation of trouble-makers was common. In such cases, a communal assembly was surrounded by cavalry and compelled by officials' pressure, threats, or mass flogging to pass resolutions exiling its own militants and leaders. These were then at once, before the eyes of their kin and community, rounded up by an army detachment and driven like cattle out of the village on the way to the next railway station and then into permanent exile in Siberia.[31] All this left behind bewildered and decapitated villages, rendered momentarily docile, and peasants whose hatred was well hidden behind a show of servility. The authorities were doing their best to 'put the fear of God and the tsar' into the peasants and there was indeed enough to fear. The executions were swift where the *agrarniki* – those arrested because of 'agrarian disturbances', were concerned.[32] Bad as it was in Russia proper, it was worse still in the Baltic provinces. Throughout the country, repression of the peasants went hand-in-hand with the arrests and exile of the rural intelligentsia. By the end of January 1906, the Jacquery and any rural defiance seemed to have been laid low.

Yet by now the revolutionaries and the government knew better than to believe that the peasant struggle had come to its end. For the Russian revolutionaries, it was increasingly the one remaining hope. Their urban forces were now in retreat and disarray after the bitter defeats in winter 1905–06. The tsar's army was still reliably putting down rebels and mutineers. Hope was now more and more placed on a Jacquery in the summer of 1906 which could raise morale in the towns and unsettle peasant soldiers. The next stage of the Revolution was expected to assume 'peasant colouring' in the words of a Marxist writer of the period.[33] On the other side of the barricade, Witte's report to the tsar on 10 January 1906 ran as follows:

It is my view that the expressions of revolution in townships and elsewhere, with the exception of the agrarian movement, are by now sufficiently repressed not to reappear with any strength . . . The agrarian disturbances, however, not only have not come to an end, but have only entered their first phase. One should expect in the Spring their reappearance with added strength if no adequate steps are taken.[34]

After Witte's dismissal, the newly-appointed Minister of the Interior, Stolypin, clearly endorsed a similar view in designing his programme for the suppression of revolutionary activities in 1906.[35] They were right.

During the winter of 1905–06 the only peasant attacks reported were those of the forest invasions, but in the spring of 1906 a full-scale peasant assault was launched again. By the summer, it had risen to the levels of intensity recorded in autumn 1905. Half the *uezds* of European Russia were again on fire. The peasant rebels were less active in some of the old areas but in others, for example, in the West Ukraine, their attack had only now begun in earnest. With the decline of urban strikes, the struggle of most of the 'peripheries' crushed by the end of 1905, and with the Russian middle classes increasingly hostile to the revolutionaries, the Russian peasants – more or less alone – faced the forces of order, heavily reinforced. In the words of S. Shestakov, the SD specialist on peasants who usually understated their vigour, by 1906 'the workers' masses could not any longer effectively resist the increasing reaction. Only the peasantry went on with its war for "land and liberty", in all the ways it could and the best it knew how'.[36]

Many of the descriptions of the new wave of destruction of manors in the summer of 1906 closely resembled those of November 1905. 'Rumours of destruction by peasants spread rapidly . . . They took everything they could and burnt the rest . . . Everybody [?! T.S.] panicked . . . For two weeks all the *uezd* lived in this way . . . A terrible picture: in the villages the bells ring, columns of smoke are everywhere, and at night the horizon is ablaze'.[37] The scope of the destruction was more limited now (about half the 1905 figures) and it was centred further south, especially in the Voronezh *guberniya*. In many areas the dominant form of attack became rural strikes, which trebled in comparison with the figures of autumn 1905. Strikes also spread to the areas in which the 1905 destruction of manors had been particularly prominent, such as the central agricultural region. The new peasant tactics were duly acknowledged by the government, in an urgently passed decree, imposing harsher punishment on the leaders and organisers of rural strikes (on 15 April 1906).[38] Simultaneously, a considerable number of rent strikes began and the invasion of grazing land returned to the levels of autumn 1905. The number of cases in which arable land of the manors was invaded and put to peasant use was still small, but on the increase.

The convocation of the first Duma in April 1906, the government's refusal even to consider the peasant land demands, and the eventual dissolution of the Duma correlated with an increase in the intensity of the peasant attack. It reached its climax in July. By now the punitive army expeditions were increasingly resisted by force. In various places, usually as a reaction to the arrest or maltreatment of a neighbour, villagers assembled at the sound of the church bells ringing the alarm, to fight pitched battles with the forces of order. At times they actually routed small units of mounted police. Single policemen and soldiers were ambushed. There were attempts to rescue prisoners by force. Small-scale guerrilla action was reported from some areas (for instance, the northern *guberniya* of Vyatka) and Robin-Hood-like robbers were supported by the peasants in the *guberniya* of Perm'.[39] In a new show of resistance, growing numbers of communes passed resolutions forbidding their members to serve in the police or refusing to rent houses to policemen and their families. The records and reports increasingly speak of the bitter animosity (*ozloblonnost'*) of the peasants. For the summer of 1906 Veselovskii recorded about 120 cases of violent confrontations between peasants and the forces of order, with 200 peasants killed and many hundreds wounded as a result.[40] Losses to the police and the army recorded by him included thirty-three killed and forty-two badly wounded – not a large number but twice the figure of government losses in the suppression of the Moscow uprising in December 1905.

This growing resistance by force, mostly defensive, did little to change the final results. With the battle in the cities all but won, peace with Japan signed, the army back from the East, its mutinous units rapidly suppressed or demobilised and with the state finances strengthened by the French loan, the state administration and the squires were the clear victors in that battle. During 1906 they also markedly recovered their nerve. The clamour of the Association of United Nobility, the newly-established trade union of the squires, for the 're-establishment of order in the countryside' and for a 'no compromise' stand over matters of land, as increasingly well received by the topmost authorities. The heavy-handed rural pacification continued and there was now less of an attempt at appeasement. By the end of the summer, the peasant struggle was once again in decline. This was not yet the end of the matter, however. During the winter of 1906–07, the figures of forest invasions and rural strikes in various parts of Russia were actually higher than ever before in that season. In the spring of 1907, grazing lands were massively invaded for the third year running. Some destruction of manors was reported in 1907 in the south. Arson by individuals unknown – the major weapon of vengeance of the peasant communities,[41] had increased sharply to reach its peak for a century in 1907. By now, it was aimed not only at the squires, but also at peasant neighbours, mostly at those suspected of acting as police stooges. (The houses of a few *kulaks* and of a number of known radicals were also burned.) These cases of arson even took on a particular organisational structure. Often it was a commune assembly which decided to employ it, and then proceeded to choose executors from among its members by drawing lots, with all its members committing themselves to silence.[42] The peasant struggle reached another peak in the summer of 1907, although lower than that of 1906. It then declined, finally to disappear, or rather, to attain its pre-revolutionary levels.

To recapitulate, in 1905 the peasants of Russia rebelled. Their rebellion took different forms and lasted until 1907. It presented a major challenge to the government, badly bruised in 1904–05 by external and internal enemies and facing a country with a large peasant majority. The rebellion was ultimately defeated by the harsh, punitive methods of the army, predominantly peasant in its social origins. It was as if *Pugachevshchina* had brought back the old times. These were not the old times, however, and even 'the same things' would not be the same in a new social context, with new classes and new forces on the political scene. But there is more to it. There is something wrong when an attempt is made to fit the tale of rural Russia 1905–07 into the persistent image of Jacquery. Peasants rose and kings trampled on them – so far the tale rings true. The same goes for the peasant columns marching across the Volga steppe in the blaze of burning manor-houses. However, the peasant attack was outstandingly bloodless, and on the strength of evidence of other times, this cannot be explained away simply by the good-heartedness of the Russian peasant. Also, peasant action was to a remarkable degree orderly in organisation, not at all like the mindless hunger-driven violence of hate and vandalism anticipated by its enemies and by some of its eulogisers. It also showed major similarities of goals and means which were particularly striking in view of the lack of an accepted leaders or ideologists, an all-encompassing organisation of long standing, an established unifying theory of social intervention or national networks of communication. It may be that it was, after all, not so unlike many original *Jacqueries* of Europe before the executioners and the chroniclers of the nobility turned their participants into monsters.[43] We know far too little about it. What we do know on good evidence is that the peasant rebellion in Russia 1905–07 was not the Jacquery of the images and expectations which this word conveyed. To answer 'How so?' and 'Why not?', one has to look at the peasant rule and the peasant dream.

B. THE PEASANT RULE

Examined more closely, the peasant revolt of 1905–07 displays a variety of goals and perceptions as well as of tactics consistently preferred by the different constituencies among the peasants who rose. Regional and ethnic divisions, wealth and socio-economic differentiation were the more obvious aspects of this heterogeneity. However, there was another basic duality which cut across regions and strata even, though it was often related to them. There were those peasants who acted mainly in response to an immediate physical need: hunger, dying livestock, freezing cold in an unheated hut or the only slightly-less-urgent incentives such as inability to set up a son on his own without a new house, which required timber from the squire's estate. On the other hand, there were those with an awareness of long-term and broader demands, which at times seemed vague but were often worked out very clearly in the endless village debates. The All-Russian Peasant Union and the Labour Faction in the Duma articulated these views on a national scale and we shall turn to these organisations shortly. The long-term demands were, first of all, to turn over all land to the peasants. This was particularly strong in the area where land was scarce and supplementary incomes limited and the old grievances concerning land ownership and rights of usage mixed with the new needs of a growing population. But there was also the craving for political power and civil rights, even though this meant something very different to peasants than to urbanites and only a few of the peasants would use those words.

Land was liberty but so was power – liberty from hunger and

insecurity and also a place of respect within the village. In another sense, it meant liberty from the total and obnoxious tutelage of, and oppression by petty officialdom, with its local protégés, allies and masters: the *kulak*, the clergy, the squire, and the dignitaries of the province. The Russian situation has produced quite a list of terms to designate the official or officially sponsored systems of arbitrary violence against its people, of the violations of their moral code and their helplessness against it: *proizvol, bezpravie, bezzakon'e*. This was by now at the core of the peasant political demands for change. The demands were seldom expressed as a wish to rule the Russian state in a peasant way or as a clear overall ideal of national political strategy over and above the basic demands for land reform, a 'charitable government', some general 'liberty' and being 'listened-to' when most fundamental needs were concerned. Power mainly meant local power, the running of the village or the district by the peasants and for the peasants. It was mainly that type of power as against the overwhelming powerlessness of day-to-day life which was in question. A small step to an outsider's eye but one which entailed a tremendous shift within rural Russia.

The relative significance of the various goals: immediate *versus* long-term, and land against political power, divided the peasants who were involved in the events of 1905–07. The division was manifest to the participants themselves. Both the peasants and the rural intelligentsia often spoke of a peasant mass of 'dark people' (*temnye lyudi*) – illiterate and drunken, helpless and brutal, conservative even while engaging in revolt, open to the persuasion of the Black Hundred's xenophobic appeal. On the other hand stood those peasants who were 'conscious' (*soznatel'nye*), that is, literate, capable of advanced farming, politically astute and radical in their demands – a peasant political 'class for itself' in the process of formation. In 1905, it was their impact in the villages which was rapidly on the increase. Tan quoted a description of it overheard in one of the villages. The difference between the 'conscious peasants' who joined the Peasant Union and the 'hooligans' who drank their time away, was described to him as that between peasants with patched clothes and those with clothes full of holes.[1]

The attitude towards the state monopoly of liquor and its shops may indeed exemplify this basic duality within the peasantry. It can also show a direction in the changes which occurred. In the 1902 Poltava revolt, the peasant rebels studiously advoided the liquor shops – it was the 'tsar's property' and was not to be touched. During the *pogroms* and acts of destruction in October 1905, liquor shops were often broken into, with subsequent drunken orgies lasting for days. The reports indicated, however, that in the areas of pre-eminence of the All-Russian Peasant Union, the local peasant revolt and/or collective action usually began with the peasant pickets sealing off the liquor shops or even burning them down altogether. This aimed to secure the villagers against drunken disorder and police provocation. It was also a declaration of war on the 'state monopoly' of vodka. Finally, at the end of 1905 when its Peasant Union leaders were arrested, the assembly of the village Krivorozh'e ruled as follows: 'In these sorrowful days of the imprisonment of the brothers Mazurenko, it is resolved not to drink vodka altogether and not to permit its sale'. This remarkable piece of applied political ethics was closely followed by a further decision, which showed how far the peasants had progressed in their political education: 'Those of the local squires who will not sign [a demand for the immediate release of those arrested] . . . will be boycotted. From 1 January until the acceptance of our demands, we are taking away from them all their workers and house servants'.[2] A self-assured and imperious 'we are taking away'.

The very existence of peasant general political goals in rural Russia of 1905–07 was doubted by many. First, it was said that it was over land, and land only, that the struggle was taking place. Second, peasant struggle was equated with immediacy and violence. Finally, it was said that in their political declarations peasants were no more than a tool in the hands of the rural intelligentsia, who wrote their lines for them.[3] We shall consider the first two issues here and turn to the last in Chapter 4.

The example of the Vyatka *guberniya* may explicate and document the significance of other-than-land issues for the Russian peasantry. This northern province, a former colony of the Great Novgorod, had its autonomy suppressed only in the fifteenth century. There was never any 'private', that is, squire-directed serfdom there and only a few nobles. The population of the province was highly homogeneous – 97 per cent were peasants by 'social estate', 89 per cent farmed as their main occupation and nine-tenths were ethnically Russian. The wide expanses of the province's land were not very fruitful. Accordingly, the local peasants engaged quite extensively in sup-plementary crafts and trades. They were also known to be relatively literate and independent. At the November 1905 congress of the All-Russian Peasant Union, the Vyatka delegate put their position clearly: 'The land problem is of no import to us, but our life is terribly difficult all the same'.[4] The development of the All-Russian Peasant Union in the province was spectacular, with mass meetings in many of its villages and a provincial conference of 200 delegates in November 1905. When, in December 1905, their next provincial conference was banned by the authorities, hundreds of peasants 'took apart' some stores of weapons and descended on Vyatka to defend their congress by the force of arms. In the resulting street battle between the army garrison and the peasants supported by some of the local revolutionaries, seven men were killed and twenty-four wounded on both sides before the army won the day. The colonel in charge, who displayed particular ruthlessness in the execution of his duties, was subsequently shot by one of his own soldiers, a peasant son.[5] During 1906, the Peasant Union, despite suppression and arrests, proceeded to operate very actively in the province and there were even some beginnings of guerrilla struggle. With no serfdom to remember, no land to fight for and no manors to burn, and therefore low on the scale of all the accepted indices of Jacquery, the peasants of Vyatka had little doubt that struggle was necessary and knew clearly which side they were on. For 'life was terribly difficult all the same'.

The primary attention of the government, the contemporary press, and later historians was naturally focused on the spectacle of burning manors, land invasions and armed confrontations – the Jacquery as understood. In the case of many of the Soviet scholars, this view was also related to their interpretation of Lenin's brash comment in 1917 that the only trouble with the peasant rebellion of 1905–07 was that they did not quite finish the job, burning down only part of the Russian manors.[6] Consequently, the burning of manors was turned into the major index of peasant revolutionary spirit and deed. Yet these studies note, often with surprise, that a high level of peasant organisation and radicalisation dampened rather than increased the violence in the area. Indeed, in 1906, the burning of estates in a new locality often followed, rather than preceded, the arrests of its peasant militants and leaders. Another comment which Lenin made earlier and on the spot, in 1906, that the destruction of manors was a sign of peasant weakness and of a lack of belief on the part of the peasants that they could hold onto what they took, seems much closer to the mark.[7]

Those peasants who had discerned the significance of the shift in power relations also knew the overwhelming strength of the state and the army which faced them, dispersed and mostly unarmed as they were. The local squires could be disposed of by force; the state was quite another matter. The total disappearance of tsardom was not within the scope of possibilities then envisaged by most of the villagers. Also, when defeated, a rebellious peasant could not easily run away or abroad – land and family could not be left lightly. As long as all that was so, the alternative to a riot was to minimise violence while organising politically – a rural equivalent of the SDs and SRs urban tactics which in actuality used as its main weapon political mobilisation, backed up at times only by limited violence.[8] The strategy differed, of course; the urban revolutionaries aimed at an eventual national uprising resulting in a republic, the contemporary peasant activists usually did not.

To be sure, there was little objection on the part of the 'conscious' peasant to violence *per se* on, say, moral grounds. The use of arson and armed invasion were often enough accepted as long as it was plausible that they would work, in other words, would produce a shift of land ownership or in political power in the localities. They did not break ranks when their villages chose violence. Nor were they necessarily averse to fighting, arms in hand, especially in self-defence (*dat' otpor*) or when the strength of the revolutionary wave in the region and/or weakening of the army's grip made the chances for victory look possible. More or less clearly, more or less spontaneously, the majority of the 'conscious' peasants were trying to work out an effective tactic of struggle for land and for local power. This 'political line', or more precisely the peasant political intuition based on collective experience, reached its fullest expression and climax with the establishment of alternative peasant governments in some of the rural localities, and on the other hand, in the nation-wide organisations of Russian peasantry – the All-Russian Peasant Union and the Labour Faction of the First and Second Dumas.

The alternative peasant government – the 'peasant republics' – spread rapidly by the end of 1905, to be destroyed by the victorious counter-revolution. We shall briefly review Georgia, Latvia and Russia on that score before returning to the national scene.

*   *   *

The first appearance of peasant alternative rule was in 1903 in Guria, at the Georgian periphery of the Russian state. The story made a considerable impact on contemporaries and is well worth telling. The name Guria came from that of a principality abolished by the Russian conquest in 1810 and since renamed the Uzurget *uezd* of the Kutais *guberniya*. The area consisted of a complex of valleys in the south-western corner of the Russian Caucasus (Transcaucasia in fact; see map on page 270) crossed by the Kutais–Batumi railway to Turkey. It held two tiny townships and seventy-nine villages within a territory of about 40 square miles. With few exceptions its population of some 100 000 was Georgian and peasant. A number of impoverished nobles blended into the peasantry and there were also a few rich noble landholders and some state officials. The local peasants were left particularly badly-off by the terms of emancipation from serfdom. (In Georgia, this turned most of the peasants into share-croppers.) The rural population of Guria was more than usually literate and had a reputation for independence of thought and deed.

In 1902, Georgii Uratadze, a local boy, a drop-out student and a committed SD, initiated peasant action against the local squires in the village Nigoiti, close to the rural school in which he taught.[9] Their demands were: a decrease in the landowners' share of the crops, freedom of grazing land and participation of the nobility in the budget of local expenses, paid until then by the peasants only. What followed had a touch of tragi-comedy at first. The peasants refused to act without taking a collective oath of loyalty to the struggle and to each other. The embarrassed young rationalist was pressed into acting the way a priest would, administering an oath in a religious ceremony of a most solemn nature. Next, the closest SD Committee, in the city of Batumi, was approached by Uratadze to guide him and take charge. As a point of principle it took a dim view of political action in such a petty bourgeois environment. (There was not one single industrial enterprise in the whole of Guria.) It was K. Chekhidze, the future spokesman of the RSDWP faction in the Duma, who delivered the verdict: 'We are Marxists. Marxism is a philosophy of the proletariat. A peasant and a small proprietor are unable to assume the philosophy of the proletariat. As a petty bourgeois he is closer to the bourgeoisie that to the proletariat. That is why we cannot have a peasant movement under our banners'. The Committee was particularly upset by the rumours that an oath had been taken by the peasants – no Marxist could condone such metaphysics. The young man was flatly refused SD sponsorship and chastised for 'adventurism'.[10]

The tragi-comedy rapidly turned into high drama. Rumours about the peasant action and the oath of loyalty in Nigoiti spread rapidly through the valleys and legends formed. The response was overwhelming and shook both government and revolutionaries alike. In village after village of Guria and in some areas further away, peasants congregated, worked out demands, selected leaders, and took mutual loyalty oaths. Faced with this wave, most of the local landowners rapidly and meekly gave in to the demands. The authorities' search for the culprits, if anything, facilitated the spread of peasant political action. The oath-taking villagers refused to hand over the 'instigators' and the repression which followed transformed the peasant struggle into a broad confrontation with the Russian authorities. The peasants of Guria and some other districts emerged from it more united than ever before. The Georgian intelligentsia, the urbanites and some of the nobles lined up on the side of 'their' peasants, invoking both socialist and nationalist slogans. The SD organisations were eventually swept into accepting leadership of the rising peasant movement. To save some face a 'Rural Workers Committee' of the SDs was established in Batumi and put in charge of the Guria trouble-makers. (There were, of course, practically no 'workers' in Guria in any strict class sense, though as usual in peasant populations, especially where land shortage is acutely felt, many peasants engaged in supplementary wage-labour. There were also men there who had formerly worked in Batumi and had been deported back to their villages after a strike in 1902 – an important input of political experience for the years to follow but neither a 'proletarian stratum' nor the leading group in the district.) When, in 1903, an autonomous SD committee consisting of peasants and local teachers declared itself to exist in Guria, the RSDWP Party accepted it into its fold without a whimper.

By the end of 1903, a systematic boycott by the whole population threw the official authorities of Guria into limbo.[11] The SD Committee of village representatives and of the 'propagandists' became for a couple of years the only authority accepted by the population. Freedom of speech, weekly political mass meetings, new controlled rents, new public courts and a local militia were introduced *de facto* throughout the area. The 'official' authorities were, for the most part, terrorised, bewildered or disregarded, while the few of them who tried to fulfil their duties were attacked, killed or forced out of the area. They were hunted even behind the grave as in the case of Prince Nakidze, killed in January 1905. His burial had to take place outside the region because of a boycott by the gravediggers. For a long time, government intervention by force was held back by the political situation in the rest of Caucasus and the sympathy for Guria in the whole of this region. Some of the richest noble landlords petitioned against army intervention. In 1905 a sympathetic governor of Kutais province adopted a *laissez-faire* attitude towards the peasant self-rule and even visited Guria, escorted by the local 'red' militia. The news of this exceptional, unexpected, indeed outrageous socialist rule of the Georgian peasants spread surprise and new thoughts not only in the Caucasus. From 1903, extensive reports of it in *Iskra* and other newspapers reverberated throughout the revolutionary community of Russia.

With the beginning of the 1905 revolutionary events all over Russia, the militancy also increased in Guria. The local militia (the 'Red Hundreds') was expanded and trained in preparations for an armed struggle against the tsarist regime. Police stations of the area were no longer disregarded, but attacked and burned down. The policemen, soldiers and guards were disarmed. A detachment of Cossacks and police which ventured into the area was ambushed and routed at Nasakerai.[12] The district town Uzurget was eventually taken by the armed villagers, and a new rule declared at a mass meeting in November 1905. The region was now universally known as the 'Guria republic'. In the words of a government supporter, 'the Guria Committee actually ruled Guria; without their permission you could not move a step in its streets'.[13] In 1905 the creation of alternative authorities along similar lines proceeded in a number of other areas of rural Georgia, for example, in the *uezd* of Senak (the 'Senak republic'), in Rachinskii *uezd*, in Mingerlia, in the village of Orbeli, etc.

At the beginning of 1906 the counter-offensive of the reaction reached Guria. The liberal governor of Kutais was arrested and the whole of Western Georgia harshly pacified by the forces of General Alikhanov and Colonels Krilov and Tolmachev. Guria was treated with particular severity by the invading army. The 'republic' disappeared, with its leaders arrested or in flight and its armed detachments dispersed after a decision not to challenge the regular army head-on. The repressions, arrests and the deportation of 300 men to Siberia, however, did not change the political stand of the peasants in the area. Nor did twenty days of flogging force the villagers of Lonchaty to name 'instigators'. In 1906 preparations were still being made for an armed uprising once the revolution was renewed in Central Russia. More significantly, while the villagers of the area duly declared submission, they voted overwhelmingly time and time again for the SD Mensheviks who led the Guria republic. This peasant support was to show remarkable consistency well into the 1920s.[14]

Politically Georgia was to proceed in its own particular way. As to the SDs the unity of the Mensheviks all over Russia was formally maintained, but the differences between their Georgian and non-Georgian contingents were to play a constant and increasing role in the years to come. The leader of the Georgian Mensheviks and a native of Guria, N. Zhordanya, led the SD faction eventually created in the first Duma. The Georgian Mensheviks proceeded to win elections to all the Dumas. In the 1917 election to the Russian Constitutional Assembly, it was Georgia, with its nine-tenths peasant population, which proved to be the only non-Russian region in Russia were declared Marxists and Mensheviks at that (that is, members of a party which polled only 2 per cent of the all-Russian vote) received an absolute majority. But all that was still to come. Immediate and shocking in its insights, the 'Guria republic' was the first case in history of a peasant rule by consent led by a Marxist elite and in direct confrontation with a state represented by foreign officials and soldiers.

*   *   *

At least to the SDs, the rural revolution in the Baltic provinces (especially in Latvia) was less outrageously odd than Guria. There was a large class of rural wage workers there. A considerable part of this workforce was employed in the manors of the German landed nobility, to whom half the land belonged. Since the 1880s, major strife along class and ethnic lines had been reported there, partly facilitated by the state policies of Russification, which for a time encouraged the Latvian villagers' opposition to the German landlords' grip. By the end of the nineteenth century, the urban organisations of the Latvian SDs began to extend their impact into the countryside. This party was to stand close to the Bolsheviks in its sympathies, but with an autonomous organisation of its own. It lacked altogether a specific agrarian programme, yet clearly and increasingly drew considerable rural support, from wage-workers as well as from smallholders. By 1904, the politicisation of the Latvian countryside and the impact of the SDs in it was very much on the increase.

The 1905 revolution resulted in Latvia in a wave of rural revolutionary demonstrations and confrontations which reached a peak in the July general strike of the rural workers.[15] Despite the strongly proletarian composition of the rural strikers in Latvia, there was a considerable peasant flavour to what took place. A major demand of the strikers was for the large estate lands to be sold or rented to them. The wage-workers employed by the local peasants did not join in the general strike which developed as an anti-manorial and anti-German affair. The rural Latvian communities usually acted in unison, smallholders and wage-labourers alike. The local church and congregation were used as the major focus for revolutionary meetings and demonstrations of the Latvian-speakers in the locality (one of the demands was to remove the German clergy appointed by the local barons). The authorities knew it, and came to refer to that struggle interchangeably as a 'peasant *bunt*' or as a 'rebellion of the Latvians'. The State of Emergency declared in August 1905 consolidated the opposition and made it truly national. By October 1905 Latvia as a whole faced the tsardom, urban workers and intelligentsia faced German patricians, and rural Latvia confronted German landowners defended by the Russian cavalry and by ethnically German vigilantes and paid guards. The Latvian SD was generally accepted as the major national political force which called the tune of the revolt *in toto*. Similar features characterised events in Estonia,[16] although to a lesser degree.

On 17 November, a congress of Latvian peasants met in Riga. The delegates of 600 villages present called for the establishment of alternative local authorities in the countryside. They then proceeded rapidly to do just that. Within days, about 100 self-governing cantons were set up. In all of them, the old authorities were removed or put under total boycott, while the village meetings set up their own organisations to administer the area. New courts were created, liquor shops and public houses (*korchmy*) closed and an armed militia set up. The new rule was fully effective and based on the total co-operation of the whole of the ethnically Latvian rural population.

Throughout 1905, the organisation of armed detachments of the revolutionary parties was also taking place. A major part of these were rural, linking with the newly-organised local militias. During the summer, a large number of attacks were made upon policemen and on local police informers. By autumn, the detachments had begun to attack the manors systematically. These were often defended by the German nobles, their retainers and guards, turning the battle into mini-civil war – an important part of the process of the establishment of alternative rule in the localities. Within weeks, 459 manor houses were destroyed in Latvia and a further 114 in Estonia, with the estimated financial losses to the local nobility reaching one-quarter of the all-Russian figure for 1905.[17] The rural revolutionary militia rapidly increased in size. By the end of November 1905 nearly 2000 armed men, mostly villagers, stormed and occupied the city of Tukkum, while others occupied the small townships of Gazenup and Vindava. In Ruene, up to 10 000 partially-armed villagers were reported in a confrontation with the army. Temporarily, most of the countryside of the Baltic provinces was under a revolutionary regime, with government army units locked in the main cities. It took a massive military operation to reconquer the Latvian and Estonian countryside by the end of February 1906, laying much of those countries waste. The remainder of the armed revolutionaries, the 'forest brothers', proceeded to wage a bitter rearguard guerrilla struggle for two more years.

A comparison between the Georgian and the Latvian rural confrontations leaves them open to contradictory interpretations. Both took place at the ethnic periphery of Russia – could they simply represent ethnic specifity or ethnic strife? Both were led by the SDs – was peasant alternative rule related to the Marxist outlook of its leaders? A look at central and south Russia will help to clarify these questions.[18] There an alternative peasant rule was established in a number of areas in which the population was ethnically Russian or Ukrainian and where there was no leadership by the SDs, or any other political party for that matter.

*   *   *

During 1905–06 a number of 'peasant republics' came into being in different parts of European Russia. They were never systematically and comparatively studied. The evidence is scarce and patchy, but it is of major significance. It shows that Guria represented a spectacular expression of a more general type of peasant organisation and struggle. The best-documented of the 'peasant republics' of Russia and the probably latest to survive was the 'Markov republic' in the Volokolamsk *uezd* of the Moscow *guberniya*, about which a small collection of articles and recollections was published in 1926.[19]

The sub-district (*volost'*) of Markovo was fairly typical of the

non-Black Earth parts of central Russia. It consisted of six villages
with about 1000 peasant households in them. The soil was poor and
partly waterlogged. The distance from Moscow was 150 km only, but
access to the area was difficult. During the 1861 emancipation, only
about 2 *desyatinas* of land per 'registered soul' (in other words,
a mature male at the time of the last 'Revision') was granted, clearly
insufficient under the prevailing system of agriculture. The peasants
supplemented their income by crafts and trades, with different
villages specialising in different categories of these. (In one of the
villages the main supplementary income was carpentry; in another,
shoemaking and so on.) Also, some additional farming land was
rented from the local squires. In fact, during the 1890s the
impoverished peasant farmers outbid the squires where use of land
was concerned. At the beginning of the century, only five of the
squires still farmed directly in the whole of the *uezd* of Volokolamsk.
All the others had sold off or else rented-out all their land to the
peasants.

Despite these unpromising conditions, the area stood out as
advanced as regards the adaptation of new methods of farming. Also,
it showed higher than average levels of literacy. A small group of
non-party radicals within the local intelligentsia, especially teachers
and agronomists, was doing its usual best to spread literacy and
political dissent there. To them, the *volost'* of Markovo was known as
a 'conscious' one – interested in news from the larger world and
defiant of the authorities.

By the summer of 1905, the peasants of the area watched with
growing excitement the unfolding of the revolution. Leaflets and
newspapers were read out and discussed at illicit meetings by the
peasant literates and the local intelligentsia. After the October 7
manifesto was published, the district agronomist Zubrilin, known and
respected for his professional success in introducing locally the
multi-field rotation and grass farming, was asked by peasants to
address the assembly of the Markovo commune. The subject was that
of the newly-granted freedoms and the possible place of the peasants
in the political developments. On 31 October 1905, the assembly
gathered with a considerable number of peasants from other villages
present (many of them having travelled long distances 'to hear about
things'). The assembly turned into a mass meeting. After a debate, it
voted on a resolution, worded at the peasants' request by Zubrilin.
This demanded democratic freedoms, extra land for the poor
peasants, education for all and amnesty for political prisoners. Many

such resolutions were, of course, voted in those days all around Russia. But the assembly of Markovo also proceeded to decide, with immediate effect, to refuse to obey the existing authorities, to stop the payment of all taxes and not to provide the army recruits until their demands were met. The resolution was then duly signed by all the heads of households and sealed by the commune's leader, Burshin, who was promptly elected 'President of the Markovo Republic'. In November, the *volost'* assembly adopted a similar resolution for the whole of the *volost'*, and extended it by a call for a Constitutional Assembly and 'an end to autocracy'. The whole *volost'* declared its collective adherence to the All-Russian Peasant Union.

What followed was a period of distinctive peasant self-rule by consensus. Its substantively anti-government nature was well-described by a historian of the period as 'a peculiar form of a general strike'.[20] The members of the radical local intelligentsia (inclusive of Zubrilin) were on the run or under arrest by 1906. What proceeded to happen was a direct expression of the peasants' own political intuitions and preferences. The peasants ran their *volost'* under their elected leadership and in open defiance of the state authorities, the orders of whom were simply ignored. Five men were elected as the local committee of the Peasant Union – a secret closely guarded from the authorities. It was they who made all major decisions. Rents were controlled and the work of the schools and the local authorities reformed. The loyalist elders and the local policemen were dismissed, boycotted, disregarded or scared out of the area. The peasants were unarmed and yet the provincial governor flinched from calling in the troops. The attempt to regain control by persuasion failed. The official dismissal of the revolutionary *volost'* elder was met by a good 'Schweikian' device – the peasants refused to elect a successor while the elder declared that to his sorrow he could not relinquish powers, for there was nobody to hand them over to. In the middle of the Moscow *guberniya*, in the Russia of 1906 with its reactionary offensive and violent repressions, a peasant 'free territory' proceeded to function for most of the year. It came to an end only in mid-July, 1906, seven months after the end of the Moscow uprising. Ryzhkov – the revolutionary *volost'* elder – was arrested by a trick, the police moved in, and the alternative authorities melted away. The boycott of the government appointees went on for quite a time afterwards.

One can quote other cases to show how similarity of context bred similarities of peasant response all throughout Russia. For example, a particularly powerful branch of the Peasant Union came into being in 1905 in Sumy *uezd* of the Kharkov *guberniya*.[21] The population of the district was about 250 000, of which nearly 90 per cent were peasant, Ukrainian and Orthodox. The Union was led by A. Shcherbak, a well-to-do peasant who returned to his village with his savings after twenty years of farming in California. Against his advice the peasants of the district decided to begin with a petition to the tsar, complaining about poverty and the disrespectful treatment of peasants. They requested the tsar 'to free us from officials . . . who cost a lot and do not give us order, only disturb our life and work and offend us daily . . . understanding nothing of peasant problems'. They demanded that all officials should be elected 'for we have enough men who are wise . . . who will cost less and do a better job'. Shcherbak duly presented this petition to Witte. He was arrested on return and after regaining his freedom, proceeded to organise the Peasant Union in Sumy. He was to become known nationally, for addressing a meeting of the St Petersburg Soviet with a call for unity of workers and peasants against the autocracy. He was also one of the major orators at the national congresses of the Peasant Union.[22]

In October 1905, the peasants of Sumy resolved to forbid all trade in land, and to take into the collective ownership of the neighbouring peasant communes the local sugar factory (Sumy was a sugar-beet-growing area). They also demanded a Constitutional Assembly and proceeded to elect L. Tolstoy and M. Gorkii – the major anti-establishment writers – honorary members of their organisation. The local centre – the town of Sumy (26 000 inhabitants) subsequently witnessed a demonstration of 40 000 peasants under red flags. The contemporary reports agree that: 'In November and the first half of December 1905, all the *uezd*, inclusive of the city, was in the hands of the committees of the Peasant Union'.[23] The officials were replaced by re-election, the factories put on strike, the Land Chiefs and local police officers rendered ineffectual by boycott. The *uezd* committee of the All-Russian Peasant Union ordered into the town a peasant detachment which took over local policing. The Peasant Union also established its own courts, initiated a newspaper, legislated new administration arrangements, etc. Despite the growing repressions the third *uezd* conference of the Peasant Union took place on 18 December 1905 and was attended by 350 delegates. It still represented the real power on the spot. It took numerous further arrests, the exile of the leaders and massive repression to bring it all to an end. Similar developments were reported from different places all over Russia in 1905–06, especially so in the other major centre of Peasant Union influence – the Saratov and the Don provinces.[24]

Nor was it a matter of the All-Russian Peasant Union or of the Russian and the Ukrainian peasants only. For example, in the Vasil'kov *uezd* of the Kiev *guberniya*, the peasant assembly of the Rakitiniskii *volost'*, with no relation to any national institution, simply elected a committee of 'twelve peasants and two Jews' to run the area as the sole authority acceptable to its inhabitants. The local correspondent of the Free Economic Society reported that the committee remained in full control for a few months.[25] The list of measures undertaken was similar to those elsewhere where the peasants took charge. The report stated also that 'the impact of the committee was immense. For example, drunkenness stopped at its request and so did theft'. The 'rightful authorities' effaced themselves completely. The local Forestry handed over timber to those in need, in accordance with the committee's written instructions. Eventually, a police officer arrived with a cavalry escort of 120 men. In what followed, some of the local activists were arrested and others fled, bringing the alternative authority to an effective end. Reports of such authorities being established by peasants of different ethnic groups, came from several regions, for example, the Mari and Chuvash villages in the Pomyalovskaya *volost'* on the Volga.[26]

A few cases of peasant self-rule were initiated and/or led by the revolutionary parties in central Russia. Local party activisists of the PSR and RSDWP (often in close coalition – to which the central party authorities tended to object) were involved.[27] Along the Volga and in Tambov and in the Chernigov *guberniya*, the SR Peasant Brotherhoods were particularly powerful and active. In western Ukraine, an effective group of rurally focused SD Mensheviks who used the Ukrainian language in propaganda – the *Spilka* – initiated similar take-overs which reached their climax in 1906.[28] Most of those events were limited and locally generated.

To conclude, cases of rebellious rule by consensus, with the 'rightful authorities' rendered helpless or removed by boycott, and an alternative local leadership deriving its power from peasant support, appeared all over Russia. The demands, methods of administration and tactics of defiance were fairly similar. The aim was to control non-peasant lands and to establish peasant communal rule in the countryside. An outstanding measure of unity between the diverse peasant households was displayed. On the whole, communal assembly and the *volost'* formed the kernel of such organisations in

Russia and the Ukraine. (Re-election of their officers 'without permission from above' formed a part of the struggle for change.) In Latvia, the parish played this role and in Georgia, the village meeting and the SD party committee.

Resident outsiders who neither farmed nor held land were usually left out of the direct confrontation, but a *volost'* clerk who dared, on his own initiative, to send a loyalist telegram to say that 'land holdings in the area are sufficient' was immediately dismissed and deported from the area by the local peasant authorities, as were some families of rural guards and policemen. The communal and *volost'* authorities were putting their 'offical powers' to this unexpected legal use as yet another act of defiance of the 'higher' authorities of the province and of the state.[29]

At the ethnic peripheries, cases of peasant self-rule were more numerous and on a larger scale. Those involved were better armed, more ready to use their weapons and usually led by a revolutionary party. There, the particular ethnic context turned such confrontation into a form of national liberation struggle, often – but not always – led by different branches of the SDs. In most of the places where peasants of Russia, the Ukraine and Byelorussia attempted to organise, they preferred to affiliate themselves with the All-Russian Peasant Union – a non-party organisation.

*   *   *

For the first time in the history of Russia, a national organisation of peasantry came into being in 1905. The nature of the All-Russian Peasant Union and its history explains the incompleteness of evidence about it. Much of its actions was never recorded. Its local activities, in particular, were often carried out without any documentation whatever, as much for reasons of secrecy as because of the limited literacy of many of its supporters. The union was smashed without leaving a successor to claim its direct heritage and hence to advance its memory. Even the precise number of national congresses of the All-Russian Peasant Union is not quite clear. Two of them, in July–August and November 1905, were fully documented. Two or three more were said to have taken place in 1906 and 1907.[30]

The single Soviet student of the activities of the All-Russian Peasant Union in 1905, Kiryukhina, offered at least some idea of the extent to which the Union structure grew during less than a year. She was able to ascertain for the end of 1905 (that is, six months after the congress at which the Union was erected) the existence of no fewer than twelve *guberniya* committees, four inter-provincial ones, numerous *uezd* committees and 470 local branches with 200 000 members.[31] Yet, these considerable figures were still badly understated in her view, because of lack of direct evidence. In 1906 the Union itself claimed a membership figure approaching one million.[32] Activities of the Peasant Union were reported by September 1905 in at least forty-two *guberniyas*. The delegates to its Congress in November 1905 represented seventy-five *uezds* of twenty-seven *guberniyas*, but quite a number of those elected to it did not reach the congress because of arrests. Some of the areas in which the Union was particularly active were not represented at all. For example, three out of the five guberniyas with delegates at the December 1905 regional conference of the Peasant Union's organisations in the north (St Petersburg, Pskov and Novgorod) did not have any representatives at all at the November national congress.[33] In November 1905 delegates of a number of *volost'* in Siberia met and decided to join the Peasant Union, but, once again, did not manage to have their representation reach its second congress. Moreover, the actual influence of the union's existence and of its statement reached way beyond its membership.

The best-known expressions of the All-Russian Peasant Union were its congresses of July–August and November 1905, broadly reported by the press. Their official protocols were published and their message spread all around Russia.[34] In November 1905, at the larger of them (and the only legal one), there were 187 delegates, two-thirds of whom had been elected by commune and *volost'* assemblies.[35] The government pounced on the Union within days. The national leadership (the General Committee) was arrested. Mass repression followed, yet at the next clandestine congress in March 1906, delegates of new *guberniyas* came and reports indicate that the organisations of the Union were still continuing to grow.[36] The Union reached its full influence between mid-1905 and mid-1906. Its decline was as dramatic as its rise. By the end of 1907 it disappeared entirely.

The protocols and reports from the 1905 congresses of the All-Russian Peasant Union left a powerful feeling of drama, of colour and of the epic – the descriptions and speeches sounded at times like a peasant legend, the lives of the saints and a meeting of a village assembly rolled into one. Most of the speakers were peasants, their imagery and argument drawn from the experience of rural life as much as from the Bible. Political, economic and ethical considera-

tions were fused in their argument. Some expressed themselves
clumsily, others were born orators. An immensely attentive and
active audience listened to them all with grave seriousness con-
tinuously commenting and supplementing their speeches from the
floor. It was only when some members of the intelligentsia took the
floor to offer long-winded arguments that this audience reacted by
shouts of 'enough', 'talk sense!' and often stopped them short. A
single squire among the delegates to the November congress spoke,
making clear why it was he who had been elected and sent by the
peasants of his neighbourhood: he called for a peasant take-over of
all lands, for the distrust of government intentions and for sending
armed escorts with the peasant deputies to the Duma to defend them
by force, should the need arise. We have some striking visual
descriptions of this congress: a wall of peasant costumes (*poddevki*)
and beards, two women in shawls (representing an assembly of
peasant women from a village near Voronezh), a legless delegate who
came all the way on crutches and addressed the congress virtually
from the floor, some jacketed intellectuals (mostly rural teachers), a
priest in black (shortly to be defrocked and sent into monastic
imprisonment for 'defiance'), and a single parade-uniform of a
retired army officer of peasant origin – a village delegate who created
a scare by coming to the great occasion in his 'Sunday best', of which
he was proud.[37]

While the exact scope of the All-Russian Peasant Union's influence
and activities is hard to ascertain, the nature of the organisation is less
in doubt. We shall discuss the full context of their demands in the
next section, but the call for 'land and liberty' summed it up
adequately. Geographically it spread mostly in what the tsar's
government called Russia, that is, Russia, Ukraine and Belorussia.
(The ethnic 'others' in it were mostly Latvians and Ugro-Finns, that
is, the Mordva and the Ests.) There were relatively few representatives from the western provinces, which also meant that the
organisation spread mostly in areas where the repartitional communes were pre-eminent.

Socially, a clear majority of the delegates to all the Union's
congresses and of its local leaders were peasants, and 'middle
peasants' at that, that is, smallholding family farmers.[38] The debate
about the scope of the membership of the union, mainly, whether
non-peasants should be permitted to join it, was inconclusive. (At the
July–August congress a considerable body of opinion preferred it to
be for *bona fide* peasants only.) For both the 1905 Congresses, the

study of the social composition of the delegates indicated that about 25 per cent of them were non-peasants – mainly members of the 'rural intelligentsia', mostly local teachers elected by the peasant *volost'* or communal assemblies to represent them.[39] Kiryukhina also studied the composition of thirty local committees of the Union, arriving at a result which gives a rough idea about its local activists. Eighteen of those committees consisted of peasants only. Peasants formed a clear majority in all the other twelve committees, but these also included teachers (in six of them), doctors (in three), clerks (in four) and clergy (in two). In three of the thirty committees there were also '*kulaks*' (unspecified by the author but singled out from the peasant majority). Of 317 local organisations of the All-Russian Peasant Union for which the relevant evidence was available, 224 (70 per cent) were set up by the decision of the local communal assembly (*skhod*).[40]

In terms of party political affiliations, the overwhelming majority of the Union members, delegates and leaders alike, were 'non-party' even though in some places a strong SR presence was reported. Of the 187 delegates to the November 1905 Congress, eleven were described as members or supporters of the PSR, five as SDs and two more belonged to *Spilka*, while none were KDs – a grand total of 9 per cent for those who were party-affiliated or related.

During 1905, Committees of Support were established in several places, initiated by the Union of Unions (which the Peasant Union had joined) consisting of urban intelligentsia and aiming to help the Peasant Union with contacts and publications. The arrest of the Peasant Union's national leadership made these bodies grow momentarily in importance but the police rapidly caught up with them also. Most of the members of the Committees of Support were arrested in early 1906 and their work ceased.[41]

The destruction of the All-Russian Peasant Union offered an interesting lesson in the political sociology of the peasantry. Despite its massive support, the All-Russian Peasant Union disappeared in less than two years of its climax and all attempts to revive it failed. The question 'why did it disappear?' must be asked. Heavy repression after November 1905 contributed to the decline of the organisation. Specific orders had been issued to the police to suppress the Union and to arrest all its activists. In the single *uezd* of Sumy, the Union's area of particular strength, 1100 peasants and members of the intelligentsia were arrested and/or exiled. Yet extensive and energetic activities of the Union were still reported in 1906 in many areas. Weakened though it was (as were all the anti-government organisations by that time) the All-Russian Peasant Union was alive, no less so than other organisations which survived. Why the eventual difference?

Peasants encountered more difficulty in organising themselves and/or being organised for a number of socio-political reasons which are well enough known: their dispersion, the 'vertical segmentation' into households, factions and villages, their relatively low political know-how, etc.[42] Conditions of illegality in Russia put any national organisation without professional cadres at a disadvantage. Yet the experience of other Eastern European countries (particularly of the Green International's parties) defy the simplistic 'peasants cannot organise politically' explanations. The major reason for the rapid disintegration of the Peasant Union was political rather than one of inherent qualities, of suppression or of organisation. That is indeed why the local committees of the Peasant Union also disappeared while any peasant political activity which survived the counter-revolutionary offensive reverted to the communes and the *volost'*.

The answer seems to lie in the dual interdependence between the All-Russian Peasant Union's leaders and their revolutionary allies and on the other hand, with their peasant support. In a peculiar way (and contrary to what was said of them then and since) the Peasant Union leaders were too *avant garde*, and too revolutionary to survive as organisers of the peasants during the period of the reactionary offensive. Almost to a man the revolutionary intelligentsia of Russia was against 'the electoral farce' of the first Duma, and preached electoral boycott. The gut feeling of the peasant mass was for voting in this election. Their belief that an assembly of the people of Russia must draw the obvious conclusion about land and liberty for the majority of its people was overwhelming. So was their grasp of the significance of the fact that, for one, national elections would actually take place in Russia with the peasants participating in them. So too was their appreciation of the strength of the government and of the relative solidity of the army. Yet the Peasant Union leadership decided to stand shoulder-to-shoulder with its allies from the rural intelligentsia, the workers' Soviet, the Union of Unions and the revolutionary parties in supporting the electoral boycott. The arrest of the Peasant Union General Committee made that stand all the more rigid, for who was going to reconsider it?

When the election came, the peasants voted overwhelmingly in it. They elected mostly 'non-party' peasant delegates who carried to the

Duma the message which the All-Russian Peasant Union refused to carry for them. By the time the revolutionary parties smartly admitted that the electoral boycott was 'a tactical error' (also admitting, as it were, to the realism of the peasant 'gut wisdom' as against their own mental constructs) there was no recognisable leadership of the All-Russian Peasant Union left to follow them in this U-turn. More importantly, an ideological equivalent of the Union – a Labour Faction created by the non-party peasant deputies – was doing a creditable job. The basic Peasant Union demands were repeated by this group. Russian peasants then proceeded to demonstrate their indifference to the tag as long as somebody claimed what they wanted, that is, land and liberty, and spoke the peasant tongue representing peasant unity and particularity in the confrontation with the state and the squires. The few Peasant Union activists who refused to follow the policy of boycott and were elected – for example, S. Anikin of Saratov – simply joined the Labour Faction, as did the few 'anti-boycott' SRs and SDs (the latter were eventually to set up a faction of their own).

The fact that under the leadership of the Peasant Union, of non-aligned local leaders or of some very diverse political parties (the RSDWP, the PSR, an alliance of both,[43] the PPS, even the Bund) peasants of different areas fought for essentially similar demands and adopted broadly similar strategies, is central here. Under the bewildering pressure of appeals, explanations and orders by the government and its enemies, often misinformed and always suspicious, facing complex political situations, most of the Russian peasants kept a remarkably level head. Their attitude to goals and organisations was pragmatic, based on experience, and on the whole politically wise. They were also remarkably consistent in their goals. The fact that all this was not clear to so many of Russia's officials and intellectuals had to do with the intellectuals and the officials rather than with peasant thought. A century earlier, a brilliant analyst and the Russian revolutionaries' man of inspiration described the peasants' entrance onto the contemporary political scene thus: 'clumsily cunning, knavishly naive, doltishly sublime, a calculated superstition . . . an undecipherable hieroglyphic for the understanding of the civilised'.[44] So it was, when considered in the light of somebody else's needs, views and prejudices. To understand it on its own terms, one has to look at the peasant needs, and more closely, at the way peasants perceived them, that is, to proceed further with the consideration of peasant thought and peasant dreams.

C. THE PEASANT DREAM

Dreams matter. Collective dreams matter politically. That is a major
reason why no direct or simple link relates political economy to
political action. 'In between' stand meanings, concepts and dreams
with internal consistencies and a momentum of their own. To be sure,
their structure bears testimony to the relations of power and
production in which and by which they are or were embedded and
shaped. However, such interdependencies are never one-sided.
Patterns of thought, once established, acquire a causal power of their
own to shape economy and politics, often decisively. In particular,
the political impact of ideology, and at its core the image of an ideal
society in relation to which goals are set and the existing reality
judged, is major.

Doubts have often been expressed as to the very possibility of
studying peasant ideology or thought. Such an analysis can never be
ascertained, so the argument runs, for lack of convincing evidence.
Peasants differ between regions and between villages as well as within
every village: the rich and the poor, the farmer and the part-
craftsman, the man and the woman, the old and the young – how can
one generalise about 'the peasant mind?' To make things worse, most
peasant lore is oral, while most of those who write of peasantry are
outsiders – how can one trust such testimony? Anyway, collective
thought is notoriously difficult to express, to record and to define.
Nor does it quantify easily – a major sin to those for whom
mathematics is synonymous with true scholarship.

Yet on the other hand, a prudent refusal to generalise about
peasant thought would also mean giving up the full analysis of
peasant political action, for there can be none without considering
peasant goals. Nor could the problem be resolved simply by
narrowing the analysis to a specific peasant stratum or to a single
village. The same argument would apply to each sub-division until
one was left with many single, different and unrelated personas – a
caricature of social reality if ever there was one. That is why the
alternative often adopted by analysts is simply to deduce patterns of
consciousness from the structures and/or interest of classes, groups or
societies. Such a short-cut, substituting for actual consciousness its
presumed causes, is tautological and on its own resolves little. The
causes and context of consciousness must be explored, not postulated.

A debate on the epistemological limitations of knowledge could go on endlessly, exercising sophisticated minds, yet marching on one spot. To move forward, one must take such questions down a few pegs as regards the level of abstraction. The relevant introductory questions, re-stated more specifically and in direct relation to our topic, are: can one provide meaningful and significant generalisations about the collective thought of the Russian peasants during the period discussed? If so, is there sufficient evidence to study the peasant political ideology which concerns us here? Should the replies to both questions be positive, one may proceed to the issue in hand.

A major case in point may help us answer the first of these questions. The rules of inheritance within the Russian peasantry from 1861–1911 were never legislated, but explicitly left, after Emancipation, to 'local custom', as understood by the peasant magistrates of every community. Our knowledge of the procedures which actually resulted is fairly reliable. Several studies of the decisions made by peasant courts were undertaken by the Russian Court of Appeal. These massive studies concerned the decisions of peasant magistrates in numerous villages, differing in their history, climate, riches and type of agriculture as well as their interaction with the nobility, the urban society and the broader economy.[1] Besides diversities, the studies revealed the repetition of the basic principles of inheritance and property-relations throughout the Russian peasantry. This evidence is all the more striking in that these principles differed consistently from the corresponding relations operating within the other social classes of Russia as well as the 'national' – that is, non-peasant-directed – legislation. We are talking here of family property (as opposed to either private or collective ownership), the non-admissibility of the will, the equal division of land among all resident sons and sons-in-law, the specific 'female property' and so on. It goes without saying that these generic characteristics of the Russian peasant norms and procedures concerning property were linked with the structure of the peasant households and villages. However, this was, once more, a link of mutual interdependence and not a simple reflection of the one in the other (whichever the 'one' and whichever the 'other'). In this sense the Russian peasant common law (*obychnoe pravo*) was central in its significance to the peasant economy and its dynamics. To conclude, this major example should suffice to show that generalisations about the particularities of the Russian peasant mind are possible and, when justified by the evidence, provide considerable illuminations.

To proceed to the issue of data. Despite the fact that the majority of the Russian peasants were illiterate, extensive evidence relevant to the study of peasant collective thought in Russia and representing in particular the political views of the peasantry during 1905–07, is available. Thousands of petitions, resolutions of communal assemblies (*prigovory*) and instructions to delegates (*nakazy*) were recorded. They were addressed to the tsar, to the government (especially after the decree of 17 February 1905 which actually called for their submission), to the deputies of the Duma and to the All-Russian Peasant Union. The Peasant Union congresses debated and passed a number of major resolutions. Later, the peasant deputies addressed the Duma, putting to it the case of their electorate. A number of relevant reports by observers as well as by police and army chiefs and by state administrators about the peasants' views and moods are also available,[2] and so are some memoirs of officials, nobles and the intelligentsia. The evidence is rich, if uneven, and within the heterogeneity of expressions shows considerable consistency of content.

One may begin the review of the peasants' wishes as to the type of society they would like to see, with the debates and the decisions of the two congresses of the All-Russian Peasant Union in 1905 to which we have already referred.[3] A broad consensus was clearly established at both. While well aware of the limitations of their capacity to impose their will on the tsarist state, the peasant delegates showed considerable unanimity in their preferences and expressed them clearly. The ideal Russia of their choice was one in which all the land belonged to the peasants, held in a roughly egalitarian division and worked by family labour, without the use of wage-workers. All Russian farming land would be assigned to the peasant communes and the land-holding equalised by them in accordance with the size of the family and/or a 'labour norm', that is, the number of labourers in each family. Trading in land was to be abolished and private ownership of land brought to an end. The local authorities, elected to represent equally the entire population, were to be invested with extensive powers to oversee division of the land and to run the public services, among which free education for all was particularly emphasised. At the state level, a parliamentary monarchy rather than a republic was vaguely envisaged, with civic equality, freedom of speech and assembly, as well as 'compassion' as a major principle guiding state policies – a rudimentary formulation of an idea not unlike that of a 'welfare state'. All officials were to be elected. Women were to be granted an equal vote ('which may help to fight against drunkenness'). Solidarity was strongly expressed with 'all of our brothers' engaged in the confrontation with the government: the workers, the soldiers, the intelligentsia and the ethnic minorities.

There was also a fair consensus at the congresses of the All-Russian Peasant Union as to the delineation of the evil forces which stopped peasant dreams from coming true. These were first and foremost the state officials (*chinovniki*), described succinctly in an initial manifesto as 'malevolent to the people' (*narodu vredny*). The squires, the *kulaks* and the local Black Hundreds were also named (in that order) as enemies, but ran a clear second to the 'apparatus of the state'. In the major transformation aimed at, the squires were to lose their land, the *kulak* 'commune-eaters' their disruptive ability to exploit neighbours and the Black Hundreds their capacity to perpetuate terror in conjunction with the local police. Some of the decisions voiced a moral–political consensus, relevant once more to the peasant ideal of society: rejection of the death penalty, a demand for general political amnesty, a denunciation of drunkenness and condemnation of the anti-Jewish pogroms as 'shameful and sinful'. Much of the debate was couched in moral, often biblical terms of the fundamental rights and wrongs assumed to be as evident to all good men and women as the difference between day and night. An endlessly repeated statement, 'The Land is God's', is an example and a crucial case in point – a *Weltanschauung*, a moral judgement, a political stand, a strategic demand, all in one.

The many disagreements within the All-Russian Peasant Union congresses concerned mainly the road towards the realisation of these goals and not their nature. The arguments related particularly to the issues of the private land redemption and the form that the struggle should take, that is, how far it should be carried by revolutionary violence. To begin with the first issue, everyone agreed that the lands of the state, the tsar and the church should enter the redistributional pool free of charge. A majority of the August Congress preferred the peasantisation of Russia's land to include also the possibility of a partial 'buying-off' of some of the private land owners, to be financed by the state. A substantial minority objected to any such payments (for 'land was created by the holy spirit' and, not being man-made, should not carry a price-tag).[4] An image of orderly transformation of land and power with a new consensus safeguarding the stability of that change was often expressed and was clearly at the root of the tactical preferences of the majority of the delegates where 'land redemption' was concerned. So was the wish to keep the state at an arm's length in the future administration of local affairs and of land use.

The awareness of confrontation with the combined weight of the state machinery and the landed nobility was strong in the minds of the peasant delegates. The issue of political tactics was central to the Peasant Union's debate. The agreed methods of struggle were both legal and illegal. They included the boycott of state officials and their appointees, the removal of loyalist elders by holding new elections, the establishment of Peasant Union committees called upon to take over local affairs and the passing of resolutions formulating demands (*prigovory*) by the assemblies of peasant communes and *volost'*. The very spread of the Peasant Union branches, district organisations and conferences was a direct challenge to and pressure on the authorities. The November Congress also banned the sale or rental of lands and declared that the suppression of union activities would be countered by a refusal to provide taxes and draft recruits. In line with the position taken by all the revolutionary parties, the Union of Unions and the St Petersburg Soviet of Workers' Deputies, the November Congress decided to boycott elections to the Duma until a fully democratic electoral law was introduced. At the same time, the Peasant Union disassociated itself from the 'taking apart' of the manors, which was declared counter-productive if understandable in view of peasant grievances, bitterness and disorganisation.[5] The division of land, further progress in peasant organisation and an amnesty for all political prisoners were to take care of that.

The next step planned in the possible escalation of the struggle, should the government prove obstinate, was a general peasant strike (doubtlessly with the fresh recollection of the October urban strike in mind). The general peasant strike meant to them the withdrawal of peasant labour from the manors and the refusal to pay rent and taxes. Many of the speakers called for resistance by force (*dat' otpor*) to punitive measures and expeditions – as a way to keep the 'forces of order' under some constraint. The possibility of a massive invasion and *de facto* take-over of all manorial and state lands in the Spring was seriously discussed. A call for an armed uprising was considered but refused.

Attitudes toward the tsar were one of the major issues in which the particular mixture of peasant radicalism and peasant conservatism (or caution) found its expression. The state and its officialdom were rebuked and abused constantly, yet the tsar was usually 'left out of it'. Some of the delegates, doubtless representatives of a sizeable part of the peasantry, still held the belief that the tsar must be misled by wicked ministers not to understand what was so self-evident to them. Although an increasing number of the peasant activists clearly knew better, they still voiced suggestions (especially at the November Congress) to continue 'not to touch *him*' as their villagers might not be ready for such a challenge and a peasant split over the issue of monarchist loyalties might be disastrous. For nearly all the delegates, while struggle for the peasantisation of all lands and a change in the local power were central, the attitude toward the state, the big cities and the national symbols was more distant. One peasant delegate expressed this in a half-jocular, half-serious report to the November Congress. He proudly told about his *volost'* assembly's reply to an official, who, after listening to their debate about the future, demanded to know 'where did you place the tsar in all that?' The peasant's blank-faced answer was 'of him we do not speak at all'.[6] Soldier Schweik's wit and tactics of avoidance were still the old and tested peasant weapons, a fine way to confront a puffed-up outsider and to draw a quiet grin of appreciation from one's neighbours.

The intellectuals watching peasant congresses often expressed surprise or dismay at the discrepancy between the powerful rhetoric and the moderation of the actual decisions.[7] Members of the revolutionary parties craved revolutionary action. Peasant violence was reported throughout Russia. At their congresses of 1905, peasant delegates spoke sharply of grievances and demands, but did not endorse armed action (although the majority never rejected it either). Yet this contradiction lay mostly in the intellectuals eye. Every peasant assemblyman knew the difference between a genuine desire (carefully hidden from the outsiders, yet forcefully expressed to unite the assembly round him) and the recognition of the realities with which one had to live. Every peasant also understood the simple tactics of any peasant market: to bluster and press, then try to settle by a compromise which secures a concession, is acceptable to all and 'right' within the peasant code of propriety (*po-chestnomu*). There were in such attempts neither surrender nor despair. The delegates of the mostly unarmed and land-bound villages decided on a political attack, but were not ready (yet?) to adopt the tactics of armed struggle.

Peasants also knew the limitations of their own political organisation. To unite peasant power nationally and to do it effectively, one needed either an outside base, for example, a revolutionary army ready to march against the peasant's enemies, or else some measure of legality which would secure communication, unity and leadership. With the first not in evidence, the peasant activists of Russia tried to make use of and extend the second, while building up inter-village unity and power. They brushed aside advice offered by the revolutionary parties, both the SD representative's proposal of a republic and the SR delegate's call for an armed uprising. The majority of the peasants, in whose eyes power (and particularly local power) was central, clearly strove to minimise violence, that is, to use it limitedly, selectively and on the whole defensively.[8] These choices were not, however, the consequences of manipulation by some distant leader playing parliamentary games of respectability. The local reports showed the consistency of the opposition to the destruction of manors by the mass of the 'conscious' peasants on the spot. There was no lack of courage in it either, for the extent of calm bravery shown by many of the peasant activists in the face of the pacification squads, prisons, executions and trials was impressive,[9] and these were the very villages from which the Russia infantrymen went to fight well in the later foreign and civil wars. The sober realism of recognising the superiority of the regular army in any face-to-face engagement was well proven by the entire experience of 1905–07.

That is also why, all in all, the delegates and activists of the All-Russian Peasant Union seemed to have represented the 'conscious' peasants' grasp of their own interests well. It was characteristic that the great realist, Lenin, admitted to just that.[10]

The representative nature of the Union's view for the Russian peasantry at large was challenged at once by its contemporary critics. The popular press supporting the government and financed from its 'secret funds' ('loyalist' in government designation, 'reptile' to its enemies), promptly denounced the All-Russian Peasant Union as an organisation of arsonists and its congresses as a conclave of intelligentsia dressed up as peasants. At the other end of the political scale, an SR delegate to the November congress (Studentsov) claimed that the congress was dominated by its presidium which represented the intelligentsia and/or rich peasant delegates. That was how he explained the November congress's moderation.[11] Shestakov of the SD Bolsheviks subsequently explained, in a similar way, the refusal of the July–August congress to declare its support for a republic and its decision to partly compensate private landowners.[12] He treated similarly the rebuke by the November congress of the demand of the RSDWP workers' delegation for the privilege to address the congress on a par with its elected delegates (since, it has been said by the SDs, the peasants should learn from the workers' superior revolutionary experience). Maslov, the contemporary Menshevik theorist of rural society, eventually accepted, together with Lenin, the assumption that the peasant congresses of 1905 accurately represented peasant political thought, but he claimed it to be a particular expression of the peasant repartitional commune, and therefore restricted to the areas where those existed.[13]

It so happened that these doubts and comments of contemporaries were brought speedily to an acid and spectacular test. As already mentioned, the mass arrests and the All-Russian Peasant Union's decision to boycott elections meant a veritable purge of its activists from the first Duma. The peasant deputies actually elected were mostly unattached to any national organisation or political party. During the election campaign, the arrests and deportations of the rural intelligentsia, together with the boycott, produced as pure a case as possible of peasants' choice free of interference from the political organisers of the day. In the language of a 1906 report about the pre-election atmosphere, 'all of the political life in the villages seemed dormant'.[14] The KDs, the only party which carried out a nation-wide campaign, did little in the countryside and gained the support of less than one-sixth of the peasant-elected deputies.[15] On the other hand, the impact of the authorities was felt through pressures against candidates deemed unreliable, rather than through organising a loyalist faction of their own.

The resulting first Duma, with its massive 'non-party' peasant representation, produced a sigh of relief from the Establishment: the Duma's conservatism seemed assured.[16] The parties of the Left fully agreed with this anticipation, and so did the liberals. What actually followed sent a shock of surprise through the Russian political scene, for a moment drawing attention from the triumphant reaction which followed the defeat of the revolutionary challenge at the end of 1905. The largest group of the 'non-party' peasant deputies promptly banded together into the Labour Faction (*Trudoviki*) incorporating representatives from all over Russia (including a number of delegates from the western provinces where the repartitional commune did not exist). Within a month, the labourites produced demands, both 'agrarian' (the 'Project of 104') and more general, concerning political amnesty, democratisation, etc., which were indistinguishable from those of the All-Russian Peasant Union.[17])

Any notion that some hidden agents of the Left (or of the Peasant Union) had hijacked the peasant vote was dispelled by the political position of those peasant deputies who stayed outside the Labour Faction. To the total surprise of the authorities, of the KDs' leading faction in the Duma, as well as of the Duma's radical critics in the boycott camp, the peasant deputies 'spoke' what was described by a major Soviet historian of the period as 'the language of the populists-of-intelligentsia, supporting ideas of the nationalisation of land and raising the banner of equal land redivision and of the "labour principle" in doing so' – a fact which 'shook to the core the social-democratic doctrinaires'.[18] Even the self-declared peasant conservatives and monarchists among the peasant deputies supported the agrarian programme tabled by the Labour Faction. Some of the peasant deputies from the ethnically non-Russian areas joined the national minorities' factions (the Autonomists) which stressed the demand for self-rule along ethnic lines. They consequently objected to the All-Russian pool of land demanded by the Labour Faction, but once again agreed with the rest of the programme. The peasant deputies who joined the KD faction, unlike the Labourites, supported redemption payments for *all* private lands due to be taken over but also wanted the requisitioning of land, and its distribution to the landless and smallholding peasants. Cutting across boundaries of party allegiances, regions and ethnicity, the peasant land demands were stated particularly well somewhat later, during the second Duma (1906–07) when the villagers learned more about the new institution and the divisions in it. In the words of instructions (*nakaz*) given by the otherwise conservative and nationalist Krasnichinsk Orthodox Parish of Lublin province to its deputy in the second Duma: 'You may compromise on all other issues but in the question of land you should join the extreme tendency, that is, without fail demand the transfer to peasants of lands and forest' (*nadelenie*).[19] For a major part of the peasantry, the parallel resolution (*prigovor*) of the assembly of the village Shnyak in the Kazan' *guberniya* was clearly as relevant: 'Worse than poverty, more bitter than hunger is the suppression of the people by absolute powerlessness in the face of arbitrary officialdom (*bezprav'e*). Without a permit, you cannot take a step, say a word or else it is a fine, prison or exile to Siberia . . . Instead of the courts it is the local police which pass all sentences'.[20]

The homogeneity of the positions taken by the peasant communities and the peasant deputies increased after the government's declaration of intent at the opening of the first Duma, by which any redivision of privately-owned land was flatly rejected. As the work of the 1906 Duma proceeded, the opposition of the peasant deputies to the government solidified. This did not make them dissolve into a general opposition line-up or simply accept the guidance of the existing political parties. A Labourite left wing moved closer to the PSR, rallying round the 'Project of 33', which called for the abolition of land property in Russia and the 'socialisation' of all Russian land. This was added to the milder 'Project of 104'.[21] On the other hand, the consciousness of a particular peasant interest together with the 'psychological isolation' of the peasant deputies – a mixture of apprehension and plebeian pride – was well expressed in a letter of a Labourite deputy to his village in the Poltava *guberniya*. It said: 'Our project concerning land is good . . . but it is only a project and what will happen in the Duma one cannot say, for of us, the peasants, there are only 141 present here, while the rest are any manner of trash' (*a to raznyi sbrod*).[22]

The next stage, and one more test of peasant consistency of views and demands, came when the government banned the majority of the deputies of the first Duma from re-election. The second Duma, which met in 1907, carried a new slate of deputies. Despite the heavy pressures on the electorate by the provincial governors, etc., this Duma proved even more radical in membership than its predecessor. The peasant vote went even more against the government. Of the fifty-three deputies elected directly by peasant representatives – that is, not via the provincial assemblies of representatives – forty-seven supported the opposition and only three defined themselves as loyalists. The Labour Faction was almost totally new in its membership. Despite the lack of an effective extra-parliamentary organisation to secure consistency and electoral drive, it nearly doubled and promptly repeated all the initial Labourite demands (especially the agrarian projects). Meeting directly after the enactment by decree of the so-called Stolypin and Agrarian Reform, promoting the privatisation of communal land, the Labour Faction also showed unqualified hostility to it. Equal hostility was expressed in the many instructions to the Duma deputies voted by the villagers throughout the whole of Russia.[23]

In the second Duma, the other substantially peasant factions, such as that of the Cossacks, once again came out in full support of the land demands of the Labour Faction. Significantly, even the deputies of Volyn' – the one place where the Black Hundreds swept the peasant vote, presented agrarian demands not unlike those of the peasant radicals elsewhere. (In the ethnic context of Volyn', as in Krasnochinsk already mentioned, such demands were directed

against the Polish nobles and Jewish merchants. This secured support
for the Black Hundreds' xenophobic appeal.) Even in the depressed
and cynical mood which prevailed by the end of 1907, the elections to
the third Duma still produced a major peasant vote for opposition.[24]
The new electoral laws precluded it, however, from substantively
influencing the actual composition of the Duma. The few Labourites
who found themselves elected stated once again in this preserve of
conservative squiredom their insistence on the basic peasant demands
for land redivision, as much as the election of all the state officials
and their total objection to the Stolypin agrarian reform. Once again,
in their demand for land redivision they were joined by otherwise
conservative peasant deputies.

The response to those peasant demands, and a proof of the surprise
and fury they caused, was offered by a sequence of vitriolic attacks on
the Labour Faction by the right-wing parties. To exemplify, one such
publication described the Labour Faction of the Duma as a group
consisting of people with:

1. arrested natural abilities resulting from incapacity as much as
from a lack of consistency which can be acquired only by good
education; 2. incredible self-esteem resulting from supremacy over
one's own ant-hill, that is, an environment which is lacking even
more in any culture; 3. untrammelled Utopianism determined by
the mixture of half-education and insolence; 4. a hate of everything
which is cleaner, whiter, more sophisticated – a type of hate
without which the impudence and the Utopianism would lose any
meaning or justification.[25]

The author clearly knew all one could know about class hatred and
the depths of the deepest class gulf in Russia. His fury centred,
typically, on the plebeian elite representing the mainstream of the
Russian peasant movement and which was supported also by large
numbers of workers and some of the 'ethnic minorities'.

*   *   *

While the deputies and delegates to the peasant congresses and to the
Dumas argued about the demands and dreams of the Russian
peasantry *in toto*, every village proceeded throughout 1905–07 with
its own never-ceasing debate. Scraps of news were endlessly retold,
discussed and embellished, printed sheets were read and read out,
the thirst for knowledge seemed infinite. A rumour that a meeting

was to be held or that a 'knowledgeable man' was visiting a village brought over neighbours on foot, in carts and on horseback from many miles away. The villages also sent out delegates 'to find things out' and numerous deputations to invite 'an orator' from the local towns or neighbourhoods. A village in the south specified such a request, ordering its messengers 'to bring over a student or a Jew to tell of the news', while another village voted to offer payment of an 'orator's' wages from the communal purse,[26] and so on. At the centre of this immense process of communication was not propaganda sent or brought from elsewhere, but rather a grandiose and spontaneous effort at political self-understanding and self-education by millions of illiterate and half-literate villagers. In an endless, slow, often clumsy and ill-informed and ever-heated debate, masses of peasants looked at their life and environment anew and critically. They conceived and expressed what was often unthinkable until then: an image of a new world, a dream of justice, a demand for land and liberty. For, once again, it was not only land which was in question.

It is usually the local evidence which is the most difficult to come by where peasant movements are concerned. However, in Russia 1905–07 much of the peasant thought was expressed publicly, formulated and written up. An Anglo-Saxon parliament in which its members once elected are free to act as they deem fit would have struck the Russian peasants as distinctly odd. The experience of communal self-management taught them otherwise. A deputy was to be told specifically what he was sent to say – hence the *nakaz*, a document somewhat along the lines of the *Cahiers de déléances* of the French Estates General in 1798, but more direct in regard to the legislation demanded. The authorities and especially the Duma were to be told of the peasants' hardships and needs – hence the communal decision (*prigovor*) and the petition. Major waves of these documents corresponded to (i) the government's official call for legislative suggestions in early 1905, (ii) the All-Russian Peasant Union only legal congress in November 1905, (iii) the first, and (iv) the second Duma, in summer 1906 and spring 1907 respectively. The communal and *volost'* assembly offered a ready-made machinery for such actions, while for once, the newspapers and the analysts publicised them broadly. The revolutionary parties, especially the SDs, opposed the petitions to the government and the Duma as Utopian and reformist but failed to make any headway on that score.[27]

The direct and representative nature of the peasant petitions and instructions was manifest. The documents declared it time and time again ('we wrote it ourselves' – *sami sochinili*), to which the language used readily testified. So did the signatures, which usually began with that of the village elder (the document 'certified true' by his stamp) and continued with those of all the village literates. Then followed a long line of crosses made by the illiterates declaring not only support of a view formulated by somebody else, but direct participation in the decisions. The sophistication of some of these tracts, especially in areas from which every politically active member of the intelligentsia had by then been removed, showed to what extent knowledge of politics is not chiefly a matter of books or of universities.

A contemporary published collection of documents addressed to the first Duma from the villages of the Samara *guberniya* offers a fair example of the species.[28] Of the seventy-eight items, thirty-eight were addressed to individual deputies, thirty-one to the Duma *in toto*, and nine to its Labour Faction collectively. They asked for land, for lower rents, for agricultural credits and for progressive taxation of incomes. They also demanded 'liberty' in general, amnesty of political prisoners, election of all of the officials, free education for all, state salaries for the clergy (which would free the peasants from the necessity to pay their keep) and courts whose proceedings would be 'equal, prompt, just and merciful'. The most frequent complaint, next to that of the shortage of land, was one concerning *proizvol*, that is, official lawlessness and the arbitrary nature of the local authorities' rule – the peasant's main antonym to liberty, self-management and good order. One village also told the deputies that it did not take over the land of the local manors by force 'which could easily be accomplished' because 'a law is needed'. Many others called on the deputies to stand fast and not to yield over the basic demands. The villagers clearly appreciated more realistically than the Russian liberals what might happen to the peasant deputies who would do just that: they were told 'to bear their cross for they are the last hope' and that 'God and their people will stand by them'. Last, a village assembly announced to the Duma its decision to close the local church 'for if there were a God, he would not permit such injustices to continue'.[29]

A single letter to the Duma may be of particular interest here, representing as it did a deep stirring of the most neglected half of the peasant population. It came from the peasant women of three villages in the Tver' *guberniya* who met in secret. Once again, no rural intelligentsia was involved – the text was written down by a teenage pupil of the local primary school. The letter addressed to the members of the Duma protested the fact that while 'our men are quite ready to entertain themselves with us (*guliat' s nami rady*) they refuse to talk to us about the land and the new laws . . . Before now they admittedly beat us at times, but serious matters were decided together. Now they say that we are not partners any more, for only they elect the Duma'. The women asked for an equal vote which is necessary 'to handle matters in a godly manner'. The Duma 'must offer expression to all: the rich as well as poor, the women as well as men, for otherwise there will be not truth on earth and no peace in the families either'.[30]

Russia historians, especially in the last generation, have attempted to analyse quantitatively the large numbers of peasant petitions and instruction available in the archives. Such a content analysis was performed on the above documents from the Samara *guberniya*, on 146 instructions from branches of the Peasant Union, on the 458 instructions and on some 600 village petitions related to the second Duma and so on.[31] Once again the fundamental homogeneity of the results, concerning documents originating from different peasant communes and groups over a huge country, is striking. The instructions of the local branches of the All-Russian Peasant Union as summed up by Dubrovskii can be used as an example.[32] The demand for a transfer of all the land to the peasantry and for the abolition of private land ownership was total (100 per cent of the documents in question) and a large majority wished it to be performed by the Duma (78 per cent). The demand for a law to ban the use of wage-labour within agriculture was also made by a clear majority (59 per cent). Views were split with regard to possible compensation for the lands of the private landowners (very much as at the Peasant Union congresses). General opposition was expressed to indirect taxation and the demands for progressive income tax were very strong (84 per cent). On the political side, most of the documents demanded free and equal elections (84 per cent), accountability and often the election of all officials (73 per cent). Amnesty to political prisoners was listed by 87 per cent, while free education for all as always topped the list of the peasant 'non-economic' demands (100 per cent).

Another study undertook a content analysis along fairly similar lines of the already mentioned seventy-eight petitions to the second Duma from the *guberniya* of Samara. The results were broadly similar to those of Dubrovskii. Additionally, the peasant attitude to the government policy in general and to the Stolypin Reforms was considered – the new major issue of 1907, showing that these were not supported by even one of the documents. An attempt to delimit consistent differences between the petitions of villages in the poorer (northern) part of the Samara gub. as against those of its richer region was also made.[33] It showed a more intensive participation of the relatively richer areas in the 'petitions campaign', these areas also laying more stress on the political demands. In terms of the socio-economic indices, the participants in the petition movement were said to be mostly 'middle peasants', that is, both poorer family farmers (but neither the landless nor the destitute *golyt'ba*) and the better-off (but not the richest) within the rural population. The inhabitants of the larger villages were shown to be more active than those of the smaller ones. Comparison of all these studies of local evidence leaves the impression of overwhelming similarities – a unified ideology, a dream remarkable in its consistency, overriding the local differences.

The terminology of peasant political thought is itself interesting. Some of it has been mentioned already. Words to express the new experiences and demands were sought and found in tradition or in legend as much as in the new vocabulary of the newspapers and of towns. Some of it was produced by the intelligentsia, other terms came from the peasants and entered the language of the educated. The 'golden manifesto' and the 'second freedom' expressed the hope for a decision by the tsar to divide the rest of the nobles' land among the peasants. The concepts of 'equalisation' (*uravnitel'nost'*) and of the 'labour principle' (*trudovoe nachalo*), that is, the adjustment of the land grant to the extent of the labour of each family unit – were used by peasants and the intelligentsia alike. The 'Black Repartition' (*Chernyi peredel*) and the global all-embracing commune (*Vselenskii mir*) embodied the most radical designation of change – a world of peasant righteousness, of total and equal redivision of all land and of Russia as a commune of communes, with very little social space left to the non-peasants. There were some words which declined in usage signalling the new times. The word 'humbleness' (*smirenie*) so often used in the descriptions and self-definitions of the Russian peasants of old, was fading away. The term 'strike' came to symbolise a class attack and a challenge – 'we have struck (*zabastovali*) the grazing lands' the peasants said of the land invasions in the south of Russia. The word student became synonymous with 'revolutionary'. The government press referred to all this as the infestation of the peasant mind by the rural intelligentsia or else a proof of illiteracy or miscomprehension on the part of the peasant mass. But these were new ideas finding expression in new words. One could not make up such words synthetically any more than one could produce by stealth the political dreams which came to move masses of Russian peasants in those days.[34]

The nature of the peasant dream of a good society which surfaced in 1905–07 was linked with and generated by the way of life we refer to as peasanthood: the specific economy, power structures and communal life as well as the cognitions involved. This was the essence behind the stubborn consistency and generality of peasant dreaming. Both comparison with other peasant societies of the day and consideration of Russia's past made it clear. The slogan 'land and liberty' expressed those dreams remarkably well as far as slogans ever do, that is, pinpointed the essentials without quite exhausting their content. Production on the land, usually operating within a three-field system, with family labour as its main input, related directly to the demand: all land to those who till it and to them only. The focus on the consumption needs and the idiom of survival were characteristic of and necessary to a way of living in which survival had been the essential goal for milleniums. It meant also the deep suspicion of all other landholders in the area. The considerable tensions in every community went together with overriding unity when facing outsiders. Liberty was envisaged mainly as the freedom from external restraints. It was to a decisive degree the image of self-management known to the peasant communities, writ large, improved and idealised. Education was mainly the access to literacy and the skills of a village scribe or teacher – a badge of equality with the non-peasants as much as a way to new non-farming jobs for the 'surplus' son or daughter, who could be 'educated out' in that way. It was, therefore, definitely a good thing and to be open to all of the peasant youth. The demands for charitable government, 'fair and merciful courts', the election of officials and popular control came as much from peasant legends and the lives of saints as from the mostly negative rural experience. Past traditions mixed with new characteristics of the peasantry in crisis – the type of crisis described today as that of the so-called 'developing societies'. The forms in which it was expressed have shown it clearly: terminology of conservatism, conventionality, patriarchialism, religion and often of parochialism and semi-magical beliefs injected with new and radical words, views and experiences, and put to use to grasp and shape a rapidly transforming society and to understand a revolution in which the peasantry was massively involved.[35]

The Russian peasant rebellion carried many generic signs of the twentieth century peasantry on a war-path:[36] 1. the 'crisis of authority' linked to the ecological and demographic crises as much as to the impact of markets and 'monetisation' associated with socio-economic polarisation and pauperisation; 2. the external context of an extra-rural confrontation which weakened, split and immobilised the powers-that-be, affecting their ability to dominate peasants; 3. the typical points of socio-political strength and of weakness of peasant populations – their size, spread and monopoly of food production as against segmentation, limited formal education and low 'classness'.

The non-economic goals and aspects of peasant struggle must be seen to understand its characteristics. The Russian peasant struggle of 1905–07 has clearly shown what was called, in a different time and place, the peasant 'moral economy' – peasant ideology of righteousness as central to their revolt.[37] That is where cognition and dreams linked directly into peasant political confrontations and wars. That is also why the ideas, words and symbols of the Russian peasants during the revolutionary epoch would have been more easily understood by other peasants from far off, than by most of the well-educated Russians of their own generation. The basic disunity of the *literati* and 'their own' peasants, that is, peasants of similar ethnic origin, often hid from the Russian officialdom and intelligentsia the consistency and the rationale of peasant demands and dreams. The affected love of peasant dress or verse, from *chastushka* songs to the poems of Klyuev or Esenin, was but a part of a fundamental misconception. In all that, once more, the Russian peasantry was not exceptional.

Finally, the issues of consciousness and political struggle cannot be disconnected from the Russian peasantry's history. Peasant demands were often legitimised by reference to the good old times, true and mythical, to past rights lost unjustly – *das alte Recht* for which the peasants had fought in *Bauernkrieg* of the sixteenth century Germany and often before and since. The old generation still remembered the Russian emancipation from serfdom in 1861, both the dramatic change and the many disappointments. However, one can and should go further into the past. There is enough evidence to show that, well hidden from 'official Russia', the memory of great peasant rebellions of the sixteenth and seventeenth centuries was never quite extinguished in some of the areas, especially in the mid-Volga, for example, in areas particularly active also in 1905–07 peasant rebellions like the province of Saratov.[38] For centuries the state meted out punishment even for remembering Razin and Pugachev, the church anathemised them, yet legends were told, ballads sung and millenial dreams woven – well described by a recent writer as a veritable 'samizdat of the illiterate'.[39] These songs and legends carried the message of peasant defiance but also some basic ideas around which a new ideology could take shape. The image put forth by Razin and Pugachev alike of turning all the peasants of Russia into Cossacks – independent, free and self-ruling peasant communities – did not die. Nor did the idea of land for all and war on the officials, the squires, and the corrupt clergy. Some of it was carried through centuries by the Old Believers' sects who added to it a specially xenophobic dimension – to them Tsar Peter was not only the beginning and the symbol of all oppression but also of devilry – an anti-Christ invented by the Germans.

Peasants did better out of the 1905–07 revolution than some other social groups. Yet, the majority of the Russian peasants were neither molified nor ready to give up what to them was theirs by right. Nor were they ready to accept Stolypin's Reforms as a fair substitution for what they fought for. They had accepted the reality of the state's force, but that was all. Within a decade this peasant awareness and self-awareness, deeply rooted within peasant praxis and crystallised by the 1905–07 experience, were to play a decisive role in a new revolutionary war which ended differently and made Russia for a while more peasant than ever before or after.

Two major questions concerning the 1905–07 revolution are left open. They reflect the two alternative senses in which conclusions may be drawn. The first is the question: 'Who led whom?' in so far as the present majority of the Russian population was concerned. This represents mostly the analytical worries of the further generations attempting to make sense of the peasant struggle of 1905–07 and to make it fit broader historiographies of Russia. The second and more general question is, 'Who learnt what?' This refers to the consciousness of the revolution's contemporaries, the consistency and the change within it and what these meant to the future of Russia. We shall tackle them in the order indicated.

4 The Peasant War 1905–07: Who Led Whom?

At the very least, statistically,
by what they do or leave undone
it is the led who lead.

Berthold Brecht

The interrelation, confusions and infections of human
consciousness are, for history, reality itself.

Mark Bloch

A. QUESTION AND CONTEXT

From the moment when the twentieth century struggle of the Russian peasants undermined the late nineteenth century assumptions about their essential meekness, stolid conservatism and incapacity for revolutionary action, a debate commenced over who led them or enticed them into rebellion. The very fact of the debate bears evidence to the surprise of the contemporary Russian peasant-watchers, in the face of peasant political behaviour which defied any manner of prediction. The passing of time has not banished this discussion or its significance. The reasons for its persistence involve both analysis and ideology. The assumed mode of interpretation forms a necessary centre-piece of any historiographical and/or structural analysis of the 1905–07 and 1917 revolutions and consequently of the history of modern Russia. Its significance for understanding the peasant economy and political action elsewhere had been also considerable, for Russia was often used as the model and as decisive evidence for these matters, especially by socialists. The issues around which the debate centred have played a strategic role in the reproduction and construction of the ideological images of Russia, reading back into history the concerns, the justifications and the strictures of both the 'establishment' and the 'dissent' in each consecutive generation. The long shadow of that particularly vehement argument about the past extended all the way to the recent Polish or Chinese agricultural crises, to the critique of India's last five-year plan, and to the collectivisation of Soviet agriculture, if not to the last crop-failure in a nearby *kolkhoz*.

That is also why the stacks of new evidence, much more of which has been gathered and published in the USSR since the late 1950s, does not necessarily add illumination here.[1] Indeed, the complex problems involved may become incomprehensible or be altogether lost in an avalanche of new documents and figures, pushed and pulled by those who shape and present them.[2] To make sense of it all, one must go back to the roots of the debate and, while questioning facts and relating them to the perceptions of the different generations, proceed then to question the questions themselves. Without such investigation, essential aspects of the 1905–07 rural revolution would remain unclear.

Out of the heterogeneous list of the potential culprits or claimants who were said in those days to lead or to edge peasants into revolution – the anarchists and the SR Maximalists, the students and the criminals, the Jews, the Polish nobles and the Japanese – only a few deserve to be treated seriously. In terms of social strata, these are the rural intelligentsia (mainly the *zemstvo*'s 'third element') and the urban industrial workers. On the map of political parties, the honours were claimed mainly by the SRs and the SDs and, since the inception of the USSR, by the heirs of the SD's Bolshevik branch. One more alternative would be to assume that no external agency played a decisive role in the peasant struggle, that it was essentially self-generated and autonomous. In the more sophisticated studies, the question has usually been presented as that of a hierarchy of causes, that is, of their relative significance and interdependence, rather than of monocausal explanation. Even then the essential question of 'who led whom?' persists and links into the very core of the historiography of Russia and the Russian revolution.

The link between the general theories of society or strategies of its transformation and the preferred answers to the question 'who led whom?' were already evident to the political leaders during the 1905–07 era. These operated both ways. A general social theory implied the plausibility of some particular pieces of evidence or interpretation and the more persistent selection of data which suited one's pet theory. There were also cases of open falsehood, of evidence faked to argue a case. Even such data has its analytical uses for, to follow Mark Bloch's memorable maxim, 'Above all, a fraud is in its own way a piece of evidence'.[3] On the other hand, strategic, stubborn and unexpected evidence concerning the peasant struggle produced changes in the very fabric of the social theories and political strategies of the day, even though such processes have usually been less explicit and less immediate than the impact of theoretical presumptions on the selection of data. Also, there is no simple and absolute way to deduce unique empirical predictions from a given theory, with the result that even within the orthodoxy of a given school of thought, debate has never ceased, even though some major assumptions were being taken for granted by the bulk of its practitioners. To quote Bloch again as to what it means: 'The interrelations, confusions and infections of human consciousness are, for history, reality itself'.[4]

B. CONTEMPORARIES: RIGHT AND LEFT

The central image of the direct causes and substantive 'chain of command' within the 1905–07 rural revolution in Russia, as adopted by the monarchist establishment and its press, was that of a mostly non-Russian intelligentsia, possibly in the pay of foreign powers, provoking into riot 'rootless' elements, especially workers. In those Russian villages where no 'students, Jews and anarchists' were evident, it could have been outside agitators or the political suspects exiled into the provinces under police supervision (*podnadzornye*) who would have stirred up trouble, beginning with the rootless-within-the-village, that is, the marginal farmers, landless wage-workers and the local youngsters, who did not yet know any better.

Those senior state administrators who took pride in their self-image as men with a realistic and balanced appreciation for political and social matters (as against the paranoia of the monarchist press and the unbecoming panic of the provincial squires) were also certain that it was the intelligentsia and especially the third element which was to blame. To them also, the rootless elements of the villages were the connecting link between the radicalism of the rural intelligentsia and those peasants who were misled into rebellion. The administrative stratum differed mostly in their more sophisticated understanding of the political crisis as well as of the 'anti-state elements' with whom they shared much cultural baggage. In 1904, Stolypin, the clever governor of Saratov and a man 'on the make', expressed it well in reporting to the tsar about the dangerous radicalism of the 'most influential and powerful element in the Saratov *guberniya*, referred to as "the third" and consisting of the employees of the *zemstvo*, the teachers, the medical personnel and recently even some of the lawyers.' He proceeded as follows:

> In these times of military defeats, of disclosures of the govern-ment's ills (*yazv*) and its alleged weakness, the third element has raised its head . . . One cannot deny their courage, energy, knowledge and capacity for hard work but, on the other hand, they show prejudice, deep antipathy to the historically established ways and forms . . . love of destruction and instinctive preference for the revolutionary ways over those of legality and reform . . . The only power which stands in the way of the third element is by now the [state] administration.[1]

For once – and new in the history of Russia – members of the intelligentsia resided constantly, legally and in some considerable numbers in the countryside and in small provincial towns. It was no longer the tsar's order of exile for misdeeds – true or assumed – or the wish to retire from the world which placed them there. An estimated 70 000 of them worked there as teachers, agronomists, medics, social scientists, etc., relating daily with the peasant populations.[2] It was to them in particular that the Minister of the Interior, Durnovo, referred in 1905, saying that 'Russia can do without intelligentsia' – the 1905 pattern of arrests and deportations showed clearly what he meant. Not only the political stand, but the 'student-of-social reality' attitude and skills usual to those people seemed pregnant with danger. In his 1906 report Witte singled out the very pursuit of rural statistics as menacing and in need of immediate restriction.

Once accepted, this view seemed to establish the rural intel-ligentsia as the true masters and activists of the All-Russian Peasant Union. To the monarchist press, these were simply members of the intelligentsia dressed up as peasants. Once again, the top administra-tors of tsardom knew better and understood that peasants were actively and extensively involved, but even to the brightest of them and writing with the benefit of hindsight, 'the leading role in this Union' was 'clearly played by intellectuals close to the Socialist Revolutionaries'.[3]

The question of why and how the 'third element' was capable of corrupting peasants into radicalism was a matter of debate. To many within the reactionary wing of the monarchists, it was Witte who was to blame both in his 1890's strategy of promoting industry at the expense of agriculture and his appeasement of the mutineers in 1905. However, to an increasing number of squires and bureaucrats it was the backwardness of the peasant society and economy which gave the radicals of the rural intelligentsia their ability to stir up trouble. As manors burned and the first and the second Dumas met to heap abuse and demands on the government, the Russian peasant commune was increasingly singled out as the reason for the rural rebellion. In the writings and speeches of the monarchist camp, the peasant commune was rapidly transformed from the kernel of stability and the preferred tool of social control into the chief bogey – the root of economic stagnation, social backwardness, political collectivism and effective radicalism which must be defeated and demolished at all costs.

Most of the Russian dissenting liberals accepted the essentials of the official view about the leaders and *provocateurs* of the peasant uprising. They differed from the state administration mainly in stressing the facts of the peasants' just grievances, especially the shortage of land, and in accepting the need to offer some immediate solution which would appease rather than repress both the peasants and the 'third element'. As against the crassness and incompetence of the tsar's administration and the parochial egotism of the majority of squires, that could be done only by an enlightened government responsible to the Duma. On the other hand, they agreed that the dissolution of the peasant commune was a natural and necessary element of Russia's 'progress'. Especially in the eyes of the KDs, a combined solution, increasing peasant landholding (with full indemnity paid to its owner) and promoting the de-communalisation of rural Russia, was necessary to establish the social base for consensus politics in the British style – their manifest ideal and point of reference.[4]

Turning to the revolutionary parties, an assumption of the spontaneity of the peasant struggle would have suited most of the populists and the Bakuninists of old, but the new political map of Russia differed. The PSR 'official heirs' to nineteenth-century revolutionary populism, were, by all contemporary accounts, the most influential of the political parties within the peasant countryside of Russia proper.[5] They began earlier to build up a peasant following and set up particular peasant organisations in some of the *gubernya's*. By 1905, their major theorists had developed a theory concerning peasant participation in social revolutions and the political goals particular to the rural scene: the 'socialisation of land', that is, the confiscation of all private land without indemnity, its egalitarian redivision via the peasant communes and the banning of land sales and rural wage-labour.[6] All this did not make them into a peasant party in any direct sense. Some peasants admittedly joined the SR Peasant Brotherhoods but the main rural influence of this party in 1905–07 lay with the rural intelligentsia, especially the teachers, the 'statisticians' (social scientists engaged in rural research), the medics and even some clergy.[7]

Russia's right-wingers with a tendency for 'cloak and dagger' explanations often substituted the revolt of the peasantry by the alleged misdeeds of the government's terrorist enemy. To them, the peasants involved were merely stooges of the rural intelligentsia which was, in turn, manipulated by the SRs. The agrarian disturbances of 1905–07 were no more than the SR's clever plot. The other wing on the same side of the barricade, the SDs, never tired of explaining the PSR's total political irrelevance: the SRs could not possibly lead a peasant revolution, even though their rural connections could not be denied. Put with a suitable rhetorical flourish by Trotsky, while speaking about propaganda among the peasants at the 1903 Congress of the RSDWP: 'this soap-bubble which, out of courtesy, one calls the PSR, is not serious enough . . . Lack of serious rivals makes our task easier'.[8] SRs were blamed in one breath for being too radical (for example, calling for armed rural struggle) and not being radical enough (for example, in their readiness to co-operate with other opposition parties as against the harsher exclusivity of the RSDWP).

As against their detractors, the PSR was caught in the ambivalence of its own stand.[9] The rural intelligentsia was often theirs in its sympathies, but it was unseemly to assume that they pulled the peasant masses by the nose. The main revolutionary force within Russia was to the SRs, the 'labouring class', with peasants as its majority and with the workers and intelligentsia incorporated in it. Contrary to the populists of the 1870s who tended to treat workers as peasants on temporary leave, the PSR increasingly viewed the impoverished peasantry as workers. The peasant revolutionary spirit and quest for socialism were to that view natural and in harmony with the true interest of the entire labouring class led by the revolutionary parties which fought to destroy tsardom and to make Russia just. The PSR was the best representation of this quest. Yet, while doubtlessly on the warpath, with the manors burning, alternative authorities being set up, demonstrations with red flags, etc., most of the peasants still refused republicanism or armed uprising, and even showed

ambivalence as to the take-over of all private lands without an
indemnity. The peasants did not quite set their goals and means in
relation to their true interests as expressed by the PSR, but did what
they did most energetically. That was puzzling.

In consequence the PSR did not claim for itself the decisive role in
the peasant action. Contrary to its later images, many of the SRs
were not 'peasantist' in their 1905 analysis, aspirations or hopes
(following in the People's Will tradition). In 1905–07 much of their
political effort and actual impact rested, besides the intelligentsia,
with the urban workers and with the military.[10] As for the nature of
the actual peasant struggle, it was mostly viewed as that of a peasant
mainstream lagging behind its PSR vanguard on the path toward the
people's social revolution. Chernov has described this revolution as
popular–labourist (*narodno-trudovaya*), i.e. as an intermediate stage
preceding a socialist revolution. As to the diversity of positions
between the revolutionary rural intelligentsia and the peasants, it was
only a transitional state of affairs that time would cure. Others within
the PSR ranks took a grimmer view. A number of delegates to the
1906 congress doubted the use of joining the All-Russia Peasant
Union and even objected to it *in toto*, treating it as a reformist
organisation competing with their own revolutionary efforts.[11] Their
argument matched closely the earlier attack of the SD's *Iskra* against
the 'Economists' and against relying on popular spontaneity.

To turn from images and self-images to the facts, the rural
intelligentsia without doubt played a major role in the radicalisation
of the Russian peasantry – propagating socialist views, spreading
criticism, informing the villagers of happenings elsewhere, or simply
teaching literacy and reading out leaflets and news to an illiterate
audience. Their sympathy was clearly with the government's enemies, the PSR most of all, but also with some milder version of
populism, the SDs and the KDs. The most committed among them
organised local peasant groups, helped to set up branches of the
All-Russian Peasant Union, and, on occasion, initiated SR Peasant
Brotherhoods or the SR and SD branches. Some of the nationally-
known figures of the Russian intelligentsia, such as Tan (Bogoraz) of
People's Will fame,[12] or Peshekhonov – a major 'rural statistician' of
the *zemstvo* – were also quite central in the peasants' nation-wide
attempts at self-organisation, especially in the 'Committees of
Support' of the All-Russian Peasant Union. Chernov and Vikhlyaev
of the PSR were invited to advise the Labour Faction caucuses in the
days of the Duma. The brothers Mazurenko, teachers known only
locally in the Don area, emerged as leading lights at the 1905

congresses of the All-Russian Peasant Union and were elected to its General Committee. To 'conscious peasants', the 'village literates' with 'patched clothes', the rural and rural-related intelligentsia with its strong radical sentiment acted as natural allies and guides.

However, all that is no proof that the rural intelligentsia or leaders popular with them actually led the peasant revolt in 1905–07. The only way that assumption can be tested is by relating political goals to political action. By that decisive test, the image of an intelligentsia-led peasant revolt falls to the ground. When the actual political influence of the 'third element' was at stake, it manifestly failed to swing the peasant masses. Most of the rural intelligentsia in the south tried very hard to prevent 'excesses', such as the burning of the estates, as counter-productive to the true peasant and/or socialist and/or broader anti-monarchist interests. Yet the peasants laid waste thousands of manors. In 1905–06 a decisive majority of the rural intelligentsia, and especially the revolutionaries, hotly supported the boycott of the first Duma but the peasants voted overwhelmingly for it. The intelligentsia, on the whole, was republican. For the most part, the peasants stayed vaguely monarchist (the major case of a peasant anti-intelligentsia pogrom in 1905 in Kamyshin, near Saratov, had to do with an 'enemies of the tsar' allegation). In the case of the SRs, one can also compare the distance between their strong belief in terrorist and armed action and the positions actually adopted by the large majority of the peasants.

Within the upheaval of 1905–07, the literacy of the 'third element', their worldly knowledge and critical faculties were treated with respect and called upon by the peasants, who in those days listened thirstily to new images, ideas and words. But it was disregarded when it ran contrary to the peasants' established preferences, prejudices and choices. When a massive police purge of the 'third element' took place at the end of 1905, it was not followed by a decline of the peasant struggle – the peasants fought on. Contrary to claims of the government and the self-image which many of the rural intellectuals would love to cherish, the rural intelligentsia did not lead the Russian peasantry in the politically decisive issues. The same holds for the specific interpretation which saw the SRs manipulating the peasants via the rural intelligentsia.

*   *   *

In the assessment of the peasant revolt, the orthodox Marxists of the

two main factions of the RSDWP had 'a much longer way to go', both
conceptually and tactically, than the monarchists or the SRs. In 1896
the senior party of the Second International, the German SDs,
rejected the very idea of a Marxist Agrarian Program. It was Kautsky
supported by Engels – to the Russian RSDWP, the highest
theoretical authorities – who defended this position and explained
it.[13] Human progress was assumed to show a number of absolute
law-like determinations: large units of production were more
effective than small; peasanthood meant poverty and stagnation;
industrial capitalism represented improvement (bound to exploitation, however). Agriculture was unable to progress and transform at
the all-societal speed, but industry would take agriculture in tow. The
forces of production must rise, the proletariat must increase in size
and strength, and peasantry must eventually disappear. The rise of
capitalism and knowledge would reflect in the growing political
impact of the working class and its party, eventually resulting in
socialism. On the road to it, the party of the most advanced class and
of the only scientific social theory, the party of the future, must not
engage in back-sliding compromises with other social and political
forces. That was particularly true of peasants who both represented
the past within the present and held property and thereby could not
be a socialist force. Strategically, the only possible attitude to their
demands was neutrality – a party of socialist progress had nothing
more to offer to the peasants than the realism of accepting the facts of
life, that is, their demise under capitalism and hope for a better future
under the proletarian leadership. At the same time, tactically,
peasants and especially the peasants' sons in the army uniforms,
should be shielded from anti-socialist influences. The dual persona of
the poor peasants, that is, their selling wage-labour while holding
land, should facilitate socialist propaganda aimed at them for that
purpose.

In the Russian context all this seemed for a time to make perfect
sense. The formative period of the Russian Marxist movement,
between the mid-1880s and 1902, was the nadir of the peasant
struggle. In the words of a Marxist analyst, the peasant 'suffered
silently . . . and was left by the Social Democrats to his fate'
(*rukoi na nego makhnuli*).[14] The vicious famine of 1891 increased, if
anything, the peasant apathy. Not only the populists' hope of the
1870s for a peasant revolution, against which Plekhanov established
his initial Marxist positions, but even Plekhanov's own declaration in
the 1880s that Russian Marxists 'do not intend to sacrifice the

countryside', by now looked romantic and naive – a surrender to earlier populist prejudices. In the 1890s, pessimism about the peasant revolutionary potentials went hand-in-hand with the evidence of the actual capitalist transformation of Russia and the belief (shared with the Russian liberals) in its liberating potentials as against the reactionary straitjacket of the feudal survivals, of which the peasant commune was one. Plekhanov's essential position, adopted then by all Russian Marxists ('orthodox', 'revisionist' and 'legal'), assumed that capitalist economy was already established in Russia and by now stood in contradiction with its superstructure – the autocratic state – as well as with the backwardness of the peasant communes. These were to be brought into correspondence by a democratic revolution. In this confrontation, the weakness and the ambivalence of the Russian bourgeoisie made proletarian hegemony necessary to make the struggle effective, but its results must be a bourgeois state. A peasant war was neither expected nor desirable – it would reflect the backward impulses of the petty bourgeoisie scared of the inevitable progress. In Plekhanov's view, the Marxist approach to an agrarian programme had to proceed from 'a view of socialism being the result of the development of the forces of production in a capitalist society'.[15]

Despite Lenin's initial readiness to be somewhat more open to peasant demands than his Iskra partners, the first agrarian programme presented by him and accepted by the RSDWP congress of 1903 was the tactical expression of this SD view of the 1890s. The peasants were offered little and were expected to play a limited role in the coming struggle. The rural proletariat was to be the mainspring of revolutionary action in the countryside. Groman expressed this well in saying that the agrarian programme of the RSDWP second congress (substantially limited to the restoration of the lands 'cut-off' in 1861) represented 'the lack of belief in a serious and imminent peasant struggle'.[16] In 1906, at the fourth congress of the RSDWP, Lunacharskii treated it *ex post factum* similarly on behalf of the Bolsheviks when he spoke of 'the old colourless (*blednaya*) agrarian programme' and charged Plekhanov with admitting that it was adopted 'out of the fear of a peasant revolution . . . [and thereby] of a victory for the populism'.[17]

The period 1905–07 was one of a major and dramatic confrontation-cum-transformation of the view of peasantry in the SDs' camp. It was expressed in a debate developing under the direct impact of the rural explosion of 1905–07 and the strange news from

Guria, which had been broadly publicised since 1903 by *Iskra*.
Increasing demands for a new rural strategy came to the fore. The
shift in perspective was uneven. Different activists of the SDs were to
support in varying degress the revision of the initial Agrarian
Programme of 1903, which, until 1906, had united them all. Few of
them considered a new theoretical approach. To others, the issue was
mainly tactical: a trade-off between the wish to gain peasant support
in the struggle against tsardom and the fear that a peasant victory and
an egalitarian land redivision would retard capitalism and delay
proletarisation, that is, act regressively within post-revolutionary
Russia.[18] Finally, there were those who did not see any reason to
change anything at all – attempts to court the peasant petty
proprietors were contrary to the true proletarian interest. All agreed
on the urgency of setting up autonomous organisations and the
leading role of the rural proletariat – the village equivalent of the only
consistently revolutionary class of the Russian bourgeois revolution
and a seed of the future socialist one. The debate was coloured by the
old suspicion of claims about the revolutionary capacity of peasants,
which sounded populist to many of the party's old hands who had
argued themselves hoarse in the 1890s to dispel the 'romantic
Utopianism' of all those who doubted Russia's being capitalist and/or
'still' expected peasant uprisings.

At the root of the issue lay a fundamental contradiction between
the 1903 theoretical stand of the RSDWP concerning the development of capitalism in Russia's agricultural sector and the political
facts or tactical needs of 1905–07. If Russia and its agriculture were
substantially capitalist, as Plekhanov assumed since the late 1880s,
the rural class-split into bourgeoisie and proletariat would preclude a
specifically peasant revolution. If there was a peasant revolution,
capitalism could not have prevailed in the Russian countryside. In the
words of the Lenin, who was the author of the 1903 Agrarian
Programme of the RSDWP and was now calling for its revision, a
new strategy had to assume that 'the economy of the squires in Russia
is based on repressive-enserfing and not on capitalist system of
economy. Those who refuse to see it cannot explain the contemporary broad and deep peasant revolutionary movement in Russia'.[19]

Factional boundaries between the SDs did not fit neatly the front
lines of the new agrarian debate. In addition, attitudes oscillated
rapidly, as could be clearly seen among the delegates to the party
congresses, who shifted within days between very different agrarian
strategies. The Bolshevik third congress (in April 1905) left the issue

of a possible change in the 1903 Agrarian Programme ambivalent,[20] as did the Mensheviks at their parallel conference in Geneva. For a while, the political programme aiming to tap the peasants' revolutionary capacity, by accepting the demand for total abolition of private land ownership and for the egalitarian redivision of all land among Russia's smallholders, was held only by minorities within each of the factions of the RSDWP. Mensheviks, such as V. Groman, and, in his own way, N. Zhordaniya, were closer to Lenin's views over that issue than most of the senior Bolsheviks.[21]

At the fourth congress in 1906, Lenin's and P. Rumyantsev's suggestion of 'nationalisation of all land' (which stood as close to the positions of the All-Russian Peasant Union and to the PSR's 'socialisation' idea as one could venture in those days) was not only defeated by the Menshevik majority of the delegates but also refused by the majority of Bolsheviks. Most of the Bolshevik delegates (including Rozhkov, Stalin and Borisov among others) objected to the Menshevik agrarian programme of land municipalisation but voted for a programme converting all lands into peasant private property, to facilitate the development of capitalism. Lenin's views in that matter were at that time being questioned in the *Proletarii* – his own faction's newspaper. Local activists were clearly as divided. At the very centre of the peasant Jacquery, the Bolshevik organisation of Saratov described even the half-step taken by the third congress towards the revision of the agrarian programme as an unacceptable retreat from the Marxist positions.[22] A. Shestakov, in charge of the Bolshevik rural action in the Moscow *guberniya* and his party representative at the first congress of the All-Russian Peasant Union, went further, questioning Lenin's suggestions in an open letter as a 'step backwards in terms of capitalist development'.[23] In November 1905 the conference of the RSDWP's northern committees decided 'under no circumstances to admit into the party programme' peasant demands for the confiscation and redivision of all land. Similar views by Bolshevik writers appeared throughout the SD press.[24] At the fourth congress Plekhanov put it more poignantly: 'Lenin looks at nationalisation [of land] with the eye of an SR. He even begins to adopt their terminology, for example, talks of popular creativity [of political forms T.S.]. Nice to meet old acquaintances but it is unpleasant to see how Social Democrats adopt populist points of view.'[25] Many of the SRs cheerfully agreed with that evaluation.[26]

Despite these differences and changes of attitude, the place given to the working class in historiography offered to the Russian SDs a major point of unity and consistency. To the SDs, the only intrinsically revolutionary class was the industrial proletariat. The RSDWP was spared the PSR doubts and the monarchists' certainties concerning the role of 'rural intelligentsia'. The intelligentsia was to them neither a specific social entity nor an analytical unit, but only part of the petty bourgeoisie (when challenging the SDs) or else it was conceptually absorbed into the proletarian vanguard. The revolution's bourgeois–democratic nature made it naturally appealing to different social classes and groups, including the peasants. The marked tendency to substitute for 'true proletarian interest' the SDs' views and organisation also meant the gradual repositioning of the peasants' struggle as against the RSDWP itself. The fact that the party's agrarian programme of 1903 was over-pessimistic in so far as the peasants' revolutionary potential was concerned, was by now admitted by most of the SDs and explained by the extent of 'feudal survivals', as being greater than initially expected. The Mensheviks and Bolsheviks fought bitterly over the anticipated revolutionary potential of the bourgeoisie and the possible class alliances for which the proletariat should strive. The image of the chain of command in the rural struggle was less of an issue. To all of them it was the industrial workers of the large enterprises, especially the highly-skilled metal-workers, printers, etc., in the largest cities, who led the workers' camp, including the rural proletariat. It was mainly its proletarian struggle, especially strikes, which triggered off the 'agrarian disturbances' of the poor and 'middle' peasants, with some of the richer peasants possibly drawn in.

Following that line of argument, the peasant-workers and the rural proletariat provided a 'transmission belt' between the countryside and the main urban scene of political struggle. The peasants were mainly fighting their own class enemies – the squires – and could therefore support revolution only at its pre-socialist stage. That was, however, Russia's actual stage. The Bolsheviks on the whole were more optimistic than the Mensheviks about both the chances of revolutionary victory in general and the peasants' revolutionary capacity. Lenin did not remain in the minority there for long. His reconstructed agrarian programme became part and parcel of the Bolshevik political platform and terminology. This new strategy of nearly unconditional support of the peasant demands was conceptualised as promoting the 'American road' to capitalism under a victorious revolutionary regime – the democratic dictatorship of the workers and the peasants. In that view the egalitarian land redivision for which the Russian peasants fought was to be treated not only as politically advisable in challenging the tsardom but also as economically progressive in clearing the way for the fullest flourishing of capitalism. It also explicitly accepted the views of the All-Russian Peasant Union and the Labour Faction in the Duma as the genuine expression of the peasants' will.[27]

Lenin's new position meant that the merger of the proletarian and the peasant revolution was the core condition of the forthcoming revolution's victory and a corner-stone of the optimal post-revolutionary regime. The supreme qualities of the proletariat were assumed and its leading role declared essential for the success of the revolution, but the peasantry was by now treated as a *bona fide* social class on a par with the workers and not a dated notion (to be put by good Marxists in quotation-marks).[28] Its revolutionary struggle was accepted as progressive, its alliance sought and the political organisation which expressed it treated as natural partners. Even more dramatically, Lenin by now accepted the PSR as partners in the ongoing revolutionary struggle.[29] Quite a difference from the second congress of the RSDWP!

It was the alliance with the peasants and those who in his view represented them which Lenin now defended as the alternative to the RSDWP 'block' with the 'Westernisers' of the bourgeois parties, especially the KDs. This strategy of a Left Bloc was to become a major dividing line between the Bolshevik and the Menshevik mainstreams.[30]

C. THE POST-REVOLUTIONARIES: THE DRIFT OF THE INTERPRETATION

The October Revolution of 1917 put the state–institutional seal of approval on the SDs' version of the 1905–07 events in what was accepted to be its Leninist interpretation. It has since formally guided the work of Soviet rural historians and other social scientists. For the generations to follow, it meant a considerable pool of researchers available and privileged access to evidence and publication. Outside the USSR little interest has been shown in what seemed but a shadowy and unsuccessful version of 'the real thing', which actually happened in 1917. All this makes the Soviet literature and versions central for any review of the issue in hand.

A major characteristic of them was the iconisation of Lenin, the acceptance of his views as the 'clinching' argument in any debate.

Discussion would be permitted only over the different interpretations of his primordial text (some of the recent sycophant texts even spoke of Leninology). In our case, there are two major approaches, with two periods in Lenin's political biography accentuated and two sets of texts involved. The first is rooted in the corpus of Lenin's writings in the 1890s, explicating Plekhanov's line of 'capitalism now' and of merciless war against the populists' blindness. The second follows the more action-bound writings of 1905–07 in which strategy was reconsidered and transformed but theoretically the *t*'s were mostly left uncrossed and the *i*'s undotted. Mostly for reasons of party politics, Lenin did little to resolve the resulting analytical 'contradictions', and in particular, despite the decision to drop the first agrarian programme of the SDs did nothing to adjust his *Development of Capitalism in Russia*, on which, after all, this agrarian programme was based. This was made explicit in the classic anecdote of the revolutionary generation: Yu. Steklov (in the 1903 argument about the cut-off lands, etc.) and his party comrade Skvortsov-Stepanov (in 1909) used in their debate against Lenin the work of 'Ilin' – his own work published under this pseudonym in 1899.[1]

From the mid-1920s onwards, it was not Lenin's new strategy established in 1905–07 which was predominantly reflected in the orthodox (and increasingly streamlined) historical studies within the USSR. To be sure, Lenin was constantly quoted, but it was mostly the 'young man' Lenin. It was also Shestakov's simplistic and defensive book of 1926 rather than Lenin's 'democratic dictatorship of workers and peasants' of 1905–07 or his political strategy of 1919–23 which underlied the next generation of Soviet historical interpretations by those who identified with the ruling party.[2] Pokrovskii, who came to define then what orthodoxy is for the Marxist Russian history, made it all simpler by decreeing the tsardom (since the days of Muscovy) to be the creature of mercantile capitalism.[3] Dubrovskii, to whose work in the 1950s we shall return presently, made his debut then, strenuously fitting the rural struggle in Russia of 1905–07 into Lenin's early writings.[4] Elsewhere, a special effort was made in the 1920s and thereafter to gather any scrap of evidence of the 1905–07 rural activities of the SDs.[5] Soviet historians increasingly repudiated the revolutionary influence of any movement other than the Bolsheviks on the peasants. Even the impact of the Mensheviks in Guria was denied by a few already in the 1920s, a view eagerly repeated by Shestakov. The All-Russian Peasant Union increasingly came to be treated as a fake peasant assembly, manipulated by *kulak*s and bourgeois opportunists – a peculiar shadow-picture of the 'official' views held in 1905–07 by the monarchist propagators of tsardom. By the 1930s, with Stalin's collectivisation in full swing, any peasant self-organisation was firmly presented as reactionary or else as manipulated by evil forces. The first post-revolutionary generation of Soviet rural historians perished or were silenced in a fratricide of mutual accusation and purges in the new period which began in 1929. Those quotations from Lenin which did not fit the 'anti-peasant' tendency, then sweeping the theoretical field, were simply forgotten or mislaid. To quote an example:

in class terms the Moscow congress of the All-Russian Peasant Union was a *kulak* congress. The interests of the poor peasants and middle peasants were totally alien to it . . . Its voice was not that of the peasant masses but that of the rich upper stratum within the villages – the peasant bourgeoisie increasing its power in that period.[6]

Against these forces of evil stood the revolutionaries of the countryside led by their proletarian elder brother, led in turn by the Bolsheviks. The revolutionary *Guria* was dominated by an even longer chain of command: the Georgian peasants were led by the local proletariat, led by the Russian senior proletariat, led in turn by the Bolsheviks, led by Lenin as advised by Stalin.[7]

The post-Stalin era saw a renaissance of interest, both genuine and formal, in Lenin's original writings. Some of it simply enhanced and streamlined the past dogmatism of quotations and legitimations, but much of Lenin's revival in the last 1950s to early 1970s was used as a vehicle for a more realistic appreciation of the issues of the Russian revolution. The field of our interest has benefited particularly from the political realism of Lenin's 'on-the-spot reporting' in 1905–07 and the courage with which he championed new unorthodox tactics against his own comrades. A new look at his work has helped to restore some measure of realism and immediacy to the discussion of the prevailing conditions and of the 1905–07 peasant struggle. To take an example from the text used earlier, the All-Russian Peasant Union was rehabilitated and once again admitted to be a genuine political expression of the Russian peasantry and of the revolutionary and democratic spirit of the 1905–07 peasant revolt. Some of the work produced by Soviet historians was excellent in its content and its insight. I shall avoid embarrassing its authors by personal praise. Yet within a decade or so, a new paradigmatic general line recrystallised to define what is acceptable or preferable in that field. It is linked once more to the heritage of a submerged Plekhanov, and to a very early Lenin as expressed in the views of Shestakov, Dubrovskii, in the 1920s, treated as 'orthodox', that is, good. Three questions arise from this. What was this case and the evidence presented in its support? What was the root of the 'drift' of the interpretation during these sixty years? What are the conclusions concerning the matter at hand?

In its most current form, the essence of the 'orthodox' views and the evidence marshalled in their support is expressed by two major and related claims concerning the hegemony of the working class in the peasant revolution of 1905–07 and the direct leadership of the Bolsheviks in the peasant uprisings. There is a third weaker claim, stressed to a much lesser degree, which concerns the impact of the class division in intra-village relations. The works of Dubrovskii (in 1956) and Tropin (in 1970) offered a general, up-to-date summation of those views, eventually providing the textbook guide for students and a framework for further research, for the clearance of Ph.Ds and for easily acceptable publications.[8] The monotonous nature of most of the studies of the different regions of Russia published in the 1960s and 1970s has been very much the result of such a procedure: a given framework of analysis, annotations and conclusions into which diverse local figures and names are poured each time.[9]

The first of the major contentions of that paradigm has been empirically expressed by the claim that the agrarian disturbances followed directly and necessarily the vicissitudes of the workers' struggle. The view that the peak of agrarian disturbances was reached in November 1905 (after the general strike) and not in June 1906, expressed that claim directly. Particular rebuke was reserved for the idea that while peasant struggles were indeed influenced by some extra-rural political confrontation, they were not influenced by the one assumed to be decisive, that is, strikes (for example, that it was the agrarian debate in the first Duma of 1906 boycotted by the Bolsheviks or the activists of PSR which triggered off a wave of peasant rebellions). The second contention was expressed by the claim that it was the Bolsheviks and the Bolsheviks alone, who, led by Lenin, presented before the revolution the only realistic ('scientific') analysis and anticipation of the peasant uprising. Consequently, their party played the decisive role in the peasant struggle, organising it and leading it. Proceeding with that line of argument, the many failures of the peasant struggle and its final defeat were due not to the tsardom's strength but to the ambivalent class nature of the peasants and, mostly, to the treasonable intrigues of the Mensheviks, the SRs and the KDs, who tricked the peasants away from the revolutionary struggle. Finally, the main way intra-peasant class analysis enters that paradigm is through the claim that all along the measure of revolutionary militancy and struggle stood in direct relation to the presence and the initiative of the rural proletariat or at least to its semi-proletarian substitutes. It was admitted, however, that (in Lenin's terminology) while the 'first civil war' of the peasants against the nobles was central, the 'second civil war' of the rural proletarians against the peasant capitalists was 'still' at a very low stage.

This interpretation of the events of 1905–07 is not in its entirety the view held by the Bolsheviks who watched them directly. Lenin expected the peak of the peasant uprising to be reached in the summer of 1906, and counselled delaying the armed urban uprising until then. Writing about it in 1917, he still assumed that the peak of the peasant struggle had indeed been reached in 1906, a view in evidence also in the official history of the Bolshevik party published as late as 1935. Also, the historical studies published in 1925 during the celebration of the twentieth anniversary of the event, and with most of the leading participants still alive, documented the weaknesses of the Bolshevik rural policies of 1905 and of their impact. Few have claimed then that it was the Bolsheviks rather than the SRs or the Mensheviks, who were particularly active in the countryside. The nature of the drift from these positions towards the views which currently prevail is an issue in itself to be discussed elsewhere. Tropin's book, the latest of the Soviet general 'directing' texts and one incorporating the main claims of Dubrovskii (in the 1920s and again in the 1950s), will be used to present the currently prevailing view. This view of the rural political struggle links ideologically with the 'capitalism already' approach to the economic history of rural Russia at the turn of the century which is discussed in Chapter 4 of *Russia as a 'Developing Society'*.[10]

The claim of a direct and decisive impact of the Bolshevik party on the peasants in 1905–07 is the more recent and the less substantiated. Much of it rests on brazen inexactitudes of admission or omission of which the authors must be aware. To exemplify, Tropin's attack on the left alternatives to the Bolsheviks forms a major part of his argument: the Bolsheviks' policies appear as the antithesis to the ways in which the SRs and the Mensheviks were sabotaging the revolution. Tropin accordingly charged the SRs both with the anti-revolutionary policy of objecting to the use of force at the congress of the All-Russian Peasant Union in November 1905 (p. 131) and with the provoking of the 'agrarian terror' (p. 55).[11]

Such charges contradict one another. More importantly they contradict direct evidence for November congress, where the call for an armed uprising (rejected by the majority) came only from the delegates from Saratov. They appeared, like all the other delegates, under cover names ('Saratov's first, Saratov's second', etc.) which are, however, easy enough to decode as those of N. Rakitnikov and I. Rakitnikova and A. Studentsov. All are identifiable as members of the PSR and, indeed, agitators (*razezdnye agitatory*) within that party, in other words, its professional revolutionaries. The first was a member of the PSR Central Committee.[12] None of the RSDWP members present at the congress (that is, at least two elected delegates plus the Ukrainian *Spilka* plus the official representatives of the party) suggested anything as radical. On the other hand, the PSR consistently rejected 'agrarian terror' and even expelled its proponents – the separate party of SR Maximalists. (This small group, mostly destroyed by the police in 1906, operated in 1917 as the Bolsheviks' ally against the PSR.)

The Mensheviks have been treated even more cavalierly. Following the massive rewriting of Caucasian history in the 1930s, led by the then Georgian chief-of-police and later its party boss, L. Beria, Guria was simply appropriated and turned into a Bolshevik preserve and success story.[13] Documents were censored and memoirs rewritten. All this established an incredible tale of a revolutionary boyhood for Beria's boss and by 1938 helped Beria to earn his ticket to Moscow, to Stalin's side, as his chief of police. When the thief, Beria, was shot, the loot was never quite returned to the owners–Tropin simply repeated Beria's tale without giving him as source. Yet as late as 1926 the official Bolshevik historian of his party work among the peasantry testified thus: 'In rural organisations of Georgia, the increase in the impact of the SDs [during 1905–07] was reflected within the party membership by the increase of the share of Mensheviks in it, until the whole leadership of the movement was totally in their hands'.[14] The evidence of elections to Duma and to the SD party congresses supports it fully. Another trick – the impact of the Mensheviks elsewhere in the Russian countryside (for example, the *Spilka* in Western Ukraine) was being subsumed under the general heading of 'the RSDWP', while specifically Bolshevik work was carefully singled out.

Even Lenin and his considerable input into the 1905–07 debate did not escape such cosmetic treatment. In particular, much effort was made to document that the idea of a 'worker–peasant alliance' as 'the main method to overthrow the tsardom' was more or less always in his mind.[15] There was, of course, no sign of it at the RSDWP Second Congress only eighteen months before the 1905 explosion (and already after the Poltava peasants rose and the peasants and teachers of Guria set up their revolutionary organisation).[16]

On the whole, clairvoyance and orthodoxy-to-one's-own-views are consistently claimed for Lenin. Yet his point of strength among the Russian SDs was the exact opposite, namely his capacity to learn, challenging the 'holy cows' of his closest lieutenants, as well as his own earlier beliefs. He usually refused to admit to his own theoretical non-conventionality, but that is another matter. The change in his attitude to the revolutionary capacity of the peasants, resulting from the experiences of the 1905–07 revolution, was just such a major turning-point, ranking with the introduction of the NEP in 1921 in its significance and in its radical challenge to the majority of his followers' views. Both were met with stupefaction or dissent by some of his closest supporters.[17] The Fourth Congress (where Lenin's agrarian programme was defeated not only by the Menshevik majority but also within the minority faction of the Bolsheviks) marked the lowest ebb of Lenin's capacity to command his own following. There is, in fact, much to admire in this tale of vision and leadership, challenging both in-built prejudices and one's own infallibility in the service of a cause. The shamefaced way in which Lenin's 'inconsistencies' are treated brushes aside his most valuable asset as a leader – the ability to think anew, the courage to change and the capacity to convince or cajole.

As for the substance of this argument, the crucial test of the Bolshevik impact on the Russian peasant is not, however, in what happened between or within the Russian revolutionary parties. Nor can it be defined by Lenin's pronouncements. It lies in the direct evidence of the extent to which party organisations actually led the peasants in terms of action and in formulation of their demands. A general conclusion that no party had enough resources to influence peasants nationally in that way is right there. The PSR Brotherhoods with 18 000 peasant members (by their own estimates) operated by that time in a number of the *gubernii* of central Russia: Tambov, Saratov, Samara, Chernigov. The SDs' impact in the villages at some of the peripheries was clear, but there were no RSDWP party organisations consisting mainly of peasants within Russia proper. The SD's rural organisations, mentioned obliquely and without substantiation by Dubrovskii in 1956, to the extent to which they existed at all, were not peasant in their membership.[18] There were political and organisational as well as ideological reasons for it. Most of the SDs then would have been outraged by an influx of petty bourgeois members into 'the party of the proletariat'. Also, seventy years of subsequent research has not produced one name of a Bolshevik who was a peasant leader of substance in 1905–07. The SDs' 'work in the villages' was mainly that of distributing leaflets and sending out a few speakers (once again it was different at the ethnic peripheries, especially in Latvia, Georgia and to a lesser degree in those parts of the Ukraine where the *Spilka* was active). The counting of those leaflets, often undertaken of late, is beside the point in so far as actual leadership within the countryside was concerned. They were, indeed, often the proof the exact opposite, namely of an incapacity to reach the peasants in any other way. The leaflets and speeches were received in the villages with curiosity or indifference, sympathy or hostility, but the resulting dialogue must have resembled the Russian tale describing conversations between an old man and God: the old man talked to the icon which did not answer back.[19]

It is the response to the leaflets, speeches and appeals which has to be proven or disapproved as the bottom line of an argument about a party's political impact. To judge it we must apply once more the test we have already used for the rural intelligentsia. The Bolsheviks, in line with the other revolutionary parties, advocated a republic, the boycott of the first Duma and the extra-legal distribution of all manorial lands. The Russian peasants said and did the opposite.[20] Until 1906 the RSDWP, including its Bolshevik faction, offered an agrarian programme of restitution of the lands 'cut-off' in 1861 only, and insisted on the necessity of building within the countryside an autonomous and parallel organisation of the rural proletariat (while discouraging proletarians from committing themselves too far on the side of the 'middle' or rich peasants). The Russian villagers did not refer to it at all. At the peak of Russia's largest peasant revolt in centuries, the number of peasants within the cadres of the Bolsheviks was about zero, as was the number of Bolsheviks elected to the second Duma by the 'electoral college' of the peasantry. The same goes for the separate organisations of the 'rural proletariat'. The story about the Bolsheviks leading the Russian peasants in the 1905–07 revolt dissolves once the relevant evidence is considered.

The second element of the view discussed – the claim of the political impact of the urban workers on the Russian peasants – was introduced earlier; it is better substantiated and within limits doubtlessly correct. Most Russian workers were of peasant origin and connections. News coming from an urban kinsman was undoubtedly more plausible than an oration by a party propagandist or the exhortations of a police officer. Evidence shows that the peasant-workers (and likewise the ex-servicemen, the travelling craftsmen, the local literates and other villagers who were particularly exposed to external influences) often brought radicalising information and/or led the peasant communities in the struggles of 1905–07. The general strike of October 1905 had a powerful impact throughout rural Russia.

This is not what is at issue, however. To begin with, the question 'who led whom?' is not quite that of 'who learned from whom?'[21] Moreover, the process of learning was not uni-directional either in fact or in its political consequences. While the peasants undoubtedly learned from the urban experience of proletarian struggle, the opposite was also true. For example, much argument took place within the RSDWP about the origins of the Soviets: to Martov it followed the Menshevik call for workers' political self-management, while Lenin spoke of it as the workers' spontaneous political creativity and later related it as far back as the Parisian commune.[22] Not too many workers would have known particulars of the SDs' organisational debate and fewer still would have heard about what had happened in Paris in 1871. But every Russian worker knew what a *volost'* assembly was – a meeting of representatives of the villages which was exclusively one-class (with the state officials and other 'outsiders' usually kept out), discussing issues of common interest under its own elected executive. The reason why an all-city organisation of representatives, elected only from workers in their main enterprises, was set up with such ease and spontaneity was directly related to forms known and accepted. This closely resembled also the experience of the All-Russian Peasant Union 1905–06 and of the workers' and soldiers' Soviets of 1917.

Proceeding to the more demonstrable and, indeed, demonstrative, the capacity and the wish of the Russian peasants to go their own way, as opposed to the idea of leadership by a proletarian vanguard, was laid dramatically bare at the November congress of the All-Russian Peasant Union. A delegation of SD workers of Moscow demanded rights equal to those of the elected delegates to address the debate, for 'you can learn a lot from the workers' struggle'. (They 'rejected as offensive' the observer status granted to the non-elected representatives of the all radical parties and groups.) The congress shouted down and voted out that demand because 'we have just got rid of self-appointed teachers and supervisors'. As a result, the official SD delegation left the congress altogether. The congress proceeded to pass a resolution of full *solidarity* with 'our brother workers' (as well as with the soldiers and the students) in *their* struggle.[23]

The centre-piece of the evidence for the claim that peasants followed where workers fought has been statistically a comparison of the chronology of workers' strikes with that of the peasant agrarian disturbances. The Addendum to Chapter 4 which follows presents the analytical model and evidence involved. In short, Dubrovskii based his argument in 1956 on the monthly reports of 'agrarian disturbances' in the 1905–07 police files. He argued that, contrary to the assumptions of contemporaries (including Lenin), the peak of agrarian disturbances was reached in November 1905, directly after the general strike, and not in June 1906 when the intensity of the workers' political struggle was at a much lower level. A generation after the victory of the Chinese revolution, two generations after Zapata of Mexico and the 1903–06 Guria republic in the Russian Empire itself, and while the struggle in Vietnam was moving toward its climax, Dubrovskii concluded with a general social law (*zakonomernost*) by which contemporary peasants must follow workers in revolutionary struggles.

Tropin used a different set of figures to underpin similar theoretical assumptions. He began from the 1912 study by Prokopovich which measured the intensity of peasant attacks of 1905–07 by the percentages of districts (*uezds*) in which agrarian disturbances were reported. (Dubrovskii scoffed at those figures because of their limitations, duly acknowledged by their author, and in particular the fact that they provided no way of gauging the intensity of disturbances in every given *uezd*.) Tropin added the figures of E. Morokhovets for the Baltic provinces and his own count for the Caucasus to arrive somewhat triumphantly at the conclusion that the peak of the peasants' struggles was reached in 1905 (53.3 per cent of *uezds* involved) and not in 1906 (47.6 per cent only).[24] Once again, it followed, as it should, the climax of the urban struggle.

The Addendum to Chapter 4 which follows will show that on the strength of the very evidence of Dubrovskii and Tropin, contrary conclusions should be drawn. It also indicates why Dubrovskii's figures cannot be fully trusted. However, it is the very question of when the peasant struggle reached its peak which misses the point. Indeed, the extent of effort to make the 1905 figures overtake those of 1906 must arouse considerable suspicion. Classes in revolution are not horses at a rally, with the first horse over the pole getting the medal or winning a bet for its owners and backers. On its own, a month, a season or a year of agrarian disturbances even if correlating with workers' strikes and following them directly, proves nothing. Indeed, by those standards, the 1903 workers' struggle in the south of Russia would be 'hegemonically led' by the peasants of Poltava, Guria or Saratov, who, of course, rose in 1902.

By the evidence available and mostly accepted, the majority of the politically active workers in Russia fought in 1905–07 not only for their livelihood but for the political destruction of tsardom and followed in this struggle the revolutionary and socialist parties on the national scene. By the evidence available and mostly accepted, the militant Russian peasants, during a roughly similar period, fought for land, while their demands for power were mostly locality-centred. The peasants' direct participation in the life of the political parties of the day was remarkable by its absence. It is ultimately the political content which defines revolutionary struggle, not blanket correlations of events or of numbers and 'incidences'.

Finally, the last and the least-accentuated component of the supra-model reviewed is a kind of class analysis, relating militancy to the availability of the proletariat (and of capitalism), nationally or regionally – that is, the more of the second (and the third), the more of the first. During the revolutionary period, that expectation was very much in view – a tribute to the Marxist scientific analysis of society, as understood. Martov explained in this way the revolutionary *élan* of rural Latvia.

Maslov expanded it to a full-scale regional analysis in 1907, an approach which Pershin tried later to advance further within the Soviet historical analysis.[25] The evidence of Guria proved, as already said, the exact opposite to the 'proletariat equals revolutionary action' formula. So did the most spectacular and symbolic event during the 1905 mutinies in the south of Russia. The Russian sailors were often recruited from urban population. Of the Black Sea Navy only one ship was manned mostly by peasant conscripts and that one happened to be the battleship *Potemkin* of revolutionary fame. The same applies to the comparison between the relatively limited struggle in the villages of the more 'proletarianised' and industrial

north as against the rebellious Black Earth centre of Russia. Inside
the villages, Dubrovskii's own figures showed an actual drop in the
share of the 'second war' during the 1905–07 period (despite the fact
that in his study all the rural strikes were subsumed, quite wrongly,
under the general heading of 'the proletarian struggles'). No actual
militancy of a rural proletarian vanguard – the main expectation of
the Russian Marxists and a central focus of their tactical decisions –
was ever identified in 1905–07 in Russia proper. Indeed, the
permanent labourers (*batraki*) were consistently reported to be the
least active there. Moreover, most of the attacks against the 'Kulaks'
and/or incidents of inter-peasant class war came not from the rural
proletariat but from family farmers.[26] Both the leadership and the
membership of those involved in the 'agrarian disturbances' or the
peasant self-organisation was solidly peasant and mostly 'middle',
that is, placed economically close to the mean of peasant households
in the region involved. Even at the north-west periphery with its
distinct character, cases were reported in exact opposition to the
'proletariat = revolution' (and Marxism?) equation, for example, the
particular support given to the SDs by the richest (and most literate)
strata of the peasants in Lithuania. No evidence of specifically anti-
capitalist (or 'anti-*kulak*') struggle was reported from the 'more
capitalist' south-east of European Russia.

Consequently, ambivalence permeates the work of most of the
contemporary Soviet historians of 1905–07. The proletarian revolutionary potential in the Russian countryside is sharply declared and
any other view rebuked. Unsuitable evidence is then substituted by a
rhetorical phrase, for example, when the 'rural paupers' become 'The
Path-Blazers (*zastrelash-'chiki*) Of The Revolution'.[27] Elsewhere,
rural strikes are still being counted as incidents of 'specifically
proletarian struggle' which on the next page are described as
organised by the local peasant communes and aiming at specific
peasant goals (demanding the use of meadows, land to rent *and*
better wages, together with the exclusive use of the communes'
landholders as labour on the local manor).[28] Once the rhetoric is
over, all this is usually soft-pedalled and quietly abandoned, while the
analysis of the rural political scene is continued along unrelated lines.

Two more points before leaving the issue of the Soviet interpretations of the 1905–07 peasant struggle, a semantic one and a
substantive one. As to the first, 'massaging' terms to transform their
meaning or to show division between the 'good' and the 'bad' in
factional struggles has often been done when evidence did not

substantiate a pre-assumed model. The words, which can be treated as particular pointers to such operations, were: 'peasant committees', 'nationalisation of land' and 'essentially'. The two which begin the list are taken from Lenin's programmatic suggestions at the RSDWP congresses (second, third and fourth, respectively). The first is suitably vague. Any extra-communal group of peasant activists (and there were many) may be treated as 'a committee' and thereby as the peasants' keen response to Leninist leadership.[29] The second is as suitably close to what most peasants demanded, what the All-Russian Peasant Union and the Labour Faction presented and what the PSRs formulated as 'the socialisation of all land'. The Utopianism of the PSR and the naiveté of the peasants in doing so were declared often enough before the RSDWP's Fourth Congress, which then found itself bound to adopt it in part or in full. The way to keep the claim of infallibility while admitting change is to state that the clear inadequacies of the second congress's 'Agrarian Programme', the ambivalence of the third congress, the divisions at the fourth and what the peasants actually demanded were but the logical unfolding of the initial axioms of the science of society which, as such, differed totally from the PSR's view. 'Nationalisation' with egalitarian land redivision under the control of peasant representatives (which is good) as against 'socialisation' (which was roughly the same, but bad, being terminologically introduced by the SRs), was used in such a manner. When there were difficulties with such arguing of cases, the term 'substantively' (*po sushchestvu*) was liberally used, not to designate the crux of a position reviewed, but its critique or reinterpretation to suit a presupposition, that is, instead of 'to my view' (or 'it would serve my pet theory better'). For example, peasant demands for the land take-over under their communes was *po sushchestvu*, Lenin's nationalisation programme, which was *po suschestvu* what the orthodox Marxists always had in mind; poor peasants were *po sushchestvu* proletarian when radical-for-us and '*kulak*' when radical in other ways, and so on. If not actually, then at least 'substantively', everyone's views but Lenin's and those who followed him at each stage, were wrong, even when Lenin admitted to his own error. As 'substantively', the Bolsheviks led the peasants in 1905–07 (and until Stalin's death the Peasant Union was a Kulak organisation).

Finally, a related but different dimension of the debate was expressed via the assumption about the most significant units of peasant political action. The core of the evidence showed (and the representatives of the different views between the Soviet historians usually accepted) that peasant communes operated as such units.[30] A major subsidiary division and conflict–dimension was the capitalism-related class distinction. (Dubrovskii expressed it in Lenin's words as the assumption of the 'first war' against the squires exceeding the 'second war' against the rural bourgeoisie.)[31] This polarity often hid some other dimensions of rural strife. While the conflict of the peasant commune (and its 'middle-peasant' core group) with the squires and the local state authorities was indeed the most significant of confrontations in 1905–07, there were at least five more inter-peasant conflicts unfolding, the divisions by age, gender, ethnicity, the segmentary factions and the 'ideological' ones. In the 1905–07 records, 'old men' and women were often reported as a conservative and restrictive force in local confrontations, while young males were named as the most active.[32] (This was not universal – cases of particular female activism were reported, as mentioned in Chapter 3 of this volume.) Ethnic heterogeneity often divided neighbouring villages and, less frequently divided the villages themselves. Local 'vertical' segments or factions of mutual support by kinsmen, neighbours or friends (*shabry*) were known to operate and to clash in many places, but their significance in the life of a Russian village was, on the whole, much less than in the case of the Arab *hamula*, the Chinese clan or the Latin American *compadradze*. Finally, some of the Russian peasant communities have known ideologically-defined factions, a rough equivalent of the Black *versus* Red divisions between families which lasted for generations in the countryside of nineteenth or twentieth century France and Spain.[33] In rural Russia, one side defined itself as the Black Hundreds – loyalist, monarchist, anti-intelligentsia, and anti-Jewish. The other side was formed by those described as 'the conscious ones' (*soznatel'nye*). While the communal peasantry *versus* non-peasant power-holders and the class divisions offered analytical categories which, on the strength of evidence, can be properly described as substantively central, other dimensions of strife must be considered as we move from the general level and from the first approximations to the detailed studies of specific localities and regions.

D. PEASANT WARS AND THE 'INFLECTIONS OF HUMAN MIND'

Decades of a sustained effort by the Establishments' historians to substantiate a view contradicted by evidence should not be left with its simple negation. The question 'Why?' when it concerns 'the inflection of human mind', is for history, indeed, reality itself. Also, once understood, patterns of bias help us to use more realistically the evidence gathered and the analytical work already undertaken. For that purpose, the gradual drift of the mainstream explanation and the drive behind that, must be related to the more general character-istics of society and to the patterns of thought of its historians. Let us look in that way at the general view which currently prevails among the Soviet historians of the period.

The task of defence and legitimation of the Soviet Union and its leaders has been formally adopted by Soviet scholarship as part of the 'principle of party partisanship' (*partiinost'*).[1] In this framework some authorities are accepted and defended come what may. On the other hand, some views, some authorities and some data are simply refused at the outset as hostile or slanderous. Our particular interest, however, is not with the resulting silences or self-righteous lies of expedience. Those appear, of course, throughout the world and regularly overspill into research, but even under heavy pressure to conform, scholars' work is seldom simply reduced to crude or ingenious lies. However selectively, it attempts to put to use verifiable facts and to relate them by logical argument. To abandon those anchors of scholarly pursuit defeats the long-term purposes even of those who try to manipulate social sciences. Lies are often less convincing to people trained in analytical skills. Worse still, a tissue of lies does not offer the information which political leaders and administrators need for effectively going about their business. Also, some of those who choose scholarship are not cynical, and some, fewer still, are ready to pay the price for defiant inflexibility in the pursuit of the truth as they see it.

To understand the logic of a 'false consciousness' and the direction of the analytical 'drift' in our case, we must consider why some views and data are more admissible and/or plausible than others and see them in relation to the context and content of the analysis offered. At its most general, the context of the discussion reviewed, as against that of the generation contemporary with the Revolution, is that of the rapid development of the USSR into a superpower engaged in a global confrontation. In that capacity it faces a polarised 'capitalist world', with centres of power and enviable abundance synonymous with the older industrial civilisations linked to the areas of particular economic difficulties and a politically 'soft underbelly' – the so-called 'developing societies', usually with a strong peasant presence. It faces also the ideological challenge of China (and used to face Yugoslavia), that is, countries of large rural populations and genuine peasant movements, which were socialist by self-definition and led by communists. Second, there is the intra-societal context of ever-present and acutely-felt agricultural crises of production – a major impediment to the USSR's economic advance. As for the content of Russian history as a discipline of the Soviet social sciences, it has been established as applied Marxism, defined through the writings of Lenin. Under Stalin, it incorporated a powerful undertone of Russian nationalism. All of this combined in the growing emphasis on the supremacy and global primacy of the Soviet people, of the Soviet Union as a society as well as a state, of the Soviet Communist Party and of Marxism–Leninism as interpreted and practised by its leaders. At the apex of this system of legitimation stands Lenin – the creator of the Soviet people, society, state and party as officially understood, the ultimate interpreter of social reality, and also, in himself, a major reason why his most direct followers can and must guide mankind *in toto* towards the ultimate well-being – communism.

The theoretical structures most effective for revolutionary action are not usually the ones most suitable in the legitimising of a post-revolutionary state. The political and conceptual elements listed correspond much better with the Marxist interpretations of the pre-1914 Second International than with the iconoclastic departures from them in Lenin's strategic turns which followed the experiences of 1905–07 and again, 1917–21 revolutions. Progress, understood as an unilinear and necessary evolution from one mode of production to another – the vision of Kautsky and Plekhanov, means that the USSR is singularly at the forefront of world history (in Brezhnev's wording, at the 'stage' of 'advanced socialism'). It also means that once true socialists have gained political power and the state ownership of the means of production is established, a simple increase in the forces of production (that is, further industrialisation) produces communism. Lenin's unfortunate slogan equating socialism with 'Soviet power plus the electrification of the country' would mean just that – after all, 'Soviet power' was, in that sense, already established in Lenin's own lifetime. Kautsky's erudition and Stalin's crudity have carried in this sense a remarkably similar message.[2]

Moreover, Marxism understood as a science leads to an expectation of the possibility to deduce social processes from given assumptions. Consequently, the axiomatic authority from which one proceeds acquires extraordinary status. Moreover, it means that the correct theory is validated by a political victory and vice versa. Those defeated are, by definition, analytically wrong, unless treason interfered with reality. The concept of science (interpreted in a Positivist sense) also implies its exclusive validity while any other view is transformed by definition into prejudice, utopia, bad-will or sabotage. That is 'objectively true' even when those who reject or doubt the wisdom of the supreme Marxist authority, that is, a party leadership, are 'subjectively' (that is, actually) the soul of decency, evidently devoted socialists and/or the best of scholars. By the same token, ethics is defined as service to science, that is to progress, and therefore the organisations which represent it, and vice versa, an organisation which represents progress is ethics institutionalised and should define what is right or wrong to the specialist in any field.[3]

The fact of an un-capitalist Russian peasantry engaging autonomously in the 1905–07 revolution upsets the evolutionist scheme described. By the historiographical clock adopted, Russia would have been thereby very 'backward' (or 'Asiatic', or both) and its leap to the top of the international league not easy to explain. The same applies to Lenin's role as the propounder of a theory valid for the whole world, especially its more industrialised parts. To explain it all by accident, choice or will sounds unscientific. The analytical tools developed by the Left to address these matters, for example, the concepts of 'uneven development', 'permanent revolution', etc., come mostly from unacceptable origins (the Populists, Parvus, Trotsky, etc.). In any case, as long as the logic of evolutionism is consistently assumed, they offer metaphors rather than answers. Also, images of their own backwardness *vis-à-vis* Europe have been deeply offensive to Russian nationalists' sensibilities. As long as the assumption is kept that what happened must have happened (and represents the inevitable laws of evolution, with the Soviet history marking out the path to mankind at large), this presents one more problem of legitimation. In political terms, the revolutionary characteristics of a peasant class expressed in the capacity for autonomous action would have also justified, a two-party system, at least for the 1920s (actually, for a while, envisaged by Lenin in 1917). An image of a socialist revolution which stripped of direct representation the plebeian majority of the population is not an image to cherish (especially so with the 'developing societies' of today forming a major ideological battleground between the superpowers, in which the USSR's potential allies call for the support of the social underdogs).

It would be much more satisfactory to find the Russia of the 1890s to 1917 well-'developed', with capitalist agriculture and a 'dissolved' peasantry, explaining the socialist potential, the most advanced theory, the 'proletarian dictatorship' and Russia's place in Europe. The period of NEP is easier to justify then as a very short transition only, despite Lenin's contrary statements.[4] So is the character of the 1929–38 collectivisation in the USSR. The collectivised Soviet agriculture and the form it took can consequently be treated as a technological necessity, on a par with industralisation and with all the resulting problems definable and resolvable by technical means.

The drive toward such a supra-model of Russian rural history was ever present in those groups of the Russian intelligentsia which gained their education and intellectual distinctiveness from Plekhanov. It increased considerably in the USSR of the post-NEP era. In an inverted manner it corresponded with the view of Russian *émigré* historians that Stolypin's reforms *must* have succeeded in following the natural, that is, all-European steps of advance towards de-peasantisation (and failed only because of the accidents of death or war and of the ill-luck of the Bolshevik Revolution). While Kautsky's name is dirt in the USSR and Plekhanov treated with suspicion, the theoretical framework which they designated in the 1890s (and shared then with the very young Rosa Luxemburg, Martov and Lenin) could not be bettered as long as the logic of consistent evolutionism is adopted as Marxist orthodoxy. The second congress of RSDWP faithfully reproduced these views. When his time came to challenge them, Lenin did so by claiming that Russia was *not yet* as capitalist as expected, that is, he stayed within the earlier theoretical structure but 'moved the clock back'. Plekhanov called this populism all the same – not without foundation. The fundamental question and alternatives of our own time are still those which were set out in 1905–07. For reasons suggested, one of the views reigns supreme, linking writers who otherwise differed in their specific topics of interests and ways of presentation. It is ever challenged but cannot be defeated. In the given political and intellectual context any dominant view is designated as Leninism, true, unambivalent and ultimate. Lenin's most fruitful ambivalences of a creative mind are simply denied.

Contradictions between the prevailing view and the evidence available have their own laws of motion. Once the Stalin-like methods of resolving such contradictions by the physical destruction of any opposition were put aside, the institutional logic of this matters made the USSR's mainstream research more similar to that of the West than both sides care to admit. Self-perpetuation of a prevailing view, especially when it seems to serve state interests and ideological needs, is in the short term fairly unproblematic within scholarly practice. Patterns of selection and self-selection of the employees-in-charge ('cadres') minimise 'disorder', as intellectual rebels lose access to ranks, budgets, printing presses, graduate students and therefore, seemingly, to the future. Social sciences are usually underprivileged compared with the natural sciences in so far as major correctives of unrealistic views are concerned: the test of laboratory and the immediacy of technological usage and needs are absent. But creative arts, of which social sciences are one, have the peculiar ability to subvert structures of intellectual control, as well expressed by Andersen's tale 'The Emperor's New Clothes'. Kings and kings' scribes are usually naked. The more sizeable their realm the more unclad they tend to be. In every generation anew a bright child is destined to cry out regardless of the consequences: 'the king is naked'. Bright grown-ups usually know it too, but bide their time or speak in whispers. Then, all of a sudden, 'a hundred flowers bloom' and for a while a society comes to terms with its own characteristics, problems and doubts. When such blossoms subsequently freeze or are pruned, social life seldom goes back to where it all began. But a step was made, however small. For that to happen, stubborn long-term intellectual work from those who gather 'facts as they actually are' and from analysts who persist in their unorthodoxies, form a necessary ingredient of the periods 'in between'.

Looking at the scholars' thought is ever speculative and open-ended. One is permitted a metaphor in doing so, as long as its limits are clear. Andersen's tale of the naked king is a good point at which to stop and sum things up.

*   *   *

In 1905–07 Russian peasants mostly followed their own inclinations rather than those of the radical intelligentsia or the proletariat. They rose against the squires and policemen but eventually fought the tsar's government and its soldiers too. Within the bulk of central Russia's villages there was no visible socialist leadership, yet a mass revolutionary movement for social justice took place. The fundamental proof of the extensive spontaneity and the essential autonomy of the peasant struggle of 1905–07 lies in the specificity of its goals, expressed in confrontation with the squires and with the Russian state, but also in the manifest contradictions of their deeds and views (some mutual sympathies excepted) with all the political parties of the day. The actual social composition of the peasant movement sustained that view. So did the rhythms and forms of the peasant struggle. The relation between the Jacquery, the peasant fight for political power and the peasants' dreams of a better society further illustrate the spontaneity and autonomy of the peasants in 1905–07. The revolution of 1905–07 was rightly recognised by contemporaries as several overlapping struggles: that in the cities, that of the peasants, that at the 'ethnic peripheries' and possibly one more within the army and the navy. The fact of a common enemy – the Russian state of the day – should not overshadow the distinctive and particular dynamics of these major composites. In particular, the claim that the Russian peasants were 'led from the outside' does not stand up to serious empirical examination. The Russian peasant war of 1905–07 was mostly of the peasants, by the peasants, peasant-led and aiming for peasant goals.

That is not to replace one 'social law' – by which peasantry facing advancing capitalism is necessarily reactionary, that is, backward-looking in its goals, ambivalent, disjointed and 'led from the outside' – with a contrary statement, once again elevated into an absolute law. Revolutionary tendencies and capacities of social classes are not absolute but always subject to historical and social context. Nor do those tendencies or capacities grow or decline in a straight line, either up and up or down and down. More specifically, peasant choices of, or openness to, the radical or socialist goals and ideologies as well as their ability to act militantly, autonomously, unitedly and effectively is subject to internal and external determination which cannot be postulated but must be studied in each case. Recent comparative analysis is helping to establish it more clearly.[5] The comparative perspective can also help to define more specifically the characteristics of the Russian peasant struggle and its pattern.

As was often the case elsewhere, the Russian peasants' militancy and capacity for autonomous political action and the extent to which the peasants stood united in 1905–07 against enemies and well-wishers had its roots in the family farming and the communal structure within which they lived. Patterns of self-identification and ideology linked with it, establishing a coherent social system. The acute crisis of this system was central for the rural history. The interest of the rich and the poor in each of the villages differed considerably, but the community of fate and/or conflict when facing the forces of nature, the state, the squires, and even the market (for agricultural and non-agricultural produce as well as for seasonal wage-labour) provided then powerful, and on the whole, overriding reasons for co-operation and mutual support. The experience of centuries had taught the villagers that such unity was necessary for most of them to survive. Both the cohesion of the communes and the peasants' self-identity were sustained and reinforced by the deepest cleavage and exploitive diversity within the Russian society, its peasant countryside facing the combined and closely-knit forces of 'upper Russia': its state and officialdom, its squires and nobles, its moneyed urbanites and its many tools of social and political control.

When compared with other peasantries or other times, the front-line of conflict and defiance can be stated more specifically. It was, for the most part, a war against the local squires and/or state representatives, developing into a confrontation with the state at large. The hostility toward the urban, moneyed classes was then usually dormant, the attitude toward the intelligentsia ambivalent but rather positive and particular community of fate was felt with other plebeian groups repressed by the authorities. As to the organisation, the land repartition within the Russian peasant communes caught the particular attention of its analysts, which explains why Maslov, Groman and many others insisted that peasant political action and the All-Russian Peasant Union were the creatures of, and necessarily limited to, the specific regions where the repartitional communes were active. That view clearly underestimated how much village communality was neither specific to Russia nor simply a tool for land redivision. The complexity of peasant village life, its social, political, cultural and welfare needs and the agriculture of the day were most effectively approached collectively and locally. Informal communal hierarchies, unity and organisation were one way to make such a collectivity work. The Russian commune formed a flexible and ready-made framework of organisation for whichever large-scale tasks were accepted as necessary, besides functioning as a major unit of identity. There were considerable conflicts in the communes, and many members complained rightly about its restrictive tendencies and fumbling ways. All the same, most of the Russian peasants knew that without the commune things would be worse still. As against an international taxonomy of the peasant societies, running from those where communal cohesion is strong to those where it barely exists at all (and is replaced by atomisation or by an inside class confrontation), the Russian communities were high toward the cohesion pole. What Le Roy Ladurie said about the communal unity as the major element of 'the bloody dignity of rustic wars' was true also for Russia in 1905–07.[6]

All the specific aspects of peasant cognition – its conservatism and the institutionalised suspicion of strangers, its conventionality and acceptance of the collective will – were relevant to and fairly effective within the context of village life. New ideas and newly-perceived needs were mostly integrated into the existing patterns, which made them the stronger for it. The nation-wide similarity of reaction to the agrarian crisis and the ability to construct specific peasant organisations and to secure meaningful political representation was not surprising in those conditions. Neither the peasants nor the intellectuals of the day knew it then, but it was part and harbinger of a new wave of rising peasant identity and peasant political impact in Europe and elsewhere.[7]

The 'middle-peasant', that is, the fully peasant nature of the core of the peasant leadership and the Russian peasant marching army in 1905–07 was not accidental. It reflected the nature of most of the contemporary Russian peasant communities. The middle peasants, in an exact definition of this word, were a decisive force in the Russian countryside and its communities. The landless and 'household-less' (in the sense of not having a family farm to which to relate) did not carry enough weight in the villages, nor could they offer singly long-term resistance in a rural confrontation. The revolt was perpetrated not by the uprooted but by those who were refusing to be turned into such. The power of the communal assembly was such that the richest usually failed to control these communities. As for the *kulak*s of the Russian countryside, at least in the peasant meaning of this term, these were neither the richer farmers nor the employers, but the 'not quite peasants' who stood apart or against the commune.[8] (The closest rural synonym of the term '*kulak*' was indeed *miroed* – 'the commune eater' – which indicated not only what was considered evil by the villagers but also what was to be defended and what was to be used in self-defence.) While the Russian intelligentsia engaged in the never-ending quarrel about the nature of the Russian peasant commune, its ups-and-downs or its very existence, the Russian peasants 'voted with their feet' for it every time when sustained and radical collective action was necessary. It happened in 1905–07 and again in 1917–20. In all probability, this also happened before, even though nobody bothered to document it.

The times of peasant revolt (and more generally 'times of troubles') were also the times of the particular flourishing of the peasant commune. The decline of one made the other shrink.[9]

One more way to test the social structure of peasant politics and war is to look at the historical continuities of peasant political action. Much was made of the depth of rural social transformations under the impact of dramatic state intervention in 1906–14 – the so-called Stolypin Reform. Yet when 1917 came the peasant demands and action were remarkably similar to those in 1905–07. They were led locally by peasant communes which resurfaced 'with a bang' throughout Russia. The major inter-peasant struggle reported in 1917–19 was not the rich–poor confrontation but the massive attack on the 'splitters off', that is, those householders who left their villages to set up separate homesteads under Stolypin's provisions.[10]

Whatever his earlier view and later comments and constructions, Lenin was one of those few within the Russian Marxist camp who drew radical and merciless political conclusions from the Russian peasant struggle in 1905–07 and the way it did not fit accepted predictions and strategies. That was certainly why, by the end of 1905, Russia was to him no longer overwhelmingly capitalist as in his book of 1899. He expressed this transformation not by rewriting his earlier theoretical text but through the strategic admission of the peasant revolutionary *élan* in party programmes and tactical pronouncements. The new approach was expressed in statements defining the All-Russian Peasant Union as no less than 'an embryo of a peasant party' representing a social class of political allies,[11] rather than in re-writing the initial chapters of *The Development of Capitalism in Russia*, which contradicted the very possibility of it being so.

Despite the many disclaimers, that picture of the Russian peasantry in 1905–07 as 'a class for itself', capable and indeed prone to political action, was accepted as a fact by all the most effective political leaders of Russia. The Stolypin reforms acknowledged it, on behalf of the tsardom's authorities which proceeded at once toward a major attempt to try and dismantle it as a political danger. Lenin's revolutionary programmes acknowledged it for the Bolsheviks. It has been mainly the ideological needs of subsequent generations which put it in doubt. As such, this belongs also to the history of Russia. But it pertains to different times, much later than the revolutionary period which we are discussing here.

ADDENDUM: PEASANT AND WORKERS' STRUGGLES IN 1905–07: THE STATISTICAL PATTERNS

In the 1920s and again in the 1960s and 1970s a concentrated effort was made by a number of Soviet historians to prove statistically a close and specific interdependence between the urban proletarian and rural peasant struggles during the 1905–07 revolution. The hypothetical model, presented on the whole as a cast-iron social rule, had its origins in the Marxist interpretations of the Second International in the 1890s, especially by Kautsky, Plekhanov and Engels. At its roots lay a deductive and highly generalised political sociology which treated the proletariat, that is, wage-labourers, especially within the manufacturing industries, as the only consistently progressive and revolutionary class of the current world. It was moreover necessarily and naturally revolutionary, whichever the context, and destined thereby to lead all other oppressed groups in the political struggle toward socialism. As part of this analytical scheme, the rise of capitalism and the simultaneous decline of the pre-capitalist classes, especially peasants, was assumed to provide a necessary stage of the human evolution. That being so, the peasants of Russia, where capitalism evolved at neck-breaking speed, were assumed to be naturally reactionary and/or politically ambivalent in their wish to parcel up land of the squires and in being unable to accept the necessity of capitalism which spelled their social demise as a class. These impediments – together with the well-advanced socio-economic differentiation of peasantry into capitalists and rural proletarians meant that no autonomous peasant-class struggle in Russia was expected by the Marxist theorists of the 1890s. Their model arch-party in the more advanced Germany, with which Russia was seemingly catching up, had refused even to set a specific 'agrarian programme' aimed at the peasant population. As Engels put it: 'in brief, our small peasant, like every other survivor of the past modes of production, is hopelessly doomed. In view of the prejudices arriving out of their entire economic position, the upbringing and the isolation . . . we can win the mass of small peasants only if we make them a promise which we ourselves know we cannot keep'.[1] The first agrarian programme of the Russian Marxists in 1903 accordingly aimed to neutralise peasants rather than to attempt the impossible task of drawing them into the forthcoming revolution. Particular virulence was added to this argument by the SD confrontation with the Russian populists (who assumed the peasantry's different prospects) over who represents socialism in Russia.

The massive peasant uprising in 1905–07 and the peasant political attack on both the squires and the government were not expected by the theorists of the 1890s. It could still be accommodated into the analytical scheme described via the assumption that Russia was not yet capitalist (or else that political 'inertia' reflecting the peasant pre-capitalist past, reinforced by a pre-capitalist state, made them act as a class which they were not any longer). A shorter cut was to assume that the main explanation of peasant rebellion can be found in its being led by the revolutionary proletariat. With no signs of rural proletariat playing the leading role in the countryside, that could only mean that the rural peasants were following the urban proletarians, which is the point of the statistical exercise we are to consider.

In defining and ideologising this general model of theory-cum-statistics in the last generation, the most important were the books by S. Dubrovskii and by V. Tropin, in 1956 and 1970 respectively. The explosion of regional studies, theses and books about the 1905–07 revolution in contemporary Soviet literature has usually followed the supra-models established by these authors, simply injecting them with different figures and names. Simultaneously, studies of broader scope and statement of ideological relevance treated Dubrovskii's and Tropin's conclusions as facts or even as the natural expressions of social inevitability.

Figure 4.1 and Table 4.1 present the gist of the argument. In the 1920s Dubrovskii counted the monthly incidence of cases of 'agrarian disturbances' on the tsarist police files for 1905–07.[2] He concluded that the peak of 'agrarian disturbances' was reached in November 1905 when 796 cases were reported, and not in June 1906 as previously assumed (736 cases only). The curve of peasant militancy was therefore related to and said to follow that of the workers' strikes which reached their all-time peak in October 1905 and were much lower in 1906.[3] A different method to quantify peasant struggle (by accounting for the percentage of *uezds* in which 'agrarian disturbances' were reported) was put to similar use by Tropin (Table 4.2, page 176). Some

TABLE 4.1   *Dubrovskii's comparison of striking workers and 'agrarian disturbances' 1905–07*

	1905		1906		1907	
	Peasant attacks[a]	Workers on strike[b] (thousands)	Peasant attacks[a]	Workers on strike[b] (thousands)	Peasant attacks[a]	Workers on strike[b] (thousands)
January	17	444	179	190	72	65
February	109	293	27	27	79	56
March	103	73	33	52	131	25
April	144	105	47	221	193	90
May	299	221	160	151	211	212
June	492	156	739	101	216	21
July	248	152	682	169	195	36
August	155	104	224	40	118	19
September	71	38	198	88	69	23
October	219	519	117	32	27	43
November	796	326	106	13	14	142
December	575	433	88	18	12	9

[a] Number of incidents of the 'agrarian disturbances' reported by police as estimated by S. Dubrovskii, *Krest'yanskoe dvizhenie v revolyutsii 1905–1907 gg.* (Moscow, 1956) pp. 42–3.
[b] Number of workers on strike taken from the reports of the Factories Inspectors for which see V. Varzar *Statistika stachek rebochikh ha fabrikakh i zavodakh* (St Petersburg, 1910) pp. 15–19.

regional discrepancies were admitted by Tropin, for example, that the peasant struggle reached its peak in the Western Ukraine only in 1906. All the same, he fully agreed with the way Dubrovskii summed up his statistics as a general 'social law' by which contemporary peasants are bound to follow workers in any revolutionary struggle.

In a number of ways Dubrovskii's figures did not meet the standards of presentation of evidence to which such major significance is given. In particular, as noticed already by a Soviet scholar of the field, its sources are not open to inspection.[4] More importantly, the consideration of the figures Dubrovskii offered is statistically faulty and actually defies the analysis attached to them. The division of the statistical series into months (or else into quarters, beginning with January) is misleading, not to say ridiculous. An analysis of the tendencies in question cannot be based on formal calendar units. Either the realities of peasant life must be allowed into the picture by a seasonal division which is agriculturally meaningful, or else one must be statistically consistent and 'smooth down' the curve by one of the accepted methods, while undertaking the analysis of the trends. Once a realistic seasonal division is introduced (Figure 4.2 and Table 4.2, page 176),[5] Dubrovskii's own figures show the monthly average of incidence of 'agrarian disturbances' to be 548 in the summer of 1906, as against 362 in the autumn of 1905. (Even if we take the months of the 1905 uprising, October to

TABLE 4.2 *Comparison of the striking workers and 'agrarian disturbances' 1905–07[a] (seasonal)*

	1905		1906		1907	
	Peasant attacks	Workers on strike (thousands)	Peasant attacks	Workers on strike (thousands)	Peasant attacks	Workers on strike (thousands)
Winter[b]	63	369	260	217	80	46
Spring	182	133	80	143	178	104
Summer	298	137	548	103	176	25
Autumn[c]	362 (530[c])	294	104	44	37[b]	69[b]

[a] The division into seasons is adopted from M. Leshchenko, *Selyanskii rukh na pravoberezhnoi ukraine v pervoi revolyutsii 1905–1907 gg*, Kiev, 1955 and follows the agricultural cycle.
Winter – December to February
Spring – March to May
Summer – June to August
Autumn – September to November.
[b] The averages for Winter 1905–06 and Autumn 1907 are based on the sole available figures, i.e. January and February 1905 and December 1907.
[c] The exceptional impact of the October 1905 general strike following the September 'low' make the Autumn 1905 'Seasonal Average' less meaningful. The figure in brackets indicates an average for October, November, and December 1905, that is, when the 1905 Revolution was at its height.

December, the monthly average of 530 incidences of peasant struggle is still lower than in the summer of 1906). Consequently, once Dubrovskii's figures are presented in a realistically seasonal way they actually tell us that the 1906 'highest peak' of peasant struggle coincides with a relative low in the workers' political action flattened out in 1906 by repressions and the defeat of 1905. If on the other hand statistical considerations are to reign supreme and a 'moving average' is used for the presentation of the trend to remove the impact of 'a month' as an arbitrary time-unit, the 'workers-lead-while-peasants follow' relation is still much weaker than correlation with seasonality for both trends, with the single exception of October 1905. (See Table 4.3 and Figure 4.3.)

As stated, the argument about the supremacy of the 1905 'peak' of peasant struggle over that of 1906 was carried over into a different way of quantification – the accounting of the *uezds* involved in 'agrarian disturbances'. A major study by Prokopovich published in 1912 (see Table 4.4) has shown two peaks of the peasants' struggle with 48 per cent and 52 per cent of the total number of *uezds* in European Russia involved in September–December 1905 and May–August 1906 respectively.[6] In 1926 Morokhovets took a step to bring the Prokopovich-like figures into line with Dubrovskii-like conclusions. He added to the initial figures of Prokopovich the numbers

TABLE 4.3 *Comparison of striking workers and 'agrarian disturbances' 1905–07 (using a 'moving average')*[a]

	1905		1906		1907	
	Peasant attacks	*Workers on strike (thousands)*	*Peasant attacks*	*Workers on strike (thousands)*	*Peasant attacks*	*Workers on strike (thousands)*
January	63[b]	368[b]	260	217	80	46
February	76	270	80	90	94	49
March	119	157	36	100	134	57
April	182	132	80	143	178	109
May	309	160	315	160	206	108
June	346	176	527	142	207	90
July	298	137	548	103	176	25
August	158	99	358	70	126	26
September	148	220	180	53	71	28
October	362	294	140	44	37	69
November	530	426	104	21	18	64
December	513	316	80	32	13[c]	75[c]

[a] For every month, an arithmetic average is taken, of the figures for that month, the preceding month and the following month.
[b] The figure for January 1905 disregards December 1904 for which no data is available.
[c] The figure for December 1907 disregards January 1908, for which no data is available.

TABLE 4.4 Uezds in which 'agrarian disturbances' were reported (% of total)

	1905			1906			1907		
	Jan–April	May–August	Sept–Dec	Jan–April	May–August	Sept–Dec	Jan–April	May–August	Sept–Dec
Prokopovich's figures	14.8	18.2	47.9	25.1	52.1	15.1	9	6	1
Morokhovets' figures	17	21	52	24	50	14	8.8	5.6	0.6
Tropin's figures	18.8	20.7	53.3	23.8	47.6	13.4	8.2	15.0	0.7

Sources:
S. Prokopovich, *Agrarnyi krizis i meropriyatiya pravitel'stva* (Moscow, 1912); E. Morokhovets, *Krest'yanskoe dvizhenie i sotsial-demokratiya v pervoi russkoi revolyutsii* (Moscow, 1926), p. 10; V. Tropin, *Borba bolshevikov za rukovodstvo krest'yanskim dvizheniem v 1905 g.* (Moscow, 1970) p. 155.

for the Baltic provinces to arrive at the figure of 52 per cent for September–December 1905 as opposed to 50 per cent in May–August 1906.[7] In 1970 Tropin proceeded to do the same with figures presumed to represent the rural struggle in the Caucasus. Once that was done, the 'peak' of the peasants' struggle in the summer of 1906 (which 'scored' 47.6 per cent) was overtaken to an even more satisfactory degree in the autumn of 1905 (ranking 53.3 per cent).[8]

The main weakness of the procedure adopted by Morokhovets and Tropin to make their point lies in the relation between the qualitative and the quantitative side of such an analysis.[9] Statistically, to mix heterogeneous populations is to bias the results or to render them meaningless. To add the geo-ethnic peripheries with their fundamental differences in social structure, ethnic context and political leadership to the provinces of European Russia would have been doubtful in any case. The bias becomes decisive once the different regional history is taken into account. By the end of 1905 the outstandingly massive and brutal military intervention made the rural populations of the Baltic and Caucasian provinces drop out of sight in terms of overt mass action. The fact that both those 'peripheries' and the major townships of the Empire were laid low by oppression before the summer of 1906, reinforces rather than puts in doubt the strength and the relative autonomy of the peasant revolt in Russia and the Ukraine during the summer of 1906. It once again offers evidence to support the exact opposite of the point Tropin was making.

In fact, the rhythm of the peasant struggle represented in Dubrovskii's and Prokopovich's and Tropin's seasonal figures offers another interesting insight, if studied more closely. Once the powerful (and doubtlessly significant) impact of the October 1905 'all-Russian' general strike is 'subtracted' and the influence of the use of repression from November 1905 to January 1906 is considered, we are left with a clear agrarian seasonality of the peasant revolt, a trend which was often repeated elsewhere: the Chinese plain, the Kurdish hills, Mexico, India, and so on. Summer is the time to rebel and autumn and winter the time to retreat. (See Figure 4.4.) This rhythm of the Russian peasant struggle proceeded for three years. It reached its most direct and strongest expression in mid-1906. The multi-year picture indicates a gradual build-up of the peasant fighting spirit, despite the severity of the 1905 repressions. While the deformation of the statistical curve from October 1905 to January 1906 manifestly represented an impact of the urban struggle on the peasants, the multi-year trend with its 1906 climax has shown the strengths of causality generated within the peasantry itself. The complaint of many Soviet historians (and their explanation for the revolutionaries' defeat) that the peasant struggle came 'too late' (*zapozdal*) and did not merge with the urban struggle (*ne slilsya*) has expressed just that, without saying it directly.[10]

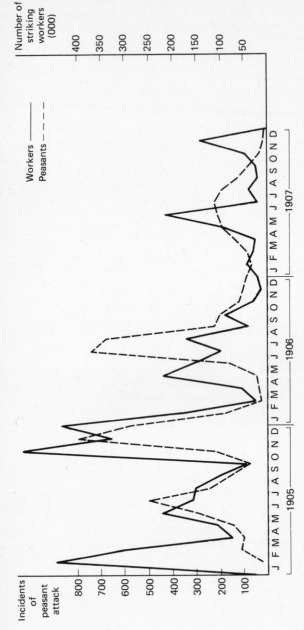

FIGURE 4.1 *Dubrovskii's comparison of striking workers and 'agrarian disturbances' 1905–07 (monthly)*

Source:
S. Dubrovskii, *Krest'yanskoe dvizhenie v revolyutsii 1905–1907 gg.* (Moscow, 1956) pp. 42–3.

181

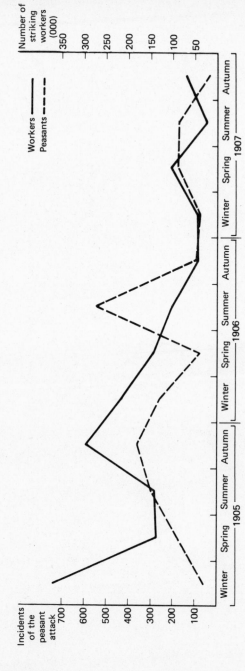

FIGURE 4.2 *Comparison of the striking workers and 'agrarian disturbances' 1905–07 (seasonal)*

Source:
As in Table 4.1.

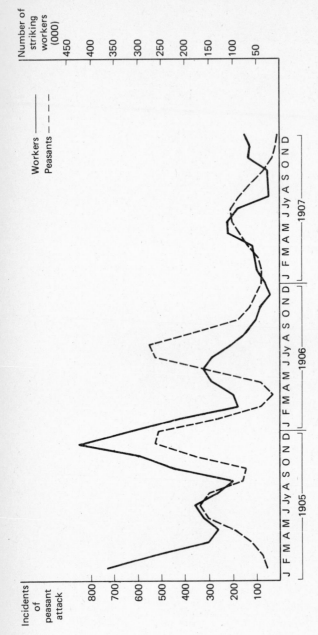

FIGURE 4.3 *Comparison of the striking workers and 'agrarian disturbances' 1905–07 (using a 'moving average'[a])*

[a] For every month, an arithmetic average is taken, of the figures for that month, the preceding month and the following month. The figures for January/February 1905 and November/December 1907 are in each case the average of the two months only.
Source:
As in Table 4.1.

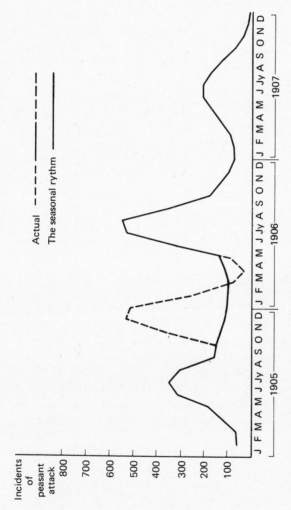

FIGURE 4.4   *The general rhythm of 'agrarian disturbances' 1905–07*[a]

[a] The intensity of peasant attacks was 'smoothed down' by the use of a 'moving average' and 'extracting' the impact of the general strike, the manifesto promising a Duma with legislative powers, and the events which followed, that is, the October 1905 to January 1906 peak in urban struggle (the actual curve is marked by a broken line).
Source: As in Tables 4.1 and 4.3.

5 History Teaches: Learning, Unlearning, Non-Learning

like a blue flame I shall ingress the soul of the people
like a red flag I shall roam through their towns
while everybody sleeps I shall cry out – liberty
but different content will give to each of them
                                    Maximilian Voloshin (1905)

A. MOMENTS OF TRUTH

For its participants a revolution is a moment of truth. It is so not only metaphorically, in the sense of supreme confrontation with political enemies, but also most directly, in the sense of looking at one's own pre-assumptions, images and beliefs in the merciless light of experience. The stakes are high, the lessons harsh and there is no time for leisurely meditation about chessmen and alternative moves. Nor is there time for a replay. The results are final.

Within the process of revolution, images and realities confront and shape each other in a massive and fundamental process of learning. The major break of continuity rips the veils of the taken-for-granted, common sense and party rhetoric, offering an objective, hard and un-negotiable political lesson, the most dramatic of them all. How far were the lessons of 1905–07 taken up and 'taken in' by the people of the Russian Empire, its political activists, administrators and leaders? Did history teach?

In the most general sense, the many maxims about 'learning from history' are neither true nor false. The truth is that some groups and some individuals 'learn from history' while others patently do not. In the aftermath of the revolution's defeat in 1905–07 in Russia, the primary issue was the capacity or failure to learn, unlearn and relearn by its survivors and suppressors – that is, who learned what, who failed to learn and what were the reasons for both.

To begin with a recapitulation, the 1905–07 test of theories and models of revolution inherited from nineteenth century Europe (and based mostly on the experience of the 1848 revolution and on the extrapolation of economic processes which followed it in western and central Europe) produced several pieces of evidence which did not fit the structures of self-understanding which were well-established in Russia in the 1890s, especially so, within its socialist and liberal political dissent. Let us enumerate the most significant of those 'pieces'. The *peasantry* acted as a major revolutionary force and showed considerable unity of political purpose despite the evident difficulties of doing so over the immense territory and under an oppressive regime. The SDs' expectation of radicalism or particular socialist inclinations on the part of the rural wage workers was not fulfilled (with the possible exception of Latvia). The *ethnic periphery*, inclusive of areas which by no stretch of the imagination could be defined as advanced in the terms of industrialisation, urbanisation or proletarianisation, for instance, Georgia, outstepped the metropolis in the intensity of revolutionary struggle. Moreover, the political dissent there was usually led by the local Marxist. (This phenomenon was symbolised by the struggle in Guria – the longest and most consistent territorial control by the SD 'orthodox' Marxists in pre-revolutionary Russia, based on the mass consensus of the population in a peasant, mountainous, frontier region – a clear predecessor to Shensi, Viet Bac and Naxalbari in China during the 1930s, Vietnam in the 1940s, and India in the 1960s, respectively.) The *internal contradictions within the power elite and the state apparatus* of Russia could not easily be assigned to different class interests, and yet emerged as a major determinant of the revolutionary history. The effective capacity of *armed citizens* to challenge an army in direct confrontation in the streets and on the barricades proved next to nothing as long as the army did not waver. But massive political pressure was very effective, especially when the authorities were incapacitated or ambivalent as to a full display of military force while the dissent stayed broadly united. Unheard-of patterns and scale of *political mobilisation* showed the significance of the sudden 'explosion of legality' – the temporary loosening of the government's grip, enabling the open expression of views by the mass of the people otherwise silent. It has also accentuated the outstanding importance of the *alternative bases of authority* and of organisations established *de facto* – that was the main significance of the general strike and its committees, the political parties, the trade unions and the associations, the workers Soviets and the Union of Unions, the All-Russian Peasant Union and the peasant 'republics'.

Turning to the less surprising, in terms of the then broadly-
accepted class analysis of the social forces expected to play a major
political role, by 1906 the *squiredom* came to exercise a powerful
conservative impact. The *industrial and transport workers* on the
whole also bore out the Marxist's and the brighter policeman's
expectations in so far as their revolutionary capacities were concerned, but the *bourgeoisie*, in the classical sense of capitalist owners
of enterprises, did not offer a substantive bid for power while a
'professional' stratum very much did, presenting constitutional and
liberal demands (and coming to be treated thereafter by most of the
theorists of the Left as a substitute bourgeoisie). The ideological
confrontation between the revolutionary and the reformist tendencies *within the intelligentsia* became a major dimension of the
revolutionary struggle, shaping the political movements and divisions. *Students* played a particularly important role, their militancy
often linking the workers and the 'educated classes' by direct political
action. But the main marching army of those who fought in the city
streets and paid for it by the prisons and gallows, consisted – by a
clear majority – of young workers in heavy industry or transport but
also in the small workshops and merchant enterprises (inclusive of
the salesmen – the *prikashchiki*) especially in the west and south of
the country.

As for the monarchist forces, the defensive reaction of the
rightwing gut-populism on the loyalist side of the fence, expressed in
pogroms and formalised in the Association of the Russian People,
was – at least to the Left and to the liberals – unexpectedly strong. So
was the control of the tsardom over its army, despite the considerable
number of local mutinies. Once in uniform, peasant conscripts did
not, on the whole, act as their brethren in the villages. To be sure, in
some of the units, soldiers, sailors and NCOs faced officers for the
first time in a 'class-against-class' scenario, but they were brought to
heel within hours or days. The loyal obedience of the large majority
of *the rank-holders (chinovniki)* in the civilian state service and the
army's officer corps was less surprising. Also unsurprising was the
fact that a few of them 'went over' to the side of the opposition.
Internationally, while no tsar's ally considered it suitable to offer 'to
send in the marines' to help out the Romanovs, it was the financial
capital of republican France which in 1906 helped to re-establish the
Russian state and its repressive capacities through a large loan.
French public opinion supported Russian constitutionalists and/or
revolutionaries, but the appeal by the Russian liberals for interna-

tional solidarity of their counterparts in France in refusing resources to the tsar was simply brushed aside.

Some reactions to the formidable list of 'the unexpected' consisted in refusals to admit evidence, or in claims of its transitory, accidental or extra-social nature (be it in the 1905 famine, administrative mistakes, imported revolutionary propaganda or the pernicious impact of the non-Russians *in toto*, who used the defeat in war to try and destroy the fabric of the truly Russian, truly loyal society). Alternatively, the novelty and the contradictory nature of the evidence encountered led to partial revision and adjustments of aspects of analysis which did not fit some particularly obnoxious facts, without, however, putting the more general theoretical understanding to question. That was the essential attitude expressed in Kautsky's image of a self-contradictory revolution 'which in its essence *must and can be* bourgeois only, *and yet*, is taking place in a period when in all of the rest of Europe only socialist revolution is possible'.[1] In its further development by a main Soviet historian of the period, Pankratova, this line of thought defined the 1905–07 experience as the expected bourgeois revolution with 'a rider' of specificity added as a point on a time-scale, namely, that it was the first such revolution to take place in the period of imperialism and was thereby 'mass-democratic' in its *form*.[2] But she insistently kept the initial pre-1905 theorising via a statement of a linear equation in which the stage reached by Russia in 1904 equalled that 'of Germany in the mid-nineteenth century', in other words of course, that of 1848. At their extreme, such attempts to keep explanations orthodox and continuous while admitting to the unexpected, have taken the tortuous and unintentionally humorous form of Dubrovskii's summing up of the vicissitudes of the SDs' agrarian programmes of 1903–17: 'In so far as 1905 fully proved the correctness of . . . [the Bolshevik Party's views and policies T.S.] it was decided to change [those views and politics T.S.]'.[3]

The third alternative is to treat the deviations from the expected not as an itinerary of exceptions and points of amendment, but as a syndrome representing social reality systematically different from the conceptual models used. In our case, it would be to admit the specificity of what came to be called 'developing societies' as a type of societal structure and the fact that Russia carried its major characteristics, which first came fully to light in the 1905–07 revolution. Peasant radicalism, radical nationalism, the power and autonomy of the state apparatus, the massive state economy, the

significance of alternative bases of authority and of mass mobilisation
of immense proportions, the political weakness of the bourgeoisie,
the particular significance of the intelligentsia, of the army, and of the
revolutionary movements together with the particular international
context, can be approached and explored more realistically in this
conceptual framework. It would also put the undoubted revolutionary potential and tendencies displayed by the Russian industrial
working-class in an historical setting, as a matter of social context and
stage of development rather than of absolutes – a point well and truly
disregarded with disastrous results elsewhere by the Third International in the 1920s and 1930s. It would finally lay much more
analytical stress on the significance of the global system, and the
structural inequalities and the uneven developments within it, for the
definition of the nature and the outcome of revolutionary situations.
That is probably the only way to grasp fully the new realities of the
1905–07 revolution in Russia. Russia, at the turn of the century, can
best be understood neither as exceptional nor as yet another case of
the 'general' development following Western Europe – a delayed
carriage rolling along a well-known track. It becomes less peculiar
once compared not only with Western Europe but also with Asia, but
Lenin's pet abuse of 'Asianness' (*aziyatchina*) where Russia was
concerned, is once again, only an aspect of the truth and too
'narrow'. Put in a nutshell, at the turn of the nineteenth century the
Russian Empire displayed the characteristics of a 'developing society'
without yet recognising itself as such.

So radical a reconceptualisation is not accepted even today, a
tribute no doubt to the power of the Modernisation Theory in the
West and of the combination of Russian evolutionism and nationalism, but an increasing number of interpretations recently have been
reaching out towards it or beginning to adopt it, often in terminolo-
gical disguises. Necessarily, all this was even less clear to the
revolution's contemporaries. The furthest a radical analyst was then
ready to go was to the 'neither . . . nor' denial of the self-assured
conservatism of ideas and of solutions, rooted in nineteenth-century
experiences and theories, that is, to the acceptance of the 'dinstinc-
tiveness of the process' without nailing its actual nature and structural
causality. This held true for the Left and the Right alike. To say so is
not to sneer at them. The difficulty of radical reconceptualisation
flying in the face of customary wisdom and the prevailing analytical
tradition is staggering. Even a partially new analysis narrowing the
gap between the unexpected reality and its theoretical expression

gave immense political superiority of vision to those who were ready to proceed with it, especially when new political crises took place. There is an old tale about the one-eyed man in the country of the blind. He was king.

B. COLLECTIVE MEMORIES, PLEBEIAN WRATH, HISTORICAL FUTURES

The political learning from history is not the abstraction of pure wisdom nor the establishment of a scientifically detached final proof. It is always partial and composed as much of manifest conclusions as of tacit understandings, patterned plausibilities and emotional preferences. Systematic misunderstandings – Frances Bacon's 'idols which beset human mind' and Karl Marx's 'fetishisms' – also belong there. The meaning of 'learning' differs at the different levels of closeness to the centres of political power, of action, of information and of systematic thought. In particular, it is not easy to talk meaningfully about the lessons learned by broad social categories or groups – that is, generations, genders, ethnic entities and social classes – except in terms which are in turn broad, and to a considerable degree speculative and circumstantial. On the other hand, there can be no doubt that the revolutionary drama of 1905–07 left a powerful impact on the collective consciousness of the Russian society and, selectively, on its main components, extending far and wide from the core of those politically active. This is particularly important because when the next revolution began only a decade later in 1917, it was still part of the direct memory of the majority of mature Russians. It was therefore directly relevant then to what they did and what they did not do.

The strengths and the 'density' of historical recollections relate to their context. In the words of Mark Bloch 'peaceful continuity of social existence is much less favourable to the transmission of memory'. He also said of the historians that 'a good cataclysm suits [their] business better'.[1] Dramatic historical experiences establish persistent recollections, models and visions as well as particular cognitive bonds, a *Zeitgeist* linking those involved in them most directly and energetically which thus shape a political generation. The core of such a political generation is usually formed by an age-cohort of those who were young-but-mature when a political storm hit the land or, better still, matured under its impact. Such an age-cohort often represents a calendary half-generation, say, a decade. It was this phenomenon which was expressed by the Russian term *shestidesyatniki* – the people of the 1860s, that is, those who came to political maturity and action (often as part of their university experience) in the period 1860–69. In particularly dramatic days such age spans shorten down to a few years only. Russians referred to as men of the 1880s (*vos'midesyatniki*) were mostly those who matured during the existence of the *Narodnaya Volya* – the Party of the People's Will, especially during its main challenge to the tsardom in 1879–83.[2] The term 'sixty-eighters' was used similarly in the US for those whose campus lives coincided with the events of 1968. The generation-shaping impact of the 1905–07 experience was powerfully expressed in the social images of Russia, of its possible futures and its potential revolutions. Those images were once again negative as well as positive for, as noticed by a wise observer, 'revolutions destroy as many hopes as they fulfil'.[3] One should add that this holds true as much for the revolution that succeeds as for those that do not.

The political thought of Russia has consistently singled out ethnic groups and social classes as the fundamental units of social classification, self-consciousness and analysis. These identifications appeared in the legal designation of everyone, in the government's projects as in the opposition's demands. Before considering the significance of these categories to the issues at hand, let us look at a few alternative divisions.

Age strata have already been mentioned. A major study of the 1905–07 'agrarian disturbances' singled out a number of cases in which in the villages the old men (*stariki*) as well as women were those who opposed and at times prevented the attacks on the manorial estates.[4] The particular militancy of the young men in the villages was mentioned simultaneously. Our companion volume indicated the extent to which these divisions were defined by the social characteristics of family farms and village life for the peasant majority of the Russian population.[5] The 'old men' who were able to control political action were, no doubt, not the elderly village paupers or loners (*bobyli*), but household heads (*bolshaki*), while the rebellious young men were mostly those who were unmarried and subjugated to their households' heads. Yet, not all of this diversity is translatable into socio-economic categories, or into polarities of power, for the impact of age-cohorts on political consciousness also had a logic of its own.[6] Those in their sixties when 1905 came had grown up under serfdom and witnessed the immovable rule of

Nikolai I followed by the emancipation through Alexander II's decree and the counter-reforms of Alexander III.[7] The pre-eminence of the tsar's will was to them absolute, defining continuity as much as any possible change. The young men of 1905 knew all this only by hearsay. Their exposure to the multiple social changes of the 1890s was high, their literacy more extensive, the urban scene closer, and the impact on them of the political activists, especially the rural teachers, more pronounced. Those between the ages of 15 and 25 in 1905 were 28 to 38 in 1918 – by which time many were ex-servicemen and most were heads of household – the communal assembly's core group. The major lesson learned by them in 1905–07 was that of the hostility of the tsarist state towards their main demands, the brutality of the army response, and of their own estrangement from the Russian urban 'middle classes'.

We know little of the workers' 'generation of 1905–07' but, significantly, when the next wave of political strife rose in 1912–14, a split was reported between the older trade-union activists who supported the Mensheviks, and the younger men, who had watched the events of 1905–07 as teenagers or children (and were often rural migrants, in 1912–14 fresh from the villages). The younger men supported Bolsheviks and the SRs.[8] It was their victory which established the powerful Bolshevik presence in the St Petersburg factories during the period 1912–17, a decisive factor in what was to happen in the last fateful year. It is still mostly speculation as to the reasons for this hold but, relevantly, the experience of the defeat and disappointments of 1905, the heavy unemployment of 1906–10 and the spectacle of the failing efforts of the socialist activists to hold on to some influence meant little to this group. They were now keen to challenge head-on the 'politics of small deeds' and the related moods which the revolutionaries branded as 'liquidationism'. Theirs were the boyhood dreams of revolution, not its defeat.

For the intelligentsia and especially the small political elite of party leaders we can do more than speculate on the impact of 1905–07 on the age groups. Their typical age differed significantly as shown in recent studies.[9] The KD leaders of 1905–07 were mostly the non-socialist and non-revolutionary 'men of the 1880s', who – while objecting to the political regime – kept aloof from the People's Will challenge to it. They had been shaped by the experience of Alexander III's counter-reforms and the ongoing struggle to defend public institutions autonomous from the state, that is, the *zemstvos*, universities, professional associations, a 'free judiciary', etc. The SD

leaders came mostly from the 'generation' of the 1890s – the days of
the industrial boom which followed the 1891 famine. A small and less
reliable sample of the PSR cited in Emmons study referred to two
groups in its leadership: the people of the 1870s' 'going-to-the-
people' who survived, and those much younger who joined at the
beginning of the twentieth century as the revolution unfolded. As for
the intelligentsia *in toto* and especially those who were in their teens
in 1905 and in their twenties or early thirties when the next revolution
came, the effect of the political ideas and leaderships on them was
also rooted in the collective memories of 1905–07, real or mythologised. In the words of the already-quoted poem by Pasternak (who
was born in 1890, by twenty years – take or leave two – the junior of
Lenin, Gershuni, Struve, Martov and Zhordaniya):

> this night of guns,
> put asleep
> by a strike
> this night – was our childhood
> and the adolescence of our teachers.[10]

Within the hierarchical and repressive Russian society, women
appeared still as the lower and still more oppressed part of each social
category. Russia's first book of manners, the seventeenth century
Domostroi, made wife-beating a necessity and a virtue. Women were
usually expected to display the nobility's self-discipline without its
powers, merchants' servility without their property-hold, and
peasants' labour without the charge of a farm and the right to voice a
view at the communal assembly. Informal influences and arrangements amended up to a point those handicaps, but the actual
inequality of the Russian women was severe. The 1905–07 revolution
stirred up some of the resoluting tension. A Russian equivalent of the
suffragettes developed in the 'professional' circles and their organisation joined the Union of Unions. It disintegrated within a short time.
Peasant women attempted to organise in some villages, as mentioned
but that was seldom and did not survive for long. Mostly, the social
mechanisms of gender control held intact and autonomous female
action seldom appeared. Most of the women who participated in
political struggle did so beside their men and led by their leaders. We
mentioned the persistent reports of the peasant women's caution in
the face of the authorities – a conservatism of the oppressed, rooted
in realistic pessimism about the fate of anti-government defiance as
much as in lack of access to broader social visions, abstract ideas or

simple literacy. Among the urban wage-workers, women were mostly engaged in personal services which were never unionised, while the metal industry and railways which were central to the political defiance of those days, had no women at all.

The 1905 reforms gave nothing in particular to Russian women; they did not receive the right to vote, and the inheritance and divorce laws stayed intact keeping them disenfranchised. Russia's political parties, since the 1870s, had a number of illustrious female members and leaders. But no long-term organisations or modes of action struggling for particular feminist causes were established in 1905–07, with significant results for the goals, nature and social composition of the 1917–21 political organisations. The place of a social underdog does not necessarily mean being a social rebel or even dreaming the dream of social justice. Nor does it necessarily mean drawing meaningful political lessons from a manifestly revolutionary situation. No specific 'female lesson' was drawn from the 1905–07 revolution, at least, not explicitly.[11]

*   *   *

The 1905–07 revolution reinforced political expressions of the ethnic divisions within the Russian empire. Old grievances and new offences came into focus while hopes for amiable settlement or compromise solutions declined. This sharpening of edges was expressed, first, in the relations between the Russian tsardom's loyalists and its non-Russian subjects. At the western and southern 'peripheries', the memory of the patriotic outburst mixed with bloody repression by the Russian army and state, made the wishes for autonomy or independence stronger. The argument of those who did not believe in the possibility of leaving the Russian realm by challenging directly its power seemed to have been vindicated, yet those who thought so found themselves ideologically and morally in the position of preaching the continuation of a foreign rule which proved once again its brutality. The repressions, merciless enough toward the Russian rebels, were much harsher when aimed at the non-Russians. Also, within a short time it became clear that the tsardom's most solemn promises could not be trusted when non-Russians were concerned. The government acted as a bully would. Faced with rebellions, it retreated and promised amends. Once back in the saddle, it revoked projects of reform and even generated new xenophobic policies.[12] The sharp drop in the representation of the 'peripheries' in the Third

Duma, the renewed moves to abolish Finnish autonomy, and the official russification of the Khelm district (which belonged beforehand to the ten Polish provinces) followed in quick succession. All the Russian 'minorities' lived under constant threat of arbitrary curtailment of their rights. National independence seemed the one way to defend oneself from the bully by putting a state frontier between one's people and its power. For those – like the Latvians, the Jews and the Georgians, respectively – who were too small in size, too dispersed or else too fearful of other hostile neighbours to conceive of independence easily, autonomy and legal equality were now a major demand. These demands went together with sympathy or tolerance towards the most radical of the political organisations operating in Russia because of their tough anti-tsarist, anti-Russian-nationalist and 'defeatist' positions.

As for the public opinion of the Russian loyalists and monarchists, the extensive participation of non-Russians in the revolution reinforced all of their xenophobic fears and prejudices concerning ethnic disloyalties. The Sukhotin discussion, already quoted, was a fair example of those views.[13] The popular expressions were usually cruder and more violent. Russia united and undivisible was to be kept by force against the naturally treasonable tendencies of the Jews, Poles, Armenians, Finns, Sarts (the central Asian 'natives'), etc. Even the old Slavophiles' dreams of Slavic unity against everyone else were now rejected by the vocal nationalist Russian camp whose interdependence with the government and the tsar's court was evident. To secure the tsardom's future, Russia was simply to be russified. The only questions left were those of timing and the means for uprooting of all alien cultures.

The next 'ethnic' lesson of the revolution was the confrontation between the different non-Russian nationalisms as well as between the nationalists and the socialists of the 'peripheries'. In the revolutionary days, the divisions of goals and views were no longer a matter of leisurely disputation for there was an issue of actual power control over territories, resources and people. The harshness of struggle increased accordingly. The Polish provinces of Russia offered an exemplary case in point. As long as the conflict was less pronounced, different anti-tsardom forces co-operated or, at least, ignored each other. That stopped once the 1905–07 struggle began. The National Democrats (ND) in close alliance with the Catholic hierarchy and some industry owners fought a merciless battle of political confrontation and physical assault against aliens (particularly, the Jewish *Bund*) and against the unpatriotic and ungodly Polish socialists of the SDPK and the PPS Left. The Polish nationalist movement and the ethnic frontiers of hostility defined in those battles were to play a central role in the decade which followed, and, even more so, in the First World War and in the Polish Republic established in its wake. The same held true for the Baltic provinces, the Caucasus, the Ukraine, the Volga provinces, etc.

Two more 'ethnic' lessons or ideological reinforcements related to the events of 1905–07 were less clearly cut, yet as significant in the long term. The interdependence of ethnicity, class and attitude to the revolution, or at least the guiding stereotypes of those, were reinforced in the social consciousness of Russia: Jews–intelligentsia–socialists, Poles–petty nobility–nationalists, Latvian–rural workers–social democrats, etc. The exceptions to each of those ethno-class images were, of course, extensive. Jewish craftsmen were as active as the Jewish students, numerous Poles were industrial workers with strong Marxist convictions and so on. All the same, the entrenched assumptions of the existing correlations were to influence in future both the 'minorities' involved and the loyalist administrators and officers.

Finally, there were the implicit political lessons learned from the tactical experience of struggle by the leaders and activists of the strictly internationalist revolutionary movements of Russia proper. Most of the orthodox Marxists and radical populists in the RSDWP and the PSR had no doubts that similar substantive interests existed between the ethnically-different proletariats or 'labouring classes' of the Russian empire. All-Russian parties encompassing all the ideological soul-mates in Russia were the logical conclusion. Yet, despite numerous efforts and lengthy negotiations it never quite worked out in this way in the days of 1905–07.

Formally the Latvian and the Polish SD as well as the Jewish Bund had eventually joined the RSDWP but, in fact, all of them kept their own organisations. The Georgian SDs, mostly Mensheviks, kept their own council, never fully adopting the All-Russian leaderships' views. The Ukrainian SRs operated separately from the PSR. And so on. In addition, all the factions were regionally and ethnically skewed in a consistent manner. For example, among the workers, the Bolsheviks were particularly strong with the Russians of Urals and St Petersburg, the Mensheviks more influential with the Georgians, the Jews and the Ukrainians in the south. The PSR had a clear Russian majority in its ranks and was particularly strong along the Volga, but also had a large Jewish component, especially in its terrorist arm. Whatever the ideological claims or long-term hopes, astute leaders could not but be cognisant of all this in their designs on those facts of political life. These considerations tended to reinforce further the existing ethnic patterns of appeal, support, self-selection and organisation.

*   *   *

As for the major social classes, to the workers of Russia's industries, crafts and railways, the aftermath of the revolution was depression and crisis. By 1906 unemployment reached the 300 000 mark and stayed high. Massive arrests by police went hand-in-hand with lockouts organised by the associations of industrialists in the major cities. Workers' demands were now rejected and many of their 1905 achievements withdrawn. Prisons, deportations and employers' blacklists decapitated workers' communities by removing from their midst those politically most active. Others reacted to unemployment and persecutions by the age-old practice of retreating to their villages or by moving to a different city to sit out the bad days.

There were some achievements left when the revolutionary wave subsided. Since the manifesto of October 1905 trade unions were legally permitted and quite a number of them kept operating despite daily police intervention and harassment. There was a small parliamentary representation in the Duma of deputies elected by the workers' 'electoral college'. Some specifically workers' newspapers were being published. The government eventually legislated for insurance and pension rights to industrial wage workers and left unionisation and the newly-prescribed elections for the Insurance Boards to workers' own initiative – a Bismarck-like, rather than a Zubatov-like strategy.[14]

The immediate lesson learned by the workers from the revolutionary drama was the extent and the limitations of their power. They could stop the country from moving but they could not defeat an army nor win a long-term battle with a combination of police and employers. The state was against them, the promises of equal treatment a sham. The urban middle classes, especially 'the educated' talked sweetly but in the real fight from November 1905 to January 1906 and after, turned hostile to workers' militancy. Only the activists of the socialist party and the intelligentsia's radical minority in the Union of Unions stood fast and went down in defeat together with the workers.[15]

By 1912, when the next upswing of the workers' strike movement came after a dark half-decade, it related to the 1910–14 economic upturn which extended the urban wage-labour force by one-third, reducing unemployment, and drawing on the rural population.[16] Once again the workers' challenge was preceded by a year of student-demonstrations and peasant famine in places. It was triggered off by a piece of government brutality: the 1912 Lena goldfields massacre of its strikers. This news was answered by an explosion of 'solidarity' strikes. There was also a growing number of 'economic' strikes demanding improvement of wages, shorter working days, etc. More of them were turned 'political' by police repression. The number of strikes remained high also in 1913 and in the first half of 1914 became reminiscent of the 1905–07 intensity and vigour,[17] but this time the workers' movement did not link with the other urbanites and was greeted by 'liberal public opinion' with unease rather than with the unlimited support and delight of early 1905. Also, from the word 'go' the workers' movement had now a clear anti-monarchist edge. Besides the strike wave its major expression was the electoral transfer of the boards of legal workers' organisations, that is, the trade unions and the Insurance Boards, from the hands of those more inclined to compromise to those more militant and aggressive.[18] A sharp swing of workers' support was reported not only from the Mensheviks to the Bolsheviks and the SRs but also farther still to the left, for in the 1914 strike the Bolshevik committee of St Petersburg found itself outflanked by the more radical 'wild' activists who refused its calls to bring the strike to an end.[19] Haimson's recent well-documented analysis of the social composition of the workers' movement concluded that this political shift represented a victory for the young and those drawn into towns in the recent economic upsurge (contrary to the standard view of the Soviet textbooks which treat it as representative of the advance of well-established and definitely urban *potomstvennye* workers-for-generations).

Socially linked to the workers but engaged in a different battle, the Russian peasants were left at the end of the 1905–07 revolution with more tangible results than any other group which rebelled. Unemployment was hitting hard at the urban workers, those who fought for the republic seemed utterly defeated, the liberals' parliamentary dream was caricatured and rendered powerless by the third Duma. The Russian peasants received neither all the Russian land for which they fought, nor all the liberties they demanded, but rents did go down and rural wages did go up.[20] Also, most of the peasants' debt was cancelled by the state. The panic sales of land by the squires (who within a couple of years disposed of nearly one-third of their properties in seven of the most rebellious provinces)[21] gave access to new land to quite a number of peasant households and communes. The extensive sales did not lead to a sharp drop in land prices mostly because of the state-owned Peasant Bank's massive purchases, but the sale of land by the Bank to the peasants peaked dramatically from 1906 onward, admittedly benefiting more those who were better-off but not exclusively so.[22] Farming production was on the increase and so were the prices for agricultural goods. Some state finance was made available for agricultural extension, land colonisation, etc. Most importantly, the authorities were taught a political lesson with regard to peasants' anger, their potential strengths and something about the limitations of their patience, a lesson which no one was likely to forget for a while. Despite the decline of the great hopes of the revolutionary days an important leap in peasant self-esteem took place also and was due to play its role in the days to come.[23]

The main 'practical' conclusion was still the fact that contrary to the dream of two generations and more, the tsar was not going to grant more land in a 'second freedom'. He was not, after all, the peasant saviour and defender against the officials and nobles; the punitive expeditions of 1906–07 were never quite forgotten. As for the land, it had to be taken or bought. It could not be taken – the power of the state proved too formidable. The most active of those who could afford it, tried harder than ever before to purchase land or to receive it through colonisation. Others began to get rid of land when it was neither sufficient nor extendable, provided of course that there was some alternative employment.

At the same time, the Stolypin reforms – the government's major response to the revolution – were encountering stiff opposition in many peasant communities. In most of them there were some householders who could benefit from the reforms and now tried to put them to use. Only in a few cases, however, were members of communes permitted by them to disengage or, more radically, did a communal assembly decide to privatise all its land. Mostly such steps were forced by the order of the authorities.[24] The wish of local officialdom to gain favour with their superiors by a show of brisk execution of what 'the top' wanted to see (*vysluzhitsa*) was the main force for the reforms, the peasant communes' opposition, the main obstacle to it. The majority of the peasant households refused to believe that 'splitting off' without any extension in land or further substantial investment could possibly improve their lot and, on the whole they were right. At the same time, dismantling the commune would remove the minimal security and support it offered. Put in the peasants' own words 'should the commune be violated (*narushena*) there would be nobody whom one could even ask for alms'.[25] The attitude towards the reforms often reported was 'like to the plague'.[26]

*　　*　　*

The expression 'common people' (*narod*) was often used in Russia as a synonym for peasantry. It closely overlapped with the historically-grounded Russian legal concept of the 'tax-paying classes' (as opposed to the servitors),[27] or simply with those engaged constantly in manual labour as opposed to those who did not. Peasants formed a large majority in all these categories, which the wage-workers and the craftsmen entered also. Those who used this term usually assumed a fundamental division between the privileged inhabitants of Russia and its plebeian masses – Russia's human base of producers, foot-soldiers, body-servants, etc. The ethnic aliens (*inorodtsy*), especially the non-Slavs, were usually excluded, explicitly or implicitly, from such categorisation.

The differences between the workers and peasants of Russia in their gaols, political positions, leaders and allies in 1905–07 were already spoken about. These differences were considerable, but did not make fundamental links and similarities between worker and peasant disappear. Most of the workers of Russia were peasants by origin and/or by legal designation. The great majority of them were farmers' sons. In 1905 not less than half of the male wage-workers held land and often went back to the villages to help with the harvests or simply to visit the families they had left behind in the country-side.[28] A major part of them lived singly in urban lodging-places, and either had wives and children in the village or else intended eventually to marry and resettle there, that is, to re-peasantise. On the other hand there was a constant flow of peasant sons into the towns, especially in times of economic upswing. In his language, way of life and looks an industrial worker differed more from the other urbanites than from his village cousins. It was this which made plebeians a social reality in Russia: not so much the similarity between the workers and the peasants as the overriding nature of their common dissimilarity from the middle and upper classes, however defined.

The experience of 1905–07 made these similarities and diversities stand out. The workers' attitude toward the urban middle classes became more hostile, the peasant trust of the tsarist government was undermined. Retreating into their 'natural' shells in the face of the triumphant reaction, peasants and workers mostly met each other. The 'psychological distance that separated the St Petersburg workers from educated privileged society'[29] was as true also for the country's peasants. On the other hand, the old deep-seated peasant distrust of and alienation from all outsiders made sense to the urban workers in 1906–07 and afterwards. In 1914, just before the war, a major newspaper reported army and police detachments with drawn bayonets patrolling deserted cities of shattered street-lights, torn-up telegraph poles, strike-bound factories of industrial St Petersburg and the 'monstrous anger' of workers alongside the city centre in which, 'the usual traffic, the usual life, and the trolleys are moving about as usual'.[30] Workers knew it too. Clearly, in Russia's villages and towns not only land, wages and abject poverty were at issue but also the societal division, fundamental and sharp, into the plebeian 'us' and the variety of 'them': the state and the nobility, the manor houses and the 'clean quarters' of the city, the uniforms, the fur coats the gold-rimmed spectacles, or even the elegantly-rolling phrase.

The proof of the pudding is in its eating and the particular 'pudding' of plebeian wrath was to be served in the 1917–21 war and revolution. Much has been argued about the reasons why the 'White Cause' (*Beloe delo*) was defeated by the Reds who lacked, at least initially, the state-administrative know-how, the organised military forces, foreign support, basic equipment and international legitimation. Leaders of the old Russia, socialist competitors for power and the foreign specialists, gave the Reds a few weeks to survive at the most. The reasons since offered for the Bolsheviks' victory ranged from the stupidity of their foes and the marvels of Lenin's party organisation, to geography (the centrality of Moscow and the country's size) and the mistaken military tactics adopted by the White Generals. All this, relevant as it may have been, disregards the fact that the civil war was fought not between Bolshevik party members and monarchist officers, but between armies in which both these groups were in minority. In the conditions of civil war those armies' loyalty could not be taken for granted and thereby became a decisive element in defining the outcome of the battles. The ability to mobilise resources necessary for army operations was equally important: the acquisition of food and fodder, horses and labour teams, ammunition, uniforms, and even the crude footwear still in use by the Russian infantry (*lapti*). Largely, the recruits and the resources were not volunteered, but the question continually was how much would be volunteered, how much effort would be spent taking the rest, and how much was eventually at the disposal of the armies' command.

Despite stringent methods and cruel punishments, the Whites failed to mobilise substantial numbers of plebeian soldiers to fight their battles. Despite the frequent mutinies and mass desertion the Reds proceeded to do so and this eventually secured their victory.[31] By all reports, the White Army units acted mostly as a conquering army against the workers and the peasants of the areas they controlled. As they moved on through the Ukraine, south Russia and Siberia, rebellion spread in their rear. A White military historian described it as 'a wave of rebelling plebs' (*volna vostavshikh nizov*).[32] The 'anarchist' forces, the 'green' bands of peasant rebels, etc, made war mostly on the White Armies and did not challenge the Red Army to the same degree during the decisive period of 1918–19. The reason for this lay in what was described by the White Army's leader, General A. Denikin, in his memoirs as 'hatred accumulated over the centuries, the bitterness of three years of war, and the hysteria generated by the revolutionary leaders'. He also spoke about his personal experience of travelling incognito through revolutionary Russia:

> Now I was simply a *burzhui*, [member of the bourgeoisie in the popular Russian slang of those days, T.S.] who was shouted and cursed at, sometimes with malice, sometimes just in passing, but fortunately nobody paid attention to me. Now I saw real life more clearly and was terrified . . . I saw a boundless hatred of ideas and of people, of everything that was socially and intellectually higher than the crowd, of everything which bore the slightest trace of abandon, even of inanimate objects which were the sign of some culture strange or inaccessible to the crowd.[33]

He neglected to say that in civil war this hatred and sense of estrangement were mutual. Caught in the historical logic of this confrontation, Denikin and his partners could not in the face of it all change the social strategy of their army and this sealed the destiny of their struggle. They were nearly as unable to recognise a major element of the historical causality which was less general than 'centuries of hatred' but less immediate than 'the bitterness of . . . war', that is, the 1905–07 lessons of class confrontation and the political realignments which followed. Also, in the light of the civil war the answer to the question of realism on the part of the plebeian inter-class camp as a socio-political entity seems straightforward. It was the common people's plebeian distrust and hate of the *burzhui* and the *epoulettes* which in 1918–19 brought about their grudging adoption of the Soviet regime. In the last resort this decided the civil war.

One way to document this 'lessons of 1905–07' aspect of Russia's political history through 1917–19 is to list the toughest components of the Red forces then. Resolute, totally devoted, armed and merciless units, even when relatively small, were decisive in the revolutionary days. Their list resurrected the 1905–07 roll of the groups, social and ethnic, which had been most harshly treated by the punitive expeditions, deportations and executions. The sailors of Kronstadt and the metal-workers of Nevskaya Zastava were crucial in the battles of St Petersburg (both in 1917 and in 1919). The grim loyalty of the Latvian riflemen who guarded the Sovnarkom in Moscow in 1918 and put down the Left SR rebellion there, became famous.[34] Their colonel, Votsetis, a Latvian peasant's son who by strength of will and natural ability had succeeded in getting to the tsar's Academy of the General Staff, went over together with them to become the first Commander-in-Chief of the Red Army. The Poles, Jews and Latvians of the Cheka were well-represented by the names of its most significant leaders: Dzerzhinskii, Menzhynskii, Uritskii, Unshlikht, Peters and Latsis. In the most decisive moments of the civil war its chronicles name on the Red side Russian railmen of Irkutsk and Tashkent, Jewish boys from Minsk and Odessa, Finns from Vyborg, industrial workers from Rostov, Kharkov, Lugansk and Ivanovo Voznesensk. The only major amendment to the 1905–07 list was offered by some newly created nation–states: in Poland, Georgia and part of the Ukraine national loyalties often refocused or overrode 1905–07 revolutionary origins and recollections.

As for the peasant majority of Russia and the bulk of its plebeian 'masses', the *narod*, those who entered the revolutionary ranks did it mostly via the service in the Red Army. The whole process of its recruitment was shot through with the unfocused, volatile preferences and moods of the villagers. When in 1918–19 the villagers of the Russian plain, flogged and 'pacified' in 1905–07, had to enlist or choose politically 'their side' in the war they usually preferred the localised 'green' bands who came from their own midst. When this option was not there or the fear of insecurity put anew a premium on state-directed (that is 'national', in the accepted English idiom) forces and organisations, they supported the Reds rather than the White officers or the Cossacks. The same was true for the most significant 'third road' peasant units, like the forces led by Makhno. In 1918 and 1919 the efforts of both the Reds and the Whites to draft soldiers, to eliminate desertion and to make their units of conscripts fight rather than disintegrate at the first clash, were all decisive. By 1920 the socio-military map of the Civil War changed. The Red Army was now massive and professional. It was establishing its stratum of new loyalist leaders and disciplinarians composed mostly of peasant sons and few other underdogs of the ex-tsardom, for whom the new regime opened unbelievable careers to the very top. This new officer corps and its trainees, the *komandiry* and the *kursanty* of the Civil War, began to replace old revolutionaries, as well as the professional officers of pre-revolutionary vintage drafted by the Soviet regime.[35] With a fine feel for symbolism it was the *kursanty* and not the 'Iron Latvians' who came now to guard the Kremlin (as well as put down Antonov's peasant rebellion in Tambov and to crush the sailors of Kronstadt – Trotsky's 'pride and glory of the Revolution', who rebelled for 'a free, independent, non-party Soviets of workers and peasants, without the Cheka and the commissars'). But the Red/White contest was by that time over and a new Russia was set in a mould which was to define it for the next decade.

*   *   *

For the privileged Russia, that is the human antonym of the plebeian masses and manual labour; the experience of 1905–07 focused and dramatised long-term concerns particular to its major social components. These concerns were often articulated by political leaders, official spokesmen, writers and parties to which we will turn presently. But the impact of the revolution affected also those who were politically indifferent until that time. The fundamental concerns in question were land and order for the squires, order and good management for the bureaucrats, riches and profits for the wealthy, rule of law, public representation and principled justice for the intelligentsia. Implicit and ever-present was the assumption, particularly strong with those less sophisticated and less-versed in the complexities of the political programmes and ideologies, that while improvement in the life of all social groups and categories was desirable, their own group privileges must stay intact.

Of the privileged Russians, the experience of revolution was probably most traumatic for its 30 000 'squires', their families and dependents.[36] Their post-Emancipation economic decline and, the late nineteenth century wave of 'return to the provinces', the Witte anti-agricultural strategy, the *zemstvo* clashes with the government and the war defeat against Japan made for their growing political sympathies with constitutionalism.[37] Bureaucratic incompetence was now to be amended by Russia's best families' participation in the political process. The common people (that is, mostly 'their' peasants) were to be led towards political Europeanisation or else towards a revival of their Slavic virtues, while opposing those who clearly mishandled Russia's interests and its tsar's authority. Bureaucratic harassment and orders of exile for its reform-minded leaders were met by the growing *Fronde* of the Russian provincial nobility.

What followed was more painful and disturbing by far: cities filled with red-flagged demonstrations, peasants on the rampage burning manorial estates, army units refusing to obey their officers' commands. When the Duma election came peasants were not ready to be led by their nobles, even the most liberal of them. At the same time, the *zemstvo's* most outspoken leaders of the best noble pedigree, now in the KD party, seemed to have turned traitors to the squires and the tsar alike by opting for compulsory purchase and peasantisation of private lands while allying with dangerous subversives. The explosion of dismay of the 'squires' 'silent majority' swept forever the KDs from leading positions in the *zemstvos*, transforming and urbanising thereby the face of Russian constitutionalism. Simultaneously, the government's *coup d'état* gave the Russian squires incredible parliamentary powers – the Duma deputies representing 30 000 of them were now more than twice as numerous as those representing the nearly 20 million peasant households. The third and fourth Dumas with the built-in majority of squires were as conservative, nationalistic, monarchistic, and apathetic as the class which now controlled them. With peace returning to the rural regions, the squires' readiness to ally with the Black Hundreds or to support unconditionally state dignitaries dropped sharply, but they did not return to the mood of the 1903–04 *Fronde* either. The national leaders of the squires were now particularist and conservative. The 'squiredom's' political will was mostly limited to its own welfare and advancement.

To the dignitaries (*Sanovniki*) and the middle ranks of the managers of the Russian state and its armed forces, the first impulse following the revolt was the restoration of 'order', that is, of obedience to the hierarchies of tsardom. The bases of resistance and defiance were reduced one by one. Force was the main method for doing so. Reforms were treated as appeasement mostly, and when convenient, were disregarded.[38] Some were withdrawn when their appeasement value declined. The *coup d'état* by the government on 3 June 1907 against its own legislation and contrary to the tsar's firm promises, exemplified these characteristics of state policies, but also the dilemmas thus presented. One cold cut through some immediate problems by force but others – those more substantial – would not go away as a result. The job of the bureaucracy was to manage and the question was how to proceed to manage a state machinery which had just proved so outrageously inadequate to its tasks. The brightest of Russia's state managers saw now the solution and the way towards the long-term stability of the realm in a massive overhaul of the state and the society – a 'revolution from above'. As consistent and as emotionally grounded in its links to the 1905–07 experience, was the bureaucratic conservative instinct of the others to sit tight, to change nothing but simply to remove from sight or office those who spoke of troubles and who proclaimed the need to change matters; radical socialists as much as radical monarchists, constitutionalists as well as those of the state officials who were considered too clever by half. The strengths of the conservative view lay not only in the whole structure and training in state bureaucracy but also in its links with the squires and the impacts of the growing discontent with parliamentary experiments in the tsar's own circle. It was the conservatives who consequently won the day. For the state bureaucracy most of the decade which followed the revolution was well described by Soviet historians as one of curtailment (*svertyvanie*) of the reform programmes.[39] Its essence for the Russian state apparatus was the defeat of the bureaucracy's radical impulse and the growing dismay of those who put their hope in it.

As with the squires, the rank and file of the Russian state bureaucracy and professional armed forces had its loyalty, solidarity and stereotypes of enemies dramatised by the revolution. Their entrenched dislike and distrust of alien Jews and rebellious students, non-Russian nationalists, riotous workers and barbaric peasants was deepened and new fury was generated against politicians, journalists and academics. 'Politician' became a particularly dirty word to the state officials and to the army officers, including those majors and captains who as generals and admirals were to command the Whites in the 1918–19 battles. The list of those whose repression by the White Army helped to seal its doom was as explicit as the composition of the Soviet marching army of plebeian hate, and as clearly defined by the 1905–07 experience. The bogies, victims and – often by necessity – the enemies of the White Cause were not simply Bolsheviks, but all socialists, many constitutionalists, all Jews as well as the Poles, Georgians and Ukrainians struggling for independence, the non-Cossack farmers of the Don region (*inogorodnye*) the workers of Rostov, Kharkov, Odessa and Irkutsk, the peasant 'Green' fighters throughout Russia. Also, nearly all the politicians were rejected as such. In the days of the 1919 march on Moscow, in Denikin's temporary capital, Ekaterinodar, the extremely right-wing Gurko was shown the door as also was the radical anti-Bolshevik ex-SR Savinkov. The attempts to broaden the political appeal of the White forces came only when their defeat was final and for all to see – the last days of Kolchak and the last battles of Wrangel.[40]

Those in Russia whose access to riches resulted neither from the landowning remains of the days of serfdom, nor from state ranks and privileges, came mostly from the merchant dynasties of Moscow – such as the Morozovs, or from the major speculators, Russia's robber-barons of the nineteenth century, like Putilov.[41] Industries which were neither state- nor foreign-owned belonged mostly to the merchant families, while lesser merchants controlled much of Russia's small enterprise and crafts. There were in Russia endless tales about its merchants' propensity to cheat (*plutovstvo*) as their main qualification for trade, and about the conservative cere-moniousness of their daily life, punctuated by orgies as much as by outbreaks of religious frenzy. An educated minority with a broader outlook and ambitions of its own, people like Ryabushinskii, Konovalov or Tretyakov organised clubs, initiated and directed newspapers, promoted the arts and at the beginning of the twentieth century tried to lift their brethren by class into the political arena (which for Russians usually meant some measure of opposition to the government). They met with little success. By the end of 1905 even those of the Russian capitalists who did show some political interest mostly retreated from such unconventionalities and put their trust in the tsar's omnipotence and the bureaucrats' order. The effort of their organisations in Moscow and St Petersburg centred now on defeating strikers and the defence of profits. Later attempts by the few politically-minded members of the Russian capitalist strata to overcome the political indifference of their class and to defend some semblance of constitutionalism likewise ended in failure. Dispirited by those refusals on the part of the bourgeoisie to act as a class, the small vocal minority of the Russian capitalists moved by 1912 farther to the left, joining, promoting or creating oppositionist factions, 'blocs' and Masonic lodges. For the mass of the Russian 'entrepreneurs' the lessons of 1905–07 were that party politics was not for them, that radicals were dangerous, workers volatile and that one should stick to one's status in life and concentrate on manipulating the forces of order – in other words, officialdom – to one's best advantage.

Those who stood above the plebeian masses by reasons of land-ownership, rank or capital, beginning with the tsar's courtiers and Russia's millionaires but inclusive of the patriotic petty officials and little merchants, never forgot the 1905–07 nightmare and the great fear of the 'beast unchained', of the avalanche of red flags, marches, general strikes and burning estates, the collapse of respectability and certainty – the world itself, their world, on the verge of falling apart. The great fear mingled with hate and with 'never again' resolution. There was however one privileged stratum in Russia which could not quite share in this singleness and unity of perception and emotions.

The Russian intelligentsia's nature, characteristics and ideological tendencies were already discussed.[42] The ambiguities of this delimitation must be kept in mind because many of the Russian nobles, bureaucrats and merchants shared much of its intellectual baggage. Some consequent interdependence existed but the mainstream of the Russian intelligentsia displayed significant characteristics of its own. To begin with, its views and moods were more complex, ambivalent and heterogeneous. They were also deeply moralistic. Put into the ideological language formulated by its most influential spokesman in Russia of the late nineteenth century, Mikhailovski, the issue of truth as knowledge (*istina*) was inevitably linked to the issues of truth as justice (*spravedlivost'*). For nearly a century, the elevation of the common people was treated by the best of them as a self-imposed duty. State bureaucracy and autocratic rule linked to the illiteracy, poverty and powerlessness of the people, were the impediment and an evil. The 1905–07 revolution shocked the intelligentsia, but could not be easily rejected or dismissed as alien. Revolutionary struggle was the intelligentsia's own, even while many of them condemned it as utopian or irresponsible. The repressions, executions and the reactionary wave were particularly hateful to them and hurt many of the nearest and dearest even to those who were politically indifferent or vague. In the days which followed the revolution's defeat the Russian intelligentsia was swept by despair – tragic motives, decadent literature, religious revivalism and 'looking for new gods' – an idiosyncratic variety of reactions to the bloody end of the 'days of freedom' and the big dreams. Those politically active who 'kept the faith' were now mostly in prisons, in Siberian exile or in emigration. (Yet, importantly, when the period of political depression and reaction began to lift, this was first indicated by the late 1910 and 1911 demonstrations by students – the intelligentsia's customary 'first-line' troops).[43] At the opposing pole stood those converted by the revolution to conservatism, religion or nationalism tinged with acrimonious hostility toward the Russian intelligentsia's revolutionary dream.[44] A leading constitutionalist of the early days of the 1904–05 'banquets campaign', son of the upper crust of the nobility and a university professor of law, Trubetskoi, went to the core of this bitter dismay describing the Russian intelligentsia's admiration of and commitment to the common people as an 'idolatry of the brutes' (*zveropoklonstvo*).[45]

Between those who remained revolutionaries and those who turned violently against them, stood the majority of the Russian intelligentsia which reacted to the revolution's defeat mostly with careerism, subjectivism or legalism. The first of those categories gave up the public and public-spirited goals to focus on personal well-being. They settled, grew fat, politically docile and apologetic for the mad days of their 1905 youth. The next category created works of arts, often brilliant, and bohemian environments, usually bizarre. Of those who refused to give up all hope but rejected the revolutionary creed, a large group concentrated now on legality in two different senses of the word. They tried to use legal means to expand public welfare, popular organisations and personal rights. They also tirelessly elaborated upon and tried to extend the legal order (*pravovoi poryadok*), a process increasingly treated by them as the one realistic way to help Russia follow the European road to common good. This elaboration and adoration of legal argument and constitutionalist debate was particularly prominent with the Russian 'liberal professions'. It put them increasingly at odds with those who represented in Russia the political power, or the social mass or else the revolutionary challenge. Legalism of the Western liberal type – that is, a rule of law formalised and defined – contradicted Russia's full-blooded monarchists' belief that the country's strength lay in its tsar's standing above the law. As for the Russian plebeian masses, legal argument left them indifferent, if not openly suspicious of the phrases involved and those who spun them. The Russian revolutionaries treated this argument mostly as desertion – a verbose way to surrender to and co-operate with a repressive regime.

In the post-revolutionary days – the twilight of tsarist Russia – the revolutionaries retreated into the squabbles of emigration, the Russian artistic intelligentsia into symbolism and sex, while the careerist young people grabbed and usually got their goodies. The 'legalists' got nothing; but with their eyes on Western Europe they did not understand it.

C. RETREAT INTO PROGRESS: THE KDs AND THE MENSHEVIKS

Evidently, conclusions about the lessons drawn from the revolution by the leaders of the main political parties and by the state authorities can be more direct than those pertaining to Russia's social classes, ethnic groups or age-cohorts. Speeches, declarations, books and protocols abound in which the post-mortem of 1905–07 was conducted. In Russia its debate by political leaders never subsided, at least not until a new revolution in 1917–21 posed new challenges and established new conditions. Among those whose lives were then suddenly put in limbo by the defeat and subsequent 'second' emigration, it proceeded much longer than that. The differences in the content and coherence of such conclusions from the 1905–07 experience were extreme, relating both to the theoretical positions of the respective movements and to the individual capacities and idiosyncracies of its leaders. Some of the summations were manifestly untrue, aiming to hide or to explain away embarrassing facts, and known to do just that. But besides lies of expedience and propaganda half-truth, deep convictions and analytical certainties were being established on which further political decisions were to be based.

To grasp the role of leaders and their ideas one must accept not only that they matter greatly in the political life of societies, but also that their impact cannot be understood on its own. Political leaders provide a most significant social agency in the crystallisation, dispersal and change of mass ideologies, but their influence is subject to the broader social context and the dynamics of their political organisations. It is this social and political context to which Brecht referred in saying that, in a major sense, 'it is the led who lead'.[1]

As for the political organisations, in Russia their most fundamental diversity lay between the state apparatus and the political parties which opposed it. The power and the bureaucratic nature of the Russian state made for a seemingly unlimited capacity to execute all its master's wishes and to self-perpetuate its own characteristics and personnel in the face of any internal opposition, but for reasons already discussed it was markedly less effective and eager when reforms were concerned.

Compared with the age-long stability and extensive resources of the state, the party organisations of the post-revolutionary period looked weak and undernourished. Most of them, even the KDs, were never fully legalised by the tsarist government which meant that they had to operate on the sufferance of the police or else in a clandestine manner. The revolutionaries' clandestine networks were now deeply penetrated by police stooges and often uprooted by arrests and exile of its activists. The membership of all the Russian political parties was in sharp decline from mid-1907. The quality of the central leadership was now paramount to a party's survival (and to its ability to regenerate and go once again into political battle when the post-revolutionary reactionary wave came to its end). A significant difference between the political parties of Russia was the extent to which their local organisations survived at all. The survival ability of the main constitutionalist and socialist parties active in 1905 during the 1907–12 half-decade closely followed those parties' capacity for using overt – that is, legal – action; despite sharp decline, the KDs did best in keeping their members, the PSR became nearly extinct, the factions of the RSDWP stood somewhere in the middle. As to the revival ability, when in 1912–14 a new wave of opposition began, the Bolsheviks benefited most in terms of newly-acquired supporters.

The back-impact of 'followers' on the leaders' abilities to lead was more limited in the period of reaction, but grew sharply once it was over. We have already mentioned the political influence of the radicalisation of workers, especially in St Petersburg, in 1912–14 and of the plebeian antipathies in the civil war.[2] Isaac Deutscher has described what followed as 'the revenge of . . . past over the present . . . the reassertion of national tradition in a revolutionary society'.[3] One can call it also the revenge of the followers over the leaders and over their theoretical constructs in the context of a post-revolutionary society.

As the leadership of the Russian political parties entered the next revolutionary period, 1917–21, its outlook was strongly influenced by the experience of Stolypin's attempt at 'revolutions from above' (1906–11) and by the First World War, but the initial impact which shaped their ideas and defined them as leaders was that of the 1905–07 revolution. Put at its most general, this had resulted for the majority in what was well-described by one of them as the 'retrogression of . . . political thought'.[4] But it was those who moved in the opposite direction, defying their theoretical origins, who were to define government strategies in Russia's decisive ten years of 1906–11 and 1917–22.

* * *

The leadership which 'retrogressed' fastest was that of the Party of Popular Liberty – the KDs. Historically they represented the fully developed evolutionist view of Russia's nineteenth-century 'westerners'. Theirs was also the legalist outlook at its strongest. In the Russia context at the turn of the century they refused to describe themselves as 'liberals', but used the term 'constitutionalists' instead, stressing in this way that they were intent not only on civic liberties but also on social justice, extensive welfare provisions and a limited agrarian reform. At their first congress, in the midst of the revolutionary October of 1905, when everything seemed suddenly possible, they passed decisions which sounded republican and revolutionary. Their tactic was defined then by the catchy phrase about 'no enemies on the Left'. The peasant rebellion, workers' uprising, the anti-constitutionalist turn of the Russian nobility and the power of government repressions shook them badly and as from the second KD Congress in early 1906 they declared themselves for a constitutional monarchy and dissociated themselves from revolutionary action. They were aiming now to become an 'open political party' in the European sense of the word.[5] Yet, in their eyes The Revolution, in the vague sense of equating it with political emancipation and social transformation, but not with revolutionary violence, still belonged to them as the natural leaders of the 'Liberation Movement'. The experience of Western Europe which they considered so often, seemed to indicate it clearly.

As a result the KDs made a consistent political effort of offering their leadership to the Russian people, especially to the peasant four-fifths of the population. Their failure to be accepted as such in the first and the second Duma led to the next stage in the KDs' recoiling. They were now putting an increasing emphasis on the

necessity of stage-by-stage evolution, on educational process,
Europe-like democratisation, government reforms and some type of
understanding between the opposition and the government. Their
veneration of law was aimed now not only against the arbitrariness of
the government, but also against revolutionary tendencies and
agrarian radicalism. They did not retreat from their programmes for
public welfare and control but came to mistrust much more the
populace and what universal suffrage could bring to Russia, should it
come before its people were civilised and educated.[6] All this was
expressed with particular strength when the countryside was concerned. 'Between the party leadership and the countryside lay a
chasm (*propast'*)' sadly testified A. Naumov, one of the party's
important local activists.[7] Growth of a 'statist' tendency could be also
recognised now within the KD ranks, that is, a return to the
assumptions of the early Russian liberals of the 1860s, such as B.
Chicherin or K. Kevelin, as to the benefits of a powerful state in any
effort to have Russia transformed (in line with the views of the
liberals, of course). These high hopes relating to state centralism a
'strong-hand government of liberal measures', stood in contradiction
to the self-images usually associated with the liberals of Western
Europe. Anarchic popular tendencies and socialist maximalism were
increasingly being blamed by the KDs for the sorry end of the
expectations of 1905.

Factional divisions within the KDs as well as the views of the
parties to their immediate 'right' made more manifest the ideological
dilemmas which the KDs faced. A powerful right-wing faction existed
in this party from its inception. They attacked the KDs' links with
socialists, were sharply hostile towards the Labourites in the Duma,
condemned the Vyborg Manifesto, consistently pressed for alliance
with the liberals-to-the-right and for new efforts to find a mode of
co-operation with the government.[8] Their further shift to the 'right'
was expressed in the growing accentuation of the positive significance
of the Russian state, a position defined earlier by Struve as the 'true
nationalism'.[9] To him the danger of popular revolution was now that
it might destroy the achievements of Russia's westernisation (that is,
europeanisation), reversing the progress which had been achieved
mostly by the powerful intervention of the Russian state and
following the patterns set by Peter I. The political instincts and
reactions of the majority were dangerous because the Russian people
were barbaric still. In the same spirit, Count Haiden, who was to join
the KDs at a later stage, described the 'agrarian movement' as

'harmful because of its reactionary nature . . . it is without as much as a shadow of legal sense'.[10] The socialists unleashing of the popular movements were, therefore, a spearhead of barbarism bent to destroy Russia and the very social environment from which most of the revolutionaries came.

In the harshest post-1907 attack on the Russian intelligentsia, mounted by Struve and several of the important theorists of this tendency inside and outside the KDs, the *Vekhi* collection of essays, Gershenzon made the point that it was only the tsarist state which defended the Russian intelligentsia from plebeian destructive fury.[11] Others spoke of necessity to repent, morally and religiously. The resulting row finally destroyed both Struve's reputation as a left-of-centre liberal and his claim to lead the KDs. It also showed how deep the fissures in the 'Liberation Movement' of 1903–05 became after the experience of revolution and its defeat. When the new political crisis surfaced in 1912, the failure to establish any political rapport with the government or a viable opposition in the Duma made the KD mainstream leadership move to the 'left'. The KDs' right-wing faction increasingly turned then against its own party.[12]

The KDs went on to play a major role in the Progressive Bloc in the days of the First World War and became a major partner in the Provisional Government of 1917 – its right wing. They offered the only serious centre-right challenge in the 1917 election to the Constituent Assembly but did fairly badly with only about 4 per cent of the total vote. Only in some larger cities was their influence strongly felt. They closed ranks in the revolution and the civil war between November 1917 and 1920 (which were to all of them a confrontation of the 'state principle' with anarchy and the separatism of the popular beast, utilised by German agents – the Bolsheviks). But the final conclusions differed once again, explicating the essential ambivalence of the KDs' stand. Maklakov, Tyrkova, Struve and other leaders of the right-wing KDs put the blame for what had happened squarely on the shoulders of their own mainstream party leadership, especially of Milyukov, for failing to co-operate with the more open-minded dignitaries of the tsarist government in 1906–07. In the last days of the KDs the conclusions drawn from the 1905–07 experience were restated by them with all the bitterness of the civil war – a new Tsar Peter was needed to bring to Russia enlightenment by force before its people could be entrusted with liberalism. Struve, ever the brightest and most ready for experimentation with ideas, made the next conceptual step in his analysis of the Russian civil war. In his view it had nothing whatever to do with the 'common people' who as ever remained indifferent, self-centred and inert. Their only expression, if at all, were the 'Green' bands, equally hostile in Struve's view to the Whites and to the Reds. The results of the civil war were defined by military causes only: it was the superiority in numbers of Red horsemen over their White equivalents which was the explanation as to why Bolsheviks held on to their rule in Russia even after their German puppet-masters were defeated.[13] By that time Milyukov reached an opposite conclusion: the revolution was clearly what the masses of the Russian population wanted; a political party sworn to democracy had to follow popular will. The leader of the KDs' mainstream left the 'middle ground' to adopt the position advocated earlier by its left-wing, that is, the support of fundamental social reforms, the peasantisation of all lands and eventually, the Red Kronstadt's 1920 slogan of Soviet regime without the Bolsheviks. As a result, the KD party in exile finally split in 1921. By that time it mattered little politically, but defined well, *ex post facto*, the KDs' political course and its contradictions.

In the leadership of the KDs there was always a left wing, some of the supporters of which described themselves as Marxists. Their conclusion from the experience of 1905–07 broadly preceded that of Milyukov later on. It was the call to try and re-establish the Alliance of Liberation, that is, to turn back to the brotherhood of the centre-left intelligentsia of 1902–04. In the inter-revolution period this view was supported by a number of provincial activists, but effectively 'kept out' or marginalised by the party's leadership.[14]

The main political organisation to the 'right' of KDs was the Octobrist brand of liberalism. Their name spoke of their adoption of the tsar's manifesto of October 1905 as the new base for Russia's political structure. In fact, they went still further toward a rock-solid monarchism. They first demonstrated their separate identity and loyal nationalism by attacking the KD programmes for autonomy of the Polish provinces. They then supported the government in the 1906–07 issues of 'law and order', inclusive of the establishment of the military tribunals. Under the leadership of Guchkov the Octobrists clearly jostled for the position of the tsardom's government party in the third Duma. Eventually they failed both to co-operate with a government, which did not wish for any real partnerships, and to secure the goodwill of the tsar's circle, to whom the very idea of Duma was wrong. A consequent attempt by

Guchkov to return to opposition was to cost him most of his battle-shy troops of Octobrist Duma deputies. His faction split between those who were to stay pro-government come what may and those who opted for the tactics of mild defiance (and moved closer to the KDs). Conceptually, Octobrists had little to add at any stage of their existence. What was in their hearts and minds was put in words and programmes much better by Struve or Maklakov of the KDs, or else, by Stolypin. The same was true for most of the ever-changing factions 'in between' the two major organisations of Russian liberalism. Of those, the most energetic were the Progressivists, led by Konovalov, who represented yet another attempt of the educated capitalist minority to have its voice heard.[15] They came into being in the face of the 1912 elections to IV Duma, political strikes and the growing right-wing attack on Prime Minister Kokovstov as too accommodating to the 'public opinion' of the middle classes. Their main effort went into the establishment of an united liberal front of constitutionalist opposition – eventually to take shape in 1915. The Octobrist and all the Liberal middle groups were to disappear in 1917, transferring their support to the KDs and later, during the civil war, to the White Cause.

To recollect, the experience of 1905–07 revolution crystallised the Russian liberal movement, but also uncovered its fundamental dilemmas. The one lesson learned by them was about themselves, mainly, that they were not revolutionaries. Some of them knew it from the outset. Most of the others moved from 'marching', in the early-and-radical Struve's words, 'beside and not against the Social Democrats', to the absolute condemnation of the revolutionary use of force and to 'defending the Duma' at all costs while calling for the farther democratisation of Russia. But then major dilemmas surfaced. A gradualist approach could not work against a government which was intensely autocratic and held the reigns so tightly. Legislative activity needed an effective parliament, but the Duma was badly curtailed by the tsardom. Democratisation unleashed popular forces for which respect of law and individual liberty meant little. Social reforms which were orderly and aimed to hurt no-one were opposed by nearly everyone. To the right-wingers the KDs' views were dangerously radical, to the left-wingers they spelled surrender to the tsarist status quo. Yet in the words of one of the major theorists of the moderate liberals 'autocracy would lead to a revolution. To sustain the dynasty and the monarchy these must be restricted'.[16] The one hope left was to trust history, interpreted in evolutionist spirit, that is, to assume that time and education would turn Russia eventually into a piece of Western Europe. But Russia was not turning into Western Europe. The views and the words of Western Europe liberalism acquired different meanings in this different social and historical setting, as the KDs eventually came to recognise.

In the face of a crushing defeat and of a reality which refused to meet their understanding, the Russian liberals regressed in two opposing directions: towards a 'statist' Westernism with a strong 'anti-popular' accent, and towards the hope for a non-class radical unity of people of good will, a new Alliance of Liberation (but able to attract peasants). Both views led their supporters away from the classical tenets of European liberalism. Neither worked.

*   *   *

In the period which followed the 1905–07 revolution, the belief in and the hope for progress defined by the laws of evolution was true not only for the mainstream of Russian liberals, but also for the Orthodox Marxists, especially the Mensheviks. Indeed, their 'orthodoxy' was in its essence evolutionist and Westernist in following the views and prescriptions of the majority of the German SDs. In 1905–06 many of their 'holy cows' were challenged and some new ideas arose, but after the revolution came what was to be described by one of their main leaders (in a phrase already quoted) as the 'retrogression of Menshevik political thought under the impact of the decline of the revolution'.[17]

The ideological starting-point of the RSDWP as it emerged in 1903 was the set of views agreed by its dominat *Iskra* faction. Put succinctly, this meant an 'orthodox' – that is, Kautskian – interpretation of Marxism and a particular historiography of past, present and future. It assumed for the present a necessary and speedy advance of all Europe towards a socialist society, determined by the mounting forces of production, expressed in the proletarian class struggle and illuminated by the Marxist science of society – all linked to the inevitable rhythm of 'progress'. This consistently evolutionist creed incorporated necessary stages of historical advance: feudalism – capitalism – socialism. Also, Kautsky was the first to reform Marx's view of the essential spontaneity of the proletarian move towards power in the context of capitalism.[18] Lenin was to develop it farther. In this view, to advance promptly or even, to advance at all, one had to inject the working class with science, hence the supreme significance of Marxist intellectuals and the social democratic parties which were about to lead the working class.[19]

Plekhanov positioned Russia within this historiography as a society lagging behind Europe, and in which the growth of capitalism was being contradicted and delayed by pre-capitalist social structures. These were, mainly, the tsarist state (defined by him later as a partly-demolished form of Oriental Despotism) and the Russian peasantry. Capitalism in that view was well advanced in Russia of the 1890s. A bourgeois revolution was imminent, but Russia's capitalists were too weak to secure it. The only way forward was to do so through what came to be called after 1900 a 'proletarian hegemony', that is, to use the might of the proletariat, its organisations and its social alliances to establish the full-fledged bourgeois society and political democracy typical of it. This new social context would let the Russian working class grow into a German-like force of massive numbers, splendid organisation and scientific sophistication, enabling them to proceed to the next stage – the establishment of the socialist mode of production. Two fundamentally different stages and two revolutions, separated by a considerable period of social transformation and economic growth, were considered necessary. Put with flair by Rosa Luxemburg during the revolutionary days of 1905, it meant that:

> the Russian revolution will, formally speaking, bring about in Russia what the February and March revolutions [of 1848] brought about in Western and central Europe half a century ago. At the same time . . . because it is a belated and struggling fragment of the European revolution . . . it will have a more pronounced proletarian class-character than any previous revolution'.[20]

Kautsky's battle for scientificity, as he understood it, was translated in Russia into the outstandingly vitriolic language of supreme arrogance introduced by Plekhanov against any socialists who were 'unscientific' and therefore as reactionary and as obnoxious as the practitioners of witchcraft would be to true scientists (the more so, if laying claims to the science itself). Plekhanov's young allies in Russia, especially the most dramatic love–hate couple of the 'orthodox' Marxist leadership, Lenin and Martov, adopted and enhanced all those views, adding to them organisational accents and *élan*, faith bordering on obsession in party organisation and tough political will. Their practical programme was in turn adopted by Plekhanov and Axelrod in Geneva and eventually by the SDs' movement *in toto*.[21]

The division which came to light at the 1903 Congress of the RSDWP and split it down the middle, concerned party organisation, tactics and style rather than theoretical substance. Lenin and Martov disagreed over the extent of party centralisation which should be aimed for. To Lenin it should be total, including the rights of the central leadership to disperse, restructure and appoint every local committee. To Martov it was nearly total, but he was becoming wary of what super-centralisation might mean to the political mobilisation of working-class activists. Tactically, Lenin and his supporters were more confrontational towards class enemies, Martov more inclined to take over and use the existing legal institutions. Lenin's description of himself in those days as a Jacobin linked to the working class was shrewd in a double sense.[22] His faction, its disciplinarian tendency and hierarchy of leadership had attracted particularly the SDs of a 'hard-nosed' and tough-minded disposition who were ready to obey and ready to assume command of 'their' class and of anybody else. The term also implied the Girondist tendency of Martov's Mensheviks – that is, of one of 'honest pedants'[23] given to formal dispute rather than to a merciless drive for power (and as prone as the Girondists to lose a duel with political toughs).

The leaders of Bolsheviks and Mensheviks alike did their level best *ex post facto* to present the disagreements of 1903 as already evident a decade earlier. It was only too easy (and ideologically profitable) to see things in that light after the division became final. The truth, however, was that while in 1903 both sides searched high and low for doctrinal reason to justify the split, their theoretical differences were 'still so subtle'[24] that they could not be effectively defined. As a result, while leaders of the factions ranted, quarrelled and suspected, the rank-and-file began spontaneously to re-establish RSDWP party unity 'from below' in autumn of 1905 and by 1906 forced the leaders to reunite – to the majority of Russian SDs there was no ideological reason for them to stay apart.[25] Indeed, the grand ideological cause declared eventually by both factions to be the explanation of the 1903 party split, was Lenin's tough formulation of Section 1 of the party statute, yet, at the next congress of the united RSDWP in 1906 the Mensheviks, who fully dominated it, calmly and painlessly voted this very formula into the party statute.[26] The definite Bolshevik–Menshevik division came not in 1895, as a Menshevik historian would have it, nor earlier still as Lenin was to declare nor in 1903 when they packed one against the other's committees and boards, nor in the 1904–05 factional struggles either. It happened when they were formally united in one party during the period 1906–12, that is, when the different conclusions from 1905–07 took final shape.

The first irreconcilable division between the factions of the RSDWP came to light in the tactical debate at its 1906 and 1907 congresses and conferences. To the majority of the Mensheviks, a bourgeois revolution meant the natural alliance with what was to them the party of the bourgeoisie – the KDs. For Lenin the need to secure proletarian hegemony in a bourgeois revolution, in a country in which the bourgeoisie was weak and fearful, meant that the KDs must be kept from attaining a position of influence and that the only allies could be the peasants, or in party-political terms, the Labour Faction of Duma and the PSR. For the Bolsheviks, the former view was an opportunistic surrender to the bourgeoisie, to the Mensheviks the latter view was a Utopian surrender to the populists. Different attitudes toward the peasantry were linked to different perspectives of political action, especially the tactics of insurrection (Bolsheviks held on to them for much longer than the Mensheviks), the elections, the alliances preferred in the Duma, etc.

By 1908 and under the shadow of defeat and mass arrests, not only the RSDWP but also each of its factions became deeply divided. Among the Mensheviks there were now the Liquidators, the Trotskyites, the Party Loyalists etc; among the Bolsheviks, the *otzovisty*, the *ultimisty* and other groups. The majority of the members of the Bolshevik central committees in 1903–07 were no longer with Lenin. Many SDs withdrew from struggle altogether. As for those who kept at it, two views emerged from the profusion of factions and were eventually to offer the axis of regeneration of the Bolsheviks and Mensheviks as parties with separate ideologies and organisations. This new development and the major conceptual changes and political reconstructions were marked by massive exchanges of supporters between the RSDWP's initial factions. Symbolic of this, by 1917, in Petrograd, Aleksinskii – once a member of the Bolshevik Central Committee, but now a spokesman for a right-wing faction of the Menskeviks – faced Trotsky, once a leading radical Menshevik, but now a member of the Bolshevik Politburo and there second only to Lenin. One can proceed with a long list of such changes among the lesser lights of the SDS.

We shall turn later to the Bolsheviks and Lenin. As for the Menshevik mainstream, the analytical response to 1905–07 which was to define them in the years which followed was set out by Axelrod and Martov and supported by a number of less-prominent leaders

operating inside Russia, while Plekhanov retreated into sulky
isolation calling a plague on both houses. This rethinking was set in
motion by Axelrod's 1906 call for a worker's congress to advance a
legal, broad and massive workers' party along the European lines.
Mensheviks were increasingly wary of clandestine organisations
which were badly mauled by arrests; they wished to move from such
organisations to viable 'on surface' trade unions, co-operatives, etc.
In the face of the 1905 defeat they saw as their aim the development
and education of an elite of workers' leaders, the organisation of the
proletariat around specific and limited aims and the rebuilding of the
badly-damaged RSDWP from below on this new basis. They aimed
also at a new and 'amphibian' (able to act simultaneously legally and
clandestinely) cadre of party activists – a kind of 'Third Element' but
serving mainly the working class and mostly recruited from it.[27] Their
inter-party foes promptly called it 'Liquidationism' (of the clandestine revolutionary party) and charged those who supported it with
retreat from the path of revolution to that of reform. Martov
furiously rejected that accusation of treason to Marxist orthodoxy
and to socialist revolution. Indeed, one could rightly claim that the
exact opposite was true, for what was happening was his faction's
regression to the positions of the Emancipation of Labour Group of
the 1890s, from which the *Iskra* 'orthodox' offensive began. They
were also going back to the tactical insights of Kramer in his 1896 call
to move 'from propaganda to agitation'.[28] To understand Axelrod's
and Martov's view one must see the impeccable logic of their
response, for it was neither inconsistency as Marxists, nor lack of
courage, nor surrender to class enemies that one could charge them
with, but rather the insistence on following a line of thought whatever
the context and the political experience. As for their essential logic,
in Haimson's excellent description it was 'the broad perspectives of
the immediate future [as] . . . pre-ordained [by the] bourgeois
revolution'.[29] Or put otherwise in the words of a leading Menshevik
theorist of agriculture, I. Chernyshev, 'in the 1848 revolution . . .
each country got a constitution it "deserved" for its economic
"success" '.[30] Russia was not yet at the sufficiently advanced stage,
but then time was to solve it.

  In that light, the reason for the revolution's defeat seemed clear to
most of the Mensheviks, at least, once its excitement was over. The
revolution began too early, the country was still too backward,
under-capitalised, subsequently under-cultured and with too weak a
proletariat to carry the day in the face of the reactionary elements.

The very existence of the Bolshevik and the PSR extremism was to L. Martov explainable in terms of Russia's backwardness, which was prone to produce such utopian thinking. (This argument of course, closely followed Plekhanov's attack on the People's Will Party in the 1880s.) In similar spirit P. Maslov described Lenin's idea of dictatorship of 'workers and peasants' as contradicting the process of economic development. One had now to fight off in the RSDWP the excessive utopian demands, the Blanqueism and premature action as well as the attempts to give comfort to reactionary peasants – for the SRs' subjectivism clearly infested also the ranks of the SDs. Russia's specificity was fully defined by its backwardness and that alone. All political action had to be defined by the fundamental aim to Europeanise Russia and its workers' movement. As for the tactics, the ranks of the SDs had to be proletarianised, and related to the day-to-day workers' needs within a new 'policy of small deeds' bound to re-education in class terms. The working class would naturally support this stage-by-stage effort to build its organisations and to defend its immediate aims. Most importantly one must remember that the goal of a scientific socialist movement is general progress plus the proletarian parties' autonomy in it. All tactical steps, alliances and enemies had to be defined accordingly.

The Mensheviks proceeded to act in the light of their best logic. The times were grim, persecution rampant, the cadres weakened and dispirited – but slowly, stubbornly the Mensheviks built up legal trade unions, and influence in the new Insurance Boards, cultural clubs and other organisations of the working class.[31] Then came the test – a new radical wave of workers' defiance and strife in 1912–14. To the dismay of the Mensheviks, their workers' leaders rapidly lost command of the unions and organisations built up with such effort to the local Bolsheviks, to SRs or even to non-party 'wild' men, often fresh from their villages.[32] Mensheviks were hard at work to upgrade the working class to the best of the German standards. But it was proving the wrong working-class for what they tried to achieve. The Mensheviks believed they knew scientifically the history of Russia's future – it was like Europe's past. It was, however, the wrong history to know for what they were encountering. The developments of 1914–20 were to make it all clearer still. The split between the internationalist and radical Martovites and the other brands of Menshevism, especially the 'defencists', added to the disarray. If a 'judgement of history' can be quantified at all it was passed in the 1917 elections to the Constitutional Assembly of Russia in which the

SD Mensheviks' vote was only 2.3 per cent of the total (6 per cent in towns), and lesser still if their exceptional political fortress of Georgia was excluded.

There is one more analytical test which one may apply to trace the logic of the Menshevik analysis. It is to look at its further extrapolation by the major theorists in the 'new exile' relating it to the actual history which we now know. In the 1904s F. Dan, a major leader of the Mensheviks and Martov's heir in their ranks, considered the history of the Bolsheviks and of his own faction in a book from which we have already quoted.[33] Looking back he admitted to many mistakes on the part of the Mensheviks, particularly their refusal to struggle for direct political power at the 'bourgeois stage', their attitude toward the KDs, etc. He also cited some parallel failures of the political predictions made by the Bolsheviks, in particular the fact that no peasant revolutionary party came into being in Russia and therefore, in his view, no peasant-workers' revolutionary democracy could ever become the basis of the post-revolutionary regime. He pointed out that the USSR was built by the cadres of all of the RSDWP, both Bolsheviks and Mensheviks, for many loyal Mensheviks became the 'experts' of the new regime in its Gosplan, VSNKh and other leading economic institutions and without them the new government's ability to manage the country would have been badly impeded.[34] He then proceeded to interpret in this terms the Russia of the 1930s. The only way Russia used to be particular (its *svoeobraznost'*) was its being belated (*zapozdalost'*). Now Stalin's collectivisation put the country right. 'As is well known the Soviet Regime resolved the problem of moral and political isolation of the *Kulaks* and drew the middle peasant into the *Kolkhoz* system', securing this by 'the advantages of the large-scale collective economy able to use machinery and more advanced methods'.[35] Simply that. As for the future, the country progressed so economically and socially as a result of collectivisation that now, inevitably, a new stage was approaching. The reason for the 'dictatorial metamorphosis' of the Bolsheviks – the lack of possible peasant democracy in Russia and its peasants' backwardness, was no longer a major causal force. Stalin's constitution of 1936 (that is, one year before the *Ezhovshchina* purge) was, according to Dan, the consequent and necessary 'major step . . . toward democratisation'. By the laws of the Marxist social science Russia was now rapidly moving toward a democratic society.[36] The fundamental logic was still that of the 1890s, re-established in the aftermath of 1905–07. It was still impeccable in its consistency. It was as much out of touch with the object of its application.

D. CONSERVATIVE MILITANTS AND MILITANT CONSERVATIVES: THE SRs AND THE 'UNITED NOBILITY'

In the list of Russian political parties the Party of Socialist Revolutionaries was exceptional, as much in the extremity of its rise and fall as in the related characteristics of its leadership, party organisation and political stand. The harsh trajectory of the history of the PSR was to climax in the one awesome year of 1917 when in March its members witnessed the victory of a remarkably bloodless revolution, then the creation of a republic, a government led by SRs, an absolute majority won by the PSR in the first democratic election to the Constituent Assembly and, in November, their final defeat and decline into oblivion. This exceptional piece of drama and bad luck was not only a matter of the final result, for the party seemed afflicted by it during the decade which preceded 1917 as well as the years which followed it directly.

Bad luck is not an easy explanation to adopt when social scientists consider their data. It runs contrary to their fundamental training, knowledge and prejudices which call for the seeking out of causality in conscious programmes and/or the social forces which lay outside the realm of accident. Yet 'bad luck' may play its role and to deny it at the outset would be to brush aside evidence of possible major significance. The history of the leadership of the PSR is a case in point.

A comparison with the RSDWP may help to make it more clear. The effective political leadership of the SDs in 1905–20 was consistently in the hands of a remarkable 'middle generation' of those whose age in 1905 was roughly 35. The most prominent among them were V. Lenin (born in 1870) and Yu. Martov (born in 1872). They gained their political spurs in the late 1890s and were often referred to by the SDs of Russia in 1899–1903 (together with Potresov, born 1869) as 'the old men' faction (*stariki*). With the help of the party's true 'aldermen' Plekhanov, Axelrod and Zasulich, then in their fifties and settled abroad, they first fought and defeated a 'younger generation' of SD activists – the 'Economists', who were less 'orthodox' in theory, less radical in aims, less disciplinarian in

organisation and less exclusivist in self-definition. The top echelon of
the PSR began in a remarkably similar way. Its equivalent 'middle
generation' of leaders who established the united party were S.
Gershuni (born 1870), M. Gotz (born 1866), V. Chernov (born 1873)
and E. Azev (born 1869). Their next 'generation' (which in those
dramatic days meant five to ten years) consisted of S. Sletov, A.
Gotz, V. Zenzinov, N. Avksentev, and B. Savinkov, all eventually to
join the PSR right-wing faction. The PSR was less inclined than
RSDWP to ideological uniformity, which led to a lesser ability to
secure inter-generational continuities, but also, importantly, 'luck'
took its turn in this case. M. Gotz, the PSR tough man of strategy,
tactics and organisational abilities, who harshly drummed into his
comrades the significance of power and called for a direct drive
toward a socialist revolution (he was also first to call this political
perspective 'the permanent revolution') was gravely ill by 1903 and
dead by 1906. The party's charismatic leader, Gershuni, able to keep
it united by sheer strength of personal appeal, was imprisoned in a
fortress in the decisive days of 1905. He escaped in 1906, but died in
March 1908. In December of the same year E. Azev was unmasked as
a police stooge.[1] That left Victor Chernov as the only survivor able to
speak on behalf of the Lenin–Martov leadership-generation in the
PSR. To make things worse, the Populists' outstanding leaders and
minds of Plekhanov's and Axelrod's 'generation' – people such as A.
Mikhailov, N. Kibal'chich, or A. Zhelyabov who would have been in
their late forties in 1905 – died young on the gallows or in prison.
Many others were broken by prison and some turned indifferent or
hostile to the cause of their youth.[2] Those who survived the long
incarcerations and came back and joined the PSR were well-
represented by E. Breshkovskaya and M. Natanson – outstandingly
brave, ever-active, well-loved, theoretically mediocre and tactically
inept.

With the initial core of the effective leadership of the PSR all but
gone and the rest of it put to shame by the way Azev's affair was
handled (the party leaders refused initially to admit to the possibility
of his guilt and let him slip away), the Central Committee of the party
by the end of 1908 held little authority. The PSR disintegrated into a
number of warring factions and writers. When it reconstituted in 1917
it was mostly in the hands of the 'young men of the 1905 generation',
that is, men of different shades of 'moderate' pragmatism such as A.
Gotz and N. Avksentev, to whom Kerensky was now added – an
extra piece of poor luck in the days of revolutionary change when

radicalism of thought, deed and imagination of the leaders was at the highest premium.[3]

Of course, not only luck, but the party's membership, strategy and theory were at issue. During the heyday of 1905–07 the cadre of the PSR was socially and tactically fairly similar to that of the Bolsheviks: militant and young workers and intelligentsia and strongest in the major centres of ethnically Russian population. (The SRs were more influential in the rural provinces of Saratov or Tambov while the Bolsheviks were stronger in the industrial Urals. Both had consider-able followings in the cities of central and western Russia and in St Petersburg.) But the characteristics of PSR party organisation provided for its particular vulnerability. The multi-class self-image led to extensive diversification of effort which spread the party cadres thin at each of the 'fronts' of its activities and promoted diverse tactics and factionality. The efforts to penetrate peasantry and army were particularly costly in 'human investment'. Strong roots in the rural intelligentsia also meant fewer 'cadres' elsewhere. The price of terrorist tactics was heavy, many of the party's best activists were lost, to be sorely missed in the years to come. Other activities suffered likewise; in particular, workers' trade unions were given low priority while many worker supporters of PSR left the factories to join the terror squads of the BO PSR. The party's considerable impact in the industrial St Petersburg of 1906 was mostly squandered. (The attempt in 1909 to re-establish a clandestine PSR workers' organisation in this city – the Workers' Alliance, was effectively destroyed by extensive police arrests in 1910.) The PSR refused to make use of a major venue for legal action by boycotting the third and the fourth Duma (once again, not unlike the left Bolsheviks led by Bogdanov) which weakned the PSR further still. While all the clandestine revolutionary movement declined and distintegrated under the blows of the police, their party declined still faster.

By 1909, the discovery of Azev's treason was as much as the PSR structure could take. Attempts to rejuvenate the party from abroad failed.[4] There was little exaggeration when in 1916 A. Spiridovich, the police chief turned historian of revolutionary movements, sum-med up the collapse as follows:

> By the beginning of 1914 no party organisation [of PSR, T.S.] in its strict sense existed in Russia. There were the Socialist Revolu-tionaries spread throughout the country's different cities and dreaming about such organisation and about party work. There

were also emigrants abroad, split into factions, and there was a
Central Committee and its publications . . .

With a fine anticipation of the future, he added 'there are therefore
party cadres ready to begin revolutionary activities, once called upon,
following a definite programme'.[5] The memoirs of the party leaders
substantiated this summation for 1909–16. Also, for the second time
in a quarter of a century (it first happened in 1887–1900) the defeat of
its revolutionary wing made the populists' message pass by default
into the hands of a politically milder milieu of sympathisers,
especially those active in a variety of *zemstvo*s social services
attending to the peasantry's needs in the legal profession or in
journalism. Their impact was to play a central role in the reaction of
the SRs to the First World War and the characteristics of the PSR
1917 party regeneration.

Finally, to get the picture right one must look at the conceptual and
ideological characteristics of the party which, after all, delimited it in
the most direct sense from other political tendencies in Russia.
Conditions made V. Chernov into the party's top interpreter of
ideological matters. (The death of Gershuni also left him, beside
Breshkovskaya, its best-known leader.) The PSR rejected in principle any obligatory authority outside its own ranks, for example,
Kautsky's role to the Iskrites of the RSDWP. This made Chernov's
stature as a theorist grow still more. He was an able writer and
polemist with a tendency for synthesis of different points of view
('eclectic' to those who did not like his work). As a leader he was
predisposed to appease people rather than to cut through the party
problems. Out of the several strands of the revolutionary populist
traditions of the 1880s Chernov, aided by P. Vikhlaev and N.
Rakitnikov, developed mostly its peasant-directed prong. He related
it explicitly to the 'revisionist' wing of the Marxist analysis of the
Second International, but his own position and that of his party's
official leadership in 1905–17 were polarly opposed to the German
'revisionist' support of evolutionary solutions.[6]

The main concept developed by Chernov to form the hard-core of
the PSR agrarian programme was that of 'lands' socialisation',
crystallising a view which linked revolutionary goals and peasant
wishes and therefore did a considerable amount of good to the SRs'
peasant support, expressed at its strongest in the 1917 elections.[7] It
assumed the total take-over and equalising redivision of Russia's
land, executed by its peasant communes, and a total ban on the land

market and on any permanent wage-labour within agriculture. Examined *ex post facto*, this concept was as realistic as one could be in the predicting of the actual state of affairs in Russia in 1918–28. While developing in this way the PSR's analytical thought and long-term planning, Chernov and his aides did remarkably little in so far as the other aspects of the revolutionary populist creed of 1850–80s were concerned – the issues of power, state and political control, the struggle against the state-and-capitalism combination, or the issue of revolutionary dictatorship.[8] The major problem raised by Tkachev – in the focus of attention of the People's Will Executive Committee and still later discussed by M. Gotz in the PSR itself – of forcing history's pace by a revolutionary state-intervention and of the direct move towards socialism (as opposed to the SDs' insistence on the transformation of Russia through a necessary 'bourgeois stage') were mostly avoided. In fact, Chernov had eventually grafted a 'stages theory' onto his own historiography of the future. The tsardom was to be defeated by a 'social' revolution, which would be more than the bourgeois revolution but less than a socialist one. The socialisation of all lands by the peasants would restrict the capitalist system, but not dispose of it. Two things followed. Little was offered to the working class in the forthcoming period in terms of tangible changes, especially in so far as the direct control of their conditions of production was concerned. Nothing was said of the post-revolutionary state versus the PSR. Also the adopted rag-tag description of the revolutionary class of Russia (workers, peasants and intelligentsia, but usually interpreted tacitly as 'all the people of good will' facing 'the autocracy') was not the effective way to mobilise plebeian hostility against the country's 'haves' – a political tool the Bolsheviks were to put to use with such effect in their 'class-against-class' policies of 1917–19.

As for the PSR theoretical lessons from 1905–07, those can be explained in part by what I shall call the 'abacus principle', to put to use what J. Needham suggested as one of the reasons why China's mathematics did not advance as did that of the Europeans since Galileo. In Needham's view this was because of the earlier Chinese advancement in the theory of this field (a Leibnitz-like grasp but much before his time) while the parallel discovery of the abacus effectively solved the practical problems of accounting. This led to stagnation while the very fact that Europe was backward, together with the pressure there of practical needs like seafaring, led to the outburst of 'new' – that is, Galilean mathematics and science.[9] Early advances and simple solutions which 'work' for a while often become reasons for subsequent sluggishness of critical thought.

The experience of 1905–07 fitted better the anticipations of the early revolutionary populists, whose thought the PSR overtly adopted, than the expectations of other parties: peasant rebellion, the soldiers' mutinies, the eventual plebeian clash with the 'society' of educated middle classes evident in 1906–07, the particularities of the Russian revolution as against the 1848 European patterns, etc.[10] By 1906, Marxists such as Lenin, and Constitutionalists such as Milyukov, were reconsidering their programmes and often stole much of the Populists cloth (Lenin took it from its revolutionary wing while the KDs adopted the views of its reformists). Both were to take over more of those programmatic elements in 1917.[11] While the political competitors adjusted and changed their strategies in the light of new experiences, the PSR did little on that score from the moment the concept of 'land socialisation' was established. Their second congress of 1907 simply reaffirmed the views of the first one. The party conference in 1908 repeated it once again, as did the conference in 1913 – each of them restated what had already been said with a consistency akin to self-hypnosis. Of the recent historians, Hildermeier called it pointedly a 'mixture of complacency and unreality'.[12] The main theoretical news of the PSR mainstream in 1907–17 was the unfolding by Chernov of a new interpretation by which even if the Stolypin reforms succeeds in destroying the commune, the agrarian programme of PSR – that is, land socialisation – can still be effective and *should not change*. The particular weaknesses of the PSR positions concerning power, the working class, etc, were left mostly unattended by the party's leadership. Non-learning was the major characteristic of the way this party learned its lessons. Its main modification was further retreat into the 1870s' 'land and liberty' organisational naivety about the State and political power.

With the official PSR leadership holding rigidly to its initial views, the pending political and ideological issues were raised mainly by the factions of the PSR internal opposition. On the left, the *Revolyutsionnaya mysl'* journal and group provided continuity between the SR Maximalists, who departed from the party in 1906 and were rapidly destroyed by police action, and the left-wing SRs who were to ally with the Bolsheviks in late 1917. They called for the direct struggle for socialism (the 'permanent revolution' of M. Gotz) and in consequence, for the immediate 'socialisation' of the factories – that is, the control of industry by the working class. By 1909 some of them departed from the PSR altogether. More powerful in its impact was the offensive of the party's right-wing faction which began with the establishment of the *Pochin* publication in 1911.[13] It assumed the possible success of Stolypin's reform and called for the party's readjustment, but it was their type of adjustment which defined the faction. Radkey described them as the 'tired revolutionaries' and as radicals who 'grew older' in spirit. The solution they offered was to transform the PSR into a peasant party – that is, to turn it into the class representation of smallholding farmers only, rejecting the revolutionary multi-class stand as well as PSR manifest preference for communal land structure and production. As with the other political parties of Russia, the factions of the PSR between 1907 and 1917, as well as in 1917–21, were mostly defined by the diverse lessons extricated from the 1905–07 revolution. The revolutionary experience and the defeat of 1905–07, mercilessly exposed ambivalences of the catch-all programmes, frailties of leaders, and weaknesses of organisation.

In 1914 the right-wing of the PSR adopted a 'defencist' political stand. Chernov, who refused to bow to the nationalist wave, joined the socialist conference of objectors to war in Zimmerwald. By 1917, many of his party comrades, struck by the patriotic bug, spoke darkly of his treason.

A quick aside concerning one of the impacts of the war-generated nationalism is necessary here. Any attempt to uncover a line of causality between the lessons of 1905–07 and their results in 1917–20 must also take into the consideration of causes, the impact of the intermediate period and especially the First World War's optimistic beginning and its sorry aftermath. Most of the Russian socialists were ill-equipped to deal with the nationalist wave which struck Russia in 1914. The 1903–05 war against Japan produced fairly little excitement or patriotic vigour. Little was expected in 1914, while the belief in power of the Second International to unite the socialist parties of Europe and to secure peace was strong in all of its Russian sections. The war and the collapse of the Second International led in Russia to an immediate split between the 'internationalists' who still refused to support their government in a world war and the 'defencists' like Plekhanov, Potresov or Sletov who rapidly turned into a left-wing of the broad patriotic camp committed to victory over the German enemies. Later, in 1917, this group was increased by a number of Zimmerwald supporters, like A. Gotz and I. Tsereteli, who opposed the war until then but now came to interpret the new Russian

Republic's alliance with the West European powers as a united front of great democracies of the world, and therefore, for all socialists and democrats the thing to support. All along the KDs and the Bolsheviks had no particular ideological problems to resolve *vis-à-vis* the 1914 or 1917 patriotic claims. The former at once joined the national camp focusing their criticism of the tsardom on the inefficiences of the way in which the war was conducted; the latter stubbornly stuck by their 'defeatist' stand. (In his exile in Switzerland Lenin went a step farther calling for the global turning of the national wars into a social war – a direct transfer from world war to a world revolution.) As for the Mensheviks, a group of the activists in Russia joined the war effort and seemed smugly pleased with the fact that their Bolshevik competitors were now hampered by the nationalistic moods of many workers. Others refused any support for war. Many of the PSR supporters in the Russian intelligentsia, and the more so, the less radical populist groups, were also loudly patriotic. Others and especially the PSR workers–activists majority in Petrograd and some of its intellectuals were sharply anti-war, laying a foundation for a future split and the creation in 1917 of the party of Left SRs. In exile, the brightest theorists of the divided parties and their living symbols, Martov and Chernov, joined the internationalists' anti-war effort of European socialists. The immediate political impact of it was minute, the impact of it in 1917 was major. In that time, both parties were split wide open between a 'defencist' majority (now joined by some ex-internationalists) and a stubbornly 'internationalist' minority. It was enough for Lenin to come back and read out his unexpected *April Thesis* calling for immediate struggle for peace and for power, in order to take command within days of his party and its Central Committee. Milyukov commanded (or, at least, manipulated) the KDs nearly as well. Martov and Chernov were out of control and their parties split when the theoretical re-tooling, radical politics and imaginative leadership as well as unity were particularly necessary to make them act as an effective force.

*   *   *

The fourth of the organised political camps which in the wake of the 1905–07 revolution experienced what could have been called 're-treat . . . in thought', or at least its deadening immobility, was the core group of the Russian 'squires'. In the ideological, political or social sense their camp extended to many of the Russian top bureaucrats, to the right-wing Duma deputees and, to some of the 'popular' extremist leaders and organisations of the 'hard' Right, as well as to most of the *Camarilla* – the tsar and his immediate environment of kinsman, friends and hangers-on. The views of the other sub-groups of Russian legitimism were on the whole less consistent or expressive as to the long-term policies concerning the future of Russia. Once the Revolution was over, the state apparatus was reluctant to declare any opinions over and above those of loyalty and obedience to 'those above'. The Black Hundreds were now losing coherence, impact and members while government subsidies were being used to discipline them.[14] The *Camarilla* seldom produced positive plans over and above the dispersal of the Duma.

As to the 'squiredom' the revolution and especially the 'agrarian disturbances' had rapidly made it produce an overt political organisation – the Council of the United Nobility.[15] In its demands as much as in the 'blind spots' of its programmes and declarations, the United Nobility was to act as a class organisation *par excellence*. There was considerable consistency in its views. To them there was no 'agrarian problem' in Russia and no land shortage, only the issue of peasant backwardness and the consequent need to increase agricultural productivity as well as to improve the peasant moral sense of property-holding, solving thereby the self-inflicted peasant plight. There was also no revolutionary situation in Russia, only the pernicious agitation of the 'revolutionary mob which goes under the name of intelligentsia' and which 'with the help of instigators (*podstrekatel'i*) and the lies of the newsmen produced murders, robberies, and hooliganism'.[16] The main long-term problem lay in the disloyalty of non-Russians toward the Empire and the way they used the naivety of some Russian people for their dark designs. This was helped by the ambitious and disloyal schemers inside Russia's nobility and its better folk – the KDs. What was needed was to restore order, to punish offenders, to cut-off unreliables, to toughen up the loyal forces, to restore the natural and patriotic leadership of Russia's peasants to its nobles, while abolishing the commune – the organisation of the Russian peasants' separatism which now proved its dangerous potential. The manorial land property was 'unalienable' not only because this best suited the landholding nobility, but also, because it was naturally in the best interest of Russia.

The United Nobility's bid for political power was first to encounter a major political defeat. The leaders of the Russian squires assumed, with the government of the day, the natural conservatism of the

peasant core of the true Russians. This view gave the nobility a
self-evident position as leaders of the loyalist peasantry in the
countryside and in the Dumas to come. In due course these forces
were to face and politically to defeat the restless elements of the
realm. Consequently, steps were taken by the United Nobility to set
up a general landowners' union aiming to give form to the
squiredom–peasantry alliance. (Germany was often used as an
example to explain how natural such unity would be.[17]) The failure of
this attempt in the summer of 1905 and the results of the election to
the first and second *Dumas* led to what was well described as the
'brutal realisation that peasants do not want nobility to represent
them'.[18] On the whole, the peasants treated the local squires as class
enemies. With bitter taste in their mouths the leaders of the squires
had to recognise that in the Russian countryside they were on their
own. This also meant that in the given context, universal suffrage and
democratic rule would spell their doom. Plans had to be laid
accordingly. They coincided and linked with the government's coup
of 1907, which produced a heavily biassed electoral law and the third
Duma. Its majority was as much a replica of the United Nobility as
they could ever have hoped. Through the tsar's appointments a
faction of similar ilk was rapidly increasing in the State Council.

Despite the evidently reactionary nature of the United Nobility's
moods and designs, the image of simply 'marching back' must be
qualified when their actual strategy is concerned. True, there were
demands to conclude the military victory over the 'internal enemies'
by going back to pre-Duma or even pre-Witte Russia, to repeat the
counter-reforms of Alexander III. But the reactionary views of the
bulk of the Russian squires and their allies were now modified by a
new interpretation of goals and a distinct tactic which signified the
new times. As to the goals, in the nineteenth century the ideological
representatives of the Russia's Right were hostile to all 'Western'
ideas as such, associating liberalism with parliamentarism, *laissez-
faire* with an unsavoury merchant predominance (*zasil'e*), universal
suffrage with anarchy and mob rule. To them Russia was unique and
supreme in its true religion, organic unity (*sobornost'*), and God
blessed autocracy. In particular, the unlimited nature of the Russian
tsardom saved the country from the horrors of demagogy and from
universal bureaucracy, as well as from the instability rooted in the
evil of men and the 'fanaticism of logic', associated with the moral
nihilism of modernity.[19] Their images often adopted the Slavophiles'
terminology, but without its radical edge, that is, without the belief in

necessity of reform which informed the Slavophile vision of Russia's unique destiny.

What was new was an admixture of Westernism in the views and assumptions of the conservative circles. This was expressed in the growing support of a *laissez-faire* economy and the wish to advance property laws in line with those of Western Europe (while at the same time totally rejecting their association with parliamentary democracy, an assumption which was universally adopted by contemporary European social theory, both liberal and Marxist). The brighter among the Russian conservatives now wanted to untie the bundle of West European characteristics and to select out of it a few elements only, such as the privatisation of peasant land and the dissolution of the peasant commune. Their reactionary cravings for non-parliamentary policy and the 'strong-hand' of the good old times was often informed by 'good education', which inevitably meant some learning from and about the West. This found its anecdotal expression in the explanation given to the *Daily Telegraph* reporter as to why the tsar appointed the Grand Duke Vladimir to take charge of St Petersburg on the Bloody Sunday of 9 January 1905. The Duke was very well read in the history of the 1789 French Revolution and 'would not permit therefore any crazy indulgence' – so the explanation ran.[20] Russian conservatives were not totally immune to the lessons of history, but they were selective about it to the point of turning it into a caricature, and wished to make it work for the status quo as against a changing world, which was bursting at its seams. It was still the case of 'non-learning'.

The new tactic which increasingly entered the policies of Russia's right-wingers was their attitude toward the government. Strictly monarchists and violently hostile to all 'enemies of the throne', the Russian right-wing lobby attacked with remarkable consistency the tsar's ministers and prime ministers of the period. This started with Witte, who was firstly blamed by the squires for his anti-agricultural policies.[21] In 1905 the charge became treason and the placation of the mutineers. He was now blamed for the October Manifesto of 1905, for the revolution and even for the result of the elections to the first Duma. The removal of Kutler from the Ministry of Agriculture and of Witte as Prime Minister, together with the need to close ranks in the face of revolutionary attack, seemed to have united all Russia's monarchists in their support of the government. Yet, within one year from Stolypin's appointment as the Prime Minister, he was also encountering growing conservative opposition, on a par with that by the socialists and the constitutionalists. This proceeded until Stoly-pin's death in 1911. His successor, Kokovtsov, a man of lesser ambition and reformist zeal, rapidly came under similar attack, to be dismissed – to the right-wingers' open glee – in 1914. The way the legislative machinery was now set up gave exceptional power of veto to the conservative squires.[22]

As a result, a parliament met, debates continued but little legislation of significance emerged. As years went by the parliamentary life of Russia was increasingly described as pointless, aimless and boring even by those who fully participated in it. Nor were even the tsar's ministers fully in control. Power moved increasingly into the hands of a narrow circle of courtiers, the tsar's wife and kinsmen, Rasputin, and the *Camarilla*. To them, it was the Duma which was to be blamed for all the ills of the Russian state. Adopting the posture of a man ill-advised and hurt in 1905 by his bureaucrats and one who nurses a just grudge against 'the educated Russia' but is well-beloved by 'his people', the tsar presided over this retreat from orderly bureaucratic, let alone parliamentary, procedures. Witte's earlier memoirs concerning the tsar's court were admittedly shot through with the bitterness of a dignitary who fell from grace, but shrewd all the same. He spoke of the tsar's contempt towards his government and the arrogant ignorance of his close environment, while its top bureaucrats systematically ignored laws and 'gave two thirds of their time to intrigue'.[23] By 1915 many of the United Nobility chiefs and other right-wingers found themselves also in open opposition to the tsar's servile government, which their earlier 'hunting down of the prime ministers' helped to produce. In the face of the incompetence shown by the state administration in running the war, the Duma deputies' opposition to the government became once again, as in the second Duma, nearly total. Yet it was a deeply legitimist parliament, elected under electoral laws which gave massive preference to the conservative squires.

Despite deep differences, in the days which followed the 1905–07 revolution, most of the political activists of Russia shared the tendency to retreat to pre-1905 fundamental assumptions – that is, to understand what happened and to plan the future accordingly. The KDs shifted toward the type of Westernism which informed the Russian 'statist' liberals of the 1860s while the Mensheviks moved closer to the views of the Emancipation of Labour Group of the 1880s and 1890s. The SRs stayed put or else adopted a version of the Land and Liberty policies of 1870s, while the United Nobility looked back to the good old days of Alexander III (with a new approach to the peasant commune added). A minority of Russian leaders, once again deeply divided in goals and ideological premises, shared in those days another major similarity: their conclusions were substantively original and radical, that is, focused on newly-perceived particularities of the Russian context. They consequently attempted to establish new political strategies responding to the nature of Russia's social crisis by moving into uncharted (or at least untried) waters. In the chapter to follow, an outline of these views will be suggested – a step to lay out and open up for further exploration a set of problems linking the political and intellectual history of Russia and of the world at large.

6 History Teaches: The Frontiers of Political Imagination

> Without the 'dress rehearsal' of 1905 the victory of the October Revolution in 1917 would have been impossible.
>
> Vladimir Lenin

> History has to do with beings who are by nature capable of pursuing conscious ends.
>
> Mark Bloch

A. STOLYPIN AND REVOLUTION FROM ABOVE

To hammer home a point, the originality claimed for the strategies of those political leaders of Russia whom we are now to discuss was not a matter of some abstract 'newness', full of coherence or finality. Elements of views already expressed and borrowed were integrated with new ideas, as well as with pragmatic devices and tactical compromises. The result was very often contradictory and ever in flux. What united them, made them particular and provided for their political impact was their analytical vitality – their ability to leave behind the reigning assumptions of the past and to move into uncharted waters while reacting to the unexpected Russia which came to light in its revolution. On a personal level, this ability was underpinned by the capacity to be merciless enough towards (or distanced enough from) one's own social and intellectual origins and to 'think big', that is, to be able to go beyond intellectual tinkerings toward grand designs of social reconstruction. The outcome depended on the general social context but also on the ability of the leaders to pursue effective political tactics and in particular to tie together a coalition of allies and lead them in the harsh political confrontations which inevitably resulted from challenging holy cows and their loyal cowmen.

As from 1906, this stand was associated on the government's side

236

with Peter Stolypin. Much has been said by his aides, enemies and biographers to show the extent to which his programmes were borrowed from other people's views and from the many projects which gathered dust in the archives of the Russian Ministry of Interior.[1] The point is well taken, Stolypin was not the inventor of the substantive elements of the reforms associated with his name. What he did was to give them particular integration and justification in the light of a revolution, to back them up with the authority of a man who as the counter-revolutionaries dragonslayer had become for a moment the darling of Russia's rulers, and to put at their service the combined administrative resources of the Prime Minister's office and the Ministry of the Interior. All this was linked with a powerful personality which basked in public drama. Vigorous, youngish (at 43, he was Russia's youngest minister), hard-working, ambitious and proud, a splendid parliamentary rhetorician of unbending monarchist loyalty, he was to be remembered by friend and foe alike as the 'last great defender of the autocracy'.[2]

Stolypin's general design for leading the Russian tsardom into a new era (and becoming its 'second Bismarck' in the parlance of his days) was defeated in its major parts by Russia's conservative lobby. Of the inheritance and debris left, only one major piece of actual legislation was passed and followed up by administrative efforts – the landownership and land-consolidation measures. They consequently came to be referred to as 'The Stolypin Reform'. In fact, as recently stressed by a major Soviet historian of the period, what was at issue was 'a package of reforms' linked by internal logic (*stroinost'*) into a new political course.[3] The package carried a vision of a new Russia – the 'great Russia', which in a famous speech Stolypin contrasted with the 'great upheavals' which in his view were professed and preferred by the radicals and the revolutionaries.[4] At its core was as much the transformation of Russia's rural society – that is, of 80 per cent of its people – as the design to transform and make more effective the machinery of its state. Simultaneously, the foreign relations of Russia were to become more pacific, the ethno-religious 'merchant minorities' of Russia (as prominent in it as in many of the contemporary 'Developing Societies') were to be brought closer into the national political and economic processes,[5] public education was to improve and a national welfare system was to be established for the urban wage-workers. Once the administration was overhauled and the rural society transformed (and the ground thereby cut from under the feet of the SRs, whose impact on the communalist peasantry Stolypin

considered the main direct danger to the tsardom)[6] Russia would
move toward what later generations would call a 'self-sustained
growth' of wealth, efficiency and culture and of the associated
political might. Then as before, social spontaneity was to be linked to
energetic government intervention. A short and clearly-defined span
of time was assigned to this programme – 'twenty years of internal
and external peace' after which by Stolypin's promise 'one will not be
able to recognise contemporary Russia'.[7] Stolypin's initial plans were
spelled out in the Prime Minister's opening speech to the second
Duma in 1907. The steps proclaimed most urgent were to be not only
the repression of revolutionaries but also, the dismantling of
communal landholding and administrative reforms, which included
(besides the officialdom of the Ministry of Interior) that of the
elected municipalities, the courts and the police. This was to be
linked to, or followed by, a number of other provisions concerning
the rebuilding of the army and navy, the elevation of the legal rights
of the Old Believers (the 'sectarians' to the official Orthodox church)
and of the trading rights of Jews, the extension of the railways, a
wage-labour insurance and pension scheme, the eventual introduction of compulsory public education, the formalisation of new civic
rights and a tax reform.[8] Stolypin's hard-nosed monarchism and 'law
and order' zeal was the most visible. ('You will not scare us' he
barked back at the furious onslaught from opposition deputies which
followed his promise of further repressions by a government which
would be 'unyielding' and 'purely Russian').[9] He made his point clear
as much by setting up Military Courts and mounting executions as by
dispersing the Duma in a governmental *coup d'état* which changed
the electoral law. But this full-scale counter-revolutionary was well
aware from the outset that 'reforms are necessary in times of
revolution because the revolution was born to a considerable degree
from the shortcomings of the social system. Only to fight revolution is
to remove the results and not the causes . . . In places where the
government defeated the revolution [Prussia, Austria] it did so not by
the exclusive use of force but by using its strength to place itself at the
head of the reforms'.[10]

   In 1906, during the period which passed between the dispersal of
the first Duma and the convocation of the second one, Stolypin's
government legislated by decree major elements of its agrarian
reform. The tactic adopted was to show clearly that the initiative
came from the government and not from the parliamentarians, whose
unreliability had by now come to be expected. Under Section 87 of

the new Fundamental Law such decrees had the power of law as long
as they were presented to the Duma when it reconvened and until
they were decided in the ordinary process of legislation (that is, voted
on by the Duma and the State Council, and authorised or refused by
the tsar). In one of his last speeches, in 1911, Stolypin bitterly
described the actual legislative process as a repetitive sequence in
which a government project was presented to the Duma – was
accepted there but suffered radicalising amendments – was sent to the
State Council for confirmation – and was thrown out by its
conservative majority, never to become law. According to this
testimony, the result was a 'kingdom of macaroni' (parliamentary
slang for the multiplication of insignificant laws), where nothing was
done regarding the passage of fundamental reforms.[11] But that was
still to come. The major part of Stolypin's decrees of 1906 evolved
painlessly enough into the agrarian law of 1910. By that time it was
actually being implemented for more than three years. The sequence
of 'agrarian' degrees began on 12 and 27 August 1906 with the
transfer to the Peasants' Bank of tsar-and-crown lands to be sold to
peasants at 80 per cent of their market value. In October the
peasants' duty to seek communal permission for inter-family partition
of land and for a passport to travel outside the village were cancelled.
The right of the Land Chiefs to arrest and to fine peasants at will was
also abolished. On 9 November came the most important ingredient
in this line of legislation – the rights of the heads of every peasant
household to privatise the communal lands which they held in use.[12]
Simultaneously came the right to demand the transformation of land
strips into consolidated holdings (or else to receive money compensa-
tions from the commune for those strips which could not be united).
A decision by 2/3 later allowed that one half of its households was
now sufficient to have a repartitional commune abolished altogether
with all its lands becoming the private property of their holders. On
15 November mortgaging of peasant communal land was permitted,
opening a new dimension for the activities of the Peasants' Bank,
whose funds were considerably extended. A number of additional
steps were to complete those reforms. A project was put in motion by
which family land property was to give way to private ownership.[13]
An administrative network was set up aiming to advance communal
and inter-communal land-divisions and land-consolidation measures
and especially the establishment of homesteads (*khutora*). Such
single-plot farms separated from the villages were officially declared
the optimal form of smallholding agriculture.[14] They were favoured

when land sales by the state-owned Peasants' Bank were conducted, when state credits were granted, and when communal land was privatised. State land was offered for colonisation in Asian Russia and the Caucasus, which was now to benefit from some financial support. Later, in 1910, in the process of turning the decree of 9 November 1906 into law the State Council 'stiffened it up' by adding a provision by which all communal lands which had not undergone land redivision since 1861 were privatised at once and the communes which held them declared extinct. The smooth passage of Stolypin's agrarian decrees into laws was due to the fact that for once the bulk of the Russian bureaucracy, the squiredom and the tsar's immediate social circle (the *Camarilla* to the Russian literate public) the Russian monarchist reformers as well as most of its conservatives were in accord.[15] Even the main constitutionalist opposition in the Duma, the KDs, objected mainly to the way the reform was implemented – its imposition on the peasants – but not to the principle of land privatisation, the establishment of homesteads or the colonisation efforts in Siberia.

The second leg of the initial stage of Stolypin's grand project was to be the administrative reform. Part of it was explicitly related to the pending privatisation of peasant lands and to the declared wish 'to absorb' the Russian peasants as a consequence into 'society at large'. To do so, all the particular institutions related to the peasant social estate such as the peasant *volost'* and its court would have to be replaced by generic, that is by non-social-estate authorities.[16] The aim of the administrative reform, however, was much broader than simple adjustment to the new land-holding scheme. It was also explicitly seen as 'not only a pragmatic but a political reform'.[17] It was to form a major step in a line of prolonged changes in the nature and organisation of the tsardom.

The administrative reform project included for every province (*guberniya*) the establishment of a provincial executive and the extension of the governor's authority. The senior provincial staff, their training and salaries were to be enhanced. Authorities due to be elected not by the peasants only were to be established in each *volost'* and in the larger settlements. A major change was to take place at the district (*uezd*) level of administration bridging the province and the *volost'*. Every such district was to receive an appointed governor instead of the existing system in which the local Marshal of Nobility was considered the senior official of a vague coalition of *uezd* authorities. The *zemstvos'* franchise was to be extended. Even more radical changes were considered but shelved in view of the tsar's hostility toward decentralisation (in particular the idea of dividing Russia into nine major regions of considerable autonomy not unlike the USA 'states' or the German *Länders*).[18]

Further steps were to complement these reforms. A new lowest ring of elected Judges of the Peace was to be established. The police were to be shaken up and reformed, their status and salaries improved, their executives to link directly with the more sophisticated *gendarmerie*. The elected *zemstvo* authorities were to be spread to those provinces in which they did not yet operate. This was particularly significant for the thorny issue of the western provinces where their extensive landownership, under the existing regulations would have given a majority to those elected by the Polish nobility. To counter this Stolypin championed ethnic electoral colleges and further extension of popular franchise in these areas which would extend the representation of the mostly Ukrainian and Belorussian peasantry there. Restriction of the electoral strength of the massive Jewish population was to enhance simultaneously the relative status of the Poles in the towns as the extension of elected urban authorities took place in western Russia.

Other legislative projects of Stolypin's government were put forward simultaneously. These were to abolish the legal handicaps of the Old Believers, and some of the restrictions concerning Jews. The administration of the Orthodox church was to be improved. Some welfare provisions were also considered: the state-supervised health insurance, the pension for the workers, and a law concerning universal primary education, began the long process of becoming laws.

The turning points of the Stolypin era were his defeats over the legislation concerning the administration reforms and that of the 'minorities' rights. Both were engineered by the right-wing opposition to his government, who treated the reform of the local authorities with open hostility. Early in 1907, the delegates to the third congress of the United Nobility and many members of the State Council declared their opposition and offered systematic arguments against these projects. A leading figure in both these institutions, an ex-minister of state, Stashinskii, suggested that such changes would promote the take-over of the local authorities by 'people of the grasping entrepreneurial type' who would ally with the inteligencia's 'third element' – a coalition of all ills in the eyes of conservative nobility.[19] As explicit was the reported surge of salon gossip within the right-wing society circles of St Petersburg the gist of which was that 'one should not expect anything good from Stolypin and what is needed is a different government headed by P. Durnovo'.[20] By 1908 a coalition of Stolypin-haters was clearly visible in Russia's political Right. It consisted of powerful groups within the State Council and the United Nobility as much as of the senior Orthodox clergy, many top-ranking bureaucrats who felt themselves out of place *vis-à-vis* the new political experiments and most of the *Camarilla*, allied with the extreme right-wing politicians of the Duma and some journalists close to them. The ambivalence of the position of a Prime Minister who was to act as the tsar's servant, a bureaucrat and also a parliamentary politician, was fully exploited. The tactic of attack chosen was to undermine the tsar's support of Stolypin by the claim that the Prime Minister sided with the conservative Duma against the hostile opposition to it by the super-conservative and truly loyal reactionaries – in other words, positioned himself against the monarch. At the same time, steps were taken to demolish Stolypin's tacit alliance with the Octobrist majority of the third Duma to make his government helpless all along the institutional network of Russian official politics. The prerogatives of the crown were chosen as the main focus of the anti-Stolypin political gossip and challenge.[21] This attack was to succeed on all scores.

Despite the sound and fury of Stolypin's effort he was gradually losing ground and retreating under the right-wing pressure. For his authority and position he depended on the tsar whose eventual attitude toward Stolypin was well defined in the tsar's 1911 conversation with Kokovtsov about the functions of a Prime Minister in Russia. 'Do not follow the example of Stolypin', the tsar said, 'who in some ways has always tried to outshine me' (*'menya zaslonyat'*).[22] The tsar was only too ready to accept the whispers that Stolypin did not take the necessary steps to defend the prerogatives of the crown; time and time again he censored Stolypin and refused some of the laws passed with government consent, thus making it clear who was the master.

Stolypin fought back by argument and pressure, by administrative devices and by the use of the newsmen (especially the government's newspaper *Rossiya* set up for that purpose). On the other side, the right-wing lobby engaged in increasingly public anti-Stolypin campaign. In March 1908 Stolypin's project of administrative reforms (watered down first by his own government colleagues and then in committee) was publicly declared by the fourth congress of United

Nobility to be not only 'inadvisable' but 'actually harmful'. The hierarchs of the Orthodox Church loudly attacked the extension of tolerance to the Old Believers. Prince V. Meshcherskii, a journalist who had the tsar's ear, argued in his newspaper against the reform of the local courts. None of these reforms were eventually to become legislation – some stopped by the Duma, others by the State Council. The extension of the trading rights of Jews managed to scrape through both houses, but at its signature stage was refused by the tsar. In the meantime, attempts were being made to get rid of Stolypin himself. He survived, but at the price of what was sadly summarised by one of his closest aides who wrote: 'at the end of the day he dissipated himself in compromises'.[23]

Things came to a head in 1909 when Stolypin submitted his resignation after being accused of lack of zeal in defending the tsar's authority. The tsar did not accept this resignation, but Stolypin's weak spot was clearly exposed. He reacted by an attempt to appease his right-wing critics and the tsar's court by transferring the accent of his declarations and new legislative proposals to the Russification of the 'peripheries' – playing the nationalist card.[24] The autonomy of Finland was attacked and badly diminished. The area of Khelm was separated from the Polish provinces (in answer to the demands of the local xenophobic clergy of the Orthodox church). Steps were being taken to tighten up on the execution of the regulations restricting Jews from residing outside their Pale of Residence, that is, the districts to which they were legally limited. The tactical accord between Stolypin, the Duma majority, the State Council, and the tsar was re-established with remarkable speed while the project concerning Finland was becoming law. However, it failed to re-establish Stolypin's credibility with the right wing or to soften the legislative passage of his other proposals. With growing encouragement from royal kinsmen, friends and dignitaries within the tsar's closest environment, the hunt of Stolypin continued, while many of those who were friendly to him in the Duma found it increasingly difficult to support him in his 'turn to the right'.

Stolypin's enemies eventually 'got him' next time in March 1911 over the legislation concerning the establishment of the elected *zemstvo* authorities in the western provinces. The project seemed an easy one to pass and indeed was accepted by the Duma and sent to the State Council which showed every sign of intending to accept it in turn. But an ambush was laid there for Stolypin by a coalition led by P. Durnovo and V. Trepov. The argument used was that ethnic electoral colleges would promote the tsardom's disunity while the extension of franchise was too democratic to accept. The law was rejected demonstrating to all and sundry the Prime Minister's weakness.

Stolypin reacted furiously, demanding that the tsar should prorogue the Duma and the State Council and enact by decree the freshly-rejected legislation. He also demanded the punishment of those who tripped him up, threatening resignation. For a moment his will prevailed – the tsar signed the decree and had Durnovo and Trepov ordered out of St Petersburg. Then all hell broke loose. The tsar was furious at his hand being forced. The anti-Stolypin right wing was indignant with the way its leaders were treated and plotted vengeance. Stolypin's Duma allies were outraged at such blatant anti-constitutional use of a legal trick.[25] Stolypin's enemies were closing in for the kill. By mid-1911 he was politically dead and he knew it. His removal was only a matter of time and even the manner of it was picked by the tsar's circle – Stolypin was to become the next Viceroy of the Caucasus, far enough from St Petersburg and any real policy-making. This was prevented by his death. Two controversial pieces of evidence relate to the last months in the life of Stolypin. In 1953, A. Zenkovskii informed Stolypin's daughter who lived in the USA that he had discovered notes dictated to him by Stolypin in May 1911 which concerned a long-term project for the further political reconstruction of Russia. It was apparently a draft of a memorandum to the tsar, possibly planned as a last shot before or at Stolypin's dismissal. Stolypin's family accepted the authenticity of those notes.[26] Some historians have been sceptical but no clear-cut argument has been presented to refute this text.[27] In its essential part the memorandum further extended what Stolypin attempted to achieve during the five years of his prime ministership and would indicate that his retreat in 1909–11 was against his better judgement. The core of this proposal was: (i) to treble the state budget [from 3 to 10 million roubles per annum] and use this increase in the state's economic power for major structural investments, the improvement of administrative machinery and for welfare provisions; (ii) to decentralise the administration by extending considerably the powers of the *zemstvo* and to offer full legal equality to the non-Russian groups in the population of the empire; (iii) to extend the Prime Minister's authority by ensuring that all ministers report to the tsar only with the PM's knowledge and must be appointed with the PM's consent.

Second, Stolypin was killed in September 1911 by a double agent, D. Bagrov, a man who was both an *okhrana* (political police) employee and also a member of the anarchist movement.[28] His killing and the amazing incompetence of the officers in charge of security came to be believed by many (including Stolypin's own family) to be the result of a deliberate plot by the police officers. The man particularly charged with this plot was P. Kurlov, the Vice-Minister of Interior in charge of the Gendarmerie. Kurlov was appointed against Stolypin's will by the tsar's order and was aware of Stolypin's wish to have him dismissed for incompetence. Also, the Chief of Gendarmes was known to act behind the back of his minister and against him.[29] The senators who carried out the preliminary investigation of Stolypin's death decided to charge Kurlov and three more police officers with *prima facie* gross negligence but all the accused were given the tsar's pardon before the full investigation began. Those who have since tried to untangle this affair were divided sharply between some who assumed police provocation and others who believed Bagrov to be a genuine loner, who, in his wish to redeem himself with anarchist comrades whom he betrayed, killed Stolypin on his own initiative, after having led the *okhrana* by the nose. The most recent review of evidence, by A. Avrekh, made him conclude that a police officers' plot was indeed hatched and that in the shooting of Stolypin Bagrov acted as their tool.[30]

* * *

The half decade of political drama associated with Stolypin has been open to various interpretations. His image in the works of historians outside Russia varied from that of a patriotic defender of new democracy based on Russia's peasant smallholders, to an early version of xenophobic fascism in the service of the Russian tsar, a true scion of Russia's reactionary nobility. The Soviet historians inevitably began their discussion of the man and of the period by defining them after Lenin, as 'Bonapartist',[31] but it was the interpretation of that usage which varied. The most significant division has been expressed in recent years in the debate between V. Dyakin and A. Avrekh. Dyakin believed Stolypin to represent monarchist reformism reflecting the 'relative autonomy' of the state apparatus and its specific goals and self-images as the final arbiter of the interest of Russia. Stolypin's reformism would confront not only the Left opposition but also a Legitimist reactionary bloc of interests and tendencies entrenched in the formal and informal political institutions of Russia.[32] This view was refused by Avrekh to whom Stolypin represented the same reactionary forces as the United Nobility, rooted in both cases in the similar class interests of the squiredom. The right-wing attack on Stolypin was in that view no more than a squabble of little significance ('of tenth magnitude' in Avrekh's words), a rift between the more parochial members and those more capable of a broader outlook within the same single camp.[33] Stolypin himself, according to this view, was a mundane and accidental man at the top (and nothing like the truly outstanding Witte). His defeat was insignificant and created barely a ripple as far as the history of Russia was concerned.

The vehemence of Avrekh's retort to Dyakin was remarkable, he charged his adversary with repeating 'Octobrist views' while 'having neglected an accepted position of Soviet historiography'[34] – quite a claim if one remembers its political meaning. This must have expressed some connotation far remote from the issue in hand and the days of Stolypin. It would also have to do with the scanty evidence sustaining Avrekh's image of a singularly reactionary Stolypin. Leaving aside guilt by association (Guchkov of the Octobrists could be awesome, yet still right on this particular point), the main evidence cited against the assumption of a substantive division between Stolypin and the United Nobility was the later claims that it was they who dictated Stolypin's policies where agrarian reform was concerned. Such self-images or propaganda despatches mean little in isolation. The bitterness of the anti-government attacks mounted by Russia's reactionaries and the counter-measures by Stolypin (as well as his attempts at a compromise which they shunned) do not appear as a partners' tiff while sharing out common loot. The overt goals of Stolypin and of the reactionaries differed substantively and consistently.[35] They fought each other bitterly. If self-evaluation by contemporaries is to be taken into account it should begin with Stolypin himself and his closest aides. By 1909, while pursuing policies consequent on the lessons drawn from the 1905–07 revolution and the wish to avoid its repetition, none of them had any doubts as to who in the 'Establishment' tried to destroy Stolypin and why.[36] Nor did they doubt that Stolypin was attacked from the Right by those who 'did not learn a thing and did not forget a thing'. The Russian ruling elite also knew that the fight between Stolypin and his right-wing opponents was a fight to the death and that its result could be central to Russia's destiny. So it was, unless one is to assume that the Russian nobility and its tsar were engaging in a class suicide pre-ordained by inevitable laws of history.

My own general view of that matter has already been expressed.[37] In a world in which Franco could rule Spain for a generation only to die in bed of a presidential palace and while Khomeini still leads a Persian *Jihad*, to deduce actual history from evolutionist Laws of Progress is unwise. While historiography has its place, specific results of political battles and particular 'roads' and 'turns' which societies follow are not deducible from it. Also, looking at the patterns of social change, one can see in addition to those which are general and those which are unique *several* significant, different and typical roads leading from pre-capitalism. Of those, the one we tend to describe today as that of 'the developing societies', possibly still an over-generalisation, was typical of Russia at the turn of the century. In 1904-06 Stolypin discovered this Russia which differed from all he had been taught by his peers and his teachers to accept and he had the courage to face that. Consequently, he fought for a post-1906 Russia which would move substantially from the one in which he grew up and which his own social class and his tsar still preferred. The question is: what was the significance of his way? Also since then Stolypin-like reforms have stubbornly reappeared all around the world.[38] Why should it be so? Finally, Stolypin was defeated not by laws of history, but by actual political forces. What were they?

The essentially pragmatic turn of mind of Stolypin and his close aides meant that the theoretical content of what he attempted was never fully spelled out as a coherent theory. They lacked an Adam Smith or Friederich List who elsewhere had established the general principals underlying the economic strategies, present and future of the respective governments and rulers. Russia's best theoretical minds were otherwise engaged. Yet, in their own practical way the policies of Stolypin and his team were to make theoretical history for their country and for countries far away (it was to be mediated by people such as A. Gerschenkron of Harvard or critically by P. Baran of Stanford at the very core of the 'development theory', 'modernisa-tion', and 'dependency' debates defining economic strategies the world over in the 1950s to 1970s). By this test as well as that of the consequent struggle for the structural transformation of society, Stolypin was a revolutionary in thought and deed, even if such a compliment would make him blink. Also, the possibility of his success should not be excluded purely on theoretical grounds.

Stolypin's strategy took into account not only European past history and a wish 'to catch up with Europe' but also some major elements of Russia's particularity in doing so. The classical political economy of Adam Smith and Ricardo reflected and explored the first capitalist surge in Europe. It was this theory's *first amendment* by Friederich List which has come to define the policies of 'the second wave' of industrialisation in Germany and Japan. The same holds for the government policies of Russia under the stewardship of Witte. The essence of this approach lay in the policies of state intervention via 'protectionism', that is, the partial control and stimulation of markets, investments, credits and profits in order to secure the growth of the 'infant industries' before the benefit of world-wide free-market economy could be reaped by the country in question. The lessons of the 1899–1907 crisis of economic downturn, military defeat and revolution taught a few of the brightest Russian bureaucrats (including Witte, who was not, however, given the opportunity to put his new understanding into practice)[39] that a second amendment to classical economics must be introduced if the country was to achieve the coveted economic growth and 'modernity'. In that view, only then could the 'first amendment' economic strategies begin to work as they did in Germany, leading in turn to a stage at which the classical economic prescriptions and goals could be put to use while Russia would emerge as an equal partner in the world capitalist market. The *second amendment* of the Classical School of political economy was the new understanding that the radical social transformation of rural society and state apparatus – a Revolution From Above – must take place before (or at least simultaneously with) the protectionist industralisation policies. To leave this to spontaneity (the protectionist defences accepted) would produce a bottleneck and a crisis, bringing the country's economy to a standstill. While never stated in those terms by its authors, Stolypin's 'package of reforms' and the further steps consequent to it, aimed at 'the second amendment'. This programme to resolve the Russian crisis makes good logic for the contemporary context of many 'developing societies'. This is why it still has the power to captivate planners and politicians. But good logic alone does not determine political outcome. During the period 1906–11 the question was that of the ability of Stolypin 'to make his strategy stick' – to demobilise its enemies and to mobilise social power to execute what he had in mind.

Against Stolypin 'the hangman', stood all those forces which fought the autocracy in 1905–07. To the radicals he personified the tsardom's repressive nature. For the non-Russians he also symbolised

Russian nationalism. But against his revolutionary designs for extensive reform stood also the reactionaries and the conservatives of officialdom and squiredom, made more powerful by the defeat of the revolution and the personal preferences and characteristics of the autocratic ruler who sulked in the Winter Palace. The peasant 'separators' did not show political support for Stolypinite progress either, while the opposition of the peasant communes was at times desperate and often effective.[40] The agrarian component of the reforms produced a wave of privatisation and colonisation of lands, but by 1911 both were tailing off while the government's pet homesteads were established on less than 1/10 of the land privatised.[41] In party political terms, Stolypin's administration was tacitly allied with the Octobrists. When by 1909 Stolypin was forced to turn to the right, his main support in the Duma became the so-called Nationalists, a parliamentary faction with little coherence and without any real organisation in the localities. This meant a shift from a party which was manifestly weak in its political and intellectual resources to a group with no such resources at all.

Stolypin's programme was a 'revolution from above' without major social classes, parties, or public organisations to back it. The incredible aspect of the tale, therefore, was the paper-thin nature of the political support Stolypin commanded while striving for a major social transformation. It rested with a remarkably small number of people who nevertheless decided, to put it into practice.[42] What made them ready and, up to a point, able to face this challenge was their high office in an extremely powerful bureaucracy and the arrogance of Russian dignitaries who believed themselves representative of 400 years of Russia's uninterrupted growth and of an autocratic monarchy. Like some of the Russian liberal intellectuals of the nineteenth century they believed that the main virtue of autocracy was its ability to disregard social circumstances and any 'particularist' visions, to stand above law and to challenge the course of history by bending circumstances and imposing what is 'best for Russia'. However, to achieve their goal of social transformation they needed 'cadres', an effective 'general staff' of specialists with theoretical imagination and a sufficient army of executors whose zeal would exceed simple bureaucratic orderliness. Some shift in the nature of the staff which directed the agrarian reform could be noticed: from parochial and patriarchial Land Chiefs to the better skilled, more 'modern' and more professional officials of the new Ministry of Agriculture (the GUZZ).[43] But the focus of this effort was narrowly agricultural and local, the numbers of those involved working for the GUZZ small and their loyalty suspect. To be able to use the force of the state to transform Russia in the face of formidable opposition, Stolypin needed not only the tsar's good will, legislative support and economic resources, but an equivalent of the *oprichniki* of Tsar Ivan IV, or of the Land and Liberty intelligentsia 'going to the people', or else, of the peasant sons komsomolites and policemen of Stalin's drive in 1929–37. Neither the core of Russia's political activists nor the conservative nobles, nor the supposed peasant beneficiaries provided it. As for Stolypin, he did not even understand that one needs a corps of revolutionaries to make a revolution.

The period which followed indicates how much of Stolypin's failure to use the state to restructure Russia was not accidental in terms of the political forces involved. Under Kokovtsev the momentum given by Stolypin's initiatives proceeded for a while, the law of workers' insurance was finally enacted. The new Prime Minister was greeted in a friendly enough manner by the right-wing press, but within a short time the reactionary attack on him began along lines fairly similar to those of the hunting down of Stolypin. Men and ideas representing even partly the 'revolution from above' were out of the question. The Legitimists who made the running wanted nothing less than a return to the pre-1905 ministers acting as the personal executives of the tsar, and parliamentary institutions limited to advisory functions only. With the imposition of a Minister of Interior to whom Kokovtsov objected (in 1912) and Kokovtsev's eventual dismissal (in 1914) the first of those aims was achieved and the Prime Minister's authority reduced. A new governmental *coup d'état* aimed at further restricting the Duma's functions was under intensive consideration in 1914 when the First World War began. No other suggestion of a substantial legislative change surfaced within the Establishment during the last years of the tsardom.

The experience of the First World War showed the tsar's government for what it was – as incompetent and corrupt as it had been reactionary and servile. By 1915 the conservative fourth Duma was united against the government policies to the same extent to which the second revolutionary Duma of 1907 had been. So was the clandestine opposition. On the government side there was no-one of Stolypin's calibre as a policeman, an administrator and a 'revolutionary from above'. The war was being lost, with the army command and the state apparatus demoralised accordingly. Outside the palaces and 'clean quarters', the offices and the command posts, a plebeian resentment was growing as was the dismay of 'the educated public' and the unease of the rank-holders. When the next revolution came in 1917 it did not come as a bloody battle of major forces locked in combat. The monarchy simply fell apart at the lightest push. There was nobody and nothing of social substance to stand by it.

B. TROTSKY AND THE PERMANENT REVOLUTION

Seen from the vantage point of a different world half a century later, it was the Marxists of Lenin's brand who offered the one alternative both to the tsardom's reactionaries and to the monarchist radicals. The literature available and the usual biases involved in reading history backwards reinforce that view. In fact, the picture was much more complex, the more so when seen through the eyes of contemporaries. To Stolypin, the most dangerous challenge to the tsardom came, as stated, from the SRs and their possible ability to move politically the commune-bound peasants. To many others, a powerful parliament led by the KDs – Russia's most accomplished rhetoricians, lawyers, academics and writers – was the natural sequence to the autocracy as Russia proceeded to modernise and civilise. In the actual political life of the crucial year of 1917, it was the PSR's peasant electoral support which gave the absolute majority of Russia's 'one man, one vote' Constitutional Assembly of 1917.

The people who came to rule post-revolutionary Russia were its 'orthodox' Marxists – indeed, proudly and insistently so, but to say that does not yet sufficiently define the victors of the 1917–20 revolution and war. Of Russia's orthodox Marxists who in 1901–03 delimited themselves as 'the *Iskra* supporters' many did not all belong to the winning side of 1917–20. Nor did the 1903 factional divisions of the RSDWP provide a clear-cut explanation for it. To be sure, those who came to rule Russia defined themselves as Bolsheviks, but their leadership and cadre included by then a massive dose of those who were Mensheviks in 1903, while their political 'line' differed extensively from the one adopted by the 'majority' at the second congress of RSDWP.[1] At the same time, the latter-day Mensheviks who opposed the new regime (while consistently refusing to fight it weapon-in-hand) included in 1917–20 many leading Bolsheviks from the early days. Georgia in those days was ruled by the local SDs who defined themselves as Mensheviks, but whose politics differed considerably and increasingly from their Russian namesakes.[2]

A more meaningful way to divide the different 'orthodox' Marxists of 1903–17 is to single out those whose political strategy prevailed in 1917–20 – that is, those who succeeded in attaining, managing, and, at least for a time, retaining state power then. Such grouping clearly correlates with the nature of the political lessons drawn from the 1905–07 revolution by singling out an otherwise heterogeneous category of those 'orthodox Marxists' who were capable of supreme heresies. There were three major sub-categories of these drawn from three different sections of the RSDWP of 1903–17; the inter-faction group which strove for the party's reunification (*primiriteli*), the Mensheviks and the Bolsheviks. Using single names to define political approaches and groupings these can be identified by the names of Trotsky, Zhordaniya and Lenin.

The Marxist wave of 1890s represented a major cultural revolution within the ranks of the Russian radical opposition.[3] The ideological drive at its inception came from the insistent efforts of Plekhanov and his allies to establish a clear dividing line between themselves and the Populists and, particularly, the Revolutionary–Populist tradition which was treated by them as the utopian pre-history of Russia's revolutionary movement, now coming of age. The most important elements of the new Marxists historiography which came to underlie the political strategy and tactics of the Russian SDs were:

1. The acceptance of progress, understood as the inevitable rise in the forces of production market relations, mechanisation and in the size of the capitalist enterprises, paving the necessary road toward bourgeois democratisation and eventual socialism (as opposed to the moralising criticism of capitalist development by the Populists).

2. The scientific necessity to assume a two-stage development of Russia in which a bourgeois revolution and the subsequent blossoming of capitalism under a parliamentary regime must first lay the necessary foundations for a socialist mass movement and the socialist revolution (as opposed to the classical Populists' belief in the possibility of 'jumping a stage' and proceeding at once to reconstruct Russia in a socialist way).

3. A class analysis which singled out the industrial proletariat as the only consistently revolutionary class of our times. It was also the only force unequivocally supportive of the eventual socialist transformation, equated with the proletarian rule at the second stage of Russia's future history (as opposed to the Revolutionary–

Populists' assumption that in the face of the capitalism-creating state, the peasants and the intelligentsia may be as revolutionary as industrial workers, and that all of these should be treated as different wings of the same labouring class striving for socialism).

4. The stern tactical objection to terrorist attacks. (It was still accepted as possible strategem by the Plekhanov-led Emancipation of Labour Group in the 1880s, but came to be treated later by the Orthodox Marxists as a specific Populist badge and as a misdirection of the party efforts and cadres from the necessary day-to-day work of agitation within the working class.) The alternative goal was to work for the establishing of a mass party of the proletariat, for which the German SDs acted as a model.

5. Another tactical conclusion by the Orthodox Marxists was to lay particular stress on the separation of the working-class organisations and SD leadership from any 'bourgeois or petty bourgeois' organisation. (In a similar spirit, the Marxist parties throughout Europe refused until 1917 to join governments presiding over the bourgeois stage of history.)

This characteristic of organised Marxism in the Russian context as against their PSR fellow socialists (and eventually, fellow members of the Second Socialist International) were central to the way RSDWP reacted to the 1905–07 experience. Already in its early days it became clear that compared with the other parties of the International it was more doggedly 'orthodox', more militant, and more vituperative in its language of factional confrontations, to which the otherwise lordly Plekhanov was the first to contribute with gusto.[4] Also, the most prominent 'Russians' inside the German SD party and the leading lights of the second International, Rosa Luxemburg and Parvus, led there the challenge to any political strategy limited to parliamentary advance. In that light, Karl Kautsky expressed then the hope that the revolutionary élan and ideological puritanism of the Russian Marxists would rejuvenate the whole of the European Social Democracy. The Russian daily context of harsh repression met by the all-sacrificing political action, the total challenge and deep commitment, defined the RSDWP's high revolutionary qualities. The other dimension of its particularity were the nineteenth-century ideological roots from which Russian Marxism grew. In ethnic Russia it was the revolutionary experience of the People's Will party which was consistently argued against by the Orthodox Marxists, but which deeply affected their positions just the same.[5] At the 'peripheries' of the empire these earlier roots could be found in the traditions of independence struggles and/or the confrontation of the ethno-classes there.

*   *   *

The main position associated with Trotsky's 1906 contribution to unorthodoxy was the 'permanent revolution' thesis. It had its direct beginnings in the analytical work of Parvus (and, if one is to assume silent borrowing, also in the writings of M. Gotz of the SRs).[6] A. Helphand, known by his pen-name Parvus, was a brilliant and controversial journalist who grew up in Odessa. In common with many in his generation he received his initial ideological education from the Russian populist literature and later became a Marxist. He emigrated and found his second home in the German SD party.[7] Parvus shared with Rosa Luxemburg and very few of the other German SDs a more internationalist and 'globalist' grasp of capitalism as well as socialism, and stressed, to the obvious surprise of his more parochial colleagues, the significance of the changing equation of international power between Europe and the new 'rising' countries – which, in his view, were Russia and the USA. Again unusually he often spoke about the particular problems of colonialism and stressed the possibility that a war (not just an economic crisis) could lead to a social revolution. To him, the nation-states had outlived their days; it was the international interdependence and especially the global economy which was all-important now. A Russian revolution would also have to be treated in terms of the general European processes. In the German SD, which adopted Parvus, he made his first mark by the violence of his attacks on the 'revisionists', especially on Volmar and Bernstein (he astonished his German comrades by asking for the expulsion of E. Bernstein from their party, a view in line with that of Plekhanov). Parvus's tactical suggestions aimed to radicalise the party's activities. In particular, he called for the use of workers' strikes as an intrument of political attack. Parvus often acted as a major interpreter of the Russian Empire for the German SDs.[8] The characteristics of Russia, in his view, were defined mostly by its multi-level backwardness. The Russian urban society was particularly underdeveloped even when compared with Russia as a whole. Its 'China-like' cities, did not incorporate the mass of craftsmen and small capitalists who formed the class base from which the radical bourgeois struggles and regimes of Western Europe drew their strength. That and the major significance of foreign capital in Russia made its native capitalists exceptionally weak. The Russian peasantry (and the rural craftsmen within it) was numerically massive, but too disjointed and conservative to become a political force. The proletariat was therefore the only revolutionary power in Russia, a point which was true not only for the socialist stage of its future history, but also for its immediately forthcoming bourgeois transformation. He concurred in his view with the 1900 position of all the '*Iskra* group' members, but gave it a stronger sociological grounding. He was also ready to draw from it more radical conclusions.

While residing in Germany, Parvus maintained his links with the Russian revolutionaries. He wrote for their publications and helped them in a variety of ways (eight issues of *Iskra* were actually printed in a clandestine workshop established for that purpose in Parvus's personal flat in Munich). In 1904 he met Trotsky and they embarked on a few months of intensive discussions. Parvus, then 37 and a major *enfant terrible* of the German SDs, and Trotsky, then 23 and a rising star of the RSDWP but at the time in conflict with both its Bolshevik and Menshevik factions,[9] struck up a friendship. As time went by the differences between them asserted themselves – Trotsky's powerful political leadership capacity (but with a particular blind spot for the working of party apparatus), his arrogant charisma and tightly focused energy, as against Parvus's egocentricity, inability to take effective command in day-to-day political actions, and his erratic multiplicity of moods and purposes. For the moment they suited each other. After 'Bloody Sunday' – 9 January 1905 – they met hastily again and while Trotsky departed immediately for Russia, Parvus proceeded to publish Trotsky's earlier booklet which developed the idea of massive and offensive political strikes as a way towards revolution. Parvus added to it a lengthy introduction arguing on behalf of himself as well as of Trotsky his 'backwardness' model and, as its conclusion, the view that because of the weakness of the Russian bourgeoisie it is the proletariat which must assume at once power by establishing a revolutionary workers' government dominated by the SDs – a shockingly new view which directly challenged the two-stage historiography of Russian orthodox Marxism.[10]

By the end of October Parvus went to Russia to join Trotsky, who was by then the vice-chairman and the moving spirit of the St Petersburg Soviet. After the arrest of the Soviet Trotsky proceeded to impress Russia with a spectacular speech at its trial. He then escaped from imprisonment to return to the very centre of Russian revolutionary politics in exile. After Trotsky's arrest, Parvus chaired a clandestine 'second Soviet' (which moved to take the place of the arrested members), but it failed to make much headway. Its members were rapidly rounded up by the police. Parvus was also arrested, managed to make his escape and left Russia and its politics for good. Trotsky's and Parvus's co-operation came to an end. Parvus was eventually to re-emerge in the public eye in the days of the First World War as a war-made millionaire and an agent for the German imperial government who was later to advise the SD ministers of the 1918 German republican government. He still considered himself a Marxist, but seemed the only man in Europe to believe it.[11]

In later days when Parvus became a dirty word in the socialist movement (and a 'non-person' to its literature), some historians came to believe or to pretend that the substance of 1905–17 Trotskyism was in fact fully authored by Parvus. That was not so, for while Trotsky adopted most of Parvus's general analysis he added to it some major conclusions specific to himself. Advancing from where Parvus's thought had stopped, he went on to establish an alternative strategy which was to play a major role in the Russian store of Marxist ideological unorthodoxy. Its essence was part of the political masterplan which the Bolsheviks adopted in April 1917.

Trotsky was one with Parvus in the assumption that 'the principal distinguishing characteristic of Russia's historical development was its limited nature'. They agreed as well that Russia's backwardness was 'determined by unfavourable natural conditions [which] delayed the process of social crystallisation and stamped the whole of our history with the features of extreme backwardness'[12] and that Russia lacked the marching army of radical capitalists because of the underdevelopment of its urban society. At the same time, neither of the erstwhile friends had much concern for things rural and especially for what Trotsky called 'the peasant knot of backwardness'.[13] As for political tactics, both sided with the Bolsheviks in objecting to any alliances with the KDs (which in view of the weakness of the Russian bourgeoisie became in this view its ideological substitution, but without the economic drive and the power of 'the real thing'). Only a proletarian attack could dislodge the tsardom and only a working-class revolutionary government dominated by the SDs could lead a post-revolutionary Russia. Trotsky gave greater emphasis to the significance of state power in defining the nature of Russian backwardness. Throughout his political life his attention to problems of state power remained particularly intense.[14]

Decisively for future political strategy, while Parvus's imagination stopped at a workers' post-revolutionary government which would accomplish the most democratic version of capitalism (the first bourgeois 'stage'), Trotsky made a further decisive step of suggesting that once set in motion the proletarian rule would necessarily intensify and would transcend bourgeois democracy and directly attack capitalist property. This would mean 'proletarian dictatorship' by a minority and a quick, direct march towards socialism, while the two-stage history of the future would not materialise at all in Russia. It also meant that the workers' rule would necessarily lead the capitalists elsewhere to move against it, to try to strangle it 'from the outside' (as in the case of France in 1789–93). The only way for the Russian revolution to succeed then would be to cross national frontiers, and to become an all-European revolution. Once set in motion the Russian revolution therefore was envisaged as ever-extending both in the depth of its social radicalism and in the broadness of its geographical spread, until the world at large was driven into it – a 'permanent' revolution. Fully understanding how far his views put him at odds with the reigning evolutionism of the Second International, Trotsky attacked head-on the 'stupid mistake . . . [of] historical analogies by which liberalism lives', that is, the use of the examples of 1789–93 and 1848 instead of the 'social analysis' of actuality (especially of the evidence of particular strengths of proletarian impact in 1905 as against the earlier European revolutions).[15] He knew well enough that he was not talking of liberals only.

The main reason why this astonishing conclusion was not dismissed at once by the SDs as an anti-Marxist relapse into Populism or as Utopian mysticism was Trotsky's clear 'Westernist' stress on the proletariat and on the supreme significance of economic progress as the guiding principle of political strategy. He even launched a sharp attack on Lenin's suggestion of 'the democratic dictatorship of workers and peasants'. In Trotsky's view, under no circumstances could peasants play an independent political role and/or form a party of their own, which made Lenin's idea backward-looking and unrealistic. The only viable revolutionary regime could be a workers' dictatorship, 'resting on' the peasant majority of the population and its good-will-cum-indifference, but in no way treating peasants as partners in state power. The fact that the transformation to socialism was to him an immediate aim made it all the more imperative. In the light of what was happening before Trotsky's eyes, his short-sightedness concerning peasants was quite remarkable. To him the 1905–07 revolution was defeated not through the strengths of the state or the weakness or mistakes of the revolutionaries, but by the stupidity (*tugodamonst'*) of the peasant soldiers.[16] In that view peasants did little of political substance in 1905, somewhat more in 1906, but their significance was altogether meagre. Expectations of a peasant uprising in 1906 simply proved Lenin's unrealistic attitude towards the peasantry. The PSR idea of 'socialisation' of all land was contrary to the peasants' real wish to hold on to their particular properties, which made the PSR claim to rural influence bogus. The Labour Faction of the Duma was to Trotsky but another proof of the fundamental social law of the city's hegemony over the countryside – the Labourites were simply led by the KDs, and when disappointed by them, began to follow the Social Democrats.[17] (He did not even bother to consider seriously the massive 1906 vote for the PSR in the workers' electoral college of St Petersburg, that is, Trotsky's 'own backyard' in terms of his most recent political action.)[18]

In the period of the post-1907 political decline of Russia's revolutionary movement Trotsky found himself essentially an out-sider. As for the main factions in the RSDWP, he proceeded to call for their unification while the actual gulf between them grew steadily. He was considered a Menshevik, but was at war with all of the Mensheviks' major leaders. In his distrust of the KDs he outdid the Bolsheviks. At the same time, his harsh anti-populism and anti-'peasantism' put him with the most conservative of the Mensheviks who harped back to the 1890s. His vision of a proletarian dictatorship aiming at socialism at once, to follow the end of the autocracy, was treated an oddity by both. Even the PSR moved away by then from such a view under the impact of its 'Marxisation' and its own brand-new two-stage theory produced by V. Chernov.

Yet it was the concept of 'permanent revolution' to which Deutscher was referring in concluding – justly – that Trotsky, 'for the rest of his days as leader of a revolution, as founder and head of an army, as protagonist of a new International and then as a hunted exile' was to 'defend and elaborate' after having it 'put in a nutshell in 1906'.[19] As for the RSDWP, Trotsky's ideas were too dramatic and, eventually, too relevant to be simply put to rest. So was the experience of the Soviet of St Petersburg as an embodiment of direct proletarian rule, a period and an experience about which the Russian socialists learned mostly from the writings of Trotsky and the publications which he edited.

By 1914 Trotsky was also becoming less isolated. Slowly a small but brilliant group of RSDWP activists and writers who disagreed with the Bolsheviks as well as with Mensheviks had grown up. The confrontation over the attitudes toward war led to further realignment which crystallised them still more. A number of them centred on the anti-war *Nashe slovo* published in Paris – Lunacharskii and Manuilskii of the ex-Bolsheviks, Trotsky, Antonov-Ovseenko, Ryazanov, Chicherin and Kolontai of the ex-Mensheviks.[20] All these were to play leading roles in the October revolution and the post-revolutionary Bolshevik regime. In 1917 this group came partly to overlap with the *mezhraiontsy* – the so-called Inter-Borough SDs of St Petersburg, who considered themselves neither Bolsheviks nor Mensheviks and adopted Trotsky as their leader on his return from exile.[21] They rapidly allied with and in July 1917 joined the Bolshevik/Communist party and its Central Committee.

In November 1917 it was Trotsky who, on behalf of the Bolsheviks, presided over the Soviet of St Petersburg while Antonov-Ovseenko was the secretary of its Military Commission, about to command the uprising which brought the Bolsheviks to power. (Of its three-member executive, two were in fact ex-Mensheviks.) During the 1917 major season of mass meetings in which the power of the Bolsheviks took shape, Lunacharskii and Trotsky were the chief Bolshevik public speakers on a par with Lenin.[22] The immediate political plan which they all followed was the scrap of paper on which Lenin made his notes while his train was bringing him back to Russia – the 'April Theses'. Lenin read them out immediately on his arrival to the astonishment and open opposition of the majority of his leading supporters in St Petersburg. Within days he gained their acceptance of his plan to which we shall return later. Relevant here is that the crucial change in strategy was Lenin's call for 'immediate transfer to the second stage of revolution which should give power into the hands of the proletariat and the poorer strata of the peasantry' and the decision to use the Soviets for this purpose as the new national and local plebeian authorities.[23] In the new political world of 1917 with its unbelievable changes and opportunities which outran plans, strategies and imagination, Trotsky's principle conclusion from 1905–07 about the possibility of 'the great leap' into immediate socialist-led and socialism-aimed transformation of Russia was now the strategy of its main revolutionary party. It was shortly to become the ruling one. The Lenin–Trotsky 'ticket' at the top of Soviet Russia high command during the civil war was not only a combination of the Bolsheviks' charismatic party leader and its outstanding strategist with the bright and brittle political war chief of its armies and the great orator, the 'Danton of the revolution'. It carried also the deeper logic of a meeting of ideological streams of the RSDWP which now combined in their long-term search for the revolutionary roads and agencies of change.

How strong then was the political impact of the intellectual–ideological history of revolutionary leaders as opposed to that of the force of the circumstances? Do politicians use already-established analytical tools and conclusions, or do they design them anew each time? Both are true (and the way 'circumstances' are seen are ever influenced by the concepts available and the plausibilities established). More directly, Trotsky's argument about the 'permanent revolution' was spelled out loud and clear at the 1907 fifth congress of the RSDWP and in a sequence of his writings. It was overtly adopted by few, but it must have sunk deeply also into the minds of its Marxist detractors. The way in which its major elements were put to use in 1917, when political reality began to outrun imagination, strongly supports this view.

Trotsky's step forward in his concept of revolutionary state-power and political transformation coexisted with massive orthodoxy concerning the other elements of his Marxism. The intellectual breakthrough was clearly one-sided. He never stopped repeating his belief that in Russia *all* the universal social laws *fully* applied and that any claim of the country's exceptionality was a lie. (One is nearly drawn to Shakespeare's comment about 'the lady "who" protests too much'.) Russia's ability to transform itself without a major technological and ideological input from the genuinely civilised countries was to him out of the question. Also, Trotsky was superficial, indifferent or hostile in regard to a number of central problems of analysis and politics of Russia, such as ethnicity or peasantry. Those were treated with disdain or solved dismissively by a phrase drawn from Marxist rhetorics of the nineteenth century. His image of the revolutionary camp was simple: a proletariat led by a small cohort of revolutionaries with the rest given to the enemy and its tails or else obediently following, indeed, being swept by, the proletariat.[24] Linked to it was the extent to which he was behind the times in the way he understood the internal dynamics of party organisation – his major weakness in 1903–17 and his undoing in 1923–27.

C. ZHORDANIYA AND THE NATIONAL FRONT

Despite some manifest similarities, in most of his personal and ideological characteristics, Noy Zhordaniya was the polar opposite of Lev Trotsky. Like Trotsky, Zhordaniya was an 'orthodox' Marxist who supported the Mensheviks at the 1903 Congress, but was nearly always at odds with their all-Russian leadership. But Zhordaniya persistently referred to himself as a Menshevik throughout his life – a *Georgian Menshevik*, and his overt unorthodoxy and flashes of tactical genius related mostly to what Trotsky tended to 'brush under the carpet', that is, what the Marxist circles described then as the National Question, the Party-building Question and the question of the 'class alliances' with the non-proletarians. As to the Peasant Question both would agree on the grand theory but their strategies and practices differed.

Zhordaniya began his political education with Herzen, spent much of his life in Western Europe and Poland, in St Petersburg led the SD faction of the first Duma and served on the All-Russian Central Committee of the SDs. But he felt at home only in Georgia and was barely known elsewhere. In Georgia, he fully mastered the SD party organisation which for a generation dominated the Georgian political scene. As a leader Zhordaniya showed courage of conviction and the charismatic ability to make his followers time and again change an ideologically-entrenched 'political line' while keeping their organisation intact. As for his unorthodoxies, they had neither Trotsky's flourish and thunder, nor his theoretical and global sweep. On balance, in matters theoretical, he was a conservative rather than a rebel (and his placement in our Chapter 6 rather than Chapter 5 is open to an argument which will follow). Singularly unimpressive at the All-Russian RSDWP congresses, Zhordaniya was nevertheless Georgia's most effective politician. Kautsky was to say, in the highest praise he knew to offer, that 'Zhordaniya did even more for Georgia than Plekhanov for Russia, because he remained in the country instead of working from a place of exile and united the talents of the practical fighter with the activities of a thinker and a publicist'.[1]

Something more must be said here of Georgia, hidden as it has been behind the Caucasus mountains from its St Petersburg masters and from the Europeans' public eye and standard education. Georgia's history stretched back to ancient Greece and Rome – in the west the Colchis of the Argonauts, and in the east the Iberia of Strabo's history of Rome and of the Roman frontier garrisons.

Christianity reached there in the fourth century AD and eventually took the 'Eastern' that is 'Orthodox' interpretation following Byzantium. A Georgian kingdom attained its political and cultural peak in the eleventh and twelfth centuries. Destroyed by the Mongols, Georgia came later under the sway of Turkey and Iran, to be time and time again devastated by wars, robbers and slave-traders. Eventually, in the eighteenth century, in an attempt to defend the country from extortions and raids (the seizure of children for slave-trading in Muslim lands was a major issue), a Georgian king asked for the help of his Russian co-religionists. Under Catherine II Georgia became a Russian protectorate, and later in 1701, in open breach of the tsardom's undertakings, Paul I ordered its annexation. Together with the neighbouring territories of Transcaucasia, Georgia became the Caucasian Vice-Regency of the Russian Empire under a Viceroy who resided in Tiflis. (See Map 3 on page 270.)

At the turn of century the Georgians lived mostly in a fairly compact area on the Turkish frontier of the Empire where their population often intermixed with those of the Christian Armenians, the Muslim Azerbaidjanis usually known as 'the Tatars') and with the Ossetins, the Abkhaz and other hillmen. The 1897 census has shown somewhat more than 1 million Georgians,[2] of whom 9/10ths lived in villages, mostly as peasant shareholders. Six per cent of the Georgians – a very high proportion – were members of the 'social estate' of the nobility, but the landholdings of most of the Georgian nobles were so limited that many of them had to work manually on their land, or else find employment in government service, the army and the liberal professions. In towns there was also a small and growing working-class, but there were very few Georgian capitalists – the rich merchants of Tiflis were mostly Armenians and the larger enterprises were usually theirs or foreign- or state-owned. Standards of literacy and education, which were among the highest in the Empire, were linked in Georgia with a flourishing literature and impressive intelligentsia, often of noble descent. The Georgian intelligentsia formed a relatively large group in the cities and acted as the custodians of the sense of ethnic identity which was powerfully felt despite the particularism of the separate mountains and valleys. To many of its natives Georgia was an ancient island of high culture in the ocean of the barbarian Turki, Slavs and mountaineers.

The political life of the Russian Transcaucasia was active despite severe police restrictions. Circles of SDs and of Georgian and Armenian nationalists were operating in the early 1890s throughout the region. In 1898 Zhordaniya took over the Tiflis editorship of the well-established *Kvali*, and together with his friends turned it into a legally-published Marxist journal. The growing structure of clandestine SD circles and committees with strong workers' participation was being linked with the *Kvali* editors' efforts at Marxist education. This began to alarm the authorities and mass arrests came in 1901–02. As often happened in those days, joint imprisonment enabled the SDs of the different districts to meet and helped to establish a recognised leadership. In 1902 a Transcaucasian Joint Committee of SDs was set up.[3] At the second congress of the RSDWP in 1903 there were four representatives of Transcaucasia, three of whom came from Georgia.[4] Ever since, the Georgians were to play a major role in the RSDWP, but their leading figures were sharply divided between those whose focus of loyalty and attention lay with the All-Russian party and its affairs, such as Tsarateli, Chekhidze, Stalin or Ordzhonikidze, and those who centred on Georgia like Zhordaniya, Dzhibladze, Ramashvili or Makharadze. With the impact of the Bolsheviks both weak and in decline (which made some of them move elsewhere, for instance, to Baku), the RSDWP of Georgia was increasingly a Menshevik preserve. All delegates of Georgia to the 1906 'unificatory' Congress of RSDWP were Mensheviks. But the Georgian Mensheviks differed considerably from their Russian namesakes and allies.

During the period 1903–07, as the Georgian SD was introduced into the mainstream of the All-Russian organisation, the peculiarities of the Georgian contingent became increasingly apparent. It was linked to local political conditions and was expressed as much in their attitudes to the peasants, the urban bourgeoisie and the 'national questions' as in the particular tactics which combined broad alliances, extensive 'use of legality' and uncompromising militancy and discipline of action.

Chapter 3 described the way Georgian peasants imposed themselves on the Georgian SDs. By 1906 there were 5000 paid-up members of the RSDWP in rural Guria alone – a membership as large as that of the two major industrial cities of Ivanovo Voznesensk and Odessa combined. This force of peasants committed to 'orthodox' Marxism was a source not only of astonishment and of theoretical outrage, but also of the Party's strength.[5] It could not be explained away historiographically by the use of the 'Russian prescription', that is, simply declared a typical anti-feudal struggle. The most militant of the SD peasant Marxists, as in Guria, came from the rural areas with the most advanced economies, highest levels of literacy and fewest 'remnants of feudalism'. Despite the socio-economic differentiation in each of them, regional peasantries of different parts of Georgia acted in unison, proclaiming for the socialist cause in its orthodox Marxist interpretation. The SD Mensheviks of Georgia became the world's first Marxist mass party outside Europe of which the members consisted mostly of workers and peasants. The party's support involved also the radical section of the intelligentsia (which was usual throughout the Empire). That was not all, for this party's social sustenance extended farther and, once again, in a socially astonishing way. The petty traders of Tiflis and Batum acted in 1905–07 as a disciplined force at the call of the RSDWP. Their financial support, but even more so, the trade strikes (the closing of all the shops), played a major role in the confrontations with the Russian authorities.[6] Even farther afield in a social sense, many clergymen of the Georgian church, state officials, members of the bourgeoisie, and even some of the squires came to the aid of the RSDWP which they treated as the main liberation movement of the Georgian people. It was this broad national front which secured the party's revolutionary 'punch' in 1905–06 and its electoral successes to all of the four Dumas. It also helped to keep its clandestine and legal organisation alive during the period of the Reaction.

This brings us to the next major particularity of the Georgian SDs – the significance attributed by them to the 'national problem'. The 1903 Congress of the RSDWP gave it little attention over and above declaring a very general and unspecified 'right of self-determination of all nations',[7] and the rejecting of any party organisations established on an ethnic rather than a territorial basis.[8] To the Georgian SDs the national problem was central. It held three major dimensions. First, the Georgians were ruled by a Russian administration which displayed strong russificatory tendencies. The local clerks and policemen were under a Russian viceroy, local clergy was under a Russian bishop, the language of schooling and official business was Russian, that is, a language which was unknown or barely-known to most of the population. Second, most of the Georgians believed the Russians' sovereignty over their land to be the lesser of two evils, when compared with damage from Turkish and Persian attacks which were still vividly remembered. Zhordaniya's memoirs record the comment of a Gurian peasant who sharply opposed independence demands by saying 'We do not want to go back to the time when our children were sold' (to the Turks).[9] The reports of the way

Armenians were treated in Turkey reinforced those fears. Third, there was the problem of the non-Georgians in the midst and on the perimeter of the Georgian population as well as of the ethnically-different Georgians, for each valley developed its own specific characteristics and identification.

Not surprisingly, Zhordaniya's first piece of theoretical writing was devoted to the 'national problem'.[10] (The same could be said about another Georgian SD, and similarly a drop-out from a clerical seminary, Josep Dzhugashvili – Stalin.)[11] In this paper Zhordaniya concluded, in line with Kautsky, that it was the capitalist development which was now necessarily uniting Georgians into a nation, while at the same time dividing them along class lines. The ideological battle which initiated the self-definition of the Georgian SDs as a party (parallel to the orthodox Marxists' confrontation with the Populists in Russia) was the SDs' argument with the Georgian Federalists. The Federalists called for the unity of all Georgian peoples in the struggle for specifically Georgian national autonomy (linked to Russia by a federative arrangement). The Georgian Mensheviks sternly opposed independence, as well as federative autonomy and any related slogans of ethnic unity. Zhordaniya explained this by the party's peasant constituency, claiming that a call for the national unity between sharecroppers and landlords would make his party lose its peasant support and thereby also demoralise its workers' membership. As for the Georgians' liberty, it was to come as part of the Russian revolution. In the new democratic Russia, the Georgian Mensheviks wanted a Transcaucasian Parliament, possibly based on Electoral Colleges (*Kuriyas*) representing the region's different ethnic groups. This ethnically informed and militant anti-independence stand with an orthodox Marxist explanation were linked in the 1905–07 struggle to the highly unorthodox tactics of a united front which accommodated the majority of the Georgian population, included representatives of all of its major social classes, and was led by the SDs. Their Georgian anti-independence patriotism was well received by many; it was hostile to the tsardom but not to Russia, took account of the local anti-Turkish fears, provided for the interests of the massive plebeian majority, and promoted *de facto* unity by being adopted by Georgia's largest political organisation.

The peculiarities of the Georgian comrades did not endear them to the Russian Menshevik leaders. It was gratifying to have such a disciplined constituency ready to fight tsardom and to vote at the

RSDWP Congresses, but the roots of their Menshevism were suspect. Zhordaniya and his friends certainly objected to Lenin's demands for extreme discipline and centralisation, as damaging the working-class initiative. But they also refused them because a more decentralised party structure would better fit autonomous regional organisations, including Lenin's own. In contrast to the Bolsheviks of 1905, they strongly advocated participation in all legal activities, organisation or election as facilitating their cause (including election to the so-called 'Bulygin Duma'). But at the same time, together with the Bolsheviks, they opposed any alliance with the KDs and adopted a sharply confrontational line towards the state authorities. Their armed Red Hundreds were numerous and ready to do battle. The party did not rule out 'terrorist' action, and indeed several senior Russian officers, such as General Gryaznov, were killed by the SD armed detachment in 1905 and 1906. This 'un-Menshevik' militancy on the part of the Georgian Mensheviks was duly acknowledged by Lenin, who at the fifth congress in 1907 apparently offered Zhordaniya a practical 'alliance of militants' against Martov and his friends.[12]

The Georgian Mensheviks successfully withstood the period of Reaction. Despite the harshness with which Georgia was treated neither their clandestine nor their overt organisations were uprooted. Their broad constituency proceeded to stand by them. In tactical terms, Zhordaniya supported first the Axelrod's call for a Workers' Congress (rejected at once as the SD party's liquidation by Lenin and Plekhanov). But in 1909 he turned sharply against what he called the 'spinelessness' (*beskhrebetnost'*) of the Russian Mensheviks expressed in their 'policy of small deeds', alliances with the liberals and in the pessimism of their general strategy and political will. In the years leading up to the First World War, Lenin, Plekhanov and Zhordaniya found themselves for a time in alliance attacking the 'Liquidationists' of RSDWP from radical positions.

As for the analytical retooling in consideration of the lessons of the 1905–07 revolution, it was particularly uneven in Georgia. Indeed, one could claim a considerable measure of 'un-learning' in the days which followed. The 'abacus principle' suggested above had its impact. Successes of practical politics precluded critical self-appraisal and theoretical advance. It had also to do with the personal style of Zhordaniya's leadership which was pragmatic, direct and consistently avoided (or was incapable of) innovation in the 'orthodox' theoretical language of analysis and cognition. All through the 1907–17 decade the Russian SD leaders bombarded each other with theoretical books attempting to make better sense of Russian history, yet not even one such study came from the pen of the Georgian Mensheviks leader. There were instead the Marx and Kautsky quotations which were to explain all that needed explanation in the social analysis of Georgia. There was also the experience of the French Revolutions of 1789 and 1848, used by Zhordaniya to specify the problems and the possibilities of the stage at which Russia and Georgia found themselves (differing mainly in the nature of the 'national problem'). The 'two-stages' theory reigned unchallenged: the road of an underdeveloped society like Georgia was necessarily one of bourgeois political revolution, rapid economic advance and socialist transformation, following each other in necessary sequence.

Peasants remained the point of largest discrepancy of theory and practice. The surprise occasioned by the massive peasant militancy and influx of 1903–05 subsided, to be explained away by the catch-all phrase about the 'bourgeoisie stage' or simply to be taken for granted as the Marxist birthright to lead the less-progressive social forces. At the congress of 1906 Zhordaniya described peasants as a section of bourgeoisie. So they were to stay in his language of political theory, be their support of the RSDWP what it may.

As against these powerful blinds and orthodoxies the Georgian Mensheviks and their leader adopted one major element of a perspective which was new and directly related to their 1903–07 political experience. Unlike the Russian Mensheviks who looked for a bourgeois leadership of the bourgeois stage of history, with the proletariat enclosed in its own party and institutions, the Georgian RSDWP was ready to assume authority, to control territories and to rule. This linked to the debate on the National Problem, to that of inter-class tactics and to the Georgian SDs' sophistication in this fields.[13]

In the Transcaucasia, the February revolution brought to surface political parties and a variety of new organisations along lines roughly similar to the developments in central Russia.[14] The region received a pale representation of the Provisional Government – the OZAKOM, but the real political power and authority were in the hands of the Soviet organisations. A network of workers' Soviets was established first as well as their unified executive – the Centre of the Workers' Soviets in Transcaucasia. Set in Tiflis, it was dominated by the Georgian Mensheviks and chaired by Zhordaniya. A parallel organisation of soldiers, mostly Russian and dominated by the SRs, set up its own Centre. Some peasant soviets and their Centre were also eventually organised, but played a subsidiary role to the Menshevik-led Workers Soviets. A joint committee of the three Centres – the Regional (*Kraevoi*) Centre was for a time the main authority of Transcaucasia. The best organised Georgian Mensheviks played a decisive role in it while Zhordaniya defined most of its programme. The first new armed force at their disposal, replacing the tsarist police in Tiflis, was a militia unit brought over from Guria by the local Menshevik leaders.[15] Within a short time a Red Guard was set up, based on the workers of Tiflis.

The October Revolution in Petrograd led to the next stage in the political transformations of the area. Throughout 1917 Zhordaniya increasingly heaped abuse on Menshevik policies in Petrograd (as St Petersburg was named since 1914). By September 1917 he demanded an end to coalition governments with the KDs, 'active struggle' for peace and 'deepening of the Revolution' as the one way to meet the Bolshevik challenge.[16] When news came about the new revolution, the Transcaucasian authorities refused to recognise the new regime, and set up their own government – the Transcaucasian Commissariat and a Parliament (*Seim*), to hold power 'until the Constitutional Assembly receives full authority over all of Russia'. The Commissariat and the Soviet Regional Centre faced a complex array of forces, divisions, and conflicts. In the new elections to the Soviet of Soldiers' Deputies, the Bolsheviks and the Left SRs received a slim majority. Consequently the mostly-Russian Soldiers' Soviets pledged loyalty to Lenin's government. The Tiflis Red Guard, a *de facto* Menshevik workers' militia, took then the city's arsenal by force from the soldiers who guarded it, and used the weapons to secure the Workers' Soviet and its leading party control over Georgia. In Baku the conflicts exploded in the bitter street battle in which a coalition of Bolsheviks, SRs and Dashnak Armenian nationalists won the day against a Muslim militia, establishing the rule of the Soviet (which was chaired since February 1917 by Shaumian – a Bolshevik who was now appointed by Lenin as Commissar Extraordinary for Transcaucasia). In different places local governments were popping up daily. At the Turkish Front the army now wanted to go home. So it did, and trains full of armed soldiers began to move through Transcaucasia towards Russia, clashing on the way with a variety of militias. The Bolsheviks tried to use some of these regiments and their supporters to establish control over Georgia, but failed in face of resolute action of the Tiflis Soviet and his Red Guards. In an incident which made history the Red Guards arms were used in

February 1918 to suppress a Bolshevik demonstration in the Alexander Park at Tiflis – an upside-down version of St Petersburg of those days.

Against this picture of power struggle, divisions and strife, one of the nightmares of the Georgians and Armenians in Transcaucasia began to materialise. The Turkish Army was advancing, pushing aside the slight resistance it now faced. The Brest–Litovsk Peace Agreements between the governments of Russia, the Ukraine and Germany (the Transcaucasians were not represented), granted the cities of Kars and Batumi to Turkey. Negotiations were taking place, but the Turkish Army proceeded to move. The rag-tag Georgian volunteers who assembled to defend Batumi were easily defeated by it. The Azerbaidjani Pan-Islamic leaders called for a full Turkish take-over. Panic and despondency was growing in the non-Muslim part of Transcaucasia. In the 'everybody for himself' scramble which followed, the Georgian leaders moved rapidly, choosing an unexpected solution. They called for German mediation in their conflict with Turkey. (Germany was of course Turkey's ally, but their interests differed.) On 26 May 1918 the independence of Georgia was proclaimed, and the newly-created government of Georgia called in the Germany Army (which was now in the Ukraine) to protect the country from further Turkish advance. For the next few months the new government of the Georgian Republic headed by Zhordaniya, operated with the German Army on its territory, but with little German intervention in its internal affairs (very different from the way the Germans acted in the Ukraine). The Turkish advance was indeed halted. With the end of the First World War, British military units replaced the Germans. A new armed conflict developed, this time between the Georgian Republic and the British allies in the Russian White Army in Sochi to whom Georgian independence was a scandal and treason. Once again, this lasted only for a short while. In 1919 the British departed and the Whites disappeared from Georgia's immediate frontiers, but international relations proceeded to play an extraordinary role in its existence. The country was situated in a hub of conflicts and disputes – with Turkey, independent Armenia, Azerbaidjan, the Russian White Army now in Crimea, the Russian Red Army and a variety of smaller groups. Also, the territories which Georgia now controlled there were numerous 'minorities', both ethnic and religious – the Ossetin, Adjar, Abkhaz, Armenian, Azerbaidjanies and Russians.[17]

Internally the evolving political and economic structure of Georgia

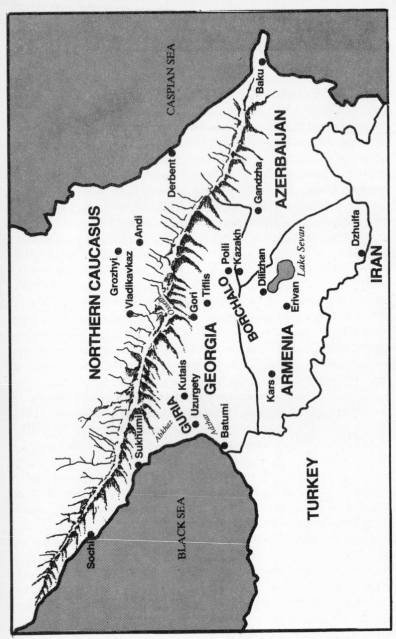

MAP 3 *Transcaucasia, 1917–21.*

of 1918–21 provided an opportunity to express in fact the creed of its dominant political party. Zhordaniya all along declared the agrarian reform to be the linchpin of a long overdue social progress. It was now to be introduced at once. With minimal opposition from the big landowners, a sweeping agrarian reform was carried out, in which more than 1 million acres of arable land and 8 million acres of forest and pasture were taken over by the government. This included 4000 private estates which were expropriated without compensation. The maximum permitted landholding per household was legislated at 15 *des* of cereal-producing land, and half this amount when more profitable cultures were concerned.[18] Some of this land became the property of the state or the regional authorities, but most of its arable section was sold at once on credit to the landless or smallholding share-croppers. No steps were taken to promote the collective effort of rural communities, inside or outside agriculture. The government also nationalised the mines (which provided the country's main export), hydro-electric power, mineral springs, habours and railways. By 1920 52 per cent of Georgian wage-earners were state-employed, 28 per cent worked for municipal or co-operative enterprises or organisations, and only 19 per cent were private employees.[19] A state monopoly of international trade was proclaimed, aiming in particular to control the major source of the Armenian merchants' speculative gains. In this as in many other issues of the day, Georgian nationalist and socialist goals and rhetoric combined and intermixed.

As for the newly-established authorities, democratically elected *zemstvos* were established throughout Georgia after the February Revolution. The controls of the Georgian Church by a Russian bishop was brought to an end. Experiments were made with National Councils in order to establish the formal representation of the ethnic minority groups and to look after their cultural and educational needs – akin to O. Bouer's conception of extra-territorial 'cultural autonomy' in Austria. Numerous trade unions and cultural associations were being set up.

The political supremacy of the Georgian Mensheviks was maintained throughout the independence period, as was the characteristic National Front of a loyal supporting constituency of workers and peasants providing the core of a broader multi-class unity of the 'defence of the Motherland' type – all led by an 'orthodox' Marxist party. Even the most loyal Bolsheviks admitted *ex post factum* the rock-like Menshevik support by the Georgian workers.[20] Electorally the Mensheviks were stronger still in the countryside. In the 1919 election (which was also a *de facto* plebiscite on the reforms introduced), the Georgian Mensheviks received 72 per cent of the general urban vote and 82 per cent of the rural one, with a resulting absolute majority of 109 of the 130 seats in the country's parliament. (Of its deputees, 32 were classified as workers, Mensheviks all.) The power of Zhordaniya's party was in fact still larger than its electoral expression. It fully dominated the trade unions, much of the national economy, and most of the country's cultural and social organisations. Besides the newly-created Georgian Army, there was the militia of part-timers – the Red Guard, which was now renamed the National Guard – which consisted mostly of Menshevik workers, and was used as the main armed force of internal control. When their Bolshevik and right-wing enemies complained as they did about 'the Menshevik dictatorship',[21] they had a point, despite the fact that the ruling party had the clear support of a majority of the population. There was in its ranks a growing arrogance of power. Its forces repressed – often mercilessly – dissent by ethnic and political groups. Non-Georgians were treated with suspicion. The Bolsheviks were prevented from functioning legally most of the time. This we-hand with parliamentary niceties and some genuinely democratic procedures.

There were in fact some weak joints in what was to the Georgian Mensheviks the revolutionary transformation of their society in the light of the prescriptions of their own and of their theoretical masters.[22] Difficult objective circumstances must be remembered: the economic shortages concomitant with war and the loss of the traditional markets and suppliers, pressure at the frontiers and finances in disarray. But at least three political issues reflected a political 'line' adopted by the ruling party as to the peasants, the 'national question' and the state.

Peasants provided most of the Menshevik electoral strength of Georgia and gave stability to their rule, but in 1918–21 there were hardly any SD peasants in the parliament or in the party councils. Little was done to mobilise the peasantry politically or militarily. The privatisation of land without any collective projects attached or considered led, if anything, to the peasants' political demobilisation. Nothing like the Red Guria of 1905–07 was called into being in the Georgian republic, with significant results for its fate. The workers' Soviets, unions and militia held the centre-stage, to be supplemented, and substituted by state institutions. The peasant majority which gave its loyalty to the revolutionary leaders of 1903–07 was told to stay at home, till its land, vote once in a while and leave politics to the hegemonic classes of the bourgeoise stage of history. A peasant minority in some hills or valleys, which did challenge the new government for reasons which had to do not only with ethnic conflicts but also with Georgia's rural-dwellers' dissatisfaction in several districts (for example near Gori) concerning social, political and economic issues was put down by force.[23]

As to the 'national problem', both inter-state and intra-state, Zhordaniya initially called the dissociation from Russia 'a major disaster which has befallen us', and tried later to preclude the collapse of the Transcaucasian Federation. However, the mobilisation against external dangers increasingly came to be reflected in xenophobic policies toward Georgia's neighbours and the local 'minorities'. Duly dressed-up in the orthodox Marxist terms of 'progress', 'class interest', the 'necessary stage', Georgian nationalism was gaining momentum of its own. As part of it, Georgia was now increasingly being represented and self-defined as the European rampart against the Asian Russia and Turkey.[24] Internally, the use of force for the purpose of ethnic 'pacification' was broadly accepted, against the Ossetin hillmen-villagers, the Adjar landlords, the Azerbaidjani urbanites etc. There were also the ethnic mini-wars against Armenia and the Russian White Army over matters of territory. The *Borshalo* district, where Georgians were a clear minority in relation to the Armenians and the Azerbaidjanis, was occupied by the force of arms.

Finally, 'statisation' of the revolutionary authorities was taking place – authority was now being transferred from the Soviet to the government institutions. The significance of the professional officers, officials and diplomats, mosly trained in the tsarist bureaucracy and indifferent or even hostile to the socialist images of the new regime grew considerably. The *de facto* political marginalisation of the massive peasant majority, nationalism and the 'statisation' of political structure of Georgia increasingly combined to distance the Menshevik leadership from their popular support, revolutionary antecedents and capacity to handle major crisis by an appeal to mass action.

Such a crisis was in the making. During the 1920s most of Transcaucasia became a *de facto* part of Soviet Russia. In May 1920 the Georgian Bolshevik rose and a few Red Army units crossed the frontier in an apparent effort to establish Bolshevik rule in Georgia. The loyalist forces managed to hold their own. A peace treaty and diplomatic relations followed between two neighbouring states – one immense the other small – both claiming a common Marxist heritage and representing for good or ill its most politically vital elements in Russia.[25] But this peaceful coexistence was not to last.

In February 1921 a new rebellion broke out in the mostly non-Georgian frontier district of Borchalo. The insurgents established a revolutionary committee which called for the intervention of the Red Army. Commanded by Zhloba, one of its most famous cavalry commanders in the civil war, it crossed the frontier at once, this time in considerable force. It moved rapidly toward Georgia's heartland. The Georgian regular army and its generals proved remarkably inept and dispirited. There was no attempt to arm civilians, to offer a stubborn challenge in the streets of the main cities, to start guerrilla warfare or a systematic boycott of the invaders – in a word, to put to use the revolutionary experience and the political loyalties of the population. After two weeks, on 25 May, Tiflis was taken, and shortly afterwards the Georgian capitulation document was signed.[26]

That was not the end of the Georgia-related Marxist idiosyncrasies. The demise of Georgia's independence now led to a major confrontation within the leadership of the Bolshevik Party – and formed a major part of Lenin's last political struggle of 1923–24.[27] His attitude to this first war between 'orthodox' Marxist governments put him at odds with his closest supporters who included both Trotsky and Stalin.[28] On 29 May 1921 Lenin ordered Ordzhonikidze (Stalin's friend who was sent from Moscow to supervise the Red Army and the local political scene) 'to seek an acceptable compromise for a bloc with Zhordaniya or other such Mensheviks who even before the rebellion were not absolutely averse to the idea of a Soviet regime in Georgia under certain conditions'. Lenin proceeded: 'I must ask you to remember that the internal and international situation of Georgia require not of the Georgian communists the application of the Russian stereotype'.[29] Ordzonikidze did not comply. Compromise was brushed aside also by the Georgian Bolsheviks as well as by the Menshevik government, which chose to go into exile. But the struggle at the top of the Bolshevik Party continued. The systematic misinformation concerning Georgia and the disregard of his instructions played a crucial role in Lenin's final wish to have Stalin removed from the Party Secretariat and to bring to heel what he now came to treat as a clique representing 'Russian nationalist moods typical of the Russified non-Russians' – that is, particularly Stalin,

Ordzhonikidze and Dzerzhinskii.[30] He was by that time too ill and too isolated to carry the day.

As for Georgia, the early years of Bolshevik rule were marked by open hostility between a minority government supported from elsewhere, and the majority of the population. Georgia-based Bolsheviks were trying to find a working compromise by accepting some of the population's wishes. The alleged report to the Central Committee in Moscow in December 1921 by the leader of Georgia's Bolsheviks, P. Makharadze (who came back from exile to chair its Revolutionary Committee – the *Revkom*), makes this context particularly dramatic:

> The arrival of the Red Army and the establishment of Soviet power in Georgia had the overt appearance of a foreign occupation because in the country itself there was nobody who was ready to take part in a rebellion or a revolution. At the time of the proclamation of the Soviet regime there was, in the whole of Georgia, not even a single member of the party capable of organising action or providing leadership and this task was accomplished mainly by doubtful or sometimes even criminal elements . . . We must realise that the Georgian masses have become accustomed to the idea of an independent Georgia . . . it is impossible to deceive the masses in a political question of this nature, and especially the Georgian people, who have gone through ordeals of fire and water in recent years.[31]

He was charged with 'social–nationalism' by Stalin and overruled. There was now constant tension between the 'local' leaders of Georgian Bolsheviks and Ordzonikidze as 'the man from Moscow'.[32] Local leaders led by Mdivani appealed to Lenin against him and the tension was high.

Lenin became totally incapacitated in mid-1923 and died early 1924 leaving the field to his successors. In the same year there was an armed rebellion in Georgia directed by the Menshevik government in exile. As in 1905 the majority of those who fought in it were workers and peasants while most of the Georgian intelligentsia, and other social strata supported it – the National Front was still holding and the customary militancy of the Georgian Mensheviks had its day once more. The uprising was defeated and bloody repressions followed, eventually uprooting by arrests and executions the Georgian Mensheviks' impact. By now the local Bolsheviks were also being increasingly charged with counter-revolutionary nationalism, and the persecutions spread to them. This was eventually to destroy on charges of treason nearly all the initial small group which represented local Bolshevism in Georgia of 1921, with only Makharadze spared by recanting. The man in charge of the avalanche of arrests and executions was a police chief, destined to become the Georgian Bolshevik Party's first secretary – L. Beria, who eventually went on to greater things.

*   *   *

For Zhordaniya and his friends the revolutionary experience of 1903–07 resulted in some lessons of major significance in the power struggle to come as well as some notable failures to learn, which contributed heavily to their eventual defeat. One lesson learned from history was the acceptance of the need, the possibility and the political potential of a multi-class national front led by a Marxist party and operating as the main revolutionary agency of change for Georgia. The inter-class enmity towards the Russian State under-scored this strategy, the workers of Tiflis were its main striking force, while the peasant majority of Georgia's population provided the numerically superior ingredient of political strength. Trivial as it may sound today, a socialist government at a 'bourgeois stage', benefiting from some consistent support of propertied classes was a dramatic innovation. The Georgian Mensheviks' preoccupation with the 'national problem' facilitated the multi-class coalition they were to lead. Yet analytical insufficiencies in that very field were catching up with them during the period of Georgia's independence. The international context of 1917–21 and the realities of power combined to increase the emphasis upon the national creed. This emphasis was sliding into an unrestricted nationalism which the Mensheviks did not know how to handle and indeed, often refused to recognise.

The attitude which did not change and was clearly supported by experience related to the working class. The Georgian Mensheviks' fundamental theory told them to expect class-consciousness, militancy, discipline and consistent support of the SDs from the workers. It was so throughout the first two decades of the century. The hard-core proletarian support and its air of resolute militancy made the Georgian Mensheviks akin to the Russian Bolsheviks of the day rather than to the Mensheviks in Russia. But in Georgia there was much less 'battle for the soul' of the working class. They belonged in mass to the Mensheviks and that was that.

The persisting 'blind-spots' related to the 'theory of stages', to 'progress' and to the peasants. The major lesson to be drawn from the 1848 revolution, discussed by Zhordaniya as directly significant to the context of revolution in which he was living, was that the impatient and premature attempts of the Parisian workers to introduce socialism in June 1848 necessarily led to a reactionary relapse.[33] Early in 1917 he spoke of his differences with Bolsheviks as 'tactical' only, they were to him still the 'hard' wing of RSDWP with whom he felt much sympathy in contrast with the 'spineless' one. When Bolsheviks reached for power refusing parliamentary democracy, his hostility to them became total. They knew that 'June 1848 policies' must lead to reactionaries' victory, yet, irresponsibly and unscientifically took this road! Zhordaniya condemned them now as the voluntarists and the Blanqueists of a barbarian land; it was the backwardness of Russia which explained this utopian relapse.[34] His strategy was now based on the certainty that the Bolshevik rule must collapse and lead to the rebuff of socialism both in Russia and the world over. The authorities whom he quoted with particular relish on the definition of scientific attitude which must prevail were Marx and Kautsky. And it was Kautsky's book about Georgia which offered all he needed for a sound historiography of past, present and future. 'To how great an extent socialism can be introduced must depend upon the degree of ripeness which the country has reached . . . The government of Georgia has chosen the method of masterly limitation . . . [a] backward country can never become a pioneer in the development of socialist form'.[35] East of Elba there was, of course, little ripeness of the type Kautsky required.

Directly related to the issues of 'progress' and of 'stage' in the Marxist analysis of the unripe lands was that of the peasantry – 9/10 of the Georgians. On the face of it, the experience of the rural struggle under socialist banners in 1903–06 should have changed the earlier theoretical constructions by the local Marxists, but, in this case, conceptual resilience proved stronger than revolutionary dreams. The new post-tsardom regime was defined by Zhordaniya as one established by workers, soldiers and progressive bourgeoisie and to be directed by the proletariat and the bourgeoisie.[36] In an offhand phrase the 'three main classes of contemporary society' were the nobility, the bourgeoisie and the proletariat.[37] Adjusting history to the needs of the day, the participants in the 1905 struggle were now described as a 'motley mass (*pestraya masa*) led by the proletariat'.[38] He sounded not unlike Chekhidze facing 'the problem of Guria' in

1903 (even though there was always more emphasis on direct party political action in what he had to offer). All this clearly did not go down well with some of his party activists, for Zordaniya was driven to attack the tendency of 'talking too much of the peasants' as contradicting Marx. He also reminded his followers that Georgia's main internal dangers are peasants and the fact that peasants twice buried the French republic.[39] The Russian peasant commune was the sign and the reason for the country's backwardness. Marx's comparison of peasants to potatoes was duly quoted to explain why peasants are incapable of democratic self-rule.[40] Finally, the anti-government rural rebels were simply defined as Georgia's counter-revolutionary Vandee of peasant backwardness (but the peasant majority was still progressive – the point proven by obedience to the Menshevik government). The place assigned to peasants in the republic, the way the agrarian reform was carried out, the way the republic chose to defend itself, were thereby defined. The Georgian peasants continued to trust their SDs, and the Georgian SDs honourably granted them land, but they refused to treat peasants as fellow socialists and fellow fighters for social justice and a better future.

A peculiar comparison suggests itself here relating Georgian political experience not to Europe, as Zhordaniya came to claim so insistently, but to China. The first-in-the-world peasant rebellion led by the Marxists of Guria in 1903–06 was preceded by a revolution carried out by a Georgian 'national front' in which a workers' marching army, a peasants' mass of supporters and a non-plebeian rear were led by a highly militant and disciplined Marxist party. Eventually there was in Georgia a government of 'orthodox' Marxists which rested on extensive popular support in a massively peasant country. The banner which the Chinese People's Republic adopted and Mao declared on its official inauguration carries five stars on a red field, one large and four small. It was to symbolise the Communist Party of China *vis-à-vis* the class ingredients of the national front it led: the workers, the peasants, the petty bourgeoisie, and the national bourgeoisie – a fair description of Zhordaniya's Georgia. The differences were of course as significant as the similarities. The Georgian Mensheviks like the majority of the orthodox Marxists of their era assumed that Georgia's economic backwardness precluded its advance to socialism and that as a class, peasants could not be socialists. (Indeed, were they a class at all?) Their class mobilisation, political and military, was discarded as dangerous to the progressive regime lead by Marxist. Mao and his friends thought otherwise. While carefully keeping up the ideological fiction and rhetorics of proletarian revolution, they substituted it in fact by a mass peasant uprising and a popular army led by cadres – a substitute proletariat engaging in revolutionary socialist trans-formation. In a bizarre or paradoxical manner the next act of the peasant rebellion in Guria against the landlords' oppression as well as tsardom's cruelty and the next challenge to the particular 'orthodox' Marxist brand of peasantophobic stupidity, was played out not in Georgia but in the fields, hills and jungles of Asia.

Returning to the history of the territories of the Russian empire, there were only two streams in its RSDWP leadership, deep differences excepted, which drew from the revolutionary experience of 1905–07 their own tactical versions of the 'face-to-the-peasants' policy. That is, they adopted the crux of peasant demands as they stood, in 1905 and again in 1917, without identifying with their cause or their drive. Once again differences accepted – it was Lenin and Zhordaniya, who emerged in 1918 as the absolute leaders of their parties, and the only Marxist leaders who commanded plebeian mass loyalty within the respective countries which they came to lead as heads of State. It was eventually they who were also to face directly the first version of war between states governed by movements which had officially adhered to 'orthodox' Marxist doctrine, originated from the same party, and shared the brotherhood of arms in earlier struggles – offering in 1921 lessons which even now are not digested or fully understood.

D. LENIN: REVOLUTIONS AND THE POST-REVOLUTIONARY STATE

It is difficult to see Lenin, the man and the leader of a victorious revolutionary movement, beneath the mummy of the creator of a post-revolutionary state. This is so, not only because of the endless stream of propaganda and counter-propaganda in which Lenin and Leninism undergo endless declensions by friend and foe, as the synonyms of the ambivalent mixture of revolt and excruciating discipline, of tactics of liberation and of the policies of a superpower. Also, Lenin's image has been 'iconised' at a deeper level of human and social response by two characteristics of what amounts to a cult. First, together with St Vladimir, Ivan 'the Terrible' and Peter 'the Great', Lenin has become a symbolic forefather, a patron-saint of a state and a nation, and is treated as part of the intimate ethnic identity of its people and of their claim for a place in the sun. That is true also for those to whom these people and claims spell abomination. Second – and again in friend and foe alike – there is the deeply-set and often unconscious admiration for the carriers and symbols of immense will, grand-scale success and limitless power, nearly any success and nearly any power, which make those facing it bow down or stand tall. Lenin represented plenty of all of these.

The resulting distortion of vision where the actual Lenin and his views are concerned has also been not unlike those of an icon of a Russian saint or a medieval fresco of a devil. It has been one-dimensional, ahistorical and unequivocal. The vision was there-fore unrealistic, but serviceable in the establishment of sacrosanctity or when functioning as a legitimating or delegitimating device. Lenin's image has been made ahistorical in that all Lenin's pronouncements and actions were treated as one, regardless of his personal biography and the political conditions and accidents which associated with it. It was therefore devoid of actual context which could then be grafted *ex post factum* by smart historians in the many official biographies, in which a presupposed model systematically prevailed over the actual events. It was one-dimensional in that it was assumed to be either totally right or totally wrong. As with gods, Lenin's thought did not change, it could only unfold what was already there (and, of course, was predestined to emerge). In Soviet textbooks the exceptions permitted were the few cases when Lenin himself set out his own past mistakes (usually as part of a new programme he was defending). Even this was usually disregarded when Lenin's personal story was concerned. To his iconographers and diabolisers he was also totally unequivocal – his moments of doubt, ambivalence and zig-zag, usually related to major changes of view, have been consistently 'ironed out' or played down.[1] So were the moments when Lenin failed to convince his closest associates or, more generally, to play the assigned role of the ever-incisive leader of an ever-trenchant and loyal faction, who knew everything about everything, or else invariably got it wrong.[2]

The political biography of historical Lenin falls into three main durations, dramatically and consequently divided by the revolution-ary explosions of 1905 and 1917. One can describe the periods as that of young Lenin, of revolutionary maturity and of state power. These can be subdivided further into a number of stages, focusing on the viewpoints of his contemporaries and on the criteria of 'the principal enemy' of Lenin's choice, rather than on his self-descriptions or on those of his eulogisers. A rough taxonomy is presented in Table 6.1.

TABLE 6.1   *The historical Lenin: a taxonomy*

Period		Stage	Dates
(i) *The young Lenin*	(A)	The deferential Lenin	1895–1901
	(B)	The Jacobin Lenin	1902–05
(ii) *The drive for power*	(A)	The 'peasantophile' revolutionary Lenin	1905–07
	(B1)	The parties' decline and the proletarian hope	⎰ 1909–11
	(B2)		⎱ 1912–14
	(C)	The internationalist Lenin	1914–17
	(D)	Lenin's power drive	1917 March–October
(iii) *The state power*	(A)	The Republic of Soviets	1917–18
	(B)	The civil war	1918–20
	(C)	The beginning of construction of a new regime	1921–22
	(D)	Lenin's last struggle	1922–23

The political context of each of these stages differed as did Lenin's response, but we should guard against relating these simplistically, as cause and effect in an unproblematic model of rationality. A choice between alternatives *and* a set of contradictions were involved in each case and the results stamped by a particular personality which was in turn shaped by their impact – a dialectical loop. In his immediate goals, the targets of his attack and the audience at which he directed his effort, Lenin's political stance changed sharply as he moved from one stage to another. Some of those changes he declared, others can be spotted if we watch Lenin's change of emphasis in the choice of the political enemies. Parallel and partly related to this were his changes of tactics and style of leadership. At a different and 'deeper' level lay the issue of Lenin's *Weltanschauung*, the basic theoretical models through which he perceived Russia and world and the long-term strategies of socialist revolution and transformation he adopted. With regard to these, there were some profound consistencies throughout his life while the transformation was slower, responding to the three 'periods' rather than to the 'stages' of the taxonomy suggested. Our particular interest lies in the period 1905–17 which led to the October

Revolution but cannot be limited to it. The selective nature of the biographical notes to follow is evident, it is the issue of the learning and new frontiers which interests us.

The first stage of Lenin's initial biographical period can be best described as one of the *deferential Lenin*. This clashes with the standard images of the man, but may be the more illuminating thereby. In his late twenties Lenin was in his first flush of discovery of a 'Science Of Society And of Revolution', which was to illuminate as well as to resolve rapidly all the ills of Russian society and of the world at large. In this, he was part and parcel of the mass conversion of Russian radical intelligentsia to Marxism during the 1890s. The new truth was seen as fully evident, the failure to adopt it by all and sundry as a matter of underdeveloped minds, entrenched interests, woolly thinking or sheer stupidity. To Lenin, the refusal to compromise in any way with those given to such deviations and a militant defence of the triumphantly emerging science – that is, of 'Marxist orthodoxy', went hand-in-hand with the deepest deference to its masters and sages. This extended not only to Marx himself but to his main earthly representatives, Kautsky and Plekhanov, with Engels (who died in 1895) acting as the human bridge between them and Marx himself. All the fundamental laws of the new science were seen as already established, unarguable and due now to be put to use. Their interpretation of Russia was also established and self-evident, along the lines described above.[3] What was still to be done was to change the world which the philosophers had so satisfactorily explained, that is, to facilitate effective political action aiming at the overthrow of regime which was delaying the natural evolution of Russia. The first evident step was to develop the necessary organisation – that is, a Marxist party of the proletariat. The scientific truth was to be applied, popularised and propagandised by the latter. As a necessary part of the process of establishing and of spreading scientific knowledge, constant punishment was to be meted out to the spokesmen of the medievalist tsardom, to the corrupting bourgeoisie and to the Utopian witch-doctors, thus to the 'establishment' and to the opposition of the liberal and the populist type.

At the age of 23, Lenin joined the Alliance for Struggle in St Petersburg ('for the Liberation of the Working Class' was subsequently added to its title). Strenuous engagement, clandestine organising and political writing followed. Lenin was active in Marxist circles for education and self-education and later in the Alliance's propaganda-and-agitation effort in the workers' quarters as well as in its attempts to establish an SD nation-wide organisation, including the Russian Marxist exiles.[4] Lasting personal contacts and conflicts were established in this group which included Lenin, Martov, Potresov, Kryzhanovskii, Krasin, Radchenko, Krupskaya, Zaporozhets, etc. By the end of 1895 the police closed in, arresting the Alliance's leading members. Lenin (now 25) and most of the others were imprisoned and eventually sent to a Siberian exile. The authorities clearly did not consider them much of a menace, it was mostly the 'terrorists' they were hunting. The arrest of Lenin was mild and his sentence of exile short – it expired by 1900. Then, almost immediately, he left Russia.

Lenin's writings of those days mirrored his political views and concerns. The major goal of his analysis was to translate Plekhanov's thesis about the already-capitalist nature of the country into agrarian economics, central to the majority of Russians, and to give a lie to the view that rural impoverishment could have precluded it from happening. The principal enemies of the related polemical effort were the publicists of the milder wing of Populism who were treated to a virulent barrage expressing what struck a current writer as 'Lenin's fanatical anti-populism'.[5] A short aside was also aimed at Struve who began to construct out of his progressist and 'legal' Marxism a creed of 'progressist' liberalism.[6] The 1896–99 period of arrest and exile was mainly used by Lenin to work massive statistical data into an extended version of his 1893 model of market-induced capitalism, now broadened to the country at large – Lenin's first book, whose aim was to establish firmly the economists' case for capitalism in Russia as championed by the whole 'Plekhanovists' camp.[7] In particular, in view of the advanced socio-economic differentiation of the Russian rural inhabitants (massively documented from the sources of the *zemstvos* statisticians) peasants were to be treated not as a social class but as a notion, a turn of speech related to the past (the term 'peasants' was subsequently used only in quotation marks in Lenin's early writings). To a Marxist the political conclusion from the book was inescapable – the establishment of the proletarian Marxist party along 'European' lines was to proceed at once, to promote the belated bourgeois revolution which was to make Russia's political system congruent with its political economy.

There is of course no way to divide Lenin's life neatly into totally separate seasons; real biographies never do. But if the recollections of his contemporaries are to be considered, in 1901–02 a new Lenin became increasingly visible – a *Jacobin Lenin*. This shift was marked in his political writings – a new principal enemy of the not-so-good Marxists took pride of place, that is to say, the revisionists, the opportunists, the 'soft' faction of his own ideological camp. For a time the external enemies of the SD, inclusive of the Populists, were to be attacked in an off-hand way, '*en passant*' one might say. Signs of this new turn began to emerge with the angry 'anti-credo' letter of the Siberian exiles aimed at Russian adherents Bernstein's revisionism. It matured with a furious onslaught by *Iskra* upon the '*Economist*' defenders of workers' spontaneity. In 1902 Lenin's second book laid down on behalf of the *Iskra* supporters an absolutist defence of party discipline and centralism – a major attack on the primitive amateurishness (*kustarnichestvo*) of the past and a call for a supreme organisation of professional revolutionaries, a 'Leninist' party of 'cadres' in the language of today.[8] At the same time Lenin drew up the *Iskra's* agrarian programme eventually to be accepted by the Second Congress of RSDWP. By now his growing division with Plekhanov became the *Iskra* editorial board's major headache – from a 'Plekhanovist' Lenin was rapidly becoming his own man. Trotsky described the related change of Lenin's political persona as 'a decisive crisis of . . . political self-evaluation . . . [marked by a new] firmness and self-confidence' and the feelings of the other editors of *Iskra* as one of 'perplexity' at 'this sudden self-confidence'.[9] Other recollections concur as to this sharp growth in Lenin's confidence and stature. It was this personality which was acquiring increasing fascination in a camp committed to revolution, who saw present and future very much in the light of the French Revolution. 'From such stuff Robespierres are made' – that is how Plekhanov explained to Axelrod one of his temporary realignments with Lenin. When to the painful surprise of all of the *Iskra*-ites the 1903 Congress of RSDWP ended in a split, Lenin emerged as the undisputed leader of the uncompromising disciplinarian wing of SDs – the Bolsheviks. His faction saw itself still simply as the 'hard' wing of the Orthodox Marxists of Russia – the Jacobins of the proletarian camp. In the acrimonious factional dog-fight which followed, Lenin worked out an explanation of the split which was very properly rooted in Marxist social analysis and suitably hurtful to his newly-acquired enemies. While sharing common principles, theirs was the vagueness of the petty-bourgeois Russian intelligentsia while his was the truly proletarian militancy.[10] There were only two proletarians out of the 43 actual delegates at the RSDWP second congress and a similar proportion at most of its local committees, but no matter, the charge hit home. As the preparations for the third congress have shown, while most of the Party's luminaries and émigrés preferred Menshivism, the majority of the local party activists at its committees in Russia sided with Lenin's faction. By the time the congress and the alternative conference of those SDs who followed the Mensheviks met in 1905, the whole political context was changing dramatically, as were Lenin's outlook and concerns – the 1905–07 revolution had begun.

The next change in Lenin's approach was deeper, more original and fundamental in conclusions, more decisive for the nature of the strategy he was to espouse to the end of his life. It was eventually to make Bolshevism into a separate ideological creed of global appeal embedded in the Third International and the USSR. Once again it was signalled by a change at the top of Lenin's list of political groups singled out for damnation. The hatred of tsardom and the commitment to destroy it were of course there as before, while the populists and the 'soft' Marxists were still being held up repetitively for ridicule. But it was the KD liberalism, and the KDs' attempt to monopolise the leadership of the 'liberation movement' and especially its peasant constituency which was now central to Lenin's political effort. The issues were: who was to follow the tsardom as the rulers of Russia and what was to be the nature of the post-revolutionary Russian society? The dispute with the Mensheviks over correct tactics was finding a new and programmatic substance in the analysis of the struggle for power and, linked with it, of peasantry and its newly-discovered militancy. To Lenin, the proletarian party had to aim for state power and therefore for a place in the Provisional Revolutionary Government, which was due to emerge with the defeat of the tsardom and preside over the forthcoming bourgeois revolution. To achieve its natural aims this revolution had to rest on the majority's will while checking the vacillations of the bourgeoisie (which, if permitted to do so, would have compromised with the tsardom). Peasant radicalism was fortunately showing the way for a solution. To finalise the 'bourgeois stage' of the Russian history and to do it radically, that is 'in a plebeian way', the new regime had to be a 'democratic dictatorship of the proletariat and the peasantry'. The term 'peasantry' emerged then from between quotation marks to remain as from that time on the list of Lenin's legitimate concepts, and to play a central role in Lenin's future analysis. It was no longer a fiction but a social class. The Marxist legitimacy of these was established through the declaration that Russia was after all less capitalist than expected and the assumption of two parallel 'social wars', an immediately relevant struggle of all peasants against 'the remnants of feudalism' and the struggle between capitalists and proletarians of the countryside, still mostly in the future. In party political terms all this meant, shockingly, the need for an immediate revolutionary alliance between the SDs and the PSR as well as the Peasant Union against the tsardom's rule and the KD's compromises.[11] That was precisely what Lenin came to demand as 1905 unfolded, referring back to the experiences of the Parisian Commune of 1871.[12] In line with that the limited and limiting 1903 agrarian programme of RSDWP had to be changed at once. The RSDWP elders accused him of *peasantophilia*; he saw it as *revolutionary* common sense. Through 1906 and 1907 Lenin proceeded to argue, to quote extensively examples of the radicalism of the peasant Labour Faction in the Duma and to taunt his SD colleagues with 'fear of peasants' which in the Russian context of the day amounted to crippling political pessimism and revolutionary paralysis. In the same spirit he now declared the significance of 'popular revolutionary spontaneity' – until then a phrase strictly reserved for the revolutionary populists. Lenin, the leader of a future successful revolution was beginning to establish his own formula for the revolutionary agency of change.

By 1907 Lenin had also turned against the electoral boycott and called for the use of the Duma as a legal platform for revolutionary propaganda. Stolypins 'governmental *coup d'état*' and de-democratisation of electoral system did not change, indeed reinforced, Lenin's view of this matter. His party was to work hard to secure representation in the third and fourth Dumas.

In his abrupt turn and the rapid development of a new strategy and analysis Lenin faced two consequent political problems. The more immediate and dramatic was the surprise and dismay that his new views, so far from the '*Iskra*-ite' beginnings of 1900–03, created in the ranks of the activists of RSDWP. Second was the way in which Lenin chose to handle the question of fitting those changes into contemporary Marxist theory and the historical experience of his party. We have already mentioned the 'Populist' label to which he was treated by Plekhanov at the 1906 Congress and the fact that Lenin found himself in the minority there even among the Bolsheviks over the crucial issue of post-revolutionary land-use. Within a few months he had recovered the control of his faction and his 'land-nationalisation' programme was adopted by them, but not without tensions which contributed to the creation of Bolshevik internal opposition. By the time of the 1907 RSDWP Congress, the upturn of grass-root radicalism was serving the 'hard' SDs well, with Lenin as the major benefactor. A coalition of the Bolsheviks with the Polish and Latvian SDs and some of the left-wing Mensheviks won the day on most of the issues as against the Menshevik-led central committee.

This success was due to extraordinarily energetic tactical leadership, the growing Robespierrian image of Lenin with the SDs' rank and file and the feeling of many Bolsheviks that he was irreplaceable. It had also to do with the superb understanding of party organisation which Lenin had acquired (which was, at least at this stage, much in advance of his ability to lead the extra-party activities of the SDs – his impact on the Soviets remained slight).[13] Lenin's growing influence reflected also the adroit and effective way he came to handle issues of Marxist legitimation. Extensive knowledge of texts, remarkable capacity for hard work on matters of ideology, skill of logical advocacy and a merciless publicist pen served him well. He must have reminded many of the Russian intellectuals of the indefatigable Chernyshevskii, whom Lenin and so many of them admired (but a version much quicker at the draw and more 'practical' and harsh). In a context in which for the first time his strategy was in no way deducible from Engels', Kautsky's or Plekhanov's interpretation of Marx – that is, from the 'orthodox' Marxism – he was establishing a consistent way of handling ideological discrepancies. Tactical change (for example, concerning the electoral boycott) were admitted in passing but total continuity with The Classics proclaimed as well. A growing discrepancy between strategy and theory resulted, but its recognition was sharply refuted. We shall return to this issue. For the moment its context and content are simply to be stated.

By 1908 the revolution was defeated. Stolypin was in the midst of his drive to modernise the tsardom and to make it immune to any new attacks by the revolutionaries. The revolutionary movement was in sad decline and disarray. Prisons were full. Russian political emigrants quarrelled endlessly about the causes of the defeat. Factions blossomed and interfactionary scandals followed each other in quick succession. The Bolsheviks split also. A left faction demanded the continuation of major preoccupation with armed struggle and boycott of the Stolypin's Duma. They deplored Lenin's new anti-boycott position as 'half a turn to the right' – a mild form of 'liquidationism'. With the single exception of Lenin, this group (eventually called *Vpered*, after a publication they issued) included the most significant Bolshevik intellectuals, their main speakers at the earlier party congresses, many members of the central committee and leaders of the Moscow and St Petersburg organisations: Gorkii, Bogdanov, Lunacharskii, Aleksinskii, Vol'skii, Shentser (Marat), Lyadov, etc. Lenin promptly labelled it 'desertion typical of the intelligentsia'. What sustained him now was his hope of the necessary revival of the natural proletarian class militancy as against the flimsy socialist emotions of the intelligentsia. Also, it was the extent of the realisation of this hope which may help to sub-categorise this period in Lenin's biography: until 1912 and after. For the moment, the SD's and specifically the Bolshevik's losses of working-class members were in fact as severe, but they retreated more often into apathy than into the more visible pursuit of careers or into the factions which rent apart the Russian émigrés. To Russia's secular moralists of the day, there was a decisive difference there to be recognised and remembered.

The new stage of Lenin's biography was marked, as before, by the change in the main focus of his publicistic attack. It was now, once again, aimed mainly at the alternative groups in the RSDWP. He heaped abuse on the liquidationists like Axelrod, that is to say, those who intended to rebuild the party on the 'broad basis' of legal unionism, a view gradually adopted by a majority of the Mensheviks. He hit with particular strength at the non-Leninist Left SDs who claimed Bolshevik credentials. His next book 'Materialism and Empiocriticism' aimed at Bogdanov and Lunacharskii's epistemological experimentation with Mach's theory of knowledge. Although not very substantial philosophically, this book carried a powerful ideological charge – the tactical non-Leninists were also philosophical non-Marxists. Lenin was never delicate in his attack on political ex-friends-become-foes, but the abuses he aimed then against *Vpered*, against 'liquidationists', and also against those who attempted the thankless task of party reunification (especially Trotsky, who promptly became 'Judas–Trotsky') reached levels never to be surpassed in his career. Even the elders of the Second International were drawn into the Russian squabbles, and Lenin's relations with them, particularly with Kautsky, cooled perceptibly.

In part, Lenin's fury of abuse and his factionalist vigour were related to the bitter test of revolution's defeat and to the fact that he was never as personally lonely as in those days. Contemptuous of what to him was cowardice, philistinism, empty phrase-mongering and treason from nearly all those with whom he shared the early days of the RSDWP, he became aloof as never before. In the circle of those who stayed with him or joined him now to become the core of the reconstituted Bolshevism on the eve of the First World War, he stood head and shoulders above the others in his knowledge of Marxism and of party dynamics as well as in broadly-established authority. Those days of endurance and the way Lenin stood fast then were decisive for the way he was later to dominate intellectually and morally, those who stood with him in 1908–14 as well as those who were to join or rejoin him in 1917.

He was particularly impressive within a mood and an environment of 'émigré blues', through his phenomenal capacity for sustained hard work and tightly focused energy. Beside the tactical tug-of-war of the factional struggles and the unceasing efforts, punctuated by arrests, to rebuild the SD's networks in Russia, Lenin never stopped his studies of texts, his analytical work and political writings. Besides two major excursions into philosophy (the spell in the British Museum preparing his attack on the 'Machist' and the period when he systematically worked his way through Hegel in 1914–15), Lenin concentrated mainly on the topics raised and questioned in the heat of the 1905–07 revolution. In 1908 he studied the history of the Paris Commune 1871 and wrote about the Russian agrarian problem at the end of the nineteenth century. He watched Stolypin's reform closely and did so with a cool eye answering his own friends' claims of the impossibility of its success with a curt 'You are wrong. It may' (*Net, mozhet*). In 1909 he studied the German agrarian census (and in 1916 did the same with that of the USA), with a particular eye on the patterns of the development of capitalism. He eventually accepted much of the optimistic reports about the results of Stolypinite agrarian reforms relating it clearly to the lack of signs of 1905–07-like rural rebellion, the disappearance of the Peasant Union and the decline of the PSR in 1909–17. The times of the Russian peasant revolution may have passed after all, which would mean a new agenda of 'capitalism-now', and the 'next' type of class struggle. But even if so, the experience of 1905–07 would not have lost its significance fully – it would simply 'move East'. In 1912 Lenin praised the militant democratism and the 'subjective socialism' of Sun Yan Tse as representing just that, and followed it up in 1913 by an article about 'Backward Europe and Progressive Asia'.[14] To Lenin's view China was now producing its own Herzens that is, non-proletarian revolutionaries involved in a struggle for liberation from social but also national oppression, who were therefore 'progressive', that is, natural allies of the proletariat. So were the peasants there, offering a massive base to a struggle which would be at once anti-feudal and patriotic. Two books about the rights of the nations to sovereignty ('self-determination' was the word) and about the differences between the nationalism of the oppressors (to be universally condemned) and of the oppressed (potentially positive), followed in 1913 and 1914. The Russian experience combined with that of other countries at the 'peripheries of capitalism', and the attempt to put it to revolutionary use, helped to produce in 1916 Lenin's 'Imperialism As The Last Stage of Capitalism' – a theoretical statement of a newly-integrated 'globalist' Marxism and an anticipation of a process in which the combination of the most backward Europe and the most advanced Asia – that is, Russia – might play a particular role.[15]

As to the Party work in its narrower sense, the student demonstrations in 1911 but especially, the waves of workers' militancy, which commenced in 1912 marked the time when Lenin moved to establish a Bolshevik Party totally separated from the other elements of RSDWP, yet using its name. This usurpation led to a furious row and an attempt by 'all the rest' to build an alternative. It foundered on the rocks of SDs' heterogeneity. Lenin's main tactical slogan was now the building of his proletarian organisations in Russia, harshly separate and 'without obscuring ideological diversities' (*ne zatemnyat'*) with everybody else. His party's success at the 1912–14 stage of working-class politics was beginning to transform the political map of Russian dissent, but it was the First World War which turned it upside down. The old political shape and shadows, the Second International, the RSDWP, the Russian 'Liberation Movement' were now well and truly dead. The overriding new division, and, one can say rightly, 'blood alliances', were now between the 'patriots' and the 'internationalists'. Within this division, Plekhanov and Potresov found themselves together with SRs like Sletov and the whole of KD in a coalition of a 'defence of the motherland' type, which reached as far as Guchkov if not to the tsar himself. On the other hand, most of the Russian socialist leaders of the 1905–07 revolution met in Zimmerwald to try to re-establish socialist unity against nationalism and war: Lenin, Trotsky, Martov, Axelrod, Chernov, but only Lenin had the command of a party which with few exceptions followed him. After his 1908–14 period of loneliness in the socialist camp Lenin was now seemingly out of isolation yet he dissociated himself from most of the 'Zimmerwaldians' by his merciless 'defeatism' and the call to turn the World War into a civil war and a world revolution (rather than to try to end it by a 'just peace').[16] This 'left-Zimmerwaldian' position was to serve as the beginning of the Third International (which Lenin had actually proposed at once). A Western biography of later days described this stand then as 'preposterously grandiose'.[17] In the revolutionary days to come it was the grandiose which was to impress, to mobilise and to lead. In the meantime, in these days, terrible for internationalists and socialists, a disciplined party organisation ready to do battle against the 'patriots' and led by a resolute and unbending leader was at the highest premium. Lenin's uniqueness was now established on the international scene.

This was also the time when the last link of deference to any of the living Marxist authorities snapped so far as Lenin was concerned. His relations with Kautsky had been eroded earlier,[18] but it was now that Lenin's genuine incredulity followed by blaze of indignation in what concerned the behaviour of the German SDs in the face of war, made him turn his back on its main theoretician, the 'pope' of the Second International. Lenin now regarded him as another spineless phrase-monger. His attack in 1919 on the 'renegade Kautsky' had its beginning in 1914.[19] What concerns us here is that while there were still some political allies in Germany (especially in its prisons for war-objectors, where Leibknecht and Luxemburg found themselves) there were no masters there. Lenin was on his own, in Marxist theorising as much as in socialist politics of the day.

When the Russian revolution came in February, Lenin's response was as resolute as it was unexpected both to his socialist fellow émigrés and to his Bolshevik supporters in Russia. Yet in what followed he was every much the man shaped by the experience most of them had shared, especially the 1905–07 revolution, and the 1914 collapse of the Second International. The difference was in the nature of learning. Lenin learned more radically and was by now ready and able to impose his own interpretations, against anybody else's views.

At first he made a furious effort to return to the scene at once – the delay in homecoming of January to June 1905 was not to be repeated. In the meantime his 'Letters from Afar' laid out, in rapidly-drafted articles for the Bolshevik newspapers in Petrograd, the essentials of a breathtaking new strategy. It was to be the total refusal to accept the 'defencist' Provisional Government or to co-operate with the other socialist organisations which supported the new regime. 'The only road to peace is power . . . we need proletarian rule and (for a transitional period) a state' as an expression of the 'revolutionary dictatorship of workers and the poorest peasants'.[20] The road to it was through the maximum use of the new and unheard-of democratic opportunities opened in 1917 as the larger version of 1905 'explosion of legality', and especially the plebeian democracy expressed in the Soviets. The slogans he put foward while still abroad were 'peace at once', 'workers' armed militia', 'no co-operation with other socialists' and 'immediate agrarian reforms' following the 1906 Labourite 'programme of 104'. More shocking was the general objective which, put in a nutshell, meant the drive for power aiming at 'socialism now'.[21] Those in the Bolshevik Party leadership who were first to arrive in St Petersburg and were now in charge – Kamenev, Stalin, Molotov[22] – simply disregarded those messages which sounded as much in contradiction with the Marxist essentials of the 'theory of stages' as with the mood of euphoria and socialist brotherhood typical of those days. The 'Old Man' was clearly out of touch with the actualities of new Russia. But in April Lenin was back and within days his will and his authority prevailed over – one can say, compelled – the Central Committee, and then the hastily summoned seventh conference of activists to change radically the Party's 'line', its programme and even its name.[23] The aim was now the combined struggle for peace and for socialist rule. The global context assumed was of a revolutionary epoch for Russia and the world at large – the February revolution was not the end but only the beginning of war-created revolutions.[24] The political form it was to take was the establishment of a Republic Of Soviets along the lines first represented by the Paris Commune in 1871. The road towards it was what Lenin called 'full democratisation' – that is, the substitution of the tsarist state by plebeian organisations and by elected officials and officers, while full equality was secured for non-Russians. A parliamentary democracy 'would be a step back' and even the 'democratic dictatorship of workers and peasants' as defined in 1905, was treated as 'overtaken by the events' – the aim was a socialist revolution led by socialists and supported by the class forces capable of sustaining socialism.[25]

Peasants were now a doubtful proposition, possibly hostile, because of what Stolypin seemed to have achieved: 'What are the peasants like? We cannot really know'.[26] But opposition to war from the peasants in uniform could be expected as well as the good will of the 'poor peasants' to a party ready to support the Labourite Duma faction's 'programme of 104'. That would be sufficient to change the balance of power between the political forces now in contest, but the historical conditions of the 'second stage' that is, moving toward socialism at once, meant to Lenin that Soviets or rural wage-workers (*batraki*) were now central and had to be promoted urgently (besides and separate from those of the poor peasants, once again divided from Soviets of peasants at large). This was to secure a reliable working-class representation in the countryside. The neutrality of the Russian peasant majority and the spread of European proletarian revolution were the two pillars necessary to sustain a dictatorship of the proletariat – urban and rural – engaged in pre-socialist *and* socialist transformation of a backward country.

Throughout 1917, Lenin's slogans and Lenin's vision were rapidly gaining adherents, as much in the freshly-politicised mass of the Soviet's supporters as in the radical wings of the SDs, the SRs and the Anarchists. Both the membership of Lenin's party and its impact were growing in leaps and bounds. The party's effective high command rapidly changed its face, absorbing the most militant and tough elements of the 'internationalist' SDs and reversing some old alliances and hostilities – Lunacharskii was back, Trotsky, Kollontai and Antonov-Ovseenko in, while Zinoviev and Kamenev became a new inter-party opposition. When the Russian Right Wing and 'the defencists' of the army under C.-in-C. General Kornilov attempted a *coup d'état* against the provisional government and failed, the Bolshevik drive for simultaneous power, peace and social trans-formation became overwhelming. The take-over in October–November 1917, a Soviets-based coalition government with the party of Left SR as a junior partner, and the latter's eventual defeat and disintegration, established a new political system – the one-party Soviet state. This, together with extensive social reforms, land redivision and the nationalisation of industry began a new political era of Lenin's parties rule and his personal pre-eminence, unquestioned and unquestionable in his camp.

As the Civil War unfolded, the major issues discovered or reformulated in 1905–07 came back one by one into focus. Within a year Lenin learned what by his own admission had still puzzled him in 1917 – that is, the actual extent of the Russian peasantry's transformation under Stolypin. As often before, his conclusions were expressed in the language of political tactics rather than in theoretical re-analysis. By 1919 the Committees of the Poor were dismantled (the separate Soviets of rural workers or of 'poor peasants' never came into being) and a mild variant of 'face-to-the-peasants' policy was introduced – an important element in the Red victory as the tide of civil war turned finally in their favour in the second half of this year. In 1920–21 in the face of the now-growing peasant rebellion related to compulsory grain deliveries, another major step was made in the same direction, a full-scale conciliatory policy of the 'give-the-peasants-what-they-want' type, the introduction of the NEP. Simultaneously, Lenin also watched with particular attention the 'ethnic peripheries' and the vicissitudes of the 'national problem' there, its uses and its limitations in the Bolshevik's struggle for power. His attentiveness and flexibility toward the 'self-determination' issues was once again of major importance for the Bolshevik victory in the war, especially in the face of the rigidly nationalistic 'One-and-Indivisible-Russia' position taken by the White Armies' commanders. (Actual solutions were never simple and conflicts over how to handle them filled the period with the case of Georgia and Zhordaniya matched by more 'political' resolutions elsewhere.)[27] Next, in 1919–22 there were the issues of relations with 'the educated Russia' – Chernyshevskii's 'the society' and the SDs' substitute bourgeoisie of its earlier debates. (The actual landowners and owners of factories had disappeared by then as had the rulers of the tsarist state.) This linked to the problem of fellow-participants in the 'liberation movement' and in the RSDWP of 1903–12. The related uncertainties, ambivalences and diverse opinions between the Bolsheviks found their expressions in the many policy changes, the de-legalisations and re-legalisation of the alternative socialist parties and of alternative intellectual traditions. (By 1922, the final decisions to suppress Martov's Mensheviks, to put on trial the SR leaders and to expel *en masse* from Russia many of its top academics who refused to choose emigration brought this to an end.) There was finally the constant reconsideration of the problems of 'stages' of development and, related to that, of the nature of state power, its content and its form, its goals and restrictions, its opportunities and its pitfalls.

The trial-and-error steps toward the establishment of a new regime lasted from the civil war until the end of Lenin's life and after. His party was singularly ill-equipped, in its concepts and its 'cadres', to preside in peace over the transformation of an industrially backward society, which was neither capitalist nor socialist, was composed mainly of peasants and situated at the peripheries of global capitalism. By 1923 the shape of the political regime of the new state was becoming clearer and unleashed one more attempt by Lenin to change radically his 'party line' and its executors – a 'stage' never quite completed and well-described as that of 'Lenin's last struggle'.[28]

*   *   *

Three major lessons concerning political reality and one defining his attitudes to it, were drawn by Lenin from the 1905–07 experience. The most immediate concerned peasants. He declared it himself, fought over it with his closest supporters, and came to define it as central to his split with the Mensheviks. While the freshly-discovered peasant radicalism made the Mensheviks freeze and the KDs become more conservative, to Lenin it opened up new unthought-of revolutionary possibilities. The significance of peasant presence and impact was also clear in Lenin's view of the social context of the Civil War and his optimism about its outcome (even though the second reason for his optimism – the European revolution – failed to materialise). Considerations of peasantry also defined the sharpest turn of state strategy over which he presided – the introduction of NEP. It was as significant, in his last struggle and, one can say, posthumously, when his political Last Will designated the workers-and-peasants alliance as the issue on which the future and the nature of the Soviet regime would depend, as well as the fundamental social context of the factional struggle due to follow his own death.[29]

Although on the face of it, the significance of this issue seems both self-evident and overstated, it was neither. Peasants were the large majority of the population of Russia, its production forces and its armies. But the conclusions to be drawn from this were not simple, nor did the full complexity of the issue strike the eye at the first glance. In particular, the creators of the RSDWP did not consider the Russian peasantry's bulk to be a decisive factor in its analytical assessment. Their mind was on the concept of progress and therefore upon capitalism and on the scenario of the proletariat confronting the bourgeoisie. All the rest was assigned to the dissolving, and thereby naturally conservative and secondary, vestiges of the past. Of those, the police uniforms of the tsarist state were a political actuality which could not be easily disregarded or treated as marginal. Peasants could be so disregarded and often were. That is why peasant political significance for the future history of Russia was yet to be discovered as also were the potentials of their political militancy, revolutionary *élan* and capacity to tip the scales, especially when other political forces were locked in combat over who would rule Russia. Also to be discovered, beside the power of peasant political action, was the impact of its focused inaction, the peasant ability to exercise political pressure by obstinate passivity when food, labour, tax and conscripts were concerned. Finally, as noticed by the brightest of the contemporary Soviet students of Lenin's intellectual biography, what needed to be recognised was that 'Russian peasantry at the beginning of the twentieth century not only persisted as a class but . . . it was also in process of class formation'.[30]

Second, behind the debate on 'the agrarian problem' – that is, in the Russian context, mostly about peasants – stood a number of further political and ideological issues of broader significance. Contrary to restrospective impressions, the Russian socialists and revolutionaries were democrats almost without exception. The designation as 'Social Democrats' used by their major strand, accurately represented all of them. The fundamental assumption held was that the autocratic rule of the Romanovs could be broken only by the majority will and effort – a revolution – and that the regime to follow it would necessarily be a majority rule (even if to the 'orthodox' Marxists it represented a stage, which in its class context had to be a 'bourgeois dictatorship' resting on the petty-bourgeois consent). Majority will would be necessary for the survival of the new Russia as much because of the power-struggle entailed, locally and internationally, as because of the fundamental democratic legitimation upon which popular support would be conditioned once the tsardom was destroyed. The main alternative, held by few, was a version of the People's Will model, particularly unacceptable to the orthodox Marxists, by which an organised minority must first break the tsardom's grip, but would then turn the power over to the people. In a country containing a clear peasant majority, the form which the resolution of the peasant problem would take defined also the fundamental issues of the power-shift and of the nature of any future democratic state and the cadres of its anticipated rulers.

That is why Lenin's change of mind as to the very existence and revolutionary tendency of the peasantry as a class, expressed in the image of 'the democratic dictatorship of workers and peasants' also put under strain in 1906 a number of 'non-rural' fundamental assumptions of the Iskraites. Lenin was now advocating a type of state never before implemented, with a radical peasant party alongside the SDs; both representing a plebeian class-coalition at the core of the democracy which would rule Russia. In such a regime, the peasants and their party would be treated as equal partners, subject to the ideological interpretation that they are not and cannot be socialists proper, and that the alliance is therefore necessarily limited to the capitalist stage (expected, however, to last for generations). In his argument Lenin consistently divided between the 'good' and the 'bad' of the 'petty bourgeois' political preferences and action. He often assigned the first to actual peasants or their representatives within the Labour Faction of the Duma and the second to the 'peasantists' of the PSR.[31] His eventual solution in face of the 1917–20 revolutionary crisis was to adopt, lock, stock and barrel, the PSR agrarian programme and to declare his own party rule to be representative of the actual interests and the alliance of two classes: the hegemonic workers and the peasants.[32] It was the NEP which was to uncover the substantive political meaning of this formula.

In so far as the political placement of the Russian peasantry *vis-à-vis* the Russian revolution was concerned he was of course not the first on the Left to change his mind. We know by now that Marx did.[33] However Lenin did not know this, nor was he simply catching up with the late Marx of 1877–81. What made them differ was on the one hand the rigid Second International interpretation of Marxism which Lenin adopted as The Science of Society and on the other hand, his direct experience of two revolutions. As to the differences, first, in his analysis Lenin consistently disregarded the peasant community and the peasant commune, that is, the Plekhanovites' major target for derision as 'running contrary to class theory'. It was also the major unit of political action of the Russian peasantry in 1905–07, in 1918–20 and in 1921–22. Lenin's insistence that the peasants should set up Peasant Committees, to direct the political action (never a success) was but another expression of this peculiar blind-spot. Contrary to it, in the late writings of Marx, Russian peasant commune and locality was central to the understanding of the context in which peasants could participate in revolution, also in a socialist one.[34] Second, throughout his life Lenin treated socialist peasants as a logical aberration (even though peasant paupers could in his view support socialists because of a *de facto* proletarianisation). Despite his shift in agrarian programme in 1905 Lenin was still uneasy *vis-à-vis* the idea of peasant revolutionary struggle against the Russian state; his training and statistical evidence told him one thing, his tactical sense and the political reports often told him something quite different. Before 1917 he was beginning to assume that Stolypin's effort had made the Russian countryside catch up with the 'orthodox' Marxist – that is, scientific theory of capitalism in agriculture which Lenin presented so impressively in 1899. In

1919–21 he once again adjusted his theory to experience, but this
time there was going to be no retreat but a steadily deepening
recognition of the problem of peasantries non-disappearance (no
eternal stability is indicated, of course) and its political significance
for a socialist Russia; 1919–20–21, and further on, stretching as far as
his last letters and articles. Marx was less intent than Lenin on being a
Marxist; which helped him in 1881 to reach more explicitly similar
conclusions.

The reformulation of the peasant problem undercut the two-stages
theory of revolution. Lenin proceeded to hold fast to it in his
statements but knew a problem when he saw one. When the First
World War and the new theory of global capitalism at its final stage
made the issue acute, he moved to the assumption of immediate
dictatorship of the proletariat (and the 'poorest peasantry' understood as a *de facto* rural proletariat 'one step behind' on a historical
scale).

Next and linked to 'the agrarian problem' was the 'national
problem'. As to its significance Lenin had shown his tactical insights
already when stating in 1905 that a 'Riga-like' level of workers'
militancy in the Russian towns would have brought the tsardom then
to its end (very offensive that to the Russian nationalists of today and
seldom quoted). Non-Russian nationalism clearly 'worked' as an
anti-tsarist weapon, but the full-scale strategic and theoretical
conclusions from it had to wait for a few more years. By then they
were becoming linked to the issue of global capitalism and of the
neither-proletarian-nor-capitalist radicalism in the countries of its
periphery. Once again, when the theoretical transformation came, it
came quickly and decisively. The right of nations and major ethnic
groups to sovereignty was fully admitted by Lenin in 1912 but put in
the context of (and relative to) the attack against capitalism. To see
the significance of this move one must relate it to the Russian SDs'
gamut of views, from Plekhanov's early objections to the issue being
raised at all (because 'the proletariat has no motherland') to the
demands of the Bund for an 'non-relative' and extra-territorial
national autonomy. Most of the 'national sections' of SDs in Russia in
1912 objected to Lenin, but their diversity over national issues made
a stable anti-Lenin coalition impossible – their positions still ranged
from those of Bund to those of many radical SDs, notably
Luxemburg, Radek and Bukharin, who supported a version of
Plekhanov's earlier view. Lenin took a pragmatic view and a middle
position, focusing on political alliances and their utilisation in

revolutionary struggle against a common enemy, but with a sharp reminder that one cannot equate the nationalism of the oppressing nations with that of the oppressed. The first had to be condemned and Lenin was to keep to this view in an absolute manner, while the nationalism of the oppressed was to be treated on its revolutionary merits.[35]

The concept of imperialism 'as the last stage of capitalism' has eventually drawn it all together. A new and broader formula of an international revolutionary camp was established to define and promote the twentieth century socialist offensive that was to change the world and make Lenin's name as international as the image he came to project now. The tactical sub-formula was a party of revolutionary cadres *plus* a socialist-directed industrial working class, and/*or* a massive radicalised peasantry, and/*or* national liberation struggle, resulting in a post-revolutionary state of a new structure, logic and momentum, coming into being at 'the peripheries of capitalism'.[36] A long-term socialist strategy particular to what we call today the 'developing societies' was thereby established, on a par with its right-wing equivalent – Stolypin's 'revolution from above' by a modernising state bureaucracy advised by the Western experience and/or specialists.

The Civil War and its aftermath justified Lenin's first fundamental assumption concerning the context of power transfer in Russia – the ability of his party in 1918–19 to secure peasant sympathetic neutrality or even spontaneous armed support (especially behind the backs of Denikin's and Kolchak's White Armies). As to the second pillar on which his plans rested, Lenin went on to believe that socialism cannot be established otherwise than internationally. The position defined in 1905 and still held in 1917, was that 'the Russian revolution has sufficient strength to win but insufficient strengths to hold the fruits of its victory . . . To hold on to our victory, to defend us from Restoration, the Russian revolution needs a non-Russian reserve . . . the socialist proletariat of the West'.[37] An all-European revolution – the socialist 1848, was confidently expected. As the hope for the European revolution faded away it was gradually supplemented by the hope that the next significant revolutionary upheaval would come from the 'toiling masses' of Asia, fuelled by the cravings for independence and a peasant rebellion combined, for 'the fact that Russia, China and India represent the majority of mankind is decisive for the world's future and its socialist transformation'. The 'non-Russian reserve' was increasingly being seen as the 'colonial and semi-colonial people of Asia' which as time went by became synonymous with the Third World at large.[38]

The third major lesson of 1905–07, enhanced in the light of further revolutionary experience but remarkably consistent, was Lenin's trust in 'popular' that is proletarian or, more broadly still, plebeian spontaneity and 'creativity' (*tvorchestvo*) of political forms. (He usually spoke of the 'revolutionary proletariat' but on a number of occasions extended it to 'the common people' that is the *populus* of Russia.) As consistent was the essential ambivalence of two lines of thought and two emotions, both characteristic not only to Lenin. As to his biography there was the brilliant student, the worshipper of science who despised Russia 'un-culturedness' (*nekul'turnost'*), the believer in the right and the duty of a disciplined revolutionary elite to impose its wisdom on the unstructured proletariat and to tell it what is good for it – the author of 'What Is To Be Done'. On the other hand, there stood the man who believed in the good sense of 'the masses', especially the readiness to right political wrongs in a revolutionary manner, beginning with the first defence of the *narodnoe tvorchestvo* at the 1906 party congress and as far as his 1923 projects of state reform – the diligent student of the Parisian commune who authored the 'State and Revolution'.[39] The first emotion was hatred – of the Russian backwardness of 'the masses'; and on the other hand of soft-minded social reformism and phrase-mongering of the intelligentsia. (One can speculate as to whether its nineteenth-century roots were in populism or a pre-Marxist subculture of the Russian intelligentsia or somewhere else). These two hatreds were present also in Chernyshevskii about whom Lenin said that the reading of his book 'ploughed him over' in his youth.[40] More important is that to Lenin all this had been not a matter of propaganda, but of deep conviction, and that the trust in potentials of 'popular creativity', hedged and ambivalent as it had been, was to play a major role in Lenin's plans and to influence deeply his self-image and identity as a leader. This went beside his rigid disciplinarianism and uncompromising trust in 'the party' as the carrier of 'the science'.

In 1905 for the first time Lenin saw Russian workers and peasants on the march, their ability to organise collective nation-wide action in rudimentary and yet remarkably effective ways, their distrust of the 'top dogs', their stubbornness and courage, their faith in the possibility of what more sophisticated minds dismissed as Utopian – a kingdom of absolute justice, the *Opon'skoe tsarstvo* and the

Vselenskii mir of the Russian peasant fairy tales. He saw the ambivalences and the potentials of it, the way the Russian 'masses' swung between rebelliousness (*buntarstvo*) and the readiness to accept absolute authority, but also the rapid way they learnt political self-reliance under conditions of harsh confrontation and violence. In the bitterness of defeat, loneliness and post-1907 emigration squabbles Lenin stuck to his belief in the revival of popular fighting spirit as the only solution to the deepest crisis of his revolution. He saw it come as a proletarian new challenge within five years. He banked on it again in 1917 in his direct appeal to workers and peasant–soldiers, over the heads of the established political parties, and won the day. In 1922 in his dissatisfaction with the conceptual and political tools at his disposal and in growing dismay at the incapacity of many of his comrades to face the new challenge of peace and gradual social transformation, he turned once more to the same source of hope. Rightly or wrongly, to Lenin the main chance of a socialist future for Russia lay once again with the faceless mass of popular supporters, mostly workers but increasingly peasants too. Lenin's notes dictated from his death-bed bear final testimony to this. They consist of a letter and six short articles/notes addressed to his party's leaders and activists. Let us look at them as Lenin's life was drawing to a close.[41]

His letter of December 1922 to the party's congress became best-known because its scandal-value, prescient suggestion to remove Stalin from the position of party's General Secretary because of his brutality and the shrewd commentary about some of the other leaders: Trotsky, Kamenev, Bukharin, etc. But Lenin also recommended in the same text a more than tenfold increase in the size of the Central Committee and the Party Commission for Control, drawing their new membership from the workers. These new members were to be charged with the task of inspecting and restructuring the administration of the post-revolutionary state. He added two major provisos, (i) 'including, when speaking here of workers, also peasants' that is, as close to the revolutionary populists basic concept of *narod* (common-people, *plebs*) as he ever came, and still, reinforcing it even further (ii) that 'the ranks of the new members of the Central Committee should mostly consist of those who come from social strata lower than those which advanced in the last five years . . . [and who are] close to the ordinary workers and peasants'. The new members of the Commission for Control were 'to be present at all meetings of the Central Committee and the Politburo and read all of their documents'.[42] He also offered a fundamental socio-political context to the suggested reform: the Communist party rule was based (*opiraetsa*) on two classes – the workers and peasants – and on their mutual agreement.

Other of Lenin's last notes suggested new steps to secure cultural contacts between workers and peasants as well as major efforts in popular education, condemned the tendency to stress too much the administrative aspect of state planning; spoke of deseperate need to reform state administration, and called for a major effort in advancing 'grass-roots' rural co-operatives (which in Lenin's view 'the context of the new regime would equal socialism').[43] He attacked once again, for the last time, the 'pedantry' of the Second International, its failure to understand 'revolutionary dialectics' – that is, in this case, to see the need of combining peasant and workers struggles and the unrealism of its orderly 'theory of stages'. He spoke again and again about the un-socialist tendencies of the state apparatus. Finally, Lenin discussed anew the national cravings of the non-Russians in the republic of Soviets, relating them to the forthcoming revolutionary struggle of the 'colonial and semi-colonial people of Asia'. In that light he condemned the new symptoms of Russian nationalism, justified now as the needs of administering a centralised state, and did so with particular reference to Georgia. The sentence with which he began this note reflect the tenor of much of his last notes: 'I think that probably, I bear considerable guilt before the workers of Russia by not intervening [earlier] with the necessary energy and sufficient harshness . . .'.[44]

As to the issue which interests us here, two conclusions can be drawn. Lenin's last struggle still followed the fundamental itinerary which was first considered, if not fully, in the light of the experience of the 1905–07 revolution. As against young Lenin's views, there was now a new formula of global social transformation which stood at the junction of the peasant, the national, the plebeian spontaneity and the party-building lessons of 1905–07, enhanced in 1917–20, and set against the unexpectedly low will-for-power and political drive of the European and US working class. Time was to prove the high realism of these assumptions and anticipations. Second, when related to the history of post-Lenin Russia, his predictions and fears proved remarkably apt, but clearly understated. Put otherwise, he was an able learner but there were limits to his imagination.

To see Lenin in the context of his experience is not to resort to another form of Plekhanovist political behaviourism: 'give us the conditions and the leaders will necessarily "pop-up" '. The availability of leaders of capacity and vision cannot be taken for granted and their personalities do matter, even if also they 'do not make history just as they please'. At the same time their characteristics and appeal are never abstractly 'right' but are interdependent with the cultural patterns and histories of different societies. That is why Plekhanov's (and many other contemporaries') comparison of Lenin to Robespierre so clearly lacked a Russian dimension. As already noted, Lenin was much more 'like' Chernyshevskii enhanced, in his dogged stubbornness, factional cantankerousness and in his hatred of 'liberals', who symbolised all he despised in his own social background, especially the Oblomov-like phrase-mongering of the educated Russians. In an angry mood Gorkii once likened him to the Old-Believers grim martyr and saint Avvakum who, merciless to any compromise, died to the glory of God and of the Old Books. The life-long love–hate relationship of Lenin with Martov represented in part this issue of personal identity as against tragic paralysis which the Russian Mensheviks so typically displayed when faced with the intellectual and moral contradictions of revolutionary politics. The reprehension of 'spinelessness' was the common heritage of the nineteenth century Russian intelligentsia this term was designed to shame. This central anti-vision – a major heritage of Chernyshevskii and People's Will, together with Hertzen's condemnation of self-satisfied small-burgher *meshchanstvo* and Pisarev hate of the soft-hearted obscurantism – defined a collective *Weltanschauung*. So was Tkachev's anti-evolutionist and anti-reformist Jacobin prescription to grasp the helpful event – 'the art of the moment', for a political opportunity may never repeat itself. By undercutting the tenets of social distance, respect and respectability outside the narrow stratum of the 'educated' the wars and the revolutions taught similar lessons to plebeian Russia. To the extent to which revolutionaries of the Russian intelligentsia exercised influence of 'the masses', the message they transferred or reinforced was similar. To most of its people – the intellectual elite and the 'masses' of Russia – the power of Lenin's attraction was very much that of his boldness and of his merciless and often unscrupulous, yet personally disinterested and modest, drive for power, and the feeling that he always knew what to do next and was ready to stand by it, come what may. History taught the Russians to respond to such appeal with particular strength.

It is also in this context that one must see the growing discrepancy between the Lenin of theory and the Lenin of political strategies and tactics. Throughout his life Lenin was to admit some of the past tactical mistakes (and at times to stress them particularly, to make a point). At the same time he resolutely claimed that no changes in theory were involved, even when the opposite was dramatically true. His insistence on theoretical unoriginality was total.[45] When pressed he usually answered with abuse or simply restated that the principles of his view were ever and absolutely right. At times he shrugged his shoulders or used the terms (or code-word) 'dialectics', which on such occasions his critics were said to lack. He minded less the resulting ambivalences than the ever-clear Plekhanov, as long as simplification was justified by action. From 1905 onwards a gap between the two Lenins, the populariser of orthodoxy and the strategist of originality has grown steadily to bedevil generations to come. So did his versions of historiography of the Bolsheviks[46] *vis-à-vis* what was then known by many from personal experience to have happened. In terms of academic properties much of it is outrageous or incomprehensible. Its logic, for good or ill, lay elsewhere, in the dynamics of political struggle and the style of leadership which Lenin offered to those who followed him. Yet Lenin was not the Machiavellian pragmatist depicted by many of his hostile biographers. His aim was not power as such but power to transform Russia in accordance with his lights. He also treated his Marxist heritage with deep concern, even in the midst of revolution and government duties engaging not only in political polemic but also theoretical inquiry.[47] The self-image of the custodian of the revolutionary spirit and a leader of revolutionary proletariat matter deeply to him. Tactical flexibility went together with some theoretical and ethical thresholds which Lenin never crossed.

Finally, as to the content of leadership rather than to its rhetoric and legitimations, 1905–07 was also a period when Lenin learned to learn. The brilliant deductions, the evidence laboriously put to use to explicate given theories, and the lawyer-like briefs of accusation against any critics, which formed the main content of his early writings, received a new dimension. After 1905–07 Lenin was much more attuned to the unexpected (it was this, together with the search for the contradictions which came to define his usage of the term 'dialectics' and of 'concrete'ness' he used synonymously to it). In the heat of inter- and intra-Party confrontations he usually failed to mention the moments when strict adherence to the theoretical assumptions of his youth had led to political mistakes. But he never seemed to have forgotten those experiences and never lost the sense of their possible reappearance in the practice even of those who like himself seemed to have mastered the 'Science of Society'. He did not treat this as licence to stop his studies or as 'freedom from Marxism', but was now much more ready both to think anew in the face of political experience and, most importantly, to borrow political solutions from people whose general analysis he thoroughly rejected. He was also aware of the fact that he borrowed from the SRs most of all – to him this found its explanation in the correspondence of their 'petty bourgeoisie', views and prejudices with those of the majority of the Russians. To incorporate it was a democracy of type.

If 1900–03 and again 1908–14 were the times when both Lenin's confidence and inter-party experience grew, making his authority tower even over the most senior and effective of his political partners, 1917–20 was a lesson of war and 1921–23 was a lesson in state formation. The revolution of 1905–07 was the time when Lenin learned – during his first direct struggle for revolutionary power – about peasant rebellion, about nationalism, about mass movements and about learning from political experience (and how to be taciturn about doing so).[48]

Postscript: Matters of Choice

This book is at its end. Its text has drawn a picture of a society and of an epoch presenting an argument as to their characteristics, contradictions and motions. It then proceeded to discuss a half-forgotten revolution to reclaim it as a decisive moment in the history of Russia and of mankind. The Preface set out the book's point of departure and stated its conclusions. A Postscript permits a brief statement about what the author has learned in the process of study about study itself – that is, not about Russia and its revolution but about sociologically informed history and the historical sociology of societies, states and revolutions.

There has been masters of historical craft who have dealt with it broadly, and my particular admiration of Marc Bloch's descriptions and prescriptions has been manifest in what has already been said. To re-read Bloch's work, together with a few more historical and analytical writings of highest quality, be it Marx, Kluchevsky, Wright Mills or Broudel, and farther away in time and space, Thucydides or the classical Chinese historians, is to rest from prejudiced banalities so often paraded as academic sense, 'media' wit or laymen's self-evident facts. To re-read the masters is also a lesson in intellectual humility. One is less inclined consequently to speak of things which have already been said by them so well.

In what follows there is no attempt at a general statement concerning the pursuit of intellectual ventures and of the academic disciplines discussed. What will be said here aims to single out, to focus or to recollect in short something less generic, referring to the *Zeitgeist* of a limited period and to a diminutive group – a few decades of the current time within the social sciences and the particular issues and pitfalls involved. It has to do with the growing contradictions between the views assumed and taught for a century or more as against the analytical tendencies and styles emerging within some of the contemporary works concerning social living. More specifically and personally, it is about what a generation of students of societies learned to assume from its textbooks, teachers and leaders, in confrontation with the lessons of their own research work and teaching, of arguments within small bands of friends, of staggering surprises so typical of our times and of the painful efforts at making sense anew. This book has considered at length the lessons drawn from history and the failures to draw historical lessons by social classes and by political leaders of the revolutionised Russia of the 1890s to the year 1919. What are the lessons which can be drawn from the process of studying this for the contemporary sociologists' and historians' own work? In which way does the content of their work link with the general presumptions concerning their trade.

Of these issues, still immense in scope, I shall consider four items, one may say 'blinkers', the impact of which struck me as particularly acute. This will be followed by a strategic suggestion and an existential one. As to the blinkers, the first is the assumed interdependence between the conscious will and the impersonal causes of human action. Second is the accepted causal hierarchy of social institutions and units of analysis. The third is the impact and variance of the models of historical time implicit in the social sciences. The fourth is that of labels and of tolerance. All those are related by a common mode of misinterpretation – a tendency which can be defined at its shortest as reductionism. This particular 'idol of the human mind'[1] has found expression as much in formally adapted epistomology and methodologies as in unfocused moods, 'common sense' and the patterned plausibilities consequent upon it. While our general assumptions reflect particular findings such assumptions shape in turn the questions we ask, the data selected, its analysis and the conclusions. Those who believe that they can dodge the related theoretical concerns and to avoid verbose complexity and 'philosophising' by talking 'simply' of 'facts' are particularly prone to fall into the trap. Conceptual naivity is no alternative to woolly imprecisions.

Simplification forms a necessary part of any analytical effort and of the pedagogical processes of transferring knowledge. Without it no conceptual model could be set and no general tendency explicated, but, as an already quoted maxim has it, the price of usage of such analytical tools is 'eternal vigilance'.[2] At the core of this warning stands the danger of becoming prisoners of the techniques we devised, losing sight of what is the object of our study as against its approximations designated as steps by which it is to be explored. Reductionism is a mode of misinterpretation when a well-warranted simplification or a transitional over-statement adopted as an exploratory step takes over our field of vision to become treated as if it were the reality it was summoned to explore. This turns an heuristic procedure into a blinker.[3]

The first of the blinkers in question has been the tendency to reduce human will to its material or structural determinants. This omits choice and disregards accident. The economists commit this error through the exclusive focusing upon the flows of monies and goods; historians are led into it by an 'obsession with origins' as the particular 'idol of the historians tribe',[4] sociologists (and some others) worship likewise structures and systems. In an inversion which reminds of Freud and his 'displacement mechanism' the alternatives often took the form of professing pure subjectivity – a phenomenological society as an a-historical construct without the everness that people construct their world with resources which are extra-subjective and mostly drawn from or imposed by the past. While lip-service is often paid to the image of society as an *inter*dependence between human choice and extra-human determinations, the actual descriptions and theories of social action have been for a century or so losing sight of this interdependence.

The advance of the social sciences has led to an increasing de-accentuation by its mainstream of the particularities of the field of human action. While in the twentieth century the crude materialism of the eighteenth and nineteenth centuries was being supplemented through extending focus on the structures of human action and interaction,[5] human activity has continued to be treated in analysis as no more than a necessary reflection of circumstances and inputs (that is, of both the material resources *and* the social structures). What resulted was a puppet-theatre-like model of human history, legitimated as 'science'. Quantification, statistical averages and computing games in which the qualitative diversity was left unattended have been used likewise. As to the alternative explanations of social history, the one most often used, especially by the 'media', was the presentation of its decisive moments as outbursts of human pathology, 'crowd behaviour' or subconsciousness, possibly triggered off by a 'charismatic personality'[6] (until things settle into what is once again open to 'science' – behaviour which is no more than a vector of 'objective' forces, mechanically repetitive, fully predictable and boring in the deepest sense of the word). This alternative of assuming a history of pathological lapses is, even for the 'charismatic' moments, as deterministic as the view it challenged. It has substituted irrationality for the total causality of 'the objective', but refused the existence of human choice, whatever its restrictions.

Against these images/presumptions concerning human reality a different view has been reasserting itself if very slowly. Its intellectual origins lie in the turn of nineteenth-century German 'critical philosophy' which fertilised Marx's 'Theses on Feuerbach' as much as G. W. Mead's 'social psychology' of the Chicago School, and offered intellectual context at once to Max Weber, Sartre and Gramsci.[7] The crux of this particular message was that interdependence between material circumstances, tightly patterned behaviour and collectivities on one hand, and on the other individual and group choices and perceptions, never operate as a simple sequence of cause and effect. Nor are behavioural responses repetitive only. At the core of human collective being stands intersubjectivity which is Janus-faced – a process of choices between alternatives as much as a set of impositions, social controls and limitations. Moreover, those restrictions are never static, nor simply reflective of material circumstances but in a continuous process of structuration and destructuration in which the 'subjective' and the 'objective' are links of an endless chain. Human response is a combination of the necessary, the imposed and the learned with the creative and the dissenting solutions of the problems of human existence. Reductionism undermines our understanding of these contradictory processes by 'suspending' some of their links. It also makes us loose the appetite for asking questions concerning actuality as against the schemes of it or the construction of its lifeless substitutes, as the eye freezes on the performance in a puppet theatre with gods or the fatality of inputs and circumstances as the puppet masters.

We have been living through a period of extensive scientific pretence matched by a deplorable predictive record of the analysts of societies. This could have been a source of hilarity (akin to the pre-'satelite' jokes concerning the meteorologists), but too much depends nowadays on such errors.[8] The resulting debris of the presumed necessities and of the planning disasters all round us – modernising zeal turned famine, liberal dream spawning fascist regimes, revolutions of saints which have brought hell on earth. All those were not only matters of the entrenched interest of selfish elites but often *also* of choices which in the long run contradicted the paramount interest even of those who made these choices. Our text documented it clearly. Global problems are unresolvable if treated only as issues of cognition, but with issues of understanding and of the consequent choice forgotten they cannot be resolved either. For a century politicians and activists of outstanding resolve tried to change the world. The point is to interpret their failures, better still, to make re-interpretation into a necessary part of any future political deeds.

To look anew at the ways we look at history is one of the 'methods' to rectify our analytical procedures. In choosing the 'points of entry' our steps would best be guided by a deceptively naive suggestion from the nowadays unfashionable Mao, clothed as it was in the jargon of the day. To the question 'which "deviation" from party line, the "Left" or the "Right", is the more damaging?', he once answered 'the one you fought least against'. Social sciences suffered from a heavy reductionist over-accentuation, one may say being hypnotised by the doubtless proposition that we inherit our social world ordered and most of our knowledge comes 'second hand'. That is why considerations of history must begin with the rebalancing in our minds and analytical practices of the assumed interdependence of consciousness, choice and accident as against the material and structural determinants of human reality. This also means the acceptance of deep and changing contradictions between the 'elements' from which human reality is constructed. Put in another way and in the language of the philosophical origins of the debate, following the spell of determinism, or, better still of fatalism presented as science, we must regain the dialectical balance – the understanding of human history and especially of the revolutionary processes in it must be 'dialecticised'. To 'dialecticise' would mean here not only to re-accentuate the endless chain of causalities, its contradictions and essential historicity, but to do so also for the human will (within limits to be specifically researched), the issues of choice (not a 'free' one, but between alternatives to be defined) and the problematic nature of understanding (in which the fetishisms and 'idols' form an integral part). Will, choice and error are no 'black boxes', and stand in need of constant study, but they cannot be simply reduced to 'causes' considered 'more real'. Even though 'they do not make it just as they please . . . men make their own history' – one can scarcely say this better than Marx did.[9]

The significance of such issues to this book is direct. Without it, the view suggested above as to the relations between the 'developing society' called Russia and the moment of truth in the 1905–07 revolution will remain an oddity. With it, it is a contribution, one of many attempted and still needed, to move from the facile optimism of the end of nineteenth-century theories of the inevitable progress, to the twentieth-century acceptance of tragic realism, without surrender of the values of the Renaissance, so well expressed by Gramsci as the 'pessimism of intellect, optimism of will'.

Second, and closely related, is the issue of the hierarchy of social institutions used to explain history. The problems and the solutions discussed above carry significance which is broader than those of the relative autonomy of choice and accident. Unidirectional models of cause and effect, often mono-causal, concerning the interdependence between social institutions, easily turn into vehicles of reductionism and/or abstraction which forecloses study. An example and a major case in point has been the nature of the state *vis-à-vis* Marx's metaphor of 'base' and 'superstructure', turned by so many of his followers into the synonyms of cause and effect in a unidirectional scheme. This made the state into an epiphenomenon of some real and final causes placed elsewhere – a particularly pernicious misconception in a world in which the significance of the state machineries increases daily.[10]

Mutual causality, its contradictions and the need to 'dialecticise' anew our understanding apply here as well. And once again, the matter rests not only with the admission of historicity and mutual impact but also with the acceptance of particular characteristics of major social institutions, their motions and rules of the game, which are irreducible to each other or to something else. The very way questions of 'last-instance' final causes were set, too often provided for the loss of sight or, at least, de-accentuation of the riches of social reality, its historicity, its contradictions. Nor can the alternative be the methodological capitulation of admitting that 'everything' is important within the huge and unstructured pile of 'facts'. On the contrary, social analysis centres on hierarchies of significance and determination but it must treat them as specific instances. The point is not to declare which hierarchy is necessary, deductively and eternally, for 'causes' are moments of an endless causal chain. A society cannot be deduced but must be studied. Nor can the major social institutions be reduced (into 'simply' economics, 'not more' than power or 'only' consciousness). The intrinsic inelegance which creeps into theory and conceptual models of society as these became more realistic is rooted in the nature of human reality, not in the inadequacies of social analysis. An admission of contradictory complexity, without surrendering to it or running away from it in despair, belongs to the very core of the trade of the social sciences. The 'triangle of social determination' suggested in the text above was an example of admission of such complexity and a step to define a substantive hierarchy of significance, specific to a time and a place.

This brings us to another bridge between what was referred to as the first and the second sets of 'blinkers'. The significance asserted for the status of alternative or choice in social history *vis-à-vis* the material and structural determinations is not static, it is not a substance but a flow and a phase. The extent of *alternativity* in history, to build some flexibility into a stubborn English noun, is relative to context and conjecture, which offers one more reason to 'dialecticise' our understanding (rather than simply to invert it or to alter the ratio of the elements in the assumed interdependence).[11] Material constraints are seldom unrelated to human experience and cognition, and thereby, potentially, to human will and choice. This is the more explicitly so for social institutions. Nevertheless, long periods pass during which material circumstances (as well as our images of them) and social institutions (reflected in individual cognitions) facilitate the high consistency of social reproduction and forclose fundamental changes. During these well-patterned, repetitive, socialisation-bound and sociologically explicable stages the historical processes behave themselves in a nicely predictable manner, the 'alternativity' of history is low. Then, once in a while, comes a period of major crisis, a revolution, an 'axial' stage.[12] The locks of rigidly patterned behaviours, self-censored imaginations, and self-evident stereotypes of common sense are broken, and the sky seems the limit, or all hell seems let loose. The 'alternativity' of history, the significance of consciousness, and particularly the scope for originality and choice, increase dramatically. The 'turning' taken then by a society establishes its pattern of development for decades or centuries. This was the essence of the Russian revolutionary epoch 1905–38, to the beginning of which our study was devoted.

Reconceptualisation and re-institutionalisation rather than 'charisma' or mass pathology provide the mental texture of an axial stage – a revolution, a 'moment of truth'. Later, the social structures with its 'common-sensical' plausibilities, hardened by the 'big stick' of coercion, and entrenched privileges, new and traditional, resume their grip, as history proceeds for a while along a road of few possible 'turning-points'. The admission of a constantly changing extent of dependence between social structure and human choice – the changing extent of what we have called 'alternativity', as well as of the shifting hierarchies of social institutions, are fundamental to our understanding when considering social history and historical sociology.

Third, our historiographies carry implicit yet highly significant assumptions concerning the nature of the historical time. Its arch-model, an ideal chronology used as a *chronogrammar* in Corrigan's expression, is usually treated as self-evident and becomes the more deceptive for it. By now much has been done to explore the particular breach between the ancient assumptions of natural cyclicity and the Judeo-Christian linear vision of the creation, the fall and the redemption (to which the first coming of Christ added its own Christian particularlity – a point from which historical time is counted forward as well as backward).[13] Contemporary historians and philosophers have explored also the ways the theological linearity of time-perception served to advance (and was eventually transformed into) the arch-model of evolutionism and progress as the decisive self-image, legitimation and point of origin of the political ideologies and social sciences of today. The human praxis underlying those assumptions was analysed, for example the cosmological and agricultural cycles beneath the ancients' perception of time or the industralisation at the root of the evolutionary theories of the nineteenth century. Some further social characteristics were linked to the different time perceptions, for example the prevalence of pessimistic ethics in ancient philosophy *vis-à-vis* the optimistic philosophical anthropology of nineteenth-century Europe. The reverse impact of the prevailing perception of time on human praxis was also studied, if to a much lesser degree.

Such considerations are more clearly perceived *ex post factum* but it seems that we are living through another paradigmatic change – the collapse of or at least a major challenge to the theory of progress as an arch-model of historical time. What is slowly taking its place is a conceptualisation of no agreed name which substitutes for the models of linear rise those of multi-directionality and unevenness of related changes – a more complex but more realistic organising concept (which is also more open to the impact of multi-directional causalities, discovery, accident and of alternative strategies adopted). Its analytical origins are rooted in the ideas of 'uneven development' as explored first in early nineteenth-century Russia,[14] but the term may deceive us if treated too directly. The essence of this view lies not in quantitative 'unevenness' of speeds but in qualitatively different roads, i.e. what Paul Sweezy called 'a variety of fates' of the different contemporary societies[15] – as much the different societal actualities as different potentials for them. This means also simultaneous, different and irreducible clocks and *zeitgeists*, of which

Braudel 'unresolved debate', of 'division of history into slow- and fast-moving levels, structure and conjecture', is but a part.[16] What all that does or would mean it its global impact is outside our brief, but to disregard the problem is to misread the text above. Full-blooded 'progressism', focused only on the records of speed and on the impediments to the advance along a necessary and known historical road, would make this book superfluous. If another view of historical time is taken, the argument of this book becomes central to our understanding of Russia and its revolution together with their relations to the world at large.

Fourth and last is the issue of labels and of epistemological tolerance. Admission of the high complexity of societies and multiplicity of ways to study them has been antithetical to bureaucrats, policemen and many others who were inclined to substitute for it simply dualities of 'us' (good) and 'them' (bad). The 1968 radical wave produced on the Western campuses a wave of Marxophilia. This mood is now rapidly swinging 'the other way round' to an anti-Marxist beating of the drum. What has linked the early 1950s' US Joe MacCarthy's and the latter-day anti-Marxist crusades with the shrill Marxisms for fools and some other *ideologues* has been one more category of a reductionism – the yes-or-no crude model treated as reality itself. It is as far as one can go both from real Marxs' life and research practice as from that of the real fathers of liberal thought which both sides usually swear by. Rooted in the academic environments these are not even oversimplifications for the purpose of political action, but rather ways to enhance a self-image or a career for oneself and one's friends.

Those who refused to join these versions of medieval Mystery Plays or angels and devils have usually earned the label of 'liberalism', on the Left with the prefix 'bourgeois', on the Right with the suffix 'fellow-travelling' (to which 'rotten' could be added to accentuate the point for the less literate). The word 'populist' (less bad) or 'revisionist' (awful) were being used for similar mental manipulation, especially so on the academic left in the 'developing societies'. Factually, we are dealing here with misnomers – there are few factory owners who are liberal and few liberals who followed Marx. The issues of personal liberty raised by nineteenth-century liberals are substantive enough still today and more than one of them died for his beliefs – one should not mistake liberalism for liberal rhetorics used as a cover for opportunism or for moral cowardice. Also, those named today 'populists' seldom professed or preached a smallholders' monopoly of the future while questions raised in the nineteenth century by their European theorists are still very much with us. And everybody 'revised' masters. Something else has been clearly at stake – labelling via reductionist, finite and dualistic models and yardsticks (with a half-way purgatory attached).

Such issues have been discussed endlessly, so let us make our comment brief. Theory and the pursuit of knowledge mix here with politics and ethics. What clearly needs to be restated first is that tolerance is not just a matter of political or of ethical choice. When facing infinite, complex, contradictory and changing reality, tolerance without a refusal to take a stand is a major epistemological device, while its opposite serves reductionism, with all its 'blinkers'. Epistemological tolerance is necessary for the effective analysis and learning from experience. It is also necessary to optimise the training of analytical skills. Monasteries, barracks and asylums can close gates, universities cannot without undermining their purpose. As our book has shown, neither do effective political leaders facing major crises.

Proceeding from the 'blinkers' to a general suggestion, a strategic conclusion concerning the contemporary historical sociology, put at its shortest – it is the need for greater admission of diversity, complexity and contradiction within the human reality and, at its core, of the particularity of it, expressed in the phenomenon of human consciousness, creativity and choice. This is what we called the 'dialectisation' of our understanding. It treats reductionism as the major self-inflicted injury of the modern historical understanding. It assumes a historiography which centres on potentials, alternatives and diversities and not only on necessities or totalities.

As to existential conclusions, these cannot indeed rest only on analytical findings but relate to political goals and applied ethics – a complex interdependence and a badly underdeveloped dimension of our understanding. Little as we understand it, we cannot do without it, for it is where our thought and action meet. Scholarship is as much a way of life and a system of values as an occupation. This statement is not one of self-congratulation; the best supportive evidence has been the hit-lists of the dictatorships, making this point plain. Those who claim the title of scientists who study society should keep therefore in mind a value-judgment and a warning about what he called the 'social-ethical ends' by the greatest contemporary scientist. 'We should be on our guard not to overestimate science and scientific method when it is a question of human problems', wrote Albert

Einstein in 1951. He proceeded, 'Man is, at one and the same time, a solitary being and a social being . . . what to me constitutes the essence of the crisis of our time concerns the relationship of the individual to society. The individual has become more conscious than ever of his dependence upon society. But he does not experience this dependence as a positive asset, as an organic tie, as a protective force but rather as a threat to his natural rights or even to his economic existence'.[17] Assumptions of human creativity, actual and potential, of alternatives and multi-directionality of developments, of multiplicity of time and of different relevant visions of truth are not only more realistic but also offer better weapons in facing the crisis of our times depicted by Einstein and still advancing.[18] This can be expressed as yet another non-deterministic, irreducible, dialectical chain where rigid division into cause and effect are spurious.

As long as there is choice, there is hope. As long as there is hope, people search for truth, dream of a better world and fight for it. As long as people search, dream and contend, there is hope.

Abbreviations used:

ES	*Entsiklopedicheskii slovar'*, Brokhauz and Efron (St. Petersburg. 1891–1906).
KA	*Krasnyi arkhiv* (published in Moscow, 1922–41 by the Central Archive Department of RSFSR, later of USSR).
NES	*Novyi entsiklopedicheskii slovar'*, Brokhauz and Efron (St Petersburg/Petrograd, commenced 1910 (unfinished)).
PSS	V. Lenin, *Polnoe sobranie sochinenii* (Moscow, 1967–9 (5th edn)).
SD	Social Democrat (group or party, i.e. the RSDRP).
KD	The Constitutional Democrats, i.e. the Party of Popular Freedom.
SR	Social Revolutionary (group or party, i.e. the PSR).

Notes and References

The references to each section (1A, 1B etc.) form a separate unit, i.e. the signs op. cit. and loc. cit. refer to items already listed in that *section. See opposite for abbreviations used.*

INTRODUCTION

1. B. Pasternak, '1905', *Stikhi i poemy 1912–1932* (Ann Arbor, 1961) vol. I, p. 110.

1 A REVOLUTION COMES TO BOIL

1A The 'neither . . . nor' Revolution

1. N. Stone, *Europe Transformed 1878–1919* (London, 1983) Part II, reviewed this evidence and summed it up as 'the ghost of 1848' brought about by 'the bankruptcy of the right, and the challenge from the left' in the wake of 'the strange death' of the European liberalism. Russia is treated in this interpretation simply as part of these European developments. For a Soviet discussion of the related international context see also *Istoriya sssr*, 1968, vol. VI, pp. 250–6 which speaks in a similar vein of 'the working class of Western Europe "learning to speak Russian" ' in those days. Ibid., p. 252. See also E. Hobsbawm, *The Age of Capital* (London, 1975) chap. 16.
2. The dating is used to signpost these revolutionary processes rather than to do justice to the full complexity and length of each of them. The Iranian 'constitutional revolution' began in 1908 and lasted until 1911 (1909 is the date when the Shah was dethroned). The Mexican revolution began in 1910 and lasted until 1925 (or even until 1943 if the Cardenas presidency is to be considered). For further evidence relevant to this line of comparison see I. Spector, *The First Russian Revolution* (Englewood Cliffs, 1968).
3. With as many as 200 000 Iranian workers in the Russian Caucasus, Iran was a case in point of direct contacts. Russians participated there both on the side of the revolutionaries and in the ranks of the monarchists. There were no Russians in India or Indians in Russia, but B. G. Tilak explicitly used Russian experience and tactics while establishing his version of

militant Indian nationalism. Spector, op. cit., pp. 39, 46–7, 98–100. In Mexico the impact of 1905–07 revolution was even less direct.

4. For discussion see T. Shanin, *The Rules of the Game: Models in Scholarly Thought* (London, 1972).

5. This line of analysis is actually often used in the comparative history of today, e.g. Stone, op. cit.; also T. Stockpol, *States and Social Revolutions* (Cambridge, 1979) (see especially Tables I and II which compared revolutions in France 1789, Russia 1917 and China 1911). For the reasons why I find these views useful but insufficient see the text which follows as well as Chapter 5 of the companion volume *Russia as a 'Developing Society'* (London, 1985).

6. For example, the record of 10 February 1905 of the proceedings of the Russian government shows that 'the sedition (*kramola*) of 1881' was used as the main point of reference in the discussion of contemporary revolutionary struggle. KA, vol. 32, p. 217.

7. See, for example, Lenin's 1905 explicit model and periodisation of the revolutionary process which he expected for Russia in PSS, vol. 12, pp. 154–6. It was based directly on Germany in 1849 and France in 1871.

8. The full text ran as follows: 'It will be best in so far as the Russian revolution [of 1905–07] and our task in it is concerned to look at it neither as if it was a bourgeois revolution in the usual sense, nor a socialist revolution, but a distinctive process taking place on the borders of the bourgeois and socialist societies, serving the liquidation of the first, promoting conditions for the second and offering a mighty push to the total development at the centres of capitalist civilisation'. The quotation provides a fair example of a new insight coupled with the refusal to react to the admittedly distinctive reality by re-conceptualisation of sufficient depth. Kautsky's claim to 'orthodoxy' was clearly well-founded. K. Kautsky, *Dvizhushchie sily i perspektivy russkoi revolyutsii* (Moscow, 1926) p. 29 (first published in Russian in 1906 with an admiring introduction by Lenin).

9. See Shanin, op. cit. (London, 1985) Chapter 5. It defined, as the 'first amendment', F. List's ideas concerning the industrialisation of Germany as well as their implementation in Russia (especially by S. Witte). 'Stolypin's reforms' (referred to as the 'second amendment') recognised that the 'Listian' policies of transitional and selective protectionism will not suffice in a country of the Russian type. In this interpretation a massive state-induced change in social structure had to be secured to make these policies work – a 'revolution from above'. See also below, Chapter 6, Section A.

    The basic conceptual elements of the so-called Stolypin reforms were already present in the discussions between senior officials and the scholarly nobles of Russia since mid-nineteenth century.

10. Lenin, PSS, vol. 41, pp. 9–10.

1B A Revolutionary Situation: Masses as Actors

1. The relevant literature is too extensive for a marginal comment. A. S. Cohen, *Theories of Revolution* (London, 1975) offers a reasonable

bibliography. Of the relevant items published since, the most interesting are T. Skockpol, *States and Social Revolutions* (Cambridge, 1978) (once again with a good up-to-date bibliography); C. L. and R. Tilly, *The Rebellious Century, 1830–1930* (Cambridge, 1975); E. Hobsbawm, 'Revolution', *XIX International Congress of Historical Sciences* (San Francisco, 1975) and an article particularly rich in context by R. Aya 'Theories of Revolution Reconsidered', *Theory and Society*, 1979, vol. 8, pp. 44–5 (for discussion of multiple sovereignity). Elements of all these insights are incorporated in the text. For further discussion of the view adopted see T. Shanin, Class, State and Revolution: Substitutes and Realities, in H. Alavi and T. Shanin, *Introduction to the Sociology of 'Developing Societies'* (London, 1982).

2. See T. Shanin, *Russia as a 'Developing Society'* (London, 1985) chap. 5.
3. Ibid, section D. For immediate reference see also P. Lyashchenko, *Istoriya narodnogo khozyaistva SSSR* (Moscow, 1948) vol. 2, chap. 8 and M. Simonova, *Problema 'oskudneniya' tsentra* etc., in *Problemy sotsial'no-ekonomicheskoi istorii rosii* (Moscow, 1971).
4. The expression 'ethnic group' is used in the sense of the Russian term *natsional'nost* which differs markedly from the west European concept of nationality. For discussion see T. Shanin *'Natsional'nost'*: The Case of a Missing Term' in H. Alavi and F. Halliday *State and Ideology in West Asia* (London, 1986).
5. Yu. Martov, *et al.*, *Obshchestvennoe dvizheni v Rossii* (St Petersburg, 1910) vol. 1, pp. 273–80; V. Leikina-Svirskaya, *Russkaya intelligentsiya v 1900–1917 godakh* (Moscow, 1981) chaps. 1, 7.
6. For example, in 1902, near Poltava, peasants attacked a police station, demanding them 'to set free their student', that is, a barely literate local peasant who led their protest and was arrested as a result.
7. V. Veselovskii, *Krest'yanskoe dvizhenie 1902 goda* (Moscow, 1923). See also S. Dubrovskii and V. Grave, *Krest'yanskoe dvizhenie nakanune revolyutsii 1905 goda* (Moscow, 1926).
8. Veselovskii, op. cit., p. 103.
9. Ibid, p. 58.
10. Ibid, p. 8.
11. For that messy affair see 'Zubatovshchina', *Byloe*, 1917, no. 4 (26); KA, vol. 1, pp. 289–328. Also M. Lyadov, *Kak nachala skladyvat'sya rossiiskaya kommunisticheskaya partiya* (Moscow, 1925) chap. XXX. For a view from the monarchist side see P. Zavarzin, *Rabota tainoi politsii* (Paris, 1924) Part II. Zubatov himself was eventually disgraced and exiled by his superiors. A bizarre epitaph ends this tale of an intelligent gendarme and a loyal monarchist facing the tsarist establishment. Zubatov shot himself on the day the abdication of Nicholas II was announced. None of his superiors did.
12. V. Varzar, *Statistika stachek rabochikh na fabrikakh i zavodakh za trekhlet'e 1905–1908* (St Petersburg, 1910) especially p. 7, gives the basic evidence of the matter. This report did not record mining, crafts, agriculture and the workers outside European Russia, that is, it was representative of the total wage labour but covered only a part of it. For further discussion see note 1 of Section 2A to follow.

1C A Revolutionary Situation: Leaders and 'Grey Peasant Workers

1. A. Spiridovich, *Revolyutsionnoe dvizhenie v rossii* (St Petersburg, 1914) vol. 1.
2. T. Shanin, *Russia as a 'Developing Society'* (London, 1985) chap. 5, section D.
3. M. Lyadov, *Kak nachala skladyvat'sya russkaya kommunisticheskaya partiya* (Moscow, 1925); L. Haimson, *The Russian Marxists and the Origins of Bolshevism* (Harvard, 1955); J. H. C. Keep, *The Rise of Social Democracy in Russia* (Oxford, 1963).
4. The booklet 'Ob agitatsii' was written by A. Kramer. See *Albom po istorii vkp(b)* (Moscow, 1928) pp. 19–21; Lyadov, op. cit., chap. VIII.
5. Quoted from the party manifesto, 1897, Spiridovich, op. cit., Appendix I, p. 216.
6. Ibid, chap. II; Lyadov, op. cit., chaps. XXIII–XXXIV; *Albom*, p. 25.
7. V. Lenin, 'Chto delat', PPS, vol. 6, pp. 1–192 which, on behalf of the Iskra, put the case for a closed organisation of professional revolutionaries as a necessary condition for successful revolutionary struggle. It was the extent of the strikes of 1902–03 which triggered off the SD's fear that 'the conscious activists are being swallowed (*pogloshcheny*) by workers' spontaneity', Lyadov, op. cit., p. 119.
8. See I. Belokonskii, *Zemskoe dvizhenie* (Moscow, 1914); I. Gindin, Russkaya burzhuaziya i tsarism v period kapitalisma, *Istoriya SSSR*, 1963, no. 3; V. Dyakin, *Russkaya burzhuaziya i tsarism v gody pervoi mirovoi voiny* (Leningrad, 1967); E. Cheremenskii, *Burzhuaziya i tsarism v pervoi russkoi revolyutsii* (Moscow, 1970).
9. Belokonskii, op. cit., pp. 80–2. Also Yu. Solov'ev, *Samoderzhavie i dvoryanstvo v 1902–1907 gg.* (Leningrad, 1981) chap. 1. For extensive documentation see *Arkheograficheskii ezhegodnik za 1974–9* (Moscow, 1975) pp. 285–95.
10. S. Sletov, *K istorii vozniknoveniya partii SR* (Petrograd, 1971); G. Gershuni, *Iz nedavnego proshlogo* (Paris, 1908); V. Chernov, *Pered burei* (Berlin and New York, 1953).
11. *Pamyatnaya knizhka sotsialista revolyutsionera* (Paris, 1911) Part 1; Spiridovich, op. cit., vol. 2 (Petrograd, 1916); Sletov, op. cit.
12. Spiridovich, op. cit., pp. 82–3.
13. *Vtoroi ocherednoi s'ezd rsdrp* (Geneva, 1904); Also the sources in note 4 above. Albom, op. cit.; *Istoriya kpss* (Moscow, 1966) vol. 2.
14. Ibid, Appendices.
15. Quoted from the speech of Martynov in Congress on 31 July. Ibid.
16. 'Resolution about the Socialist Revolutionaries', Ibid, appendices.
17. Haimson, op. cit., p. 183.
18. Belokonskii, op. cit.; M. Simonova, Zemsko-liberal'naya fronda, *Istoricheskie zapiski*, 1973, vol. 91.
19. The tenor of the political conclusions reached by the more radical members was well expressed in the following statement: 'Autocracy is the road to a revolution. To save the dynasty one must restrict its power'. Belokonskii, op. cit., p. 289.
20. *Osvobozhdenie*, no. 2 (18 June and 1 July 1902).

21. Ibid. For the organisation programme and statute see *Arkeograficheskii et., loc., cit., pp. 294–6.*

22. There has been considerable literature comparing Russian parties' programmes, tactics, membership etc. See, for example, L. Velikov, *Tablitsa russkikh politicheskikh partii* (St Petersburg, 1906).

23. See Shanin, op. cit., chap. 5, section D.

24. E. Tarnovskii, Statisticheskie svedeniya o litsakh obvinyaemykh v prestupleniyakh gosudarstvennykh, *Zhurnal ministerstva yustitsii* 1906, no. 4, pp. 64–5, 72–5, 91–3.

25. Lyadov, op. cit., p. 156. The workers' pre-eminence in the lists of political prisoners was there to stay. See, for example, A. Shcherbakov's study of Siberian exiles in 1908–11 in *Ssylnye revolyutsionery sibiri* (Irkutsk, 1973) (especially pp. 222, 237). The percentage of those charged with 'crime against the state' whose occupation was agriculture increased in 1907 to twenty-four while for those charged with 'crimes against administrative order' was eighty-two. (The parallel figures for industrial workers were twenty-one and three, respectively.) *Rossiya 1910* (St Petersburg, 1911) pp. 310–11.

1D The Forces of Order and the Force of Anger

1. S. Vitte, *Vospominaniya* (Leningrad, 1924) vol. I, p. 23 quotes it as Pleve's expressed opinion and claims its adoption as directly responsible for Witte's own dismissal. The quote is clearly malicious and possibly apocryphal but it correctly represents the spirit of the times and the logic of the political strategies adopted.

2. For particulars concerning the war, see *Letopis' voiny s Yaponiei 1904–1905* (St Petersburg (?), 1904–05) Parts 1–8; M. Pavlovich, *Russko–japonskaya voina* (Moscow, 1925); A. Sorokin, *Russko-yaponskaya voina 1904–1905 gg* (Moscow, 1956).

3. I. Belokonskii, *Zemskoe dvizhenie* (Moscow, 1914); E. Cheremenskii, *Burzhuaziya i tsarism v pervoi russkoi revolyutsii* (Moscow, 1970), chap. 1; Yu. Solov'ev, *Samoderzhavie i dvoryanstvo v 1902–1907 gg* (Leningrad, 1981) chap. 1.

4. KA, vol. 43, p. 110.

5. For a description see V. Nevskii, the Bolshevik contemporary and historian of the revolution in *Rabochee dvizhenie v yanvarskie dni 1905 goda* (Moscow, 1930), pp. 61–128. He commented that the SDs let it all 'slip between its fingers' (*prozevali*) mainly owing to the factional struggles in which they were involved. See also G. Gapon, *Istoriya moei zhizni* (Leningrad, 1925) and the official reports in *Pravo*, 1905, nos. 1 and 2. Also, P. Anatol'ev, *Devyatoe yanvarya* (Moscow, 1925) chaps. V, VI, VII.

6. The contemporary figures varied from an official admission of 128 dead and 333 wounded (with no losses to the forces of order) to the opposition's claims of up to 1000 killed and 2000 wounded.

7. For a rare example of appreciation of those issues see E. P. Thompson, 'The Moral Economy of the English Crowd in the Eighteenth Century', *Past and Present*, 1971, no. 50.

8. L. Tolstoy, *I Cannot Stay Silent* (New York, 1915) pp. 395–411.

2 THE REVOLUTION FROM BELOW: DOWN WITH AUTOCRACY!

2A   A Tale of a Revolution: January 1905 to April 1906

1. The contemporary data available for 1895–1904 and 1906–08 is based mainly on the works of V. Varzar. His figures recorded only the workers of 'registered factories' in European Russia, that is, did not include miners, railwaymen, workers in services, and industrial workers of Asian Russia who would add about 50 per cent to his total figures. Nor did it reflect the rural wage labour. All the same, the trends indicated by these studies are without doubt a fair representation of reality *in toto* and were universally used by the representatives of different ideological camps. V. Varzar, *Statistika stachek rabochikh na fabrikakh i zavodakh za trekhletie 1906–08 gg* (St Petersburg, 1910). See also L. Haimson and R. Petrusha, *Strike Waves in Imperial Russia (1912–14, 1905–07)* (a conference paper quoted with the permission of the authors). See also section 2C.

    The statistical data were usually divided by provinces (*guberniya* abbr. *gub.*) or multi-provincial regions such as European Russia, often referred to as 'the fifty *guberniyas*'.
2. Strikes of significant strength were also reported in January and the beginning of February in Yaroslavl, Kharkov and Nizhnii. For the regional diversity see in particular V. Nevskii, *Rabochee dvizhenie v yanvarskie dni goda* (Moscow, 1931) and a considerable number of regional monographs published close to the 1955 period of the 'fifty years since . . .' celebrations.
3. 600 000 strikers altogether were reported in the Polish provinces inhabited by only 7.5 per cent of the population of the Empire and in which about 10 per cent of its wage-workers lived. Yu. Martov, P. Maslov and A. Potresov, *Obshchestvennoe dvizhenie v rossii v nachale XX veka* (St Petersburg, 1909–12) vol. 4, book 2, p. 160.
4. I. P. Belokonskii, *Zemskoe dvizhenie* (Moscow, 1914) pp. 266–82.
5. S. Vitte, *Vospominaniya* (Leningrad, 1934) vol. II, pp. 157–8.
6. KA, vol. 8, pp. 49–69.
7. V. Nevskii, *Revolyutsia 1905 goda* (Kharkov, 1925); A. Pankratova, *Pervaya russkaya revolyutsiya* (Moscow, 1951); V. Obninskii, *Letopis' russkoi revolyutsii* (Moscow, 1906); H. Seton-Watson, *The Russian Empire 1801–1917* (Oxford, 1967); Martov *et al.*, op. cit., vol. 2, book 1.
8. S. Kirpichnikov (S.S.K.), *Soyuz soyuzov* (St Petersburg, 1906); D. Sverchkov, Soyuz soyuzov, in *Krasnaya letopis'*, 1925, no. 3, pp. 149–63. V. Leikina Svirskaya, *Russkaya intelligentsiya v 1900–1917 godach* (Moscow, 1981). In terms of party affinities P. Miliukov of the future KD, V. Groman of the SD Mensheviks and S. Mitskevich of the Bolsheviks were among the initiators of the Union of Unions.
9. Martov *et al.*, op. cit., p. 30.
10, *Istoricheskie zapiski*, 1975, no. 95, p. 41.
11. See Nevskii, *Rabochee dvizhenie v yanvarskie dni 1905 goda* (Moscow,

1930) for description of the conditions, the moods and the difficulties of those times. Active in the period 1905–07 as a Bolshevik, Nevskii became one of the party's historians in the 1920s. He reported that it was Gapon who led the workers of St Petersburg at the end of 1904 while 'the life of the party masses was mainly that of mutual squabbles'. Ibid, p. 160, also pp. 76–82, 93.

12. Martov *et al.*, op. cit., p. 64; A. Spiridovich, *Revolyutsionnoe dvizhenie v rossii* (St Petersburg, 1914) vol. 2, chaps. XIII, XIV.

13. The SD elected delegates to its Fifth Congress of 1907 and this gives the membership figures agreed on by the different factions (which carefully double-checked each other). See *Istoriya kpss* (Moscow, 1966) vol. 2, p. 215. We assumed arbitrarily that half the membership of the Bund (27 000 *in toto*) came from the Polish provinces. For the PSR estimates see M. Perrie, 'The Social Composition and Structure of the Socialist Revolutionary Party Before 1917', *Soviet Studies*, 1972, vol. 24, no. 2, pp. 224–5. See also V. Ginev, *Bor'ba za krest'yanstvo i krizis russkogo neonarodnichestva* (Leningrad, 1983) pp. 138–9. The PSR's own figure reported at the Second Congress (1907) was 50 000 in Russia without the Ukraine, (which would account for 7000 to 10 000 more). There were also reported 18 000 members of the PSR 'Peasant Brotherhoods'. The SDs often ridiculed those PSR membership figures as overstated (see Lenin, PSS, vol. 14, p. 173 etc.) but available data substantiate the claim that the membership of PSR was then higher than that of their Bolshevik or Menshevik competitors taken singly (it collapsed in a later period). For figures of exiles and people arrested see A. Shcherbakov in *Ssyl'nye revolyutsionery sibiri* (Irkutsk, 1973) pp. 218, 237, 241. Also V. Leikina Svirskaya, *Russkaya intelligentsiya v 1900–1917 godakh* (Moscow, 1981) pp. 250–4. For somewhat different estimates of membership of RSDWP see D. Lane, *The Roots of Russian Communism* (Assen, 1969) p. 13, whose total figure for SDs all over Russia is 150 000 – that is, fairly similar to that of the source we used.

The international community of socialist parties adopted a broadly similar view. The seats awarded to the representatives of Russia at the 1907 Stuttgart Congress of the Second International were RSDWP (Bolsheviks and Mensheviks jointly) 37, the PSR 21 (*Mezhdunarodnyi sotsialisticheskii kongress v shtutgarte*, St Petersburg, 1907, p. 8).

14. *Vtoroi period russkoi revolyutsii* (Moscow, 1957) Part I, pp. 317–19; M. Akhun and V. Petrov, *Bolsheviki i armiya v 1905–17 gg* (Leningrad, 1929); Spiridovich, op. cit., chap. XVII.

15. The extent of spontaneity in the actual commencement of the rail strike is a matter of dispute. See S. Chernomordnik, *Piatyi god* (Moscow, 1925) pp. 93–117; V. Pereverzev, 'Vserossiiskii zheleznodorozhnyi soyuz 1905 g.', *Byloe*, 1925, no. 4/32; I. Pushkareva, *Zheleznodorozhniki rossii v vserossiiskoi oktiabroskoi politicheskoi stachke* (Moscow, 1959) (dissertation).

16. M. Pokrovskii, *1905* (Moscow, 1925) vol. 2; E. Krivosheina, *Peterburgskii sovet rabochikh deputatov v 1905 g.* (Moscow, 1926); A. Pankratova, *Vserossiiskaya politicheskaya stachka v oktyabre 1905 g.* (Moscow, 1955); Martov *et al.*, op. cit., vol. 2, pp. 1–120.

17. *1905 god v Peterburge* (Moscow, 1925) for records and reports of the city's Soviet. Memoirs of its members were extensively published during the 1925 celebrations of the 1905–07 revolution, for example, A. Pisarev in *Krasnaya letopis'*, 1925, no. 4. The best known of these memoirs by the vice-chairman of the St Petersburg Soviet was L. Trotsky, *1905* (London, 1971). See also its chairman's memoirs, G. Khrustal'ev Nosar' in *Istoriya soveta rabochikh deputatov* (St Petersburg, 1906). Also 2A, note 16.

18. For the text and the tale see the sequence of documents published in KA, vols 11–12. For text see B. Dmytryshyn, *Imperial Russia* (Hindsdale, 1974) p. 383.

19. For consistent reporting see *Pravo* – the main newspaper of the Russian legal profession, with strong constitutionalist tendencies. Also V. Obninskii, *Novyi stroi* (Moscow, 1909).

20. See the memoirs of the then Vice-Minister of the Interior in charge of these payments, G. Kryzhanovskii, *Vospominaniya* (Berlin, n.d.) pp. 152–9. For the Black Hundreds see Martov *et al.*, op. cit., vol. 3; Obninskii, Novyi, op. cit., pp. 268–77, 9–22; S. Smirnova, *Chernaya sotnya* (St Petersburg, 1906). See also section 2C, note 5.

21. See, for example, the recollections of the SD Bolsheviks' leader in Kronstadt, A. Aleksandrov, 'Kronshtadskie vosstaniya v 1905–06 gg', *Krasnaya letopis'*, 1925, (3) 14.

22. Obninskii, op. cit., which compiled the relevant facts and figures. The liberal press had documented it month by month especially in *Pravo* and *Vestnik Evropy* for 1905–07, and in the newly-created legal socialist press, for example, *Novaya zhizn'*, *Syn otechestva*, etc. The official nature of unofficial execution was enhanced by Durnovo's order to punitive expeditions 'not to hold arrestees'.

23. V. Vodovozov, Tsarskosel'skie soveshchaniya, *Byloe*, 1917, nos. 3–4; KA, vol. 31, pp. 81–102.

24. For example, B. Pares, reported on the spot about that rapid change of mood and the 'disgust with violence' which spread after October 1905 in the middle classes. See his *My Russian Memoirs* (London, 1935). See also E. Cheremenskii, *Burzhuaziya i tsarism v pervoi russkoi revolyutsii* (Moscow, 1970) chaps. VI, VII.

25. Nevskii, Revolyutsiya, op. cit., pp. 152–161.

26. A Soviet source claimed as many as 2000 armed fighters in the 'detachments' of Moscow, that is, the PSR and the SD Bolsheviks 250–300 each, SD Mensheviks 100 with more than half in non-party units. N. Yakovlev, *Vooruzhonnoe vosstanie v dekabre 1905 g* (Moscow, 1957) pp. 117–18.

27. See in particular the report of D. Gimmer of the Moscow 'Military committee' published in S. Chernomordik, *Pyatyi god* (Moscow, 1925) vol. I. Also Nevskii, Revolyutsiya, op. cit., pp. 88–95.

28. See *Agrarnyi vopros v sovete ministrov* (Moscow, 1924); KA, vol. 31, pp. 94–102.

29. For the background and particulars see V. Vodovozov, op. cit., nos. 3–4.

2B   A Tale of the Revolution: The First *Duma* to Winter 1907

1. *Vestnik evropy*, 1906, no. 4, p. 762.
2. V. Vodovozov, 'Tsarskosel'skie soveshchaniya', *Byloe,* 1917, nos. 3–4, p. 227. (The quoted view was that of P. Shvenbakh) and *Petergofskoe soveshchanie o proekte gosudarstvennoi dumy* (Berlin, (?) p. 191 (for the views of Bobrinskii). For general discussion see Y. Solov'ev, *Samoderzhavie i dvoryanstvo v 1902–1907* (Leningrad, 1981) pp. 180–6.
3. *Gosudarstvennaya duma, sozyv I* (St Petersburg, 1906) vols. I, II; *K desyatiletiyu 1-oi gosudarstvennoi dumy* (Petrograd, 1906); P. Semenyuta, *Pervaya gosudarstvennaya duma* (St Petersburg, 1907); N. Borodin, *Gosudarstvennaya duma v tsifrakh* (St Petersburg, 1906).
4. The figures of workers on strike were about 2 900 000 in 1905, 1 100 000 in 1906 and 790 000 in 1907 and those on political strike 1 700 000, 650 000 and 540 000 respectively. (The figures are a summary of monthly reports, for instance, striker who proceeded to strike for two months would be twice accounted for.) V. Varzar, *Statistika stachek rabochikh na fabrikakh i zavodakh za trekhletie 1906–08 gg* (St Petersburg, 1910), p. 7.
5. Both Lenin and Plekhanov increasingly urged their followers against pliancy (*ustupchivost'*) and compromise (*primiren'chestvo*) towards the other faction.
6. For example, on the SRs' side Gershuni in his letter from prison to the January 1906 PSR party congress, on the SDs' side Larin (then a Menshevik, after 1917 a leading Bolshevik economist).
7. For socialist parties see section 2A, note 13. For police estimates see also A. Spiridovich, *Revolyutskonnoe dvizhenie v rossii* (St Petersburg, 1916) vol. 2, chaps. XII–XV. In the Polish provinces SDKP claimed 22 000 members in 1907, to which an estimated 13 000 of the Bund and 50 000 for the PPS should be added. (The last figure was given by this party at its Eleventh Congress in late 1905. It would have grown but some of the PPS members were expelled or left with the Revolutionary Faction of J. Pilsudski.) The membership of the KD then reached about 100 000 members, for which see E. Cheremenskii, *Russkaya burzhuaziya i tsarism v gody pervoi mirovoi voiny* (Leningrad, 1967) p. 416.
8. *Agrarnyi vopros v pervoi gosudarstvennoi dume* (Kiev, 1906); *Svod agrarnykh programm* (St Petersburg, 1907).
9. *Byloe*, 1907, no. 2, pp. 29–35.
10. V. Obninskii, *Letopis' russkoi revolyutsii* (Moscow, 1907) vol. 3, pp. 5, 36, 42; G. Kryzhanovskii, *Vospominaniya* (Berlin, n.d.) pp. 101–4, 142–4.
11. NES, vol. II, p. 210. During the whole period 1905–07 a constant stream of restrictive legislation aimed at any form of opposition was published. As an example, the issue of May 1906 picked at random of the official legal publication *Zhurnal ministerstva yustitsii*, carried the following legislative items:
    a) increases in the maximum punishment for the publishing of anti-government materials
    b) a new decree about the criminal responsibility for slanderous rumours about the activities of state administration and state officials

c) regulations to speed up legal procedures

d) further delimitations of the areas of exile (*ssylka*)

12. For example, Obninskii, *Novyi stroi* (Moscow, 1909) p. 157. The British diplomatic services reported the numbers of Russian state officials killed by the terrorists to be 1126 in 1906 and 3000 in 1907. *British Public Records FO 371, vol. 726, no. 21149* (June 1909).

13. M. Perrie, 'The Social Composition and Structure of the Socialist Revolutionary Party Before 1917', *Soviet Studies*, 1972, vol. 24, no. 2, pp. 227–9, based on an analysis of *Politicheskaya katorga i ssylka* (Moscow, 1934).

14. Ibid, pp. 321, 238–9.

15. See this volume, Chapters 3 and 4.

16. P. A. Stolypin, *Sbornik rechei* (St Petersburg, 1911) pp. 75–7 (speech on 5 December 1908).

17. A. Smirnov, *Kak proshli vybory v gosudarstvennuyu dumu* (St Petersburg, 1907); A. Levin, *The Second Duma* (New Haven, 1940) pp. 65–9. *Gosudarstvennaya duma, sozyv 2* (St Petersburg, 1907) vols. I, II.

18. Smirnov, op. cit., pp. 238–9, 250–1.

19. ES, vol. 4/D, section devoted to electoral laws and to the *Duma*. For discussion see A. Avrekh, *Tsarism i tret'eiyun'skaya sistema* (Moscow, 1966) chaps 1, 2; G. Hosking, *The Russian Constitutional Experiment* (London, 1973); L. Haimson, *The Politics of Rural Russia* (Bloomington, 1972) pp. 9–25, 285–92.

20. For an important insight into the way it was produced see Kryzhanovskii, op. cit., pp. 93–141.

21. 'The Russian revolution lingered on in the form of sporadic workers strikes in 1906–07. In the countryside the activity among the peasants against landlords actually increased . . . [which] leads some historians to extend the dates of Russian revolution from 1905 to 1907'. *The Modern Encyclopaedia of Russian and Soviet History* (Indiana, 1983), vol. 31, pp. 68–9.

2C   The 'Internal Enemies of Russia': Revolution as a Composition of Forces

1. KA, vol. 32, pp. 229–33.

2. Lenin, PSS, vol. 23, pp. 237–9, 249.

3. For discussion see Chapter 1 of the companion volume, T. Shanin, *Russia as a 'Developing Society'*

4. A decree was passed urgently by the government, permitting and encouraging the creation of private militias to defend the manors, but remarkably little came of it in Central Russia.

5. The expression 'Black Hundreds' was initially used to define the non-privileged strata of the medieval Russian city. (The first two 'Hundreds' were the organisations of guilds of the merchants described as 'Of White Bone' while lesser, that is, the plebeian 'Hundreds' were 'Black'.) For a self-description of Black Hundreds see, for example, *Rukovodstvo chernosotentsa-monarkhista* (Saratov, 1906) which defined the abolition of the Duma as the aim of the movement and its enemies as: constitutionalists, democrats, socialists, revolutionaries, anarchists and

Jews (p. 6). For the movement's activities see Obninskii, *Polgoda russkoi revolyutsii* (Moscow, 1906).

6. See V. Gurko (then the Vice-Minister of the Interior) *Features and Figures of the Past* (Stanford, 1937) pp. 433–8.

7. For example, the bishop Illidor, the journalist Gringmut and also numerous booklets of personal abuse and vilification as, for example, N. Vasil'ev, *Chto takoe trudoviki* (St Petersburg, 1907) concerning the Labour faction at the Duma as noted in Section 3C, note 14). Anti-semitism was a particularly important element of ideology. For example, of description, of Dumas deputee V. Gessen as 'a KD, Jewish in extraction and in political beliefs' *Sinodik chlenov vtoroi gosudarstvennoi dumy* (St Petersburg, 1907) p. 38.

8. As in note 3 above.

9. For example, the memoirs of A. Polovtsev, for May 1906 reported that an extremist monarchist plot in some army units had to broken by the arrest of a number of the officers, KA, vol. 4, p. 110.

10. M. Akhun and V. Petrov, *bolsheviki i armiya v 1905–1917 gg* (Leningrad, 1929); V. Obninskii, *Novyi stroi* (Moscow, 1911) pp. 111–29, 167–8; *Vtoroi period revolyutsii* (Moscow, 1957) pp. 317–19; A. Spiridovich, *Revolyutsionnoe dvizhenie v rossii* (St Petersburg, 1916) vol. 2, chap. XVII.

11. L. Trotskii, *1905* (Moscow, 1922) p. 263. He added by way of explanation that it was the 'peasant-like slow thinking' (*tugodumnost'*) which made the same men burn neighbouring estates but, once dressed in uniform, to shoot his own likes as well as urban workers.

12. See the diary of Prince Constantine, KA, vols. 44, 45.

13. Trotskii, op. cit., p. 115, quoted affirmatively in Witte memoirs.

14. V. Obninskii, *Letopis' russkoi revolyutsii* (Moscow, 1907). See also Obninskii, *Novyi stroi* (Moscow, 1909); B. Veselovskii, *Krest'yanskii vopros i krest'yanskoe dvizhenie v rossii* (St Petersburg, 1907); *Revolyutsiya 1905–1907 v gruzii* (Tiflis, 1956) (includes the report by the Assistant Governor Kipshidze about repressions by universal rape in the village Makhuri of Kutais province).

15. The largest number of those executed by court martial was reached in 1908. S. Usherovich, *Smertnye kazni v tsarskoi rossii* (Kharkov, 1933) p. 492.

16. Those reports and the comments by the tsar are filed in the TsGIAL of Leningrad, and under each of the comments in blue pencil runs the neat calligraphic handwriting 'by His Imperial Majesty's own hand it has been inscribed . . .' with the signature of the chief of the imperial chancellory. They make unforgettable reading – a kind of Nixon tapes exposed to the public eye.

17. KA, vol. 32, p. 167.

18. Obninskii, *Novyi*, op. cit., p. 114.

19. A. Shestakov, *Krest'yanskaya revolyutsia 1905–1907 gg. v rossii* (Moscow, 1926) p. 46.

20. Yu. Martov, P. Maslov, A. Potresov, *Obshchestvennoe dvizhenie v rossii v nachale XX veka* (St Petersburg, 1909–1912) vol. 2–1, pp. 117–18, 299.

For a similar assessment by a Bolshevik historian and contemporary see Nevskii, *Revolyutsiya 1905 goda* (Kharkov, 1925) pp. 337, 510.

21. Lenin PSS, vol. 16, p. 275.

22. See Gurko, op. cit., pp. 286–7.

23. In *Istoriya SSSR* (Moscow, 1968) vol. IV, p. 25.

24. In this note and also in notes 23–5, only the sources specifically devoted to the region are annotated. Additionally, much of the information comes from Nevskii, op. cit.; Martov, op. cit.; ES; NES; V. Stankevich, *Sud'ba rossii* (Berlin, 1921); *Revolyutsiya 1905 goda i samoderzhavie* (Moscow, 1928); *Revolyutsiya 1905–1907 godov v natsional'nykh raionakh rossii*; *Istoriya SSSR*, 1968, vol. VI. For particular sources concerning Latvia see *Revolyutsiya 1905–1907 v latvii* (Riga, 1956); *The Revolution in the Baltic Provinces* (London, 1907) etc.

25. V. Kalandadze and M. Kheidze, *Ocherki revolyutsionnogo dvizheniya v gurii,* (St Petersburg, 1906); *Katorga i ssylka* (Tiflis, 1925) (1)3; *Revolyutsiya 1905–1907 v Gruzii*, op. cit.; N. Zhordaniya, *Moya zhizn'* (Stanford, 1968). See also Chapter 4 of this volume.

26. *1894–1905 revolyutsionnoe dvizhenie v rossii* (St Petersburg, 1907) pp. 161–226; Martov etc., op. cit., vol. 3, pp. 227–70; *Historia Polski* (Warszawa, 1960) vol. III.

27. *Deyatel'nost bunda za poslednie tri goda* (1903); N. Bukhbinder, *Istoriya evreiskogo rabochego dvizheniya v rossii* (Leningrad, 1925); H. J. Tobias, *The Jewish Bund in Russia* (Stanford, 1972).

28. L. Haimson and R. Petrusha, *Strike Waves in Imperial Russia, 1912–14, 1905–07* (a conference paper) which has also shown the most significant correlation to 'strike intensity' was the urban concentration of enterprises and workers while the size of the enterprise mattered little. For the figures of the Russian industrial inspectorate see V. Varzar, *Statistika stachek na fabrikakh i zavodakh* (St Petersburg, 1910) discussed by Haimson and Petrusha as well as by A. Amal'aik in *Istoricheskie zapiski*, 1955, no. 52, pp. 142–85.

29. *Istoricheskie zapiski*, 1975, no. 95, p. 41. For an interesting discussion of the trade-union movement see P. Kabanov, *Rabochee i profsoyuznoe dvizhenie v moskve* (Moscow, 1955).

30. Map 1 is based on the figures of Varzar, op. cit. pp. 15–19. Most of the contemporary maps and tables over-accentuate the strike intensity in central Russia by using absolute figures (and not proportions of the population of wage workers).

31. For discussion see Shanin, op. cit., Chapter 5, section C.

32. K. Kautsky, Slavyane i revolyutsiya, *Put' k vlasti* (Moscow, 1959) (first printed in Russia in 1902 by *Iskra*, no. 18).

33. For example, memoirs of P. A. Baryshkin, *Moskva kupecheskaya* (New York, 1954); E. D. Cheremenskii, *Burzhuaziya i tsarism v pervoi russkoi revolyutsii* (Moscow, 1970).

34. For discussion see V. Leikina-Svirskaya, *Russkaya intelligentsiya v 1900–1917 godakh* (Moscow, 1918) chap. 7. S. Kirpichenikov, *Vserossiiskii soyuz inzhenerov i tekhnikov* (St Petersburg, 1906) and also his

pamphlet *Soyuz soyuzov* (St Petersburg, 1906); J. Sanders, The Union of Unions (New York, 1983) (unpublished dissertation, Colombia University, New York); P. Milyukov, *Vospominaniya* (New York, 1955) vol. I, pp. 285–91.

35. Quoted after Leikina-Svirskaya, op. cit., p. 231. The attitude to the Union of Unions adopted by the SD leaders and especially by their Bolshevik brand was usually hostile. A typical view was that this organisation because of its class characteristics could not but be dominated in class terms by KDs. For example, V. Vorovskii, *Izbrannye proizvedeniya o pervoi russkoi revolyutsii* (Moscow, 1955) pp. 364–71 (written in 1905). Also, Sanders, op. cit. With his usual flourish Trotsky described the Union of Unions as an 'organisational apparatus to make the heterogeneous dissenting intelligentsia into political slaves of *zemstvo* liberalism', Milyukov, op. cit., p. 281.

36. For discussion see Shanin, op. cit., Chapter 5.

37. Martov *et al.*, op. cit., vol. 2, part 2, p. 264. Martov has also spoken of an optical illusion of a purely proletarian struggle and victory in the general strike of October. To his view the victory came precisely because the struggle was not solely proletarian (op. cit., p. 232). A measure of overstatement accepted (the polemic zeal was part of the debate about the attitude to the liberal opposition) he doubtless put his finger on a most important characteristic of the 1905 struggle.

38. The initial Bolshevik distrust of the Soviet is admitted in *Istoriya kpss* (Moscow, 1966) vol. 2, pp. 104–7. These feelings were still stronger where the Union of Unions and the All-Russian Peasant Union were concerned.

39. See A. Anfimov, *Krupnoe pomeshchich'e khozyaistvo evropeiskoi rossii* (Moscow, 1969); R. Manning, *The Crisis of the Old Order in Russia* (Princeton, 1982); *Trudy s'ezda upolnomochennykh dvoryanskikh obshchestv* (St Petersburg, 1906); Yu. Solov'ev, *Samoderzhavie i dvoryanstvo v 1902–1907 gg.* (Leningrad, 1981); M. Simonova, 'Zemsko-liberal'naya fronda', *Istoricheskie zapiski* (1973) no. 91.

40. The dissent within the Russian nobility had never disappeared altogether. At the very time when the reactionary tendency was gaining the upper hand a squire from the Don region petitioned the Minister of the Interior in 1906 against the repressions in his area, saying of those responsible for them 'They have infuriated the whole of Russia, filled all its prisons with no reason, arrested the teachers leaving children without schooling . . . after shamefully losing to Japan they now torture the helpless peasants . . . Every policeman flogs peasants and because of those bastards, we peaceful noblemen will eventually find our life unbearable'. Quoted after Shestakov, op. cit., pp. 57–8.

41. For a comparative discussion of the European scene see A. J. Mayer, *The Persistence of the Old Regime* (New York, 1983).

42. From a petition of landowners quoted in KA, vols. 11–12, p. 156. See also Belokonskii, op. cit., pp. 50–104, 263–397 for the steady backwards progression of the government under these pressures. Also V. Vodovozov, Tsarskosel'skie soveshchaniya, *Byloe*, 1917, nos. 3 and 4 (25/26).

3.   THE REVOLUTION FROM BELOW: LAND AND LIBERTY!

3A   The Jacquery

1. *The Concise Oxford Dictionary* (Oxford, 1901) p. 542; *The Encyclopaedia Britannica* (London, 1938) vol. 12, p. 861.
2. Quoted after J. le Goff, 'The Town as an Agent of Civilisation' in C. M. Cipolla, *The Fontana Economic History of Europe: The Middle Ages* (London, 1977) p. 71.
3. A. Peshekhonov, *Agrarnaya problema* (St Petersburg, 1906) p. 46.
4. For the discussion of the issues of the 'bearable' and the 'unbearable' in the exploitation of peasantry and of place of the moral outrage at the roots of rebellions see Chapter 1, section C. See also J. C. Scott, *Moral Economy of the Peasant* (London, 1976) following in this matter E. P. Thompson, 'Moral, Economy of the English Crowd in the Eighteenth Century', *Past and Present*, 1971, no. 50.
5. See P. Longworth, *The Cossacks* (London, 1969).
6. See I. Smirnov *et al.*, *Krest'yanskie voiny v rossii XVII-XVIII v.* (Leningrad, 1966); P. Avrich, *Russian Rebels* (New York, 1972). For the rebellion of Pugachev also see P. Longworth, 'The Last Great Cossack Peasant Rising', *Journal of European Studies*, 1973, 3, which carries an extensive bibliography. For a major contemporary Soviet study of the Pugachev rebellion, V. V. Mavrodin, *Krest'yanskaya voina v Rossii v 1773–1775 godakh* (Moscow, 1966–70).
7. J. Bloom, *Lord and Peasant in Russia* (New York, 1964) pp. 551–8, 591; P. Silver, *Peasant Disturbances in Russia, 1826–1917* (an unpublished M.A. thesis, Columbia University, New York, 1977).
8. For example, Avrich, op. cit., pp. 256–63. It clearly contradicted claims of the total lack of historical memory by Russian peasants as voiced by, say, M. Gorkii, *O russkom krest'yanstve* (Berlin, 1924).
9. E. Wolf, *Peasant Wars in the Twentieth Century* (New York, 1969). In the same context Barrington Moore commented that modernisation begins with peasant revolutions which fail and continues with peasant revolutions which succeed. For discussion see his *Social Origins of Dictatorship and Democracy* (Boston, 1969).
10. *Agrarnoe dvizhenie v rossii v 1905–1906 gg.* (St Petersburg, 1908) vols. 1 and 2, analysed in S. Prokopovich, *Agrarnyi krizis i meropriyatiya pravitel'stva* (Moscow, 1912).
11. S. Dubrovskii and V. Grave, *Agrarnoe dvizhenie v 1905–1907 gg.* (Moscow, 1925) followed up by S. Dubrovskii, *Krest'yanskoe dvizhenie v revolyutsii 1905–1907 gg.* (Moscow, 1956).
12. For such compilations see P. Maslov, *Agrarnyi vopros v rossii* (St Petersburg, 1908) vol. 2, V. Veselovskii, *Krest'yanskii vopros i krest'-yanskoe dvizhenie v rossii* (St Petersburg, 1907). A. A. Vasilev etc., *Krest'yanskie nakazy samarskoi gubernii* (Samara, 1906); Dubrovskii, *Krest'yanskoe*, op. cit.; Also notes 28 and 31 in section 3C.
13. Especially the *Protokoly delegatskogo s'ezda vserossiiskogo krest'yanskogo soyuza* (Moscow, 1906).
14. For example, a general study by V. Tropin, *Bor'ba bol'shevikov za*

rukovodstvo krest'yanskim dvizheniem v 1905 g. (Moscow, 1970), and a long list of regional studies discussed in M. Simonova, 'Krest'yanskoe dvizhenie 1905–1907 gg. v sovetskoi istoriografii', *Istoricheskie zapiski*, 1975, no. 95, pp. 204, 252; and in L. Sen'chakova, 'Opublikovanie dokumentov po istorii krest'yanskogo dvizheniya 1905–7 gg., *Istoriya SSSR*, 1979, part. 2.

15. E. Zhivolup, *Krest'yanskoe dvizhenie v kharkovskoi gubernii v 1905–07 godakh* (Kharkov, 1956) pp. 106–7.

16. Prokopovich, op. cit., p. 35; Veselovskii, op. cit., pp. 116, 121. *Agrarnoe dvizhenie v rossii*, op. cit., vol. I, pp. 52, 364–5, vol. II, pp. 22, 30, 59, 371 etc.

17. Dubrovskii, op. cit., p. 63.

18. See sections 1C and 2C in this volume.

19. *Ezhegodnik rossii 1906* (St Petersburg, 1906) pp. 210–11 reported the drop of winter crops in European Russia, as against the five years which preceded it, to average more than 20 per cent. In the particularly hard-hit Penza *guberniya* the drop was more than by one third. Also Veselovskii, op. cit., pp. 85–95.

20. V. Nevskii, *Revolyutsiya 1905 goda* (Kharkov, 1925) p. 186.

21. For the compilation of the relevant contemporary reports see in particular Veselovskii, op. cit., pp. 32–3; Prokopovich, op. cit., pp. 29–30 (based mainly on the newsmen's reports for example, that of A. Maximov in *Russkie vedomosti*). Also Maslov, op. cit., pp. 150–3; N. Lavrov, 'Krest'yanskie nastroeniya vesnoi 1905 goda', *Krasnaya letopis'*, 1925, no. 3 (14). For a relevant record by a foreign witness see B. Pares, *My Russian Memoirs* (London, 1935) pp. 148–57.

22. A Shestakov, *Krest'yanskaya revolyutsiya 1905–1907 gg. v rossii* (Moscow, 1926) p. 46.

23. Maslov, op. cit. 1, pp. 161–2; Veselovskii, op. cit., p. 32; Prokopovich, op. cit., pp. 42–5; *Historia Polski* (Warszawa, 1960) vol. 3.

24. *Protokoly delegatskogo . . .*, op. cit., (the quotations come from its Appendix and pp. 139–41).

25. For a vivid contemporary description, A. Studentsov, *Saratovskoe krest'yanskoe vosstanie 1905 goda* (Penza, 1926) pp. 3–8.

26. M. Bok, *Vospominaniya o moem ottse p.a.stolypine* (New York, 1953) pp. 147, 151, 152.

27. Ibid. pp. 151, 152.

28. Simonova, loc. cit., pp. 214–15.

29. Studentsov, op. cit., pp. 17–41. Saratov *guberniya* was one of the areas where the peasant organisations of the SR were initiated (see I. Rakitnikova, 'Revolyutsionnaya rabota v krest'yanstve v saratovskoi gubernii', *Katorga i ssylka* (Moscow, 1928). By 1905 up to 200 Peasant Brotherhoods were reported as operating there – one of the strongest PSR organisations within the Russian peasantry. Maslov, op. cit., p. 243. The SR were also strong in the central Russian *guberniyas* of Kazan', Simbirsk, Tambov, etc. Tropin, op. cit., pp. 53–54. Also V. Ginev, *Bor'ba za krest'yanstvo i krizis russkogo neonarodnichestva* (Leningrad, 1983) pp. 41–79.

30. E. Morokhovets, *Krest'yanskoe dvizhenie i sotsial-demokratiya* (Moscow, 1926) pp. 60–1.
31. See for example the reports of Admiral Dubasov, tsar's special envoy sent 'to pacify' the Chernigov *guberniya*, KA, vol. 2–3 (69–70).
32. For a vivid recollection of such a prison see T. Sushkin, *Agrarniki: siluety 1905–7 gg.* (Moscow, 1927) who reports the sentence of death and the actual hanging of a peasant lad condemned for the 'expropriation for revolutionary purposes' – at which nobody was hurt – of the sum of 2 roubles 75 kopeks, that is, about $1.
33. B. Gorn, *Krest'yanskoe dvizhenie za poltora veka* (Moscow, 1907) p. 80. Martov spoke of the 1906 expectations and hope of radical workers' circles for a peasant revolt to change the political scene. Yu. Martov, P. Maslov and A. Potresov, *Obshchestvennoe dvizhenie v rossii v nachale xxgo veka* (St Petersburg, 1909–12) vol. 1–2, p. 254. Lenin expressed same views in PSS, vol. 12, pp. 154–7, 176.
34. *Agrarnyi vopros v sovete ministrov* (Moscow, 1924) pp. 70–1.
35. See Stolypin's circular, KA, vol. 32, pp. 158–82.
36. Shestakov, op. cit., p. 44.
37. Veselovskii, op. cit., pp. 111–12 (based on newspaper report). See also Shestakov, op. cit., pp. 125–32.
38. *Zhurnal ministerstva yustitsii*, June 1906, pp. 17–18.
39. Pares, op. cit., pp. 150, 158.
40. Veselovskii, op. cit., pp. 125–32. See also Maslov, op. cit., p. 325 and the documents gathered in *Vtoroi period revolyutsii* (Moscow, 1957).
41. For example see the report by Zhivolup, op. cit., p. 102, about the village Dmitrievka being burned after its inhabitants refused to participate, together with the neighbouring villages, in the attack on a local manor.
42. Maslov, op. cit., p. 381. See also *Agrarnoe dvizhenie v rossii*, op. cit., vol. II, pp. 271–8 etc.
43. For an example of such 'interpretative journalism' of the olden days see the report about the 'cruel, terrible and inhuman insurrection of the common peasant folk' in Tyrol of 1525, whose leader 'a malicious, evil, rebellious but crafty man' demanded most scandalous things, namely, the abolishment of the exclusive legal privileges of nobility and clergy as 'contrary to the word of God', the election of judges and jurors, a regional university, the turning of the monasteries into hospitals and asylums, fair prices for food and the public ownership of mines. (Quoted after J. S. Shapiro, *Social Reform and the Reformation*, New York, 1909.) Our own chroniclers have learnt since not to spell out in such detail malicious demands of peasant leaders on the well-justified suspicion that these may sound to some of the readers attractive, reasonable and even surprisingly mild.

3B   The Peasant Rule

1. Tan (Bogoraz), *Novoe krest'yanstvo* (Moscow, 1905) p. 39.
2. B. Veselovskii, *Krest'yanskii vopros i krest'yanskoe dvizhenie v rossii* (St Petersburg, 1907) p. 96 (following a report in *Russkie vedomosti*).

3. For example, the report of the governor of Saratov, in KA, vol. 17, p. 86.
4. *Protokoly delegatskogo soveshchaniya vserossiiskogo krest'yanskogo soyuza* (Moscow, 1906) p. 31. The province of Vyatka and its peasants were consistent in electing left-wing deputees to all Dumas.
5. KA, vols. 11–12, p. 173; Veselovskii, op. cit., p. 82. Also *Protokoly pervogo severnogo s'ezda vserossiiskogo krest'yanskogo soyuza* (St Petersburg, 1907) pp. 13–15. Also A. Popyrina, *Krest'yanskoe dvizhenie v vyatskoi gubernii v revolyutsiyu 1905–1907 godov* (Kirov, 1958).
6. Lenin, PSS, vol. 23, p. 241.
7. Ibid, vol. 13, p. 319.
8. The PSR actually split over that issue. While the majority accepted individual terror against limited and clearly defined targets (for example, senior officers in charge of the 'punitive expeditions' or those accused of spying), the minority – the SR Maximalists – demanded unlimited terrorist action inclusive of agrarian terror and set up a separate political party to do so. The other divisive issue was that of the so-called 'Minimum Programme' which SR Maximalists refused.
9. G. Uratadze, *Vospominaniya gruzinskogo sotsial-demokrata* (Stanford, 1968). His recollections are supported by extensive quotations from memoirs of Bolsheviks, P. Makharadze and A. Kalatze, published in 1927 and 1923 respectively. For evidence and extensive quotations see ibid, pp. 190–5, 204–11. (The rewriting of Georgian history by L. Beria in the 1930s has made such sources disappear from the libraries.) For an example of the official version of today see M. Tservadze 'Krest'yanskoe revolyutsionnoe dvizhenie v gurii v 1905 gody', *Voprosy istorii*, 1955, no. 12. For further discussion see Chapters 4 and 6 of this volume.
10. Uratadze, op. cit., p. 41.
11. See the relevant parts of the above quoted sources by Veselovskii, Maslov, Morokhovets, Groman (Gorn) and Uratadze as well as of the regional sources reviewed above. Also S. Abeliani, *Krest'yanskii vopros v zakavkazii* (Odessa, 1914).
12. The revolutionaries spoke of seventy Cossacks killed in that battle while the government admitted to six killed, five unaccounted for and thirteen wounded. Kalandadze, op. cit., p. 74; G. Zateryannyi, 'Myatezh na zapadnom kavkaze', *Istoricheskii vestnik*, 1911, vol. 26, pp. 643–4.
13. Zateryannyi, loc. cit., p. 644.
14. Morokhovets, op. cit., pp. 193–205, 210. Also *Vtoroi period revolyutsii* (Moscow, 1957) Part 3, p. 415 (for report about the 'reintroduction of order' in Lamchaty).
15. See the police report in KA, vol. 11–12, especially pp. 263–76 which documented nearly 100 peasant republics or 'cantons' (p. 276) as well as the fact that the major demand of the wage-workers of rural Latvia was land (p. 264). Also see *The Revolution in the Baltic Provinces of Russia* (London, 1907); *Revolyutsia 1905–7 gg v latvii* (Riga, 1956); and *Revolyutsiya 1905–7 godov v natsional'nykh raionakh rossii* (Moscow, 1949).
16. See note 15 above; also *Revolyutsia 1905–7 gg v estonii* (Talin, 1956).
17. KA, vol. 11–12, especially p. 271.

18. See also Chapter 4 of this volume.
19. I. Pavlov, *Markovskaya respublika* (Moscow, 1926).
20. V. P. Danilov, M. P. Kim and N. V. Tropina, *Sovetskoe krest'yanstvo* (Moscow, 1973) pp. 15–16.
21. In the Kharkov province of central Ukraine.
22. A. Shcherbak, '1905 v sumskom uezde', *Proletarskaya revolyutsiya*, 1926, vol.(54)7. Also Danilov, *et al.*, op. cit., p. 252; Shestakov, op. cit.; Maslov, op. cit., p. 252; V. Groman, *Materialy po krest'yanskomu voprosu* (Rostov, 1905).
23. Shcherbak, op. cit.; Also E. Kiryukhina, 'Vserossiiskii krest'yanskii soyuz v 1905 g.', *Istoricheskie zapiski*, 1955, no. 50, p. 131.
24. For developments similar to these in Sumy see discussion of another centre of activities of the All-Russian Peasant Union led by the brothers Mazurenko in the area of Don, by Kiryukhina, op. cit., p. 101. For the discussion of other areas see M. Simonova, 'Krest'yanskoe dvizhenie 1905–1907 gg.', in *Istoricheskie zapiski*, 1975, no. 95. The evidence for Saratov is gathered in the unpublished work of T. Mixter.
25. Maslov, op. cit., p. 252.
26. *Revolyutsiya 1905–7 godov v natsional'nykh* op. cit, pp. 700–4 etc.
27. Morokhovets, op. cit., pp. 61–8. F. Vodovatov, *Krest'yanskoe dvizhenie v samarskoi gubernii v period revolyutsii 1905–1907 gg.* (Kuibyshev, 1957) pp. 113–120.
28. The organisation was created by a Marxist minority which left the nationalist-populist PUP in 1904 and associated with the Mensheviks of RSDWP. Its most prominent member Yu. Larin was later to join the Bolsheviks and to become for a time one of the major 'agrarian specialists' of the early Soviet regime. The activities of *Spilka* reached their climax in 1906. The mass arrests in 1907 brought it to an effective end. See Morokhovets, op. cit., pp. 124–45, also M. Leshchenko, *Selyanskii rukh na pravoberezhii Ukrainy v period revolyutsii 1905–1907 rr.* (Kiev, 1955).
29. The richest evidence to it remains the study by Vol'noe ekonomicheskoe obsshchestvo, *Agranoe dvizhenie v rossii* (St Petersburg, 1908) vols I, II. For a good recent review of it see M. Perrie, 'The Russian Peasant Movement in 1905–1907', *Past and Present*, 1972, no. 57.
30. One more congress met in March 1906 in Moscow. There was a meeting in May 1906 in Helsinki and possibly one more meeting in 1907. Maslov, op. cit., p. 231; Dubrovskii, op. cit., p. 110.
31. E. Kiryukhina, 'Mestnye organizatsii VKS v 1906 godu', *Uchennye zapiski* (Kirov Pedagogical Institute, 1956) no. 10, p. 139, for the way the estimate was made.
32. *Chto takoe krest'yanskii soyuz*, (n.d., 1906) The source was a propaganda leaflet which could overstate actual figures. Most of the membership was collective, that is, represented communes and *volost'* which joined *in toto*. On the other hand, on the government side the report of Durnovo, then Minister of Interior, on 29 January 1906 to the tsar speaks of the 'tremendous impact' of the All-Russia Peasant Union. *Vtoroi period revolyutsii* (Moscow, 1957) vol. I, p. 961.

33. *Protokoly pervogo severnogo oblastnogo s'ezda vserossiiskogo krest'yanskogo soyuza* (St Petersburg, 1906).
34. *Uchredinel'nyi s'ezd vserossiiskogo krest'yanskogo soyuza* (Moscow, 1906) (the July/August Congress); *Protokoly delegatskogo soveshchaniya vserossiiskogo krest'yanskogo soyuza*, op. cit., (for the November Congress).
35. Kiryukhina, *Vserossiiskii*, loc. cit., p. 134.
36. Maslov, op. cit., pp. 227, 230–31.
37. See protocols as well as reports of observers, such as by Tan, op. cit.; Groman, op. cit. etc.
38. Ibid; Kiryukhina, loc. cit., pp. 103, 115.
39. Kiryukhina, *Vserossiiskii*, op. cit., pp. 103, 115.
40. Kiryukhina, *Mestnye*, op. cit., tables 4, 5. Also in Vsserossiiskii, loc. cit., p. 116.
41. See report of court proceedings against the Committee of Support in Petersburg in *Pravo*, vol. 1907, pp. 3104–7.
42. For comparative discussion see T. Shanin, *Peasants and Peasant Societies*, (Harmondsworth, 1971) part 3; also Scott, op. cit.
43. For evidence of such SR and SD rural alliances see Simonova, op. cit., p. 240.
44. Karl Marx, 'The Class Struggle in France 1848–1850', in K. Marx and F. Engels, *Selected Works* (Moscow, 1950) vol. 1, p. 159.

3C The Peasant Dream

1. See the codification of peasant common law by V. Mukhin, *Obychnyi poryadok nasledovaniya u krest'yan* (St Petersburg, 1888). For discussion see also T. Shanin, *The Awkward Class* (Oxford, 1972) Appendix B and *Russia as a 'Developing Society'*, Chapter 2.
2. For example, the reports of the governors of the provinces and of the officers in charge of pacification and of the punishments expeditions published in *Revolyutsiya 1905 goda i samoderzhavie* (Moscow, 1928).
3. *Uchreditel'nyi s'ezd vserossiiskogo krest'yanskogo soyuza* (Moscow, 1906); *Protokoly delegatskogo soveshchaniya vsrossiiskogo krest'yanskogo soyuza* (Moscow, 1906). Also Tan (Bogoraz), *Novoe krest'yanstvo* (Moscow, 1905); V. Groman (Gorn), *Materialy po krest'yanskomu voprosu* (Rostov, 1905). Also, an *ex post factum* description, for example, the one by a Bolshevik speaker there, M. Vasilev-Yuzhin, *V ogne revolyutsii* (Moscow, 1934) pp. 133–83.
4. *Uchreditel'nyi s'ezd*, p. 27.
5. 'When strong, we get our way by peaceful means, when split we turn to arson and similar means. As long as we are not organised, arson and bloody means will continue.' Report of a delegate from Minsk *guberniya*, *Protokoly delegatskogo, etc.*, p. 61.
6. Ibid, p. 8.
7. See for example Tan, op. cit., p. 45.
8. *Protokoly delegatskogo*, pp. 18–26; *Uchreditel'nyi s'ezd*, p. 32; E. Kiryukhina has quantified it all by dividing the speakers at the November

congress into thirty who spoke against armed struggle, fifteen for it, and twelve for a display of force 'by means other than the use of arms'. See here *Vserossiiskii krest'yanskii soyuz v 1905 g.* (Autoreferat) (Moscow, 1950). Her figure of supporters of the armed struggle is sharply overstated.

9. See for example T. Sushkin, *Agrarniki: siluety 1905–1907 gg.* (Moscow, 1927).

10. 'It was a truly popular mass organisation, which has shared, of course, many of the peasant prejudices . . . but definitely 'of the soil', real organisation of masses, definitely revolutionary in its essence . . . extending the framework of the peasant political creativity'. Lenin, PSS, vol. 10, pp. 232–33.

11. A. Studentsov, *Saratovskoe krest'yanskoe vosstanie 1905 goda* (Penza, 1925) p. 42, 46.

12. A. Shestakov, *Krest'yanskaya revolyutsiya 1905–1907 gg. v rossii* (Moscow, 1926); V. Groman, *Materialy po krest'yanskomu voprosu,* (Rostov, 1905).

13. P. Maslov, *Agrarnyi vopros v rossii* (St Petersburg, 1908) vol. 1, pp. 277–281.

14. B. Veselovskii, *Krest'yanskii vopros i krest'yanskoe dvizhenie v rossii,* (St Petersburg, 1907) p. 138.

15. Yu. Martov, P. Maslov and A. Potresov, *Obshchestvennoe dvizhenie v rossii v 1nachale XXgo veka* (St Petersburg, 1909–12) vol. 2, part 2, p. 265. By that account, of the deputies elected by the peasant electoral colleges to the first Duma 24 belonged to the KD, 68 to the Labour faction, 15 to the 'Autonomists', 59 were 'non-party', that is, not defined all through the session as belonging to any specific faction; one was an *oktyabrist.* See also M. Krol', *Kak proshli vybory v gosudarstvennuiu dumu* (St Petersburg, 1906) and T. Emmons, *The Formation of Political Parties and the First National Election in Russia* (Cambridge, 1982) Part III.

16. For example, Prince Constantine on the peasant deputies to the Duma; KA 45, pp. 130–46; also Martov, op. cit., vol. 4, part 2, p. 2, etc.

17. For the text and the debate of the 'Project of the 104' see *Agrarnyi vopros v pervoi gosudarstvennoi dume* (Kiev, 1906) pp. 5–9. More than 4/5 of deputies of the Labour Faction in the first and the second Duma were peasants, the rest were workers and intelligentsia – mostly of peasant origins and elected by peasant vote. For figures see *Istoricheskie zapiski,* 1975, pp. 95, 257.

18. M. Gefter in *Istoricheskaya nauka i nekotorye problemy sovremennosti* (Moscow, 1969) p. 22.

19. The archives of the second Duma quoted after E. Vasilevskii, 'Sotsial'no-ekonomicheskoe soderzhanie krest'yanskikh prigovorov i nakazov', *Uchennye zapiski MGU,* 1956 (*Natsional'naya ekonomiya* series) p. 132.

20. Ibid, p. 130; See also Tan, op. cit., pp. 115–26.

21. *Svod agrarnych program* (St Petersburg, 1907). Also D. Kolesnichenko, 'K voprosu o politicheskoi evolyutsii trudovikov v 1906 g.', *Istoricheskie zapiski,* 1973, no. 1973.

22. Quoted after M. Simonova in *Istoricheskie zapiski*, 1975, no. 95, p. 270. The expression 'psychological isolation' is gratefully borrowed from L. Haimson, *The Politics of Rural Russia* (Bloomington, 1979) p. 291; he used it to express the particularism of Russian peasant politics. For the extent to which it 'worked' politically see reports of the systematic voting down of middle-class and squire deputies by the peasant electoral colleges (*zabalotirovat' gospod*) while choice by lottery of the deputees was at the same time suggested. *Vestnik evropy*, 1906, no. 4, p. 369.

23. For results of the election to the second Duma (and especially its peasant component see A. Smirnov, *Kak proshli vybory vo 2-yu gosudarstven-nuyu dumu* (St Petersburg, 1907) (especially chaps III, VI, VII, XI). For the peasant attitude to Stolypin reform see I. Chernyshev, *Obshchina posle 9 noyabrya 1906 g.* (Petrograd, 1917) and speeches of the Labourite delegates in the second Duma.

24. Maslov, op. cit., p. 395 claimed a persisting peasant vote for the opposition also in the third Duma election; L. Haimson has recently noted anew the continuous strength of the opposition in the peasant electoral colleges in most of the centres of peasant movement, Haimson, op. cit., pp. 291, 298.

25. N. Vasil'ev, *Chto takoe trudoviki* (St Petersburg, 1917) p. 4. The booklet proceeded to discuss individually leading members of the Labour faction. To exemplify: speaking of S. Anikin it described him in the following terms: 'He is a Mordvin [a small Ugro-Finnish ethnic group, strongly russified, but here clearly accentuated as alien and backward, T.S.], and terrible to look at. With an unpleasant voice as of glass grinding he has eyes which count every penny in everybody's pocket and are disturbed by it. His education is most typically "Labourite" that is, a rural school and a craftsman college. His most recent occupation was that of a rural teacher, often arrested for political activities. His speciality is the tendentious agitation among the peasants'. (p. 85).

26. Maslov, op. cit., p. 323.

27. Maslov, op. cit., p. 214; Shestakov, op. cit., p. 59; Lenin, PSS, vol. 13, p. 121. To quote some chapter and verse, the whole petitions movement was described as 'the fruit of the governmental demagoguery and of the political underdevelopment of the peasants' by the future president of the USSR, Kalinin, in the main Bolshevik newspaper *Proletarii*, 9 August 1905.

28. *Krest'yanskie nakazy samarskoi gubernii* (Samara, 1906) pp. 6–80. See p. 40 for a petition which carries forty signatures and 280 crosses to represent all households – a literacy index of 12.5 per cent for the heads of households.

29. Ibid.

30. Quoted after Maslov, op. cit., p. 308.

31. See Bukhovets, 'K metodike izucheniya 'prigovornogo dvizheniya'', *Istoriya SSSR*, 1979, part 3. For the Peasant Union, Dubrovskii, op. cit., pp. 111–13. Also for sources concerning the first Duma see V. Mikhailova, 'Sovetskaya istoricheskaya literatura o krest'yanskikh naka-

zakh i prigovorakh', *Nekotorie problemy otechestvennoi istoriografii i istochnikovedeniya* (Dnepropetrovsk, 1972). The second Duma found a much better coverage. See the works of Maslov, op. cit., pp. 282–8; E. Vasilevskii, op. cit., and V. Nil've, *Razvitie V. I. Leninym agrarnogo voprosa v teorii nauchnogo kommunizma, 1897–1916* (Moscow, 1974).

32. S. Dubrovskii, *Krest'yanskoe dvizhenie v rovoloyutsii 1905–1907 gg.* (Moscow, 1956) p. 112.

33. Bukhovets, op. cit., pp. 101–5, 108–11.

34. For an interesting relevant work about the Russian peasant ideology and its early semantic expressions see H. Wada, 'The Inner World of Russian Peasants', *Annals of the Institution of Social Sciences* (no. 20) (Tokyo, 1979) and his not yet translated book 'The World of Peasant Revolution'. Wada's article drew partly on the recent works concerning peasant culture published in the USSR by A. Klibanov, V. Khristov and M. Gromyko. In this underdeveloped field, the work, now in progress by V. Danilov (for the somewhat later period of NEP), is keenly awaited.

35. For comparative context see E. R. Wolf, *Peasants* (Engelwood Cliffs, 1966) part 4; T. Shanin, *Peasants and Peasant Societies* (Harmondsworth, 1971) part 4; G. M. Foster, 'The Peasants and the Image of Limited Good', *American Anthropologist*, 1965, vol. 62, no. 2; J. Berger, *Pig Earth* (London, 1979); E. Le Roy Ladurie, 'Peasants', *The New Cambridge Modern History* (Cambridge, 1979) XIII.

36. For consideration of these matters see E. Wolf, *Peasant Wars of the Twentieth Century* (New York, 1969); Shanin, op. cit., part 3; also H. Alavi, 'Peasant in Revolution', *Socialist Registrar*, 1965, no. 2; E. J. Hobsbawm, *Primitive Rebels* (London, 1963) etc.

37. N. Kibal'chich of People's Will commented already in 1880 about the Russian peasant rebellions to say: 'no village revolted merely because it was hungry . . . the fundamental condition of nearly all those popular revolts has been material suffering. But the actual occasion has always been some violation of law (real or false) by the authorities or a revolutionary initiative taken by an organised nucleus close to the people and its interests'. T. Shanin, *Late Marx and the Russian Road* (London, 1983) pp. 217–18 (the translation differs slightly). The term 'moral economy' is used as it was by E. P. Thompson, while J. Scott, talks specifically of the place 'subsistence ethic' and its violation in the peasant revolt in south-east Asia in his *Moral Economy of the Peasant* (London, 1976).

38. See P. Longworth, 'The Subversive Legend of Sten'ka Razin', in V. Strada, *Russia* (Turino, 1975) vol. II. Also Avrich, op. cit. One can document considerable similarity in that matter between the Russian peasant oral lore and that of other peasantries of Europe, for example, Hobsbawm, op. cit. versus a major collection of relevant Russian legends, A. Lozanova, *Pesni i skazaniya o razine i pugacheve* (Moscow, 1935). Historical continuities of peasant 'rebellious tendencies' have been poorly studied.

39. Longworth, op. cit.

4 THE PEASANT WAR 1905–07: WHO LED WHOM?

4A Question and Context

1. In particular the 'fifty years of . . .' celebrations of the 1905–07 revolution in 1955 and later have led in the USSR to a new wave of publications of sources and to some analytical discussion. A book by S. Dubrovskii, *Krest'yanskoe dvizhenie v Rossii, 1905–07 gg.* (Moscow, 1956) has laid down what has seemingly become at that stage the proper general position to be held by all. It has guided most of the regional collections and studies published. Another wave of relevant publications materialised a decade later aiming to document Bolshevik rural political action with V. Tropin, *Bor'ba bol'shevikov za rukovodstvo krest'yanskim dvizheniem v 1905 godu* (Moscow, 1970) playing then a role similar to that of Dubrovskii before. The ideological underpinnings were spelled out in S. Trapeznikov, *Agrarnyi vopros i leninskie agrarnye programmy v trekh russkikh revolyutsiyakh* (Moscow, 1967). For discussion see section 4C and the Addendum to Chapter 4 of this volume.
2. A particular dimension of it has been the way some Western scholars professing strong anti-Soviet sentiment were led by their noses by Soviet tables and figures, the content of which was left out of consideration.
3. M. Bloch, *The Historians' Craft* (Manchester, 1954), p. 93.
4. Ibid, p. 151.

4B Contemporaries: 'Right' and 'Left'

1. Quoted from the 1904 report by P. Stolypin in KA, vol. 17, p. 86. For a markedly similar report by the public prosecutor in the Kharkov *guberniya* see L. Owen, *The Russian Peasant Movement 1906–1917* (London, 1937) p. 229.
2. A figure concerning 1908, given by R. Manning, *The Crisis of the Old Order in Russia* (Princeton, 1982) p. 91. For the nature of the 'third element' see ibid, pp. 51–6. Also T. Shanin, *Russia as a 'Developing Society'*, Chapters 1, 5.
3. V. Gurko, *Features and Figures of the Past* (Stanford, 1939) p. 389.
4. *Agrarnyi vopros* (Moscow, 1906/7) vols. I, II; M. Gertsenshtein, *Zemel'naya reforma v programme partii narodnoi svobody* (Moscow, 1906); A. Shingarev, *Kak predpolagala nadelit' krest'yan zemlei partiya narodnoi svobody* (St Petersburg, 1907). For the understanding of the selectivity of the human mind it is interesting to note that the KDs' leader Milyukov claimed in his memoirs (written much later) that the All-Russian Peasant Union failed completely and that only the peasant Jaquery expressed their action. P. Milyukov, *Vospominaniya* (New York, 1955) vol. I, pp. 405–10.
5. A. Spiridovich, *Revolyutsionnoe dvizhenie v rossii* (St Petersburg, 1916) vol. 2; V. Tropin, *Bor'ba bol'shevikov za rukovodstvo krest'yanskim dvizheniem v 1905 g* (Moscow, 1970) pp. 53–4; *Nachalo pervoi russkoi revolyutsii* (Moscow, 1955).

6. *Protokoly pervogo s'ezda PSR* (nd, 1906) (especially V. Chernov's report); V. Chernov, *Zemlya i pravo* (Petrograd, 1919); P. Vikhlyaev, *Pravo na zemlyu* (Moscow, 1906); O. Radkey, 'Chernov and Agrarian Socialism before 1818', in E. Simmons, *Continuity and Change in The Soviet Thought* (New York, 1967).

7. This claim should not be overstated. At its peak of influence the PSR reported 18 500 members of the Brotherhoods (as against 50 000 in the party organisation. V. Ginev, *Bor'ba za krest'yanstvo i krizis neonarod-nichestva* (Leningrad, 1983) p. 139. A current study of over 1000 SRs exiled for political offences, mostly as the result of the 1905–07 revolution, shows that 235 of them were involved in rural revolutionary activity. Of this category forty-two were peasant cultivators of peasant parentage and thirty-two workers or artisans of peasant parentage, that is, 18 per cent and 13.5 per cent respectively. Of the other categories the largest were that of fifty teachers and forty students. M. Perrie, 'The Russian Peasant Movement in 1905–1907', *Past and Present*, 1972, no. 57, p. 151.

8. The session of 1 August 1903, *Vtoroi ocherednoi s'ezd* (Geneva 1904).

9. See *Pamyatnaya knizhka sotsialista revolyutsionera* (Paris, 1911) especially pp. 15–70 for a summary of SR programmatic and tactical decisions in the first decade of the twentieth century. Also Spiridovich, op. cit.

10. The SR controlled some of the powerful trade unions, especially that of the railwaymen and recorded considerable successes in some elections to the second Duma within the workers electoral college (40 per cent in St Petersburg and a straight majority in Putilov works as against the combined strengths of the Bolsheviks and Mensheviks, that is, the united RSDWP). A study of SRs exiled between 1901 and 1916 has shown that 44 per cent of them were workers and artisans. M. Perrie, The Social Composition and Structure of the Socialist Revolutionary Party Before 1917, *Soviet Studies,* vol. 24, no. 2 (1972).

11. See *Protokoly pervogo s'ezda PSR*, pp. 164–7 for these doubts about the All-Russian Peasant Union. A number of SR local organisations actually boycotted it as reformist. Also V. Yudovskii, *Nashi protivniki* (Moscow, 1929) vol. 2; Ginaev, op. cit., chap. 2.

12. V. Bogoraz (psuedonym Tan) was a leading member of the *People's Will* organisation in the 1880s. Exiled to Siberia he became an authority on the northern tribes of Chukcha and an ethnographer of international renown. After serving his sentence he went to the US but returned in 1904. A member of the central strike committee during the October 1905 general strike, he was arrested in 1906. After 1917 he became the creator and curator of the museum of ethnography in Petrograd.

13. K. Kautsky, *the Agrarfrage* (Stuttgart, 1899); K. Marx and F. Engels, *Selected Works* (Moscow, 1973) vol. 3, pp. 460–9; A. Hussain and K. Tribe, *Marxism and the Agrarian Question* (London, 1981) vol. 1. The SD party of Germany refused on Kautsky's bidding the very idea of declaring an 'agrarian programme' out of fear that it would mean surrender to the petty-bourgeois interests and views of the peasants. This decision was considered by some as a victory of the 'orthodox' majority over the 'revisionist' minority within the party but the actual factional

divisions did not quite fit that view. Bebel, the leader of the party, manifestly hostile to 'revisionism', spoke sharply against Kautsky's position on the agrarian problem and described the decision as setting back the achievements of the party.

14. V. Groman, *Materialy po krest'yanskomu voprosu* (Rostov, 1905) p. 65. The study offers a good general summary of the debate concerning peasantry between the Russian Marxists of the nineteenth century.

15. Quoted after M. Yakobii, *K agrarnomu voprosu* (Moscow, 1906) p. 18, which carried an SR critique of the RSDWP agrarian debate.

16. Groman, op. cit., p. 101.

17. *Chetvertyi ob'edinitel'nyi s'ezd rsdrp* (Moscow, 1959) pp. 211–12.

18. The SDs of Latvia and of the Russian Poland, followed the German example of not having an 'agrarian programme' at all. The same solution was suggested by Strumilin at the fourth congress of the RSDWP and supported by a considerable number of delegates.

   The fear of surrender to peasant proprietary tendencies and the belief that egalitarian land redivision is economically regressive, and therefore politically impermissible, remained strongly entrenched within the European Marxist movement. In 1918, Rosa Luxemburg defined the egalitarian redivision of all Russia's land in 1917 as creating 'a new powerful layer of popular enemies within the countryside' and even as a 'slogan taken over from much condemned Social Revolutionary Party rather than from the spontaneous peasant movement', R. Luxemburg, *The Russian Revolution* (Ann Arbor, 1952) p. 46.

19. Lenin, PSS, vol. 12, pp. 249–50. For description of the 'non-factional' and constantly changing divisions among the delegates to the IV Congress of RSDWP in so far as the Agrarian Programme was concerned see S. Strumilin, *Iz perezhitogo* (Moscow, 1957) pp. 205–21. He recalled that the idea of division of all non-peasant lands into peasants' private possession was supported, besides the majority of the Bolsheviks (but not by Lenin), by a large group of Mensheviks. Ibid, pp. 215–16.

20. The agrarian programme limiting SD 'agrarian' demands to the return of the 'cut-off' lands to the peasants was kept, but new decisions supporting peasants struggle were adopted simultaneously.

21. For substantiation and the specific positions of the Menshevik majority, of Groman, of Lenin, of Rozhkov, of Finn-Anotaevskii (the last two of the Bolshevik majority in conflict with Lenin), see *Svod agrarnykh programm* (St Petersburg, 1907) pp. 67–78.

22. *Proletarii*, 2 August 1905 (no 30), p. 10. The decision that the agrarian resolutions of both the Menshevik conference and the Bolshevik III Congress were unacceptable was carried unanimously.

23. *Proletarii*, 14 September 1908 (no. 16) p. 1, which quoted the 'Open letter' – a leaflet by 'a leading comrade from Moscow', that is, A. Shestakov, to describe resolution about the 'unlimited support' of peasant demand passed by the third congress as 'unacceptable as long as we remain SDs' and 'representing a step backward in terms of capitalist development of our economy'. It also objected to the setting up of 'peasant' committees (quotation marks by the author) as including both bourgeoise and proletarian elements. For identification of the author see

S. Mazurenko, 'VKS pered litsom istorii', *Puti revolyutsii*, 1926, 4 (7).
The same issue of the paper reported from the countryside that 'Peasants are opting for 'Black repartition' and collective ownership of all lands by the communes'. Ibid, p. 2.

24. Conference decisions in *Novaya zhizn'*, 1905, no. 24, and articles by B. Avilov, N. Rozhkov and P. Larionov in ibid, nos. 11, 16 and 27 respectively.

25. *Chetvertyi ob'edinitel'nyi s'ezd rsdwp*, pp. 139, 59. At the fifth congress of RSDWP Martynov was to speak of 'Lenin's populist relapse'. But the full measure of Plekhanov's views and suspicions was expressed when he spoke elsewhere of Lenin's group 'marching together, in close alliance, shoulder to shoulder . . . with Socialist Revolutionaries whose banner is already that of owner-and-proletarian dictatorship (*khozyaisko–proletarskaya diktatura*) . . . and who may cry out "the Social Democracy had ceased to exist" '. *Dnevnik sotsial–demokrata*, 1905, no. 2, p. 36.

26. See for example 'Ortodoksal'nye marksisty i krest'yanskii vopros', *Revolyutsionnaya rossiya*, 1905, no. 75.

27. 'The typical member of a Labour Faction is a conscious peasant', Lenin, PSS, vol. 14, p. 25.

28. For example, Lenin, PSS, vol. 19, p. 261.

29. Ibid, vol. 14, especially pp. 179, 381, when he speaks of the RSDWP and PSR in one breath, as the revolutionary parties of Russia. Also ibid, which described the SRs as 'part of the broad and powerful river of revolutionary democracy without which the proletariat cannot even dream about the full victory of our revolution'.

30. Ibid, 'Dve taktiki', vol. 11, pp. 11–131.

4C   The Post-revolutionaries: The 'Drift' of the Interpretation

1. Lenin, PSS, vol. 47, pp. 227–9; *Leninskii sbornik*, 1932, XIX, p. 285; for a clear statement of the 'contradictory' that is changing nature of these views see, for example, PSS, vol. 3, p. 179 as against PSS, vol. 12, pp. 249–50 or vol. 23, p. 275. For a review of the recent Soviet attempt to consider and analyse this contradiction see T. Shanin, *Russia as a 'Developing Society'*, chap. 4 (especially the discussion of the works by M. Gefter and K. Tarnovskii).

2. Shestakov related together three elements which were to define an ideology: (i) Russia's agriculture being capitalist at the end of the nineteenth century, (ii) The peasant struggle of 1905–07 as but a reflection of the proletarian revolution, and (iii) The Bolsheviks' exclusive role in both confrontations. A. Shestakov, *Kapitalizatsiya sel'skogo khozyaistva rossii* (Moscow, 1924); A. Shestakov, *Krest'yanskaya revolyutsiia 1905–7 gg. v rossii* (Moscow, 1926).

3. M. Pokrovskii, *Istoricheskaya nauka i bor'ba klassov* (Moscow, 1933) vol. I. The leading 'Decembrist' Pestel' became accordingly a representative 'consciously or unconsciously, it does not matter to us' of 'capitalist farmers'. Ibid, p. 307.

4. S. Dubrovskii and V. Grave, *Agrarnoe dvizhenie v 1905–7 gg.* (Moscow, 1925).
5. E. Morokhovets, *Krest'yanskoe dvizhenie i sotsial-demokratiya v epokhu pervoi russkoi revolyutsii* (Moscow, 1926).
6. I. Drozdov, krest'yanskie soyuzy na chernigovshchine v 1905–6 gg.', *Istoricheskie zapiski*, 1940, no. 9, pp. 6–7.
7. L. Beria, *K voprosu ob istorii bol'shevistskikh organizatsii v zakavkazii* (Moscow, 1952) (9th edn, the first having been published in 1934).
8. S. Dubrovskii, *Krest'yanskoe dvizhenie v revolyutsii 1905–07 gg.* (Moscow, 1966); V. Tropin, Bor'ba bol'shevikov za rukovodstvo krest'yanskim dvizheniem v 1905 g. (Moscow, 1970).
9. That has been formalised and standardised by an explosion of books uniformly entitled 'The Struggle of the Bolsheviks for the Leadership of the Peasant Movement in . . .' with the name of a province or of a republic of the USSR to follow.
10. In particular a book by S. Trapeznikov and the works of I. Koval'chenko and his team referred to above. For a Soviet historiography of the initial stages of the debate see K. Tarnovskii, 'Problemy agrarnoi istorii rossii etc.', *Istoricheskie zapiski*, 1969, no. 83.
11. There is, of course, nothing personal in Tropin's inexactitude concerning parties other than Bolsheviks *vis-à-vis* Russian peasants. Many Soviet historians competed in such easy victories without the danger of being answered back. For example Kiryukhina's otherwise important study which made the leaders of the All-Russian Peasant Union into bourgeois liberals and charged the SRs with 'opposing nationalisation of land', forgetting to say that they were first to raise this demand as part of 'land socialisation' (Kiryukhina, op. cit., pp. 113, 127) or a regional study of the Samara *guberniya* published in 1957 which condemns the SRs (p. 159) for helping the KDs to detour the peasants of the province into the acceptance of a 'peaceful road' and then quotes as the only case of armed uprising in the province the July 1906 attempt led by the SRs (p. 165). Vodovatov, *Krest'yanskoe dvizhenie v saratovskoi gubernii v period revolyutsii 1905–7 gg.* (Kuibyshev, 1957).
12. For the decoding of names see A. Studentsov, *Saratovskoe krest'yanskoe vosstanie 1905 goda* (Penza, 1926) pp. 42–8.
13. L. Beria is best known to 'the West' as Stalin's police chief since 1938, a one-time confidant, allegedly a sex sadist and undoubtedly a claimant to Stalin's mantle when the old man was dead. His service to Stalin in purging the Caucasus of practically all the pre-revolutionary SDs (Mensheviks as well as Bolsheviks) and writing anew a history of the Caucasian Marxism, with Stalin at its centre, is on the whole less known. As part of this major operation, most of the original Georgian SD publications of 1905–17 but also of 1917–30 were removed and destroyed, archives purged, old revolutionaries made to rewrite their memoirs and so on. At its peak Beria's purge left Georgia without any of its old SD cadres while in Moscow it drew to suicide his fellow-Georgian, the 'iron Minister of Industry', Sergo Ordzhonikidze. Beria has by now dropped into oblivion but his version of history, outrageously untrue, was quietly transferred by default into new hands and provides a major

part of the official Georgian history today. The source is still Beria, op. cit.

This piece of bibliography should not be read simply as blaming Beriya or the Stalin era for 'all those lies'. Lies of political expedience began earlier – see M. Shakhnazaryan, *Krest'yanskoe dvizhenie v gruzii i sotsial'naya demokratiya* (Moscow, 1906).

14. Morokhovets, op. cit., p. 210.
15. For example, *Istoriya sssr* (Moscow, 1968) vol. VI, p. 73.
16. It was N. Zhordaniya (Kostrov), the Georgian Menshevik, who defended at the second congress (1903) what was to become the Bolshevik position much later, that is, a demand to let the peasants have all the land which they would attempt to seize and by doing so, to 'stand at the head of the peasant movement . . . not leave it to its fate'. *Vtoroi ocherednoi s'ezd rsdrp* (Geneva, 1904) (The session of 31 July.) His view was brushed aside by Lenin, who prepared and presented the 'Iskra' version of the agrarian programme. For an illuminating discussion of the analytical stages through which Lenin advanced in 1905 towards the reform of his approach see M. Gefter in *Istoricheskaya nauka i nekotorye problemy sovremennosti* (Moscow, 1969) pp. 14–19.
17. See section 4B of this volume. Also Tropin, op. cit., pp. 77–8; Interesting as a reflection of the anti-peasant and anti-populist feelings at the second congress, the SD delegate of Ryazan' and some of the others objected even to the demand for the return of the 'cut-off' lands, treating it as a populist deviation.
18. Dubrovskii, op. cit., pp. 147–8.
19. The reception was at times hostile, for example, Morokhovets, op. cit., p. 141, reported peasants objecting angrily to anti-monarchist leaflets handed out to them by the SDs.
20. The same can be said about Lenin's offhand comment about the extermination of nobles by the peasants (*rasprava*) as being a necessary and natural part of the peasant struggle.
21. G. T. Robinson rightly remarked on that score that 'if the knowledge of factory made for revolutionary spirit, the *Jacquerie* would break out in the north of Russia', *Rural Russia under the Old Regime* (New York, 1932) p. 128.
22. Yu. Martov, P. Maslov, A. Potresov, *Obshchestvennoe dvizhenie v rossii v nachale XX veka* (St Petersburg, 1909/14) vol. 2, book 2, p. 235; Lenin, PSS, vol. 35, p. 299, vol. 33.
23. Soviet historians usually refer to this accident as a provocation by the 'liberal–populist leadership of the congress'. The difficulty in explaining the case in terms of proletarian hegemony is obvious in view of Lenin's repeated insistence that the Peasant Union correctly represented peasant political interest and positions.

An SR delegate actually claimed that it was Lenin in person 'thinly disguised', who led the SD delegation in this confrontation (Studentsov, op. cit., p. 46) while the PSR was represented by V. Chernov who spoke for letting the SD workers have a hearing. Lenin's official biography seems to rule out his participation. *Vladimir Il'ich Lenin* (Moscow, 1971) vol. 2, pp. 192–205. The Soviet contemporary historians named the SD 'speaker No. 1' as M. I. Vasilev-Yuzhin, see *V ogne pervoi revolyutsii* (Moscow, 1934) pp. 172–81. The story could do with further investigation.

24. Tropin, op. cit., pp. 112, 155.
25. See Pershin, *Agrarnaya revolyutsiya v rossii* (Moscow, 1966) vol. I.
26. See the survey by the Free Economic Society in *Agrarnoe dvizhenie v rossii* St Petersburg, 1908) vols. I, II. Also its review in M. Perrie, 'The Russian Peasant Movement of 1905–1907', *Past and Present*, 1972, no. 57.
27. Quoted from one of the long line of such hack-jobs – a typical Ph.D. thesis produced in Georgia, Ya. Khatsushvili, *Revolyutsiya 1905–7 gg. v gruzii* (Tbilisi, 1958) (autoreferat). An honourable exception was the attempt of A. Anfimov directly to consider proletarians as against the rural paupers in terms of goals and to stress also the difference between the distinct categories of rural bourgeoisie. This was not followed up, however. A. Anfimov, 'Lenin i problemy agrarnogo kapitalisma', *Istoriya SSSR*, 1969, no. 4, pp. 19–21.
28. The otherwise excellent M. Leshchenko, *Selyanskii rukh na pravoberezhnii ukraine v period revolyutsii 1905–1907 rr* (Kiev, 1955) p. 210.
29. For example, Dubrovskii, op. cit., pp. 91–2.
30. For evidence see *Agrarnoe dvizhenie v rossii*, op. cit.; also Morkhovets, op. cit., and other sources reviewed in the section.
31. Dubrovskii, op. cit., pp. 64–5, 83–9. The view and even its wording have been repeated in nearly every recent Soviet study of the period.
32. See a good review of *Agrarnoe dvizhenie v rossii*, op. cit., in M. Perrie, The Russian Peasant Movement 1905–1907, *Past and Present*, 1972, no. 57, pp. 131–42.
33. E. Le Roy Ladurie, 'Peasants', *New Cambridge Modern History* (Cambridge, 1979) vol. II, pp. 153–5.

4D Peasant Wars and the 'Inflections of Human Mind'

1. As in the following complimentary description of a piece of research: 'One of the most important tasks successfully accomplished by so-and-so was to prove the vitality of the Bolshevik tactic declared at the third party congress' (*Istoricheskie zapisky*, 1975, no. 95, p. 218). To say, *it* was a task and *it* was accomplished.
2. For further discussion of the issues of evolution, progress and science *vis-à-vis* marxism see T. Shanin, *Late Marx and the Russian Road* (London, 1984).
3. Ibid, especially its concluding part 'Marxism and the Vernacular Revolutionary Traditions'.
4. The same applies to the period February–November 1917 which should have accommodated conceptually the whole of Russia's fully-fledged 'capitalist epoch'.
5. See for example, E. Wolf, *Peasant Wars of the Twentieth Century* (London, 1969); E. Le Roy Ladurie, 'Peasants' in *New Cambridge Modern History* (Cambridge, 1979) vol. 13; T. Stockpol, 'What Makes Peasants Revolutionary' in R. P. Weller, *Power and Protest in the*

Countryside (Durham, 1982) (which also reviewed and discussed other relevant texts).

6. For discussion see Wolf, op. cit. Also Le Roy Ladurie spoke of 'rural civilisation' having 'reached its peak on the continent between 1850 and 1914' (op. cit., p. 155). See also E. R. Hobsbawm, *Primitive Rebels* (New York, 1959). As for the Russian peasantry, M. Gefter has well said that at the beginning of the twentieth century 'not only was it a class . . . but at the same time it was constituting itself as a class'. *Istoricheskaya nauka i nekotoriye problemy sovremennosti* (Moscow, 1968) p. 22.

7. Le Roy Ladurie, op. cit., p. 137.

8. See T. Shanin, *Russia as a 'Developing Society',* section 4C which shows how much the expression *kulak* as adopted by the Soviet and Western professional literature, contradicted the Russian peasant usage of the term. To the peasants it meant those living on non-farming activities of a 'go-between', usury, etc., or else character traits like meanness and being unneighbourly. It did not denote farmers who were simply rich or who employed wage-labour.

9. See, for example, the discussion of the period 1917–21 in V. Keller and I. Romanenko, *Pervye itogi agrarnoi reformy* (Voronezh, 1922).

10. See G. Gerasimenko, *Nizovye organisatsii v 1917 – pervoi polovine 1918 gg* (Saratov, 1974); A. Malyavskii, *Krest'yanskoe dvizhenie v rossii v 1917* (Moscow, 1981).

11. Lenin, PSS, vol. 15, p. 334.

ADDENDUM

Peasant and Workers' Struggles in 1905–07: The Statistical Patterns

1. K. Marx and F. Engels, *Selected works* (Moscow, 1973) vol. 3, pp. 460, 469.

2. S. Dubrovskii and V. Grave, *Agrarnoe dvizhenie v 1905–1907 gg.* (Moscow, 1925).

3. S. Dubrovskii, *Krest'yanskoe dvizhenie v revolyutsii 1905–1907 gg.* (Moscow, 1956). Dubrovskii (for once without quoting the source of his methodological inspiration) followed such an exercise attempted by Lenin nearly half a century earlier. Lenin, PSS, vol. 19, p. 365.

4. The study published in 1925 (Dubrovskii and Grave, op. cit). announced in its introduction that the computation of evidence referred to is presented in a table attached at the end of the book. There is no such table and an examination of copies within different libraries of the USSR has shown that none was ever actually attached. Dubrovskii himself never explained it when he came back to use his evidence as 'hard facts' in 1956. The attempts of some of the colleagues to follow up his work in the archives of the police has failed, as many of the files are missing. There is no way to replicate those figures. Simonova defined the problem as that of 'coded (*zashifrovannaya*) evidence'. M. Simonova, 'Krest'yanskoe dvizhenie 1905–1907 gg. v sovetskoi istoriografii', *Istoricheskie zapiski*, 1975, p. 212.

5. To avoid charges of yet another personal bias, my own, the division into seasons was adopted after the work of M. Leshchenko, *Selyanskii rukh v pravoberezhnii ukraini v period revolyutsii 1905–1907 rr.* (Kiev, 1955) p. 90. It is spring: March–May; summer June–August; autumn: September–November; winter: December–February.
6. S. Prokopovich, *Agrarnyi krizis i meropriyatiya pravitel'stva* (Moscow, 1912).
7. E. Morokhovets, *Krest'yanskoe dvizhenie i sotsial-demokratiya* (Moscow, 1926).
8. V. Tropin, *Bor'ba bol'shevikov za rukovodstvo krest'yanskim dvizheniem v 1905 g* (Moscow, 1970).
9. There are other major weaknesses like, for example, the non-seasonal division adopted by the author (as discussed above in relation to Dubrovskii's figures).
10. For example, *Istoriya sssr* (Moscow, 1968) vol. VI, p. 175.

HISTORY TEACHES: LEARNING, UNLEARNING, NON-LEARNING

A Moments of Truth

1. K. Kautsky, letter to the fourth congress of the RSDWP (1906) *Protokoly chetvertogo (obedinitel'nogo) s'ezda rsdrp* (Moscow, 1934) p. 594 (italics added).
2. A. Pankratova, *Pervaya russkaya revolyutsiya* (Moscow, 1951).
3. S. Dubrovskii, *Krest'yanskoe dvizhenie v revolyutsii 1905–1907* gg, (Moscow, 1956) p. 139.

B Collective Memories, Plebeian Wrath, Historical Futures

1. M. Bloch, *The Historian's Craft* (Manchester, 1970) pp. 73–5.
2. See for example L. Lur'e, in *Osvoboditel'noe dvizhenie v Rossii* (Saratov, 1978) pp. 64–83 who spoke of 'circles of people of similar age (*sverstniki*) who display socio-psychological kinship' (ibid, p. 64).
3. I. Deutscher, 'The French Revolution and the Russian Revolution: Some suggestive Analogies', *World Politics*, 1951, vol. 4, p. 381.
4. Agrarnoe dvizhenie v Rossii (St Petersburg, 1908) vol. 1 p. 219. M. Perrie 'The Russian Peasant Movement of 1905–7', *Past and Present*, 1972, no. 57, pp. 145–6.
5. T. Shanin, *Russia as a 'Developing Society'* (London, 1985). Chapter 2.
6. This badly underdeveloped issue of social theory carries major importance for intellectual history, however conceived. For an early influential discussion see K. Manheim, *Essays in the Sociology of Knowledge* (New York, 1952) chap. VII.
7. See Shanin, op. cit., Chapter 1, section B.
8. L. Haimson, 'The Problem of Social Stability in Urban Russia 1905–17', *Slavic Review*, 1964, vol. 23, no. 4 and 1965, vol. 24, no. 1.
9. For example, T. Emmons, *The Formation of Political Parties and the First National Elections in Russia* (Cambridge, 1983) pp. 62–72. The

author studied directly the leadership of the KDs and brought into play comparative evidence concerning the SDs and SRs drawn from the works of D. Lane and M. Perrie to which reference is made in Chapter 2 of our text. (For the comparative table see Emmons, *op. cit.*, p. 71). See also the interesting 'generational' study of the revolutionary populists of the earlier period in Lur'e, op. cit.

10. B. Pasternak, '1905', *Stikhi i poemy 1912–1932* (Ann Arbor, 1961) vol. 1, pp. 110.

11. In the first half of the nineteenth century women entered the annals of the Russian Revolution mainly as the wives of the Decembrists who, to the general acclaim of 'the society', chose to join their husbands in Siberia. The revolutionary populism of the 1870s and 1880s had numerous women as its direct participants and leaders. Names such as Sofia Perovskaya (who commanded the successful attempt of Alexander II), Vera Finger and Vera Zasulich, were known and respected all throughout Russia and followed by a new female generation in the revolutionary parties of 1905–07. But both men and women of the Russian revolutionary underground insisted on female equality, refusing for that reason any particularity of female goals and organisations. For discussion see R. Stites, *The Women's Liberation Movement in Russia* (Princeton, 1978) chaps V, VII.

12. The tsarist government proceeded to play such games of 'give and take away' despite the open mistrust by those at whom they aimed. For example, once the First World War began the Russian army's C.-in-C. declared that the Russian tsardom intended to re-establish the autonomy of Poles and to secure their national interests in the future. The mass of Poles regarded it as a cynical manoeuvre of expedience.

13. See Chapter 2, section C.

14. *Istoriya SSSR* (Moscow, 1968) vol. 6, p. 369. For Zubatov's effort at police-sponsored workers organisations see Chapter 1 of this volume.

15. See Chapter 2.

16. Haimson, op. cit., vol. 24, no. 1 (especially pp. 65–7 which stressed the fact of massive rural recruitment).

17. Ibid, pp. 626–8; *Proletarskaya revolyutsiya*, 1924, no. 7 (30), nos. 8–9 (31–32S); *Svod otchetov fabrichnykh inspektorov* (St Petersburg, 1916). Figures given by factory inspectors for the strikers in the first half of 1914 were 1 254 000 strikers, of whom 4/5 were listed as engaged in 'political strikes'.

18. Haimson, op. cit., vol. 24, p. 631; *Istoriya kommunisticheskoi partii sovetskogo soyuza* (Moscow, 1966) vol. 2, pp. 443–67. The high points of this process were the electoral defeat of the Mensheviks in the election to the Boards of the Metalworkers' Union of St Petersburg and of the All-Russian Workers Insurance, in 1913 and 1914 respectively. By 1914, the Bolsheviks claimed to control 4/5 of the union boards in Moscow and St Petersburg.

19. Haimson, op. cit., pp. 640–9. The *Istoriya kommunisticheskoi partii sovetskogo soyouza*, pp. 464–5, speaks of 'politically immature' Bolshevik party members who set up their own separate and more radical organisation (eventually broken up by police arrests). For evidence of

parallel revival of PSR support see Haimson, op. cit., p. 635; *Istoriya sssr*, pp. 431.

20. G. T. Robinson, *Rural Russia Under the Old Regime* (New York, 1972) p. 263; *Agrarnoe dvizhenie v rossii*, pp. 40–3, 53, 55, 315–18; Prokopovich', *Agrarnyi krizis i meropriyatiya pravitel'stva* (Moscow, 1912) pp. 142–5. Robinson had doubted that rents actually went down but admitted to the other improvements. Primary evidence and later discovered sources documented decreases in rent, at least for a time.

21. In the Saratov and Simbirsk provinces 1/3 of all of the 'private' (that is, mostly non-peasant) land, was sold within two years.

22. Prokopovich, op. cit., pp. 142–5, 154–8.

23. M. Perrie, 'The Russian Peasant Movement in 1907–1908: A Survey by the Socialist-Revolutionary Party', *History Workshop Journal*, 1977, no. 4; Prokopovich, op. cit., p. 148.

24. I. Chernyshev, *Obschchina posle 9 noyabrya 1906* (Petrograd, 1917) pp. 133–6, etc.

25. Tan (Bogoraz), *Novoe krest'yanstvo* (Moscow, 1905) p. 14.

26. Chernyshev, op. cit., p. 165. Chernyshev's testimony is particularly valuable here because his findings run contrary to his own ideological preferences.

27. See the companion volume, Shanin, op. cit., Chapter 1, section B.

28. Ibid, Chapter 3, section B.

29. Haimson, op. cit., vol. 24, p. 2.

30. Description by correspondent of *Rech'*, 12 July, 1914, quoted after Haimson, vol. 24, p. 7; vol. 23, p. 642.

31. P. Kenez, *Civil War in South Russia, 1918*. Also see B. Startsev, *Krakh kerenshchiny* (Leningrad, 1982) pp. 37–56 for the extent and forms of spontaneous plebeian mobilisation against the Kornilov's coup in 1917.

32. A. Zaitsov, *1918 god* (Paris, 1934) p. 7. For discussion also pp. 11, 78–9, 131–4.

33. A. Denikin, *Ocherki russkoi smuty* (Paris, 1921–5) vol. 2, pp. 148–9.

34. The results of the 1917 election to the Constitutional Assembly show that Bolshevik support of the Latvian regiments was neither accidental nor particular to the military. In the electoral region of Kurlandia (a main Latvian area) the vote for the Bolsheviks was 71.9 per cent. See O. Zamenskii *Vserosiisroe uchreditel'noe sobranie* (Leningrad, 1976) p. 279.

35. By 1920 there were 26 000 of *kursanty* and about 40 000 'red commanders' as against about 50 000 pre-revolutionary officers, then in the service of the Red Army.

36. The figures are not clear-cut. Our citation follows that of recent Soviet and Western studies, for example, L. Haimson, *The Politics of Rural Russia* (Indiana, 1979) p. 293. Stolypin spoke in 1907 of larger numbers.

37. Ibid; R. Manning, *The Crisis of Old Order in Russia* (Princeton, 1982); Yu. Solov'ev, *Samoderzhavie i dvoryanstvo* (Moscow, 1981).

38. For example, the most extensive punitive flogging in centuries of the Russian rural populations directly followed the law abolishing flogging as judicial punishment, executions without trial (of people whose names were not even ascertained – the *besfamilnye*), followed the manifesto establishing a state of legal order (*pravovoi poryavok*), etc.

39. V. Dyakin, *Samoderzhavie, burzhuaziya i dvoryanstvo* (Leningrad, 1978) p. 202.

40. Konez, op. cit., p. 281.

41. P. Buryshkin, *Moskva kupecheskaya* (New York, 1954); V. Laverychev, *Krupnaya burzhuaziya v poreformennoi Rossi 1861–1900* (Moscow, 1974) especially pp. 5–10, 71–4, 157–8. Also Diakin, op. cit., and E. Cheremenskii, *Burzhyaziya i tsarizm v pervoi russkoy revolyutsii* (Moscow, 1970).

42. Shanin, op. cit., Chapter 5, sections C and D.

43. The new wave of the student disorders began with the demonstration held at the funerals of S. Muromtsev (the first Duma chairman) and of Lev Tolstoy. *Istoriya sssr*, op. cit. pp. 414–5, 418–9; V. Leikina-Svirskaya, Russkaya intelligentsiya v 1900–1917 godakh (Moscow, 1981) pp. 31–2.

44. For a particularly clear and influential declaration of those views, see *Vekhi* (Moscow, 1909) which offers a virtual compendium of negative characteristics of the Russian intelligentsia presented as charges in condemning its responsibility for the 1905–07 revolution.

45. E. Trubetskoi in *Moskovskii ezhenedel'nik*, 1907, pp. 22–3, 5–6.

5C Retreat into Progress: the KDs and Mensheviks

1. From a newly-discovered poem by B. Brecht in M. Esslini's translation (used as motto to Chapter 4).

2. See section 5B.

3. I. Deutscher, 'The French Revolution and the Russian Revolution: Some suggestive Analogies', *World Politics, 1951*, July, p. 370.

4. F. Dan, *Proiskhozhdenie bol'shevizma* (New York, 1946) p. 421.

5. P. Milyukov 'Rokovye gody', *Russkie zapiski*, January 1939, p. 119. Also C. Timberlake, *Essays on Russian Liberalism* (Missouri, 1972).

6. W. G. Rosenberg, *Liberals in the Russian Revolution* (Princeton, 1974) pp. 17–19, 28–9.

7. A. Naumov, *Iz utselevshikh vospominanii* (New York, 1954) 202; Yu Solov'ev, *Samoderzhavie i dvoryanstvo v 1902–1907* (Leningrad, 1981) p. 25.

8. R. Pipes, *Struve: Liberal on the Right 1905–1944* (Cambridge, 1980); Timberlake, op. cit.

9. P. Struve, *Na raznyya temy* (St Petersburg, 1902) pp. 526–55.

10. Heiden initially joined the Octobrist Party, politically to the right of the KDs, shortly afterwards established the Party of Peaceful Regeneration of stronger constitutionalist tendency, and eventually joined the KDs, becoming a member of its Central Committee. See Solov'ev, op. cit. pp. 155.

11. *Vekhi* (Moscow, 1909).

12. Rosenberg, op. cit. pp. 35–41.

13. Pipes, op. cit. chap. 8.

14. Emmons, op. cit. pp.75–81; Rosenberg, op. cit. pp. 32–4.

15. V. Laverychev, *Po tu storonu barikad* (Moscow, 1967) chap. 2.

16. Heiden quoted in *Arkheograficheskii ezhegodnik za 1974* (Moscow, 1975) pp. 285–93.
17. Dan, op. cit. p. 421.
18. In particular the Communist Manifesto, but also Marx's 'Addresses to the First International' in the 1860s and 1871.
19. K. Kautsky 'Franz Mehring', *Neue Zeit*, 1903; Lenin, 'What is to be done', PPS, vol. 8.
20. R. Luxemburg, in *Neue Zeit*, January 1905, quoted after *New Left Review*, 1975, no. 89, p. 41.
21. L. Haimson, *The Russian Marxists and the Origins of Bolshevism* (Boston, 1955) chap. II. *Vtoroi ocherednoy s'ezd* (Geneva, 1904).
22. Lenin, PSS, vol. 8, p. 370.
23. T. Carlyle, *The French Revolution* (London, 1913) vol. 2, p. 261, spoke of the Girondists as 'men of philosophical culture, decent behaviour, not condemnable in that they were pedants' which would have been, as good a description of the core of Menshevik leaders as could be given.
24. Haimson, op. cit., chap. 10, especially p. 183.
25. As admitted by P. Rumyantsev (Shmidt), then member of the Bolshevik Central Committee, at the 1906 Congress of RSDWP. *Protokoly chetvertogo (obedinitel'nogo) s'ezda rsdrp* (Moscow, 1934), p. 552.
26. Dan, op. cit. pp. 376–380, *Istoriya Kommunisticheskoi partii sovetskogo soyuza*, loc. cit. pp. 128–32.
27. P. Garvi, *Zapiski sotsial demokrata* (Newtonville, 1982) pp. 104–217; also L. Haimson, 'The Problem of Social Stability in Russia 1905–07', *Slavic Review*, 1964, vol. xxiii, no. 4, pp. 694–6.
28. For the significance of the distinction between 'propaganda', that is, teaching the working class Marxist ideology and 'agitation', that is calling on the workers' support for specific issues and teaching them politics by a class action which deepens revolutionary consciousness, see Section 1C, especially the conceptual breakthrough expressed by the booklet of A. Kramer summing up for the socialist activists the experience of the social democratic circles in *Vilna/Vilnius*. A. Kramer, *Ob agitatsii* (Geneva, 1896).
29. Haimson, op. cit., p. 201.
30. I. Chernyshev, *Agrarno – krestyanskaya politika Rossii* (Petrograd, 1918) p. XVIII.
31. Garvi, op. cit.; Haimson, The Problem, loc. cit.
32. See section 5B, note 19.
33. Dan, op. cit.
34. Ibid, p. 458.
35. Ibid, p. 472.
36. Ibid, pp. 488–90.

5D Conservative Militants and Militant Conservatives: the SRs and the United Nobility

1. The Bolsheviks had their own leader-spy, R. Malinovskii, who was the head of their faction in the fourth Duma and a member of the Central Committee. Like Azev, he was strongly defended by the other party

leaders (especially by Lenin) against the 'provocative rumours' about his being a police spy. But, better luck for the Bolsheviks, Malinovskii was unmasked only during the 1917 revolution, when those matters were of little significance for the party morale. The treason of Azev was particularly painful because he inherited after Gershuni's death the leadership of the BO PSR – the party's super-secret terrorist organisation on which the attention of its members and enemies centred.

2. F. Venturi. *Roots of Revolution* (London, 1960); T. Shanin, *Late Marx and the Russian Road* (London, 1983).

3. The bad luck of the PSR also held 'posthumously'. While admirers of the Bolsheviks had all the Soviet scholarly resources on their side, and the KDs as well as the Mensheviks received much sympathetic attention from the US historians, the single US scholar who gave his attention and much important research to the SRs, Radkey, came to treat them with considerable dismay. Only recently a somewhat more balanced view began to emerge from younger European historians, e.g. M. Perry.

4. A Spiridovich, *Revolyutsionnoe dvizhenie v Rossii* (Petrograd, 1916) vol. 2, chapter XX.

5. Ibid, pp. 495–6.

6. Antonov etc., *Sbornik stat'ei* (Moscow 1908); V. Chernov, *Sobranie sochinenii* (Petrograd, 1917); V. Chernov *Pered bur'ei* (New York, 1951); for a good example of PSR mainstream views and their stagnation in inter-revolutionary period *Sotsialist-revolyutsioner* 1912, no. 4, pp. 131–76.

7. O. H. Radkey 'Chernov and Agrarian Socialism', in E. Simmons, *Continuity and Change in Russia and Soviet Thought* (New York, 1967); V. Chernov, *K voprosu o vykupe* (St Petersburg, 1906); M. Hildermeier, 'Neopopulism and Modernisation', *The Russian Review*, 1975, vol. 34, no. 4; V. Ginev, *Borba za krest'yanstvo i krisis russkogo neonarodichestva* (Leningrad, 1983).

8. *Protokoly pervoi partiinoi konferentsii psr* (Paris, 1908); *Pamyatnaya knizhka sotstialistov revolyutsionerov* (Paris, 1911).

9. J. Needham, *Science and Civilisation in China* (Cambridge,1956) vol. 2, chap. 13. S. Teng and J. K. Fairbank, *China's Response to the West* (Cambridge, 1979) pp. 15–16.

10. For further discussion see Shanin, op. cit., part III. Also the companion volume of the text presented, T. Shanin, *Russia as a 'Developing Society'* (London, 1985) Chapter 5, section D.

11. In 1917 the KDs moved towards the old programme of total redivision of all 'surplus land' first suggested by the Popular Socialists. The Bolsheviks simply took over *in toto* the 'Combined Instruction to Deputies [*svodnyi nakaz*] Of 342', that is, the PSR agrarian programme of the day.

12. Hildermeier, loc. cit., p. 457.

13. *Pochin*, 1912, no. 1, pp. 1–2, 15–18; N. Avksenev 'Nashi raznoglasiya', *Znamya truda*, 1913, no. 49.

14. See G. Kryzhanovskii, *Vospominanya* (Berlin, 1925).

15. I. Vaisberg, *Sovet ob'edinennogo dvoryanstva* (Moscow, 1966) (unpublished thesis); Yu. Solov'ev, *Samoderzhavie i dvoryanstvo v 1902–1907 gg.* (Moscow, 1981) chap. 3; E. Cheremeneskii, *Burzhuaziya i dvoryan-*

stvo v pervoi russkoi revolyutsii (Moscow, 1970). A. Avrekh, *Tsarism i IV duma* (Moscow, 1981) chap. 4.

16. Quoted after the booklet by Prince M. Shakhovskii (*not* the KD leader with a similar surname) *Volneniya krest'yan* (St Petersburg, 1907) pp. 40–5.
17. Solov'ev, op. cit. p. 174.
18. L. Haimson *The Politics of Rural Russia* (Bloomington, 1979) p. 276.
19. See for the most articulate expression of that view, K. Pobedontsev *Moskovskii sbornik* (Moscow, 1897) especially sections 3, 9 and 12. The 1886 report of the Minister of Interior, D. Tolstoy explained that elected groups cannot act in accordance with principles of moral responsibility. *Ministerstvo vnytrennikh del 1802–1902* (St Petersburg, 1902).
20. Quoted after V. Nevskii *Rabochee divizhenie v ianvarskie dni 1905 goda* (Moscow, 1931) p. 106. As to what the Grand-Duke learnt from French history the report ran on as follows 'He thinks that the way to cure the people from constitutionalist attempts is to hang few hundreds in the presence of their comrades . . .' The report proceeded as follows: 'Grand duke Vladimir was given an extraordinary opportunity to show his abilities as a man of political vision and of Napoleonic abilities. He is certain of the positive results of the steps he would take'.
21. Von Laue, *Sergei Witte and the Industrialisation of Russia* (New York, 1963) chap. 3, 6.
22. For further discussion see the following section 5D.
23. Vitte, *Vospominaniya* (Leningrad, 1924) vol. 11.

6 HISTORY TEACHES: THE FRONTIERS OF POLITICAL IMAGINATION

6A Stolypin and Revolution from Above

1. G. Kryzhanovskii, *vospominaniya* (Berlin, 1925); S. Dubrovskii, *Stolypinskaya zemel'naya reforma* (Moscow, 1963) chap. 2; V. Dyakin, *Samoderzhavie: Burzhuyaziya i dvoryanastvo* (Leningrad, 1978); A. Avrekh, *Tsarism i treteyunskaya sistema* (Moscow, 1966); J. Yaney, *The Urge to Mobilize* (Urbana, 1982); V. Gurko, *Features and Figures of the Past* (New York, 1967).
2. Kryzhanovskii, op. cit., p. 221.
3. Dyakin, op. cit., p. 47.
4. E. V. *Predsedatel' soveta ministrov p.a. stolypin* (St Petersburg, 1909) p. 77.
5. Stolypin showed characteristically 'Bismarckian' limitations in his knowledge of economics and the related belief that politicians are to govern and to secure conditions for the businessmen 'to get on with the job'. Many major merchant families of Moscow were Old-believers and the same was true for the Jews and Armenians, especially in western and southern Russia.
6. E. V., op. cit., pp. 55, 76, etc. Also see the memoirs of Stolypin's daughter, M. Bok, *Vospominaniya o moem ottse p.a. stolypine* (New York, 1953) pp. 299–300.

7. From Stolypin's interview with the newspaper *Volga* in September 1909.
8. Stolypin declaration on 24 August 1906 and his speech to the Duma on 6 March 1907, for the see E. V. op. cit.
9. Ibid, p. 45.
10. From Stolypin's private notes found in his desk by the government committee which took over his papers on his death, kept in TsGIAL, Fond 1284, op. 194, d. 58, and quoted after V. Dyakin 'Stolypin i dvoryanstvo', *Problemy Krest'yanskogo zemlevladeniya i vnutrennoi politiki rossii* (Leningrad, 1972) pp. 233–4. See also Stolypin's speech along similar lines on 15 March 1910 in N. Karpov, *Agrarnaya politika stolypina* (Leningrad, 1925).
11. *Sobranie rechei p.a. stolypina* (St Petersburg, 1911) p. 100 (speech of 27 June 1911).
12. Dubrovskii, op. cit., pp. 121–5. For discussion of the peasant commune in history and its structure see also T. Shanin, *Russia as a 'Developing Society'* (London, 1984) chapter 2, section C.
13. For discussion of the differences between private and family property within the context of the Russian peasantry see A. Leont'ev, *Krest'yanskoe pravo* (St Petersburg, 1909). Also T. Shanin, *The Awkward Class* (Oxford, 1972) appendix B.
14. Dubrovskii, op. cit., chap. 5. G. T. Robinson, *Rural Russia Under the Old Regime* (London, 1932) chap. X. See also A. Kafod/Koefoed, *Khutorskoe rasselenie* (St Petersburg, 1907) and *My Share in the Stolypin Reform* (Odense, 1985). (The author, an expert from Denmark, acted as government chief advisor on issues of homestead agriculture.)
15. Some squires, members of the United Nobility and leaders of the Black Hundreds organisations proceeded to object to any change in the customary structure of Russian peasant society.
16. See the companion volume, Shanin, *Russia* Chapter 2, sections A and B.
17. Stolypin's submission to the Cabinet on 1 July 1907 as quoted in Dyakin, *Samodershavie*, p. 38.
18. Kryzhanovskii, op. cit. pp. 131–2.
19. Dyakin, *Samoderzhavie*, pp. 82–4.
20. Ibid, p. 84. P. Durnovo was the Minister of Interior in the 1905 government of Witte, before Stolypin received this post (under Goremykin). Durnovo was therefore considered, by many of Russia's right-wingers to be the true victor over the revolutionaries (and unjustly removed from his post). He was also seen by most of them as a more reliable man than Stolypin to preside over a return to the better days of pre-1905 Russia.
21. The correspondent of the *Daily Telegraph* in St Petersburg, Dillon, who often acted as a mouthpiece for the right-wing members of Russia's State Council, put it in words: 'The Russian reactionaries (conservatives have disappeared by now), find Stolypin's policies repulsive . . . he undercut the attributes of the crown giving some of them in presents to the Duma . . . which will lead to disaster'. Dyakin, *Samoderzhavie*, pp. 126–7. See also Gurko, op. cit., pp. 513–6.
22. The tsar proceeded: 'All the time him, and him alone, while I was barely being seen'. S. Shidlovskii, *Vospominaniya* (Berlin, 1923), p. 198. See also V. Kokovtsov, *Iz moego proshlovo* (Paris, 1933) vol. II.

23. Kryzhanovskii, op. cit., p. 214. Dyakin, referred to it as the period of 'reforms recoiling'.
24. A Avrekh, *Stolypin i tret'ya duma* (Moscow, 1968) Part 1.
25. For example, Guchkov, the speaker of the third Duma and Stolypin's most energetic supporter in the Octobrist party he led, resigned in protest and left St Petersburg.
26. A. Zen'kovskii, *Pravda o Stolypine* (New York, 1956) especially pp. 21–113.
27. For example, M. S. Conroy, *Peter Arkad'evich Stolypin* (Boulder, 1976) pp. 73–5.
28. Avrekh, *Stolypin*, chap. 8. Bagrov has been persistently but wrongly, described as an SR, in line with the widespread tendency to define terrorists of any type in this way. As a matter of fact, the PSR formally declared that its organisation had nothing to do with the killing of Stolypin. (The fact itself was welcomed by this party as a just punishment of the man in charge of the 1906–07 repressions.)
29. Bok, op. cit., chap. XXXIII.
30. Avrekh, *Stolypin,* pp. 384–406.
31. In this Lenin followed Marx's notion of the social determinations of Napoleon III's rule in France – that is, his ability to play on the equilibrium of class forces to secure a personal dictatorship.
32. Dyakin, *Samoderzhavie*, especially pp.16–25.
33. A. Avrekh, *Tsarizm i iv duma* (Moscow, 1981) pp. 10–17. For a general view of absolutism behind Avrekh's attitude to 'Stolypinism' see *Istoria sssr*, 1968, no. 2.
34. Ibid, p. 11, 13.
35. See Shanin, *Russia*, Chapter 5, section C. In the words of Lenin's grudging compliment, it was 'progressive in the scientifically economic sense . . . proceeding along the lines of capitalist evolution'. Note the content and the equation.
36. Stolypin allegedly went as far as to predict in his family circle that 'I shall die at the hands of the *okhrana*' (Russia's secret police).
37. See the companion volume, Shanin, *Russia*, Chapter 5, section B.
38. For example, the so-called 'White Revolution of the Shah and the People' in Iran of the 1960s and 1970s.
39. By the turn of the century, Witte was increasingly disturbed by the way Russia's agrarian crisis linked with the general economic down-turn, endangering the country's prospects. His 1900 annual report to the tsar differed sharply from his earlier optimistic view that once the industrialisation of the country was secured all the rest would follow suit. Also, since 1902 he chaired the *Consultations Concerning the Problems of Agricultural Production.* Its preliminary report can be considered an intermediary step between the Witte early economic strategy and the agrarian element of Stolypin's reforms. The 'Consultation' was brought to an end before finalising its findings. Witte himself was never again permitted to define Russia's economic strategy. Another major figure of relevance who was not given the opportunity to execute his plan for agrarian reform was V. Gurko – considered by many the true author of the Stolypin Reform.

40. See section 6B.
41. S. Dubrovskii, *Stolypinskaya zemel'naya reforma* (Moscow, 1963) chaps 4–8.
42. Dyakin expressed it by stating that while the position of Stolypin was an alternative major strategy, 'one cannot define and characterise for the moment the list of his supporters', Dyakin, *Samoderzhavie*, p. 20. The main difficulty in naming Stolypin's political faction is the fact that it never emerged at all. We are dealing with a programme designed by a few state administrators and a 'mood' which supported them in some circles. What made them able to challenge political factions, class formations and ideological positions was not their number, but their placements within the Russian state apparatus and its immense power to compel.
43. See for example, G. Yaney, *The Urge to Mobilise* (Urbana, 1982) p. 366, etc for discussion of the gradual conflict and the change in the balance of power between the Land Chiefs (*zemskie nachal'niks*) and the 'agricultural specialists' as well as the 'intellectuals' at 'the centre'. The author seems to have overstated his case but the process was rightly observed.

6B   Trotsky and the Permanent Revolution

1. For discussion of the conceptual changes see section 6D. The majority of the Bolshevik members of the Central Committees of the RSDWP 1903–12 were not in the Bolshevik ranks in the period to follow.
2. N. Zhordaniya, *My Life* (Stanford, 1968) chaps 7, 8, 9; *Istoriya SSSR* (Moscow, 1968) vol. 7. We shall discuss the issue in section 6C.
3. For the Marxist political 'break-through' in the 1890s see Chapter 1 section C, of this volume. The basic texts which put in a nutshell the new historiography at the core of their views and were most broadly used to popularise it in pre-revolutionary Russia were F. Engels, *Auty Duhring* and *The Origins of Private Property, Family and State* (especially its concluding section). These were supplemented by the avidly read books and articles by K. Kautsky and G. Plekhanov and the major Marxist periodicals, mostly in German. Of the younger Marxist generation in Russia, the writings of P. Struve, V. Lenin and Yu. Martov were particularly influential.
4. It has often been remarked in the discussions and publications of the Second International that its Russian branches produced more 'isms', describing deviations from proper socialist understanding, than the rest of the Second International combined. Trotsky even produced an essay explaining in terms of Russia's socio-economic 'backwardness' this tendency for 'fanaticism in ideas, ruthless self-limitation and self-demarcation, distrust and suspicion and vigilant watching over their own purity . . . this zeal for the latter [*bukva* – that is the hermeneutic debate of texts]'.
5. See Chapter 1, section C of this volume. Also Chapter 5, section B of the companion volume: *Russia as a 'Developing Society'*.
6. M. Perrie, 'The Socialist Revolutionaries on "Permanent Revolution" ',

Soviet Studies, 1973, vol. 24, no. 3. Also see Chapter 5, section D of this volume.

7. For a biography see Z. A. B. Zeman and W. B. Scharlau, *The Merchant of Revolution* (London, 1965); also Deutscher, op. cit., chap. IV. For the main collection of relevant writings on Russia and the 1905–07 revolution see Parvus, *Rossiya i revolyutsiya* (St Petersburg, 1906).

8. See in particular Lehmann and Parvus, *Das Hungernde Russland* (Stuttgart, 1900). Also Zeman *et al.*, op. cit., chap. 2.

9. Trotsky supported the Mensheviks at the 1903 congress of the RSDWP, but left their organisation in 1904.

10. L. Trotsky, *Do devyatogo yanvarya* (Geneva, 1905). See Trotsky's speech to the fifth congress of the RSDWP in *Protokoly pyatogo s'ezda* (Moscow, 1975). For the best historical texts about him see Deutscher, op. cit. See also L. Schapiro, *The Communist Party of the Soviet Union* (London, 1970) and L. Trotsky, *Moya zhizn'* (Berlin, 1930) vol. 1. For a more sophisticated version of the official Soviet view see *Istoriya KPSS* (Moscow, 1966) vol. 2.

11. Parvus proceeded to wield personal influence with the SD ministers of Germany after 1918. He offered his services also to the Bolsheviks, to which Lenin apparently retorted that, while they needed good brains supporting them in Europe, they could not permit dirty hands to go with it.

12. L. Trotsky, *1905* (London, 1971) pp. 4–5.

13. Ibid, p. 47. In close parallel to this view, Parvus pronounced that the peasantry 'serves the revolution by promoting the revolutionary increase in anarchy, but is unable to focus in on its own political struggle' (Parvus, op. cit.) p. 204.

14. The disproportionate absorption of economic products by the state would have meant that the tsardom sliced also into the 'share' of the privileged classes while restricting the whole society's economic progress. Trotsky spoke sharply against 'those critical socialists who seem to have ceased to understand the significance of state power for a socialist revolution' and who 'should at least study the example of the unsystematic and barbaric activity of the Russian autocracy so as to realise the immensely important role which state power can play in purely economic spheres when, generally speaking, it is working in the same direction as historical development' Trotsky, op. cit. 1971. He categorised the tsardom as 'an intermittent form between European absolutism and Asian despotism, being possibly closer to the latter of these two' (ibid p. 8). At the same time, both Parvus and Trotsky proceeded to insist that the only substantial difference between Western Europe and Russia was the *extent* of Russia's backwardness.

15. L. Trotsky, *The Permanent Revolution and Results and Prospects* (New York, 1965) p. 168. The book offered the first summary of Trotsky's position concerning the issue of 'permanent revolution'.

16. Trotsky, *1905*, p. 55.

17. The dismissal by Trotsky of peasant revolutionary potential, yes or no, has been in constant debate. Without doubt, the charge was used as a slander by Stalin's supporters and those who followed them. On the

other hand, Trotsky's most thoughtful biographer, Deutscher, dismissed this view too lightly and was even partly 'taken in' by Trotsky's interpretation of these matters. Compare for example, the evidence in our Chapters 3 and 4 with Deutscher's view – following that of Trotsky – that in October 1905 'The revolution was still a purely urban affair . . . only in 1906 did rural Russia become seriously restive', Deutscher, op. cit. pp. 91–2, 129–130. For a short but pertinent discussion of consistency in Trotsky's later attitudes to peasantry see R. Dunayevskaya, whose knowledge of Trotsky's text is superb, in *Philosophy and Revolution* (Brighton, 1980) pp. 134–6.

18. Trotsky, *The Permanent Revolution*, p. 204.
19. Deutscher, op. cit., p. 162.
20. Martov was initially a member of the editorial board but resigned out of disagreement with Trotsky and Antonov-Ovseenko.
21. The group consisted reportedly of 3000 activists, mostly workers and was led by a number of future leading politicians and diplomats of Lenin's government like Yoffe, Uritskii, Karakhan etc.
22. A Lunacharskii called it 'the golden period of meetings' between May and October 1917. See his 'Ideologiya nakanune oktyabrya', *Za 5 let* (Moscow, 1922) p. 29, which gave some vivid examples of it. See also N. Sukhanov, *Zapiski o Revolyutsii* (Berlin, 1922–3).
23. Lenin, PPS, vol. 31, pp. 113–6, 123–4. The April Thesis was adopted fully by the *mezhraiontsy*.
24. For source see this section, note 17 above and section 6C note 28.

6C   Zhordaniya and the National Front

1. K. Kautsky, *Georgia* (London, 1921) p. 18.
2. The figure quoted by the 1897 census was of about 800 000 'Georgian-speakers' but 500 000 more spoke the separately quoted but closely related Imperitin, Mangrel and Swan dialects. There were also the Adjar Muslims, who spoke Georgian, and whose ethnic status was in constant debate.
3. N. Zhordaniya, *My Life* (Stanford, 1968) chap. 3. See also *Istoriya komunisticheskoi partii sovetskogo soyuza* (Moscow, 1906) vol. 1 and G. Uratadze, *Reminiscences of a Georgian Social Democrat* (Stanford, 1968) chaps 1–3.
4. *Vtoroi ocherednoi s'ezd* (Geneva, 1904) Appendices. The committees of Batum, Tiflis and Baku were represented. Zhordaniya who was in Europe when the delegates were elected, participated in the congress as an 'observer' – a delegate without voting rights.
5. The Mensheviks who received six mandates to the fourth congress and ten mandates to the fifth from Guria, were charged by some (like Aleksinskii of the Bolshevik delegates) with representing thereby the unproletarian moderation of their petty-bourgeois constituency. The charge was ridiculous, of course; the Georgian Mensheviks were as influential among the workers of Tiflis as in Guria, while their peasant groups were politically as militant as the Russian workers–urbanites.
6. For discussion of the revolutionary activities of the 'autonomes organisa-

tion of petty bourgeoise' in Tiflis, led by Z. Chachua, see Zhordaniya, op. cit., pp. 44–5.

7. *Vtoroi ocherednoi s'ezd*, p. 3.
8. The refusal to permit ethnically-based organisations led to the decision of the Bund not to join the Party and to leave the Congress before it ended.
9. Zhordaniya, op. cit., p. 28. The Viceroy of the Caucasus, Dashkov, wrote accordingly in his report to the tsar that 'should there be a wish for separation among the different peoples of the Caucasus . . . it will be only on behalf of this (Muslim) part of it'. I. Vorontsov-Dashkov, *Vsepoddannishii otchet* (St Petersburg, 1913), p. 9.
10. 'Economic Progress and the National Question', presented at the meeting of Mesame Dasi's group in 1893. See D. M. Lang, *A Modern History of Soviet Georgia* (New York, 1962) p. 127.
11. J. Stalin, *Marxism and the National Problem* (written in 1912).
12. Zhordaniya, op. cit., p. 40.
13. We avoid as less relevant the discussion of the First World War divisions between the Georgian Mensheviks. Most of them took anti-defencist positions, few became Germanophiles or Russophiles. Zhordaniya adopted a peculiar position 'in between', that is, a milder brand of defencism 'not out of the wish to see a Russian victory but out of fear of French defeat'. The most relevant point is that, despite these diversities, the party kept its unity in 1917.
14. For discussion of the period 1917–21 see S. F. Kazemzadeh, *The Struggle for Transcaucasia* (Oxford, 1915); Z. Avalishvili, *The Independence of Georgia in International Policies* (Westport, 1940); E. Drabkina, *Gruzinskaia kontrrevolutsiia* (Leningrad, 1928); T. Makharadze, *Diktatura men'shevistskoi partii v Gruzii* (Moscow, 1921). Also Zhordaniya, op. cit.; Lang, op. cit.; Uratadze, op. cit.; Kautsky, op. cit. Particularly important is N. Zhordaniya, *Za dva goda* (Tiflis, 1919).
15. Zhordaniya, *My Life*, p. 76.
16. Zhordaniya, *Za dva goda*, pp. 35–6.
17. See Avalishvili, *op. cit.*, Zhordaniya, *My Life*, chaps V–VII. Also *Dokumenty i materiyaly po vneshnei politike zakavkazya i gruzii* (Tiflis, 1919). See also R. Pipes, *The Formation of The Soviet Union* (Cambridge, 1964) parts II, V.
18. Kazemzadeh, *op. cit.*, pp. 188–9; G. Urutadze, *Obrazovanie i konsolidatsiya gruzinskoi demokraticheskoi respubliki* (Munich, 1956) pp. 93–4, offered somewhat different figures.
19. Kazemzadeh, *op. cit.*, pp. 193–4, following the 1920 report of Georgian Ministry of Labour.
20. Drabkina, op. cit., p. 52.
21. Makharadze, *op cit.*, and on the other hand Avalishvili, *op. cit.*, 'Introduction'.
22. Especially of Kautsky who visited the new Georgian republic and proceeded to give it 'a clean bill of health' as well as friendly advice. See Kautsky op. cit.
23. See memoirs of the commander of the Red/National Guard, V. Jugeli, *Tyazhelyi krest* (Tiflis, 1920). He vividly described his unease in the face

of burning Ossetin villages, put to torch as a hard socialist duty. See also Zhordaniya, *Za dva goda*, pp. 71, 80–3, 201–4.

24. 'Our road leads to Europe, Russia's road to Asia. I know our enemies will say that we are on the side of imperialism. Therefore I must decisively state here: I would prefer the imperialists of the West to the fanatics of the East!' Zhordaniya, in a speech quoted in *Slovo* 16 January 1920.

25. See memoirs of Georgia's chief negotiator and first ambassador to Moscow, Uratadze, *Reminiscences*, op. cit.

26. For first-hand description of the regular army's incompetence and low spirit as well as Menshevik leaders putting all their hopes in state machinery, see Zhordaniya, *My Life*, pp. 105–20. Pipes, op. cit., p. 239, speaks of two weeks battle for Tiflis but this does not find substantiation in the memoirs of Zhordaniya which had direct access to information and all reason to stress this point.

27. M. Lewin, *Lenin's Last Struggle* (London, 1973).

28. Ibid. As to Trotsky's attitude, it was for once in essential correspondence with that of Stalin, see L. Trotsky, *Between Red and White* (Westpoint, 1922) (published by the Communist Party of Great Britain which presented the case for the destruction of the 'Georgian Gironde'). For further evidence concerning divisions between the leading Bolsheviks see Pipes, *op. cit.*, pp. 228–38. See also Chapter 6 section D to follow.

29. Lenin, PSS, vol. 42, p. 367 (written in March 1921).

30. Lenin, PSS, vol. 45, pp. 356–62, 343–6, 595–8.

31. Quoted in Lamb, *op. cit*, p. 240. We were unable to retrace the source but a similar text was reported seen in the un-catalogued holdings of Anna Bourgina collection in the Hoover Institution. (Personal communication from Professor R. Suny of Michigan University.)

32. Lenin was referring to it directly when he began one of the notes by stating 'It seems that I am very seriously guilty before the workers of Russia for not intervening'. Lenin, PSS, vol. 45, p. 356.

33. Zhordaniya, *Za dva goda*, p. 17. The book contains speeches and declarations and was checked and authorised by Zhordaniya.

34. Ibid, pp. 55, 67, 117. For an outlook which offered a model for Zhordaniya's general attitude to peasantry see K. Kautsky *The Road to Power*, published in 1910 (K. Kautsky, *Put' k vlasti* (Moscow, 1959) pp. 114–15, 130–3.

35. Kautsky, *Georgia*, pp. 68–9.

36. Zhordaniya, *Za dva goda*, p. 5.

37. Ibid, p. 26. Zhordaniya did at times – but not consistently so – treat peasants as part of the 'bourgeoisie'.

38. Ibid, p. 5.

39. Ibid, pp. 6, 115–19.

40. Ibid, p. 117. That is when in political sense the cards were put on the table.

6D   Lenin: Revolutions and the Post-revolutionary State

1. That is why, while the comparison of Lenin of the Soviet textbooks to an

icon can be sustained, these writings are actually inferior to the hagiography of the Orthodox Christian saints. A stereotype story of a saint assumed temptation and doubt as well as personal growth which resulted from it. Lenin's standard biographies assume none of this, which makes them as schematic as they are boring – a peculiar disservice to a man who, whatever his characteristics, was never a matter of indifference to his contemporaries.

2. As against these images Lenin admitted, for example, his being for a time 'in the mud' (the synonym of 'indecisive middle' drawn from the life of a French convent) during the 1905–06 debate of the agrarian programme, but he also knew well the standard prescription of infantry's command: 'In battle an officers order must be resolute, decisive, unchanging and clear at any time. If it is also correct, so much the better'.

3. See section 5C.

4. See section 1C and in particular the consideration of the place of A. Kramer's brochure 'On Agitation'.

5. E. Kingston-Mann, *Lenin and the Problem of Marxist Peasant Revolution* (New York, 1983) p. 42.

6. See vols. 1 and 2 of Lenin, PSS, which contain Lenin's writings from 1893 to 1897; also the closely-linked publicistic statements in ibid, vols 4 and 5 (which bring us to 1901).

7. Ibid, vol. 3. One can call it a market-subordination model of the economic transformation of Russia (first and in a partial form only in PSS, vol. 1). Lenin's free time was occupied, to earn some extra income, by the translation of the *Theory and Practice of Trade Unionism* by the Webbs and – which was much more agreeable on ideological grounds and pertinent for his future analysis – *The Agrarian Problem* by Kautsky.

8. *Chto Delat'?*, Lenin, PSS, vol. 6.

9. L. Trotsky, *On Lenin* (London, 1971) pp. 59, 62.

10. Lenin, PSS, vols 7, 8 and 9.

11. Ibid. Compare it with the resolution of the second congress of RSDWP, still in force, which denied the PSR any revolutionary substance and defined it as directly harmful to the forthcoming revolution.

12. Ibid, vols 10 and 11, especially 'The Two Tactics'.

13. For Lenin admission of this state of affairs during the decisive times of November/December 1905, see Lunacharskii's memoirs in *Proletarskaya Revolutsia*, 1925, no. 11. See also Lenin, PSS, vol. 18.

14. Lenin, PSS, vols 21 and 23.

15. Ibid, vol. 27, also vols 23, 24 and 25.

16. 'From the point of view of the working class . . . the least evil would be the defeat of the tsarist monarchy, and its armies which oppress Poland, Ukraine and other nations', Lenin, PSS, vol. 26, p. 6. Also 'objectively who profits by the slogan of peace? Certainly not the revolutionary proletariat. Not the idea of using the war to speed up the collapse of capitalism', Lenin, PSS, vol. 26, pp. 209–65.

17. A. Ulam, *Lenin and the Bolsheviks* (Glasgow, 1975) p. 394.

18. Especially when Kautsky and other 'elder statesmen' of the International tried to resolve at Bolsheviks and Mensheviks request the tangled matters of the finances and the 'grab-money' of the RSDWP.

19. See 'The Proletarian Revolution and the Renegade Kautsky', Lenin, PSS, vol. 37.
20. Ibid, vol. 31, pp. 1–6, 99–110.
21. In view of the comparisons which would have been very clear in many minds and especially of those who still remembered the 1905, Lenin was quick to dissociate from the 'views of Parvus' who was accused of suggesting a 'jump over stages' rather than 'growing through them' (*pererastat'*), whichever such comparison of gymnastics to biology could mean. Nothing was said about Trotsky's 1907 call for a dictatorship of the proletarian minority led by a revolutionary Party while 'resting on' (not 'allied with') the mass of the peasantry. A comparison of it all with the actual Russian history of 1917–28 is the best way to see it more clearly.
22. During the war the men in charge of the Bolshevik organisation in St Petersburg and *de facto* in all Russia was A. Shlyapnikov, one of its few working-class leaders. He was quickly overshadowed by the first wave of the returning exiles, who in turn, took a back row when all the exiles came back. Shlyapnikov survived in the Bolshevik Central Committee to lead its 'proletarian opposition' in 1920 and perished under Stalin's rule.
23. The expression 'overwhelmed' would not be an overstatement. The initial meeting of the Bolshevik Central Committee Lenin's views were supported by only one of its members, Kollantai. Within days it was accepted by a large majority (with fairly few exceptions such as Zinoviev and Kamenev) which then proceeded to follow it through thick and thin. See Lenin, PSS, vol. 31. *Kpss v rezolyutsiyakh i resheniyakh* (Moscow, 1953) pp. 332–353. Also N. Avdeev *et al*, *Revolyutsiya 1917 goda (khronika sobytii)*. For an observer's vivid description of the period see N. Sukhanov *Zapiski o revolyutsii* (Berlin, 1922–3).
24. Lenin, PSS, vol. 31, p. 17.
25. Ibid, p. 108.
26. Ibid, p. 110.
27. See G. Gurevich, *Istoriya sovetskoi konstitutsii* (Moscow, 1925); N. Tinashev Problema natsional'nogo prava v sovetskoi rossii, *Sovremennye zapiski*, XXIX (1926); R. Pipes, *The Formation of the Soviet Union* (Cambridge, 1964); S. Kharmadsan, *Lenin i stanovlenie zakavkazkoi federatsii* (Erevan', 1969). Also Lenin, PSS, vol. 45, pp. 256–62.
28. M. Lewin, *Lenin's Last Struggle* (London, 1975).
29. Ibid; Lenin, PSS, vol. 45, pp. 343–6, 'Letter to the Congress', which stated: 'Our party leans [is based] on two classes and therefore its instability is possible and its defeat necessary if no agreement is established between those two classes' [that is, workers and peasants]. Ibid, p. 344.
30. M. Gefter, 'Stranitsa uz istorii marksizma nachala XX veka', *Istoricheskaya nauke i nekotorye problemy sovremennosti* (Moscow, 1969) p. 22. The author who lives in Moscow, has been 'silent in print' for quite a time.
31. Beginning with 'The Two Tactics' (Lenin, PSS, vol. 11) through 'The Two Utopias' (ibid, vol. 22) and as far as his Decrees of 1917 (ibid, vol. 32).
32. See this section, note 29.

33. For evidence and discussion see T. Shanin, *Late Marx and the Russian Road* (London, 1984).

34. Ibid, pp. 16–17, 111–14.

35. At the same time Lenin distanced himself from views about unconditional national autonomy, territorial or extra-territorial, hotly discussed then in the European SD movement (especially by the 'national' sections of RSDWP).

36. For discussion see P. Sweezy, *The Post-Revolutionary State* (New York, 1980).

37. Lenin, PSS, vol. 12, (fourth congress).

38. See also Lenin's report to the third congress of his International, Lenin, PSS, vol. 44, pp. 1–61, 73–6; also ibid, vol. 45, p. 362.

39. Ibid, vol. 12, pp. 364, 366–7. Also the lecture delivered in 1917, concerning the 1905–07 revolution, ibid, vol. 30, pp. 310–14, 316, 322 and 'State and Revolution', chap. V, in ibid, vol. 33.

40. For discussion of the direct and indirect impact of Chernyshevskii on Lenin see the most interesting N. Valentinov (Volskii), *The Early Years of Lenin* (Ann Arbor 1969).

41. The ambivalence of Lenin's attitude to 'the masses' as against the 'cadres' was consistent through most of his political maturity. The author of the cadres-centred 'What is to be done?' published in 1903, suggested in 1905 a mandatory proletarian majority in every local party committee. (For Lenin's furious reaction to his comrades refusal to vote it see B. D. Wolfe, *Three Who Made a Revolution* (Harmondsworth, 1962) pp. 348–350). In the same year, he and his faction shunned the Soviet of St Petersburg as not party-directed and has seen Bolsheviks consequently lose majority in the city election to the fourth congress of RSDWP. They eventually hotly supported the Soviets. Through his life, time and again Lenin spoke in one breath about the admirable creative capacities of the masses and about the dangers of being overwhelmed by 'petty bourgeoisie flood' of this very constituency.

42. Lenin, vol. 45, pp. 343–8, 383–400.

43. Ibid, vol. 45, pp. 376. Contrary to interpretations of 1930s he clearly did not mean cooperatives of production exclusively.

44. Ibid, p. 357.

45. See, for example, Chapter 4.

46. For example, Lenin, PSS, vol. 26, pp. 243, 245.

47. Lenin, PSS, vol. 10, pp. 53–60; for discussion see Gefter, loc. cit., pp. 13–27.

48. We talked of Lenin, his leadership and his thought as expressed conceptually – through major writing, and in action – through the strategies he adopted and argued. As to 'Leninism', this concept invented at Lenin's grave by Bukharin to serve Stalin, his own future executioner, is quite another matter. Its recent description as 'ideological name of the triumphant Stalinism' is historically speaking close to mark (V. Garratano, 'Stalin, Lenin and Leninism', *New Left Review*, no. 103, 1977). As to its contemporary meanings and connotations of the term those are outside the brief of our study.

POSTSCRIPT

1. The expression is taken from and used in the spirit of Francis Bacon's *Novum Organum*, at the very origins of contemporary epistemology of scholarly pursuit.
2. R. B. Braithwaite, *Scientific Explanation* (Cambridge, 1953) p. 93. For fuller discussion of my own views (as those stood more than a decade ago) see T. Shanin, *The Rules of the Game: Models in Scholarly Thought* (London, 1972).
3. Such transformations are particularly evident when work of masters and, on the other hand, of their less skilled or less literate interpreters is concerned; Marx's view of human action becomes economic determinism, Weber's discourse on the rise of capitalism is religious monism, Chayanov peasantry is devoid of market ties, etc.
4. M. Bloch, *The Historian Craft* (Manchester, 1954) p. 29.
5. The debate of structuralism goes back to Durkheim's discourse about the substance of sociology or before. It had since changed forms and differed in impact but is part and parcel of the modern social sciences in their broadest sense. See for exemplary discussion J. Piaget *Structuralism* (London, 1971).
6. The recent 'journalistic' adoptions of the term 'charismatic' did particular harm by taking out of context and vulgarising Marx Weber's interesting insights related to this term.
7. We lack a satisfactory single text reviewing the German 'critical philosophy' of the turn of the nineteenth century and its contemporary impact. We refer here to the intellectual sequence which included Kant, Fichte, Schiller and early Hegel and proceeded in the works of the Young Hegeliens and Neo-Kantians.
8. As well put (if somewhat overstated) by J. M. Keynes: 'the ideas of economists and political philosophers, both when they are right and when they are wrong, are more powerful than is commonly understood. Indeed the world is ruled by little else. Practical men, who believe themselves to be quite exempt from any intellectual influence, are usually the slaves of some defunct economist'. (*The General Theory of Employment Interest and Money* (London 1946) p. 383).
9. 'Men make their own history, but they do not make it just as they please; they do make it under circumstances directly encountered, given and transmitted from the past. The traditions of all the dead generations wait like a nightmare on the brain of the living'. K. Marx and F. Engels, *Selected Writings* (Moscow, 1973) vol 1, p. 398.
10. For further discussion see T. Shanin, 'Class, State and Revolution: Substitutes and Realities, in H. Alavi and T. Shanin (eds), *Introduction to the Sociology of 'Developing Societies'* (London, 1982). For exemplification see P. Corrigan and D. Sayer *The Great Ark: English State Formation as Cultural History* (Oxford, 1985).
11. The neologism reflects an attempt to confront rigidity of sociological language when dynamics is concerned. A decade ago I introduced similarly the expression 'classness' while discussing peasant political action. It uses since justified the inelegance involved.

12. In the sense used by K. Jaspers, 'Axial Age of Human History', *Commentary*, 1948, p. vi.
13. See, for example, M. Eliade, *The Myth of The Eternal Return* (New York, 1959); and K. Lowith, *Meaning in History* (Chicago, 1949).
14. See *Russia as a 'Developing Society'*, chapter 5D.
15. P. Sweezy, 'Socialism in Poor Countries', *Monthly Review*, October, 1976, p. 3.
16. F. Braudel, *The Mediterranean and the Mediterranean World in the Age of Philip II* (London, 1973), vol. II, p. 1241.
17. A. Einstein, 'Why Socialism', *Monthly Review*, February 1951, pp. 5–6, 8–9.
18. It 'goes without saying' (but should be said, to avoid misunderstanding) that Einstein's short comment cannot be treated as a full-scope consideration of human goals. My own are on record in T. Shanin, 'Marxism and the Vernacular Revolutionary Traditions', *Late Marx and the Russian Road* (London, 1984).

Index of Names

Index of Subjects

THE WAR OF THE DRAGON LADY

a&b

THE WAR OF THE DRAGON LADY

JOHN WILCOX

First published in Great Britain in 2012 by
Allison & Busby Limited
13 Charlotte Mews
London W1T 4EJ
www.allisonandbusby.com

The moral right of the author is hereby asserted in accordance with

All ri   duced,
   stc   by
any   isher,
    n   er
   otl   ilar

the British Library.

10 9 8 7 6 5 4 3 2 1

ISBN 978-0-7490-1003-4

Typeset in 11/18.2 pt Sabon by
Allison & Busby Ltd.

Paper used in this publication is from sustainably managed sources.
All of the wood used is procured from legal sources and is fully traceable.
The producing mill uses schemes such as ISO 14001
to monitor environmental impact.

Printed and bound by
CPI Group (UK) Ltd, Croydon, CR0 4YY

*To Peter Jackson, editor, writer, critic,
teacher and old friend.*

CHAPTER ONE

Chihli Province, China. June 1900.

Simon Fonthill eased himself in the saddle, stood a little shakily in the stirrups – he was tired but, at forty-five and even after twenty-four years of hard campaigning throughout Queen Victoria's empire, he remained an uncertain horseman – and looked around him. The plain of Northern China presented little to see. There had been no rain that spring and no corn had been sown. Two years of drought had sucked the moisture from the rice fields and the sun's rays flinched back from the hard earth as though even they were burnt by the touch. In the distance the white road wound towards the roofs of a village, but no other living thing stirred: no people, no animals, not even a bird, for there were no trees or bushes to give it perch.

Jenkins urged his mount alongside. ''Otter than bleedin' Africa, I'd say.' He sucked in his great moustache as though to gain moisture from it. 'Don't remember it bein' as 'ot as this in the Sudan, look you.'

He sniffed. 'Can't see why we've come, to be honest, bach sir.'

'Don't let's get into that, for God's sake.' Fonthill pulled down his white topee, the better to shield his eyes, and nodded ahead. 'Should be able to find a bit of shade in that village. Stop for a cup of green tea or something.'

He relaxed back into the saddle but his mind remained on edge. It wasn't just the heat. The temperature must be well over ninety degrees, even in the shade – that which could be found – but the feeling of oppression that sat above him in the yellow sky had nothing to do with the sun. In truth, he had been uneasy since they had landed at Tientsin a week ago. China, or at least this Province of Chihli, had not been welcoming.

The teeming streets of the inland port had seemed to lack that cheerful bustle that so characterised Bombay, Alexandria or Cape Town, where white people, particularly the British, were accepted and even welcomed as traders and bringers of wealth. In Tientsin, the people had hurried by, their eyes downcast under their wide, conical straw hats and their features sullen, and the peasants glimpsed as they penetrated deeper inland seemed to share this same resentment. Fonthill had served in Zululand, Afghanistan, the Transvaal, the Sudan and Matabeleland and he recognised aggression when he met it. Here, he could almost smell it.

His unease communicated itself to Jenkins. 'There's trouble about, ain't there?' he said. 'D'you think it's them boxing blokes?'

'What, the Boxers?' He grinned. 'Well, we haven't exactly met any of them yet, have we? But something's up. I can feel it. But then, perhaps I'm imagining it. Too much sun and bloody dust.'

'Are you all right, Simon?' His wife called from the cart at the back of which she perched less than comfortably on their baggage, trying to find shade beneath a parasol. Their Chinese servant and guide slumped on the single seat before her, letting the reins leading to the mules fall into his lap. He seemed as glad as the animals to stop for a moment.

Fonthill turned his horse and let it amble back to the cart. 'Yes, fine, my love. I thought we might stop at that village up ahead and see if we can get some tea. Yes?'

'Oh absolutely. Find some shade.' She smiled at her husband.

Alice Fonthill was exactly the same age as her husband but there was very little sign of middle age in her face or figure. Dressed in a loose, white, cotton shift with sandals on her feet, she seemed neither plump nor slim but sturdy rather, with her midriff pulled in tightly by a lime-green bandana. Her face was open, her features regular and her eyes a steady grey; indeed, she could have been called beautiful if it had not been for a certain squareness to her jaw which bestowed a sense of purpose. Under her floppy white hat her hair was fair with only the lightest dusting of grey and her skin was unfashionably tanned. Not for her the protected pallor of the Raj's memsahibs. Mrs Fonthill, known to her readers of London's *Morning Post* by her maiden name of Alice Griffith, was as comfortable out of doors as her husband.

In fact, the two of them made a handsome couple as they smiled at each other in the heat. He was of middle height at five foot nine inches, though now he slumped in the saddle. His shoulders were wide and no fat had encroached to widen his waist, for a life spent farming and campaigning had made his body hard. His eyes were brown and normally showed traces of reserve, but not now as he looked at his wife with a tenderness that had survived years of sadness as well as joy. The most prominent feature of his face was the nose, broken years ago by a Pathan musket and now hooked, giving him a predatory air, that of a hunter looking for his prey. Yet his mouth, though thin-lipped, was soft and betrayed sensitivity; perhaps that rarity in Queen Victoria's great empire – a warrior with a conscience?

Fonthill jerked his head towards their guide, now seemingly asleep as he sat, hunched. 'Has he said much?' he mouthed.

She shook her head. 'Not a sausage,' she whispered. 'He's not exactly sociable, is he?'

'Ah well, we can't be far from your uncle's place. This should be the last stop. Let's get on.'

He pulled on the rein and gently leant over and gave the sleeping man a prod, pointing ahead. 'We'll stop at that village,' he said slowly.

The Chinaman opened his eyes. He said nothing but he jerked the reins and flicked his whip and the two mules shuffled ahead, hardly disturbing the dust on the road.

They had ambled barely a hundred yards when they heard the noise. It was difficult at first to tell the origin; then it became clear. Voices raised, Chinese voices, of course, but with that distinctive sing-song pattern now lost and merged into a high-pitched howl. It came from the village ahead and it personified hate and anger. The communal voice of a mob.

Fonthill turned and shouted to their driver, 'Stay here.' Then to Jenkins, 'Come on.'

They spurred their weary horses into something resembling a canter and rounded the bend that wound into what seemed like the main street of small dwelling houses, more a hamlet than a village.

The place was deserted except for some dozen Chinamen who were surrounding a youth, who stood, befuddled, as abuse was hurled at him as he twisted and turned to find a way out through the ring.

The men were dressed all alike. They were barefooted and wore the loose pyjama-type garment of the Chinese peasant. But the pastoral effect of their clothing was completely dissipated by the red cloths tied round their heads, the red ribbons that fluttered from their wrists and ankles and the scarlet girdles that circled their waists. Two of them carried swords, others large sticks.

'Boxers!' breathed Simon.

The boy in their midst was probably no more than sixteen and he raised his hands in a desperate attempt to defend himself as the blows began to rain down on him. Then the lad went down on one knee under the force of the attack from all sides and, as he did so, two of his assailants drew their swords.

'That's enough,' shouted Fonthill. 'Stop that!' He dug his heels into his horse's flanks and rode straight into the crowd, scattering them. He was conscious of Jenkins riding closely behind him as he groped behind his saddlebag for some kind of weapon. He found only the end of his ash walking stick and drew it as he burst through the crowd. Wheeling his mount around, he realised that the mob had scattered only momentarily. The boy lay dazed on the ground but the Boxers now ignored him and approached the two horsemen, fanning out to surround them.

'Watch out, bach sir.' Jenkins's vocal Welshness always seemed to increase in proportion to the danger faced. 'The buggers 'ave got swords and they'll come at our backs, look you.'

'We mustn't let them attack the wagon.' The pitch of Fonthill's own voice now betrayed the peril of their situation. 'Dammit. Shouldn't have left the revolvers with the baggage. Only one thing for it. Cavalry charge. You ready, 352?'

Jenkins's eyes were black and cold under the rim of his wide-brimmed hat. 'Most certainly. But don't fall off, 'cos I might not 'ave a chance to pick you up, now, see.'

'Rubbish. I'm as good as a dragoon now. Use your stick as a sabre. Right at 'em, then – and shout. Now. Charge!'

The two lowered their sticks, put their heads down and urged their horses into a startled gallop. As they charged, they shouted – or rather, screamed. Jenkins's was a high-pitched, Celtic cry that seemed to come from deep within him; a prehistoric place of dark valleys and hills. Fonthill's seemed half embarrassed, more a desperate appeal for a catch from first slip on the cricket field than a battle cry. Both, however, were effective, for the Boxers broke and ran. Not, however, before one of them swung his club backhandedly at Simon's horse, catching him on the rump and causing him to rear.

Fonthill, with only one hand on the reins, was unable to control his mount and he felt himself slip backwards and then crash to the ground, temporarily winding him and sending his stick clattering away. Within moments, as he attempted to scramble to his feet, he realised that Jenkins was beside him, a knife gleaming in his hand.

'I just knew you'd fall off,' muttered the Welshman. 'On your feet, boyo, they're coming at us again. 'Ere, 'ave my stick, it's better than nothing. Back to back now.'

Taking deep gulps of hot air, Fonthill tried to regain his breath. The Boxers had whirled around and the two swordsmen were advancing on them now, preparing to take easy prey. Simon noticed that neither betrayed the slightest expression as he stepped forward.

Their eyes were completely dispassionate, like those of two snakes, preparing to strike.

'Bit of dust in their faces when they come in, bach sir,' muttered Jenkins. 'Might just give us a moment. If I can get close, I'll slit their gizzards, so I will. See if you can get be'ind me, like.'

'Certainly not. I'll fight my own bloody battle, thank you very much.'

The partners knelt down slowly, as though in supplication, but each gathered a handful of dust in his free hand and then they rose equally slowly to face the swordsmen.

Fonthill's mind raced. He knew that Jenkins was a superb close-quarters fighter. He had seen him confront and subdue a strapping assegai-carrying Zulu warrior, fighting only with his hands. But he himself had no such skills. The agony was that, if they were killed, Alice would be left completely defenceless in the wagon just outside the village. The Boxers would surely take it and she, too, would perish, for their guide would be useless. He must use what skills he had. The ash walking stick would become a rapier.

Slowly, he raised it and adopted the fencing *en garde* position, as he had been taught to do so many years ago at Sandhurst, the training school for young British officers. The ridiculous posture – side on, feet planted fore and aft and knees bent, while the stick was presented, horizontal to the ground, to the opponent – caused the Boxer to pause in his advance. The man stood for a moment, his mouth gaping, perspiration pouring down his chest in the gap shown by his open vest and his pigtail moving, pendulum like, as his head moved from side to side. Slowly he absorbed the situation. Then he grinned and jumped forward, swinging his sword in a silver arc.

Fonthill moved back and immediately crashed into the posterior of the Welshman, who judging by the clang of steel on steel was now engaged in his own fight for life. Somehow, however, Simon deflected the swing of the sword with his stick, so that it passed harmlessly to his side. Moving to his left, he lunged forward classically, taking the Chinaman firmly in the midriff with the point of the stick, causing the man to gasp and fall away, holding his stomach.

Seizing the moment, Simon attacked, thrusting with his ash as though it was an épée made of finest steel. Except that, of course, it was not. With a contemptuous swipe, the Boxer swung his blade across his body, cutting Fonthill's staff in half and leaving only a shattered stump in his hand.

'Dammit to hell.' In desperation, the Englishman sprang forward and threw the sand into the face of his opponent, causing the man to clutch at his eye. Before the Boxer could recover, Fonthill thrust the stump of his stick into his face. The splintered end grazed the cheekbone, producing a cry of pain and anger.

But it was the aggression of despair, for the Chinaman was not hurt. He backed away for a moment, wiped his eye and then sprang forward, raising his sword for one last and surely fatal attack.

Suddenly a shot rang out and the man clutched at his shoulder, blood spurting between his fingers. The sword dropped from his hand and he turned and looked with astonishment at the figure of Alice, standing some twenty-five yards away, the long barrel of an American Naval Colt revolver smoking in her hand.

For a split second the scene became frozen, like some mimed tableau, all movement stilled as though the actors were waiting for applause at the end of the drama. The rest of the Boxers were standing around in various postures, waiting for the swordsmen to end the entertainment by killing their men. The youth knelt on his hands and knees in the centre of the road, his mouth open. Jenkins had somehow turned his man and now had him from the back, his long knife at the throat of his assailant, whose sword lay on the ground.

All was still and then, as though acting on some hidden signal, the scene broke up: the Boxers ran as fast as their bare feet could take them, led by Simon's wounded opponent, clutching his shoulder as he loped away. The boy stood to his feet, swayed for a moment and then approached the two Englishmen.

Incongruously, he stood before Simon and held out his hand. 'How do you do?' he asked in impeccable, if mannered, English. 'Am I right in believing that you are English, sir?'

'Bugger that.' Jenkins's interruption was low and gutteral. 'Do you want me to kill this bloke, bach sir? Might as well. He tried to kill us and I don't think I can 'old 'im much longer. Got a bit of a cut on me arm, see.'

'What?' Fonthill wiped the perspiration from his eyes. 'Good God, no. Let the swine go.'

Jenkins relaxed his grip and immediately the Boxer ducked away, like a trout returned to a stream, and ran after his fellows. In a few seconds the dusty street was deserted except for the boy and his rescuers.

Fonthill ignored the extended hand and ran towards his wife. 'Oh, wonderful shooting, Alice. I'd have been cut in half if you hadn't arrived.' He embraced her. 'Are you all right, darling? Where's the cart?'

Gently she pushed him away. She was shivering slightly, despite the heat. 'Perfectly all right, thank you. I am so used to rushing about China in this heat and shooting at the peasantry.' She handed the Colt to Simon, wiped her brow and then frowned. 'Ah, Jenkins is hurt.'

The Welshman was clumsily attempting with one hand to tie a very soiled handkerchief around his upper arm, where blood poured from a deep cut in the biceps. Alice ran to him.

'Sit down, 352.'

'No, missus. I'm all right, really. Just a scratch.'

'Sit down, I say.' Alice eased the man to the ground and knelt beside him. With a gesture of disgust, she threw away the rag, took her own handkerchief from a pocket in her skirt and folded it onto the wound, then bound it with the scarf taken from her throat. 'Hold that tightly to stop the bleeding, and we'll get back to the cart and wash the wound and dress it properly. Now, can you stand?'

Jenkins sniffed. 'Course I can. As a matter of fact, I never wanted to sit in the first place, if you remember, Miss Alice. I'm all right, thank you very much.'

Alice grinned at him. Jenkins had long since lost his hat in the affray – in her experience he rarely retained a hat for longer than a couple of hours in any one day, anyway – and, now covered in dust, he looked like some labourer from a stone mine, his thick hair standing up like grey stubble and his great moustache bristling with grit. Jenkins stood at only five foot four inches but he was not a small man. In fact, he seemed almost as broad as he was tall, so wide were his shoulders and so deep his chest. It was no surprise that he had turned the tables on the Boxer. Even at forty-nine, he was as quick on his feet as a fox, and throughout his life he had fought: in his early days in British army barrack rooms, detention centres and bars throughout the length and breadth of the Empire and then, for the last two decades, at the side of Simon Fonthill, his former subaltern, turned mentor and comrade, in a dozen adventures around the world. Formally employed now as gentleman's servant, Jenkins was part of the family. His Christian name long since forgotten, he was known as '352' – the last three numerals of his old army number, used to distinguish him from the seven other Jenkinses in his company in the old 24th Regiment of Foot, that most Welsh of army units – and he formed an essential third leg of the Fonthill stool.

Now he grinned back in gratitude at Alice as she and Simon helped him to his feet. Then Alice suddenly became aware of the Chinese youth, standing by deferentially. His shirt was torn, blood was trickling from several head wounds and swellings were appearing on his face. As she regarded him, he began to sway.

'Oh, my goodness,' cried Alice. 'Quick, Simon. He's going to fall.'

Fonthill sprang forward and caught the young man in his arms.

He lifted him easily. 'Back to the wagon,' he said. 'This chap needs a bit of shade under your parasol, darling. Here, take the Colt, Jenkins. They might come back. We need to get out of here. Alice, bring the horses.'

They hurried, as best they could, round the bend to find to their relief the cart standing at the side of the road where the mules had dragged it to find shade. Of their guide and driver there was no sign.

''E's buggered off,' panted Jenkins.

'Good riddance.' Fonthill lowered the boy onto the bags and jammed Alice's parasol so that it provided some shade for his head.

'Now, water, Alice, if you please.'

She unscrewed her water bottle and offered it to the youth's lips.

At first the water trickled down his chin and then, as his eyes flickered open, he drank.

'Good,' muttered Alice. 'Now lie still and let me bathe those bruises.'

As she did so, Simon retrieved his own canteen and, removing the temporary dressing on Jenkins's arm, began to dab gently at the wound beneath.

'Bloody 'ell,' swore the Welshman. 'That's a bit sharp, see.'

'Don't be such a baby. You said yourself it was only a scratch. Here, you do it. I'm no nursemaid. I'll hitch the horses up to the wagon. We must get moving. I don't want the Boxers back.'

Jenkins looked up. 'Why are they called that, then? They don't seem to fight by the Queensbury Rules, now do they?'

Fonthill gathered the reins of the horses and attached them to the rear of the cart. 'I'm told that they're mainly young men,' he said, 'all supposed to be fierce patriots who hate foreigners and who practise martial arts, though I don't think they include boxing as we know it.' He climbed into the seat of the wagon and cracked the whip over the mules. 'They've adopted this Japanese form of wrestling, called ju-jitsu, or something. Anyway, I don't want to fight 'em again with the stub of a walking stick.'

'Simon,' Alice called. 'Have you noticed something strange about this place?'

'Well, it's bloody hot, for one thing.'

'No. Despite all the noise we haven't seen one single person from the village. No one has come out of the houses. It's like a ghost village.'

'Ah,' the boy struggled up onto his elbow and spoke. 'That is because they frightened of Boxers. Watch from windows. They in terrible funk, you see.'

Simon grinned over his shoulder at the colloquialism. 'Goodness me, young man, your English is very good. Where did you learn it?'

'At school and at home with father and mother. They my teachers.'

'Do they live near here? Can we take you to them?'

The boy raised a smile. 'I think you go there, anyway. I think you Captain Fonthill, Mrs Alice and Sergeant Jenkins. Am I right?'

The three looked in amazement at the young man, whose smile had broadened into a grin. 'You are, indeed,' said Alice. 'Who are you?'

The lad squirmed until he was sitting upright. 'My name is Chang. There is more to it than that, of course, but it is difficult for English to say rest of name. So call me Chang.' His grin lapsed into a frown. 'But you not supposed to be here.'

'What do you mean?'

'I go to Peking last week to send you cable to ship in Tientsin, saying too dangerous to travel here because of Boxers. Cable from my father, Reverend Griffith.'

'Your *father* . . . ?' Alice was incredulous. '*My* Uncle Edward is your . . . er . . . *father*?'

'Oh yes.' The boy nodded his head, the most earnest expression on his face. 'And Mrs Griffith my mother. They buy me from warlord when I was a baby and bring me up. My real parents dead. So I think we are all cousins, or something like that. I am very glad indeed to meet you all.' And he extended his hand.

They each took it solemnly.

'Well that's solved the problem of finding the mission,' said

19

Fonthill. 'It must be near here. What were you doing when the Boxers found you?'

'I was going to buy rice, if I could find someone in village to sell.' He looked round earnestly. 'It is very scarce, because of drought. Drought a bally nuisance, you know.'

Simon smothered a smile. 'I am sure it is. But why did the Boxers attack you? I thought they were only against foreigners, and you are Chinese.' He coughed. 'Albeit a very English one.'

The boy fingered beneath his torn shirt and produced a crucifix hanging on a chain. 'Because I am Christian, follower of Lord Jesus Christ. Boxers hate Christians in particular, and they hate missionaries most of all. Reverend Father had been warned that Boxers were coming. That is why he sent me to capital to cable you not to come. Why you come, then?'

Alice resumed her treatment of the bruises. 'Your cable must have arrived after we left the ship in Tientsin – in fact, after we left the port. Now lie still.'

'No.' Fonthill turned his head. 'Can you come up here, Chang, and show us the way? If you are feeling up to it, that is?'

The boy squirmed onto his knees and crawled across the baggage until he was kneeling behind Simon. 'Oh, I am very up to it, thank you very much. Yes. You follow this way and then, in a moment, you will turn right. I will show you. Mission about five minutes away now.'

The cart with its attendant horses slowly wound its way through the barren countryside. There was no question of distancing themselves from the Boxers, for Simon could summon up nothing from the mules other than a slow trudge. But it seemed as if the insurgents had been deterred by Alice's pistol shot, for no one followed them and, indeed, the members of the little party felt as though they were the only moving life on that empty, dry plain.

Eventually, they meandered their way into another village, virtually a small town, for it was considerably larger than the place of their attack. The road led them into a warren of alleyways where, at last, people were evident, moving through the narrow streets and staring with a singular lack of benevolence at the cart and its exotic cargo of white-skinned foreigners. The party passed the open doorway of an indigo dye works, where rising steam obscured the workers within, and then a large, three-storey building, the smell of which confirmed to Jenkins, at least, that it was a rice-wine distillery.

Following Chang's very explicit directions – 'Now, cousin, pray take this next turning on the left' – they emerged into a small square dominated by a two-storeyed, wooden church, unmistakeable from the crucifix attached above the doorway. Next to it was a small house, built, like those fronting the square, of cream-coloured mud brick and featuring ochre-coloured window shutters closed against the fierce sun and a rippling roof of purple tiles. Outside the house, looking anxiously up the street and rubbing her hands together in obvious anxiety, stood an elderly woman. She was small and dressed, Chinese fashion, in a shapeless cotton garment, her smock buttoned up to the chin and her long skirt ending just above wooden clogs. Unlike other women in the square, however, she wore no straw hat and her grey hair was scraped back into a serviceable bun at the nape of her neck. Her high cheekbones and the walnut-grained skin of her face made her appear Chinese, but the set of her eyes, distinguishable to the occupants of the cart as it came closer, confirmed her as European.

Alice let out a cry, 'Aunt Lizzie!' and leapt from the cart before it had stopped, engulfing the woman in her arms. The two stood rocking together on the doorstep of the house before the old lady gently pushed her niece away and peered anxiously over her shoulder into the wagon.

'Oh, thank the Lord,' she cried. 'You've got Chang.' And she held out her arms to the lad, who scrambled down and embraced his adoptive mother. The two stayed locked together for a moment before Mrs Griffith let him go and stretched out her hand to Fonthill.

'And you must be Simon,' she said. 'Oh, forgive me.' She pulled up a corner of her apron and wiped away a tear. 'You must think me so rude but,' she smiled at the boy, 'I was so sure that something had happened to . . .' then her voice tailed away as she saw the cuts and bruises on Chang's face. 'Ah, I knew it. He has been hurt. What happened? Tell me.'

'Oh, I am all right, Mother. But I fear I would have been killed but for the intervention of my . . . er . . . my cousins. They were very brave. It was a party of Boxers, you see . . .'

'Enough,' cried the old lady. 'It is best to come inside, all of you. These are dangerous times. Simon, can you and your young man,' she indicated Jenkins, who beamed at the compliment, 'take the cart and mules into the courtyard through that door there. I will send someone to unharness the mules and take your bags. But it would be wise to get off the street as soon as possible. Come, dear Alice. This way. We tried to stop you coming but obviously our message did not get through. I thank God that you have not been harmed. Come in. Come in.'

Fifteen minutes later, they were all seated in the shade of the courtyard, drinking tea beside a large stone basin within which three white and gold koi carp circled languidly.

'Edward is making a visit to a sick parishioner,' explained Lizzie, 'but he will be here soon. Like me, he will be sorry but happy to see you. Our other son, Gerald, has been on a trip to Peking but he should be back tonight.'

'Have the Boxers bothered you, Mrs Griffith?' asked Simon.

'No, but we have been told that they have targeted us and that they are on their way here. That must have been the party that attacked Chang.' The old lady sniffed. 'Edward has refused to leave but we have just had a message from the bishop in Tientsin, ordering us to leave the mission and go to Peking.'

She put a brown-speckled hand to her brow and Simon marvelled, not for the first time, at the courage of these missionaries who spent their lives abroad, usually in discomfort and often in danger, to spread the word of their God. But Mrs Griffith was continuing, 'Mind you, I am not sure that the capital will be entirely safe, for I understand that the insurgents have burnt down the grandstand at the racecourse just outside the city.' She pursed her lips. 'It was the centre of social activity for the Europeans in the city, you know. Such a disgraceful thing to do. So uncalled for. I think we must leave now, though.'

Her voice tailed away and she looked around the courtyard. A shard of sunlight had been allowed to creep through the overhanging roof and it fell on the osmanthus plant in the corner, which she had proudly shown to her visitors and boasted that it was said to be more than four hundred years old. Simon realised what a wrench it would be for the Griffiths to leave their home, where, Alice had explained

23

to Simon earlier, they had worked for thirty-two years, building the wooden church with their own hands and confirming hundreds of Chinese into the Christian church.

His reverie was interrupted by the arrival of the Reverend Edward Griffith, who expressed both the inevitable consternation and joy at their arrival. A tall, broad-shouldered man, Griffith presented as hearty and healthy a figure as his wife offered up frailty. It was clear that, unlike his spouse, he had prospered physically in the harsh climate of Northern China and, with his side whiskers and red face, he reminded Simon very much of the dominating presence of the clergyman's brother and Alice's late father, Brigadier Cecil Griffith, also of Simon's and Jenkins's old regiment, the 24th of Foot.

It had been the deaths, disconcertingly close together, of both Alice's and Simon's parents that had prompted the Fonthills to embark on the round-the-world trip that had led them to this small town in China. Some six years before, after taking part in Cecil Rhodes's invasion of Matabeleland and surviving the clash with King Lobengula's impis there, they had returned to Norfolk to farm Alice's estate. Restive with the unaccustomed tranquillity, however, and financially buttressed by inheritances from both sets of parents, the couple had decided to make a first visit to America and visit Alice's uncle in China on their way home. They were enjoying the vastness of the prairies of North America when news reached them of the outbreak of war in South Africa. Simon was anxious to hurry to Cape Town to join in the fight against the Boers, but Alice – not unsympathetic to the cause of the Afrikaner farmers – persuaded him that the war would be over by the time they reached Africa, so they continued their journey to China.

It was only when they reached Tientsin that they heard of the Boxer Rebellion.

They were all changing for dinner when Gerald Griffith arrived, dusty from his journey to Peking. He was a tall, thin young man in his early twenties, English but dressed as a Chinaman and wearing the beginnings of a beard. He washed for dinner but did not change and seemed less than delighted to see the visitors as they assembled around the table.

'It is dangerous here, you know,' he said. 'You should not have come, for the downtrodden people of China do not like the *yang kuei-tzu*.'

'The *yang* . . . ?' enquired Alice.

'The foreign devils.' The young man spoke with a curl of his lip.

'That will do, Gerald,' said his father quickly. He turned apologetically to his guests. 'My son has grown up with the Chinese people – in fact he has never been home – and he shares an affinity with them. It is,' he shrugged, 'understandable and he has a point.'

'Of course,' said Simon. 'Perhaps you would explain a little of the background to this uprising – if that is what it is.'

'I will tell you what I know but first let us eat. Shall we say grace?'

They ate a surprisingly delicious dinner of herbal pancakes, a hotpot of fish and braised tofu – Simon surmised that Aunt Lizzie had raided what was best of her drought-denuded pantry to put on a show for her guests – and as their Chinese servant cleared away the plates, Simon repeated his request. The clergyman wiped his whiskers and settled back in his chair. 'It's all our dashed fault, really, you know,' he said.

'What?' asked Fonthill. 'Do you mean the British? The Opium Wars and all that?'

25

'Well partly, I suppose. But I really mean all the European imperial powers who have imposed themselves on this country. Dashed disgraceful, if you will pardon my language.'

'*Damned* disgraceful,' echoed Gerald. His face was flushed.

'Please watch your own language, Gerald,' Mr Griffith rebuked. 'There is no excuse for that.'

'Sorry, Father.'

Edward Griffith took another sip of rice wine and continued. 'The Manchu dynasty – it still rules, of course – always exercised a blind, reclusive xenophobia and until 1848 the only part of the Chinese Empire on which foreign merchants were permitted to set foot, and then only between October and March, was a plot of land on the Canton waterfront. Things began to change after we – the British, that is – forced the First Opium War on the Chinese in the 1840s. It was a shameful act on our part, you know.'

'Incredibly shameful,' added Gerald.

Griffith sighed and frowned at his son once again at the interruption. Mrs Griffith, however, took Gerald's hand and squeezed it. 'Let the boy speak, Edward,' she said gently. 'He has a right to his opinion.'

'Hmm. Now, where was I?'

'The Opium Wars, Reverend.' Jenkins was leaning forward, his chin on his fist, listening intently.

'Yes, thank you. Well, after the Treaty of Nanking which settled the war, the Chinese were forced to cede to Britain that barren lump of rock called Hong Kong, pay a swingeing indemnity, remove the most vexatious restrictions on commerce at Canton, open four other ports to trade and grant foreigners the right to reside in them. We had our foot in the Chinese door and we pushed it wide open.

'You see,' the clergyman filled his pipe with tobacco and stared at the ceiling, 'imperial expansion was the order of the day. China was weak.' He began thumping a large finger into the palm of his other hand in emphasis. 'Portugal had got Macao; France occupied a large part of Annam; in 1862 Britain annexed Lower Burma, just across the frontier; France then took three provinces of Lower Cochin-China and gained control of the Mekon basin; Russia then occupied a large tract of Chinese Turkestan; Japan took the Liu Chiu Islands; Britain annexed Upper Burma; and then, in 1887, the rest of Annam, Cochin-China and Cambodia were sequestered to form French Indo-China. It was a land grab of epic proportions.'

Griffith blew a blue cloud of tobacco smoke to the ceiling. 'Then came the war with Japan of 1894 to 1895 which ended in crushing defeat for this country and set off the land scramble again. It seemed as though it was China's destiny to be carved up, just as Africa has been.'

He gestured with his pipe. 'By 1895, most of the outlying dependencies of the Empire – I mean the Chinese one, not ours – had been lopped off. I don't know the figures, but the size of this vast country had been severely reduced. But it didn't stop there. The Germans were probably the worst. Two German missionaries were killed three years ago in the interior near Kiaochow. Instead of negotiating with Peking, the Kaiser rattled his great sabre and threatened war. As a result, he gained a ninety-nine-year lease of Kiaochow Bay, the city of Tsingtao, a whacking great indemnity for the two dead missionaries and extensive railway and mining concessions in that province. Then everybody jumped in.

'Spheres of influence became the thing to have. Germany claimed exclusive influence here in Shantung, Russia in Manchuria, of course, Japan in Fukien and Britain in the Yangtze Valley. Can you imagine that sort of thing happening in the British Empire? Eh?'

A silence fell on the gathering. Gerald took a deep breath to speak, but his mother laid a quietening hand on his arm.

Eventually, Simon broke the silence. 'And the Boxers?' he asked.

'Ah yes, the Boxers. Well something had to give – or more precisely something had to rise. They first appeared in this province about two years ago, when the Germans were pressing hard on the Kiaochow Bay business. They are mainly young men, often youths, and they call themselves . . . er . . . what is it, Chang?'

The youth cleared his throat to answer but a glowering Gerald intervened. 'The *I Ho Ch'uan,*' he said, as though with pride. 'The Society of Righteous and Harmonious Fists.'

Jenkins let out a great guffaw, to be silenced by a glare from Fonthill.

'Quite so,' continued the clergyman. 'Strange, of course, to us. White people called them "Boxers" because they were so fit, although they would never know how to fight with their fists in a skilled manner, as we do. Like uneducated insurgents the world over . . .' he gestured with his pipe towards Simon – 'you in particular will remember the Mahdi's followers in the Sudan—'

Fonthill nodded.

'—they all think that they are "the chosen ones" and that no bullets can harm them. They hate Europeans and particularly members of religious groups and poor devils like us, the missionaries.'

He puffed at his pipe. 'Although it is the Catholics who seem to have caught it in the neck most. I suppose you could say that the priests had it coming to them. Back in 1860, the French had negotiated a treaty under which their Roman Catholic missionaries were given all kinds of rights denied to others – rights of residence in the interior, the building of churches and the establishment of orphanages. The last bit has caused all kinds of problems, giving rise to rumours that the priests were stealing Chinese children and killing them. But it was worse than that . . .' He gestured with both hands. 'All Catholic bishops were granted the same rank as provincial governors, they were allowed to wear a mandarin's button and carry the umbrella of honour and even,' he blew out his cheeks in disgust, 'awarded the discharge of a cannon when they come and go. It had all got out of hand. As a result, we are all being tarred with the same brush.'

Mrs Griffith took up the story. 'You see, all this has coincided with terrible times here,' she said, her eyes glistening in the lamplight. 'The drought is the worst for decades, ruining the rice crop and putting water at a premium. We – the so-called foreign devils – are getting the blame for this, including the mining and railway engineers here. It is being said that the laying of railway tracks is desecrating the graves of ancestors and the new telegraph poles cause moaning in the wind, which the peasants on whose lands they have been erected say is the crying of the dead. We foreigners are being blamed for upsetting the balance of nature, as well as killing the cotton market by importing cloth and garments.'

'The British are the worst.' The truculence in Gerald's voice was evident. 'Although the Empress has banned the opium trade,' he said, 'the British traders keep it going, of course, and make much money from it. Everyone knows that.'

The visitors all looked down at the table, unsure of what to say. Then Fonthill looked up and studied the young man for a moment. There was none of his father's fortitude in his face, nor any of his mother's sensitivity. His features reflected intelligence, there was no doubt of that, but his mouth was weak and his eyes showed only antagonism.

Simon cleared his throat. 'What about the Empress?' he asked of Griffith. 'Does she approve of the Boxers or try to suppress them?'

The missionary smiled. 'A good question. She's a formidable woman. Oiled, black hair pulled straight back, skin like porcelain and long, manicured fingernails, curved like claws. They call her "The Dragon Lady". You may know that the old girl – she's actually the Empress Dowager – deposed her nephew the Emperor Kuang Hsu about eighteen months ago, for being too much in favour of Western modernisation?'

Simon shook his head.

'Well, she's as clever as a fox leading the hunt. Officially she disapproves of the Boxers, but in reality she is encouraging them, there's no doubt about that. She thinks that they will teach the foreigners a lesson or two without her getting the blame and, anyway, they would be too expensive to put down.' The old man sighed. 'They're spreading out quickly, you see.'

'And coming this way,' added Gerald, his eyes alight. 'They told me in Peking that the Boxers who burnt the racecourse pavilion are only the vanguard. It is said that the army might join them.'

'Ah, I doubt that,' said Edward Griffith. 'The Empress would never allow that. It would upset the apple cart completely with the British and the other foreign ministers at the Manchu court—'

'Who are complete ciphers,' interrupted Gerald. 'Weak men representing weak regimes.'

'Blimey,' muttered Jenkins in a whispered aside to Fonthill. ''Oos side is 'e on, then?'

Another silence fell on the little gathering. The shadows flickering across the faces of the group seemed to presage and emphasize the dangers that lay outside the walls. A sense of impending disaster permeated the room. 'Well, sir,' asked Simon. 'Will you leave your home here?'

At first it seemed as though the old man was ignoring the question. He leant across the table and took up his wife's hand. He addressed her in a low voice: 'I think, my dear, that we now have no alternative.' He nodded towards Chang, who sat listening intently to everything that was being said. 'What has happened to our son today confirms the danger. I have been stupid in delaying so long. But now, I think we must leave before dawn. These people are so close. They could come tomorrow.'

Lizzie Griffith put a hand to her mouth. 'That quickly! We can never pack in time.'

Her husband squeezed her hand. 'We cannot take much with us, Lizzie. I am so sorry, but we must leave almost immediately. Time for a little sleep and then we must away. Of one thing, I promise you . . .' He looked into her eyes. 'We shall return.'

Tears were now trickling down Mrs Griffith's cheeks. 'But where shall we go?'

'To Peking. We shall find shelter there and we can stay until this trouble blows over. It will be transitory I feel sure.' He looked up at his visitors. 'I am so sorry, dear friends, that I must ask you to leave as soon as you arrive. But there is no other choice.'

Alice stood and moved behind her aunt's chair, putting her cheek next to hers and embracing her. 'My dear aunt,' she said. 'It is lucky we are here, for we can protect you on the journey. And I shall help you pack the few things you can take. We can jettison the things of ours we don't need to make room in the cart. All will be well, you will see.'

And so the little gathering broke up. In a corner of the room, Simon detained the Reverend. 'Do you have any weapons, sir?'

The old man gave a wan smile. 'One rather old fowling piece. I fear that is all. But I do not favour violence. I speak fluent Mandarin and, if we are accosted, I think I can reason with them. I believe I am known for doing good work in this region for many years. And anyway,' he put his hand on Simon's shoulder, 'I know that the Good Lord will protect us.'

As he stepped away, Jenkins moved to Fonthill's side. 'The Good Lord,' he growled, 'plus one old fowling piece and two Colt revolvers. It's not much, bach sir, is it?'

Simon nodded and gave a half-smile. 'Alice has a small pistol, but no, not much. I fear it could be quite a journey. Gird your loins, 352, gird your loins.'

'Ah yes.' Jenkins frowned. 'D'you know, I've never been quite sure what loins are . . . ?'

'They're things that have to be girt. Bed now.'

CHAPTER TWO

They were on the road well before sunrise. There were no tears on Mrs Griffith's face now as she organised the departure with calm efficiency, as though they were merely making a summer visit to the capital. The crude cart that had carried the visitors was left behind and the Griffiths' much larger wagon was put into service to carry both sets of baggage. As the little party wound through the narrow alleyways, Simon on horseback took the lead, with a surly Gerald on his pony alongside to point the way; the Reverend Griffith drove the wagon, with Chang at his side, the two women sitting amidst the baggage and a mounted Jenkins rode behind as rearguard. Fonthill and Jenkins each carried a pearl-handled Colt revolver, and the sporting shotgun, which the missionary chose not to load, lay amongst the bags at the back of the wagon.

'How far to Peking?' asked Fonthill.

'About fifteen miles,' replied Gerald. 'The road gets better nearer the city, of course.'

'Is it open country?'

'Most of the way.'

Simon thought for a moment. 'Is there one place where we might be ambushed – where there is cover on either side?'

'Er . . . yes. Probably.' The young man's eyes widened. 'It's a small village. We have to go through its centre.'

'Can we get round it?'

'No, not really. Fields are too rough on either side.'

'Right. Tell me when we near it.'

The sun rose to make the world a heat bowl once again and Griffith stopped to stretch a tarpaulin over the rickety frame on the wagon to give its occupants some shade. The barren nature of the plain afforded them no relief from the sun, of course, but it gave them an excellent view all around, enabling them to detect any sign of pursuit, even from far away.

They skirted two villages without incident. Outside one, they met two peasants, attempting to work in the hard ground. Griffith called to them and asked for news of Boxers but the men's faces remained quite impassive and he received no reply, even when the question was repeated by Chang in a more colloquial dialect.

Jenkins rode up. 'I think people are comin' up be'ind us, bach sir,' he reported.

Fonthill whirled round in the saddle and squinted back down the road. 'Dammit. I wish I had field glasses. Can't see a sign of anyone. Can you, Gerald, you've got young eyes?'

'No. Nothing.'

Jenkins sniffed. 'Oh, they're there all right. Look 'ard. There's a bit of a dust cloud, way back.'

Simon shielded his eyes and squinted. 'Ah, yes. I see what you mean. Boxers, do you think?'

'Who else would be travellin' in a crowd, like that?'

'Gerald?'

Fear showed in the man's eyes. 'Yes. I should think so. They're coming after us, all right. We shouldn't have left. We could have stayed and spread ourselves round amongst neighbours. That way they probably wouldn't have found all of us.'

Fonthill eyed him keenly. 'Just your father, eh?'

'No. I didn't mean that.'

'Right. We'll wait here for them.'

Gerald's jaw dropped. 'You must be mad. We have four mules. If we whip them hard, we might be able to outpace them, if they're on foot.'

'Not in this heat – and mules don't like to run. Neither do I, for that matter. No, we'll wait here for them. Reverend,' he walked his horse over to where Griffith was tying up a loose part of the tarpaulin, 'it seems that we are being followed and they are probably Boxers.'

Mrs Griffith drew in her breath sharply but her husband's face betrayed no emotion. 'Very well,' he said. 'Even in this heat, the Chinese travel fast on foot, so I doubt if we can outdistance them. What do you propose?'

'I agree that we can't run. I suggest that we wait here for them. The road is narrow and there are quite wide ditches on either side, so it could be difficult for them to surround us. I think we might deter them with our pistols.'

35

'Ah no.' The clergyman shook his head. 'No violence. Let me talk to them. Some of them could be locals and they will know me. We must put our trust in the Lord.'

Simon eyed him for a moment, then nodded. 'Very well, sir. But I reserve the right to shoot if things get nasty. From what I've heard, the Boxers don't have firearms, they rely on swords and clubs, so we might have a chance of putting them off, anyway. Right. We don't have much time. Jenkins.'

'Sir.'

'Hitch your horse to the far side of the wagon – not the rear, close to the ditch – and take that shovel. See that declivity in the field over there . . . ?'

'What's a declivity when it's at 'ome?'

'Oh Lord, I do wish sometimes that you had finished that Army Certificate of Education that you started on.'

'Well, I would 'ave, wouldn't I, if you 'adn't taken me off to fight the savage Zulu, see.'

'All right. That dip in the ground over there? See it?'

'Oh yes.'

'Dig a hole in it, sufficiently deep to give you cover. Don't pile up soil, though. I don't want the Boxers to know you're there. Take ammunition for your Colt from the box in the wagon and then go quickly. There's little time. If firing starts I want you to give covering fire. But don't fire unless I do. Understand?'

Jenkins's eyes had become cold and hard again. Fonthill knew the signs. The Welshman was ready for – was about to revel in – action and danger.

'Very good, bach sir.'

'Good. Double away.'

'What do you want me to do?' Gerald Griffith's voice was querulous.

Simon looked back at the wagon. The missionary was sitting on the driving seat, slowly turning the pages of his Bible. Alice, Lizzie and Chang were now out of sight behind the tarpaulin, although, of course, the wagon was open fore and aft. Fonthill turned to Gerald.

'If fighting does start,' he said, 'we will be fairly useless on horseback, for gunfire will disturb the horses and make it difficult to fire accurately. So we will hitch the horses to the side of the wagon to stop them boarding from that side. Please tie your horse and then load the fowling piece. We will wait under cover while your father speaks to these people. But we will demonstrate that we are armed. We must not fire unless we have to. However . . .' he now spoke with emphasis '. . . Do not fire until I do. And when you do fire, aim to kill. There can be no hesitation once the fighting begins – if it does, that is. Now, tie your horse and then get into the wagon.'

Wide-eyed, Gerald nodded and led his horse to the far side of the wagon. Fonthill followed him, hitched up his own mount and climbed inside. As he did so, the Reverend Griffith stepped down and, Bible in hand, walked a little way down the road towards where the dust cloud could now be clearly seen.

'What is happening, Simon?' asked Alice. Mrs Griffith was by her side. Anxiety was reflected in both their faces. Chang, sitting at their feet, seemed quite unperturbed.

'I think there is no need for alarm yet,' said Fonthill. 'However, it looks as though the Boxers have followed us and are approaching. We cannot outdistance them so we shall wait for them here. Mr Griffith is confident that he can talk them out of violence and so there will be no shooting unless we really have to defend ourselves.'

Mrs Griffith shot a glance over her shoulder. 'I do not like Edward going among those people,' she said. 'He should stay in the wagon.'

Simon nodded. 'I quite agree. I will ask him to return. In the meantime, Alice?'

His wife nodded.

'Do you have that little popgun of yours that was so useful in the Sudan?'

'It is not a popgun, Simon. It is a very effective French officer's side arm, a very fine, eleven-millimetre Chamelot-Delvigne, that served me well in Egypt as well as the Sudan.' She withdrew the scarf that lay across her lap to reveal the little, steel-blue automatic.

Fonthill gave a smile that didn't reach his eyes. 'Good. I am sorry we can't give you a Colt, because you are probably a better shot with it than me. But have your little gun ready. Don't shoot until I do.'

Then he bowed his head. 'Sorry, Mrs Griffith. I promise that we will try and avoid violence.' He climbed down from the wagon and walked towards where the clergyman was standing, looking down the road. Their pursuers could now be seen and flashes of scarlet revealed their identity.

'I think it would be safer if you addressed them from the wagon, sir,' he said.

Griffith smiled, a little wistfully. 'No, Simon. I want to show that I am part of them. So I shall walk towards them, in peace, and speak to them from their midst. I think it is the best way.'

Simon's heart fell. If the clergyman formed part of the crowd, it would be extremely difficult to defend him if the mob turned on

38

him. He turned to his right and looked across the field. There was no sign of Jenkins, except what could be a ripple of fresh earth, some thirty yards away. Good. That flank was covered, anyway. He smiled confidently at the missionary.

'Of course, sir. Good luck. Don't be afraid to run back to the wagon if you have to. We will cover you.'

'I will.' Griffith held out his hand. 'God bless you, nephew.'

They shook hands and Fonthill climbed back into the wagon. He addressed Gerald. 'Have you loaded the fowling piece?'

'Yes, but I can't see me harming anyone with it. It only shoots pellets.'

'It doesn't matter. It will have a deterrent effect. Now,' he addressed the others, 'Mrs Griffith please keep low. The rest of us will show our weapons when the Boxers come up, I will pull back the tarpaulin to show them that we are armed. Gerald, you take the rear of the wagon, Alice you guard the front, Chang you hold the reins of the mules and attempt to quieten them if shooting starts. I will guard the side facing the road. The horses hitched on the other side should stop them climbing aboard from that side. Let me repeat – do not fire unless I do.'

'Where is 352?' asked Alice.

'He is hidden out in the field. If we have to shoot, firing coming from the flank should disconcert the Boxers.'

Gerald's face was white. 'What if they have guns? We could be mown down.'

'I doubt if they will have rifles or anything like that. If they do, shoot at the marksmen first. Here they come. Good luck everyone.'

Fonthill finished unfurling the tarpaulin, so that the interior of the wagon was revealed. As he tied the last cord, he caught a glimpse of the Reverend Griffith stepping forward to meet the Boxers, his hand upheld in the universal gesture of peace. Simon bit his lip as he watched. He tried to count the Chinamen and gave up at fourteen. Perhaps there were twenty. Far too many, anyway. A Daniel – a very old but brave Daniel – was about to enter the lion's den, with only his Bible to protect him.

Fonthill adopted what he hoped was a commanding posture: one booted foot on the sideboard of the wagon, one arrogant hand on his hip and the other holding the Colt at his side, the sun glinting on its long barrel. He nodded sharply to Gerald.

'Show your gun, young man. You too, Alice.'

Small beads of perspiration were now showing on his wife's upper lip, but she nodded and moved to the open rear of the wagon and began making a great show of loading her little automatic pistol. Gerald Griffith crept up behind her and held up his fowling piece as though about to shoot a passing bird. Mrs Griffith knelt a little unsteadily on an old leather case, her hands clasped together and her eyes tightly closed as she prayed. Chang, one of whose eyes had partly closed following yesterday's affray, had taken up his post on the driver's seat, waiting in silence.

Simon turned his gaze back to the missionary. He had now reached the Boxers, who immediately opened their ranks and allowed him to mingle with them. He stood out, tall and erect, in their midst, both hands held high, one of them holding his Bible. The Chinese had fallen silent now and the missionary's voice could just be heard, speaking quite slowly and evenly and sounding even more mellifluous in Mandarin. To Fonthill, he cut a biblical figure, as though he were a medieval preacher addressing his flock. His mind went back to an old painting that had hung in his father's study. The metaphor was made even more apt by the rapt, open faces of the young men surrounding him. Simon was reminded that they were peasants, many of them seemingly still in their teens. As far as he could see, few of them wore shoes or sandals. Violence suddenly seemed far away on this warm, sunlit morning.

Suddenly, there was a sharp report from within the wagon and Fonthill swung around to see Gerald Griffith staring at the smoking barrel of his gun.

'What the hell—?' snarled Simon.

'It just went off.' The young man's mouth hung open.

The heads of everyone in the group turned towards the wagon and the scene froze for a split second. Then a chant began from the back of the rabble, '*Sha! Sha! Sha!*'

'What does that mean?' asked Alice, wide-eyed.

'Means kill,' called back Chang. 'I think they come at us now.'

'Reload your gun,' Fonthill ordered Gerald. 'Quickly now, man, for God's sake.'

The chant was taken up by the rest of the Boxers and Simon caught a momentary glimpse of Edward Griffith holding out his hands in a placatory gesture, when a sword flashed and he disappeared into the crowd.

'Ah no!' cried Alice.

'Get to the front, Alice,' shouted Simon.

Several more swords were swung high in the middle of the crowd and then the Boxers turned towards the wagon. 'Don't fire yet, 352,' yelled Fonthill. 'I'll try and warn them off.'

He held up his free hand, palm facing outward towards the mob, and then fired his revolver above their heads.

It had the reverse effect to that intended – indeed it seemed to act like the starting gun in a race, for the front row of the Boxers immediately produced swords and began to run towards the wagon.

'Fire, Jenkins,' cried Simon. There were only about sixty yards between the attackers and the defenders and Fonthill realised that he had only six shots with which to deter the charge, for there would be little time to reload. He took careful aim, fired and brought down the leading man. Cocking back the hammer with his thumb, he fired again, and then again and again. Behind him, he heard the bark of Alice's automatic and the deeper report of the fowling piece.

The front row of the attackers seemed to melt away and the second line tripped over five bodies on the ground and the remainder halted, their swords held aloft still truculently, but their aggression now replaced by indecision.

In those few precious seconds, Simon thrust three more rounds into his Colt. Coolly, he aimed again and fired, then twice more. At almost the same time, he heard firing from the field to his right and glimpsed an erect Jenkins, hammering back the cocking mechanism of his revolver with his left hand as he let off round after round in rapid succession.

It was enough. The surprise of the attack from the right – although at too great a distance for Jenkins's handgun to be a killing piece – broke whatever resistance was left among the Boxers and they turned and fled back up the road from which they had come. In an amazingly few moments, they had shrunk to diminutive figures in the dusty distance. The attack was over almost as soon as it had begun.

Fonthill leapt down from the wagon and ran towards where he could see the Reverend Griffith lying in a pool of blood.

He bent down. 'Oh my God.' Suddenly, Alice was by his side. 'Are we too late?'

Simon gently turned the missionary over. His left shoulder bore a deep gash and his right arm had been almost completely severed at the biceps, although the fingers of the hand still clutched his Bible. Blood oozed from a sword thrust to the breast and another to the stomach. A half-smile remained fixed on the old man's face, as though something in that vicious outburst of violence had amused him. Or perhaps he was pleased at the end to be exchanging one world for another, for he was quite dead.

'Don't let Mrs Griffith . . .' began Fonthill. But he realised that he was too late. The missionary's wife was looking down at her husband, her hands clasped before her, one tear threading its way down her cheek.

Alice rose and gathered her aunt into her arms. But she was gently pushed away. Mrs Griffith gestured over her shoulder to where the Chinese lay in the road.

'Some of these poor people are wounded,' she said. 'We cannot help Edward now, but we may be able to reduce the suffering of those whom we have injured. Alice, in my main case, there is a little leather first-aid box. Please bring it and you and I will do what we can. Now, Simon,' she looked up at him, 'perhaps you would be kind enough to leave me for a moment with my husband, so that I can say goodbye. Thank you.'

Fonthill bent his head and walked towards where Jenkins was picking his way back across the field. 'A bit bloody late with your covering fire, 352,' he said. 'What happened? Did you doze off?'

'Doze off be buggered, beggin' your pardon, bach sir.' He gestured to his Colt. 'This bloody thing jammed, just as the firin' started, see. That's why, once I 'ad it cleared, like, I started blazin' away in case they 'adn't noticed me. Sorry about that, but it wasn't my fault, see.'

He gestured towards where Mrs Griffith was kneeling beside her husband. ''As the Reverend copped it, then?'

'I'm afraid so. Come on. I want a word with young Mr Gerald.'

They found the young man rather too frantically helping Alice to find his mother's first-aid box. Chang was kneeling by the front wheel of the wagon, quietly sobbing.

When the box had been found and Alice ran with it to her aunt, Fonthill addressed Gerald Griffith. 'Why the hell did you fire your piece,' he demanded, 'when I told you *not* to fire until I did?'

'I didn't fire it. It sort of went off on its own.' Gerald's eyes were staring and his mouth set hard under its thin moustache. 'It's all your fault. If you hadn't told us to show our weapons – for all the good *that* did – the thing wouldn't have gone off. I wouldn't have had to wave it about.'

Jenkins clenched his fist and took a pace forward. 'Don't you talk to the captain like that,' he growled. 'You're not fit to clean 'is boots.'

'That will do, 352.' Fonthill's voice was low with disgust. He addressed Griffith again. 'Now, I am afraid that you have lost your father and your mother will need all the help you can give her. I suggest you go to her now and help her in what she is doing – and I suggest you take your brother with you.'

'He's not my bro—' He broke off when he saw the light in Fonthill's eye. 'Oh, very well.'

Simon and Jenkins watched the two walk slowly to where Mrs Griffith and Alice were now tending two Boxers, who were sitting up in the road. 'As far as I can see,' said Fonthill, 'not one of the people who attacked us was hit by buckshot from that lad's piece. He must be a particularly bad shot. It would have been almost impossible to have missed at this range.'

'Ah.' Jenkins sucked in his moustache. 'And do you think 'e let off that thing deliberately early?'

'What?' Fonthill looked at his old comrade sharply. 'And *deliberately* cause the death of his father?'

'Hmm. Wouldn't know about that, bach sir. That's a serious thing to say about a feller, ain't it? I wouldn't know.'

'Neither would I. Come on. Let's wrap up the reverend in a sheet or something and lay him in the wagon. We can't leave him here. But we can leave them,' he indicated the dead Boxers. 'Best put them in the ditch. No time to bury them for we must be on our way. I shall be glad to be out of here.'

Simon looked around him reflectively. There was no one else to be seen, for the Boxers had long since disappeared and, for all the firing, nobody had materialised from a village that could be glimpsed about half a mile away. The fields were barren. Five dead bodies, in addition to the missionary, lay in the roadway. Alice was tying a bandage around the calf of one of the wounded Chinamen and Mrs Griffith was fixing a sling to the other's arm. Both men looked bemused but submissive. No danger there. He sighed. It had been six years since he had last experienced violence; since he had last seen men cut down in their prime. Now, within nine days of landing in China, he had experienced it twice. He wrinkled his brow in dismay. Was he born to attract it, he wondered? Did his life now *have* to be a choice between the boredom of a pastoral existence in Norfolk and the undoubted excitement of the last two days, with its concomitant sadness of the killing of a good man like the Reverend Griffith? Wasn't there a middle road he could tread? He sighed. One thing was sure: the answer wouldn't be found on this bloodstained road. Best to get out of here as fast as possible. There might be other bands of Boxers in the vicinity. Within fifteen minutes, the body of the clergyman had been wrapped in a waterproof sheet and gently placed in the rear of the wagon, and the dead Chinese rolled into the ditch. A crutch had been fashioned for the man wounded in the leg and he and his comrade had been told to retrace their steps back to the nearest village behind them – not, Simon insisted, that which lay ahead.

That, in fact, proved to be as deserted as the others they had passed through and Simon wondered whether its inhabitants were staying indoors, for surely they must have heard the sound of gunfire. Or had they fled at the threat of trouble? Chang, peering through his good eye, which was still weeping tears at the loss of his 'father', was proving to be a skilled handler of the mules and they made good progress through the village and also through that which Gerald had warned could be a place of ambush. It was as though they were journeying through a landscape torn by war, although there was no obvious sign of conflict or depredation.

The terrain changed somewhat, however, as they neared Peking. Shallow canals, which still retained a vestige of water, crossed the fields and crops of *kaoliang*, a form of millet, some of it ten feet high, were standing tall around them. They gave Simon cause for concern for they could easily conceal parties of Boxers.

His anxiety increased when Gerald was able to question one worker in the fields not afraid to talk with them.

'He says,' reported the young man, his face animated, 'that Boxers have attacked and set fire to Fengtai, the railway junction not far from here, and that the rail link has been cut. He says we are in danger.'

'Well,' snorted Jenkins from his post riding behind the wagon, 'we didn't need 'im to tell us that, now, did we?'

Alice looked up from the rear, where she was cushioning the head of Mrs Griffith on her shoulder. 'How far to Peking now, then?' she enquired quietly.

Chang sniffed and answered, 'Not far, cousin. Say three, four miles. Should soon see city.'

And so they did. It rose from the plain like some medieval fortress, surrounded with walls of stone some forty feet high and topped by castellated battlements. Towers with the distinctive flared roofs of the Chinese stood out like sentinels from deep within the city and, unlike the surrounding countryside, there was much traffic through the high gates within the walls.

'Where do we go?' asked Fonthill, riding alongside Gerald.

'We must make for the Legation Quarter in the heart of the city. This is almost a city within a city and houses the diplomatic corps.' His lips curled at the words.

'How many legations are there?'

'Eleven. All the fat birds that have been picking clean the bones of the Chinese Empire for so many years are there.' He numbered them by ticking off his fingers. 'The British, the Austro-Hungarians, the Americans, the Belgians, the French, the Germans, the Dutch, the Italians, the Japanese, the Russians . . .' He paused, attempting to recollect the last. 'Ah yes. The Spanish. They are all represented by these pompous ministers with their fancy uniforms and plumed hats. No wonder the Empress hates them all.'

'Does she?'

'Oh yes.' The young man smirked. 'If she had her way she would let her army clean them all out. But the Boxers will probably do it for her.'

At this point the wagon trundled through the deep opening of one of the gates and they were immediately among narrow streets that teemed with humanity. Fonthill frowned. The Legation Quarter did not sound like much of a sanctuary.

'Is the Quarter walled?' he asked.

'In some places. Peking is a city of walls.' Gerald became animated. 'The Legation Quarter is an enclave about . . .' He mused for a moment, his forefinger on his chin. 'Roughly about half to three-quarters of a mile square, I suppose. Part of it borders on the Imperial City – the palace and the Forbidden City, you know?'

Fonthill nodded, although he didn't know.

'Alongside the legations the *yang kuei-tzu*—'

Simon interrupted. 'The *yang* what?'

The young man shook his head impatiently. 'I told you. The *yang kuei-tzu* means the foreigners. The foreign barbarians.'

'Wait a minute.' Fonthill put his hand on Gerald's arm. 'Barbarians! Gerald, *you* are a foreigner. Your father was. Your mother is. I am. We are not barbarians.'

Gerald Griffith flushed. 'That is what the Chinese call you . . . us.

But I am not a foreigner. I was born in China. That makes a difference, you know.'

'Really. Very well. Now continue to tell me about the Legation.'

'Well, within the enclave and all around the legations the foreign commercial houses have established themselves: the Hongkong and Shanghai Bank, the Russo-Chinese Bank, two shops, Imbeck's and Kierulff's, the Peking Hotel and the Club.'

'The Club?'

'Yes. All of the people who matter – the white people, that is – are members.'

Fonthill thought for a moment. 'The Quarter – the enclave – could it be defended?'

Gerald gave a lofty smile and indicated the houses all around them. 'You see how closely the houses are built. They go right up to the edge of the Quarter. It would be difficult, I think.'

'Is the Quarter completely walled?'

'Oh no. There is the Tartar City to the north, in which the Forbidden City and the palace is built, and this is walled where it meets the Quarter, and in the south, the great Tartar Wall acts as a boundary to the Quarter, but these are the only places where you could say big walls help to protect it. But I don't know. I am not a soldier.'

'Hmm. And how many people – foreigners – are there working and living within the Quarter?'

'I think about five hundred.'

'I see. Thank you, Gerald.' But Simon was not at all reassured. A 'city within a city', with houses pressing up close to the boundaries and sides seeming comparatively open. Not exactly a fortress . . .

* * *

Soon they entered the Quarter and approached the British Legation, the largest of all the diplomatic buildings, by the look of it, built of stone but with the distinctive Chinese roof tiles sweeping low and turned up at the gutters. A Union Jack fluttered from a flagstaff outside. There they dismounted and the ladies were handed down, Mrs Griffith standing upright and firm, no tears now evident on her rough cheeks, although her eyes remained moist.

Within minutes the members of the party were seated before a large desk behind which sat the British Minister to the Chinese Court, Sir Claude MacDonald. He was a tall, raw-boned man, in his late forties, with a thin face and the ruddy cheeks of a highlander, framed by a wide sweeping moustache, the ends of which had been waxed so that they stood out like the wing tips of a bird of prey.

He listened with fierce concentration, his bulbous eyes fixed intently on Simon's face as the details of their journey, including the two encounters with the Boxers, were related. At the end, he stood, took Mrs Griffith's hand and bowed low over it.

'How frightful, madam,' he said. 'I am so sorry. I never had the pleasure of meeting your husband, but I heard much of his good works in the province. You have my deepest condolences.'

Mrs Griffith inclined her head in acknowledgement. 'We must make immediate arrangements,' he rolled his 'r's slightly on the word, 'for your husband's interment here in the Legation's cemetery. I presume, ma'am, that is what you would wish?'

'Thank you, sir.'

Sir Claude rang a bell and a Chinese servant in an impeccable loose, white tunic entered. The minister spoke to him in Mandarin and turned back to the visitors.

'I have given instructions for your things to be taken to the Peking Hotel, a short walk from here, and for rooms to be booked for you all. I suggest that you go there immediately – my servant here will show you the way – and take some rest and refreshment. I will be here at your service should you need anything. We can talk later about your future. I hope that it won't be long before you will be able to return to your house and church, Mrs Griffith.'

They stood but the tall man laid a hand on Simon's arm. 'I believe you were a captain in the British army, sir?'

'I was, Sir Claude, but some years ago now, I fear.'

'Yes, I have heard of you. Good work in Afghanistan, the Sudan and Matabeleland, I understand. I would be grateful if you could tarry a moment to talk with me.'

'Of course, sir. 352, go with the ladies and make sure they are comfortable.'

'Very good, bach sir.'

Once the two were seated, Sir Claude offered a cigarette and requested that Fonthill go through the details of the attack once again. At the end, he nodded, blew a blue cloud of smoke up to the ceiling, watching it, his head back.

At length, Simon broke the silence. 'Do you anticipate that the Boxers will attack the Legation Quarter, Sir Claude?'

The minister shrugged. 'It really depends on the Empress, Fonthill. It is rumoured that she might sit back and quietly encourage them to have a go at us, don't you know. But I rather doubt it. She wouldn't dare to flout the Foreign Powers in that way.'

'But aren't the Boxers on their way here? I understand that they have torched the railway junction near here and cut the telegraph wires.'

'Quite so. In addition to Mr Griffith, I hear that two more British missionaries have been murdered in the province. Worse than that, however, the Empress has replaced Prince Ching, a most amenable chap, as president of China, with a feller called Prince Tuan. Now, he's a reactionary of the worst kind. Hates all foreigners and he could well encourage the Boxers.'

Fonthill frowned. 'Good Lord. So it all looks rather bad?'

MacDonald stood. 'Not at all. No need for funk at all, my dear fellow. However, as a precaution, I telegraphed Tientsin and asked that a detachment of military should be sent here without delay. Some three hundred officers and men – mainly sailors and marines from European warships lying off Taku Bar – have been despatched. They should be here very soon. Should be enough to ward off any nonsense from these Boxer fellers.'

He held out his hand. 'But good to have you here, just in case, Fonthill. You could well be damned useful if we do have a spot of bother. So I hope you will stay a day or two, what?'

'Of course, sir.' They shook hands.

The minister walked him to the door and laid a hand on his shoulder. 'By the way, I have just heard some good news from home. Mafeking has been relieved.'

Fonthill stared back bleakly. 'Mafeking? What . . . where . . . is that?'

'Good Lord, don't you know? Ah, but of course. You have been travelling. The war in South Africa, this trouble with the Boers. You must know that they have been besieging Mafeking, this town in the Transvaal, for ages. Well, we've relieved the siege at last. It's been a source of great rejoicing back home.'

'Yes, of course. I know *that* Mafeking. But . . . do you mean that the war in South Africa is still on?'

'Oh yes.' Sir Claude gave a wry smile. 'My dear chap, you really must have been out of touch. These Boers gave us a terrible hiding in the first few weeks. They brought off three major victories, but the tide has turned, as we always knew it would. The matter should be brought to a close very soon now, I would think. But it was touch and go for a time.'

Simon frowned. 'Yes. I always thought that the Boer farmer was the best light-cavalryman in the world.' And then, almost to himself, 'I should have been there, dammit. I should have been there.' He looked up at the Scotsman and smiled. 'Ah well, can't be helped. Let's hope it's over soon. And this affair, too.'

'Quite so. I am sure it will be. I don't really anticipate trouble, you know. We should all be quite safe within the Legation Quarter and I trust Her Celestial Highness to sort out the Boxers if and when they get here.' He gave a paternal smile. 'Now go and get some rest, my dear chap. You've had quite a day of it.'

'Thank you, sir. Goodbye.'

Fonthill walked out into the hot sun and looked around him. Unlike the teeming streets outside, the Quarter seemed somnolent. A cluster of cream-suited Europeans wearing solar topees walked by and, despite the heat, several tight-waisted ladies, with smart straw hats tied under their chins by coloured scarves, sauntered past, holding parasols above their heads. Simon doffed his hat and they smiled back. It was all so civilised. Then he remembered the hundreds – the thousands – of Chinese on the other side of those high walls and he heard again the cries of '*Sha! Sha!*'

He strode away, a troubled frown on his face.

CHAPTER THREE

The next evening the detachment from Tientsin, mainly sailors, arrived. They marched through the streets of Peking into the Legation Quarter with bayonets fixed, a fine sight. Yet their journey had not been uneventful. They had to be transported from their ships in the bay by lighters and other shallow-draught vessels past the Chinese forts guarding the River Pei Ho to the small river port of Tangku, from which they were able to entrain for Tientsin and travel on, via the now repaired railway, to the line terminal at Machiapu, just outside the walls of Peking. There, however, six thousand Muslim soldiers from the northern province of Kansu had been concentrated by the Chinese authorities to await the arrival of the foreign force.

Throughout that day, Fonthill and his companions had grown increasingly aware that the residents within the enclave did not share Sir Claude MacDonald's sanguine view of events. Crowds could be heard in the streets outside the Legation walls chanting and shouting. It was said that many of the missionaries in their compounds out in the Chinese City had donned native dress, twisted their long hair into pigtails and prepared for flight.

It was a huge relief, then, when, at the last minute, the Kansu troops were withdrawn and the polyglot contingent was allowed to pass unmolested through to the Yung Ting Men, the main, gated entrance to the city, and then through the streets to the Quarter. In all, 337 officers and men, comprising guards specifically for the British, French, Italian, Japanese and Russian legations, marched in, led by a tiny contingent of the United States Marine Corps.

Fonthill and Jenkins watched them, silent among all the foreign residents around them who were waving and cheering the arrivals.

'It's not much, is it?' sniffed Jenkins.

'No, it's not,' Simon agreed. 'And it's a mixed bunch of nationalities, always difficult to command in action. Still, they look professional and I would back trained troops any day, however small, against a mob.'

A further contingent of fifty-two German and thirty-seven Austrian sailors arrived three days later and the presence of the troops had an almost magical effect on the city. The mobs outside the Quarter dispersed, the tension eased and those missionaries who had taken refuge within the Legation went back to their compounds in the city. Mrs Griffith, who with the rest of her party had attended the burial of her husband, began making plans to return home with her two sons.

Fonthill took advantage of this one evening to ask the old lady about Gerald. The young man had continually absented himself during the first days after their arrival, only returning for the evening meal at the hotel. Why, asked Simon, did he seem so antagonistic to his fellow ex-patriots in Peking?

Mrs Griffith smiled and nodded. 'I understand your question,' she said. 'He can be dogmatic on the point sometimes. But, you know, Simon, he is a good boy at heart, even though his father used to despair of him sometimes.'

'I'm sure he is, Mrs Griffith, but sometimes he almost seems to favour the Boxers. And where does he go during the daytime here?'

'Well, you should know that, since he graduated from university here, he has wanted to join the Chinese foreign service.' Her eyes, which had remained sad since their arrival, now briefly shone with pride. 'Gerald is a very good Mandarin speaker, you know, even better than his father. He has made some very good friends at court and has always admired the Empress. He has had this ambition to serve this country, but, of course, it is terribly difficult for someone who is not born of Chinese parents to work in the court here. But he still has hopes.'

'I see. But surely this is a difficult time to do that?'

'Oh quite. But he feels that this is when he could be of most service. Seeing both sides, you see.'

Fonthill fought back the desire to answer 'or just one'. Instead, he nodded and smiled acquiescence. 'Well, I wish him luck,' he said. 'He is obviously a bright lad.'

She smiled. 'Yes, isn't he? He will be a great comfort to me, now that . . . now that Edward is gone.'

'And Chang?'

'Ah, Chang. He has been with us since he was a baby and we have always tried to treat him as one of our own – the same as Gerald.'

Her brow clouded for a moment. 'But in the last couple of years Gerald seems to have taken against his brother. It is something that had begun to worry Edward quite a lot. We had hoped that they would both go into the ministry together, you know.'

'What now?'

Mrs Griffith pushed a stray strand of hair back into its bun. 'Chang is still quite young, of course, but he may take holy orders. Perhaps, once he is ordained, he could take over his father's mission. That would be nice, if it is God's will.'

They were interrupted by the arrival of an agitated Alice. She sat next to Mrs Griffith and took up the old lady's hand. 'Bad news, I'm afraid. We have just heard that another two British missionaries have been murdered by the Boxers at a place about forty miles south of Peking.'

Mrs Griffith put her free hand to her mouth. 'What are their names? We are sure to know them. Where, did you say?'

'I don't know, Aunt. But there is worse. The Boxers have made another raid on the railway. A heavier one this time. Stations have been burnt, the Chinese troops guarding them have fled and the rails have been torn up. The line to Tientsin is definitely broken. More and more missionaries are coming into the Legation. You can't leave now, I fear, my dear.' Alice turned her face to Simon. 'It is rumoured that the Boxers are marching on the city.'

Fonthill put his hand on her shoulder. 'That rumour has been rife since we got here, my love. But I agree. You can't leave Peking, my dear Aunt, even though this heat has got so much worse. I will try and see Sir Claude and find the true position.'

Outside, he met a perspiring and indignant Jenkins. ''Ere,' he said.

''ave you 'eard what 'appened when they burnt down that racecourse place?'

'No.'

'These boxin' chaps got 'old of one of the native Christian blokes and roasted 'im alive in the ashes of the place.'

'Good Lord. Look, I think trouble is definitely coming here.' Simon looked with affection at his former batman and his comrade in so many tight corners. '352, you once were the best scavenger in the British Army. Do you think—'

'What's a scavenger, then, like?'

'Thief. Well – more the picker-up of unwanted trifles. A taker of things from people who don't need them and the giver of them to friends who need them.'

'Well, I did my small best, bach sir, when that sort of . . . er . . . skill was needed. What do we need now, then?'

'We need rifles, 352. We need rifles. Two of them, as modern as you can get but we will put up with older ones, if need be. A couple of Martini-Henrys would be fine. One for you and one for me. If trouble comes, those Colts will not be adequate, I fear. Here, take this money. It should be enough.'

'Very good, sir. I shall go scrimmaging. Personally, I'd be much 'appier with a proper rifle than with them pea-shooters. I've made a couple of drinkin' mates who might be able to 'elp. No promises, mind you.' Mopping his brow, he walked firmly away, a sense of purpose in his step.

At the British Legation, Simon found that Sir Claude was in conference with the heads of the other delegations. John Sims, however, an aide who had once served with Simon's old regiment, the 24th of Foot, and with whom he had consequently struck up a friendship, was forthcoming about the situation.

The young man, working in his shirtsleeves in a small office as hot as an oven, was emphatic. 'We've heard that the Boxers have seized and are in the process of destroying the railway bridge at Yangtsun, just about the one irreplaceable link in the line between Peking and Tientsin,' he said. 'The heads of the legations here can't agree on concerted action and we're getting absolutely no change from the Manchu court. So Sir Claude has telegraphed to Admiral Seymour in Tientsin to send a large force to us here before it's too late.'

He held up a telegram. 'Haven't been able to show this to the old man yet, because he's still chewing the fat with the other ministers, but it says that two thousand armed men of eight nationalities have steamed out of Tientsin this morning. They should be here tonight.'

Fonthill blew out his cheeks. 'Thank God for that. Look, just in case they can't get through . . .' he held up his hand to stop his friend from interrupting '. . . it sounds as though it's going to be damned difficult to come the eighty miles by train. Just in case they have to slog through on foot, how many men do we have who could defend the Legation Quarter until they arrive?'

Sims frowned and shook his head. 'Afraid I have no idea, sir. Apart from the sailors who arrived the other day, there is just a handful of Legation guards, don't know how many.' He looked up at Fonthill ruefully. 'I know what you're thinking. There should have been some sort of contingency planning, but Sir Claude has been so busy trying to push his colleagues from the other legations into some kind of agreement . . .' His voice tailed away and he wiped his brow. 'It's been like trying to get

59

a bunch of opera prima donnas to sing all together in tune.'

He was interrupted by the arrival of Sir Claude, resplendent and perspiring in his high-buttoned blue jacket, replete with polished buttons and gold braid. He shook Fonthill's hand.

'Been to the Spanish Legation,' he said. 'The minister there is officially the doyen so we meet there, but, he is elderly and, as a leader, he is useless. We are getting nowhere with the palace. Do you know, Fonthill, when I went to protest formally about the deaths of our British missionaries, one of the Tsungli Yamen, that's a sort of Foreign Office, went fast asleep openly.'

He put up a silencing hand to Sims who was waving his telegram. 'I've been trying to get us to demand that the Empress receives all the members of the corps diplomatique in a formal audience, but we couldn't agree unanimously even on that.' It seemed as though the ends of Sir Claude's moustache were quivering in frustration. He turned to Sims. 'Yes, John, what is it?'

Wordlessly, the aide offered him the telegram. Sir Claude read it and then looked up. 'Thank God for that,' he exclaimed. He sat down on the edge of Sims's desk and eased open the gold-embossed high collar of his tunic, allowing his Adam's apple to leap, it seemed, with relief. He addressed Sims. 'Tell the commanding officer of the force that arrived the other day that I want him and his sailors and marines to turn out in force tomorrow, with carts, to march to the station to escort these troops in. Make a bit of a show of it, you know.'

He turned back to Simon. 'Well, Fonthill, we should be all right now. Two thousand troops is more than enough to put down these renegades if they attack us – and more than enough to impress the Court.' Then he frowned. 'If they can repair the railway, that is. But even if they can't, it's not a huge distance to march and I don't see a force like that being deterred by an undisciplined mob.'

Simon's face remained impassive. 'What about the Chinese army, though, sir? Would they join forces with the rebels?'

MacDonald shook his head firmly. 'Most unlikely. That would amount to a virtual declaration of war on the Foreign Powers. The Empress would never do that. No. I'm getting up early to welcome the troops in just after dawn at the station. Won't you join me?'

'Of course, sir.'

Well before dawn the next morning, Fonthill and Jenkins joined the small party of ministers, dressed in their finery, who waited, amongst a crowd of Chinese – unusually silent – for the arrival of the troops. The sailors and marines had drawn up carts to convey the two thousand newcomers into the Quarter and, as the sun came up, European civilians on horseback pushed their way through to get a better view. Also present were the Kansu soldiers, drawn up outside the city, in the park-like grounds near the Ha Ta Men Gate.

But no trains were reported as pulling into the station. The sun grew higher, the heat increased and the waiting became more and more uncomfortable for the officials and other Europeans.

'I knew it,' breathed Fonthill to Jenkins. 'The main bridge is down in the south-east, the line is up and there's no way a force like this can get through by rail. It could be some time before they get here.'

The Welshman nodded, his great moustache half sucked under his lower lip. 'Just as well, then,' he whispered, 'that I've managed to get us two rifles, ain't it?'

Simon grinned. 'Oh, well done. I knew you would. Where are they?'

'Under me bed, next to me potty. I'll show you later.'

'How old?'

'Well, I reckon they was used at Waterloo, but I think they'll do. They are only single-shot Martini-Henrys, like we used in Zululand. But they were good enough for us against them black fellers, so I reckon they should be able to knock over a few Chinks, look you. I've tested them and they fire 'igh, so remember that. I also bought two lungers – bayonets, just like we 'ad in Zululand – and two 'undred rounds of ammunition each.'

'You're a miracle, 352, that's what you are. I only hope we don't have to use them.'

'So do I. Oh, I've got some change for you.' He dug in his pocket and produced a handful of Chinese coins.

'Oh no. You keep that. As long as you don't spend it on the demon drink.'

'Who, me, bach sir? Never.'

'Well, I wish we'd got the things with us now.' Fonthill looked about him. 'There could be trouble here.'

The crowd of Chinese milling about the gate had grown now and were beginning to press in on the waiting troops. The Muslim troops from the north were beginning to stamp their feet and jeer. The crowd took up the chant and the commander of the sailors and marines looked up at MacDonald. The minister nodded his head and the troops shouldered their arms and began to escort the empty carts back through the gate. At this, the jeers grew louder but no one attempted to prevent the movement and within minutes the carts, the waiting dignitaries, the mounted civilians and the troops were safely back inside the Legation wall.

Sir Claude took off his plumed hat and wiped his brow. 'Damned disappointing,' he confided to Fonthill. 'They must have been delayed repairing the line. But they will get here – and at least we didn't have any actual trouble down there.'

The trouble came, however, that afternoon, as, back in the hotel, Jenkins was showing Simon the rifles. Once again it was Alice who was the harbinger. Her face was white.

'It's the Chancellor of the Japanese Legation,' she said. 'For some reason, he chose to go down to the station this afternoon. He went alone and was dressed formally wearing a tailcoat and bowler hat. Outside the Yung Ting Men Gate he was dragged from his cart, *by the Chinese troops*, and hacked to pieces, with the crowd all around urging them on.' She gulped and went on, 'His corpse was left lying in the gutter and they say that his heart was . . . was . . . cut out and sent to General Tung Fu-hsiang, the commander of the Muslim troops.' She sniffed. 'So much for the Empress's troops protecting us.'

Chang had entered with Alice. He nodded his head. 'It is true,' he said. 'I hear it from one of the guards at Japanese Legation. He say that commander of the guards was going to commit hara-kiri because of dishonour, but was persuaded against. It is frightfully distressing, don't you think?'

'Oh, I do, Chang,' said Fonthill. 'Frightfully distressing indeed.'

Alice looked up sharply at Simon. But there was no hint of sarcasm on his face. Instead, he took Chang by the arm. 'Sit down . . . er . . . old chap,' he said. 'What do *you* think about all this?'

'Well, old fellow,' said the Chinaman, 'I most disturbed that my countrymen should do this sort of thing. I know that they not Christians but this violence is not in Chinese religion. Confucius would not approve, oh dear me no. Not approve at all. And Empress surely cannot approve. Very, very distressing.'

Simon studied the young man's face intently. Chang looked, of course, completely Oriental. His face was oval-shaped and his eyes shone from slits set in the smoothest of skins, from which the bruises sustained in the affray with the Boxers had now disappeared. He wore a conventional pigtail and the customary white smock buttoned at the throat. A black skullcap completed the picture of a lower-middle-class Chinaman. Only the choice of the occasional, startlingly British phrase betrayed his upbringing. But these were strange times. Was he to be trusted? Fonthill decided to probe deeper.

'Gerald,' he said, 'seems to have some sympathy with the Boxers. And, indeed, I can understand his position, to some extent. The Great Powers have not behaved very well in carving up large portions of China for themselves. Some sort of uprising, given the circumstances, is not unexpected.'

Chang shook his head vehemently, so that his pigtail swung behind him. 'I not agree with Gerald,' he said. 'Manchu court has also behaved badly over years in trying to prevent intercourse with foreign traders . . . er . . . you would say, "intercourse"?'

'Perhaps "discourse" would be a better word.'

'Ah so. Discourse, yes. I must remember. Anyway, my father always say that she too old-fashioned for this year of 1900. Must move with . . . er . . . years.'

'With the times?'

'Precisely, cousin. She must move along with times.'

Simon stifled a smile at the young man's earnestness. He was sure that there was no dissembling there. Chang was a true son of his father.

He turned back to the others. 'Well that settles it,' he said. 'If there was any question of Aunt Lizzie returning to her home, that has gone now. It looks as though things are getting worse. I do hope that Sir Claude and his colleagues in the corps decide to pull their fingers out at last and begin to arrange some sort of defences. The Quarter is very vulnerable, as things stand now. And if he doesn't know that, I'm afraid I shall have to tell him.'

Despite the murder of one of their number, however, all the members of the corps diplomatique seemed to remain sanguine and Sir Claude continued to shuttle back and forth to the Spanish Legation. The streets outside the Legation Quarter's walls were now ominously quiet. From within the enclave, Chinese servants, grooms, gardeners and chair-bearers were slipping away, to be replaced by an influx of missionaries from the surrounding areas and from the many missions within the city itself. The Legation Quarter was now becoming crowded, with accommodation having to be found for the refugees, as well as the four hundred military who had arrived. The discomfort was compounded by the heat and the drought, still unbroken after many months.

Then, at last, the Boxers arrived. They burst through the Ha Ta Men Gate, to the east of the Legation Quarter. Here, there was no targeting of Christians. The red-sashed horde ran through the narrow streets, pillaging the shops and houses and killing any who stood before them. The shopkeepers and residents fled before them, crowding the streets and shrieking in fear as the Boxers began burning the buildings. The many missions, customs offices and the homes of the teachers at the Imperial University were fired and the

East Cathedral went up in flames, its old French priest and many of his flock perishing within.

The flames could be seen from the Legation and, as night fell, torches could be seen bobbing in the distance towards the Austrian Legation, which lay outside the walls of the Quarter. From the eastern wall of the enclave Fonthill, Jenkins and Chang watched the torches approaching.

'Are the Austrians still within the legation building?' Simon asked Chang, who had become the most reliable source of information about the city.

The young man nodded. 'Oh yes. But they have seven guards there to protect the building – and a machine gun.'

Fonthill grunted. 'That may not be enough. Go and get the rifles, 352. We must help them. But there is no need for you to come, Chang. It could be dangerous.'

The Chinaman looked offended. 'Of course I come, cousin. May I have loan of one of your excellent revolvers, please?'

'Er . . . yes. Do you know how to use it?'

'I watch you in the wagon. You just point and fire, yes?'

'Well, ah, something like that. I'll show you. One Colt as well, then, Jenkins. Get a move on.'

The three, now armed, slipped through the Legation gate and ran up Custom Street towards where the Austrian building stood at the north-eastern corner of the Legation enclave. Could they get there before the Boxers? They did so, but it was a close thing, for the torches could be seen bobbing down the narrow street towards them.

'Where's the machine gun?' demanded Fonthill of the young Austrian sergeant in charge of the guard.

'On zer roof, sir.'

'No. No good up there. Bring it down here. To shoot up the street. Quickly now. Er . . . *schnell jetzt!*'

The young man nodded, immediately responding to Simon's air of authority, and he doubled away, taking two of his men with him.

The Boxers were now some three hundred yards away and the cries of '*Sha! Sha!*' could clearly be heard. Fonthill clipped the old, triangular-shaped bayonet to the end of his rifle and nodded to Jenkins to do the same. With the lunger fitted, the rifle became a stabbing weapon six feet long, which even the Zulus had feared.

The Austrians had protected the door of the Legation with mealie bags. 'Drag 'em out so that they give us some protection facing up the road,' Simon shouted. 'Quickly, before they are on us.' The three laid aside their weapons and pulled six of the bags out into the road so that they formed a rough, low bastion.

As Fonthill knelt, resting his rifle on top of one of the bags, he had a momentary impression of Chang, standing very erect and extending his arm holding the Colt and pulling the trigger – with no result.

'Safety catch,' he yelled, 'just by the trigger.' Then, 'Rapid fire!'

At one hundred yards they could not miss, and three of the leading figures fell, their torches scattering across the road before them, burning on the cobbles. The Boxers halted for a moment and then came on again. But their hesitation was enough for Fonthill and Jenkins each to thrust a round into the breech and fire again and then again. Four more of the red-banded figures fell again, causing the mob to stand irresolutely.

Except for one brave man. Screaming '*Sha!*' and brandishing a large sword, he bounded forward, red bands at forehead, wrist and ankles flying behind him, presenting a terrifying figure by the light of the burning brands. Simon was still fumbling to thumb another cartridge into the breech of his rifle and Chang was clumsily attempting to reload his revolver. Jenkins, however, put one hand on top of the mealie bag and vaulted over, in time to present his rifle and bayonet to the Chinaman, who stopped, puzzled with how to deal with this strange, crouching man with the large moustache.

'Come on, yer yeller bugger,' coaxed Jenkins. 'Yer not so brave now it's not a woman or child or some poor little bugger of a clergyman facing yer, are yer? Come on, boyo.' And he made a feint to the right shoulder, which the Boxer clumsily countered with his sword. Immediately, the Welshman brought up the butt of his rifle and caught the Chinaman on the chin. As he staggered back, Jenkins reversed his rifle and plunged his bayonet into the man's chest. For a moment the two stood, seemingly connected umbilically, before Jenkins twisted the bayonet and withdrew it, allowing the Boxer to slump to the floor with a sigh.

Fonthill heard a sound behind him and swung round in consternation. The three Austrians were staggering through the doorway, carrying the heavy machine gun.

'Quick!' shouted Simon. 'On top of the bag. Come back, 352. We're going to fire.'

Laboriously, the Austrians mounted the gun on its tripod and fed the ammunition belt into the breech, while the Chinese watched, unsure, it seemed, whether to charge or run away. Then the soldier at the handles depressed the trigger and the gun chattered into life. It was enough. The Boxers turned and fled, casting aside their torches and showing the white soles of their bare feet in the flickering light.

Fonthill watched, expecting the gun to cut a swathe through the running horde. Instead, telegraph poles in the distance were severed, falling and bringing down the wires.

'You bloody fools,' screamed Simon. 'You're firing too high!'

But the Austrians paid no heed. Exhilarated by the clatter of the bullets, the gunner kept firing, bringing tiles down from the buildings at the far end of the street and causing showers of plaster to rain down on the retreating Boxers. Soon the attackers were out of sight, leaving their dead lying on the rough surface, their blood soaking into their like-coloured ribbons and sashes.

Chang was looking at Jenkins with a mixture of horror and fascination. 'You are indeed extremely good fighter, Mister Jenkins,' he said. 'You frighten me.'

Jenkins had the grace to look embarrassed. 'Well, son, it was 'im or me. I 'ad to go at 'im with the lunger 'cos I didn't 'ave anythin' up the spout, look you.'

The Chinaman was puzzled and turned his head around. 'Where do I look, Mr Jenkins? Where is spout?'

Simon sighed. 'Never mind, now, Chang. You did well.' He turned to the Austrian sergeant, speaking slowly. 'The Boxers might come back,' he said. 'Is your minister inside?'

'No, *mein herr*. He is in der Legation Quarter.'

'Very sensible of him. Well, tell him that I do not think it possible to defend this building here, outside the Legation walls. He should evacuate it.'

'I will tell him. Excuse me, *mein herr*. Who are you?'

'I am formerly a captain in the British infantry and this is my comrade, formerly a sergeant in the army. We are . . . er . . . advising the British minister. I know what I am talking about, Sergeant, I assure you. Evacuate this Legation. It is indefensible. Oh, and tell your men to fire lower with that Maxim.'

'*Ach so*. Very *gut*, sir.'

The three walked back down Custom Street, their weapons at the ready, but there was no sign of Boxers. They met, however, a small band of European civilians, armed with an assortment of sporting rifles and similar weapons. They were on their way, the Frenchman at their head explained to Fonthill, to the exposed South Cathedral, which seemed to lie directly in the path of the advancing Boxers. A cluster of Catholic missionaries were sheltering there who needed to be escorted to the Legation enclave, if it was not too late.

'We'll come with you,' said Simon. 'You may need us.'

In fact, the cathedral was not under immediate threat when they arrived. But the little party rounded up more than twenty Catholic missionaries sheltering within the venerable cathedral, plus five Sisters of Charity and twenty Chinese nuns. As they turned back towards the Legation walls they saw the glow of the Boxers' torches to the north and heard the distant chanting, growing nearer. Hurrying through the silent streets back to the Legation gates, they saw the old cathedral go up in flames behind them.

Back in the Legation compound, they were met by an anxious Mrs Griffith and Alice. Of Gerald, once again there was no sight.

Alice put her hand on her husband's arm. 'The whole commercial quarter – the richest part of the city – has been burnt down,' she said. 'All those lovely pearl and jewellery shops, the beautiful textile stores, the silk and satin warehouses have been destroyed. Simon, I would prefer it if you would not go out again outside the Legation walls. It is clear that the Boxers are starting now to infiltrate the city and, if they come at you from all sides, even you and the mighty 352 would not be able to defend yourselves. And I do not wish to be left alone in this strange country, if you don't mind.'

Fonthill seized her hand and kissed it. 'I'm afraid, darling, that we shall have to go again, although not tonight. We cannot give up the streets to the Boxers. They should be patrolled. I also think we shall have to start erecting some defences. The Quarter is very vulnerable, particularly from the south. I fear I must start laying down the law a bit with Sir Claude.'

So it was that the next morning Fonthill requested an interview with the British minister. He found the tall Scotsman very preoccupied.

'Thank you for your work last night, Fonthill,' he said. 'I knew you would be useful. I have to report to you that we are now completely cut off. Our last telegraph link, running north to Russian territory, has been severed. I have no idea what has happened to the relief contingent from Tientsin, so we are very much on our own now, I fear.'

Fonthill nodded. 'I see. This gives added urgency to what I have to say, sir.'

'And what is that, pray?'

'So far there has been no direct attack on the Legation Quarter. But if there is, it would be very difficult to defend the whole of the perimeter with the few troops we have at our command.'

'What do you suggest?'

'We should destroy those houses that come up close on the other

71

side of our wall and which would give cover to any attackers. This would give us a field of fire. From what I can see – and I do not know all of the geography of the place – there are parts of the perimeter that are virtually indefensible anyway, so we should abandon them, so shortening our line, so to speak. We should build a second, tighter, line of defence inside that we could man more adequately – digging trenches, erecting barricades and so on – and we should begin patrolling the streets outside our walls, bringing in those who are being threatened.'

The minister frowned. 'Good Lord, Fonthill. We cannot just bring in people willy-nilly. We are overcrowded as it is. Where would we put them all? And it could be dangerous. We could be importing spies and malcontents within our midst.'

'It's a risk but we can't leave people out there to be murdered. The Boxers outnumber us. So far, they do not appear to have guns. But, from what I hear of the Manchu court, they will soon get them and things will then be very different. There is also the matter of the Imperial Army. If they side with the rebels – and there have been indications of this, the assassination of the Japanese minister, for instance – if they turn on us, then we shall be in a pretty pickle.'

MacDonald mused for a moment. 'Very well. My responsibilities are heavy and I must be aware of them. I agree that we must improve our defences. The problem, of course, is getting all of the nationalities represented here to move in unison, for we are a rather uneasy coalition, you know, and it is difficult to find agreement. However, I retain some influence and I will see what I can do. I value your advice, my dear fellow.' He gave a melancholy smile. 'After all, in my army days, before I joined the diplomat service, I was only a subaltern. You were a captain.' He fluttered a mock salute. 'So – very good, sir.'

In fact, events moved quickly. Within the next few days, some two thousand Chinese Catholics found their way into the legations and the Methodists followed suit, evacuating their own compound near the Ha Ta Men. As Sir Claude had predicted, the overcrowding became acute, but one great benefit accrued. These Chinese proved to be a willing and hard-working labour force. Within the next few days, houses near the walls were burnt to the ground; barricades were erected at strategic points; trenches were dug; and shell-proof shelters were erected – all under the supervision of Fonthill and Captain Strouts, of the Royal Marines, the British Legation's guard commander.

The Peking Hotel, although it remained open, was considered by Simon to be too close to the eastern defences, so his party – Mrs Griffith, her two sons, Alice, Jenkins and himself – were given shelter inside the walls of the British Legation.

After the original sorties of the Boxers, a strange quiet had descended upon the beleaguered Legation Quarter. Rumours and counter-rumours flew. The Empress issued an edict blaming the death of the Japanese chancellor and the burnings upon 'brigands and seditious characters'. Troops of the Imperial army continued to remain passive and her ministers continued to send flowery messages to the heads of the legations assuring them of their safety and deprecating the need for foreign troops to be sent from the coast.

Then events took a dramatic turn. Each of the heads of legations received an ultimatum from the Chinese Foreign Office. It reported that the Foreign Powers had demanded the surrender of the Taku Forts at the head of the River Pei Ho, the sea gateway to Tientsin. If the demand was not met, the powers would occupy the forts by force. As a result, said the ultimatum, emotions were running high among the people of Peking and the Imperial Government could no longer be responsible for the safety of the ministers and their families in the Legation Quarter and they should leave the legations for Tientsin within twenty-four hours. Imperial troops would be provided as an escort.

These letters threw the ministers into a state of confusion – and indignation. Firstly, they had no idea that hostilities had broken out at the coast and they blamed their compatriots there for compromising their position at the capital. Secondly, and predictably, they could not agree on whether or not to surrender to the ultimatum. Equally predictably, they decided to play for time. A letter was sent, agreeing to depart but pleading for more time and asking for details of the protection to be provided and of the transport being made available.

Sir Claude, however, confided to Fonthill that, whatever the reply, he had no intention of 'moving an inch'. Nevertheless, the ministers and staffs of some legations began their packing, although in fear of what might happen once they had left the walls of the Quarter.

'It would be madness to leave,' confided Simon to Alice. 'Once out there on the plain we would all be attacked and butchered by the Chinese troops, just like the Japanese chancellor. We must stay with Sir Claude and, if necessary, concentrate our forces on defending the British Legation.'

'Wherever you are,' replied Alice calmly, 'I will be.'

The denouement of the situation, however, arrived in a quite different way. The ministers fulminated for hours around their large table in the Spanish Legation awaiting a reply but none came. Finally, the bellicose German minister, Baron von Ketteler, declared that he would wait no longer, but journey to the palace himself and demand an answer 'if I have to sit there all night'.

He set off with his Chinese secretary to the Foreign Office, both travelling in sedan chairs with canopies of red and green proclaiming their status and with two liveried servants riding on ponies as outriders. Half an hour later, his dragoman, who had been shot through both legs, dragged himself into the American Methodist mission near the Ha Ta Men Gate and declared that the minister had been shot in his chair by a Manchu solider 'in full uniform with a mandarin's hat and button and blue feather'. A patrol of fifteen German sailors went out to try and retrieve the minister's body but were driven back. The word spread throughout the legations. There was no more talk of accepting the offer of evacuation.

Instead, and with belated speed, the legations prepared to defend themselves at last.

It was agreed that the British Legation, by far the largest and, by its position, not commanded by the Great Tartar Wall but with a good field of fire, should be a kind of central redoubt. It would be a place where, if the worst came to the worst, all the defenders of the legations could fall back for a last stand. However, it was decided that it should also offer shelter to non-combatants.

As a result, the whole of the foreign community of Peking, together with ponies and mules, a small flock of sheep and one cow, gathered within the compound. An area of some three acres, which normally housed sixty people, was now occupied by nine hundred.

The separate buildings of the Legation had been hurriedly allocated to the different nationalities. The missionaries who had fled their missions in the Chinese City were crowded together in the Legation's chapel. The elegant front pavilions were stacked with all kinds of luggage, the most notable being provisions and wine; the stable-house was allocated to Norwegians; the rear pavilion was divided into small rooms for miscellaneous use, and in one of the tiniest Mrs Griffith and Alice made their new home, with Gerald, Chang, Simon and Jenkins housed together next door.

All was activity in the other legations, too. As a squadron of Chinese cavalry, in their black turbans, galloped down Custom Street past the isolated Austrian Legation, guards of all the threatened nationalities were busy strengthening makeshift barricades, laying out primitive firefighting equipment and, near the American and German legations, manning the outposts that had been erected on the Tartar Wall.

At four o'clock – the hour at which the formal Chinese ultimatum was due to expire – Fonthill and Jenkins stood on the front lawn of the British Legation, once marked out for clock golf, while Simon consulted his watch. At exactly the hour, firing broke out from the outlying Austrian Legation, which, despite Fonthill's advice, had not been evacuated.

'Well,' frowned Simon, 'I'm afraid we are now well and truly under siege. Will we be able to hold out, I wonder?'

Jenkins sucked in his moustache. 'We'll just 'ave to, bach sir. I wouldn't want to think about the alternative if them yeller bastards break through.'

CHAPTER FOUR

The ending of the formal ultimatum brought a sense of reality to the besieged foreigners and their dependents within the Legation Quarter. It was as though the defensive precautions already taken under the direction of Fonthill and Captain Strouts had been a game, the withdrawal to a secondary line away from the outer walls merely a harmless diversion to relieve the boredom of waiting for the relief column to arrive. Now, it became clear to Simon on a quick tour with Jenkins that the instructions that had been given for the erection of the fallback defences had been carried out quite inadequately. The barricades mainly consisted of overturned carts, with gaps between them, and the trenches were little more than shallow scoops in the earth. A concerted attack on the Quarter would surely have resulted in these flimsy defences being overrun.

Luckily, that attack did not come. The lull gave the defenders time to retreat from the indefensible positions outside the fallback line. After that immediate flurry of firing on the Austrian Legation, no attack was pressed home and Simon's call to leave the Legation was heeded at last and the defenders were able to scurry back to within the reserve line. Similarly, the other outlying legations – the Dutch, the Belgian, the Italian and the French – were also abandoned, as was the Peking Club and the large offices of the influential trading house, Jardine Matheson. Immediately, most of these buildings were torched by the Chinese and firing broke out, sometimes heavily, around the hastily manned new perimeter of the defences. Nevertheless, the Chinese seemed reluctant to press home any direct attacks.

'This is ridiculous,' confessed Fonthill to Jenkins at the end of the first day of the siege. The pair had spent the hours helping to direct the reinforcing of the flimsy defences: the piling of rubble upon and in between the upturned carts, the loopholing of these walls, the deepening of the trenches in the open land on the exposed sides of the line, and the making of sandbags from pillowcases and cushions. 'The trouble is,' continued Simon, wiping his brow, 'there doesn't seem to be anyone in overall charge. It's like the Tower of Babel, with everyone shouting in different languages. It's no way to conduct a defence. I have to see Sir Claude.'

'Be careful,' said Jenkins, 'don't get too close to 'im because if 'e turns round too quick, like, 'e'll 'ave your eye out with the end of them moustaches. Shall I come, too?'

'No. Get back and see if the ladies are all right.'

There was little sign of chaos, however, in the small, dimly lit office of the British minister. He sat at his desk writing quietly, his severe tunic unbuttoned at the neck and a small glass of port at his elbow.

'Ah, Fonthill,' he said, standing and extending his hand. 'Good Lord, you look a bit dusty. Take a glass of this Taylor's '79. I can commend it.'

'No thank you, sir.'

'I insist. You look hot and bothered. Now sit down and tell me what is on your mind.' He fetched another glass from an upended suitcase and filled it. 'Here.'

Fonthill took it and perched on the only other chair in the room. Then he unburdened himself of his doubts: the lack of leadership, chain of command and coordination; the still-inadequate state of the defences and the paucity of firepower. Then he took a sip of the Taylor's. MacDonald was right. It was delicious.

The minister listened without interruption, then twisted the wax more firmly into his moustache ends, as though to marshal his thoughts.

'First point,' he said. 'Leadership. You are quite right, there has been little of it, because our Spanish doyen has lacked the . . . ah . . . sense of purpose, shall we say, to provide it. This has now been recognised. I've just come back from a meeting of the corps diplomatique and I have been elected to take over the direction of the defence.' He smiled apologetically. 'Not exactly a general, don't you know, but, as I told you, I did serve in the British army years ago and actually fought in a couple of campaigns in Africa. Nothing like your experience, my dear fellow, but in the land of the blind and all that, you know . . .'

'Good. I'm delighted to hear it, sir.'

'Secondly,' he waved a languid hand to his desk, 'I am just in the middle of setting up a system of committees to delegate authority. I have already appointed a fortifications committee, under a feller called

Gamewell. A missionary, of course, but he used to be an engineer and I've got faith in him. These missionaries are the most resourceful people. We have appointed as military commander, Captain von Thomann, the captain of the Austrian cruiser *Zenta*, who is here on holiday, poor chap,' he gave a wan and rather apologetic smile. 'We're diplomats, you see, and we have to appoint on seniority. Thomann is the senior officer here, so it had to be him. But he will report to me.

'As for resources, I have drawn up here what we have. Our total strength of trained fighting men is twenty officers and three hundred and eighty-nine men, split into eight nationalities. This is the breakdown. Here, take a look.' He thrust a piece of paper towards Fonthill, who read:

	Officers	Men
British	3	79
Russian	2	79
Americans	3	53
Germans	1	51
French	2	45
Austrian	7	30
Italians	1	28
Japanese	1	24

'Very much a mixed bag, I fear,' said the minister, 'but beggars can't be choosers, what?'

Simon frowned. 'Quite so, sir. What about civilians? Can't we mobilise the fit men?'

'Indeed. I have already made them fall in, so to speak. There are two categories. The first is composed of ex-soldiers and sailors who between them have quite a bit of experience of war. There are seventy-five of these chaps, of whom thirty-two are Japanese. The second,' his wry smile returned, 'are rather colourful. There are fifty of 'em and they are mainly British students at the university. I call 'em "The Carving-Knife Brigade", because they lash these . . . ah . . . culinary objects to whatever weapons they've got: old rifles, shotguns, one elephant gun and so on. But they're rarin' to go, although,' his faint smile broadened into a grin, 'their experience of battle is confined to one chap who once saw the trooping of the colour in St James's Park, London. As Wellington said of his troops, "I don't know what they will do to the enemy, but they frighten me to death."'

Then the grin faded on the tall man's face. 'Trouble with this business of commanding the defence,' he went on, 'is that I have to observe the niceties of corps diplomatique communications. I don't exactly give orders. I must send polite little notes to the other heads of legations, requesting certain courses of action – usually written in my best French.'

Fonthill took another sip of port and suppressed a smile. 'What about ammunition – and do we have any artillery?'

'Very little, I fear. We have four light pieces, the best of which appears to be an Italian one-pounder, for which we have . . . let me see . . .' he replaced his spectacles and peered at another piece of paper '. . . one hundred and twenty shells. Hopefully it should be enough. Then the Americans have a Colt heavy machine gun with twenty-five thousand rounds, the Austrians have their Maxim and we have a five-barrelled Nordenfelt, which is almost as old as me and incapable of firing more than five rounds before jamming.'

'What about other ammo? Didn't the men who marched in from Tientsin bring reserves?'

'Not enough, I fear. The Japanese brought only one hundred rounds for each man and the rest only three hundred. Trouble is, since every contingent uses a different type of rifle, we can't create a common reserve of ammunition.'

MacDonald rose from his chair with the bottle of port and refilled Fonthill's glass, then his own. 'However,' he went on, 'there is *good* news. The most important thing is that I have nine more of these bottles left.' He smiled at his joke. 'We do have reasonable supplies of food and water. I have ascertained that we should be able to feed some three thousand people within the compounds for quite some time. There are four wells of sweet water within the British compound alone, and one shop has provided nearly two hundred tons of wheat, rice and maize and, because the spring race meeting has only just been held, we have more than one hundred and fifty ponies and a few mules in the stables to provide meat, with fodder to feed them for some weeks yet.'

He leant across the table. 'I would have liked to have put you in charge of the defences, Fonthill,' he said. 'But I must observe the damned niceties. However, I would like you to be free to approach me at any time and bring to my attention matters that concern you. As, indeed, you have already done.'

'Thank you, sir. I shall take advantage of that, when I see fit.'

'Good. Now, I have prepared a map of the Quarter, with our new line of defences marked. Come here and show me where you think we are weakest.'

Fonthill rose and stood by the minister's side and looked over his shoulder. MacDonald had marked the new perimeter that had been created by Simon and Captain Strouts. It showed a reduction of the enclave strongly on the west and eastern boundaries, where new defences had been erected along winding streets where rows of Chinese houses had been demolished to give a good field of fire, and across open spaces, particularly to the west, looking across the Imperial Carriage Park and the old Mongol Market. To the north it used fairly substantial walls and to the north-east it enclosed an open space called the Wang Fu, a traditional park. The south was dominated by the huge Tartar City Wall, some forty feet wide. Here, faced by lack of resources, Fonthill and Strouts had been forced to erect barricades across the top of the wall to enclose just the length of it which looked down on the American Legation.

Simon jabbed his finger onto the map. 'It is here, in the south, along the Tartar Wall,' he said, 'that we are weak. Those barricades must be held and, of course, they are exposed. The second point is here, to the north, where we are forced to stretch out to enclose the Wang Fu. We may have to retreat inwards here, if we are pressed hard.'

'Hmm,' said MacDonald. 'What about the canal?' This ran directly from north to south through the centre of the legations. The defences here looped southwards on each side of it from the north, with a small bridge over it, halfway down, defended. At its egress from the Quarter at the south, the canal ran under the Tartar Wall, at the very point where the barricaded 'European section' formed a bridge over it.

'Should be safe enough,' said Fonthill. 'The sides of the canal are steep and can be defended easily enough and we should be able to fire down from the two bridges if the Chinese try to enter from either north or south.'

'Good. I shall bear in mind what you have said.'

Fonthill moved away from the map. He was tired from his exertions during the day and the port, although welcome enough, was beginning to make his head throb. In addition, however, he was becoming a little impatient of the amateurish nature of the plans he was hearing for the defence of the Quarter. 'Polite notes in French' indeed! He ran his hand over his face, mixing white dust with perspiration, so that he looked clown-like.

'Do you have a reserve, sir?' he demanded.

'Reserve? What do you mean?'

'Well.' Simon exhaled in an exasperated sigh. 'There are clear weak points in the ring of defences. If one of these starts to crumble, you will need to speed reinforcements to it to prevent a breakthrough by the Chinese. How will you do this?'

Sir Claude's eyes seemed to grow more bulbous as he stared at Fonthill in silence for a moment. 'Each legation,' he said eventually, 'has the responsibility for protecting the area of the perimeter near to it. Given the circumstances you mention, I would ask the nearest commander to move troops along to defend the point of pressure.'

Fonthill nodded. 'So weakening the area from which the troops have been sent. No. It won't work. You need, Sir Claude, a small reserve of trusted troops that you can rush to the threatened points to avert the danger. Can you create such a reserve?'

The tall man put a hand to his chin. 'I see your point. As you know, we are stretched very thinly as it is. But let me see . . .' He thought for a moment. 'Look. I think Strouts could spare twenty-five of his marines from here to form such a body. I shall instruct him accordingly . . . and,' he gave a half-smile, 'I shan't have to write to him in French. Now, look here, Fonthill. Would you stay here in the Legation with your experienced chap, what d'yer call him, 325, is it?'

'352, sir.'

'Ah yes. Not far out. Yes, stay here to command this reserve and take it wherever it is needed. Will you do that?'

'Of course, sir. Honoured to do so.'

'Good man. Now. Another glass?'

'No thank you, sir. I must get back to see how my wife is faring.'

'Of course. Give her my regards.'

The next day, however, Sir Claude's system had its first test and failed it. After an uneasy night during which the Boxers had kept up an incessant, if inaccurate, fire upon the defenders – either the Chinese army had joined them or issued them with firearms – Captain von Thomann, the commander of the military forces within the Quarter, received a report that the American Legation, an important bastion in the southern defences, had been abandoned. Without attempting to confirm the report, he ordered all the defenders on the eastern side of the compound to leave their posts and fall back on the British Legation. Immediately, the Americans, still manning their posts on the Tartar Wall, joined in the retreat and took the Russians in the adjoining sector with them.

All became chaos within the British Legation, where Sir Claude, realising that great stretches of the defences were unattended, immediately ordered the men to return to their posts. They did so with alacrity and, for some strange reason, the Chinese did not take advantage of the situation, contenting themselves merely with burning down the Italian Legation and occupying one abandoned barricade.

'They're as bloody useless as we are,' observed Jenkins with a sniff.

There was one beneficial outcome, however. The inexperienced and fallible von Thomann was immediately relieved of his command and Sir Claude MacDonald, once a second lieutenant in the Highland Light Infantry, took direct command of the defending force.

It soon became clear that, whatever the pretences of the Empress, the Chinese army was now fully engaged in the attack on the Quarter, for two days after the ending of the ultimatum and the beginning of the siege, two nine-pounder Krupp artillery pieces began firing on the American and Russian legations from the burnt-out tower over the Chien Men Gate to the south-west of the Quarter.

This was a serious development, for the fire was accurately directed – clearly the work of skilled artillerymen – and if it continued and if other guns were brought into play it could bring down the makeshift barricades erected around the perimeter and the defences could be overrun. With only the little Italian cannon available there was no way the defenders could reduce the fire of the Krupp pieces.

The defences could be strengthened against shellfire, however. Under the direction of Lady MacDonald, assisted by Alice and Mrs Griffith, the grand ladies of the legations – all of whom were now sheltering within the British Legation – were set to making sandbags. There was no hessian available but every fabric that could be found was pressed into service. The result was that the barricades and hastily erected bombproof shelters were buttressed by bags made of fine silks, best curtains and lustrous satins, all in bright and erstwhile fashionable colours, so giving a surreal appearance to these patchwork defences.

For some reason, the shellfire slackened and fell away completely, but then it was replaced by fierce activity to the north of the British Legation. Here stood a mainly wooden, very old building called the Hanlin Yuan, a place venerated by the Chinese, for it was in essence a library, housing some of the great manuscripts from the past, a veritable treasure house of learning. Although this virtually abutted onto the buildings of the British Legation, the defenders made no attempt to destroy it. The Chinese respect for tradition and for learning, it was felt, would prevent any attempt to use it to burn out the British.

Not so.

Fonthill was the first to see a trickle of flame rise from the roof of the Yuan, where its eaves overhung and virtually touched those of the Legation. The wind was blowing from the north, sending sparks and smoke swirling above the Legation's roof. Simon blew his whistle, so summoning his marines, always on standby, and turned to Alice, with whom he had been sipping coffee.

'Rally the ladies, children and as many of the Chinese coolies as you can,' he cried. 'Organise buckets, chamber pots – anything that can carry water – and form a chain from the well to the wall. Tell Sir Claude, but tell him that I said we shouldn't take soldiers from the defences. That's what the Chinese will want us to do. Quickly now!'

She nodded and ran back inside. The marines, with Jenkins, had now fallen in outside the front pavilion and Fonthill led them at a run to where the flames were now leaping from the old wooden roof of the Yuan. As they neared the conflagration, they realised that Boxers and some of the Muslim infantry were firing through the smoke from nearby upper windows, so making it dangerous for firefighters to approach.

Fonthill called Jenkins. 'See those snipers,' he pointed. 'Take six of the marines onto the roof of the Legation and clear them out of those windows.'

'Very good, bach sir. What are you going to do?'

'We have got to break through and try and prevent the fire from reaching the Legation.'

When improving the defences, Simon and Strouts had taken the precaution of burrowing a hole through their own wall, leading through to the nearest of the Yuan cloisters but leaving a thin pile of rubble as a temporary closure. With his marines, Fonthill began tearing at this barrier, throwing the bricks behind them. They had soon broken through and Simon directed two marines to stand as guards in the cloister. He heard a rattle of musketry from the roof of the Legation, showing that Jenkins and his men were doing their work, and he scrambled back to meet his wife, her face blackened by smoke, leading a line of boys, coolies and some of the Legation ladies all beginning to pass water along the line in an eclectic variety of receptacles.

Alice handed him a brimming chamber pot.

'Get back,' he shouted. 'Let the coolies take this end. It's dangerous.'

'Take the damned thing,' she shouted back. 'I'm not standing here all day ruining my hair in this smoke. Come along. Here's another one.'

Fonthill frowned in annoyance but quickly ordered his marines to extend the line through the gap and into the cloister. There they began throwing the water onto the flames creeping towards them along the shingles of the cloister's low roof. For almost an hour they toiled, the line stretching some two hundred yards from well to the hole in the wall, the colourful dresses of the ladies interspersed with the dun-coloured tunics of the coolies and the shirts and shorts of the boys. Jenkins and his sharpshooters had done their work to protect the line and they slung their buckets and pots in comparative safety, but all of their efforts would have been in vain against the encroaching flames had not the wind changed. Suddenly, miraculously, it veered from the north to the east, blowing flames, sparks and smoke back towards the Hanlin Yuan itself. With a roar the old building went up in a pyre of flames.

Fonthill brought back his marines and they walled up the hole again. Then he directed them to douse the western walls of the Legation buildings with water.

At last, what was left of the Yuan collapsed in a shower of sparks. Simon became aware that Sir Claude was at his shoulder, his buttons sparkling somehow and his moustache still spiked amidst the smoke. 'Well done, Fonthill,' he said. 'Good work. The Legation could have gone up in smoke and then we would all have been finished.'

'Don't thank me, sir.' Simon nodded towards where the women, boys and coolies in the line were all slumped to the ground in exhaustion. 'Thank them. And the wind.' He looked behind him. 'At least we've got a good field of fire in this direction now.'

'Yes.' The minister's face was drawn. 'I got your message, of course, and you were right. As soon as the blaze started, firing started all around the perimeter. The American and Russian barricades on the Tartar Wall were attacked directly. So this was more than just an attempt to burn us out, it was a diversion to attract men away from our line.'

'Any breakthroughs?'

'No. We held fast all the way around. But it is quite clear that the Dragon Lady is throwing her army into the battle now. Things are hotting up in more ways than one. Where, oh where, is that damned relief column?'

Fonthill wiped a hand over his blackened face and then held it out to Alice, who now approached him. 'Have no messages got through, sir?'

'Not a damned thing . . . oh, forgive me, Mrs Fonthill.' The minister took her hand and bowed over it, with highland courtesy. 'Splendid work you did there, me dear. Way beyond the call of duty.'

Alice frowned. 'It was not that, Sir Claude. In these conditions the call comes to us all.' Her frown changed to an ironic smile. 'So we "feeble women" all play our part. We are all in this together.'

'Quite so, dear lady. Quite so.'

Alice shot a quick glance to Simon and then said, 'May I ask you a question, Sir Claude?'

'Of course, my dear.'

'You will know that I have a nephew here, Gerald Griffith, the son of Mrs Griffith?'

'Yes. I believe I have met him.'

'Have you, by any chance, commissioned him to slip outside the Quarter since the siege began, to, perhaps, gather information for you?'

'Good gracious no. That would be putting him in some particular danger, I would have thought.'

Fonthill intervened. 'What are you getting at, Alice?'

She turned a wrinkled and blackened brow towards him. 'I didn't like to tell you, Simon, but Gerald has been absenting himself from the Legation almost every day since well before the siege began. At first, I thought he was helping to stand guard at the perimeter walls, as is Chang, but my aunt tells me that is not so and that he has been slipping out of the Quarter for most of the days. She has no idea where he goes and I cannot help wondering what he is doing. Then it occurred to me that, given his fluency with the language and his contacts with the court here, he might be on some mission for Sir Claude. But clearly not.'

The three exchanged glances. 'Nothing suspicious at all, I would think,' said MacDonald, 'given his parentage.'

'Hmm.' Simon shook his head slowly. 'I'm not sure. I think I had better have a word with that young man. Come on, Alice,' he shook his wife's hand in his, 'you had better go and clean up. You look like a coal-black Mammy.'

She laughed. 'A literal case of the pot calling the kettle black. Good day, Sir Claude.'

'Good day, Mrs Fonthill.'

As they walked back, hand in hand, they passed a small man in a large white hat and elegantly suited. He was talking vehemently to one of MacDonald's aides.

'Who is that?' enquired Simon.

'That, my dear, is Monsieur Pichon, the French minister. He is universally loathed, because he is continually pessimistic, saying that we shall all be overwhelmed and beheaded. What's more, he is a coward. All of the ministers have now withdrawn to the British Legation, but most of them spend much of their days with their guards on the perimeter.' Her lip curled. 'This one is always here, usually with the women, or he takes a walk pretending to visit what's left of his legation, where his troops are. But he never arrives there.'

'What a cad!'

'Quite.' She nodded towards the Frenchman. 'Now, he'll be complaining about something, mark my words.'

Fonthill had no opportunity to talk with Gerald, for the young man did not return that night and the next day saw the fiercest fighting since the siege had begun. Early that morning Simon received an urgent message from Sir Claude: 'Americans on the Tartar Wall are under strong attack. Please reinforce immediately.'

His marines paraded at the double and, led by Simon and Jenkins, ran to the southernmost part of the Quarter, where the great Tartar Wall loomed over everything and everyone.

The road that ran along the top of the wall was forty feet wide, providing enough room for four carriages to ride along it side by side. On the western end of their sector, the Americans had piled upturned carts, splintered bunks, rubble and sandbags to cut off the road from that end, and the Germans had erected a similar barricade some two hundred yards to the east. This had prevented the Chinese from occupying all of the wall, and so from firing down on everyone in the southern end of the Quarter, and also from commanding the southern bridge over the canal. But, as Simon had predicted, it was one of the weak points in the defences and it was vital that it should be held.

Fonthill and his marines, the latter wearing their wide-brimmed straw hats so redolent of the seaside, arrived just as the Americans were involved in fierce hand-to-hand fighting on the barricade itself.

'Fix bayonets,' he yelled. 'Climb the barricade and pitch in. Come on!'

The barricade, however, although only breast-high, was not easy to climb, not least because some of the American dead and wounded had slid halfway down it on the defenders' side. Slipping and sliding on the debris, Simon climbed to the top and ducked under a sword, swung horizontally by a tall Boxer. He thrust with his bayonet and caught the man in the breast, freeing his lunger and pushing the Boxer down the barricade by thrusting with his boot on his chest.

He was conscious of Jenkins at his side deflecting a pike thrust with the butt of his rifle and spearing his man with his own bayonet. All along the top of the barricade, the marines and the remaining Americans were engaged in hand-to-hand combat with a mixture of Chinese: a sprinkling of young Boxers with their red head-and-hip bands far outnumbered by troops of the Imperial army in blood-red and green uniforms and the less-bizarrely attired Muslims from the north in their dun-coloured overalls. Looking ahead, Simon saw further troops doubling along the Chinese part of the wall to reinforce the attackers.

'Marines!' he screamed. 'Give them a volley. Fire!'

Not all of his party were able to disengage to fire but enough were able to do so and some sixteen or seventeen of the Chinese, either on the barricade or at its base, fell. 'Reload,' shouted Simon. 'Another volley. Are you ready? Fire! Reload. At the men running towards us – Fire!'

At such short range the volleys were completely effective and all the men in the first and second ranks of the reinforcements fell. Their comrades hesitated and stood for a moment irresolutely.

'Now's the time, boys,' shouted Fonthill. 'Straight at 'em. Charge!'

As one man, the marines, plus a few of the Americans, tumbled down the barricade, levelled their bayonets and ran towards where the Chinese stood. A volley from the attackers could have done incomparable damage in that small space but none came. Instead, the Chinese broke ranks, turned and ran along the road in full retreat.

'Halt!' ordered Simon. 'Reload and give them one more volley to send them on their way. Right? Fire!'

Once again the Martini-Henrys, mingled with the Americans' Springfield rifles, spat fire and more of the running Chinese fell.

Fonthill turned to look for the familiar figure of Jenkins, but the Welshman was not at his side. Whirling round, his heart in his mouth, he saw his comrade sitting on a pile of masonry at the foot of the barricade, holding his foot.

'What's the matter with you?' he called.

'Twisted me bloody ankle on this bedstead thing, look you. You can't fight a war like this, see, climbin' all over stuff. It's askin' too much.'

Grinning, Simon looked at his panting marines. 'Any casualties?' he called.

A sweating sergeant nodded to the barricade. 'Marine Robson got a sword thrust in the belly, sir. But I think that's all. I 'ope we don't 'ave to do much more charging in this 'eat, sir.'

Fonthill shook his head. 'Back to the barricade. But it looks as though we shall have to build it up a bit. I just hope the Chinese don't direct artillery fire on it, that's all.' He turned to one of the gaitered Americans who had charged with them. 'Have you been shelled?'

'Noo.' He spoke in the lazy tones of the Deep South. 'Ah guess they was afraid of knocking down this old wall an' all. Say, we all sure are thankful for your help heah. Might have let 'em in iffen you hadn't shown up.'

'Don't mention it. Do you have an officer with you?'

'Did have. But the cap'n got himself shot,' he nodded his head, 'back there. We sure took some casualties.'

'Ah. I'm sorry to hear it. Call the Legation if you get into more trouble. We're a sort of firefighting company. Come on now. Back to the barricades in case the Chinks recover their nerve.'

But they did not, and after shoring up the barrier, giving first aid to the marine with the wound in his stomach, which turned out to be only superficial, and tying a tight bandage around Jenkins's ankle, Fonthill took his men back to the British compound. There, where the Welshman's ankle was treated – despite his protests – it was found that the slight arm wound he had sustained in the affray with the Boxers near the Griffiths' village had turned sceptic. Jenkins had lived and fought for three weeks without complaining.

'It's the lack of beer, see,' he explained. 'It's poisoned me system. I've gone so long without a pint that my body is complainin'. An' so am I.'

In fact, as the days progressed under the hot sun with steady firing, some sporadic shelling and occasional direct attacks on the perimeter, the defenders' casualties increased. The little hospital that had been set up within the British Legation soon became overcrowded and the small medical staff were supplemented by the ladies of the Legation, led by Mrs Griffith, whose life as a missionary's wife had given her some basic medical skills, and Alice, who herself had acquired knowledge of first aid from her campaigns with Simon.

Pony meat and rice had become the staple diet for most in the Legation, washed down by copious draughts of champagne from the two stores within the Quarter, Imbeck's and Kierulff's. These also supplied seemingly limitless quantities of cigarettes, for now everyone smoked to combat the foul smells that rose from the bodies of the dead Chinese left outside the defences. It was no longer safe to venture beyond the perimeter to bury them – and there was nowhere to inter them, for that matter. Bathing was a thing of the past. And the sun continued to blaze down from a yellow sky.

Tensions mounted among the defenders and the non-combatants. At least the men mounting the walls and barricades had something to take their mind off the heat and the flies, for the Chinese attacks were becoming more determined, proving that the Empress had finally decided to gamble on wiping out the foreign devils so stubbornly holding out in her city.

Fonthill and his marines were called out when a mine was exploded under what was left of the French Legation and the Chinese poured through the wreckage, almost overwhelming the Frenchmen who had for so long defended their line there. The fighting was fierce there for a time – Jenkins firing, stabbing and clubbing like a wild thing, despite his bandaged arm – until the defenders gradually consolidated their bridgehead and the attackers retreated, setting fire to the ruins of the Legation as they went.

The situation was worse, however, to the east of the British compound, in the Wang Fu, where the Japanese had the responsibility of defending this rambling park, dotted with small palaces and pagodas. If it had been lost, the Chinese would have poured through the centre of the Quarter, cutting off the British Legation from the others. The original defensive line there, established by Fonthill and Captain Strouts, had had to be abandoned, and the Japanese – who were turning out, Simon judged, to be the best of the defending troops – established a series of defensive positions from which they doggedly retreated in turn, fighting over every inch of the ground. Here, the 'Carving-Knife Brigade' were proving their worth, fighting with their primitive weapons as fiercely as their smaller, professional comrades. Even so, after days of attack and counter-attack, three-quarters of the Fu was in enemy hands.

At this point, ammunition for the little Italian one-pounder – small in size but valuable, for it was the only real piece of ordnance possessed by the legation soldiers – was down to fourteen rounds. And then two pieces of great good fortune occurred to give relief to the hard-pressed defenders.

The first occurred when Fonthill and Jenkins were scavenging within an old foundry within the lines, searching for overlooked ammunition. There, lying in a corner, was a rusty but still serviceable-looking barrel of an old gun, a relic, by the look of it, of an Anglo-French expedition of 1860.

'Will it still fire?' asked Jenkins.

'I've no idea,' said Fonthill. 'I'm no gunner. But we will damned sure find out.'

A French artilleryman was consulted and, after inspecting the muzzle, he pronounced it still clearly rifled, with the firing mechanism still in place. The rust was chipped off and the barrel was mounted on a wooden base and a set of wheels originally intended for the Italian gun. Miraculously, some old nine-pound Russian ammunition was found which actually fitted.

'We have artillery,' Simon proudly announced to Sir Claude.

What's more, it worked, either when loaded with the nine-pound shells or filled with grapeshot formed of old nails and bits of iron and fired over open sights at the advancing hordes, particularly in the open spaces of the Fu. The diplomats called their gun 'The International'. To the marines, she was 'Betsy'.

The second piece of good fortune came out of the blue, from the unlikely source of the Imperial Palace.

At four o'clock on a day when every yard of the perimeter defences was under heavy attack, horns and bugles were suddenly heard from the direction of the palace, to be answered by similar sounds from all around the Chinese lines. Instantly, the firing from the attackers died away, leaving an eerie silence. A sentry on the roof of the British Legation stables reported that a large board carrying Chinese characters was being hoisted on the North Bridge. Translators with field glasses read out the message:

'In accordance with the Imperial commands to protect the ministers, firing will cease immediately. A despatch will be delivered at the Imperial Canal bridge.'

Watch was kept on the bridge, but no messenger arrived. Nevertheless, the ceasefire held and the cicadas could be heard chattering again in the Legation Quarter.

'What does it mean?' Alice asked of her husband, as she stood outside the sickbay, her sleeves rolled to the elbow and a bloodstained apron tied around her waist.

'God knows.' Then Simon's eyes lit up. 'It just could be that the relief column is nearly here at last. It would be typical of the Dragon Lady to bend the knee only when she had to and to pretend that she had the welfare of the diplomats at heart all the time. The crafty old . . . It's the only reason I can think of.'

Alice smiled. 'I wonder if he might know the reason.' She nodded her head to indicate someone behind Fonthill.

Simon whirled round. Walking by on the other side of the path, moving quietly as though anxious not to attract attention, was Gerald Griffith. He had long ago shaved off his incipient beard, leaving only his moustache, which now hung down on either side of his mouth, in mandarin style. He had allowed his hair to grow and had it gathered together at the nape of his neck and twisted in the beginning of a pigtail. He wore the loose trousers, sandals and buttoned-to-the-neck tunic of an indigenous peasant. He looked, in fact, completely Chinese.

Fonthill's previous attempts to question him on his movements during the day had met with monosyllabic replies. He went out, he said, 'to talk with friends'. While Chang had long ago attached himself to Fonthill's marines, turning out when required, still armed with Simon's revolver, Gerald seemed to take no part in the defence of the Quarter. His mother, however, would hear no criticism of him. 'He is a good boy,' she said. 'Just a little withdrawn, that's all, and does not wish to be a soldier.'

Now Fonthill walked across and caught up with the young man. 'Ah, Gerald,' he said, slipping into step. 'Been for a walk?'

'Yes.'

'It seems we have a ceasefire.'

'So it seems.'

'Do you know why?'

'Why should I know?'

Simon grasped his arm and brought him to a halt. 'Because I believe that you slip through the defences regularly and talk to your friends in the Imperial Palace.'

Gerald held up his head defiantly. 'That is not against the law.'

'It's damned near it, my friend. We are at war, Gerald. Those people on the other side of the barricades and walls are Chinese, my lad, and they are trying to kill us. Your friends. They are *the enemy*, dammit. Don't you ever consider that?'

For a moment the young man paused. 'I do not consider them to be so. They are doing what they consider to be right.'

'And do you tell *your friends* of the disposition of our defences here?'

'No. I do not know them, anyway.'

For a moment, the two men stood in silence, glaring at each other in the hot sun. In the distance, a pony could be heard whinnying from the butchery and from within the hospital a wounded man cursed in pain. Simon sighed. 'Let me ask you again. Do you know why the Empress has called a truce?'

'No. I do not.'

'Is it because the relief column is near?'

For the first time Gerald became animated. He threw back his head and laughed. 'Where did you get that idea? There's no relief column. Tientsin is surrounded and under siege – just like here. If you and these stuffy ministers think you are going to be rescued, then you are all living in dreamland.' He shook his arm free, gave a direct and lubricious grin to Alice, who had been listening to the conversation from outside the hospital, and walked on.

Alice crossed the path and grasped her husband's arm. 'Oh, Simon.

100

Do you think he's right – that there's no relief column, I mean?'

Fonthill shook his head. 'Of course not. The Old Dragon has called a halt because she's sustained too many casualties. There must have been about two thousand of her soldiers who have been killed trying to break in here. She knows she's gambled and lost.' He smiled reassuringly. 'There's no way that that cocky young devil can know more than MacDonald.'

That night the defenders on guard dozed uneasily around the perimeter, the quiet more unsettling than the continual firing had been. The next day, the shelling and the rifle fire from the Chinese resumed, with even more intensity than before.

The brief truce – called and held for no apparent reason – was over. The siege settled in once more.

CHAPTER FIVE

The brief interval, although refreshing while it lasted, had the overall effect of depressing the defenders of the Legation Quarter. It seemed as though the Empress, in her palace not so far away, was playing with them, as a cat plays with a mouse: letting it spring away for a moment and then clutching it back again in its claws. Certainly, the firing from the Chinese lines had been resumed with a fierceness that, if accuracy had been added to intensity, would have seriously reduced the defenders' capacity to resist. It was the absence of serious shellfire, however, that caused the most puzzlement.

'Why don't they use those Krupp cannon more?' Fonthill demanded rhetorically of Jenkins. 'They each give us about six rounds a day, which causes more damage than that produced by all their other pop-shooters put together. Then they lay off. It seems strange.'

Jenkins sniffed. 'Short of ammunition, p'raps?'

'Don't think so. MacDonald tells me that before all this started he saw thousands of Krupp shells stacked in a warehouse in the Imperial City. If the Chinese wake up and really begin to bombard us, I don't think we would be able to hold out much longer. The Quarter would be in ruins.'

'Why can't we make a sortie, like, and put the bloody things out of action?'

'Because they are too far away, on a roof somewhere to the south. I doubt if we would be able to get to them.' Fonthill mused for a moment. 'It's a thought, though. I'll talk to Captain Strouts about it.'

The captain in command of the British marine guard was sceptical at first, but he too began to warm to the idea. 'I know where they are,' he said, 'they're firing from the top of the Chien Men, that partly burnt-out pagoda tower on the other side of the Tartar Wall. It would be terribly risky but we might just be able to reach the place and destroy the bloody things.'

'At night, I think,' suggested Fonthill.

'I agree. A smallish party, moving fast.'

'I'll put it to Sir Claude.'

The minister was unimpressed. 'You would take the marines, I suppose?'

'Yes, sir.'

'But you know, Fonthill, they are among the most effective and best-trained of all the troops in the Quarter. If you lose them – not to mention yourself – we would be bereft. I really can't allow it.'

Simon sighed. 'I don't know why the Chinese haven't used these guns at all so far. Once they realise what an advantage they have with them and start bombarding us consistently, they could reduce virtually the whole Quarter to a heap of rubble within, say, two days. They could destroy the barricades on the wall and beyond and we would be defenceless. The siege would be over. I really feel we should try to take them out before their advantage is realised.'

'Hmm. Is Strouts with you on this?'

'Completely.'

'How will you get out?'

'Through the sluice gates at the southern end of the canal.'

'Will you need any . . . um . . . diversionary activity from us?'

'No thank you, sir. A good idea, but we will get out through the sleepiest part of the night. Nothing is ever quiet through the night here but it all tails off a bit about three-thirty. That's when we will go. Running like hell through the streets, in plimsolls, not army boots. Hit 'em before they know what's happening.'

There was silence for a time, while Sir Claude's eyes seemed to grow more bulbous by the heartbeat. Then he stood and held out his hand. 'Very well, my dear fellow. May God be with you.'

Strouts and Fonthill trained their men for two days as best they could, within the confined space of the compound. They practised running in plimsolls and sandals, carrying rifles and fixed bayonets, and they rehearsed – with the help of the French artillery officer – how to destroy cannon. 'Throw zem off ze tower as well, if you can,' he urged. 'But zey will be 'eavy.'

On the afternoon before the sortie, Simon told Alice about the plan. She stood for a moment, very still, with tears in her eyes. Then she put her arms around her husband's neck and nuzzled his ear. 'I know it is no use me trying to dissuade you from this ridiculous exercise,' she said. 'But, you know,' she pulled back her head and looked him in the eyes, 'one day you will push your luck too far. You cannot continue to get away with these ridiculous enterprises. Let someone younger go, my dear. You have done far more than your bit in this siege. I do so not want to be a widow at my age.'

He kissed her briefly. 'Don't worry. Dear old 352 will look after me. But one thing.'

'What?'

'Don't let Gerald or his mother know about this.'

'Of course.'

They assembled just as the moon was beginning to settle over the rooftops, looking like a rather exotic Chinese lantern, low in the sky.

The marines had exchanged their scoop-brimmed straw hats for a variety of knitted skullcaps and their boots for training pumps. They wore dark clothing and they had blackened their faces. Each man carried a rifle and bayonet at the trail, except for Jenkins, whose arm having recovered had volunteered to spike the guns and bore the bag of spikes and a large hammer. At his belt, however, hung his large knife. Fonthill and Strouts wore revolvers tucked into their own belts and carried naval cutlasses in their right hands, the blades blackened to prevent moonlight reflecting from them.

Sir Claude had risen to wish them Godspeed and stood shivering slightly in his dressing gown, although the night was not cold. 'You look like pirates,' he observed, with a sad smile. 'Good luck.'

The two officers saluted him with their cutlasses and Simon blew a kiss to Alice, who stood erect in the shadows. Dry-eyed but tight-lipped, she acknowledged it with the merest nod of her head. Then the little company moved away with a quick step.

Fonthill had chosen the sluice gates for their exit from the Quarter, not only because he knew it was lightly guarded from the Chinese side – the besiegers now never thought that the defenders would try to leave their ramshackle fortress – but because it was the nearest point of egress to the Chien Men, some three hundred yards away. The gates were not raised, for it would have been too noisy a process to carry out without alerting the guards. At either side of the grills, however, in the tunnel at the base of the Tartar Wall, there was a space big enough for one man to slither through. Simon took one side and Strouts – a burly, well-moustached man – the other. The rest of the party waited, huddled against the dripping walls of the tunnel.

Peering through the grill, Fonthill saw two guards, squatting on the pavement at the far side of the road. They did not move and it seemed that they were asleep. No one else was to be seen, although gunfire sounded from quite near. Nodding to the captain, Simon slithered through the gap and bounded across the road.

But, despite their posture, neither of the guards was asleep. They were, however, surprised to be suddenly set upon by two darkly dressed men with black faces emerging from the canal and they were just a little slow to gain their feet. The blade of Fonthill's cutlass wrought a slashing cut across the right shoulder of the nearest man. But he, like his fellow, was a Moslem Kansu from the north, toughened by years of campaigning for his brigand chief, Tung Fu-hsiang. He grunted with pain but rolled away from Simon's next swing and, drawing a knife from his belt, thrust at Fonthill's stomach. But it was a weak blow with his left hand and the blade point caught in Simon's cummerbund without penetrating. The next blow from the cutlass nearly severed his head.

Strouts had similarly finished his man and the two marauders stood for a moment, their blades dripping red, while they anxiously scanned the street on either side of them. There was no sign of life. Fonthill beckoned and the marines, led by Jenkins, began slipping past the sluice gates and running across the road to join them.

'Ever used a cutlass before?' grunted Strouts.

Simon shook his head, still panting.

'Thought not. Everyone uses the blade, just because it's curved. No good. The swing gives yer man time to duck. Use the point. Stupid weapon. Don't know why it's curved. Only good for thickheaded sailors.'

'Still, wish I'd got one,' sniffed Jenkins. 'All I've got is a ropey old bag.'

'You'll be lethal with that,' said Fonthill. 'Now. Everyone here? Good. Remember no firing. If we get into trouble, use the bayonet. Right. Follow me.'

They set off at a fast trot, making little sound and with no light reflecting from their blackened lungers.

No one was about in those narrow streets, although rifle fire sounded all around them. Simon realised that the musketry was coming from the upper floors of the houses, where snipers were directing a desultory fire on the American and German defenders on the ramparts of the wall. No one was looking down. It was just as well, for the raiding party would have been hard-pressed to have fought their way through the streets if met by stubborn opposition.

As it was, they found their way to where the Chinese had reduced the jewellery and fine furs quarter to blackened rubble with their indiscriminate torching of the shops earlier in the siege. It was flames from these buildings that had set fire to the fine, old brick and wooden pagoda of the Chien Men tower, leaving it a stumpy ruin of charred bricks, now some forty-five feet high. Somehow, however, the Chinese had managed to swing the two guns up to the top, giving the guns sufficient height to fire across the Tartar Wall and directly into the Legation Quarter. The two cannon could now be seen, silhouetted against the night sky.

Fonthill halted the raiding party at the end of the ruins of the shops. A scattering of soldiers lay, huddled in blankets, sleeping at the base of the tower. Others could be seen, standing by their guns at the top. To reach the tower, however, the raiders would have to cross a stretch of open ground.

''Ow the bloody 'ell do we get up there?' whispered Jenkins. 'I didn't knows we'd 'ave to do any climbin', see.'

Simon frowned. He knew that Jenkins was as brave as a lion. Hardened by a hundred fights with a variety of weapons around the world, he would take on anyone in combat. He was aware that the Welshman was as strong as an ox, a crack shot and a surprisingly good horseman. But he also knew that he was afraid of water – he could not swim – crocodiles and, perhaps most of all, heights. Standing on the smallest ladder made his legs tremble.

'For God's sake, 352,' he hissed. 'There's bound to be a ladder and, anyway, it's not very high. Just follow me – and don't look down.' He turned to Strouts. 'Will you please keep about half the party here and try and pick off the guards up on top if they see us as we climb the ladder. Stay here under cover and shoot anyone who tries to run across this space to get to us. Whatever happens, though, don't fire until we have seen off these chaps sleeping down below.'

The marine nodded. He had generously granted Fonthill the leadership of the sortie, in view of his greater experience.

Simon addressed the rest of the party. 'These men here,' he indicated about twelve, 'will come with me. No firing, now. We will double across this open space and bayonet the men sleeping. Not a nice thing to do, I agree, but it is very necessary. We don't want them to give the alarm. So everything must be done quietly and quickly. Then it will be a case of following Jenkins and me up the ladder – there's bound to be one, perhaps two – and seeing to whoever is left on top and then putting the guns out of action. Understood?'

The men nodded, the whites of their eyes standing out in their darkened faces.

'And, look you,' whispered Jenkins, 'will somebody catch me if I fall, like?'

'Stop being a baby, 352,' hissed Fonthill. 'Right. Bayonets only, remember. Get the bastards before they wake. Now, *go!*'

Like wraiths from a fire, heads down, bayonets presented, the little party sprinted across the open space towards where the sleeping figures lay. The only sound they made was the faint clunk from the spikes in Jenkins's hessian bag. The Chinamen had no chance. Remembering Strouts' advice, Fonthill plunged the point of his cutlass into the first recumbent form and then into the next. All around him he was aware that bayonets were being thrust into the sleepers, as though they were sacks of corn, being spiked before being tossed onto a pile. Two attempted to rise but they were easily cut down. It was all over within a matter of seconds. The massacre had taken place with hardly a sound being made.

Fonthill flattened himself, his back to the base of the wall. Sure

109

enough, a ladder to his right led up to the top. There seemed only one. He gulped. They surely must be seen from the top as they began to climb up and it would be so easy for the guards up there to shoot down, or even push the ladder away. They would surely shoot before he could gain the top and use his cutlass. Better to rely on his revolver – and on the marines in the shadows opposite to cut the guards down before they could shoot.

He gave a sweating Jenkins a weak and less-than-comforting grin and waved at Strouts. Then he tucked his cutlass into his belt, drew his Colt revolver and began to climb.

On the first few rungs the only sound he could hear was a muffled 'Oh my God' as Jenkins followed him. Then, a loud challenge in Chinese came from the top. Simon gave a cheery and, he hoped, a reassuring wave to whoever was above him. It was immediately followed, however, with a loud report and a bullet cracked into the brickwork near his head and pinged away. Fonthill raised his revolver and fired virtually blindly directly above him. At the same time, two rifle shots rang out from the ruins and the man above gave a grunt and toppled over, passing him and crashing to the ground.

'Keep goin', bach sir, for God's sake.' Jenkins's voice came from below him. 'I think I've peed me pants and I've got a bloke below me, see.'

Fonthill was now at the top of the ladder and, cautiously, he raised himself up and peered over the edge of the tower. Four men were silhouetted against the moonlit sky in various postures. The first, on his knees, was in the process of thrusting a cartridge into the breech of the rifle. The next two had obviously just crawled from their bedrolls and were looking around them in some consternation. The head of the fourth could only just be glimpsed between the wheels of the Krupp guns.

Gripping the top of the ladder as it projected upwards, Simon presented his revolver at the kneeling man, fired and, predictably, missed him.

'It fires high, dammit,' shouted Jenkins from down below.

The man was now on his feet, fumbling with the bolt mechanism of his rifle. Fonthill adjusted his aim and shot the man in the breast. Cocking the revolver with his thumb, he fired at the nearest of the two men standing and brought him down too. The third man held up his hands in surrender and Simon waved him aside. He looked along the sights of the Colt for the fourth but he had disappeared behind the two cannon.

'Can you get up, bach?' hissed Jenkins. It was always a sign of great anxiety when the Welshman omitted the 'sir' when addressing his comrade. 'Me trousers are soaked and me 'ead's spinnin' up 'ere. I think I'm goin' to fall.'

'No you're not. Hang on. I'm climbing up.'

Attempting to keep his revolver levelled at the standing Chinaman and wary of the man hiding behind the two cannons, Simon hauled himself over the edge and, on knees and one hand, crouched on the top of the tower. There was a clunk as Jenkins threw his bag of spikes ahead of him and a cry of 'Thank God!' as the Welshman scrambled away from the edge.

His arrival distracted Fonthill and the standing man ducked away, reaching down to pick up a rifle. Simon's first shot caught him in the shoulder, spinning him round, and the second took him in the forehead, causing him to fall.

'I keep telling you, it fires high,' grunted Jenkins, now his normal, cool self again. "'Ere, let me 'ave it.' He put out his hand and Fonthill was happy to hand over the Colt.

'Just two more shots left,' he said. 'Be careful. There's another man behind the guns.' As he spoke, he was aware of firing breaking out down below, near the edge of the burnt-out shops. Strouts and his men were obviously under attack. They must hurry.

The thought had hardly crossed his mind when a rifle barrel poked through the spokes of one of the guns and a bullet zipped through the edge of Fonthill's jacket, prompting him to roll away. It immediately galvanised Jenkins, who sprang to his feet with amazing alacrity for a man who, moments before, had been wetting himself with fear. Ducking under the barrel of the nearest gun, the Welshman fired one shot from the revolver. As the sound echoed away, he called out, 'All right, bach sir. We've cleared this top, like. The others can come up.'

Fonthill crawled back to the ladder. His men were lined up it, presenting a perfect target to whoever was attacking the marines in the ruins. 'All right,' he called. 'Climb up, as quick as you like.'

Jenkins was already examining the guns. 'Where did that Frenchie say we should stick the spikes?' he asked, perspiration dripping down his face.

'In the priming hole, at the top. Give me a spike. I'll hold it while . . .' His voice tailed away. There was no priming hole, this was a modern, breech-loading gun. One that could not be spiked.

'Damn that Frenchman,' he swore. 'Must have fought at Austerlitz.' Then he became aware that eight of his men were now on the top of the tower. 'Where are the rest of you?' he demanded.

'Got picked off comin' up the tower,' replied a corporal of marines. 'We was strung out like paper ducks at the fairground.

'Ow are we goin' to get down again, sir?'

'We'll get down all right, don't worry about that.' In fact, the thought of climbing back down that ladder under gunfire perturbed him considerably. 'Right. Four of you line the edge. See if you can get a sight on whoever is firing at us and take a few out. They'll be in the ruins. You four give me and Jenkins a hand to see if we can tip these bloody guns over the edge. Come on.'

It took some time before they could move either gun. They had been propped up by bricks to ensure that the recoil did not send them back over the edge. All of the bricks therefore had to be cleared away, together with the bodies of the dead Chinese, before the heavy guns could be shifted.

'Now,' said Simon. 'Spin them round on their wheels and simply push them over the edge – but one at a time, in case we cause the tower to collapse further. And not the ladder side, for God's sake . . . !'

All of this was being done while the four marines were delivering a steady fire on whatever Chinese they could see amongst the debris down below. Fonthill looked over their shoulders. Strouts and his men had spread out among the ruins and were engaged in a lively exchange with mainly hidden adversaries. Looking down, Simon had a sudden idea.

He turned round. The marines were on the point of tipping the second Krupp gun over the edge. 'Stop,' he shouted. 'Pull it back.'

With ill grace, the sweating men did so. 'What's up?' asked Jenkins.

'I think we can use this thing before we throw it over.'

'Ah . . . what? Fire down on them lot, down there?'

'Why not? If we can depress it enough to fire down – and if we can find out how to load and fire it.'

Jenkins wiped the back of his wrist across his perspiring brow. 'Aw, it's just a matter of shovin' in a shell and pullin' the trigger, ain't it?'

'I doubt it.' He turned to the marines, standing at the wheels. 'Anyone know anything about artillery?' He was greeted by blank faces. But one of the men firing from the edge turned his head.

'I was a gunner for a time, sir.'

'Good. See if you can load this thing. You,' he indicated the men standing, 'pull the gun back, swivel it around and build up bricks under its trail to see if we can depress the muzzle.' He looked to the east. Was the sky brightening there? 'Come on, lads. Look lively. We haven't got much time. The rest of you keep firing.'

A shell was soon found and the marine opened the breech and inserted it into the groove, slamming the breech block over it. The gun was inched carefully on its wheels toward the edge facing the ruined retail area. Then the bricks were built up under the wooden trail that would normally attach it to the harness of the horses pulling it. This, of course, depressed the barrel. There seemed to be no sophisticated sights, so Fonthill directed the men to move the gun so that its barrel was roughly aimed at the middle of the rubble and timber from which the flashes of rifle fire could be seen.

A sudden thought struck him. 'Do we have to fuse the shell before we fire it?' he asked of the ex-gunner.

'Dunno, sir. Never had to do that bit.'

'Well, we'll just have to take a chance on that.' He sighted down the barrel of the gun. 'Come and look at this,' he ordered the marine. 'Laid like this, should we be able to land a shell amongst those riflemen?'

The ex-gunner squinted down the barrel. He waved his hand. 'Bit more elevation, sir.'

Fonthill removed a couple of bricks.

'That should do it, sir.'

'What's your name, marine?'

'Oakley, sir.'

Simon grinned. 'Let's hope you're a relative of . . . what was her name? Ah yes. Little Annie Oakley. Deadliest shot in the west. Can you fire this thing?'

'Oh yes, sir. That's the easiest part.'

'Right men. Stand back.'

Fonthill looked around him quickly. The space on top of the tower was rectangular, the size of a large tennis court, but much narrower. If the gun backfired in some way, then they could all be blown off the top, for it was firing from the narrowest part. If the bricks wedged under the wheels proved inadequate, then the recoil could take the gun and Oakley back over the edge. Would it work? There was only one way to find out. He nodded at Oakley. 'Fire!'

The report was deafening and the muzzle of the gun spurted flame. The bricks were sent scattering as the whole thing recoiled – but less than a foot and it did not implode. Instead, the explosion came from the middle of the ruins below them, roughly where the gun had been aimed. An inverted triangular-shaped sheet of flame sprang up, sending a shower of debris high into the air.

The marines on the tower sprang to their feet and waved their woolly hats, cheering. A similar but fainter cheer came from Strouts' men, down below.

'Oakley,' shouted Fonthill. 'Get another shell. I'd like to give 'em one more round to make 'em think we are going to keep up the shelling.'

The shell was found and inserted into the breech.

'Right, Oakley,' said Fonthill. 'Lay the gun to fire just a little back of where the last shell landed. You three, pile up the bricks again. You lads at the edge, keep up the musketry until we fire the gun, but start shimmying down that ladder like hell as soon as we have fired. The rest of us will cover you from up here.'

Once more the barrel was adjusted and once more the shell exploded satisfactorily in the target area.

'Good shot, Oakley,' shouted Simon. 'You'll be awarded a coconut when we get back. Now, let's all tip this gun over the edge. We can't hang about up here. You others, down the ladder as fast as you can. Once down, all of you sprint across to join Captain Strouts. Jenkins and I will cover you as best we can. Off you go.'

With an effort, the gun was reversed, wheeled to the opposite edge and given a final push that sent it tumbling down to land on its mate with a satisfying, metal-tearing crash.

Simon picked up two of the rifles left by the Chinese and the bandoliers that lay by their sleeping bags. Throwing a rifle and a bandolier to Jenkins, he crouched on the edge, joining the marines waiting to take their turn down the ladder. 'Can you see any of the men firing on our chaps?' he asked the man next to him.

'They were over there, sir,' said the marine, pointing. 'But I think the shells may have got most of them.'

'Good. Get down the ladder.'

Soon, only Fonthill and Jenkins were left on the top of the tower. Dawn was colouring the sky to the east. Simon looked to his right, to

116

the south, away from the ruins, where the narrow streets criss-crossed the Chinese City. Was it his imagination, or could he see figures running along them in the direction of the open space and the tower?

'Down you go, 352.'

'No, bach sir. I'll follow, look you.'

'No. You go first. Get on that ladder or I'll push you over. Here, give me that rifle and bandolier. I'll carry them. Get onto the first rung, face the wall and hold on to the side pieces. Oh, and think of the Queen. Go on, man. I can see Chinese troops running towards us. We don't want to be stuck up here. I promise not to pee on you.'

Jenkins forced a ghastly grin. 'Very kind, I'm sure.' But his legs were trembling as he reached with a tentative foot for the top rung.

Fonthill selected a couple of rounds from the bandoliers slung around his shoulders and inserted them into the breech of one of the Mausers – a rapid-firing rifle, much better than the old Martini-Henrys they carried. He fired them in the general direction of the figures he could now see running through the nearest street. The range was too extreme, of course, but it made him feel better. Then he swung himself onto the ladder.

Climbing down that ladder was one of the most frightening and frustrating journeys of Simon's life. His progress, of course, had to be geared to that of Jenkins who, with eyes tightly shut, seemed hardly to be moving as he groped his way down, one foot slowly feeling for the rung below it. At any moment, Fonthill felt that a hail of bullets would thud into their bodies. Looking down, he could see that all of the marines from the tower had been able to reach their comrades in the ruins, some hundred yards away. And they had stopped firing, presumably because the enemy had fled. Or had they, themselves, fled? He shuddered and plodded down, after Jenkins.

At last a cry of 'Oh, thank God for that' from below him showed that his comrade had reached the ground safely. The cry that quickly followed of 'Throw me a rifle, quick' showed that the Welshman had regained his normal equanimity. He tossed a rifle down, followed by one of the bandoliers.

It was at that moment that a bullet thudded into the brickwork to his left, followed by another, high above him to the right. Immediately, they were answered by Jenkins, who was now kneeling and coolly firing at figures running across the open ground towards them from the Chinese City. At the same moment, his shooting was supplemented by firing from the ruins. As Fonthill clung to the ladder, he saw at least a dozen Chinese soldiers brought down.

'Come on, bach,' called Jenkins. 'You're only a few feet up. You can jump down now. We've got to get out of here quick, see.'

Simon, encumbered by rifle, bandolier and cutlass, swivelled round and jumped, landing on all fours next to the Welshman. 'Right,' shouted Jenkins, 'our lads over there will cover us, look you. Run like hell.'

They did so and gained the cover of the ruins, where about fifteen marines were spread out behind the debris firing steadily.

'Where's Captain Strouts?' asked Fonthill of a stout, hugely moustached sergeant.

The man nodded. 'Over there, sir. Gone, I'm afraid. Bullet through 'is 'ead. Are you all down now, sir?'

'Yes.' Simon's voice was half choked with grief. 'Is this all you've got left of the party?'

The sergeant coolly sighted and let off another round. ''Fraid so, sir.'

He nodded over his shoulder. 'Got caught from be'ind us, so to speak. We've lost about 'alf our number. If you 'adn't started your fireworks up there, the rest of us would have got it, too. I think the Chinks be'ind us took fright at that.' He wiped his moustache with a dirty handkerchief. 'They don't like artillery, y'see, sir. Pity we don't 'ave a few more guns.' He regarded Fonthill respectfully. 'If I may say so, sir, you did a good job up there. But I do suggest now that we should bugger off back to the compound.' He nodded across the space to where flashes of rifle fire could be seen coming from the streets. 'I think we've got the rest of the Chinese army comin' after us.' Then he nodded behind him. 'And a few more be'ind us still to get through.'

Fonthill nodded. 'Of course, Sergeant. Do we have any wounded?'

'Only scratches, sir. Their firin' was quite good for savages. Got most of our blokes through the 'ead.'

'Right. I'm afraid we can't stay to bury them. I will take the lead, Sergeant, and I would be grateful if you would bring up the rear, with another good man. We may have to do a couple of bayonet charges to get through.'

'Very good, sir. Quite right. The Chinks don't like the bayonets, either. After you, then, sir.'

Three abreast, led by Fonthill and Jenkins, the remnants of the raiding party began their retreat. It became clear that the troops who had closed in behind Strouts' group as the tower was scaled had not been led efficiently, for they all seemed to have dispersed as a result of the shelling. There was no attempt to hinder the party as they trotted back towards the Tartar Wall. Not until, that is, they reached the point where they could see the sluice gates to their right and just ahead of them. Suddenly, with a howl, the street ahead was filled with

Chinese troops, brandishing swords and pikes.

Fonthill gulped. 'Fall into two lines across the street. Now,' he yelled. 'Front rank, kneel.'

The mob in front of them paused for a moment, as though mesmerised by these strange movements.

'Two volleys by ranks,' cried Simon. 'Front rank, fire!' The volley from eight rifles thundered out. 'Front rank, reload. Second rank, fire! Second rank, reload.'

The front line facing the little party seemed to disintegrate, leaving sixteen bodies lying on the harsh surface of the road. Fonthill looked up and saw anxious faces peering down at him from the top of the great wall. He prayed that they would be Americans. He hailed them: 'Open the sluice gates when we charge 'em.' There was no response. Had he been heard? He felt a tap on his shoulder.

'Beggin' your pardon, sir,' said the marine sergeant, as though interrupting a conversation at an officers' tea party. 'But a party of the enemy seems to be comin' up fast be'ind us. P'raps a bayonet charge, sir?'

Fonthill swallowed and tried to answer as coolly as the question had been put. 'Splendid idea, Sergeant,' he said. 'Thank you for your advice.' Then, turning, 'Marines! One more volley from the front rank then we all charge with the bayonet. Make for the sluice gates. Now, front rank, fire!' Then, as the smoke curled upwards: 'All ranks, charge!'

The marines bounded forward as one man, spreading out across the width of the street, their rifles and bayonets extending out in front of them, like a fast-moving, prickly hedge. The Chinese facing them immediately broke. Just two sword-wielding warriors attempted to get through the bayonet wall and were cut down for their bravery. Within seconds, the British had broken through and were running towards the canal opening where, thankfully, the sluice gates guarding it were gradually being winched open. From the ramparts up above came covering fire from the Americans lining the wall.

Jenkins, the sergeant and Fonthill were the last to splash through the opening before the gates began to close. The three stood with their backs to the wall, their breasts heaving.

'No more casualties, Sergeant?' gasped Simon.

'None since we left poor old Captain Strouts, sir.' He puffed out his cheeks. 'I'd call it a well-carried-out strategic withdrawal.'

'Good, thank you. Let's all go and have a cup of horrible coffee.'

Word had got out about the sortie and, despite the early hour, the party's return was greeted at the British Legation by an applauding group of diplomats and other civilians. Sir Claude clearly had not gone back to bed since seeing off the marines and he was waiting on the Residency steps. He shook Fonthill warmly by the hand and then his face dropped as he looked over his shoulder.

'Yes,' said Simon sadly, 'heavy casualties, I'm afraid, sir. We lost roughly half of our strength, including Captain Strouts. But we did destroy the guns.'

MacDonald's drooping face took on even more the expression of a bloodhound. He said nothing but retained Fonthill's hand, continuing to shake it.

Eventually, he said, 'It was a heavy price to pay, Fonthill, but I do believe that it will prove to have been worth it. Now go and get some breakfast and perhaps you would report to me in some detail when you feel up to it.'

Alice had not slept either and he found her, white-faced and crouching in her dressing gown, outside her sleeping quarters. She had not dared to see who were among the returning party and she could not restrain her tears when she saw him. For a time they did not exchange a word, merely holding each other.

'So you see, my luck has not run out yet, my love,' said Simon nuzzling his nose into her long, loose hair. 'Dear old 352 did look after me, although I have to report that he ruined his trousers.' She looked at him in some consternation. 'I'll tell you later,' he added hurriedly. 'Is there any very old, roast pony to be had?'

CHAPTER SIX

As though incensed by the success of the sortie, the Chinese stepped up their attacks on the perimeter, particularly on the Fu, where the Japanese held on stoically, giving ground when they had to, retaking it when the opportunity occurred. The defenders' casualties grew, however, and it became dangerous to walk across open ground within the compounds. A marine, a survivor of Fonthill's sortie, was shot and killed just outside the guardhouse by the main entrance to the British Legation. The Australian machine gun and then the American were hauled back to the Legation as a final precaution.

From the general direction of Tientsin, it was reported that searchlights could be seen probing the sky. The relief expedition, at last? Two rockets were sent up from the German compound but no reply was seen in the southern sky.

Overcrowding was becoming a problem in the British Legation, which housed most of the European civilians. The Dutch minister slept in a cupboard in the small house allotted to the Russian minister and the fifty-one members of his family and staff. Forty people now sat down to dinner each evening in Lady MacDonald's dining room. Cooking itself became a problem and the ornamental rockwork in the Legation grounds became an outdoor kitchen, where large kettles and pots were used for boiling the horsemeat by Chinese cooks, incongruously wearing frilly aprons.

The strain of the overcrowding and the growing danger from snipers' bullets and shrapnel fragments was particularly hard on the women. In the case of Mrs Griffith and the Fonthills, however, this was supplemented by the latters' resentment of Gerald, causing a rift to appear between them. The young man had ceased making his mysterious disappearances during the day, and now spent his time sitting near his sleeping quarters, ostentatiously reading medieval Chinese tomes in their original, archaic Mandarin.

'If he doesn't want to fight,' hissed Alice to her husband, 'why doesn't he at least give a hand in the hospital, or in the kitchens? Chang is pathetically anxious to attach himself to your marines – he cried when you didn't take him with you to destroy those guns.'

Fonthill nodded. 'Yes, the difference between the two is amazing. You would have thought it would be Chang, the native Chinaman, who would be pro-Boxer. But it's the other way around. Have you thought of having a word with your aunt about Gerald?'

'I have tried – very delicately – to raise the matter, because the fellow just sits around all day and this has been noticed by the other ladies. Mind you,' she sniffed, 'there are plenty of others. The Italian minister, for instance, the very noble Marchese Salvago Raggi, can't be more than thirty-six years old and looks perfectly fit. Yet he sits in a chaise longue most of the time chatting to his beautiful wife. And you know about that pathetic creature, Monsieur Pichon . . .'

Simon grinned. 'Yes, but what did your aunt say about Gerald?'

'Oh, she says that he is a very studious boy who is not cut out to be a soldier and, of course, she mothers him.' Alice sighed. 'Also, of course, she is still grieving for her husband. She is doing sterling work in the hospital, which keeps her mind off things. But I can't help thinking that she is a bit jealous of me – the fact that my husband is still alive.' She put her hand on Simon's arm. 'I feel so sorry for her, my dear, but I can't help her.

'The trouble is,' she went on, 'it has been a long time since you and I – with old 352, of course – were in danger, like this. But in those days I was serving with you, alongside you, sharing the dangers. You know: in Matabeleland, the Sudan, Afghanistan and so on.' She sighed. 'Now you go off, leading bayonet charges, putting guns out of action, and I'm stuck here, trying to wash bandages in muddy water.'

Fonthill regarded his wife with surging affection. One of the reasons he loved her so much was her intrepidity. All her life, she had remained cool under pressure, whether it was scribbling under fire to record a battle for the *Morning Post* or shooting a Boxer swordsman with a Colt revolver at forty paces. Their life together had been marred by misunderstandings at first, but since their wedding more than fifteen years ago, they had loved each other with an intellectual and physical passion. Their son, conceived in the sands of the Sudanese desert, had died in childbirth and Alice had been unable to give birth again. Now, in their middle age, they had settled into a strange but loving trio, with Jenkins, as comrade and servant, sharing in their affection.

Simon tucked a lank strand of her hair back under her headscarf. 'I know,' he said. 'I'm too bloody old to be leading bayonet charges, anyway. And Jenkins says if I get on a horse I will fall off it.'

'He always did say that.'

'He did and it's true – well, partly, though I would never admit it to him.' He pushed her away to look steadily into her eyes. 'You don't need to be soldiering, my love, you are doing wonderful work in the sickbay. And,' he smiled, 'I've noticed that you've been scribbling again. A letter to your lover? How are you going to smuggle it out?'

For a brief moment, Alice looked embarrassed. 'Yes,' she said, 'that's going to be the problem. You know the tall doctor in the hospital, Dr Morrison?'

'Well, I've seen him but I've not actually shaken his hand. At a quick glance, though, he should make a very satisfying lover, I would think.'

She gave him a playful push. 'Don't be silly. I only found out recently that, apart from his medical practice, he is the Peking correspondent of *The Times* – although, of course, he can't get any stories out of here now.'

'Quite. So?'

'So, he has stimulated me to start writing again. I've been keeping a diary so that, as soon as this siege is ended, I can write features, as well as report the news, for the *Morning Post*. I can't let the opposition get away with one of the best stories for years. I haven't really had anything published in the *Post* for months, apart from the odd piece I cabled from America. Although we can't know it, I bet the eyes of the world are on this godforsaken place, now. There will be great demand for stories from inside.'

Her eyes in her perspiring face were bright – brighter than Simon had seen them in weeks. He kissed her. 'Good,' he said. 'You could outscoop the stuffy old *Times* any day.'

Then Alice's eyes clouded over momentarily and she frowned. 'There is something I feel I ought to mention to you,' she said. 'It's probably absolutely nothing at all to be concerned about but . . .' She tailed away. 'Back to Gerald.'

'Yes. What about him?'

'Well . . .' She hesitated again, in some embarrassment.

'Go on.'

'Well . . .' Another pause. Then the words came out in a flood. 'He has started to pay me some sort of . . . er . . . attention. I don't think I am misunderstanding it, but he is being very, well, friendly.'

'Nothing wrong in that. It's about time he was friendly to *somebody*.'

'No, I mean . . . He has bought me flowers, little bundles of almond blossom, although goodness knows where he gets it from. And he finds an excuse to touch my hand. That sort of thing.' She gave an uncertain smile. 'It's ridiculous, I know, but I think he rather . . . you know . . .'

Fonthill's mouth dropped open. Then he recovered. 'But that *is* ridiculous. Oh, I'm sorry. That's rude of me. What I mean is that you are more than twenty years older than him and, dammit, you're the man's *cousin* for goodness sake. And, anyway, you're married.'

Alice put her hand on her husband's arm. 'I know all that, my dear,' she said with a touch of asperity. 'And, more to the point, he knows it too. I have done absolutely nothing to encourage him, I assure you. In fact, on the contrary, sometimes I have been almost rude to him, what with him lolling about while others are fighting, and so on. I've shown my disgust. I just don't know what's come over him.'

Simon sighed. 'Well, at least he is showing good judgement. You *are* an attractive woman, my love, and I suppose, what with the heat and everything . . .' He shrugged.

'Well, I wish he'd turn his attention somewhere else. There are plenty of very pretty Chinese girls about the place.'

'Would you like me to have a word with him? Play the aggrieved husband and that sort of thing. Warn him off, so to speak?'

'Oh, good Lord, no. There's really nothing one can take exception to. And if he does get out of hand, I can handle him. I'm a big girl now, Simon.'

Fonthill smiled. 'Hmm. Yes, I have noticed.' He pulled her to him and kissed her again. Then he wiped the perspiration from his brow and looked up at the sky. 'I don't blame young Gerald for getting broody. This bloody drought is enough to unbalance anybody. If only we could have a spot of rain. I can't remember when last I had a bath.'

The next day, as though on cue, the heavens opened.

Torrential rain thundered down on Peking, flooding the trenches in the compounds and beating down the precarious shelters and many parts of the barricades. The defending troops were forced to leave their posts to bail out and repair the defences, under rain that stung them like flying pebbles. If the Chinese had not been similarly hampered, they could have attacked and stormed unhindered into the legations.

Then, as suddenly as it had begun, the rain ended and the sun reappeared, not at all daunted by what had gone before. Immediately, the temperature rose to one hundred and ten degrees in the shade and a dreadful humidity descended to torture the defenders anew.

Fonthill was helping to shovel mud out of the trenches when a messenger found him and brought a request for him to report to Sir Claude's office. After a quick douche from a bucket and a rub down with a towel he complied.

His apologies for his appearance were waved aside by the minister. Some of the old imperturbability seemed to have left the tall, elegant man, although, despite the humidity, his tie was correctly knotted and his moustache still fiercely waxed. He smiled and nodded to a chair.

'Whisky?' he asked.

'No thank you, sir. Too early in the day for me and too hot.'

'Quite right. Shouldn't fall into bad habits, despite this bloody heat and the . . . er . . . conditions here.'

Simon nodded and waited. Something clearly was to be demanded of him, but better to keep quiet and wait for it. The minister looked tired and on edge. There was no doubt about it.

'Fonthill,' he began, sitting back in his chair. 'I have something to request of you.'

'Sir?'

'I would like to make clear that it is a request, not an order, you understand?'

Simon nodded again. Whatever it was, it was going to be difficult. Still he waited.

'Yes. Now.' MacDonald leant forward. 'This morning I received a message from a Chinese who managed to slip through the enemy lines. He came from Tientsin.' He gestured to a small slip of paper on his desk. 'It seems that there has been fighting there for some weeks now, with the result that the city is under some sort of siege, not quite as tightly as we are here, but surrounded nonetheless.'

Fonthill felt his jaw drop. So Gerald had been right! He waited for the minister to continue.

'There was a force sent to relieve us, of course, some time ago, but it couldn't get through via the railway and was rather badly mauled and had to fall back on Tientsin. War has broken out – although I am unsure if it has been formally declared on either side – but the Taku Forts at the entrance to the Pei Ho river have been taken by the Foreign Powers. All is by no means lost and reinforcements are expected daily from other foreign stations. Another relief force will be mounted. We are urged to . . .' MacDonald allowed his long features to lapse into a smile '. . . hold on.'

The minister settled back in his chair. 'And this,' he continued with emphasis, 'is what we *shall do*, of course. But the pressure here is tightening. The position on the Tartar Wall is particularly difficult, for the Americans and the Germans are exposed on the skyline, as you know. Indeed,' he flipped another piece of paper on his desk, 'the American minister has today asked my permission to abandon the barricade there. I have refused, of course. It would expose all of the southern part of the Quarter to fire from the Wall. The minister has accepted this and promised to hold on.

'You will also know that we are under great pressure on the Fu. The Japanese there are doing a wonderful job and, unlike some of the other nationalities, I get no complaints from them. No panic-influenced requests from them for reinforcements. When *they* ask for men, I jump to it, I can tell you.'

'Nevertheless, the point is, my dear Fonthill, that we *can* hold on.

But I must be realistic. Food and ammunition are low – we have only fourteen rounds left for our little Italian gun, for instance. We have just enough men to man the perimeter, we don't have the space to reduce it further and our casualties are mounting. You see . . .' He let the words hang in the air for a moment. 'We really don't have all the time in the world and our people in Tientsin must be told that we need to be relieved as a matter of urgency – of *prime* urgency, in fact. They seem unaware of this.'

'Ah.' Simon nodded his head, seeing the point of the interview at last. 'And you want someone to take this message to the relief column?'

'Indeed.'

A silence hung in the heavy air for a moment. It was broken by Fonthill. 'But why me? Wouldn't it be better – safer and more effective – to send the request via a Chinese messenger? Someone who would be better equipped to slip through the enemy lines and a hostile countryside. Surely, a European would stand out like a sore thumb?'

'Quite so. These seem the obvious points. But there are strong reasons why I do not wish to entrust this communiqué to a Chinese.'

He leant forward in his chair. 'I have sent four separate messages, containing questions, to Tientsin since we have been besieged. They have been carried by native Chinese whom I thought I could trust. It seems clear to me now that none of these messages has been delivered, for this message now received seems to be singularly relaxed about the urgency of our position here and it answers none of my questions. I am sure that if these messengers had been captured, then I would have heard. There would certainly have been some references to them in this strange dialogue I continue to hold with the Manchu court.'

'So – what happened to them, do you think?'

'I believe that the messengers just absconded with them without making any attempt to deliver them. The Chinese are like that, you know.' He gave a sad smile. 'No. This time, I want someone reliable – someone resourceful – to get through to the relief column. There is an additional point in this context. I want the messenger to have a strategic appreciation of our position here. Someone with military – not diplomatic – experience, who can advise the commander of the relief column on the best way to enter the city and to attack our besiegers. I can't think of anyone who could do this better than you, my dear fellow. After all, you got through the Mahdi's hordes surrounding Khartoum to get a message through to Gordon, did you not?'

Fonthill smiled wryly. 'I was a bit younger then, sir.'

MacDonald sighed. 'My dear Fonthill, in the last few weeks you have led at least two bayonet charges against the enemy, you have climbed a forty-five-foot tower and destroyed two large guns and you have worked seemingly non-stop to keep our defences in good order. Indeed, I am told that when you received my request to come to the office, you were working with the coolies digging out a trench. I can't think of a fitter, more qualified man for this dangerous mission.'

'Well, thank you, sir. There is, however, the question of appearance. A European surely would be recognised quickly in this countryside. It would be particularly difficult to get through the besiegers here and at Tientsin.'

'I have thought of that. Both you and your man – er . . . 352, isn't it?'

'Well done, sir. Yes.'

Sir Claude gave a distant smile. 'Yes. I presume that you would wish to take him with you?'

'Yes, indeed.'

'Well, both you and he have high cheekbones and are not extraordinarily tall. That's a good start. I suggest that we disguise the pair of you as Kansu soldiers from the north. They are more Mongolian than indigenous Chinese and their facial features change considerably from man to man. We have captured several of these chaps and their uniforms are quite distinctive. They straight away proclaim that the fellows wearing them are Kansu. We can dress you up quite well.'

'What about a guide? Jenkins and I just don't know the territory.'

The minister stirred in his chair, a trifle uncomfortably. 'I can offer you your choice of a dozen or more reasonably reliable Chinese. Trouble is, I fear they are not completely to be trusted. But I agree you must have someone.'

'Ah!' Simon slapped his thigh. 'I have it! We will take Chang, the Reverend Griffith's adopted son. He is as keen as mustard, speaks the language like a native, of course, and I know has made the journey to and from Tientsin several times.'

'Good.' The faint smile returned to Sir Claude's long features. 'You will accept, then?'

'Of course. I see the importance of it, although,' he frowned, 'I know my wife won't like it.' He leant forward. 'And I have to confess that I am worried about leaving her here. Without myself and Jenkins, who would protect her if the worst comes to the worst?'

'On that point, Fonthill, you must be assured. I will personally undertake responsibility for her safety, even if the Chinese do break through. She will be as important to me as is my wife. She will be part of my family, so to speak, and, in any case, I am confident that the

Empress will not wish to see any of the ministers, or their families, harmed, in the unlikely event of there being a breakthrough. It would mean the end of the Manchu court, for the revenge of the Western powers would be punitive. The Empress will know that.'

Fonthill was not convinced but he decided to say nothing. 'Very well. When do you wish us to go?'

'As soon as possible. We have garments for you. I suggest you leave the Quarter at night, perhaps tomorrow, just after sunrise? The safest way, I suggest, is through the sewer hole in the wall. Not pleasant, I fear, but, as far as we can see, it is not guarded by the Chinese. It is quite small but men singly can slip through it easily.'

'Very good, sir. Tomorrow night it shall be.' Fonthill and the minister rose and shook hands.

As he predicted, Alice was incensed at the news. She argued strongly that two Occidentals would easily be detected, from their physical appearance and their language. Capture would be inevitable and it simply would not be possible to talk their way out of it. If they insisted on undertaking the mission, then she would go with them. A woman with the party would reduce the risk of being taken for spies and, anyway, she was damned if she was going to be left behind to become another widow holed up in Peking!

It took all of Simon's persuasive powers to induce her to change her stance. It would be far more difficult to disguise her appearance, with her fair hair and grey eyes. And the worry of having her with them, he argued, would adversely affect his ability to lead the mission.

Then the problem arose of how to explain Chang's absence to his mother. The youth was anxious enough to take part but, if Gerald, for all his new seeming affection for Alice, was, in fact, relaying information to the enemy, then he must not be made aware of the mission. In the end, it was agreed that Chang would leave a message for Mrs Griffith, explaining that he had been seconded to the American Legation for special duties and that, long after their departure, Alice would find a way of explaining, as diplomatically as possible, the real reason for his absence.

The next morning, the trio assembled in the privacy of MacDonald's office to be fitted by Lady MacDonald with their disguises. The minister's wife, tall and as elegant as her husband, bestowed as much enthusiasm for getting their costumes right as she did for dressing the participants in her very popular annual pantomimes.

None of the garments, which had been stripped from prisoners and washed carefully, fitted, but they were sufficiently voluminous for this not to matter. Each wore a canvas cap reminiscent of that of a scullery maid in an upper-class British house; long, smock-type coats, emblazoned with Chinese symbols proclaiming their allegiance to their leader, Tung Fu-hsiang; baggy cotton trousers; and single-strap sandals, through the front of which their toes poked. Heavy bandoliers were carried, either crossways or around their waists, and straight, short swords were thrust through their belts.

'What about rifles?' asked Jenkins. 'I don't fancy going halfway across China without our Henry-Martinis.'

'Certainly not,' replied Fonthill. 'Carrying two British rifles would betray us straightaway. We take the two Mausers we picked up at the tower. And Chang still has one of our two Colts. I wish to leave the other with Alice.'

'What if we are stopped?' asked Chang. 'What do I say about you not speaking Chinese? And where do I say we are going? This could be frightfully difficult, don't you think?'

Sir Claude, who had been an interested observer of the dressing-up, smiled at the young man's colloquialism. 'Some of these Kansus,' he said, 'are really Tartars from over the northern frontier who don't speak any of the Chinese tongues. I suggest you explain this and say that you are anxious to take part in the fighting at Tientsin and that you are guiding them there.'

Chang nodded. 'Yes, thank you, sir. I think I could do that jolly well.'

'You look Oriental enough at a quick glance,' said Lady MacDonald, standing back to admire her handiwork. 'Just keep your hats well down over your foreheads. And if you, Mr Jenkins, could grow the ends of your moustache so that they trail down either side of your mouth, in the Chinese style, that would help.'

'Well, I'll try, milady. But this moustache has had a life of its own for nearly forty years, now, and it takes no notice of me, see.'

'Yes, well try, there's a good fellow.'

They all shook hands, wrapped up their Chinese clothes into bundles and went to their bunks to try and gain some sleep before their departure. Then, as desultory firing marked the end of the daylight, they followed the open sewer down to where it swept through a passage in the Legation wall. Alice, who had accompanied them this far, held her nose and then kissed her husband goodbye.

'If you don't come back, I shall kill you,' she whispered into his ear.

Then to Jenkins: '352, if it looks as though he's going to try something heroic, shoot him in the leg.' She was smiling but also crying as she spoke.

CHAPTER SEVEN

The trio were able to pick their way through the tunnel on the banks on either side of the odiferous water and crawl round the low gates. There, they paused. The moon had not risen and the street was dark. To the right, in the distance, figures could be seen but there was no one to their left.

'That way,' said Fonthill. 'Stride purposefully, as though we know where we are going.'

'Mind you don't trip over my moustache,' said Jenkins. 'I'm growin' the ends, yer see,' he explained helpfully to Chang.

'No talking,' hissed Simon. 'Take the lead, Chang. Get us out of the city as quickly as you can. Will the gates be guarded?'

'I do not know, cousin. But if they are, I think they only question people coming in, not going out.'

'Good.'

Even though the hour was late, they met many people as they made their way through the narrow streets, including small groups of Boxers, distinguished by their youth and the red bands they wore round their foreheads, midriffs and ankles. They also had to thrust their way through milling crowds of garishly uniformed Imperial soldiers. But they kept their heads down and no one accosted them. In fact, they were given respectful passageway whenever there was a crowd and Simon recalled being told that the Kansu soldiery had a reputation for fierceness – to friend and foe alike.

They passed through the Tung Pien Men Gate as the moon rose, and Fonthill hardly recognised the countryside from what he remembered from their entry into the city less than a month ago. The rains, although short, had been very heavy and the fields had blossomed as a result. The road had become muddy and the ditches were now running with water.

There had been no time for a proper consultation about their route. Chang had been relied on to find the best and quickest way to Tientsin, some eighty miles away. Although making haste was imperative, it had not been possible to provide them with transport. There were now only nine ponies left within the Quarter. But there would have been no way for them to have ridden out through the defensive perimeter and, anyway, the mounts were needed for food. It was presumed that they would walk to Tientsin and somehow pick up either the relief column limping back to the town or the new one marching – for the railway link had been broken – to the north-west to relieve the legations.

Now, however, lifting one muddy foot after another, Simon had another idea.

'Where are we making for?' he asked Chang.

'We make for my home village. It is on the way to Tientsin. Perhaps we can shelter for the night in our home.'

'No. Too dangerous. You might be recognised. We march through the night and lie up somewhere during the day. It will be safer that way. But Chang, tell me: the River Pei Ho is somewhere quite near, to our left as we look now. Is that right?'

'Oh yes. Quite precisely, cousin.'

'And the river has traffic on it? Trading junks and so on?'

'Yes.'

'Where does the river come out at the coast?'

'At Taku, where ships of Great Powers lie.' Chang frowned in concentration, perspiration running down his face as they walked, for the humidity remained high. 'It is about twenty miles past Tientsin. Everyone think Tientsin is big seaport. But, in fact, it is river port, lying inland.'

Simon nodded. 'Yes, I know. Well, Chang,' he spoke deferentially, 'if you agree, I think we'll change our plans. It will take us a long time to walk to Tientsin at this rate and we are likely to be picked up and questioned at any time.'

'Quite so. Oh, I agree. But . . . er . . . what do we do?'

'We make for the river on our left. I have money. We hire a junk that is sailing south-east, towards the coast. We get off when we have news of either the old expedition retreating or of a new one advancing. With the current taking us to the sea we will be much quicker and,' he frowned, 'time is of the essence.'

Jenkins looked up and beamed. 'What, sail instead of walk? What an incredibly good idea, bach sir. 'Ere, just a minute. Are there any crocodiles in this river, Changy?'

'No, Mr Jenkins. I don't think so.'

'Good. Not that I was worried, mind you. But they . . . er . . . do tend to clog the river, look you. And we want to get a move on.'

Chang smiled. 'I think it excellent idea, cousin. We are here, I think, about six, seven miles to river. Turn off at next crossing.'

It took them, however, about another three hours of trudging through the mud before they found the turning, onto a smaller track that now wound through fields of *kaoliang* that stood well over head high following the rains. At first, this gave Fonthill a feeling of security, for visibility was now considerably reduced and he did not feel as exposed as when on the open plain. This was soon replaced, however, by unease as he realised that they could stumble upon a Chinese patrol in the darkness without warning. He called a halt.

'We are all tired,' he said, 'so I think we will try and get a couple of hours' sleep before we go on. Let us try and find sufficient space among the maize to lie down. It should be safe enough on this little road to walk in daylight, so we will press on at dawn.'

They found a gap in the *kaoliang,* on slightly higher and drier ground, big enough for them to lie down, wrapped in their waterproof capes. Before trying to find sleep, Simon had second thoughts on their story, if stopped.

'We must change our explanation now if we are accosted,' he told Chang. 'Say that we are going to the river to pick up a junk to take us to Tientsin because we have a message from our general, what's his name?'

'Tung Fu-hsiang.'

'That's the fellow. Say that we are taking a message from him to the general commanding the Imperial forces at Tientsin and that we are taking a boat at the river.' He smiled at the young man. 'If we do get stopped, Chang, we must rely on you to talk us out of it.'

'Oh yes. I do that well, I think, cousin. Rely on me.'

Simon nodded and offered up a silent prayer that the missionary's son's Chinese was less stilted than his English. Their reliance on him was total.

That reliance was called into play far quicker than he would have liked after they rose, shortly after dawn, and continued their journey. Within minutes they rounded a bend in the path and came upon three horsemen, dressed in the flamboyant colours of the Imperial cavalry, topped by black turbans, walking their horses towards them.

Taking the lead, Fonthill stepped to one side deferentially, into the maize, to allow the horsemen to pass. He gave a stiff incline of the head to acknowledge the seniority of the lead horseman and kept his eyes to the ground.

The horseman, seemingly an officer, pulled to a stop and addressed a question to Simon, who gestured mutely to Chang. The two exchanged words for a moment and Fonthill clutched to himself a half-forgotten statistic that less than nought point one per cent of Chinese people had ever seen, let alone talked to a European. He just hoped that this cavalry officer was part of that majority.

The conversation went on interminably, or so it seemed to Fonthill. Out of the corner of his eye he saw Jenkins, his black eyes gleaming from underneath his cap – no subservience here – slowly unsling his rifle.

Then, with a grunt, the officer kicked in his heels and the three horsemen rode away slowly, disappearing as quickly as they had appeared. Simon put his finger to his lips then gestured with his head and the three walked on.

After two minutes, Fonthill called a halt. 'What did he say?' he asked Chang.

A thin line of perspiration had appeared on the young Chinaman's upper lip. 'He don't seem to believe me,' he said, his eyes wide. 'He said that he had served in Peking and knew that Kansu soldiers were manning northern parts of the legations' defence and fighting particularly in the Fu, and that Kansu soldiers not allowed in the southern part of city. He asked me name of Chinese commander in Tientsin to whom we take the message.'

'Oh Lord. What did you say?'

'I invent a name – in Chinese like English Smith. I very afraid he would know man. But he rode away.'

Simon smiled. 'You did very well, cousin,' he said. 'But I think we should move quickly now and get to this damned river.'

'Shush.' Jenkins held up a hand. He was lying prone, with his ear to the ground. 'They're coming back – and galloping.'

'Quickly. Into the maize. If we have to fight, we use swords. No shooting. There might be other patrols about.'

Chang's face paled. 'Oh golly.' But he followed Simon into the *kaoliang*, while Jenkins ducked into the other side.

Within seconds, the three cavalrymen thundered round the bend, their heads low over the mane of their horses and their swords drawn. They swept by with scarcely a glance into the tall growth on either side and disappeared once again, in the direction of the river.

'They will be back.' Simon stood for a moment, deep in thought.

Then: 'Chang, you walk back a few paces and then lie face down across the path . . .'

Chang gave an exclamation in Chinese, and was joined by Jenkins. 'Blimey, why . . . ?'

Fonthill tossed his head impatiently. 'I want to disconcert them. They will stop for a moment wondering what the hell to do. You and I, 352, will be in the maize behind them by this bend. As soon as they have passed us and their attention is drawn to Chang, we will spring out behind them and bring them down. Swords, remember. No shooting.'

'Then I get up and fight, yes?' Chang's eyes were bright.

'No, be lying on your sword but don't move until we do. If you are attacked run back into the crop. Quick now. They will be back soon. Further back into the maize this time, 352. They will be looking for us in there.'

Once more the two comrades plunged into the tall crop, but this time Fonthill's heart was in his mouth. Leaving the boy out there was taking an awful risk. Would they be able to bring down the two men in the rear before the lead rider realised what was happening? And would he ride on and attack Chang anyway? The boy would stand no chance against an experienced cavalryman. He gulped. But there was no further time for introspection. There was no sound but suddenly, peering low between the stalks, he saw the officer, walking his horse slowly and looking carefully into the *kaoliang* on either side of him. Then the other two came into view, walking their horses side by side. Simon offered up a silent prayer that Jenkins had penetrated deeply enough to be out of sight.

Then he heard a loud exclamation. Chang had been seen. Simon

143

plunged through the tall stalks, crushing them, and emerged in time to see Chang, sword in hand, standing and defying the officer, whose horse was rearing. Damn! The stupid boy was fighting! The cavalryman on Simon's side of the path was trying to quieten his own horse and had his back to him. Fonthill paused for a split second and then he gulped, sprang forward and, reaching up, he thrust the point of his heavy blade through the man's side, feeling it scrape bone. With his other hand, he grabbed the man's belt and pulled him to the ground and delivered the *coup de grâce* to his breast. As he did so he felt a thunderous blow to his back, sending him pitching forward and his sword spinning away.

He lay for several seconds as the hooves of horses crashed to the ground all around him, one of them delivering a second blow, this time to his calf. He heard the cry of 'Roll over, bach, to yer right' and he did so, his hands to his head to protect his face. Half into the maize, he staggered to his feet and saw Jenkins, the blade of a bloodstained sword between his teeth, standing between the two rear horses in the narrow path, holding onto their reins and trying to sooth them. To his right and ahead, however, a far more fascinating battle was taking place.

The officer was trying to control his rearing horse and, at the same time, deliver slashing blows to Chang, who was ducking and weaving away from the blade. As he watched, he saw the boy slash at the soldier's thigh, causing blood to burst out from just above the boot. Then he slapped the rear of the horse with the flat of his blade, causing the beast to rear again, sending the wounded cavalryman sliding to the ground, where the young man thrust his blade through the man's throat.

''Old on to that bloody 'orse, Changy,' roared Jenkins. 'We don't want to walk anymore. Don't let 'im charge away.'

The boy threw down his sword and grabbed the reins of the startled beast, holding on and circling with it as it continued to rear and whinny, as though in despair at the death of his master.

Fonthill stood, his breast heaving, and surveyed the scene. The three cavalrymen all lay on the pathway, in different postures but all dead from sword thrusts. The three horses were now becoming quiescent. Chang and Jenkins seemed unharmed and Simon straightened his back gingerly and lifted his leg. There were two stabs of pain but neither was severe. Probably the result of bruising; nothing broken, it seemed. He walked forward to take one of the horses from Jenkins.

'Well done, lads,' he said. 'Bit of a bloodbath, I'm afraid. Good Lord, Chang. You fought like a dervish.'

The boy, his face glistening with sweat, grinned. 'What is "dervish", cousin?'

'I hope you never have to find out, old chap. Let's say he's just a bloody good fighter. Like you. Now, Chang, take the reins of the horses, they seem all right now. 352 – are you all right?'

The great chest of the Welshman was heaving, but he nodded. 'Yes, thank you. But I'm gettin' a bit old for this sort of thing. I think all this effort has opened up this old wound in me arm, but it's not bleedin' much. Got an earwig in me ear, though.'

'All right. You take the horses, then. Chang, help me lift these bodies into the side, out of sight into the maize. I don't want to leave any evidence. That's it. Good man.'

Within ten minutes the site was cleared, only three distinct patches of blood staining the pathway to show where three men had died.

Simon pushed dust over them with his sandal. Then he walked to study the saddles and accoutrements of the horses.

'If we are going to take these horses – and we definitely are – then we don't want us to appear to be riding Imperial cavalry mounts,' he explained. 'Here, lend me your knife, 352. I think I can cut this fancy stuff away. Rough old Kansu infantrymen wouldn't be riding like bloody medieval knights.'

In a moment the job was done. Fonthill delayed long enough to inspect the old wound in Jenkins's arm, which had now stopped bleeding, and the three of them mounted and resumed their trek to the river. Once on horseback, Simon realised that he was trembling. Killing a man at long range with a rifle shot was one thing. Stabbing him from the back with a sword was another and his lip curled and he shook his head. Was he becoming some sort of monster? What would Alice think of him if she had witnessed the mini battle on the pathway, not to mention the bayoneting of sleeping men at the tower? And was he training a sixteen-year-old boy to become a killer? He rode in silence for a while, his head down.

Jenkins noticed and gently urged his mount forward so that they rode side by side. 'She said you were to come back, bach sir,' he said, eventually. 'So you've got to think of yourself, like. It's the old story. It was them or us. Same as it always is. Goodness gracious me, we've done it enough times. Can't be 'elped. It's the life we lead, see.'

Fonthill slowly nodded. 'I suppose you're right. But I really felt that we'd left all that behind us.'

'So did I. But I knew somethin' was up as soon as we stepped off that ship. I sniffed the air, like, and I knew we was back in it. But we didn't look for it, now did we? So it can't be 'elped. An' those blokes was comin' back to get us right enough, weren't they? So don't think about it.' Jenkins paused for a moment, then he gave Fonthill a sly, sideways smile. 'Anyway,' he went on, 'you've got to admit that, for most of the time, it's fun, ain't it?'

Simon looked at him and returned half a smile. 'I wouldn't call it fun,' he said, 'though I grant that it's exciting.' Then the remnant of the smile slipped away. 'But sometimes it's just bloody horrific.'

They rode in silence for a while. Then Jenkins sniffed. 'As long as young Changy wasn't lyin' about them crocodiles,' he said, 'I don't mind a bit of a sail, see.' And he gave that great, moustache-bending smile of his that immediately made Simon feel better.

They came to the river without further incident: the brown, turgid, not-so-very-wide highway that, hopefully, was to lead them to Tientsin and – even more hopefully – the relief column. There was not so much traffic on it, as Simon had hoped, and Chang's questioning of a fisherman on the banks provided the reason.

'He says, cousin, that further down – about twelve miles, perhaps more – is where the great foreign army decided to turn back from the railway and go back to Tientsin by river. They take a lot of junks. That is why we see not many boats now.'

'Ah, so they have turned back, dammit.' Fonthill frowned. 'All that great expectancy and hope from the legations! Ask him if he knows if another army is coming to Peking.'

Eventually, Chang shrugged his shoulders. 'He don't know, but he think that army going back has been defeated many times. Many *yang kuei-tzu* killed. But he say we come to village soon. Can hire junk there, he thinks.'

147

'Good. Let's get on with it, then.'

Simon's mind turned over. How badly had the relief column been mauled? Pretty badly if they had been forced to turn back. And if Tientsin itself was besieged, what hope of another force being gathered in time to relieve Peking? The besieged in the river port would surely have enough on their plate. The prospect was depressing. He shrugged his shoulders and dug his heels into his horse's side. Their task was clear. They had to persuade somebody in command in the south that the legations' plight was desperate and that time was short.

The village was small but it was a trading point where jobbing junks called in to pick up cargoes, usually of rice or grain, to take north and south. While Fonthill and Jenkins remained watering the horses, Chang, now bearing himself with the confidence of a soldier who had killed his first man, went into the village. He came back within ten minutes, his young face carrying an earnest expression.

'There is a junk that can take us and horses downriver. He has oats for horses. It leaves soon so we must be jolly quick.'

Fonthill patted his shoulder. 'Good man. How far can he take us?'

'Ah, that is the point. He says he cannot take us to Tientsin. There is much fighting just above there. Foreign troops are there. Chinese army attack them.'

'Very well. We will go as far as we can with him. Let's go to the battle.' But Simon was not as sanguine as he sounded. Fighting! How were they going to get through the lines? If they could persuade the Chinese to let them get through to the actual combat, how to prevent the British from killing them as the enemy? He shrugged. Ah well, they would have to face those problems when they came to them.

They trotted their horses through the hamlet to a wooden loading stage that jutted out into the river, where an old junk was moored. The two-man crew was adjusting a canvas cover over the open hold and the captain, a wizened, tiny man with skullcap and pigtail, looked with trepidation at first at the three wild men of the north, with their stained clothing, rifles and bandoliers, but bowed low and smiled over the handful of coins that Simon gave him. The horses, uneasy at the swell that rocked the boat, were tethered to a rail and given a feed from a sack full of oats. The three comrades sat down gratefully at the stern of the junk and accepted bowls of rice as the square sails were raised and the boat eased out into the gently flowing current.

'Now this,' observed Jenkins quietly, 'is the way to travel.' He looked out with approval at the unbroken, brown water. 'I don't care if there are crocodiles out there, because, look you, I 'ave no intention at all of takin' a dip today. I shall just sit 'ere all day and contemplate life. I am now too old to be swimmin' about an' killin' people.'

Chang, now a fully qualified member of the trio and having, at last, begun to comprehend the Welshman's idiosyncrasies, beamed with approval. Simon scowled. 'For goodness' sake, 352, keep your voice down. We're supposed to be Kansu soldiers.'

'With great respect, bach sir, I was merely makin' an observation in a very low voice. If these Chinese blokes pullin' on the ropes 'eard me, they would just as likely think I was speakin' Kansu talk.'

'Ah, that reminds me.' Simon looked up at the blessedly weak sun. 'Which way is east? Yes, there. When we've finished the rice, it will be time for us to pray.'

Chang nodded understandingly but Jenkins's jaw dropped. 'Eh?'

'Kansus are Muslims and Muslims are supposed to pray five times a day. We must face the east, kneel, bend down with our foreheads on the deck and say something incomprehensible. It could be important later if we are stopped and the captain is questioned.'

'Ah, very good. I'll give 'em a bit of Welsh.'

They carried out their devotions, much to the consternation of the crew, and Fonthill instructed Chang to explain the reason for them. Then Simon sat in the stern, inspecting a rough, hand-drawn map of Tientsin and its environs that Sir Claude had given him.

As Chang had explained, the city itself lay some twenty-five to thirty miles inland from the Taku Forts that guarded the entrance to the river on which it lay. Tientsin itself was a native walled city but, unlike Peking, the foreign holdings or settlements were discrete and situated outside the city itself to the south. The Pei Ho and the railway wound their way in parallel north-west from Tientsin towards Peking for some twenty miles or so before parting company at Yangtsun, where the essential rail bridge had been destroyed and from which the relief column, it seemed, had turned back and taken to the river for its retreat. But it seemed that the column had not reached Tientsin. Was it being held up by the force of Chinese arms or was it simply resting and recuperating? Sir Claude's message had implied that the city was invested, but how strongly? And was it the settlements that were under siege or the city itself? Surely, it should be possible for the defenders, whatever they were defending, to link up with the retreating relief force? Depending upon how fierce the opposition was to the remnants of the British force as they trudged south, they should not be too far from the city.

Simon shook his head. Too many imponderables! It seemed to make sense for him and his comrades to try and contact the relief force, rather than try to reach Tientsin. They must surely be nearest and, depending upon how many casualties they had suffered, perhaps the commander of the column could be persuaded to turn back towards Peking, given the dire nature of the defenders there?

Right. That was decided. He folded the map. They would get through to the British force, somewhere downriver of them. But they must make haste!

All day they bowled along, swept by a following wind as well as by the river itself. Chang and Jenkins dosed intermittently, for it was soporific, lying back in the stern, their heads on their waterproofs, sleepy eyes taking in the sparse river traffic – small junks, tacking against wind and current and skiffs, flitting across the water like insects, most of them making their way upstream, away, it seemed, from the fighting. Fonthill, however, stayed awake, his hand not far from his rifle, his eyes on the banks of the river.

Soon he witnessed signs of battle. The vegetation on the banks on both sides had recently been beaten down and the soil trampled as far as he could see. Here, the river was dominated by the railway embankment which ran parallel to it and the banks on both sides were pitted by craters – shell holes, presumably, showing that the British had come under fire from guns mounted on railway carriages. Rickety buildings creeping down to the water in a succession of villages all showed bullet holes in their walls. Leaning over, Fonthill could see the bottom of the river. It was extremely shallow. Had the British junks run aground and the men been forced to land and haul them off the shoals? And it looked as though each village had had to be taken by force before the boats could continue. It must have been a hell of a journey, under fire and in the heat.

Now, traffic had ceased on the water but both banks were busy highways for Chinese troops of all descriptions, wearing various uniforms and in individual groups. Not an army, more a ragbag collection of soldiers straggling – not marching – along. They were all heading south and curious eyes were cast towards this solitary junk.

Simon felt uncomfortable, for even though he and his two companions were not easily visible, lying low beneath the deck sides of the vessel, the horses, with their military saddles, could clearly be seen. He sat up, for, faraway but clearly, he could hear the sound of shellfire. It was time to leave the river.

He roused his comrades and looked ahead. Dusk was falling but he welcomed that. It would be safer to land in the darkness, but where? He beckoned to Chang. 'Tell the captain that we must soon go ashore,' he said. 'Is there a landing place soon where it will be easy to land the horses?'

It was clear that the captain was not anxious to keep his passengers now that gunfire could be heard. 'He says, soon,' reported Chang. 'Round the bend is landing place. Road goes away from river here but about a mile to south is great arsenal of Hsiku Arsenal. He don't know what this is but he thinks British have captured it and are fighting there.'

'Splendid.' He felt in his pocket for more coins. 'Give him these with our thanks. Tell him to land us there.'

Dusk settled on them comfortingly as the junk was steered towards where another wooden landing stage leant out into the river. Simon scoured the area with his eyes but he could see no one. He turned to Chang. 'New story now, cousin,' he said with a grin. 'Now we are just three Kansu cavalrymen from the north who were sent scouting and lost their way. We are now looking for the front line to join in the fighting.'

As the sail was lowered and the boat was held to the landing stage with boathooks, the trio led their horses ashore and then mounted them. With a wave to the sailors they clattered away in the lowering darkness.

'Nice, enjoyable little sail,' observed Jenkins. 'Now what do we do?'

'We try and find where the British are fighting and then play it by ear.'

'What is this "playing by ear"?' enquired Chang. 'Is it a game?'

Fonthill grinned. 'Not exactly, old chap. We react according to the circumstances. But we must somehow get through the Chinese lines and cross the British defences without both sides killing us. Yes, well, put like that, I suppose it is a sort of game. Trouble is, I don't know the rules. Come on. Let's ride with a sense of purpose, as though we are under orders.'

They kicked their horses into a canter and rode through a shell-scarred thicket before finding the road. Most of the groups of Chinese troops had halted their journey southwards and had bivouacked for the night. Fires had been lit and bedrolls laid out. The trio rode on determinedly. Several times they were challenged – greeted? – but Fonthill gave a cheery wave and cantered by. Luckily, they met no other cavalry and saw no other Kansu soldiers.

The firing ahead seemed to have died away with the onset of darkness but, looming up ahead, on the banks of the river, they saw the blackness of a great building. Before they could get near to it they met a Chinese sentry, rifle slung across his shoulders. Chang trotted forward and engaged in conversation with the man for several minutes.

He came back grinning. 'He think I am blooming Kansu and he afraid of me, all right,' he said.

Fonthill nodded. 'Glad to hear it,' he said. 'But what is ahead?'

'Ah yes. Big building ahead is big place for Chinese weapons, ammunition et cetera. It is called Hsiku Arsenal. British have taken it and Chinese are very mad. Imperial army is now trying to take it back. So far they don't do it.'

'Good Lord! I suppose that's the remnants of the relief column. Are the Chinese attacking during the night?'

'No. Wait till morning.'

'Good, then that's what we'll do.' He turned his head. 'Let's get back into those woods and find a place to tether the horses and lie down for a few hours.'

Jenkins grinned in approval. 'Good idea, bach sir. I've 'ad a busy day. But what do we do in the morning? 'Ow do we get through the lines?'

'I don't know but I'll think of something. Come on, into the woods.'

They rested through the darkest hours, although only Jenkins slept well. As dawn was lightening the sky to the east, they rose, rubbed down the horses as best they could and mounted. The firing had not yet recommenced. They sat uncertainly for a moment.

Then: 'Have you got a spare vest in your pack?' Simon asked Jenkins.

The Welshman's jaw dropped. 'A what?'

'A spare undervest. And is it white?'

'Well, sort of. I washed it before we left.'

'Good. Get it out and tie it to this rifle.'

Jenkins shook his head in disbelief. 'Blessed and wonderful are the ways of the officer class,' he muttered as he unrolled his slender pack. He had attended Sunday school chapel as a child.

One arm of the vest was tightly knotted round the muzzle of Fonthill's Mauser and the other to the breech just before the trigger guard. Simon nodded in approval but held the rifle low so that the vest hung downwards.

'Now,' he said, 'this is no longer the disgusting undergarment of a very dirty Welsh Kansu soldier—'

''Ere, steady on,' interrupted Jenkins.

'. . . but a flag of truce, although it won't be raised until we get to the front line. There, we will ride in a V formation towards the gate of the arsenal, you two behind me, sitting very upright, and me in the lead, carrying the flag, as though we are an official delegation come to parley.'

'Ah,' nodded Chang.

'Brilliant, bach,' said Jenkins.

'Until we get to the front, though,' continued Fonthill, 'we will not display the flag and, Chang, you will lead. We shall be stopped, I'm sure, and you will explain that we have come with a message to the commander from our general in Peking, General . . . what's his name again?'

'Tung Fu-hsiang.'

'That's the chap. Explain that it is urgent and we can't be delayed. Then, when we reach the line, we will raise the flag and ride straight ahead – cantering, not galloping, mind you. Straight to the main gate of the arsenal and there we will explain that we are English and ask to be admitted.'

'What?' asked Jenkins. 'Stand there an' 'ave a chat while we get shot in the back by the Chinks and in the front by the Brits?'

'Something like that.' He grinned. 'It's risky, I admit. But I think that it's a fair bet that the English will be wary, but they won't defile a flag of truce and once they hear my voice they will let us in. As for the Chinese, I am gambling that everyone but the commander will think that it's a parley that has been ordered from on high. And once *he* realises what's up we shall be inside the arsenal.'

'Then do I get me vest back?'

'Of course. But it could have bullet holes in it. Come on, gentlemen. Let's advance.'

Once again, Fonthill's confidence was only reflected outwards. He would have felt happier if he could have reconnoitred the ground – particularly the Chinese lines – for himself. The main danger, he felt, would be getting through those lines. Chang's story would not stand up to much interrogation. Their main hope would be that the young man would argue with, not only conviction, but also with the superiority and arrogance that stemmed from being a general's messenger. He sighed. Once again, it would be a case of dipping a toe in the water to see how hot it was.

They rode back to where they had met the sentry the previous evening. He had been replaced and the new man made no attempt to stop them as they rode by. Confidence, reflected Fonthill, was all under these circumstances.

They rode on through scattered contingents of troops and heard intermittent firing from directly ahead of them. Luckily, they met no cavalry and no other Kansu troops, for they would surely never have survived interrogation from 'one of their own'. The dead cavalryman must have been correct in saying that these Muslim soldiers were restricted to fighting on the north of the Peking legations' perimeter.

They were stopped by one sentry, however, who was beginning to engage in a conversation with Chang when Simon interrupted, curtly gesturing them forward with an air of command that only an ex-British public schoolboy could call upon. They rode on and halted at the edge of a sad little thicket.

Before them loomed the huge, high walls of the arsenal, looking impregnable in the early-morning light. Stone outbuildings skirted the foot of the walls and these were manned by the defenders, who were directing a desultory fire at a line of hastily dug trenches some thirty yards away from the thicket and which curled down to the river. Smoke and cooking smells came from the trenches, as the Chinese soldiers prepared their breakfasts. The gap between the outbuildings and the trenches was some two hundred and fifty yards. The muzzles of light artillery pieces poked out from gaps in the line of outbuildings but Fonthill could see no artillery in place behind the Chinese lines. In any case, he mused, it would have taken very heavy guns to have made any impression in the walls of the arsenal.

He drew a deep breath. 'Right,' he said, 'no point in waiting. We will ride straight ahead towards that gap where the cannon is pointing out. Rifles slung behind us so that they don't threaten. We ride at a stately canter, now, and backs very straight. We are elite Chinese cavalry.'

'Even though we are Mussulmen who 'aven't said their prayers this mornin',' muttered Jenkins through clenched teeth.

They cantered out of the thicket, Fonthill in the lead, carrying his rifle high, with Jenkins's vest fluttering at its muzzle. They took the narrow trench in a leap, startling the troops below them huddled around their braziers, and set off across no man's land, in stately fashion as though they were leading the trooping of Her Majesty's colour in Whitehall, London.

Two bullets hissed by Fonthill's head from the direction of the British lines. He immediately removed his cap, coiled the reins around the thumb of his left hand and held it palm extended towards the British, in the universal sign of peace, and raised his 'flag' even higher. He heard someone bark a command from the outbuildings and the firing ceased.

They continued to ride in an eerie silence, for all firing had ceased along the lines. It was as though both sides were watching a tableau being staged for their entertainment.

When the trio had reached about sixty yards from the outbuildings, close enough to see the faces of the British soldiers, a Chinese voice rang out sharply.

'They say, come no further,' shouted Chang.

Fonthill rose in the stirrups. 'I am an English officer,' he cried. 'My name is Fonthill. I have come from Peking with a message for your commander from Sir Claude MacDonald, the British minister in the capital. We have ridden through the Chinese lines in disguise.'

Silence fell. Then a voice displaying authority came from behind the cannon: 'If you are an English officer, state your rank and regiment.'

Fonthill muttered a curse and then responded loudly: 'I was

commissioned in the 24th Regiment of Foot in 1876. I fought at Rorke's Drift and Isandlwana and I am a Commander of the Bath. If we are left sitting out here much longer presenting three fine targets to the enemy I shall make bloody sure that you are cashiered. Now, let us in. Quickly.'

There was another silence and then the voice – this time carrying an edge – ordered: 'Very well. But ride in slowly and do not touch your rifles or your packs.'

Thankfully, Simon kicked his heels into his horse's flanks and the three of them walked forward to the gap in the line. Just before they reached it, a shout rang out from the Chinese lines and a ragged volley sent bullets singing past their ears. With alacrity, they urged their steeds forward and sprang through the gaps on either side of the cannon.

Hurriedly dismounting, Simon faced a ring of rifles and a haggard-faced young subaltern, who looked at him with some unease.

'Good morning,' he said, cheerfully, extending his hand. 'Simon Fonthill. Sorry to have seemed rude but I was expecting a bullet up the arse at any minute.'

The young man shook hands, still a little warily, and then waved down the rifles. 'Good morning . . . er . . . sir. I'm afraid you took us all rather by surprise.'

'Yes. Had no time or the wherewithal to send you a letter. Ran out of stamps. Now, who is in command here?'

'Admiral Seymour.'

'*Admiral?*'

'Yes. We are the relief mission that set out to relieve Peking. The lieutenant took out a tattered handkerchief and ran it across his brow. 'I'm afraid we've had rather a rough time. We've had to fight every inch of the way back from Langfang . . .'

'*Langfang!*' Fonthill's jaw dropped. 'But that's only about thirty miles from Peking. You got so near.'

The young man smiled ruefully. 'Yes, we all know that. But I think you had better see the admiral, if you say you have a message for him.'

'Yes please, right away. Oh – I wonder if it would be possible to rustle up some breakfast for my two companions? May I introduce 352 Jenkins and Chang Griffith. I wouldn't have been able to move an inch without them.'

The lieutenant shook their hands – just a little uncertainly in the case of Chang – and gave quick orders to a sergeant. Then he walked with Simon back through a small post door set in the giant gate in the walls of the arsenal. They climbed a stone stairway and then Fonthill was kept waiting outside a semi-open door while a conversation took place within. Then he was ushered into a grand room, which, situated at the heart of the stone fortress, was blessedly cool. At the far end stood a tall, thin, bearded man, dressed in what was once the white ducks of an admiral of the British navy. Now they were creased, dirty and still covered in dust.

Seymour advance to meet Fonthill and held out his hand. His face was drawn beneath the beard and his eyes tired. 'Fonthill?' he asked. 'Are you the Fonthill of Khartoum and Matebeleland?'

Simon nodded and then grinned. 'I suppose I am, Admiral, though for the last two days, as you see, I have been a Kansu soldier.'

The grin was returned. 'So I see. No wonder we wouldn't let you into the lines. Congratulations on your disguise. We've been fighting Kansus for days and they and their general, Tung Fu-hsiang,' he pronounced it perfectly, 'have been giving us hell.'

'Really? I thought the Kansus and their general have been restricted to the siege at Peking.'

'Certainly not. They're down here in force. Now please don't tell me – *please* don't tell me – that you have come to announce that Peking has fallen?'

'No, sir. At least not when I left two days ago.'

'Thank God for that.'

'No. But I have come to urge you to make all haste to relieve the legations. They are holding out, but only just, and I don't know how much longer they can defend the Legation Quarter. Can you turn around and march on Peking? You could be there in a few days.'

'My dear fellow, do sit down.' The admiral gestured to a chair and took the one opposite. 'Fonthill,' he spoke wearily and with heavy emphasis. 'There is no question of that. We can't relieve anyone. It is *we* who need relieving. You see, we ourselves are besieged here. And, from what I can hear, so are our people in Tientsin. I fear that, at the moment, we are losing this damned war with the Dragon Lady.'

CHAPTER EIGHT

Simon Fonthill stared blankly at the admiral. 'But,' he said, 'we were told that you had set out with two thousand men.'

'So I did.' Seymour's face was expressionless but his eyes were those of a man who realised that his career had come to an end. 'Because of the need for haste, we decided that the railway was the obvious and quickest way to advance – after all, Peking was only some eighty miles away and we were being faced not by a regular army but just a bunch of peasant rebels. Well,' he smiled sadly, 'it wasn't quite like that, I'm afraid.

'Of course, we were strung out along the line in a succession of trains and we had to keep repairing the line ahead to remedy the damage done by the Chinese, so our progress was painfully slow. The Boxers first attacked us on the third day. They came on at our lead trains just a touch north of Langfang.' The admiral's voice was soft and low, as though he were telling a fairy story to a child, but Fonthill could sense the agony behind the words. 'They attacked us with supreme courage, although they were only armed with swords and spears. We brought down about sixty of them and they retreated but then they came on again, making it impossible for our chaps to get out to repair the line. In these subsequent attacks there were more of them and better armed.

'We began to run low on ammunition and water and it was damned hot. You see, as we had advanced, we had been forced to garrison every station we passed to prevent the enemy tearing up the line behind us. We were on half rations and stretched out like a thin piece of string . . .' Seymour suddenly shook his head. 'I am forgetting my manners. You would like some tea, of course?'

'That would be kind, sir. But what about your supplies?'

The admiral waved his hand. 'That is the good news. We have found that this place is stacked with weapons, ammunition, medical supplies, fifteen tons of rice and a seemingly endless supply of tea. All left by the Chinese when we shooed them off.' He shouted and a bluejacket appeared. 'A pot of tea for two, please, Jackson. Now, where was I?'

'You were stretched out like a piece of string.'

'Yes, so we were. Then the Chinese destroyed the bridge at Yangtsun and we were cut off from our supply trains, which had to retreat back to Tientsin. We thought long and hard about pushing on to Peking overland but there was no major road, we had no transport and a growing number of wounded to care for. We decided to fall back on Yangtsun, commandeer junks for our wounded and supplies, and advance up the river to the capital. But there the German force we had left as a garrison was attacked by about four thousand of the enemy and their train was pursued for some miles as it retreated back to Tientsin, from which we could now hear gunfire.'

Wearily, Seymour rose and poured tea. 'The important point here, however,' he continued, 'is that the force attacking the Germans were not Boxers but well-led contingents of the Imperial army. In other words, this rebellion was now being backed by the Chinese army, presumably on the orders of the Empress. So it was no longer a rebellion, it was war.' He sighed. 'This meant that it was impossible for us to continue towards Peking, with our wounded and cut off, as we were, from our supplies. So we took four junks and turned back for Tientsin. We have had to fight every inch of the way, deploying men at every village to take them at bayonet point and often pulling the junks containing our guns and wounded off the shoals as they grounded. We were under attack all the time. Then, suddenly, looming up out of the dusk we came upon this place, of which we had no knowledge at all. We mounted a night attack and, although it was fiercely defended, we managed to break through and send the garrison packing.'

Fonthill nodded, not quite knowing what to say, for his thoughts were beginning to turn to Alice and the beleagured defenders at Peking. But the admiral was not finished.

'Our pursuers, of course, closed in all around us, cutting us off. Here, we are only about six miles from the foreign settlements at Tientsin and we can hear gunfire from there, so they are clearly under siege. But we have not been able to make contact with them, of course. You see, Fonthill,' Seymour leant forward, 'we are dead beat. Of what was left of my small force when we were cut off north of Yangtsun, we have lost sixty-two dead and two hundred and thirty-two wounded.

We have successfully fought off a series of counter-attacks but we are simply not strong enough to break out.'

He sat back. 'There. That's our story. Every step of the way I have thought about our people in Peking and, since turning back, I have half expected to hear that they have been overwhelmed.' He smiled wanly. 'You can imagine the frustration and even the feeling of guilt. So please tell me how things were when you left and also how you were able to get through the lines.'

Simon relayed the message from Sir Claude MacDonald and then told his own story of how he and his two companions were able to reach the arsenal. At the end, both men fell silent.

It was Seymour who broke the silence. 'You've shown remarkable courage and resource, Fonthill,' he said, offering his sad smile, 'and when the people back home hear about it, you will surely get rather more plaudits than I. But that is of no account. What matters now is that we have to get out of this place.'

'Quite so.' Fonthill's mind raced. The story of the relief expedition was undoubtedly an unmitigated disaster. Surely someone – someone, that is, with some experience of land warfare, not an admiral, for God's sake! – should have realised how vulnerable to attack would be an advance through enemy territory *by train*. Cutting the advance into segments by pulling up the line and then attacking each exposed segment would be as easy as snipping a piece of string here and there. His mind flashed again to the vulnerability of Alice now and of how the defenders of the Legation Quarter had been relying on relief and expecting it daily, scanning the sky to the south-east for searchlights and listening for the distant rumbles of guns to show that a column was near. Indignation flared within him at the incompetence of it all.

Then a look into the sad eyes of the man before him, a man who had tried his best and who knew that his long and distinguished career had now ended in disastrous failure, rid him of thoughts of blame. What to do now, indeed!

'You have tried to get help, presumably, from Tientsin?'

'Oh yes. Only a Chinaman, of course, could get through and all of the reliable native people with me have refused to attempt it. I have to say that I don't blame them. Reports have come in that Tung Fu-hsiang – a vicious bandit, by all accounts – is torturing and then beheading any of his countrymen found helping the enemy. We shall just have to lick our wounds here until we are strong enough to break out.'

'Hmm.' Fonthill thought hard. 'We can tell by the sound of the guns, of course, that the Tientsin settlements are still holding out. If only we could link the two forces – here and there, I mean – then we would have a much stronger unit to attack the Kansus. Is there hope of reinforcements coming to Tientsin from the sea?'

Seymour's eyes lit up. 'Yes indeed, that is my hope. Before I left, the Foreign Powers were being asked to send troops to reinforce us from their possessions in Asia. The Russians, of course, are the nearest.'

'Good.' Simon fumbled within his long jacket and produced the rough map that Sir Claude had given him. He moved the teapot and spread the paper out on the table before them. He jabbed the map with a grimy forefinger. 'You are presumably about here,' he said, 'on the riverbank, some six miles or so from the settlements?'

'Yes.'

'And the river flows from here downstream directly past the settlements?'

166

'Indeed.'

'Then that is the route for a messenger to follow.'

The admiral shook his head. 'But a boat would never get past the Chinese, who are watching every inch of the river. Then, of course, there is the question of getting through the ring of Tung Fu-hsiang's troops who are besieging the settlements.'

'It should be possible for someone in disguise to get through the Chinese lines around the settlements. We have done it here. And I would not use a boat to go downriver.'

'What do you mean?'

'I presume you have access to the river?'

'Yes, after dark.'

'I have seen that there is plenty of driftwood that floats down the river with the current. It should be possible to pull some such detritus to the shore, take cover under it, in or out of the water, and float downstream, swimming ashore when the settlements are reached – all under cover of darkness.'

The admiral scratched at his beard. 'It's ingenious, but highly dangerous, I would have thought. But who would . . . ? You are not suggesting that *you* would go?'

'Of course.'

'But, my dear fellow. You don't know the territory, you would not be able to control your means of travel, you would not know when you had reached your destination . . . I can think of a dozen reasons why the whole thing would be ridiculously hazardous.'

Fonthill leant forward. 'I have to confess, Admiral,' he said, 'that I have a vested interest in getting you out of here. You see, I had to leave my wife behind in the Legation Quarter in Peking. I don't know how long the defenders can hold out there but their resources are running low and unless help comes soon they will be overwhelmed. If that happens, I do not wish to think of what could happen to her. If the fit remnants of your column and the defenders at Tientsin are merged – plus, of course, any reinforcements that have been able to land from the sea – then it should be possible to mount another attempt to relieve our people in the capital. But all this will take time, of course, and we have precious little of that. So I intend to leave tonight.' He paused for a moment. Then he added slowly but with emphasis, 'I need to go myself to impress the authorities of the need for haste and for care in the planning of this second relief column. It needs to go quickly – *and it must get through.*'

The two men sat gazing at each other in silence for a moment. Then the admiral stood. 'I admire your courage and your determination, Fonthill,' he said. 'Of course, I will do all I can to help. Now come over here and I will show you a better map.'

The two walked to the admiral's desk, where he unrolled a large-scale chart. 'This arsenal is not marked but we are roughly here on the right bank of the river, as you have indicated. The river flows more or less straight for about three miles, then it gets a bit complicated. Just above the Chinese City of Tientsin here, you see that the river bends back on itself and the Lu-T'ai Canal comes in from the left. Then the river itself becomes like the head of a buffalo, facing north; you come in on the right horn, so to speak, and the left horn goes to your right and becomes the Grand Canal, flowing past the city. You must not be swept into the canal because that takes you away from the settlements, which are down here, sou'-sou'-west, about another mile away. If you can get ashore at the northern extremity of the settlements, here, with the railway station on your left, that would be best. Do you speak French?'

'Yes. Well, reasonably.'

'Good, because the French concession occupies the northern end of the settlements and I assume that French sailors will be occupying this part of the defences. Now, do you intend to go alone?'

'Yes, I cannot ask my companions to undertake such a journey.'

'Very well. I suggest that you strip down but carry your Kansu clothing tightly wrapped in a waterproof. Rub down if you can find cover on the riverbank and then dress. You can't wander naked through the lines. Ah, one more thing.' He rolled the map up again. 'Just on the edge of the arsenal here, where it comes down to the river, there is a promontory, which juts out and collects driftwood. We should be able to find material for some sort of transport there.'

Simon nodded in appreciation. 'Splendid! I am most grateful for your help and advice. Now, I would welcome the chance to have something to eat and to talk to my companions.'

'Good Lord! Of course. I have been most neglectful.'

Moments later, Fonthill joined Jenkins and Chang, who were finishing a plate of rice and meat of indeterminate origin and drinking from large tin mugs of tea. Similar fare was provided for him and, between mouthfuls, he related the story of the relief column to his companions.

'Barmy, goin' by train,' said Jenkins. 'Did they think they were goin' on 'oliday to the seaside?'

Chang nodded and concurred. 'It is jolly regretful that they should go that way.'

Jenkins mopped up the remains of the rice with a crust. 'What's the plan now, then, bach sir?' He looked around him. 'I could quite enjoy this postin', out of the sun, like, an' with a bit of decent somethin' to eat. I suppose we will stay 'ere for a bit to get our breath back, so to speak?'

'Yes, well certainly you two will.' He then explained his plan to them. Chang, as usual, was imperturbable but Jenkins listened with mounting horror.

'What!' he exclaimed, his nose wrinkling and his eyebrows nearly meeting his moustache. 'We float down that bleedin' river on a bit o' wood, with the crocodiles nippin' at our balls and lettin' the Chinks take potshots at us? It's barmy, look you.'

Simon sighed. 'No, my dear old comrade. *We* don't go. *I* do. Two of us certainly would present a target and, anyway, you can't swim and you are afraid of crocodiles. I love them. Nice creatures.'

Chang broke his silence. 'Three too many, cousin. I quite agree. But you need interpreter. And I can swim and I love crocodiles too. So I come.' He grinned. 'Mr Jenkins stay behind because he is not family.'

Jenkins blew out his cheeks. 'If you go, I go. Or I shoot you in the leg, as instructed by Miss Alice. I think this counts under the 'eadin' of "stupid, brave thing", or whatever it was she said.'

Fonthill shook his head slowly. 'I am sorry,' he said, 'but I do this one on my own. Three of us are too big a party. And it is far too dangerous, anyway.'

Jenkins leant across and put his hand on Simon's arm. 'Now, listen, bach sir,' he said. 'This is no time to break up our partnership. You're as brave as a lion, I know that, and you're cleverer than General Roberts and General Wolseley put together. But you *need* me, you know you do. I can do the killin' while you do the thinkin'. We're a good team, but not so good, with respect, when we split up. Whatever you say, anyway, I shall come with you.' He turned to the Chinaman. 'An' you, Changy, should stay 'ere an' write to yer mother.'

Chang, his face set, shook his head. 'You need interpreter,' he said. 'You don't get through lines without talking. I go, too.'

Simon made one last effort. 'But you can't swim and you hate the water,' he said to Jenkins.

The Welshman shook his head. 'Who was it that swam . . . well, sort of . . . across that river in Matabellyland 'oldin' on to your 'orse's tail?' He turned to Chang. 'An' you said, didn't you, Changy, that there aren't any crocs in this river?'

Chang nodded affirmatively.

'There you are, then. What time do we go?'

Fonthill looked hard at his old friend. If there was one thing that Jenkins hated more than heights and crocodiles it was water. For him to volunteer to hang on to a piece of timber and float downstream in a fast-flowing river was the epitome of courage. But for all of his idiosyncrasies, Simon had never met a braver man than Jenkins. It was not like either of them, however, to be sentimental. So he merely smiled and nodded. 'Oh, very well, but I call this insubordination. We leave as soon as it is dark and when we have managed to pull some driftwood out of the river.'

He shook his head disparagingly. 'It's going to be a big load and it looks as though we shall need something like Brunel's "Great Eastern" now. We don't take rifles, just the Colt revolver, and we will need to pack our clothes tightly in our waterproofs. Try and get some rest now. It could be a long night.'

*   *   *

171

The three dozed intermittently through the day, to a background of artillery and rifle fire. Then, just before dark, Fonthill made his way to the rear wall of the arsenal, that which faced the river. The water lapped at its high walls but, true enough, to the right where the wall turned at right angles, a thin tongue of land jutted out, containing just enough scrub of cover to anyone watching from downriver or the opposite bank. As the water swirled up to it and round, it had collected enough driftwood to found a timber yard. Prominent amongst the detritus was the trunk of a medium-sized tree, which still had branches protruding from the base, to which a few, sad traces of foliage still clung.

Simon nodded his head. That would suffice.

As dusk settled on the river, the three set out from a little post gate near the promontory. With them came Admiral Seymour and four barefooted sailors. Fonthill and his companions had stripped down to their underpants and clutched bundles of their Kansu uniforms, wrapped in their waterproof capes. The warm air engulfed them and even the water was tepid as Chang and the four sailors waded out, their backs bent low, to retrieve the tree.

Seymour clutched Fonthill's hand. 'Remember,' he said, 'that you go to the right bank when you are abreast of the railway on your left. Be careful not to be swept to your right up the canal as you meet the "buffalo head" of the river. I don't know who is in charge at Tientsin, but tell him that we can hold out here for quite some time but that, if we hear nothing for a week, we shall try and break out to reach them.

'Good luck, my dear Fonthill. May God go with you.'

'Thank you, sir.' They shook hands as the tree trunk was pushed to the bank. Simon stole a glance at Jenkins. Despite the humidity, the Welshman was shivering. He avoided Fonthill's gaze but waded out and hesitantly climbed onto the trunk, lying prone on it, his legs slightly apart to maintain balance, with one hand clutching his bag and the other holding on to a branch that rose vertically just by his head.

'That's good, 352,' whispered Fonthill. 'The river is not turbulent so you should be quite safe if you hold on tight and spread your legs apart to keep your balance. Chang, you hold onto that branch to the right and I will take the left side. Kick with your feet if this bloody thing starts to drift to either side. Right. Here we go.'

There was a distinct muttered cry of 'Oh, bloody 'ell' as the two swimmers pushed the log away from the strip of land and the current caught it, causing it to roll a little. Then it righted itself and Fonthill and Chang kicked their feet in breaststroke fashion to propel it into the centre of the river. Once there, Simon felt the full surge of the river as they were taken up by the current.

He kept his head low, so that the water lapped his chin, and stole a glance to either side. Campfires glowed on both banks, but they were, of course, more numerous on the right bank, facing the arsenal.

He could make out no figures in the darkness and they seemed to be undetected. Thank goodness the trunk was not yawing and Simon offered up a fervent prayer that Jenkins would continue to lie supine, looking from the bank like some gnarled, knotted protrusion in the middle of the tree.

After the heat of the day, it was not at all unpleasant drifting down the river in the comparative cool of the night. They passed several junks moored for the night on the banks but nothing was moving on the river except them, as either he or Chang kicked out to maintain their position. He soon realised that the young Chinaman was like an eel in the water and, after a time, he left it to Chang to correct their position whenever the need arose.

Fonthhill became aware that their biggest danger would arise if they met shoals of shallow water, for, despite the recent rains, the long drought had severely reduced the river level. Several times he felt his feet kick the bottom as they wandered a little from the deeper channel in midstream. He took comfort, however, from the fact that Seymour had told him that there were no rapids marked on the map above Tientsin.

As they drifted, he began to address the question of when and how they would forsake their tree and gain the riverbank. He had no watch, of course, but he tried to record the position of the pale moon in the dark sky above him and also to assess the speed of the current.

Seymour had estimated that it seemed to be between one and two miles an hour, say one and a half. That meant that, given they were six miles from the foreign concessions, they should be abreast of them after about four hours. Good, that meant that they would arrive still in darkness. How he would successfully navigate the 'buffalo head' junction, he had no idea, except to keep to the left side of the river – if, that is, he knew when they had reached the junction, for little could be seen of either riverbank at the moment.

He was startled by a sudden grunt and then a low moaning sound. He let himself slip back to the rear of the trunk and raised an enquiring eyebrow to Chang, who was on his back and allowing his feet to trail behind him, fluttering in the stream, as though he always used this form of transport to travel on the Pei Ho. The Chinaman grinned and pointed forward. Jenkins, he who was terrified of water, was fast asleep and snoring!

Fonthill crept back up the log and firmly held Jenkins's ankle. He was anxious that his comrade should not suddenly wake up and upset their makeshift boat. The Welshman came to with a start and Simon hissed, 'I told you you would enjoy the trip but don't go to sleep, for God's sake.'

'Oh, sorry, bach sir.'

A light flickered from the right riverbank and then, suddenly, a rifle exploded with a crack and a dart of flame. The bullet hissed into the water behind Fonthill, who breathed, 'Nobody move. Keep perfectly still.'

Another shot was fired which splashed even further behind and then the river lapsed into silence once more. 'I think he was just amusing himself,' called Fonthill softly. 'A bit of nocturnal target practice to amuse himself on the long night-watch.'

'As long as 'e wasn't shootin' at crocodiles,' grunted Jenkins.

The water seemed to be turning cold and a shiver ran through Fonthill. He estimated that they had been in the river for about three and a half hours, although the moon had now slipped behind what seemed like a thick bank of cloud. Ah, rain would be a good thing! Under its cover they could land easily enough. But the night remained dry.

A new and hitherto hidden danger of the river, as Jenkins had discovered, however, was that their method of transport proved to be soporific and Simon felt himself drifting off to sleep, despite – or perhaps because of – the coldness now of the water. He was rudely stirred from his drowsiness when the trunk hit the bank and was immediately sent swirling around, jettisoning Jenkins in the water with a resounding splash. Fonthill immediately struck out for him and caught him by the arm, as he began to thrash the water.

'On your back and keep quiet,' he hissed into his ear. Simon slipped behind the Welshman, thrust both hands under his armpits and began kicking to take them to the riverbank. He realised that Chang was at his side, helping to hold up Jenkins, but that the tree trunk, with their bundles of clothing caught in the thrusting branches, was floating away downstream.

At the same moment, there was a babble of voices from up above them on the bank and, looking up, Simon saw half a dozen rifles thrust towards them and as many faces – Chinese faces, of course – gazing down at them in consternation.

'Chang,' called Simon. 'Tell them not to shoot.'

They scrambled ashore under the threatening rifles and Chang shouted, 'I think they shoot us now as spies.'

Fonthill's brain raced. 'Tell them that we are not spies,' he said, 'but that we are English and come from Peking with an important message for General . . . damn . . . what's his name . . . from Sir Claude MacDonald. We came by boat but it overturned in the shoals and we have been forced to swim. Make it sound good, cousin, for God's sake.'

Chang burbled away urgently while the three stood in their underpants, water dripping from them. A shamefaced Jenkins stood, clenching and unclenching his fists, his great moustache looking as though his nose had caught a water rat. 'Sorry, bach,' he murmured, 'all my fault. I'll take this lot on while you dive back into the river and get away. That's best.'

'You'll do nothing of the kind. That way we will all be shot. And, anyway, it was my fault for falling asleep. We will just have to see if we can talk our way out of this.'

It seemed that Chang was not having much success, for a rifle butt was suddenly swung into his face, knocking him to the ground.

Fonthill strode forward. 'That's enough of that,' he said, with the confident and reprimanding air of a British colonel. 'You do not hit that man again.' And he wagged his finger in the face of the antagonist. 'We are British soldiers and . . .' The muzzle of the man's rifle was suddenly thrust sharply into his stomach, winding him and causing him to bend over and drop onto one knee.

Jenkins sprang forward and delivered a perfect left hook onto the jaw of the soldier, sending him staggering, before the Welshman was felled with a rifle butt from behind.

Grimacing, Fonthill looked up at the hostile faces all around him. They were, he realised, all Kansus. Their eyes, set in Mongolian faces, regarded him quite expressionlessly. These were the toughest, most vicious soldiers in the Empress's army, little more than bandits, rapists and killers, led by the biggest brigand and foreigner-hating man in all China. As he watched, he saw the man Jenkins had struck walk forward and aim his rifle at the dazed Welshman's head and pull back the bolt.

Then the name came to him. He stood erect. 'General Tung Fu-hsiang,' he said firmly. 'Take us to him.' Then he repeated the name. 'General Tung Fu-hsiang.' He embraced the three of them with a whirl of his arm. Then gestured from his breast and then vaguely to the south. 'General Tung Fu-hsiang.'

Chang pulled himself to his feet, his eye half closed, and began speaking in Chinese again.

Whatever he said, that and Simon's firmness had an effect, for they were pushed forward with rifle muzzles. Fonthill became aware of the sound of artillery fire, much closer now, and they were being marched towards it. After five minutes they saw campfires and all three were forced to their knees by blows from rifle butts into their backs and left under a guard of two men on the edge of the camp.

'Are you all right, the two of you?' asked Fonthill.

'Me 'ead is singin' but it's me pride that's wounded mostly,' grunted Jenkins. 'Sorry, bach sir, for sleepin' at me post and fallin' off into the water. It looks as though I've got us into a fine mess.'

'Don't talk rubbish.'

Chang squinted across at Simon with his good eye. 'I think, cousin, that they now believe you that you have message for general and they go to fetch officer. But I think they will be jolly angry when they find you have no message.'

Fonthill shrugged. 'I'll think of something. I had to stop them shooting us out of hand. They're Kansus, aren't they?'

'Yes. Not very nice people.'

'By the sound of the guns, we are very near the settlements, if only we can get out of here.'

Jenkins looked down at his nakedness. 'If we get through the lines, we'll probably be arrested for indecency. Or catch cold and die of flu.'

Eventually, an order was barked from out of the semi-darkness and they were bundled forward, rifles at their backs, until they reached a large tent. Inside, a Kansu was seated at a trestle table. He was dressed and looked exactly the same as the soldiers but he was obviously an officer, for he was treated with great deference by the escorts. He spoke rapidly to Chang.

'He want our names and where we come from and why we go downstream on log,' he explained.

Fonthill nodded. 'Give our names and ranks – captain and sergeant. You are our interpreter. Do *not* say that you are the son of a missionary. Explain that we escaped from Peking with a personal message for the general from Sir Claude MacDonald, the senior minister in the legations. We made for the river, where we hired a small boat. Upriver it hit an obstruction during the night and overturned, throwing us into the water. We were all asleep on deck in just our undergarments because of the heat. We found this log floating and hung onto it, because we were all poor swimmers.'

'Blimey,' muttered Jenkins. 'There's ingenious for you, isn't it?'

Chang gave his translation, while Simon watched the officer closely to gauge his reactions. The man's face was impassive. Then he spoke curtly.

'He say, give him message and he will relay it to general.'

'No. The message is confidential and is not written. I have orders to deliver it to the general personally. Ask him to take us to him immediately.'

'He say, how you know general is here and not in Peking?'

'Word came through to Sir Claude that the general had given up his command of the troops attacking the Wang Fu to direct operations against the Tientsin settlements.'

Fonthill sucked in his breath and hoped to God that Seymour's information about the whereabouts of Tung Fu-hsiang was correct. If his gamble had failed then the odds on being shot straight away were short. But the officer's face gave no indication either way.

The Kansu fixed his gaze on Fonthill, who returned it without blinking. The two stared at each other in silence for a full thirty seconds before the officer turned and barked a command.

Chang let out an audible sigh of relief. 'We are to be taken to general,' he whispered. 'He gives orders that coats are to be found for us, for it would be insult to commander for us to appear before him naked.'

'Quite right,' muttered Jenkins. 'Well, bach sir, first round to you. But you'd better think of a good message to deliver. The general wouldn't be Sir Claude's illegitimate son, by any chance, would he?'

Fonthill frowned. 'Do be quiet, 352. I'm trying to think.'

Three dun-coloured coats were thrown around their shoulders, their hands were bound roughly behind their backs and they were pushed out of the tent. The first signs of dawn were streaking the sky to the east and they were marched away, following the officer and surrounded by a guard of Kansus. The gunfire was louder than ever and Fonthill realised that they must be near to the line surrounding the settlements, although little could be seen in the darkness.

This was confirmed as they climbed a hill and saw ahead, just out of rifle shot, a dark outline of buildings, linked by a low and indistinct line of what must be barricades. Troops were now all around them, crawling from their bedrolls and congregating around small open fires over which cooking pots were hung. To their right and behind them, cannon were firing desultorily and the sour smell of cordite hung on the air. At the top of the hill, tucked away among stunted trees, a large, low tent had been pitched, lit from within by a dim light.

'Let's 'ope that the general 'as slept well,' muttered Jenkins.

They were forced to wait for ten minutes while the officer spoke with guards outside the tent and then disappeared inside it. Then they were pushed through an opening in the canvas.

The tent seemed even larger from within and three vertical poles supported the roof. To one side, sleeping mats had been spread and three women, dressed in traditional Chinese style but looking a little dishevelled, as if they had dressed hurriedly, were folding blankets. In the centre of the room stood a table on which a large map had been spread and, at the far end of the tent, a fourth woman was ladling rice into a wooden bowl set on a smaller table, behind which sat one of the largest men Fonthill had ever seen.

Although he was sitting, it was clear that he was not tall, perhaps Jenkins's height. But he was wide – wider than the Welshman by far – and immensely fat. He was half-wearing a green tunic that had been buttoned up only to the midriff, revealing rolls of flesh. The head was either completely bald or shaven, although a long moustache adorned the upper lip, the ends of which hung down on either side of his mouth like rat's tails. The man was eating rice and meat with chopsticks, displaying a delicacy of movement that denied the grossness of his appearance.

He looked up as the trio were ushered in and gestured briefly with his chopsticks. Immediately, rifles were crashed onto the shoulders of the three, forcing them to kneel before him.

Fonthill looked with interest at the general. He knew that the man enjoyed the confidence of the Empress, because of his diligence in stamping out isolated examples of insurgency in the north of China and his oft-declared hatred of the foreign barbarians whose presence in the country was humiliating its people and the Dragon Lady herself. He was a warlord in his own right in the north but he gave devoted allegiance to the Empress and had been one of the early supporters of the Boxers. His competence as a military leader had been reflected in the fact that the Peking sector that he commanded, the Wang Fu, had posed the greatest threat to the legations, causing the diligent Japanese who defended it to concede ground regularly, if stoically. Now he regarded the three prisoners with tiny eyes, set in a round, jowled face.

Fonthill decided to take the initiative.

'Are you General Tung Fu-hsiang?' he demanded, looking directly at the general, rather than Chang, who interpreted in a diffident voice.

There was an intake of breath from the dozen or so Kansus in the tent. It was, clearly, *lèse-majesté* for a prisoner to address the general without being spoken to first and a rifle butt crashed into his back, sending him sprawling.

Chang hurriedly answered, although no one had replied to the question. 'Yes, cousin,' he said, 'this is the general. Please be careful.'

'Then tell him I have a message for him from Sir Claude MacDonald.'

The general acknowledged the statement with a wave of his chopsticks. 'Tell me the message,' translated Chang.

'No,' said Fonthill. 'I speak to no man while kneeling before him.'

There was another intake of breath, not least from Chang and Jenkins, and the general looked up, a flicker of interest momentarily lighting up his face. 'Then you will be beheaded as you kneel,' he replied, indicating for one of the guards to step forward and draw his long, curved sword.

'Then you will not hear the message,' answered Simon, still fixing his gaze on that of the general.

'Bloody 'ell,' muttered Jenkins. 'Steady on, bach sir.'

A slow smile began to spread across the general's face but he lowered his head and continued eating for a moment before looking up and growling a command to the officer. Immediately, Simon was levered to his feet.

'Very well,' said Simon. 'I wish my companions to stand also.'

Another signal was given and Jenkins and Chang were brought to their feet, rifle barrels thrust under their armpits.

'Now,' said Fonthill. 'Sir Claude MacDonald is the leader of the eleven foreign ministers who, with their staffs and families, are being kept under siege in Peking.'

'He knows that,' interpreted Chang, 'and he says that the man is a fool.'

'If he is a fool, he represents the British Empire, the most powerful empire in the world, which is three times the size of the Chinese Empire. He is also the elected leader of the ten other European powers who, with the British, have navies and armies thirty times the size of the Chinese. Sir Claude is imprisoned within the Legation Quarter but, even so, he sends his greetings to the general.'

At this, the Chinaman put down his chopsticks and leant back in his chair. Encouraged, Fonthill continued.

'He respects the general, because he knows of his prowess as a fighting man and he respects his Kansu troops, who have a similar reputation. But he is afraid for the general's life.'

Tung Fu-hsiang lifted his eyebrows and gestured for Simon to continue. 'Yes,' said Simon, 'at this moment twenty thousand Russian troops are on their way to Taku from the Russian provinces in Asia and the British are also sending troops from India. The British Admiral Seymour has captured the great Chinese arsenal of Hsiku near here and has at his disposal great quantities of field guns, machine guns, rifles, and seven million rounds of small-arms ammunition.' At this point, Chang held up his hand for Simon to slow down while he translated.

The general looked unimpressed. 'You lie,' he said. 'We have both Peking and the Tientsin settlements surrounded and there are no reports of foreign reinforcements in Taku. Even if this were so, these are matters for the Empress, not me. Why should your minister fear for my life?'

There was a muted murmur of acquiescence from the soldiers in the room.

Fonthill drew in his breath. He had no knowledge of reinforcements being imminent. They would come, he had no doubt about that. But they would probably be too late. Nevertheless, he continued.

'Because, General, the Foreign Powers, when they land and have defeated your outnumbered and outgunned army, will advance on Peking and storm the Forbidden City and the Manchu Palace. The Empress, of course, will not be harmed. She will be needed to reunite the country after the dreadful revenge that the powers will take on your people. But the generals who have supported the Boxers and led the attack on the capital and on the settlements will be killed – all of them.'

A silence fell on the room as Fonthill's words were translated by Chang, who was now speaking in a loud and firm voice, as though taking heart from the words he was conveying.

A glance from Chang showed that he had finished and Simon hurried on. 'However, because he admires your fighting spirit, Sir Claude is prepared to guarantee that you will live after punitive actions have been taken. But you must withdraw your men from the settlements immediately.'

'Good try, bach sir,' whispered Jenkins. 'Good try.'

A slow smile spread across the round face of the general. He nodded his head slowly, as if in admiration of Simon's audacity. Then he spoke slowly, giving time for Chang to translate, which he did with increasing glumness.

'He say you speak with the honesty of a snake and the wisdom of a cow,' he said. 'The whole of China is rising against the foreign pigs who have defiled our country with their religion and allowed their missionaries to murder our babies.' The general's tone rose and his words became a rant. 'None of your so-called armies will stand against the power of the Divine Empress. Just as we destroyed your pathetic attempt to relieve Peking so we will crush any further troops that land here.'

He paused. Then went on, 'As for you three, you will die the death of a thousand lashes. Tie them to the posts.'

With a yell, the Kansus ran forward and seized the trio, untying their hands and then retying the wrists of each of them behind each of the three posts. Fonthill turned his head to issue a further threat in an attempt to save them. He saw a messenger come through the opening and say something in the general's ear, then, more ominously, six long whips being produced as six of the Kansus stripped off their shirts and took post, two to each of the intruders. It was clear that the men would take it in turns to deliver each stroke, giving the flogged no respite. The coats of the three were torn from their backs in preparation for the beginning of the torture.

Jenkins groaned and, half-turning to Simon, said, 'Oh bloody 'ell. Not again.'

Fonthill, who was pinioned to the furthest of the poles on the left, turned his head. 'I am sorry, lads,' he said. 'The gamble failed. Thank you both for—'

But he was interrupted by a cry from Tung Fu-hsiang. Immediately the whips were lowered and Simon felt a finger prod the middle of his naked back. He also felt the general's breath on his cheek. It reeked of cinnamon and other spices. The Chinaman prodded his back once more and turned and shouted to Chang.

'He says, what are those marks?'

Puzzled, Simon replied, 'They are the marks of the flogging we received from the Mahdi at Khartoum, in the Sudan. My comrade next to me was also whipped. What does it matter?' The punishment had been administered more than fifteen years before but the tan which they had both received on the slow plod on the ship across the Pacific a few months ago had not concealed the scars, which now stood out like white wheals.

'He say, how many lashes you receive?'

What was this about? Fonthill sighed. Perhaps the bastard would double the dose for them – but he had already promised a thousand, which was the death penalty, so it didn't matter. 'I had fifty lashes and Jenkins twenty-five.'

'Ah!' The ejaculation came from Tung Fu-hsiang, who immediately jumped in front of Simon and Jenkins, removed his jacket and turned his back. A gasp came from the soldiers now crowded into the tent to witness the entertainment, for the general's back also bore the signature of the lash, criss-crossed and standing out whitely, like those of Fonthill and Jenkins.

'He say,' said Chang, his voice a little louder now, 'he say he got forty lashes as young man from Empress's nephew, the deposed Emperor, a cowardly man. He salutes you two as similar brave warriors. These are marks of courage. Many men die as result.'

The general, now beaming, interrupted Chang, who listened with growing disbelief and then translated with as much of a smile as his closed eye would allow. 'He say, because of this, he will release us and let us through the lines to settlements. But, he wants you to know that this is not because of minister's attempt at bribery, which he treats with scorn, but because he admires bravery. Cousin, we are not going to be whipped to death. God be praised!'

''Ere, 'ere,' muttered Jenkins. 'Tell the old bastard that I'll vote for 'im, see, when he stands for emperor, so I will.'

Fonthill maintained a straight face and nodded sagely. 'Thank the general. We admire him as a man of courage also.'

Their bonds were cut and their ill-fitting coats restored to them. Simon gave the general a half-bow, which the others emulated, and followed the officer out of the tent, amidst a hum of – what, derision, approval, disappointment? – from the assembled soldiers.

'Have you noticed something?' asked Simon. 'The firing has stopped.'

'I think I know why,' beamed Chang. 'It all bally interesting, cousin. I tell you why when we get through lines.'

They followed the officer who picked his way through the shallow trench works that constituted the Chinese forward lines. They passed hundreds of Imperial soldiers, rifles at the slope, who were marching away from the settlements. Then the officer pointed towards a low mud wall which fronted the Chinese lines some two hundred yards away. It was studded with rifles at its crest and broken occasionally by the snout of a cannon. But all firing had stopped.

'He say, there are French lines,' interpreted Chang. 'We free to go towards them.'

With a half-smile, the officer gave them a ceremonial bow and marched quickly away, to catch up with the departing infantry.

Simon turned to Chang. 'What was so bally interesting back there, cousin?'

'Ah.' The Chinaman gave a lopsided smile. 'Just as we being tied to posts a man came in and gave general a message.'

'Yes, I noticed that. Did you hear what he said?'

'Not completely. But I hear distinctly words "thousands of Russian troops" and "retreat".'

Fonthill returned the smile, slowly nodding his head. 'I thought this "comrades-in-arms and fellow sufferers" stuff was all too good to be true. The old rascal freed us because reinforcements had arrived for the settlements and he wanted to get some credit with the Allies for releasing us. The old fraud.'

'Well,' said Jenkins, 'I don't really care what 'e thought as long as 'e let us go. Now let's get moving towards the Frenchies, shall we?' And he began to stride forward.

'No!' Fonthill held up his hand. 'If we march across this no man's land wearing these coats, we are just asking to be shot by the French. Take 'em off and we will saunter across in our underpants, waving the coats. That should amuse the French and also stop 'em shooting at us. Come on – and try and smile. We could be having French onion soup for lunch . . .'

And so, barefooted, wearing fixed grins and nothing but their filthy and still-wet and virtually transparent underpants, the three comrades strode towards the defenders of the Tientsin settlements.

CHAPTER NINE

Alice Fonthill sat down outside the hospital, wiped her brow with a less-than-clean handkerchief and cursed her husband. The words came from a fruity vocabulary, built up originally in her Swiss finishing school and then honed and extended during her years of reporting for the *Morning Post* from various boundaries of the Empire on Queen Victoria's wars and also from campaigning with Simon. Alice had never lived a sheltered life and, although being shelled through most of the day and living on quarter rations of dusty rice and horse meat did not exactly represent tranquillity, she resented being cooped up in Peking and, most of all, being without Simon.

As a soldier's daughter, a war correspondent operating in a masculine world and as the active partner of an army scout and 'irregular' agent, she was used to hardship and danger. What she resented now, however, was being forced to play the role of the woman waiting anxiously for news of her man. She had done it before, of course, but rarely since their marriage. And certainly not when he had set off on any mission that so justified the term 'hopeless cause' as this one.

She jerked the brim of her canvas hat down over her eyes in a vicious movement to avoid the glare of the sun. How could he be asked to track eighty miles through enemy territory – an obvious Occidental in Oriental country – with not a single word of the language, no transport and no real idea of where he was going? And how could he accept such a task, without taking her with him? She picked up a handful of dust and threw it away again, immediately regretting it as it blew back in her face.

Alice loved Fonthill with a passion that had grown stronger with each year they had been together. They had made a false start when, impressed by his bearing and courage, she had married Lieutenant Colonel Ralph Covington, Simon's erstwhile commanding officer. Shortly after her engagement, she had realised her mistake but, when Covington had lost an eye and a hand in action, she had honoured her pledge to him. The arid years of her marriage had ended with her husband's death at the Battle of Tel el-Kebir and she had hurried into Fonthill's arms. But she bitterly regretted those lost years and the thought now of losing Simon filled her with despair. Where was he, what was he doing and why couldn't she be by his side, instead of sweating away here, changing dressings?

In the early days of the siege, before Simon had set off, morale within the legations had been kept alive by rumour of imminent relief: of distant bugles and bagpipes heard and of strange lights in the sky to the south-east. Now, these had receded and been replaced by a grim realisation that things would get worse within Peking before they got better. The fighting was static but it was relentless and casualties were mounting, usually among the most efficient and courageous of the defenders.

Practicality was the order of the day. Sir Claude was proving to be a surprisingly energetic leader, with a fine eye for detail. Typical of his range of concern was the notice he posted at the Bell Tower, written in his tiny, civil service hand. It ran: 'LOOPHOLES. Loopholes should never be left open except when being used for looking through or firing through. A brick placed at the narrowest part is quite sufficient to prevent the enemy from firing through and hitting people passing.' The ex-subaltern was proving his worth as a military commander.

The previous day had probably been the worst since the siege began. The Japanese had been dislodged from their only recently installed fallback position in the Fu and had to erect, once again, a new defensive barricade; the Germans, in their sector, had been reduced to a desperate bayonet charge to save their positions; and, as ever, the Americans were under fierce attack on the wall.

Then, just before dusk, Alice, working in the hospital, had been almost thrown to the ground by two explosions from the direction of the French Legation. Two mines had been detonated under what was left of the legation there and a howling mob of Chinese had poured through the ruins, jumping between the flames caused by the explosions.

Alice had seized her revolver and rushed to the scene. She found that the French were conducting a strenuous defence amidst the debris, kneeling in the smoke and repeatedly firing into the mass of attackers, who had now halted, daunted by the French shooting. She herself joined the French but was thrust aside by a member of what was left of Fonthill's mobile reserve, who rushed to the aid of the French, alternately firing and throwing up rubble to form a new barricade. Eventually, a bridgehead was created and held but two French sailors were buried in the debris and several others were wounded, including the Austrian *chargé d'affaires*.

Wearily, Alice made her way back to the hospital, where the day had been the busiest yet, five men having died there and ten others brought in for treatment.

Every day, however, the work in the little hospital was hard and becoming increasingly demanding. Set up in the chancery of the British Legation, it was small and inadequately resourced. It had only four small iron bedsteads and seven camp beds and most of the patients were forced to lie on mattresses on the floor, stuffed with straw in which wine bottles had been packed. The windows were sandbagged and the heat and the flies were intolerable for patients and staff alike. There were few anaesthetics, fewer antiseptics and only one thermometer.

The place was run by two physicians: Dr Velde, a German surgeon, and Dr Poole, the British Legation's resident doctor. They were given support by an overworked sickbay attendant from a British warship and an amateur nursing staff, of whom Alice and Mrs Griffith were among the earliest and most dedicated members. Latterly, Lady MacDonald, the respected wife of the British minister, had organised the ladies of the Legation to provide a deeper nursing source to assist the doctors. Dr Morrison, the *Times* correspondent, was a trained backup for the doctors but he had proved to be as brave and active a member of the defenders as any of the regular sailors and soldiers and was to be seen on the line now more than in the hospital.

He, in fact, was a factor in deciding Alice that she need not be as scrupulous a helper in the hospital as in the early days of the defence. She realised that, although he could not send any despatches back to the London *Times*, Morrison was almost certainly preparing for the day when the cable services could be reached and was making extensive notes of the incidents in the siege. She must do the same and so, given the increasing numbers of ladies to strengthen the nursing roster, she had now taken to reducing her shifts in the hospital and visiting each sector of the defences in turn.

She did so, wearing her riding breeches and boots, wide-brimmed hat and with the pearl-handled Colt revolver tucked into her belt. She had become known, in fact, as 'The Lady with the Gun' and, ignoring the protests of the officers in the line, she had several times taken part in helping to fight off attacks on her sector.

Now, squatting in the sun at the door of the hospital, Alice decided that it was pointless worrying about Simon. She rose to her feet and brushed the dust from her skirt. It was time to visit the Fu, the most hard-pressed sector of the line.

She made her way back to the tiny room – previously a store cupboard – that she shared now with Mrs Griffith, splashed a little water onto her face, changed into her breeches, thrust her revolver into her belt and picked up her pencil and notebook. As usual, she was warned not to go further as she scurried out of the Legation and across the narrow bridge spanning the central canal. And, as usual, she smiled at the sentry and continued on her way, ducking her head instinctively as the noise of the firing increased as she neared the barricade up ahead.

Alice was full of admiration for the Japanese contingent who defended the park-like space immediately to the east, across the canal from the British Legation. Of all the contingents, these little men – no more than twenty-five of them – fought the hardest and complained the least. They presented the amazing statistic of sustaining a hundred per cent casualties, in that every single man had been hit and had to leave the line at one time or another and returned, including their commander, Colonel Shiba, the Japanese military attaché. He had become a particular favourite of Alice, for he made no fuss about her helping to man the barricade.

He greeted her now with a smile and a full, ceremonial bow.

'Quieter today, Colonel?' she asked.

'Not quiet, madam. These Muslims facing us fire all the time but they usually fire too high.'

Alice knew that the defending line here had been forced to contract regularly since the Kansus had first broken through the walls of the park. Now it zigzagged across the open space, winding its way between the various small buildings and shrines, now reduced to rubble, most of them.

'Have you had to fall back today, Colonel?'

'No, Madam. And we retreat no more. If they make frontal attack, we kill them. But we stay here.'

Alice scribbled in her pad, noting that the Colonel had a bullet tear across the right shoulder of his uniform. She drew her revolver and made her way to an open loophole in the rubble that formed the barricade. She removed her hat and peered through. The Chinese barricade, similarly made of broken bricks, gravestones and the like, seemed amazingly near. They had left open a small gap, through which, presumably, they made their now increasingly rare frontal attacks, and, through it, she could see dun-coloured figures moving. They were close enough for her to make out some facial characteristics, although most of the Kansus were dressed exactly alike. She levelled the Colt. She now had no compunction at all in killing any of the Chinese troops. One less might somehow ease the danger on Simon.

She sighted down the long barrel and then froze. Into view came a white-suited figure, disconcertingly familiar, with his Occidental features, yet wearing his hair drawn back into a pigtail and affecting a long Mandarin moustache. Her jaw dropped and her finger slackened on the trigger. Then the figure had gone.

Alice pulled back away from the loophole, her eyes wide. Could it be? Could it be Gerald Griffith, mingling with the Muslim Kansus opposite this, the most tightly pressed sector of the Legation defences?

She took another look but sharply withdrew as a bullet pinged to the left of the loophole. She scurried back to find the colonel.

'Has a man – a European-looking man – in a white suit been seen on the Chinese barricades?' she asked.

The little man immediately walked along the line and barked a series of questions to his men. He came back. 'No, madam,' he said. 'All Muslims opposite us. Very sorry.'

Alice thanked him and walked away, her head down, thinking hard. The colonel had told her previously that the Kansus seemed to know which part of the defences were the most vulnerable and on which to concentrate their fire. Could it be that Gerald – *her cousin* – was relaying this kind of information to the enemy? Although he made no secret of his admiration for the Boxers and his approval of their cause, he surely would not take that attitude to the point of betraying his fellow countrymen? Or would he?

It was true that he had taken to disappearing again during the day but Alice had given up questioning him, or even of talking to the young man, for fear of encouraging his obvious admiration for her.

In fairness, this had been restricted to glances and the odd brush of the hand. No flowers now – they would be difficult to find, anyhow. Could she face him now and charge him with betrayal? It would be a heinous crime of which to accuse him. No. She would probe gently with Aunt Lizzie, although she would have to step warily there.

She found the missionary's widow sitting outside the Legation main building, sewing a piece of cotton onto an old, torn skirt.

Alice smiled at her. She had become very fond of her aunt, despite – or perhaps because of – them being thrown together in the crowded conditions of the Legation. The old lady was a strange mixture: a diffident, modest woman whose faith and love of her husband had sustained her throughout her arduous life in China; and yet also a tough, resilient pragmatist who was not above scolding a servant with the sharpest of tongues. She had taken the death of her husband with remarkable equanimity, although she visited his plot of earth in the Legation cemetery – there had been no chance of putting up a proper headstone – every evening.

'Be careful, Aunt, sitting there,' she said. 'You are not out of range of a stray bullet, you know.'

The old lady held up her handiwork in a gesture of disgust. 'If a bullet finds me,' she said, in mock resignation, 'then it will be the

Lord's will. I just can't sit inside our stuffy room any longer. And, anyway, I can't see in there.'

Alice discreetly slipped her revolver along her belt to the small of her back out of sight and squatted in the dust beside her aunt. 'Here,' she offered, 'let me do that for you.'

'No, my dear, but thank you. I can see clearly out here. Where have you been?'

'Well I finished my shift at the hospital and went for a bit of a walk.' She made a show of looking around.. 'Where's Gerald?'

'Oh, I don't know. I don't know where he gets off to.' She looked up quickly. 'No news of Simon and Chang, I suppose?'

'No, dear. And I don't expect to hear anything.' She paused. 'I am sorry we had to mislead you rather about their departure.'

Mrs Griffith came near to a sniff. 'Yes, well, I didn't feel that was absolutely necessary, although I would have tried to persuade Chang not to go, you know.' She looked at her niece with stern eyes. 'He is only a boy. Hardly sixteen. I worry about him all the time.'

'I am sure you do, Aunt, and I am so sorry. But he was ideal for the purpose and so anxious to take part. We had to dissemble to you about him because of the security risk. Sir Claude and Simon could not risk news of their journey leaking out . . .'

'You mean Gerald?'

Alice started. She had never thought for a moment that Mrs Griffith ever doubted her son's allegiance to the defenders of the legations and it was startling to see her refer to the possibility now so matter-of-factly.

'Well . . . er . . . yes. But not just him, you know. It is common knowledge that this place is riddled with spies and Boxer sympathisers.'

'Gerald would never do anything like that.' The words came out like bullets from a gun.

Alice's mind slipped back quickly to the attack of the Boxers on the cart and the discharge of Gerald's fowling piece which prompted the murder of his father. 'No, Aunt,' she said. 'Of course not.' This was *not* treading warily. The subject had to be changed. 'Is Gerald still wrapped up in his medieval texts?' she asked brightly. 'I never seem to see him now.'

A smile came at last to Mrs Griffith's careworn face. 'Oh yes. He takes *such* an interest in the history of this country, you know. He was waiting to take a postgraduate degree at the university when all this trouble started. He has such an original mind.' She paused for a moment, her needle poised. 'I suppose he is what you would call a freethinker. He has always supported the cause of Chinese nationalism against foreign intervention in this country.'

Alice decided to probe. 'And yet, of course,' she said, 'the Boxers and the people in court here who support them would blame the missionaries for so much of that intervention.'

'Certainly not!' The old lady's tone expressed extreme indignation. 'It is not the men of God who have claimed large territories of China for their own commercial ends. It was not the missionaries who encouraged the growing and selling of opium here. No. It was the politicians and empire-builders back home in Europe who made money from that loathsome trade and who have been competing against each other for years to acquire large swathes of this wonderful country, taking advantage of China's weak and corrupt central government to do so.'

She leant forward to make her point. 'You know, Alice, dear

Edward had a basic sympathy for the Boxers. He felt that they were – they are – just a bunch of uneducated young men, simple peasants, who felt that they had to stand up against this Western imperialism. No. It was their unthinking brutality, their primitive violence, that he abhorred, not their basic motives.'

Alice had never heard her aunt express these kinds of views before – indeed, she had never heard her discuss politics of any sort. But she was beginning to see what had influenced Gerald's thinking. Now, she must gently steer the conversation back to him.

'So Gerald was influenced by his father in adopting his views?'

Mrs Griffith frowned. 'Well, not exactly. Gerald was always much more nationalistic than Edward in his thinking. And,' the frown deepened, 'I am afraid that there was a gulf between him and his father in later years. They did not speak together very much. It was very sad.' She returned to her sewing.

'How, then, did Gerald acquire his views?'

'Oh, I don't really know. He read many books of Chinese history – in their original Mandarin, of course – and he began mixing with a rather regressive . . . I think that would be the word . . . group in the court here.' She looked up and stared into the middle distance, reflectively. 'He's quite a good talker, a debater, you know.'

'I wouldn't doubt it. But, Aunt, what will he make of his life now? The Great Powers will never let this siege go unpunished. Whatever happens to us here, there will be a terrible revenge invoked against the Manchu court and the government. Given his views and his ethnicity, would there be a place for him in the Chinese foreign service? Would the Empress – should she keep her throne after the war – want a foreigner like him to serve her and, indeed, would the ambassadors and ministers of the powers want to deal with someone like him?'

Mrs Griffith looked surprised at the question. 'Why ever not? He will have done nothing wrong at all in this business. He would be just the sort of young man to enter the service and help to build bridges between China and the great nations.'

Alice nodded. So '*he will have done nothing wrong*'! Her aunt clearly had no doubt about her son's basic loyalty to his country – his *real* country. Or was it his *real* country? Surely a man could decide to give his patriotism to the land in which he was born and in which he had grown up. After all, Gerald had never visited England. His parents were the only influences in his life to steer him towards allegiance to Britain and its empire. And they were completely dedicated to their work in China, an empire with a civilisation and history far longer than that of those small islands off the mainland of Europe. Alice gave a tiny shrug. She could go no further with Mrs Griffith. Her mind's eye once again threw up the distinctive image of the man in the white suit behind the Chinese barricade. She *must* discover his identity. If Gerald was a spy for the Chinese court then he was a source of great danger to the defenders of the legations. The only thing to do was to question the man himself. But – again – she had to tread warily. He must not be warned that he was under suspicion. She would catch him when his guard was down.

Gerald Griffith, however, never seemed to lower his guard, nor keep to a fixed schedule. All of the able-bodied men in the Quarter were expected to play their part in the defence, but there was no mobilisation, no formal allocation of responsibilities, except to the men and women of some standing who joined the various committees set up by Sir Claude to direct the logistics of the defence. Those down the line who shirked did become the subject of social approbation but, somehow, Gerald escaped all that. His profile, of course, was not high, unlike that of the cordially detested French minister, and he kept to himself, slipping beneath the gaze of authority, quietly reading his Chinese texts, coming and going at odd times. An evasive, slippery figure.

So it was not until three days later that Alice was able to accost her cousin. She had decided that, if he did find her attractive, despite their age difference, then, indeed, she would deploy that weapon to detain and even, perhaps, intrigue the young man – Alice had never been averse in her work to using her good looks to gain a professional advantage. As a result, catching a glimpse of him sitting reading that evening in the shade cast by the hospital, she rushed to her room, applied a little face powder and rouge and a touch of her precious perfume, and emerged to walk by him, so innocently.

'Ah, Gerald,' she smiled. 'I have not seen you for ages. May I sit with you for a minute? I think there is room on that log and that shade looks so cool.'

Gerald Griffith looked up and distinctly blushed. 'Of course,' he said, standing and taking the hand she offered to help her sit. 'I was . . . er . . . just reading.'

'So I see. What is the book?'

He snapped it shut and shuffled uneasily on their makeshift bench. 'Oh, just something from Father's old library. It wouldn't interest you. It's Chinese philosophy. I hardly understand it myself.' He gave a small, self-deprecating laugh.

Alice put a hand on his arm. 'You know, Gerald, I am so sorry about your dear father's death. Do you miss him dreadfully?'

He looked at her from the corner of his eye and, almost imperceptibly, edged closer to her on the log, so that their thighs touched. She did not move away. 'Oh . . . er . . . yes, of course,' he said. 'Although, I have to confess that in the last few years we were not close, you know.' He held up the book. 'I think he became annoyed that I did not follow his faith. I am studying the Shinto religion, you see.'

'Ah, how interesting.' She gave him a sidelong look. He was wearing a two-piece suit of dark-grey cotton. 'You always look so smart, Gerald. Goodness gracious, how many suits did you bring with you?'

He gave a slightly embarrassed smile. 'Oh, only two. The other one is a white flannel. But it is too hot, really, and it gets dirty so quickly here, of course.'

'Yes, of course. Tell me, my dear, what do you do with yourself all day under these difficult conditions?'

'Well I mainly study. And sometimes go for a walk.'

'Walk? But there is hardly anywhere to go. We are so restricted here.'

'Oh, I find places.'

The firing from the Fu suddenly rose in intensity and then fell away again. 'Another attack on the Fu,' observed Alice tentatively.

'Oh, I doubt it,' said Gerald airily. 'The Chinese there have dropped their direct attacks and decided that a process of attrition is the best way forward. With so few Japanese facing them they feel it is only a question of time before they wear down the defences there. It is better to snipe than to charge across in the open, you see.'

'Really. How do you know that, Gerald?'

He looked uneasy for a moment. 'Oh, I hear these things, you know. And it is just common sense, really.'

They fell silent for a moment. Then he looked directly at her. 'Have you heard from Simon?'

The question threw her for a moment. She had never discussed his absence with Gerald – nor with anyone, for that matter, except her aunt. 'No, I have not, nor did I expect to.'

He looked smug. 'No, I don't suppose you would, would you? Nothing gets through now from Tientsin.'

She whirled round on him. 'How would you know where he was going?'

A smile of self-satisfaction spread across the young man's face. 'Good gracious, cousin. Everyone knew that he, Chang and that ludicrous Welshman were trying to slip through the lines and impress the Foreign Powers at the coast of the need to send another relief force.'

Alice looked hard at her cousin. '*Everyone* knew, Gerald? I have told no one. Who do you mean by "everyone"?'

He shrugged his shoulders. 'A lot of people. Anyway, I saw them go.'

'Gerald, they left in the middle of the night. What were you doing out at that time? Were you spying on them?'

'Oh, I was just out walking. I don't *spy*.'

'How did you know where they were going?'

For the first time the young man looked uncomfortable. 'Oh, I just put two and two together. It was not difficult to presume that that was where they were going. They were dressed as Kansu soldiers. The Chinese certainly presumed that that was where they were heading.'

'The *Chinese*?'

Gerald had now regained his composure. He seemed now to be

revelling in his knowledge. 'Oh yes.' The pressure on Alice's thigh had now increased. 'You would be surprised at what I know, cousin. I have very good friends in high places beyond these walls, you know.'

Alice drew in a deep breath. She was amazed at his indiscretion. He was clearly keen to impress her and she decided to play along with his arrogance. 'You amaze me, Gerald. You mean you have contact with the people who are besieging us?'

'Oh, yes. They have confidence in me and I work at their friendship because I am sure that, when this ridiculous siege is over, I can be useful to both sides in settling the peace.' He took up her hand. 'I will be able to help you and Mother by interceding with the Chinese authorities, Alice. You can trust me.'

She gently withdrew her hand. 'Thank you. But you said that the Chinese knew about Simon's mission. How did they know, Gerald?'

The shifty look came back into his eyes. 'Oh, everybody knew,' he said vaguely. Then he picked up her hand again and faced her directly. His face took on a serious and troubled mien, that of a much older man, concerned for her. 'You must reconcile yourself, dear Alice, to the fact that Simon will not return, you know. The Kansus sent off three cavalrymen to apprehend the three of them and, if they resisted, to kill them. This was some time ago, so I am very much afraid that that is probably what happened. I am so sorry.'

Alice felt the blood drain from her face. She drew in a deep breath. She must retain control. She gripped the hand holding hers. 'Gerald, can you really find out what has happened to Simon? I need to know.'

'Oh, I expect so. Yes, of course. I will ask my friends. They should know by now.' The old arrogance came back to his face. 'They were so stupid, you know, Simon and the Welshman, to set out like that, expecting that my so-called brother could guide them to Tientsin.'

'What do you mean, your "so-called-brother"? Surely, he *is* your brother, even though he is adopted?'

Gerald shook his head vigorously. 'No, he is not. He is just the son of some backward peasants that were killed. My parents took him in. He is *really stupid*, with his affected accent and silly British words. He tries to be what he is not. He should be proud to be Chinese. There is no need for him to ape the British. It is preposterous. And he is so young.' His mouth turned down in contempt. 'He is the last person to guide anyone to Tientsin, let alone conduct them through the Chinese army. He is just a silly, young boy.'

Alice felt that she could not stand very much more of this. How sure could he be that Simon was dead? He did not sound altogether convinced. But she must not let her emotions take over. She must continue to indulge him, however odious the task. She pressed his hand and then withdrew her own.

'Well, thank you, Gerald. Yes, please do find out what you can about Simon.' She let her voice then assume a tone of admiration and wonder. 'It sounds as though you go freely into the Chinese lines. How on earth do you do that? It must be extremely difficult.'

He seized her hand again. 'Oh no. It's not all that difficult, if you know what I know. People do it all the time. There is a secret place that is used for smuggling. I will show you, if you like.'

'Oh yes. Please do.'

Gerald then had a moment of doubt. 'Well, I will, of course. But you must not tell anyone. Will you promise me that?'

'Of course.'

'Very well. We could go tonight. I could introduce you to some of my friends, if you like.'

'Yes, please do. That would be most interesting.'

He looked around him. He had suddenly become a furtive adventurer. 'We had better make it after dark. Shall we meet here an hour after nightfall?'

'Good, I shall be here.'

'So will I.' He now adopted a proprietorial air. 'You will see and hear things tonight that will interest you greatly. I promise.'

Alice freed her hand and stood. 'Thank you, Gerald. Until tonight, then.'

His eyes were glowing as he answered, 'Until tonight, then, cousin.'

Walking away, Alice thought of her husband. Was he dead? She tossed her head defiantly. Of course not! Simon Fonthill was indestructible. But she wished – oh, how she wished! – that he was here to deal with this odious young man, *her own cousin*!

Chapter Ten

Within fifteen minutes of crossing those two hundred or so yards of no man's land and then climbing the bales of wool, silk, cotton and peanuts that formed the main part of the French line defending the settlements, Fonthill found himself sitting facing the senior British officer at Tientsin, Brigadier General Dorward. Jenkins and Chang had been ushered away to be given soup – alas, not onion, but thin gruel – and Simon, wrapped once again in his Kansu coat, was telling his story.

'Seymour is where, did you say?' barked the brigadier.

'Only about six miles from you, upriver. He is holed up in this great Chinese arsenal. He has plenty of supplies because he has captured them, but he is completely surrounded by Tung Fu-hsiang's forces, his command is severely depleted and he can't fight his way out. Can you relieve him?'

'My dear . . . what's your name again, sir?'

'Fonthill.'

The brigadier leant forward. 'My dear Fonthill, we are not in a position to relieve anyone.'

Simon blinked. 'But the siege of the settlements has been lifted, hasn't it? I saw the Kansus retreating. Haven't thousands of Russians arrived from the coast?'

'No bloody fear. Look. We only had two thousand four hundred men to start with – to defend a five-mile perimeter against a force that we estimate to be at least twenty thousand. More came in and then we managed to get a message through to Taku, a twelve-hour ride away, through country thick with Chinese troops. Bless 'em, they responded and scraped the barrel – or rather, the ships – to produce a mixed bag of Russians, Germans, Americans and a few British. They have fought every inch of the way and managed to get through this morning.'

He wiped a hand across his chin, scraping his whiskers. 'What this means, my dear fellow, is that we have not been *relieved*. We have been merely *reinforced*. Our defenders have been supplemented, thank God, but I can't see us breaking out of here to relieve anyone. These people surrounding us are not a bunch of Boxers. They are the Kansus, fierce fighters, as we have found out, and an organised army, well equipped with artillery.'

'But I saw the Kansus retreating.'

'Not retreating. Regrouping.'

A silence descended on the room to be broken, ominously, by the boom of Chinese cannon. Weary and hungry, Fonthill felt his heart sink. He had, it seemed, escaped from the frying pan into the fire.

What hope for the Peking defenders now, with the military forces of the so-called Great Powers cooped up within rings of Chinese bayonets? He sighed.

'But Brigadier,' he said, his voice low, 'I have explained that the situation in Peking is becoming desperate. I don't know how long the people there can continue to defend the legations but it can't be long. We can't sit here and wait for them to be overwhelmed.'

The brigadier had the grace to look embarrassed. 'As a matter of fact,' he said, 'reports have come out from . . . Shanghai, I think it is, that they have already . . . er . . . capitulated. Mind you,' he hurried on, 'these are unsubstantiated.'

Fonthill put his brow in his hands. 'Oh my God. My wife is still there.'

'Ah, my dear chap.' Dorward put out his hand and touched Simon's arm. 'I am so sorry. Let me repeat that these are just rumours, and you know what China is like for rumours. Such a huge country with such poor communications. Almost sure to be rubbish.'

Simon looked up. 'Who is in command here?'

'Well . . . ah . . . nobody, really. That's the trouble, y'see. We are such a mixture. The Russians have got the most troops here but, theoretically, I suppose I am the senior officer. Look here, Fonthill. All is not lost. Let me talk to the senior chap amongst these new arrivals – Russian, almost certainly – and let us see if we can get a force to break out and get to this arsenal place. You are quite right, the effort should be made.'

'Thank you, Brigadier.'

'However,' Dorward mused for a moment. 'There is no way we could strike north for Peking without taking the Chinese City of Tientsin first. It's a walled city of about a million people and it completely dominates the way north. We estimate that it is defended by about twelve thousand Imperial troops, with something like ten thousand Boxer auxiliaries. All of which doesn't mean to say we can't knock 'em over. Now, could you lead us to this arsenal place, d'yer think?'

'Yes. Shouldn't be difficult. Skirt the Chinese City but follow the river. We wouldn't need an army but Seymour has plenty of wounded to move. We would want probably about a thousand troops who could move quickly, I would think, if you can spare 'em.'

'Hmm. Probably have to. We can't leave Seymour holed up. And we had better act quickly to take advantage of the fact that the Kansus are movin' about. Now, let's get you something to eat and wear.'

'Clothes for my two companions also, please, Brigadier.'

'Of course.'

Dorward acted with commendable speed. Early the next morning, Fonthill, Jenkins and Chang – the latter pair had refused to be left behind – set off at the head of a mixed force of men, most of them Russian, who streamed out of the settlements. The column was under the command of a Russian, Colonel Shirinsky, whose mounted Cossacks ranged ahead and either side of the infantry, who themselves marched in quick time. They were immediately opposed by a force of Imperial troops, but a determined charge by the Cossack vanguard, wielding lance and sword, scattered the enemy. The column advanced at speed and with a sense of purpose that impressed Fonthill.

The Colonel took it in a swing away from the walls of Tientsin City and then back again to the river and soon they saw the huge redoubt that was the arsenal. With a sigh of relief, Simon saw that the white ensign of the British navy still fluttered high above the walls and he joined the squadron of Cossacks who, pennants flying from their lances, cantered up to the great wooden door.

Within moments, he was introducing a weary but relieved Seymour to the red-cheeked Russian colonel.

'Thank God you got through, Fonthill,' said Seymour, pumping his hand. 'Plain sailing, was it?'

'Oh absolutely, Admiral. Pleasure cruise, really.'

While the Cossacks ranged the surrounding country, now remarkably clear of the besieging Kansus, the remnants of the original relief column were gathered, carts were loaded with supplies and ammunition from the arsenal's stores, and the wounded who could not march were led out on stretchers.

The journey back was slower, of course, but the column was remarkably unhindered, whether because of the fearsome reputation already established by the Cossacks on their advance on the settlements, or because the bulk of the Imperial troops had retreated to bolster the defence of the Chinese City, Fonthill could not decide. He was merely grateful that the first stage in the long march to relieve Peking had been successfully concluded.

As he marched at the head of the column with Jenkins and Chang, each of them arrayed in ill-fitting blue uniforms supplied by the Tientsin Office of Customs and carrying army issue rifles, his mind concentrated on the task ahead. How could he, a comparatively unknown civilian, move the massive diplomatic bureaucracy that surrounded the Allied army in the settlements to address the question of relieving Peking? Without a central point of control and chain of command to work with, how could he instil urgency and give focus to this loose collection of fighting men? Well, he shrugged, a start had been made, anyway.

It seemed almost as though the forces besieging the settlements had deliberately parted to let the Seymour remnants back within the barricades, for, the day after their return, the Chinese closed in again and launched a series of attacks along the perimeter. For more than two weeks the defenders fought savagely, encouraged by the new reserves of ammunition provided by Seymour's men and the fact that new men had arrived to reinforce those manning the low mud walls and bales of merchandise that formed the perimeter.

It was a hugely frustrating time for Fonthill, who, with Jenkins and Chang, took his turn at the barricades.

'This is a bit of a – whatchercall it – stalepiece, ain'it?' observed Jenkins, wiping his brow with a piece of fine silk that protruded from the bale over which he was firing.

'No, I think the word is "stalemate", is it not, cousin?' asked Chang. 'They can't get in and we cannot get out. It is not exactly checkmate, you see, Mr Jenkins, because either side can actually move, so—'

'Whatever it is,' growled Fonthill, 'I've had enough. I'm going to see Dorward.'

That evening he bearded the brigadier. Simon presented once more Sir Claude's message, with its plea for urgent action. The soldier nodded.

'There has been action, of a sort,' he said. 'We have formed a sort of council here, representing all of the powers involved, and I have informed them of your message. I should add that Lieutenant General Sir Alfred Gaselee, a most distinguished British soldier, is due to land at Taku any day, I understand, to take charge of troops here. At the moment, the trouble is that we have not been able to agree on an immediate course of action, when we have been under such pressure from the Chinese besieging us. But, look here.' He leant across his desk. 'There is a meeting tonight. Please come and present Sir Claude's message yourself. That should stimulate something.'

'Very well,' said Fonthill. 'But I warn you, I shall speak candidly.'

It was, felt Simon, a strange meeting. To a background of artillery fire, like a continuous and not-so-distant drum roll, eight men filed in to sit around Dorward's large table: Dorward and Seymour, two Russians, a Frenchman, an American, a German and a tiny Japanese, each dressed in the uniform of his country. With the exception of the Japanese, every man was bearded and each face reflected the strain of battle. Fonthill had dreaded that the language used would be French, the tongue of diplomacy, but everyone agreed to speak English. He had also feared that there would be a long agenda to get through before he was allowed to speak, but he was called upon to address the meeting immediately. Most of them, he reflected with satisfaction, were men of action, after all.

Dorward introduced him and gave a brief summary of how he and his two companions had arrived at Tientsin. Then Simon began.

'Gentlemen,' he said, looking round at the heavy, jowled faces, 'you have more than ten thousand men here, with the promise of more to come from the coast. You are fighting a defensive battle to protect the settlements. You have been able to evacuate most of the women and children of the settlements to Taku. You are fighting stoutly and you have been given fresh ammunition and supplies from Admiral Seymour's column. With the exception of the quick expedition to the arsenal, however, you have not moved from behind your barricades. It is time you did so.'

There was a sharp intake of breath, but he continued.

'I left Peking just over two weeks ago, getting here, as you have heard, with some difficulty. I did so because I was asked to bear a message from Sir Claude MacDonald, the British minister there, desperately pleading for help from you.' He looked around the table at each man in turn and then went on, emphasising his words.

'There are approximately two thousand civilians, including women and children and most of them Chinese, crowded into the legations there, sheltering, as you are here, behind makeshift barricades and walls. The difference is, though, that when I left, there were only some three hundred able-bodied men defending those walls. The little hospital there is full, the defenders are running low on ammunition and are reduced to half rations. The water they drink is warm and brackish. The enemy surrounding them is well armed and equipped with modern artillery. If they wished, they could reduce the whole Quarter to rubble with their cannon, but for some reason they do not do so, probably fearing the retribution that would fall on them from the Great Powers – that means from *you*, gentlemen.

'For weeks now, the defenders there – led by the formal representatives of your countries – have looked to you for relief. Their situation is rapidly becoming desperate. Whatever the circumstances here, you must set up a second relief column without delay. If you don't and if the Chinese break through and pour into the Legations, then the watching, civilised world will condemn you accordingly.

'It will take time to advance to Peking, through hostile country and without the service of the railway. But it can be done, following the river northwards. There is no time to be lost. You must break out of here *now*.'

He finished and sat back amidst heavy silence. Then the German, a large man with kindly eyes, spoke. 'Ve cannot move vizout taking the Chinese City. To leave vizout taking it vould leave the settlements at zeir mercy.'

The Frenchman shrugged his shoulders. 'It is a 'uge fortress. Do we 'ave the men to conquer it? Those big walls . . . ?'

The question hung in the air. 'Who would command the expedition?' enquired one of the two Russians.

'There must be a unified command,' declared Dorward. 'I suggest the country which provides the most men should provide the commander. And that,' he gave a deferential half-bow to the Russian, 'would be you, Admiral.'

'Ach no,' said the Russian, with a quick glance towards the silent Seymour, 'we need a soldier this time. You are the senior army man here, Dorward. You do it. You will have the Russian support.'

There was a low murmur of agreement around the table. Fonthill felt ambivalent. At least they had agreed to do *something*, but he had seen the size of the fortress that was Tientsin City. To break through those walls would need a serious besieging force. Could the besieged suddenly become the besiegers? How would they do it? But Dorward was speaking again.

'Very well, gentlemen, I am gratified to have your confidence. I take it that we are all agreed that we must take Tientsin City before we can think of mounting an expedition for the north?'

There were nods of agreement from around the table.

'Thank you. I will begin making a plan of attack immediately. Could each of you let me have, within the hour, a note of the forces you could provide for the attack? We must not, of course, leave the settlements unprotected and I suggest that, say, five thousand good men will be all that is needed. If we are to strike, we should do so quickly. There can be no suggestion of laying siege to the city. We must make a concentrated breakout which will turn into sudden, frontal attack on the gates. Let us meet again at eight tomorrow morning, when I shall present my plan to you.'

With that, the delegates stood, nodded to each other cordially, like city councillors breaking up after a municipal meeting, and departed, as the cannon still crackled in the background.

'Thank you, Brigadier,' said Fonthill. 'I hope to God you can take the city, for failure means that the legations must surely fall. Will five thousand be enough, do you think?'

Dorward tugged at his beard and smiled. 'Oh, I believe so. I have changed my mind. With the reinforcements we have received within the last few weeks and the way we have been able to repulse the attacks on the line in the last fortnight, I am convinced now that we can break out. Like a huge sortie, in fact. The city is just a couple of miles away and we can be upon it before the Chinese have had chance to prepare themselves. We now have some excellent men here in whom I have faith. You spoke well there, Fonthill. You persuaded us all.'

'Thank you. May Jenkins and I join in the attack? We don't want to kick our heels here.'

'Of course.'

Fonthill overruled Chang's protestations at being left behind – 'You are only sixteen, dammit, and although you have behaved magnificently in helping us to get here, you are not a soldier and this will be infantry work' – and he and Jenkins fell in with the 2nd Battalion of the Royal Welch Fusiliers, both of them delighted to be reunited with a Welsh regiment after so many years.

The attack took place on the second day after the meeting of the military leaders and, initially, the breakout went impeccably according to plan. Simon and Jenkins were with the British and French, held in reserve to the Japanese and Americans who led the attack, which was launched towards the South Gate in the walls, while units of Russians and Germans harassed Chinese positions on the north bank of the river.

The Japanese broke cleanly through the Chinese lines around the settlements, scattering the Kansus in their path and making Fonthill feel that a breakout could have been achieved long before this. The little men trotted along impassively behind their long bayonets, making for the South Gate, which faced the settlements.

The city, in effect, was one large box, formed by its stout walls, and with one gate on each of its sides. Without siege artillery, there was no way that the attackers could breach the walls of the city and the attack was therefore concentrated completely on the South Gate. The fault in this tactic, however, soon presented itself. The only way to reach the gate was by advancing along a causeway that ran in a straight line for approximately a mile, spanning open country crossed with canals, patches of marshy bog, irrigation channels and lagoons. The Japanese leading the attack, therefore, presented an easy target to the defenders firing down from the top of the walls. It was even worse for the 9th United States Infantry, newly arrived from fighting the guerrillas in the Philippines, who had to wade through the marshes to the right of the causeway.

Fonthill shook his head. 'Dorward is an idiot,' he said. 'This is just offering men up for slaughter. He should have attacked at night, targeting at least two of the gates. God help those Japanese.'

'Amen,' muttered Jenkins. 'To be honest, bach sir, I've never 'ad much faith in British generals, look you. What with Ishywander and all that lot in Zululand.'

'The man must never have commanded in battle in his life – he must have been stuck out here throughout his career. He's made an elementary mistake. We could be bogged down here for weeks before we get a chance to march on Peking. Damn and blast the bloody fool!'

As they watched, the fire from the ramparts of the city walls intensified and the Japanese began dropping like flies. To compound the matter, the Americans, struggling in the marshes, began moving to their left to find firmer ground on the causeway. Orders were shouted and the British and French began moving up behind the lead troops, deploying as best they could to deliver supporting fire upon the Chinese on the walls.

Fonthill and Jenkins were among the latter, crouching in the long marsh grass, attempting to target the distant and diminutive figures behind the puffs of smoke, high on the walls. The sun beat down and the humidity, intensified by the moisture engendered by the dykes and irrigation channels surrounding them, caused the perspiration to course down their foreheads and into their eyes. Their discomfort was compounded by the flies that rose from the marsh and settled on them like black snowflakes. They spent as much time beating them off as aiming and firing their rifles.

And so the day wore on, with the Japanese and Americans retreating in the face of the strong defensive fire and then surging ahead intermittently, only to fall back again.

As dusk approached, Simon met a sweating Dorward. 'Do you have any artillery you can bring to bear, Brigadier?' he asked.

'Only a couple of eighteen-pounders that we could ill spare from the defences of the settlements. Can't get 'em near enough to make a difference.'

'May I make a suggestion, sir?'

The two men eyed each other. They were roughly the same age and they might have been from similar backgrounds, except that Fonthill had formally left the army twenty years ago and Dorward, of course, had ploughed his way upwards through the officer ranks, albeit mostly in the Far East.

'You can suggest what you like, Fonthill. But may I enquire about your experience in situations such as this?'

'Of course you may. I served with the 24th of Foot and was at Isandlwana and Rorke's Drift in the Zulu affair. I did intelligence work with Roberts in Afghanistan and was in Kabul when the Residency was attacked. I was able to help Wolseley with his attack on the bePedi at Sekukuni and then at el-Kebir in Egypt. I commanded a couple of riverboats for Gordon at Khartoum, not that that did him much—'

Dorward held up his hand. 'Good Lord! Now I know who you are, Fonthill. You're the chap who got through to Gordon at Khartoum and was with Rhodes on the invasion of Matabeleland.'

Fonthill grinned. 'Well Rhodes wasn't exactly there, you know. He had a habit of turning up after the fighting was over.'

'Yes, well even so.' Dorward mopped his face with his handkerchief. 'I certainly accept your experience. Frankly, I am not sure what to do next. The Japs and the Yankees have taken a terrible beating. I've lost something like seven hundred men.'

'Yes. This looks a tough nut to crack. If I may say so, I think a frontal attack in daylight is ill-advised.'

'So. What do you suggest?'

'Wait until it is completely dark. Then, get the Germans and Russians to make a fuss, as though we're going to attack the North Gate. Have you got any sappers with you?'

'Yes.'

'And dynamite, too?'

'Well, I believe so.'

'Good. Make a big thing about retreating back down the causeway now, in the failing light. I think the Japanese and the Americans are probably a bit spent, by the look of it, so let them fall back. Then bring up the Welch Regiment quietly but hold them back. Give me enough dynamite to blow that bloody big South Gate open, then attack along the causeway with the Welshmen – they're damned good soldiers but they'll have to run fast – and break through what's left of the gate.'

'What? You would plant the explosives?'

'Yes. Well, I would take my man Jenkins with me to complete the job in case I get knocked over. It needs two men. Any more would probably be spotted, even in the dark. I do think it's the best plan, Brigadier.'

'Very well. Come with me and we'll talk to the sapper major.'

Simon explained the plan to the major, who listened, nodded and produced ten sticks of dynamite, wrapped innocuously in paper in two packets of five, each eight inches long and about one inch in diameter.

The major, a short, stout man with impressive moustaches, was pompously proprietorial about his explosives. 'Look here,' he said, 'this stuff is extremely dangerous.'

'Well,' muttered Jenkins, who had come along to be briefed, 'I suppose it would be, wouldn't it, if it's goin' to blow somethin' up, like.'

The sapper ignored him. 'These sticks,' he continued, 'are made of three parts nitroglycerine and one part diatomaceous earth, or fossilised microscopic algae, with a small addition of sodium carbonate. The point about the earth is that it makes the nitroglycerine less shock sensitive, but the sticks are still extremely volatile and have to be handled with great care. For God's sake don't drop 'em on the way, otherwise the sticks will be completely wasted – and they are hugely expensive, don't you know.'

Fonthill glared at Jenkins to prevent him from uttering the sarcastic put-down that was on his lips and asked instead: 'From what I can see of these gates, they are extremely thick and about twelve feet high. Will this stuff do the job?'

'Oh yes. Knock 'em down easily. Look. They should be detonated by using these two blasting caps fired by two long fuses, creating small explosions, triggering the larger ones.'

'Where exactly should we put the sticks?'

'Well, ideally, one group at the bottom and one about halfway up. But I don't suppose you will be able to knock nails in the gate, will you?'

'Doubt it.'

'Put them at the bottom, then, where the two gates meet. Any questions?'

'How long do we have after lighting the fuses?'

'Say thirty to forty seconds. Ensure they don't fizzle out, mind.'

'Oh we will. We will. Thank you, Major.'

'Right.' The brigadier turned back to Fonthill and Jenkins. 'I reckon you've got about an hour between now and when the moon comes up. Is there anything I can do for you before you go?'

'No, thank you. Just make sure that the Welshmen come in at the run when the balloon goes up. We don't want to give the Chinese time to shore up the gate again.'

'Of course. Forgive me now if I go and arrange things. Thank you both, and good luck.'

Fonthill gingerly deposited the dynamite in a small hessian sack and they both walked to where the men of the Welch Regiment were resting.

'Now, let me get this clear,' said Jenkins. 'When it gets really dark we just saunter up this causeway thing, steppin' over the bodies that are litterin' the place, like, an' we just pop this dynamite stuff at the bottom of the gates, ring the bell an' run away. Is that it?'

'Roughly right, old chap. I realise I've rather landed you in on this one, and I shall quite understand if you feel it's rather asking too much.'

'No, bach sir, thank you very much. I'm supposed to be lookin' after you on this postin', 'cos I promised Miss Alice, so I'll be goin' with you. I'll come just to make sure you don't drop the stuff and make that bloody little major shit 'is breeches about the cost of it an' all.'

'Don't be disrespectful about the major. He holds the Queen's Commission. Right. We'll take our rifles because we don't want to be left unarmed when the gates go down. But we'll sling 'em over our backs. Try and find us a pair of plimsolls, if you can in the time we have left. We want to move quietly – and run fast, if we have to. Off you go.'

Simon sat down and looked ahead of him. In the gathering dusk the walls of the Chinese City loomed high and impenetrable. Would the Chinese have a searchlight? They would be in trouble if they did. On reflection – and he gave a wry grin – they would probably be in trouble even if they didn't. This was a ridiculous enterprise. Everything depended upon the defenders relaxing their vigilance, having given the Japanese and the Americans a good hiding and despatching them, or so it seemed, back to the settlements; that and their attention being diverted by the faux attack on the North Gate.

Then he and Jenkins must get enough cover in the darkness to steal up to the South Gate, literally under the noses of the guards on the walls. Ah well. It seemed the only way to persuade these stuffy old armchair generals in the settlements to stir themselves for the real battle – in Peking. He thought again of Alice. He had no illusions. If the Chinese did break through to the legations, then she would stand little chance, despite the protection offered by Sir Claude. He offered up a quick prayer for her safety and then settled back to wait for Jenkins, his mouth dry, despite the heat and humidity.

The Welshman arrived, well within the hour, bringing two bayonets in scabbards, and two pairs of unlaced canvas running shoes. 'Didn't know about your size. Bigger than mine, I thought, 'cos I've got dainty little feet. 'Ere, try them on.'

'Oh, they'll do. Now. We will begin walking along the causeway at first, then, when we get nearer, I'm afraid we shall have to take to the marsh on the side of the road. The long grasses there should provide us with a bit of cover. Once we hear the sound of the diversion from the French and Russian lines, we will edge nearer and then make a run for it along the causeway. Keep the bayonets sheathed in case they flash a reflection when the moon comes up.'

'Matches?' enquired Jenkins.

Fonthill threw back his head. 'Oh, blast and damn!'

The grinning Welshman held up two boxes. 'Oh, dearie me. I 'ave to think of everythin'.'

Simon thumped him in the chest, pocketed one of the boxes, shouldered the hessian bag to hang down his back the other side to his slung rifle, then offered his hand to Jenkins. 'Good luck, old friend,' he said.

'Good luck, bach sir.'

Together, they began their walk in the darkness. The sun to the west had not long before slipped over the horizon, leaving a slight glow in the sky. But the moon had not yet risen and they made good time on the paved way, while they could. Then, to the north they heard the crackle of musketry and distant shouting.

Fonthill kept his eyes on the black walls ahead of him, dreading the sudden brilliance of a searchlight cracking open the darkness. They were now, he estimated, about a quarter of a mile from the gate.

'Time to get off the causeway,' he hissed to Jenkins. Immediately, their progress slowed as, shoulders bowed, they trudged through spongy grass and mud and then picked their way delicately through the shallow waters of the irrigation channels, stopping occasionally to freeze and listen to ensure that the Chinese had not sent out picquets to prevent just such a surprise attack. It took them more than an hour to cover most of that quarter of a mile and they were within the shadow cast by the city walls as the moon rose behind them.

The two men crouched together while Fonthill gave Jenkins his five sticks of dynamite. 'When I give the order,' he whispered, 'you run up to the right-hand side of the gate, and flatten yourself to the wall. I will do the same on the other side. When I nod, crawl up to the gate, put the dynamite as close to the door as you can, where it meets the other door. I will do the same. Trail out the fuse your way, the way you came, and I'll do the same. When I nod, light it.'

'What do we do then? Run like hell back down the road?'

'Absolutely not. It would be easy to pick us off, if they've got their wits about them. No. We flatten on the ground, as near to the wall and as far away from the bloody gates as possible. Hands over heads and just hope that the damned walls don't fall down on top of us.'

'Very good, bach sir.'

Simon took a deep breath. He could see no sign of movement on the battlements. 'Right. Off we go and good luck.'

The two men regained the causeway and, bent double, they ran towards the massive gate looming before them. Out in the open and feeling completely exposed, Fonthill realised that they were demanding a lot from Dame Fortune, if they were to reach the wall without being seen. And so it proved.

He heard a cry from up above him and then the sharp crack of a rifle. The bullet hit the paved road and pinged away, but by the time the second bullet was released, he was up against the wall, safely underneath a large stone overhang that ran all the way along, just beneath the embrasures, so preventing anyone manning the top from firing down vertically. 'Are you there, 352?' he called.

'I'm 'ere. To the gates now?'

'Fast as you can.'

The two men ran and met at the foot of the huge pair of gates. Simon placed his bundle of deadly sticks, almost touching those of Jenkins. Behind the door, the two men could hear voices shouting and the sound of running feet. Fonthill looked up and saw that there was a small post gate, set into the massive door. He unslung his rifle.

'Light your fuse and run,' he shouted.

''Ere. What are you goin' to do?'

'Never mind. Light the bloody thing.'

Throwing his rifle on the ground, Simon fumbled with a match, struck it, lit the fuse and then ran back, unwinding the fuse as it fizzed and crackled. Then he doubled back, picked up his rifle, just in time to see the post gate open. Firing from the hip, he brought down the first man to run through the gate, worked the breech bolt, fired into the open doorway, then ran back alongside the wall, hurling himself to the ground as the night exploded with a mighty boom and a thousand flashing lights that penetrated through his spread fingers. Debris, some of it blazing, rained down on him, for he had not made the comparative sanctity of the base of the wall. Then there was a great crash as the two doors forming the gate crumpled outward, shaking the ground where he lay. He became aware of a burning sensation across his leg and kicked away at a flaming ember that lay across it. His ears were singing but he could hear a faint cheer coming from far, far away, as he lapsed into unconsciousness.

He came to to find himself lying half in an irrigation channel close to the wall. Jenkins was splashing water onto his face.

'Are you all right, bach? Ah, thank God. I thought you'd gone for a minute. You were half on fire when I got to you.'

Fonthill raised his head and realised that heavy boots were pounding up along the causeway by his head as the Welch Regiment ran towards the open gateway. Cheering came from their rear but there was firing from within the city.

'Ah, thanks, 352,' he said. 'I feel a bit warm and my head's singing, but I think the fire's out. Are you all right?'

'Right as ninepence. Blimey, but you were barmy to go back to fire into that doorway. Bloody barmy, if you don't mind me sayin' so. You almost went up with the gates.'

Simon sat up and shook his head but the singing in his ears continued. 'Had to do that,' he shouted. 'Otherwise those fellers would have been through and been able to stamp out the fuses. I should have realised that there would be a post gate. Must be losing my touch. Here, help me up. I'm all right now.'

Together the two men stood, swaying slightly as the British infantrymen charged by them, their rifles and bayonets at the ready.

From within the city the firing was now muted, although screams could be heard.

Jenkins sniffed. 'I don't think there's much quarter bein' given by them Taffies,' he said, 'after bein' cooped up for so long in them settlements. An' they've 'eard what them Boxers 'ave done to the missionaries an' their families. They'll be goin' in with the bayonets, all right.'

'Let's get back,' said Fonthill. 'I don't think I'll be much good charging in there with them. My head is still singing.'

Together, the two comrades walked through the advancing troops –

the French were moving in now, behind the Welch Regiment – along the causeway and back to the settlements, where Jenkins found a doctor to examine Fonthill. His face was blackened and what was left of his Customs uniform singed and burnt, but he was found to have sustained only superficial burns and was put to bed with a soothing pill.

The next morning, he was visited by Dorward, who gingerly shook his bandaged hand. 'Congratulations, my dear fellow,' he said. 'You did a wonderful job. We stormed into the city and took it within the hour. Both the Chinese Imperial troops and the Boxers fled, streaming through the East and West Gates, those that weren't bayoneted. I fear that there was quite a bit of looting, but that can't always be helped in these conditions. Anyway, everyone here is very grateful to you.'

Fonthill waved his bandaged hand. 'Glad it worked, Brigadier. I thought for a terrible minute that we had blown it – no pun intended, you know.'

'No. The gates caved in beautifully and my sapper chap is going around saying it's all his work.' He grinned. 'And there's more good news.'

'What's that?'

'Lieutenant General Sir Alfred Gaselee has arrived from the coast with God knows how many troops.'

Fonthill's eyes lit up and he pushed himself into a half-sitting position. 'Ah, that's the best news I've heard. Now, when do you think we could put together a column and march to the north, eh?'

Dorward frowned. 'Oh, my dear fellow, not for some time yet. We have got to occupy the city and sort things out here first. Can't leave the settlements denuded. It may take some weeks yet, I fear.'

Fonthill groaned and sank his head back onto the pillow.

CHAPTER ELEVEN

Alice Fonthill dressed for that evening meeting with Gerald Griffith with as much care as she had displayed for that 'chance' meeting earlier in the day. No cosmetics this time, however. Despite the heat, which never slackened until long after the sun had gone down, she wore riding breeches, her long boots, a soiled cotton shirt, a bandana round her waist and her hair tied back severely with a scarf. From a box under her bed she retrieved the small French automatic pistol and six cartridges, which she inserted into the magazine. Then she tucked the gun into her bandana and sat on the bed, deep in thought.

What exactly was she hoping that this meeting with Gerald and his friends would reveal? Well, the first priority was to try and learn something about the whereabouts of Simon, Jenkins and Chang. She frowned. It was, of course, preposterous to think that the trio might be dead. Simon's whole life had consisted of getting into scrapes and getting out of them again. It was inconceivable to think that his time had come at last; he had so much . . . so much . . . *life* left in him. And there was 352 Jenkins with him, the Great Protector. She allowed herself a smile. No. Even if they told her that Simon was dead, then they would have to provide proof before she believed them.

Alice had to admit that the original, underlying reason why she had agreed to this assignation was to probe beneath that cool, self-satisfied demeanour of her cousin. She had learnt much already this afternoon, but the key question of whether he was an active spy, working within the Quarter for the Chinese, remained unanswered. And, if it proved that he was relaying vital information to the Manchu court, what would she do about it? She tossed her head. She would hand him over to Sir Claude, without compunction. Anyone who betrayed the defenders in their sad predicament deserved to be shot – or placed in prison. The punishment would be the minister's decision.

But what about her aunt? She had lost her husband, was she now about to lose her son – and possibly her adopted son also?

Alice put her head in her hand. Despite her great inner strength, that would surely be too much for the little widow to bear. And yet – she looked up and stared unseeingly at the wall of the room – what if Gerald had deliberately told the Chinese of Simon's mission and what if this had led to his death? She thought for a moment and then stood. It was now quite dark outside and time to go. She would face all of these questions later, if she had to.

Gerald was waiting for her, crouched by the side of the hospital from the interior of which came faint groans.

'You are late, cousin,' he said.

'I am sorry. I had things to do.'

He stood before her and seized both her hands. 'Now Alice, will you promise that you will tell no one of where we go tonight and of what you learn?'

She thought quickly, for she had already been forced to give one promise and she did not wish to compound the lie. 'Oh, come now, Gerald. You are making all this sound as though we are about to embark on a sequence from the *Arabian Nights*. You are fantasising. Or are you engaged in some enterprise which will make your mother and I ashamed of you?'

The ploy worked, for Gerald coloured and avoided her eye. 'Well,' he muttered, 'these are dangerous times, cousin, and the wrong word here or there could get us all into trouble.'

'Let us get on with it, then.' She disengaged her hands. 'Where are you taking me?'

'You will soon see. Follow me.'

They walked through to the entrance of the British Legation. The sentry there, who was used to her coming to and fro during the day, looked concerned. 'Don't go far, Mrs . . . er . . . The snipers still shoot at night, you know.'

'Just going for a little walk with my cousin, Corporal. We will be careful.'

They made their way down by the canal, past the Russian Legation, picked their way between the rubble in Legation Street and crossed to where the American Legation still stood, proudly forming the southernmost point of the defences, just underneath the Tartar Wall at the section of the wall still defended on the top by the Americans and Germans. Here Gerald turned left, crossing the little bridge over the canal, to a point just past the sluice gates in the wall. There, he put his finger to his lips, pulled back some large pieces of stone and beckoned her towards him.

'Climb over,' he whispered. 'Don't make a noise or we could be shot at by the Chinese on the wall above.'

On hands and knees, Alice scrambled over the stones to find a low opening in the great wall. A drainage pipe emerged from the ground under her feet and ran forwards into the darkness of the tunnel. She realised that it was what was left of some kind of service tunnel, only about four feet high, and running ahead into complete darkness. She waited nervously while Gerald replaced the stones, leaving them so that a chink of light shone through. He seized her hand.

'It's all right,' he said. 'Just keep stepping either side of the pipe. It's quite level. I'll go first. Keep holding my hand.'

She did so, until he paused and fumbled in the dark. With a creak, a small, wooden door opened and Alice realised that she was standing in the street on the other side of the Tartar Wall. She withdrew in consternation, for she was now outside the perimeter of the defences. But Gerald pulled her forward and they crossed the street to a house opposite, whose door stood slightly ajar.

Gerald knocked on it, pushed it open and called softly inside. He was answered in Chinese and a further door opened to reveal a room lit by several Oriental lamps. It was furnished severely in Chinese style, with tapestries and several vertical banners, decorated with Chinese symbols, covering the walls. At one end there was a kind of shrine, with candles burning at it, and also a highly coloured photograph of the Dowager Empress. Ceremonial Chinese swords, sheathed in ornamental scabbards, hung from the walls. A large wall map of the Chinese Empire caught her eye and, underneath it, what she immediately recognised as a map of the Legation Quarter. Everywhere, there were the red sashes and scarves of the Boxers – flung over chairs, hanging from pegs in the doors and lying loosely on the central table.

'Oh my God,' thought Alice. This must be the headquarters, the very heart of the Boxer movement.

Four men immediately rose to their feet as they entered. They were dressed seemingly identically in nondescript, loose-fitting garments – uniforms perhaps? – with black skullcaps, and all seemed middle-aged (Alice still found it difficult to tell the age of Chinamen). They bowed to her and Alice and Gerald bowed in return.

Then Gerald spoke quickly to them in Chinese and Alice sensed that she was being introduced. Was there an acerbic note in the response of the oldest man, who seemed to be the senior of the group? He wore a single gold epaulette and Alice noted that his hands were beautifully manicured. She caught a glimpse of silver hair swept back under the skullcap. Gerald bowed to him again and then turned to Alice.

'This is General Kuang Li, the chief of staff to General Jung Lu, who commands the Imperial army in Peking, and these gentlemen,' he waved his arm, 'are senior members of the army.' Gerald looked crestfallen. 'I am afraid that the General has rebuked me for bringing you here.'

Kuang Li bowed again to Alice and then addressed her in almost accentless English. 'Yes, Mrs Fonthill, I am afraid that Mr Griffith has compromised us and, indeed, you, by bringing you here. But, nevertheless, let me welcome you.'

'I am sorry, sir,' replied Alice, 'but I had no idea where my cousin was bringing me. If you wish, I will leave immediately.'

'Ah.' The smile on Kuang Li's lips did not reach his eyes. 'I am afraid that will not be possible – at least, not yet. Since you are here perhaps you can be of use to us. I should add,' he inclined his head towards her, 'that you are in no danger here. Would you care for some tea?'

Alice's brain whirled. The threat was clear. Gerald, the vain oaf, had blundered by bringing her here and they clearly had no intention of letting her go until she had helped them in some way. At least they obviously were not Boxers and their manners were those of cultivated Chinese. So what could they want of her?

She cleared her throat. 'I should make it clear to you, sir, that I cannot, under any circumstances, reveal details of the defences of the Legation Quarter.'

'No.' The little half-bow came again and Kuang Li shot a quick glance across at Gerald. 'I would not expect that of you, madam, nor do we need it. We have very good sources of that nature already, I assure you. No. But perhaps you can be of service to us – and, indeed, yourself, in other ways. But first . . . ah . . . do excuse me.'

He reached towards Alice and she took an involuntary step backwards.

He put out a placatory hand. 'No, if I may . . .' And, very slowly, he reached towards her cummerbund. He gently pulled down the top of it and inserted two long fingers inside it, pulling out her automatic pistol. Then, he expertly opened the magazine in the butt, shook out the six cartridges, snapped shut the magazine and, with a courteous bow, offered the pistol back to her.

'Forgive my . . . ah . . . clumsiness, but we have no weapons here.'

He gestured to the swords on the wall. 'These are just ceremonial trappings. Better that we speak without the thought of force, in any way. To repeat, madam, you are quite safe here. Now, won't you please sit down and take tea with us.'

Alice blushed and slipped back the pistol into her cummerbund. What an astute old rascal! 'Very well,' she said. 'Thank you.'

She sat at the table, which was rapidly cleared of the Boxer sashes. Tea was brought quickly. Fine, delicately scented tea, served without milk or sugar, the like of which Alice had not tasted since first they had landed at Tientsin. She sipped it gratefully and looked across at Gerald. No place was made at the table for him and he remained standing, drinking his tea.

Alice decided to take the initiative. 'My cousin,' she explained, 'gave me to understand that you might be able to give me news of my husband and his two companions, who recently left the Quarter for Tientsin. I would be grateful to know anything you can tell me about them.'

The General turned and spoke to his colleagues. A conversation ensued and Alice waited, her heart in her mouth. What would they say – and, whatever it was, would it be the truth? She stole a quick glance at Gerald, who was following the conversation with wide eyes.

He caught her glance and had the grace to look uncomfortable.

At last Kuang Li turned back to her. 'I shall tell you what we know,' he said, and she had the sudden and firm conviction that what he would tell her would be the truth.

'We know of your husband, of course, madam. He led the attack on our cannon on the Chien Men and he is clearly a . . .' He hesitated, obviously searching in his English vocabulary for the right phrase. 'I think you would call him a "doughty" warrior.' He smiled, happy that he had found the correct expression. 'Because of information given to us – but a fraction too late – we nearly cut him off on his return, but he broke through our men and was able to make his way back to the Legation Quarter.'

Alice frowned in impatience. She did not want flowery compliments – this was so Chinese, she thought – but only the truth about Simon. For God's sake, was he still alive?

The General continued. 'We also knew about his mission to Tientsin – again a little too late. So we were unable to prevent him leaving the city but we did send three horsemen after him to apprehend him and bring him back here. But, alas,' he held out his hands, almost in supplication, 'these men seem to have disappeared.

'The next we heard of this remarkable man, Mr Fonthill, is that he and his companions were fished out of the river above the Tientsin settlements by Kansu soldiers – very much alive, I hasten to add – and they were all brought before our distinguished colleague, General Tung Fu-hsiang and interrogated.'

Alice winced at the word, but Kuang Li went on. 'Then, a most remarkable thing happened. The general, who, what shall I say, has a reputation for the most intense questioning of prisoners he takes, let them go! We do not know why – he is not the sort of man one questions about these things. But he did so and, madam, your husband and his two companions seem to have, ah, disappeared. That is all I can tell you.'

Then he bowed to her across the table.

Alice felt a flush of exhilaration flow through her and she had to look down at her teacup for a moment to hide her feelings. Then she inclined her head in return. 'Thank you, sir. I am grateful for the information and for your courtesy.'

'Now,' said Kuang Li, 'may we ask something of you in return, now that,' he paused and looked across at Gerald, 'you have strayed into our house?'

'I will help you all I can, short of betraying the defenders of the legations,' said Alice firmly.

'We will not ask that of you. Now.' He leant back and put the tips of his fingers together. 'I am told that there is some puzzlement in the Quarter about why we do not unleash on you the full force of the artillery we have at our disposal.' He gave a wan smile. 'We were annoyed that your husband put our two Krupp guns out of commission but not seriously inconvenienced by his action. We have much more artillery, you see, and it is quite within our power to reduce all the legations to rubble if we so wish.'

Alice remembered Simon telling her that the Chinese had other large guns and plenty of ammunition that they did not bring into play.

'Why, then, do you not do so?' she asked.

'Ah yes. Why indeed? To give you the answer, I fear that I must now take you into the labyrinth that is Chinese politics.' The fingertips came together again and Alice formed the impression that the old man was rather enjoying himself. 'You see, despite what you see here,' and he gestured towards the Boxer scarves bestrewn around the room, 'we are not all supporters of these peasant militants. There are people within the Manchu court who have attempted to persuade the Dowager Empress that it was foolhardy and even dangerous to back these uprisings.'

He opened a small, lacquered box and, with the utmost delicacy, took a pinch of snuff, which he placed into each nostril before he continued.

'Unfortunately, these people at present do not have the ear of Her Divine Majesty. For instance, although my master, General Jung Lu, is formally in command of the Imperial army, General Tung Fu-hsiang, from the north, he who commands the Kansus, has great influence. And he bitterly hates all foreigners and wishes to destroy them. It is he who is commanding the troops that are fighting the Foreign Powers around Tientsin.'

Alice adopted a puzzled frown. 'If General Tung Fu-hsiang has the power, then why does he not shell the legations?'

'Because he does not have *all* the power. So far, General Jung Lu has been able to persuade the Empress that to order a comprehensive bombardment of the legations would be going too far, given that it would almost certainly kill all of the ministers, their families and their staffs. That kind of blind use of force would, it is feared, put the whole of the Western world against us and could even bring about the end of the Manchu Dynasty.'

Alice forbore to mention that things had 'gone too far' already and that, whatever happened to the defenders of the legations, revenge on the Chinese royal house would be severe and inevitable. Instead, she said, 'But it seems as though you are fighting only half a war, doesn't it?'

He gave a smile that was completely Chinese in its impassivity. 'If you were in Tientsin at the moment, I don't think you could say that. The fighting there is severe. But you must not misunderstand me. The Imperial forces in Peking – and you will perhaps have noticed that there are very few Boxers attacking your barricades at the moment—'

'Oh, are they in the country again, butchering defenceless missionaries?'

Kuang Li bowed his head at the shaft, but continued: 'Our forces here are determined to occupy the Legations Quarter. But it is all a question now of how that is done.'

'I am sorry but I don't quite understand.'

'The Empress is at this moment considering offering, once again, a ceasefire to the fighting here on condition that the ministers, their families and soldiers agree to leave the legations and proceed to the coast, under the protection of the Imperial army.'

'But you offered this before and it was rejected.'

The General shook his head. 'Not quite. The offer was allowed to lapse.'

'But we are at war now. The Chinese nation declared war on the Foreign Powers.'

'Quite so. Because you took our Taku Forts at the mouth of the river. But the amnesty would include the offer of an armistice.'

Alice frowned, these waters were becoming deep. 'You say the Empress is only considering this?'

'Yes. You see, she is torn between the conflicting advice she is receiving in the palace, from princes of the royal blood on the one hand who would give General Tung Fu-hsiang his head, and people like my master, General Jung Lu, on the other, who would wish this stupid war to end. Now – if you could take this message back from my general to your Sir Claude . . . er . . . MacDougal . . . ?'

'MacDonald.'

'Ah yes. So sorry. I always had difficulty with Scottish names.'

Alice stifled a grin. The complexity of Chinese names had always bewildered her. It was good to hear that there was a quid pro quo. 'But what precisely is that message?'

'We would wish to know if that offer would receive serious consideration and would be likely to be accepted. You see, it would be a great loss of face to our Empress if her generosity was thrown back in her face, so to speak. If, however, we could have Sir Claude's assurance that the offer might well be accepted – why then our people at the palace could, we feel sure, persuade the Empress to make it and so end the fighting and the war, both here and in the south.'

He sat back and a heavy silence descended on the room. It was clear that the General's colleagues present had not followed the conversation but that everyone was now looking at Alice in considerable anticipation.

'Of course I will take what you have said to Sir Claude,' said Alice, eventually. 'Naturally, I cannot say to you what his response will be. How should he relay that, by the way?'

'Oh,' that subtle smile returned, 'through the usual channels. They have always remained open throughout this conflict. But we here tonight were meeting to think of a way of putting our message to Sir Claude informally. Your arrival has seemed to meet our purpose very well. Would you care for some more tea?'

'You are kind, but no thank you. May I ask you one more question?'

'Please do.'

'What if Sir Claude rejects your invitation?'

'Ah yes. Then that would be a great pity. It would mean, you see, that the – what shall I call it? – the pro-Legation factor amongst the Empress's advisors will have lost the day, so to speak. As a result, the people at court who wish to see this war intensified will have their way and the attacks on the Quarter will be intensified. In fact, my general may be forced to initiate the terrible cannonade of which we have spoken.'

'I see. Very well, I shall take that message. And now I feel that I should leave you, unless there is anything further you wish to say?'

He held up one long, elegant finger. 'Only this – and I do hope that you will not think this rude of me. Please do not allow Sir Claude to think that he can attack this house here. After our meeting, you see, we will not be able to use it any more and it will become deserted. So any effort towards it will not be justified. Oh, and that little passage in the wall that has proved so useful to Mr Griffith will now be holed up at this end and will be of no further use to anyone.'

With that Kuang Li bowed ceremonially, followed by his companions.

Alice inclined her head. 'Thank you. Good night, gentlemen.'

She departed without a glance towards Gerald, who scurried behind her, and she crossed the street in long strides, thinking hard. She pulled at the little door but it refused to budge, so Gerald leant over her shoulder to exert pressure and pull it open. She whirled on him. 'Gerald—'

'No,' he interrupted. 'It is dangerous here, come inside.' He pushed her gently into the little opening, closing the door behind them, so that they were in virtual darkness, only relieved by the shards of moonlight that slipped through the gaps in the stone at the far end.

Gerald seized her arms, so that she could hardly move. 'Now listen,' he hissed. 'Don't believe what you heard back there about Simon. He is almost certainly dead. They softened it for you – I understood what they said – because they wanted your help. Listen, Alice.' His tone became softer. 'You must know that I love you and I have since the first moment you arrived at our house.'

She struggled to get free, but he held her tighter.

'Your life with Fonthill, from what I hear, has been one of hardship; you must have felt that you were some . . . some blasted trooper in the army, following this madman around the Empire. Even if he is still alive – and I don't think that he is for one moment – it will be easy to divorce him and marry me. Join me in a tremendous adventure in this wonderful country. You saw how highly placed my contacts are here. You would live here in Peking in great style, when I am part of the foreign office here.' He leant his head forward to kiss her.

Alice, her arms still pinioned, moved forward into his embrace and then sharply brought up her knee into his groin. Then she pulled back her head and crashed it into his nose. He howled, released her and doubled over, holding his nose.

'Now, you listen to me, *cousin*.' Alice's tone was even but bitingly cold. 'You touch me again and I will cripple you, I promise. This has happened before to other men. I know how to do it.'

She pushed him hard so that he sat down with a thud, painfully, on the pipe that ran through the tunnel.

'My husband is a *man*, not some grovelling little spy, who slithers here and there, sometimes with the enemy, sometimes with us, but always betraying those who trusted him. As for whether Simon is still alive, I would rather – much rather – take the word of that Chinaman than yours. No, don't get up. I haven't finished with you yet.

'Now, listen carefully to what I tell you because it is important. It is quite clear to me that you have betrayed the defenders here. You informed the Chinese that Simon was going to make his attempt on

242

the guns. Thank God you were – what was the phrase? – ah yes, "a little too late". You told them also about his mission to Tientsin – a little too late again, it seems. But my dear Simon could have been taken and killed out of hand.

'You hunt with the besiegers. I know this because I saw you with the Kansus in the Wu, on the *wrong side of the barricade*, cousin. You must really get rid of that distinctive white suit, you know. I now believe that you fired off your fowling piece that day in the cart on the way here deliberately to put your father – *your own father*, cousin – in danger. In fact, my dear, you killed him.'

Suddenly, Gerald was on his feet albeit stooped over in the low tunnel. His voice was high-pitched and it echoed in the confined space, bouncing back off the low walls. 'The man was an idiot,' he shrieked. 'Always was. His religion is stupid, *stupid*, I tell you, compared to the elegance and deep truth of Shintoism. He and his kind – the *missionaries*,' he spat out the word with contempt, 'were ruining this wonderful country, with its fine past and magnificent future. The Boxers were right – right, I tell you – to rise up against them.

'Now you listen, *cousin*. The Chinese, the true Chinese, like Tung Fu-hsiang, are right to fight the Foreign Powers, who just want to partition China between them. And they will win, I promise you that. And the first card to fall in the line of dominoes will be this artificial piece of foreign territory, the Legation Quarter. You will see.'

He finished, gasping for breath and holding a handkerchief to his bloodied nose.

Alice nodded. 'Now, at last, Gerald, we know where we both stand. Listen hard. I will give you half an hour – no more – to pack some

243

belongings and to tell your mother what you intend to do. I don't care what you tell her, but don't you dare make her worry on your behalf. She will hear nothing from me about tonight. You will have just thirty minutes to do that and then scramble back down this rathole to join your Chinese friends, before they wall it up. Then I shall wake Sir Claude and tell him everything that has happened tonight. So you will leave the Legation Quarter and you will not return until this siege is ended, if you value your life.' She turned to go and then turned back. 'And if you try to stop me now, I promise I will kill you. To repeat, I know how to do it.'

She scrambled back towards the shafts of light, half-fearing a sudden attack on her. She had never killed a man with her bare hands – although she had fought a few off – and she had not the faintest idea how to do it. But no attack came and she was able to reach the stones, pull them back and climb through. Then she broke into a run towards the British Legation, startling the guard on her arrival.

Chapter Twelve

If the news brought to Fonthill that it could take some weeks yet before the relief expedition could be mounted was bad, that which was brought by Jenkins shortly after Dorward's departure was even worse.

The Welshman sat on the edge of the camp stool by Simon's bed and waved the flies away. 'I don't know 'ow exactly to say this to you, bach sir,' he said.

Fonthill frowned. 'You can't find a decent pair of trousers for me?'

'No, no. It's not that. It's just, well, I can't find old Changy anywhere.'

'What do you mean, you can't find him? Where the hell did you leave him?'

'Well, we both left 'im, so to speak, when you told 'im 'e couldn't come along with our bit of gate blowin'. 'E was really fed up with that, you may remember, an' went off in a bit of a sulk. I 'aven't seen 'im since.'

Simon elbowed himself to a sitting position. 'I wondered why he hadn't been to see me. I thought he was just miserable with me for not letting him join in the attack. Have you asked around?'

'Course I 'ave. Though goin' around this place sayin' "Excuse me but 'ave you seen a Chinaman?" is a bit of a waste of time.'

'Hmm. So he's been missing since last night?'

'About that.'

'Have you made enquiries with the Royal Welch?'

'No. They're still in the Chinese City, probably enjoyin' a bit of rape an' pillagin' an' that.'

Simon thought for a moment. 'It is not like him to go off and sulk. I can only think that he would have watched us go and waited with the Royal Welch and then charged with them when we set off the fireworks. He's excitable enough to have been caught up in the glory of the charge and all that. He would have not seen us in that ditch and probably charged straight past us and gone off with the Taffies into the city.'

'Yes, but, where would 'e be now? 'E's only a lad, look you, an' wouldn't 'ave got caught up in the roisterin' stuff inside.'

'I agree. Here's what you do, 352.' Simon began scribbling a note. 'Take this to the CO of the Welch Regiment – I think he's Colonel Davies. I only met him briefly but he owes us one for opening the door for him into the city. He'll probably get a DSO for that, if he hasn't blotted his copybook by letting his lads loose on the civilian population. This explains what you're after. The NCOs might help. After all, Chang wasn't just another anonymous Chinaman – he was strangely dressed as a customs officer and there were no Chinese charging with the Welsh. Someone might have seen him. Report back to me here as soon as you can. I'm getting out of this bed.'

'No, no. You stay there. It's too early for you to get up yet. Leave this to me.'

'Very well. Off you go.'

As soon as Jenkins was out of sight, Fonthill pushed back the bed sheets and swung his legs to the floor. He had sustained burns to his right ankle and calf, as well as his hands, but he could stand and, best of all, the ringing in his ears had stopped and his head seemed clear.

A Chinese orderly bustled over. 'No go yet, sir,' he said.

'I have General Dorward's permission,' he lied. 'Now,' he fumbled in the little drawer in the bamboo table at his bedside. He produced a handful of Chinese coins. 'Can you do something for me?'

'Ah, yes, sir.'

'Good. I want some Chinese clothes. Ordinary clothes used by Chinese workmen. Something that will fit me and the man who has just left. And we shall need two coolie hats. If you can do that, I will double this. Bring them to me at my billet, at this number, as soon as possible.'

The orderly's face broke into a big grin. He bowed over Simon's hand and took the money. 'Can do that, very good, sir. Bring to you quickly.'

'Good.'

Still in his tattered underwear, Fonthill walked out of the makeshift hospital to the billet which he, Jenkins and Chang had been allocated on arrival. It was little more than a wooden shed with three bunks, but it was private and suited Simon's purpose well. There he found his and Jenkins's rifles but Chang's was missing.

Simon sat on his bunk and tried to think logically. There was no way that Chang would have run away, he would consider that to be deserting his post. He was as keen as mustard and now regarded himself as a soldier. In addition, after their capture by the Kansus and the rough treatment they had received from them, he had become their sworn enemy. Nor would he have wandered off disgruntled. One of the endearing qualities of Chang, he reflected, was his lightness of spirit and his ability to take hard knocks, both literally and metaphorically. No, it made sense that he would come after his two comrades to join in the battle in the city. And then . . . and then what? He shook his head. There was no way that he could shrug his shoulders and write off the loss of Chang as just another casualty in the Boxer uprising. He could never face Mrs Griffith – or Alice, for that matter. The boy had to be found. But where the hell to look?

Jenkins brought some news, at least. Colonel Davies had, indeed, been helpful and one of the corporals vividly remembered Chang, in his navy-blue jacket, charging by his side as the Royal Welch swept into the city. At first, they had met strong resistance from the Kansus and there had been fierce fighting, street by street, until the Muslims seemed suddenly to disappear, as they fled the city through the gates not under attack.

'Yes, but what about Chang?'

'You know, bach sir, you shouldn't be up. The surgeon major would cripple me if he felt I had encouraged you.'

'Bugger the surgeon major. What about Chang?'

'I was comin' to that, if you 'ad just a touch of patience. Now, the corporal – nice chap, from Rhyl, see, in the north of Wales, just like me—'

248

'For God's sake get on with it.'

'Well, 'e saw one of the bullets fired by the Chinks 'it the wall just above where old Changy was kneelin' an' firin', see. This bullet knocked a chunk off the wall and it fell an' seemed to knock poor old Changy out.'

'What do you mean, "seemed to"? Did it or didn't it?'

'Well, I wasn't there, was I, so I can't vouch for it. But the corporal said that Changy fell and lay still. 'E couldn't stay to 'elp 'im, because the Chinks counter-attacked an' they 'ad to retreat. When they fought their way back, Changy 'ad gone. That's all 'e could say.'

Fonthill pulled at a stray piece of bandage on his left hand with his teeth and then tucked it back in. 'Does he remember where it was?'

'Oh yes. 'E took me there. In a cobbled street just outside an 'ouse.'

'I don't suppose for a moment that you could find your way back there, could you?'

Jenkins looked indignant. 'Course I could. I marked it well.'

'Good. We'll go there tonight.'

''Ang on. You should be back in bed.'

'Balls. We'll go as soon as some clothes I've ordered arrive.'

'Brand-new suits, is it?' Jenkins grinned and looked down at his once-smart customs uniform, now burnt in patches and covered in dust.

'Not quite. I have a feeling that we are going to have to go out into the country again. And we go as Chinamen.'

'Oh bloody 'ell. Not in the river again . . .'

'We'll go where we have to. But we must find Chang.'

'Ah, amen to that, bach sir. 'E's a good lad.' But the Welshman's face darkened and he sucked in his moustache under his lower lip. 'Trouble is, as I've pointed out, this place is full of millions of Chinamen, 'cos it's their country, isn't it? It's goin' to be like lookin' for a bloody needle in an 'aystack. I mean, where do we start?'

'We start at the house where he fell, if you can find your way to it, which I truly doubt. But we are going to need an interpreter.'

The orderly arrived, the broad grin still in place, carrying two parcels. They were unwrapped and revealed two virtually identical garments: loose, pyjama-like trousers, pulled in at the ankles, high-button shirts and shapeless, cotton working overalls. Sandals and conical coolie straw hats completed the outfits, neither of which was too clean. But they fitted, more or less.

The orderly was suitably rewarded and Simon pulled him to one side. 'Are you in the British army?' he asked. 'Can you get away from the hospital for a few days? You will be well paid.'

The man's eyes lit up. 'I not a soldier,' he said. 'Work for English lady in settlements. She gone to Taku. I can leave hospital and work for you. Where we go?'

'Into the Chinese City to start with. Then we shall see. What's your name?'

'Lady calls me Sam.'

'Very good, Sam. Here, help me into these clothes.'

By the time Sam had finished with them, Jenkins and Fonthill looked exactly like a pair of Chinese coolies, quite nondescript in their earth-coloured, none-too-clean overalls. The fact that they didn't fit was of no matter. Sartorial elegance was not desired. By keeping their heads down under their cone-shaped hats, their comparatively long, Occidental faces, with their prominent noses and strong chins, could not be seen. At first glance, they looked exactly like the thousands of anonymous figures who peopled the settlements and the city.

'Do we take the rifles, bach sir?'

Fonthill sighed. 'I'd like to, but coolies don't carry British army issue rifles. Here, how well do you know the quartermaster?'

'Played cards with 'im last week. 'E won.'

'Good. Hand me that pad. Now . . .' He scribbled a note, signing it 'S. Fonthill, Major, General Gaselee's staff', and handed it to Jenkins. 'Tell him we are off upcountry on an intelligence mission. That will explain your garb. I want him to accept our rifles in temporary exchange for two Webley service revolvers, officers for the use of. It might work and we'd be better off with something we can tuck out of sight. Don't be all day.'

Simon set about unwinding his bandages and, with Sam's help, cut them down to a less unwieldy size. Jenkins returned within the hour, discreetly carrying two Mark 4 revolvers and a box of .455 cartridges. Then the three set off for Tientsin City.

A smell of cordite and smoking timber hung over the South Gate and the city itself seemed subdued, after the excesses of the night before. The streets were patrolled by a mixture of Russian, German and British soldiers but Simon and his two companions merged easily into the indigenous Chinese who walked by, going about their business, albeit with their heads down and eyes averted from those of the soldiers.

The trio halted just inside the gate, confronted by a maze of narrow cobbled streets. 'Which way?' hissed Fonthill.

'Ah. Just a minute. Bloody 'ell, these streets all look the same now.'

Simon looked up to the heavens. Jenkins, he knew, had an inbuilt inability to find his way from A to B, even if the route was marked by flaming torches. 'Concentrate, man,' he urged. 'This is important. We haven't got much time.'

'I *am* concentratin'.' Jenkins tipped back his hat and studied the streets that all opened onto the small square behind the gate. 'Ah. This one,' he said. 'I recognise that funny sign there, tho' God knows what it means. Yes, it's up this 'ill, it's an 'ouse on the left, just past an archway.'

They walked up the hill and it was clear that the street had recently been the scene of heavy fighting. Bullets had scarred the stone of the buildings and tiles were hanging over gutterings. Dark patches of dried blood showed where men had fallen and Simon was glad he had missed this part of the battle, for there was practically no shelter to be had in the terraced street, hardly a doorway in which to escape the bullets.

Jenkins stopped with confidence outside a one-storey house, roofed with the distinctive Chinese terracotta wavy tiles. He pointed to where a sizeable piece of stone had been taken from the wall. 'Accordin' to that Taffy corporal, this is where old Changy was knocked down, obviously by this stone, 'ere.'

Simon scrutinised the cobbles underneath and, indeed, there was a distinctive bloodstain. He nodded and turned to Sam. 'Now,' he said, 'knock on the door of this house and ask them if they know anything about a young Chinaman who was knocked down just here during the fighting last night. He was wearing a blue coat and carrying a rifle. And he was fighting for the British. Tell them there is a reward for information – but only if it is correct. Do you understand, Sam?'

'Understand well, sir. I talk to them.'

The door was not opened at first and when it was, after repeated knocking, it was pushed only slightly ajar. Then, when the occupant, a very old woman with tiny, bound feet, saw that it was a Chinaman and not a soldier knocking, she opened it wide. Fonthill and Jenkins kept their heads down while a conversation ensued.

Eventually, Sam turned to them with a satisfied smile. 'Yes, she remember man falling and hitting door. They afraid to open but did so when firing stopped and Chinaman on his knees holding head . . . what you say?'

'Bleeding?' offered Simon. Sam nodded.

'Young or old man?'

'Very young. He asked to come inside and bathe head, but then Kansu soldiers come before he could go inside and take him away.'

'Damn! Did she hear them say where they were going to take him?'

Sam turned and again questioned the woman, who had been following the exchange in a foreign language with frightened eyes.

'She say she think them say take him to Peitsang, where soldiers have their . . . what you say . . . ?'

'Headquarters?'

'That the word.'

'Thank her and give her this.' He handed over several coins. 'Sam, how far is this Peitsang?'

'It about ten mile north, along railway.'

'Right. Let's go there.'

Jenkins gave a frown so face-distorting that his great eyebrows nearly met his moustache. ''Ere, you know you should be in bed, and, look you, you won't be able to walk that far with that burnt ankle, see. An' 'ow are we goin' to stroll through all these Kansu buggers? They'll see we're not Chinese and then we *will* be bloody well whipped if they get another chance.'

'Don't argue. Thank you, madam,' and he gave the startled woman a most ceremonial bow. Then to Sam: 'Which way?'

'Through city and through North Gate. I take. Follow me.'

They set off, Fonthill hobbling slightly. Jenkins hissed, 'What if we get to this Pete Sang place? What do we do there? Surround it and attack from all quarters?'

'Yes. Good idea. Save your breath for the walk. It's going to take me some time at this rate.'

Sam knew his way through the Chinese City and they soon found themselves at the North Gate, a similarly impressive entrance at the opposite end of Tientsin. There were Russian guards at the gate but they paid no attention to three coolies shuffling past them, on their way to the parched *kaoliang* fields stretching away before them. Turning to his right, Sam led them to the railway track and the wide path at its side.

'We follow track,' he said. 'Lead us to Peitsang.'

Fonthill had been concerned that, once out of the city, they would be met by dug-in entrenchments of the Imperial army, but it seemed clear that, following their defeat at Tientsin, the Chinese had decided to retreat further north. They would realise that the Foreign Powers' next move would be to launch a column in some strength – not two thousand sailors this time, with officers in their white ducks, sitting in railway carriages – to the north-west to attack Peking. But Simon had no illusions. The Chinese army would stand and fight at some place – or places – along the way. Where would that be, he wondered? More to the point, was Chang still alive and, if so, how the hell would they be able to release him? As they trudged along, heads down under the burning sun, Simon recalled a maxim from his then newly opened officers' training course at Sandhurst: 'No time spent on reconnaissance is wasted.' They would have to trust to their disguises to allow them to reconnoitre the place and then form a plan. A plan. Ah yes. *A plan*. He sighed. He would have to think calmly and rationally – and hope they had a lot of luck. But would Chang be alive? From what he had seen of the Kansu, it would be unlikely. He sighed inwardly and walked on.

It took them nearly five hours to walk the ten miles to Peitsang and it was dark by the time they saw the name, written in Chinese letters of course, so Sam had to translate, on the side of the small station platform. They had followed the railway all along and had met only three people, peasants, like themselves. To their surprise, a locomotive was standing at the station, no carriages, just the engine.

Fonthill concluded that the line was still open back to Tientsin and engineers were working on the locomotive. Steam was hissing from behind the wheels but somehow it looked as though it was going nowhere, waiting, presumably, for trucks or carriages.

The town itself was little more than the rail stop and Fonthill felt uncomfortable walking through it in the semi-darkness, particularly as they passed several groups of Kansu soldiers. There was obviously a depot there for these men and he thanked their lucky stars that they would all be Muslim, otherwise they might well have been accosted by a drunken Kansu or two. But would they have Chang and, if so, where?

On the far side of the town they came upon a large field containing tents that seemed to have been hurriedly pitched. So irregular was the grouping of the tents that Simon felt sure it could not be a military camp – although they had passed nothing else that resembled one. Then he saw the rifles stacked, pyramid-style, along the rows. Two low wooden buildings stood on the periphery of the field.

'This must be the Kansu headquarters for the region,' he said.

'Yes,' said Jenkins, looking round carefully. 'But if it is that, then the old general with the fancy initials cut into 'is back ain't 'ere. 'E 'ad a damned great marquee of a tent, if you remember. There's nothing like that 'ere.'

'True. But one of those huts on the far side has got bars to its windows. And there's a guard outside. Could be a jail.'

The field had no fence or other means of delineating the boundaries for the camp, except that there was a slightly larger tent on their edge of the field, outside of which two soldiers stood guard. The guard tent?

They walked by unhurriedly, without looking at the sentries, and went round a bend in the path. Simon beckoned to Sam.

'Sam,' he said, placing an arm on his shoulder. 'I would like you to do something a little dangerous. Can you do it, do you think?'

'If not too dangerous, sir.' The young man looked nervous. 'I not soldier, remember.'

'Of course not. All I want you to do is to walk back to one of those sentries and ask him if they have captured a young Chinaman in a blue coat. Say you think he was in Tientsin. Say you come from the same village and his mother is worried about him. Do you think you could do that?'

'Ah, that easy, sir. I don't argue with guard, eh?'

'No. Just walk up easily and ask if the man is in the camp. Just say you need to tell his mother.'

'Very good. You wait here?'

'Yes.'

The young man nodded and slowly walked away. Jenkins blew out his cheeks. 'That's takin' a bit of risk, ain't it, bach sir? What if they run in old Sam as well? Then we'll be buggered and very far from 'ome, look you.'

Simon shrugged. 'We just don't have time to walk around half of China,' he said. 'If they feel Chang was important enough to arrest in Tientsin and bring back here – or wherever, for that matter – then I'm afraid they're going to torture him to find out what he was up to. There he was, wearing a British customs office coat, fighting with the Brits, remember. So we really have no time to waste. We just must take a risk.'

Jenkins nodded. 'Poor bugger. I hope he is in there and we can snaffle 'im, then.'

Fonthill's heart lifted when Sam reappeared a few minutes later, beaming.

'Yes, sir. Chinese man in blue coat taken here from Tientsin. In wooden hut.' The smile disappeared. 'They hit him, I think.'

'Is he still alive?'

'Ah yes. Wait for big officer to come tomorrow.'

Simon nodded. 'Right. That means we get him out tonight.'

'Blimey.' Jenkins's nose wrinkled. ''E's on the edge of the bloody army. They're camped all round 'im, with a guard with a rifle standing outside the door. 'Ow are we goin' to do that, then?'

'I will create a bit of a diversion and then we nip in and take him.'

'What? Just like that?'

'Yes, Just like that. We are miles from the front and they'll all be resting from their exertions in the Chinese City and the march back. By the look of it, most of the troops here are sleeping in their tents. They will not be expecting an attack and certainly not an attempt to take their prisoner. But it is vital that what we have to do we do quietly and quickly. Now listen. This is the plan.

'We are lucky in that the hut is on the edge of the encampment and that the guard tent for the camp is virtually on the other side of the field to the hut. We are also lucky that this wood seems to go to the edge of the field for two-thirds of the way round, so giving us cover when we get out with Chang. However, we are a bit unlucky that the entrance to the hut faces inwards, into the field, and that is where the guard stands, of course.' He grinned. 'That's odds of two to one in our favour.'

'Oh, bloody marvellous,' said Jenkins. Sam was listening carefully, his mouth open in concentration.

Fonthill continued: 'When we are in place on the edge of the wood, I will walk around to the guard and engage him in conversation.'

'What,' asked Jenkins, 'in fluent Chinese?'

'Of course. Now, while I have his attention, you creep up behind him, 352, and kill the bastard. Quietly – with your knife. It's important, though, that you prop him up with some kind of stick – there's plenty around in this wood – so that it appears as though he is still on guard. Got that?'

'Oh yes. Kill him and stand him up. Very easy.'

'Good. Then you, Sam . . . are you following all this?'

'Hah. Think so, sir. But not a soldier, remember.'

Fonthill sighed. 'No. We are not asking you to kill anyone. Then you, Sam, come inside with me. There will probably be a guard inside who will have the keys to where Chang is being kept. I will need you to interpret. We will threaten this man and take his keys and then . . . er . . . knock him out so that he cannot raise the alarm. Unlock Chang and escape through the woods.'

Jenkins nodded solemnly. 'An' then we all 'obble back to this Tiensingy place?'

Simon shook his head. 'No, my ankle is killing me. I can't march far. I suggest we go by train.'

A slow smile crept over Jenkins's face. 'Brilliant, bach sir. Bloody brilliant. I just 'ope we 'ave a bit of luck.'

Fonthill's face was set hard. 'So do I, old chap,' he said. 'So do I. We are going to need it. Come on. Let's go.'

They slipped off into the wood, leaving the path behind them, treading carefully in the dry timber along the edge of the field, stopping only for Jenkins to pick up a long, sturdy stick, until they came to the dark outline of the second building, nearest to the wood. Fonthill held up a hand and they stayed listening quietly. Nothing could be heard.

Simon indicated with his hand. 'I will walk around the hut this way,' he whispered. 'Give me fifteen seconds, 352, and then walk around the other side. With any luck the guard will have his back to you. I'm afraid it means stabbing him in the back, but it can't be helped. You come with me, Sam, but wait out of sight behind the hut while I approach the guard. All right?'

'Good luck, bach.' The absence of the customary 'sir' betrayed Jenkins's anxiety.

Fonthill took a deep breath and left the protection of the wood. He walked quietly round the hut and came upon the guard who was half-dozing, leaning against the door. 'Excuse me,' said Simon, his head down.

The guard immediately presented his rifle and grunted something.

'Ah, sorry to trouble you, old chap,' Simon spoke low but clearly. 'Could you tell me the Greenwich Mean Time, please?'

The question had the effect of making the soldier half-turn to face Fonthill. 'Huh?' he grunted. It was the last word he spoke. Jenkins materialised behind him, put his left hand over the guard's mouth and plunged his knife into his back, high up and slightly to the left of the vertebrae. He held it there as the man uttered a half-groan, dropped his rifle, which Fonthill caught, and began to slip to the ground as his knees buckled.

'Quick, prop him up,' hissed Simon.

Together they dragged the man to the wall. Fonthill caught a glimpse of Sam watching, his mouth open in horror, and then Jenkins had rammed the staff into the ground and put the other end under the collar of the guard, who swayed for a moment and then stayed perilously erect.

Fonthill propped the rifle against the figure and then drew his revolver. He waved it to Jenkins. 'Open the door.'

The Welshman did so and the two of them sprang inside, to be followed seconds later by the wide-eyed Sam. One man, in Kansu uniform, was sitting at a desk, his head down on his folded arms, fast asleep. Behind him were two cells, separated from the office by vertical bars. One cell was empty. In the other, lying on the earthen floor, lay the familiar figure of Chang. A familiar, but now sad figure, for he lay hunched, in the foetal position, but with blood oozing from a wound in his head and another from his upper arm. He seemed to be sleeping but his mouth was open and he was sucking in air with a rasping sound. There was nothing left of his blue jacket but a few shreds hanging from his shoulders.

'Bloody 'ell,' exclaimed Jenkins. 'I don't feel so bad about killin' that feller now. The bastards.'

'Open the outside door a fraction and keep watch, 352,' hissed Fonthill. 'Sam, when I wake this man, tell him that if he makes a sound I will shoot him.' He grabbed hold of the sleeping man's hair – cut short, so no pigtail – pulled his head back sharply and thrust the muzzle of the Webley into his nostril.

Sam spoke quickly to the man and also put his finger to his lips in the universal demand for silence. The Kansu was awake in a second and his eyes widened in terror.

'Good. Now tell him to unlock the cell door. Quickly now.'

The guard stood, wavered for a moment, and then took down a large keyring from a peg on the wall. He selected a key and unlocked the door to Chang's cell. 'Now tell him to remove his coat and his trousers.'

Before the demand could be translated, however, Jenkins called from the doorway. 'Soldier coming. From the guard tent, I think.'

'Damn! Only one?'

'Looks like it.'

Fonthill turned to Sam. 'Tell this man that I will shoot if he utters a word. Now sit him down, with his back to the door. That's it. Now, you two, either side of the door, backs to the wall. We'll grab him as soon as he enters.'

Sam was pushed behind the door, which was left slightly ajar, and Jenkins and Simon flattened themselves against the wall on the other side of the opening. There they all waited, holding their breath, until they heard a gutteral question delivered outside, followed almost immediately by an astonished 'Hah!'

Fonthill bit his lip. Would the guard immediately give the alarm or investigate inside before doing so? It was a life-or-death question.

Then, with almost agonising slowness, a rifle was pushed through the opening. Seeing the man seated at the desk must have given some assurance because the newcomer half-advanced into the room, asking a question of the seated man. Immediately, Simon grabbed the barrel of the rifle and pulled it and the soldier into the room. At almost the same moment, Jenkins sprang forward and sank his knife into the soldier's stomach, clutching the man to him as he did so. With a gasp, the guard slumped slowly downwards and Fonthill delivered the *coup de grâce* by crashing the butt of his revolver into the man's head. It was all over in seconds.

Fonthill poked his head round the door. The dead man outside was still standing, although he had lurched to one side. There was no sound from the rows of tents and, through the lines of canvas, he could see the flicker of lamps from within the guard tent. He shut the door. 'All clear, I think,' he said. 'Maybe this man was the relief. Now,' he waved his revolver at the key holder, who was visibly trembling, 'Sam, tell him he won't be harmed if he does as we ask. Tell him to remove his coat and trousers.'

With frightened eyes, the man did so.

'Now, Sam, see if you can find rope or a belt we can tie his hands and feet with. And something to stick in his mouth to gag him. I will keep him covered. 352, see if you can wake poor old Chang and bring him out here. He's got to get into these clothes, or we'll never get him out of here.'

With a heavy heart, Fonthill watched as Jenkins knelt beside the sleeping – sleeping or unconscious? – Chang and gently began to bring him to consciousness. Blessedly, he seemed only to be sleeping but it took nearly a minute to rouse him. At last he opened his eyes, immediately flinched as he saw Jenkins's face close to him, but then he smiled, as best he could. His nose had clearly been broken and his face was a mass of blood. His jaw had been injured and he found it difficult to speak.

'What's he saying?' asked Simon anxiously.

'I think 'e said that 'e's frightfully glad to see us,' grinned Jenkins.

'Get rid of those rags and see if you can help him to stand and get into the jailer's clothes.' Still covering the Kansu with his revolver, Fonthill edged towards Chang. 'We are going to get you out of here, old chap,' he called. 'But we can't have you walking naked through the streets, so we will need to have you dressed like a Kansu. Can you walk?'

His arm around Jenkins's shoulders, the boy gave half a nod and immediately almost fell over.

'Steady, lad,' said Jenkins. ''Ere, sit down at this desk a minute.'

Sam now appeared carrying what appeared to be a clothes line. 'Bind him, 352,' said Fonthill gesturing towards the jailer. 'Hands behind and feet together. Don't bother about making him comfortable. And tear his shirt up, stick part of it into his mouth and tie it in, so that he won't make a sound. We need a head start.'

Simon found a tap, returned with a cupful of water and raised it to Chang's mouth. The young man gulped it down eagerly and then spat out a little blood. Fonthill took what remained of the Kansu's shirt and, dipping it into the refilled cup, gently began wiping the injured youth's face. Chang tried to say something but was urged to be quiet. Tearing the shirt remnant into strips, Simon dipped them into the water and did his best to bind the Chinaman's wounds and staunch the bleeding, which had begun again as he stood.

Eventually, Chang was dressed and the jailer was trussed up and deposited in his own cell, with the door locked. Then, with Jenkins and Sam walking either side of the injured youth, clutching his arms, and Fonthill walking cautiously ahead, they left the jail hut and gained the shelter of the wood and, then, the path that led through the town.

'If we are challenged, Sam,' said Simon, 'say that our friend has drunk too much rice wine and we are taking him home.'

By now, however, it was approaching midnight and the streets of the little town were deserted. They were able to walk along unchallenged until eventually the hiss of steam ahead told them that they were nearing the station.

'Sounds as though the engine is still there, thank God,' muttered Jenkins. 'But will it have steam up?'

'If it hasn't, we'll get it up,' said Simon. 'The problem will be if the line down to Tientsin has been torn up. Seymour told me that they were shelled from the rail track on their way to the arsenal, so the chances are that we can get as near as dammit to the city – if, that is, we can persuade those engineers to get the thing moving.'

'Oh, I think we can manage that,' said Jenkins grimly, drawing his revolver from beneath his coat.

Chang was now staggering badly and had to be virtually carried, so Fonthill left him at the station entrance, leaning against a tree under the care of Jenkins, while he and Sam went onto the platform. Since they had first passed the station, a line of open wagons had been shunted and had been coupled to the locomotive, which was still being fussed over by two engineers, although no one else was in sight.

'Come with me,' said Simon to Sam, 'and translate for me.'

One engineer was on the footplate and the second bending down by the front bogied wheels as the pair approached. The man by the wheels stood up and truculently asked a question of them. Fonthill produced his revolver. 'Tell him to get back onto the footplate, now,' he said. 'And tell him if he makes a noise I will kill him.'

The engineer's jaw dropped and he turned and climbed up to stand beside his mate, who was now looking down in astonishment into the muzzle of Simon's Webley.

Fonthill climbed up beside them and waved Sam to come up onto the footplate too. 'Now,' he said, 'I want to know how long it will take to get steam up and if the line to Tientsin is still open. Explain that we have just killed two men and I will shoot them if they try to raise the alarm.'

Sam asked the questions and gained surly replies. 'They say they have had problem with . . . hah . . . valve but is all right now. Steam is already up. Track good to Tientsin. But they push these trucks north with soldiers at dawn.'

At this, Fonthill's interest quickened. If the track towards Peking was open again, then the destination for the soldiers could give an indication of where the Imperial army intended to make its stand against a relief column from the south.

'Ask them where they take the soldiers.'

'They say, Yangtsun. Is about ten miles to north, I think.'

'Ah, good. Now, Sam, go and fetch Jenkins and Chang. I will keep these two covered. Make haste.'

Sam nodded and scampered down the steel steps. Fonthill realised that his burnt ankle was now causing him pain and he looked around on the footplate for somewhere to sit. As he did so, he caught from the corner of his eye a quick movement. Instinctively, he turned and fired in one movement, shattering the chest of the nearest engineer, who had seized a shovel and was about to bring it down on his head. Immediately, Simon swung the revolver round to cover the other man, who fell onto his knees and raised his hands high above his head.

'Shit!' The noise of the heavy revolver had shattered the stillness of the night. How near were the nearest soldiers? He hung his head over the side of the locomotive in the general direction of Sam and Jenkins and shouted, 'Come on, quickly. We've got to get out of here.'

He turned and motioned to the engineer to get to his feet. He gestured to the controls, made a 'shushing' sound and then pointed behind him to the south. The man looked blankly at him. 'You stupid bastard,' shouted Fonthill. 'Get steam up.' He made a shushing sound again and then made a circular motion with both hands.

'Hah!' The engineer nodded and immediately turned, picked up the shovel – an action which made Simon start backwards – and then began shovelling coal into the open furnace. He turned back and adjusted a lever, which made more steam escape. Then he was back shovelling coal.

Keeping a wary eye on the man, Fonthill leant out of the cab once again and saw Jenkins and Sam, with Chang in between them, his limp arms around each of their shoulders. They were making slow progress and Simon fingered his revolver nervously. Had the shot raised the alarm? He moved to the other side of the footplate and looked along the line of trucks, stretching ahead of him. There, in the distance, he saw Kansu soldiers, rifles in hand, running towards the train. Oh hell! The two bodies and the bound jailer must have been found and the revolver shot would have given away the direction taken by the fugitives. He rushed to the other side of the footplate.

His three comrades were now some twenty yards from the steps up into the cab but, as he watched, three soldiers materialised onto the platform behind them. The nearest knelt and raised his rifle to his shoulder. Disregarding the engineer, who was now stoking furiously, Fonthill steadied his revolver with two hands and took careful aim. The shot ricocheted from the stone of the platform immediately in front of the Kansu and took him in the stomach. He clutched his midriff and fell, causing his two companions to dive into the station waiting room.

'For God's sake, hurry!' shouted Simon.

'Nearly there,' cried Jenkins. At the foot of the steps, he lifted Chang like a baby, so that Fonthill was able to reach down, clutch the young man round the waist and drag him onto the footplate, where he lay, breathing heavily.

Simon let him lie and rushed to the other side of the cab and leant out. A bullet immediately clipped off the side of the locomotive and winged its way past his head. Sighted awkwardly with his left hand, he released two shots at the advancing soldiers, causing them to duck and take cover under the trucks.

Sam at last followed Jenkins onto the footplate. 'Tell him to start the engine and reverse out of here, that way,' Fonthill shrieked at him.

'Revolver, quickly, 352. Take the other side and keep the Kansus at bay. I'll take this side.'

Their revolvers were operating at too long a range but they had the effect of keeping the Chinese from advancing along the line of trucks until, suddenly, with a lurch and a hissing of steam, the locomotive began slowly to reverse out of the station.

'Hey,' shouted Jenkins. 'We're pullin' a whole line of trucks, look you.'

'It doesn't matter. It'll slow us down a bit but it will also stop the Chinese from loading them with their troops to take up north. Keep a sharp eye, though, in case any of those Kansus have climbed onto the wagons.' Simon looked down at Chang, who was looking about him with a bewildered air. 'Chang, my dear cousin-in-law,' he shouted above the roar of the engine, 'we're taking you to the seaside – well, not far off it, anyway.'

The young man tried to force a smile. The locomotive gathered steam and soon they were rushing through the night air, with the click-clack of the rails imposing a reassuring rhythm to match the hiss from the open furnace. Sparks from the locomotive's funnel flew over them, dancing like glow-worms against the dark sky.

Suddenly, a strange 'woo, woo' made Fonthill whirl round. Sam was hanging out of the side of the cab, shouting, grinning and waving his free arm at the hidden countryside hurrying past.

Jenkins exchanged smiles with Simon. 'Enjoy yourself, son,' he shouted at the Chinaman. 'You're a soldier now.'

Chapter Thirteen

The train sped unhampered through the night, with Sam, Jenkins and Simon relieving the engineer in stoking the boiler. Their free passage convinced Fonthill that the Imperial army had, indeed, retreated en masse to the north and was about to regroup. Nevertheless, it was a great relief when the locomotive and its line of wagons steamed into an empty and echoing Tientsin station and hissed to a stop.

The engineer was given money – which further bewildered him – but was warned that his locomotive and the wagons were now the property of the Great Powers and that, under pain of death, he should not attempt to steam north again. Chang was gently eased down onto the platform and, after some discussion with passing coolies, a stretcher was produced and he was carried to the hospital and delivered into the care of the surgeon major, who demanded to know where the hell Fonthill had been. As soon as Simon was able to find his store of Chinese currency, hidden in his billet, Sam was further rewarded and returned – not without protestations – to his duties at the hospital.

The next morning, Fonthill and Jenkins sat at Chang's bedside and were relieved to be told that, although his nose had been broken, his chin was bruised and not fractured and that he had only lost two teeth. He was able to speak much more clearly now and they heard his story.

He had, indeed, charged with the Royal Welch, anxious to join in the action. Dazed by the piece of masonry that had fallen on his head, he was recognised in the street by one of the Kansu soldiers who had pulled them out of the river above the settlements.

'Damned bad luck, that,' said Simon. 'A chance in a million.'

'Your trouble,' added Jenkins helpfully, 'is that you look too Chinese. 'Ave you ever thought about growin' a moustache, a big black one? You might just pass for a Welshman then, see.'

Chang tried to laugh but it hurt him, so he was encouraged to continue to mumble his story. Convinced that he was a spy, the Kansu had marched him back with them in their retreat – 'very fast,' he said – and he had then been interrogated about why he was wearing a British Revenue coat and carrying a British rifle. This had involved having a rifle butt crashed into his face and bayonet points thrust into his ribs and upper arm. But he had stuck to his story that he had escaped from Peking and that, as a half-brother of an Englishman, he was fighting on the side of the Great Powers. His inquisitors had promised that he would be beheaded the next morning.

He gave a weak smile. 'I was so glad to see you, even Mr Jenkins.'

'Well, that's an admission,' agreed Simon. 'Stay resting, dear old

Chang, and then you can join us in the relief column that leaves for the legations – if one is ever mounted, that is.'

This remained Fonthill's greatest worry. The sense of urgency that possessed him seemed to have no echo in the comings and goings that now surrounded the military leaders in the settlements. There was no doubt that the fate of Seymour's original expedition was casting dark shadows across the preparations for the relief. Seymour himself, having failed with his enterprise, had a vested interest in portraying the strength of the Chinese forces and spoke of forty thousand troops being required. The need for even greater numbers was bandied about.

But nothing like these numbers could be found in Taku or Tientsin. Then the question of the leadership of the relief column arose. Far away, in Berlin, the Kaiser entered the fray. He claimed that, because of von Ketteler's murder, Germany must have priority in this matter and, after he had lobbied the governments of Japan and Russia, it was agreed that a commander-in-chief should be appointed in the form of the German Field Marshal Count von Waldersee. But the field marshal was six weeks' voyage away, in landlocked Berlin.

When Simon heard rumours of this, he was plunged into greater despair. Taking advantage of the fame he had gathered in the attack on the Chinese City he demanded to see the newly arrived commander of the British forces, General Gaselee. This was granted with promising alacrity and Fonthill, still wearing his Chinese coolie garments, found himself facing the general shortly after he had left Chang's bedside.

Gaselee was white-haired, wore a huge, equally white walrus moustache and had twinkling eyes set in a face that seemed always to wear a kindly, rather puzzled expression. He advanced across the room to meet Simon with outstretched hand.

'My dear Fonthill,' he said. 'Congratulations on your magnificent effort with those damned gates to the city. And I hear that you've just returned after plucking one of your chaps from the very midst of the enemy.'

'Thank you, Sir Alfred. You are very kind.' Fonthill took a deep breath. To hell with the compliments, he wanted action. 'When can you set off for Peking? We can't wait for some blasted Prussian field marshal to get here, can we? The legations can't hold out for another six weeks, that's for certain.'

Gaselee chuckled. 'Ah, I'd heard that you were a touch impatient. Now take a seat and we can talk this through.'

'Seriously, sir. We just can't afford much more talking. Lives are being lost up there.'

'I quite agree. As you know, I have only just arrived, but I have been arguing for immediate action with my international colleagues since I set foot here. And I promise you, Fonthill, that we won't wait for this Prussian to arrive. Nevertheless, there are problems.'

He held up his hand as Fonthill made to interrupt. 'Now, hear me out. My own personal problem is that the British army is not well represented here. As you know, we are still fighting a war with the Boers in South Africa – a war that we thought was over weeks ago – and that continues to make demands on our manpower. In addition, I have been ordered to put a brigade into Shanghai to defend our considerable interests there. The result is that we can muster only about three thousand troops for the relief expedition, which doesn't give me much of a voice in our councils here.

'Mind you, my colleagues have difficulties, too. The Americans, who don't have much of a standing army anyway, have got their hands full in the Philippines; in Manchuria the Russians are fighting Boxer-inspired uprisings; and the French have got internal problems in Indo-China. Only the Germans and the Japs are not involved in any overseas fighting.

'Nevertheless, I believe we can muster about twenty thousand men between us and I think that that is enough. Now, we know we can't use the railway past Yangtsun – although,' he smiled, 'it's most kind of you to present us with a locomotive and wagons. So what's your advice on the best way to get to Peking, eh?'

Fonthill smiled, half in apology for his brusqueness and half in relief at finding a senior army officer with a refreshing sense of urgency and one who was *prepared to listen*! 'There's only one way to go, General,' he said. 'Put heavy stuff on the river – you may have to pull the junks from the banks over shoals, or even to pole them – and march by its side. It goes virtually to Peking. There's no major road but in view of this drought you can cover the ground pretty well. It looks to me as though the Kansu troops have retreated or are retreating at least to Peitsang, so you should have a head start. And they were the main and by far the best of the enemy facing us.'

'Good. And I trust you will come with us and guide us when it comes to getting into the legations?'

'Of course, sir. My wife is there and I am anxious for all sorts of reasons to get back there.'

'I can well understand that. Now, are you happy to stay in native dress or shall we rustle up some kind of uniform for you?'

'I will stay "blacked up", so to speak, sir. It's been a long time since I was in uniform, anyway, and I don't think it will quite suit me to get back into it now. But thank you for the offer.'

'Good. Now, if you'll excuse me, I have much to do. I have a feeling, Fonthill, that we can get those twenty thousand men marching within the next few days, whoever the hell is in command.' His eyes twinkled. 'Perhaps it ought to be you, eh?'

'Thanks for the compliment, but I would have more faith in you, sir.'

Fonthill left with a heart far lighter than when he had arrived. At last, a general who wanted to move! Again, his thoughts turned to Alice. He knew just how self-sufficient she was, so well able to take care of herself. Yet, if those fragile defences broke, he had no confidence in Sir Claude's assurances that she would be protected. Gaselee certainly seemed to understand the need for speed, but it was clear that establishing a unified command was rather like getting an elephant to perform in *Swan Lake*. As he walked back to his billet, Simon decided that, if no real progress had been made within three days, then he and Jenkins would attempt the perilous journey back to Peking on their own. Alice could be left alone no longer.

The good news produced within those anxious few days came from the hospital. Chang had made excellent progress and was discharged after two days with light dressings on his wounds and following a successful operation on his nose that did little for his appearance but helped his breathing considerably. That same evening, Fonthill received an invitation to revisit General Gaselee.

'I know you are anxious,' said the old man, 'and you have certainly done enough down here to receive a progress report. I think I am getting agreement at last.'

'Thank God for that.'

'Quite. The Russians have a new leader here – a general named Lineivitch – and he is all for waiting, and the Yankee chap, General Chaffee, is worried that he hasn't got any artillery. But I have talked the Japanese into starting virtually straight away and as they have about ten thousand troops here, which is by far the largest national contingent, we are beginning to sway the doubters, because I have let it be known that the British and Japanese will go it alone, if necessary.' The general's eyes twinkled under his grey brows. 'This has frightened the life out of 'em because the Russians, the French and the Germans, in particular, would lose so much face in the international community back home if they didn't help to relieve Peking that I am sure they will join the party. It's blackmail, my dear Fonthill, but it's working.'

'Well done, General. So when do you think we can set out?'

'If we can't get moving within three days, that's by the fifth of August, I will eat my hat.'

'Who will be in command?'

'Can't say. We can't agree. So we will lead our own contingents and probably have a sort of council of commanders to tackle problems as they arise.'

'Isn't this a recipe for disaster?'

The general shrugged his shoulder. 'Quite probably.' Then he shot a shrewd glance at Fonthill. 'What would you rather we did, Fonthill, hang about here and sort out these xenophobic haggles or press on and get to bloody Peking as fast as we can?'

'I think you know my answer, sir.'

'Quite so.'

'So, may I enquire the size of the relief force and its breakdown?'

'Here, look at this.' Gaselee threw a sheet of paper across his desk.

'This is my estimate, but we will probably set off with less than this.'

Simon read:

Japanese	10,000
Russians	4,000
British	3,000
Americans	2,000
French	800
Germans	100
Austrians and Italians	100
Total	20,000

Fonthill looked up: 'Artillery, cavalry?' he asked.

'Should have adequate guns,' grunted Gaselee, 'but I must confess that we are light on cavalry, so we shall be hampered when it comes to reconnaissance and pursuit. The Japs have one cavalry regiment but their horses are too light and probably useless. We have some Yankee cowboys landed at Taku but their mounts will probably not have recovered in time from the sea voyage. So we shall be left, I think, with a few Cossacks and, thank God, the Bengal Lancers.'

'And your plan, sir?'

'We shall follow the course of the Pei Ho, as you recommended, taking a train of junks and sampans for our supplies. We are desperately short of road transport, although the Americans have some good mules and wagons. Most of the way there will be only one road, I understand, and God help us if it rains, because we shall be bogged down. Our strategy, my dear Fonthill, will be to launch a frontal attack on the Chinese whenever and wherever we are opposed. And our aim will be to move bloody fast, like some battering ram, until we see the walls of Peking before us.'

Simon grinned. 'At least, General,' he said, 'your plan has the advantage of simplicity.'

Gaselee gave a sad smile. 'There is no choice, Fonthill. You see, this force will be unique. Never before – except probably in the case of the Crusades, centuries ago – has there been such a polyglot, cobbled-together army. Given these circumstances, we cannot afford sophistication. We must advance as quickly as we can and go straight at 'em. I am gambling that the Chinese will not be well led and that . . .' he paused for a moment and the smile widened '. . . as always, God will be on our side.'

'Good luck, sir.'

'Be ready to march with us in three days' time.'

'We shall be ready.'

In fact, the energy of the old general proved so effective that the 'army of the nations' was brought together a day earlier and the relief column set out from Tientsin at dawn on the morning of 4th August, forty days after the siege of Peking began. Fonthill, Jenkins and Chang marched in the van. Ahead of them it was estimated that fifty thousand Chinese troops were assembled to deny them passage.

Chapter Fourteen

So it was that the three comrades found themselves retracing their steps to Peitsang – this time, though, in daylight under a scorching sun. Simon had been introduced to the council of war as someone who could guide the relief column but, in fact, his services were not needed, since it was a simple enough matter to follow the river, and he, Jenkins and Chang therefore allowed themselves to drop back through the marching men to allow Chang to walk at a less punishing pace and to join the British at the rear.

This, in fact, proved to be a mixed blessing, for the rearguard marched, not only in appalling heat, but in the dust cloud caused by the long column stretching ahead. Whenever the column halted, the weary, parched British found that all the shade had been taken and many of the wells drunk dry. It was whispered among the ranks that the amenable Lieutenant General Gaselee had volunteered to take this unenviable place on the first day as a gesture to his international colleagues.

It was the Japanese, in fact, who led throughout the day, in recognition of their numerical superiority, and it was they, therefore, who encountered the enemy first. On the basis of what he had learnt concerning the rail trucks at Peitsang, Fonthill had advised Gaselee that it was unlikely that the column would meet any serious opposition at that first small town, but the Japanese met the Chinese dug in at its front.

The engagement that followed was brief but conclusive. The Japanese advanced remorselessly in close formation, supported by artillery fire, and the Chinese, after first firing a couple of volleys, turned and fled, taking their guns with them.

At the rear, Fonthill and his companions knew little of the encounter, for the guns up ahead seemed to cease firing almost as soon as they had begun. Gaselee, riding by, paused to explain to Simon what had happened. 'They've got away, dammit,' he said. 'I knew we would have to pay for not having enough cavalry.'

The advance continued at a fast pace and by the early afternoon of the next day the column had reached Yangtsun, some twenty miles from Tientsin, where, as Fonthill had warned, a more formidable Chinese force was waiting for them, firmly entrenched in several defensive lines, supported by artillery. This time it was the British and Americans who were in the van and who consequently led the attack.

Simon, whose burns now appeared to be on the mend, had requested permission for himself and Jenkins to join the ranks for the attack, although Chang had been firmly posted to the rear. To avoid being mistaken for the enemy, they had been issued with Royal Welch jackets, although for comfort's sake they would have wished to retain their cool cotton overalls. Now, as the Allied artillery played along the Chinese positions, they waited, rifles and bayonets at the ready, for the order to advance. Perspiration trickled down their faces as they stood in the smoke and heat.

'I can't see a bloody thing,' said Jenkins, licking his lips. 'I'm just as likely to stick this lunger into a friend as into a foe. What's the plan, bach sir? Do we just march up to them trenches?'

Simon nodded. 'Looks like it.' He thought back to his conversation with Gaselee about strategy. 'I don't think there's much scope for flanking movements in this war. For one reason there's not much room, with the river on our right. And for another, we haven't the faintest idea where our support might be – or, for that matter, who they are. This campaign is going to be chaotic, mark my words.'

They exchanged weary grins and then a bugle sounded and they were off, heads down, marching through the cannon smoke, half-blinded by perspiration. It seemed almost at the last minute that the smoke cleared and they saw the first line of the Chinese trenches immediately before them. A ragged cheer broke out from the British – led, once again, by the Royal Welch Fusiliers – and Fonthill and Jenkins, with the rest of the line, broke into a shambling trot.

Simon was dimly aware of flashes of rifle fire very close up ahead and of the hiss of bullets. Then he was jumping into the enemy trench and firing at one green-clad Chinamen who rose before him, and then wheeling to engage his bayonet with that of another to his right. A shot rang out and the man slumped to the ground. Fonthill was dimly aware of Jenkins, at his side, sliding the breech bolt of his rifle to insert another round, when a sergeant's voice rang out in the mellifluous tones of the Welsh valleys. 'Don't hang about, lads. Onto the next trench. We've got'em on the run!'

Using his rifle butt as a crutch – his ankle was beginning to burn again – Fonthill levered himself up the side of the trench and lumbered ahead over uneven ground to where he could see the Fusiliers jumping down into the next line of entrenchments, stabbing and firing. He was conscious, among the chaos, of glimpsing Chinese banners in the distance and then he too was down in the trench, pausing amongst the bodies that lined its floor and realising that he was completely out of breath.

'I'm too bloody old for this now,' he gasped to Jenkins. 'Not to mention a wonky leg. Let me get my breath back.'

'Ah, bach sir. Now you know what it's like being a poor bloody infantryman.' He, too, however, was gasping for breath.

They stayed, perhaps for three minutes, at the bottom of the trench before crawling up the far side and advancing once more towards where rifle flashes through the smoke showed where the Chinese, at their third line of entrenchments, were putting up a stronger resistance. Now they were among a platoon of gaitered Americans, wearing their wide-brimmed hats, whose advance had been halted by sweeping fire from a machine gun embedded immediately ahead of them. The men were lying spreadeagled, hugging the soil, attempting to take advantage of the undulating nature of the ground but not moving forward.

Fonthill crawled alongside a corporal. 'Why don't you try and outflank the gun?' he asked.

The young man turned a startled face towards Simon. He looked him up and down, taking in the Royal Welch jacket, with no chevrons or other badges of rank and the coolie trousers and sandals. 'Who might you be, then, buster?' he demanded.

Simon sighed. 'Captain Simon Fonthill, British Army. Intelligence. Where's your officer?'

'Haven't got the faintest idea, bud.'

'Say "sir" when you speak to me. Now, take three men and follow me and Sergeant Major Jenkins here. Crawl and keep your heads down. Come on. Now!'

For a moment, the corporal considered refusing. Then the tone of command in Fonthill's voice and his air of authority prevailed. He turned to the men on either side of him. 'Foster and Schumann follah me and this . . . er . . . Limey officer. Come ahn and keep yoh heads down.'

The five of them crawled to the right, slithering on their bellies and sometimes across the front of other American soldiers, similarly taking cover. Then, when they were outside the arc of the machine gun, Fonthill led them at a tangent towards the Chinese line, again taking advantage of each patch of cover he could find: a stunted clump of millet, cut down by rifle fire; a rare rocky outcrop; or a dried-up irrigation ditch. Fonthill used every bit of knowledge he could dredge up from his days as a platoon commander, leading ground craft exercises on the Welsh Beacons.

Somehow, they managed to get within about fifty yards of a section of a Chinese trench from which only desultory rifle fire was showing. Still on his stomach, Fonthill turned to the three Americans.

'Which part of the States are you from?' he asked.

'We're all from the South . . . suh. From Virginee.'

'So you can do a rebel yell – a real yell, from Virginia?' (Simon had studied the American Civil War during his time at Sandhurst.)

A puzzled smile crossed the corporal's face. 'Sure can.'

'Right. All five of us will discharge a volley and then we'll up and attack that trench with the bayonet. But give a bloody great yell. Pretend, if you like, that you're going at a bunch of Yankees. Right?'

All three grinned and nodded.

'Right. Five rounds rapid fire and then up and at 'em.'

The resultant volley was not the most impressive that emerged from either side on that day at Yangtsun, but it caused fragments to fly from the soil bags lining the top of the Chinese trench and sent one of its defenders falling back with a bullet hole in his forehead. Then the five rose to their feet – Simon with the aid of a push from Jenkins – and charged across the intervening ground, their bayonets glinting, as the three Americans and one Welshman let out piercing screams.

It was enough to send the already demoralised Chinese – for they had seen the occupants of the first two lines of their trenches leap over them in wide-eyed retreat – drop their weapons and run to the rear.

'Where to now, bud?' cried the corporal, turning to Simon as they grouped together in the trench.

'Don't call me— Oh, never mind. To the left. Clear the trench till we come to the machine-gunner. Run on now. I have a problem with my foot but we'll be right behind. Oh, and keep up the yell. Shout for Dixie.'

Hobbling behind with the help of Jenkins, Fonthill found the trench cleared most ably by the three Americans, whose rebel yell preceded them and seemed to strike terror in the Chinese manning the line. Then he found the three Southerners crouched behind a traverse in the trench, on the other side of which they could hear the machine gun still chattering.

'Thought we'd wait for yoh heah, suh,' the corporal explained, a trifle diffidently. 'Don't know what's on the other side, yah know?'

Simon nodded. 'Dammit,' he frowned. 'Wish we had grenades. Nothing for it but just to charge round. At least the Maxim will be in a fixed position and firing forward. I'll lead. You four follow.'

'No, bach sir.' Jenkins thrust him aside. 'This is a job for a Welshman. Our yell is much better than any Yanks.'

'Hey, man.' The corporal was indignant. 'We ain't Yanks.'

But with a scream completely Celtic in its origin Jenkins charged around the traverse, closely followed by Fonthill and the three Americans. Three Chinese were manning the heavy machine gun in a specially built mini salient jutting out from the line. They stood no chance as five rifles fired as one.

'Stand guard at this other traverse,' shouted Simon to Jenkins. Then to the corporal, 'Lend me your hat.' Fonthill seized it, then stood up on the embrasure protecting the gun and waved it towards the American line. 'Come on, boys,' he shouted. 'We've put the gun out.'

Immediately, there was a cheer from the line and scores of figures rose from the ground and, bayonets fixed, ran towards the Chinese trench. Fonthill waved them on and then, exhausted, slumped onto the line of sandbags. The Americans ran by him down into the trench and then up and over, continuing their attack.

Jenkins squatted next to Simon and shouted to their three companions, 'Go with 'em, boys, we're a bit knackered, see.'

The corporal seized Simon's hand and shook it. 'Keep the hat, bud,' he grinned. 'Consider yourself an honorary Dixie Boy.' Then the three of them ran after their comrades, now all disappearing into the dust and gun smoke ahead of them.

'Well done, bach sir,' said Jenkins. 'We could 'ave been there all day in front of this bloody gun.' He turned to inspect it. 'Looks brand new,' he muttered. Then, 'Ah bloody 'ell. It says 'ere, "Made in Birmingham".'

Fonthill had no time to reply before the ground seemed to erupt all around them and they were in the middle of an artillery barrage. The two dropped to the salient floor and covered the back of their heads with their hands as earth, rocks and things indefinable rained down on them. The noise was deafening and Fonthill flinched as a piece of rock hit his injured ankle. He tried vainly to press himself further into the ground that seemed to shake beneath him.

Eventually, the barrage lifted and Simon lifted his head and reached out a hand towards Jenkins. The Welshman raised a face covered in soil and debris.

'Are you hurt, 352?'

'No. You all right?'

'Yes. Where the bloody hell did all that come from suddenly?'

Jenkins wiped soil from his moustache. 'It was a bit late, look you. We'd already captured all the bloody trenches. Do you want to carry on?'

'No. This leg is giving me trouble. I shan't be able to march if I don't rest it. Let's stay here for a minute.' Fonthill gave a wan smile.

'It looks as though the Taffies and the Yanks can manage very well without us.'

The two were clambering out of the trench when the thud of hooves announced the arrival of General Gaselee and his ADC. The general looked down on them in disapproval.

'What in God's name are you two doing here?'

'Sorry, sir,' gasped Fonthill. 'I'm afraid I couldn't quite keep up with the charge. Gammy leg and all that. Jenkins stayed behind to give me a hand.'

'Good Lord, man. I wasn't rebuking you. Well, I was. You have no right to be charging with the infantry. I am going to need you when

285

we come to Peking and try to get through those bloody walls into the legations. You mustn't risk your life at this stage. We've got plenty of damned good infantry who can do that. Now, get back out of it as soon as you can.'

'Will do, General. Where the hell did the Chinese suddenly produce that artillery barrage from? It was a bit too far in the rear to catch our chaps but it certainly caught us two.'

General Gaselee brought the head of his horse around as it tried to prance away. 'Bloody mess, Fonthill, I'm afraid. Those weren't Chinese shells. They were ours. It was the Americans in the second wave who mainly caught it. I've just come back from investigating it – the Chinese, by the way, have retreated once again. But we lost four men of the Yankees and another fourteen wounded, most of them fatally.'

'Good Lord! How did that happen?'

Gaselee pulled at his moustache. 'Two batteries involved. Ours and the Russians'. Nobody's exactly sure what happened but it seems that the Russians were unlimbering next to our battery and asked us for the range. We gave it to them in yards and it's my belief that they thought it was metres, so they dropped short before we could stop 'em. Anyway, the Yanks caught it.' He shook his head. 'This is what happens when you get a polyglot collection of units fighting alongside each other in complete bloody ignorance, without any overall coordination. Can't be helped. Probably won't be the last time it happens. Now get back and rest that leg.'

With a forefinger touch to his cap brim, he turned and galloped away. Fonthill and Jenkins exchanged glances.

'Well, there you are,' sniffed the Welshman. 'Nearly drowned in that blasted river, narrowly avoiding gettin' whipped to death by the

Chinese, nearly blowin' ourselves up with dynamite and now just escapin' by our teeth from a shellin' by the Russkies. This is a bloody dangerous war, I'm thinkin', bach sir. Too dangerous for me.'

'Rubbish. We've been through worse. Now give me a hand to get up. I wonder if the cooks are brewing any tea back there.'

The relief column spent that evening and the next day resting at Yangtsun, waiting for the supply junks to catch up and, in the words of one senior officer, 'sorting itself out'. Having been present at the council of war held at Tientsin on the eve of departure, Fonthill knew that the original plan had been to advance no further than Yangtsun until reinforcements had arrived. Some fourteen thousand troops had reached that town, a number originally felt to be insufficient to push on to Peking. But the comparatively easy victories in the two battles experienced so far had firmly put the bit between the teeth of the Allied generals involved. The old competitiveness had also reared its head.

'I fear that this is no longer going to be an advance, more a damned race,' observed Fonthill, when orders were given to break camp and resume the march on the morning of the eighth, just four days after leaving Tientsin. The field had now thinned out and of the eight starters, only the Japanese, British, Americans and Russians were sufficiently well organised in terms of transport and commissariat logistics to be able to continue. The much smaller German, Italian, Austrian and French contingents were forced to return to Tientsin and reorganise, without having fired a shot in anger.

Nevertheless, the four nations that now comprised the column were determined and quite undaunted by being outnumbered – at least in practice – by the enemy. It was, however, a gruelling march. Much of the plain now was covered in the tall *kaoliang* which provided ideal conditions for ambushes. None came, however, and it was the sun and the lack of drinking water that were the worst enemy for the column.

The British were once again forming the rearguard, with Fonthill, Chang and Jenkins marching with them. Despite the harsh conditions, both Simon and Chang had recovered from their injuries well enough to be among the 7th Rajputs of the Indian contingent when the latter marched through an American detachment.

'Blimey,' whispered Jenkins, 'look at 'em. 'Alf 'ave got their eyes closed and it looks as though they're goin' to fall over at any minute.'

'Yes, Mr Jenkins,' said Chang. 'But they're plodding along, you see. They're not giving up. They're making a splendid effort.'

The Welshman grinned. 'Yes, Changy, but you can see 'ow them Injuns beat old General Custard. Take away their 'orses and make 'em march an' the Yanks are buggered.'

Fonthill shook his head. 'Well, they fought well in that trench and on the wall at Peking. And I hope to God they're still doing that last bit.'

More and more his thoughts were turning to Alice and the Legation defenders. He was relieved and delighted when the commanders of the column decided to push on from Yangtsun without waiting for reinforcements. He kept telling himself that they would have heard if the Legation compound had fallen. But the fear grew that, as the news of the advance neared the capital, so, too, would the efforts of the attackers there. If, in breaking through, the Chinese took prisoners, then the better they would be able to bargain with the relief column outside the walls. So, despite his aching body, Simon put down his head and trudged on amongst the dust at the rear.

One night, around their campfire, Fonthill took advantage of their close proximity to question the Chinaman about his half-brother, Gerald. How well, he asked, did he know him?

These days, Chang took time to consider his answer to questions, as though in the light of the new understanding of the ways of the world that his experiences of the last few weeks had given him. His recent injuries – particularly his broken nose – had also changed his countenance, making him appear older. So, his head on one side, he pondered the question for a moment before answering.

'Well, cousin,' he said, 'he was, I think, about seven or eight when I was introduced, so to speak, into the family. As a result, there has always been a gap between us. Mainly because of age, of course, but also perhaps because of our ethnic backgrounds.'

'Yes, Chang, I understand that. Yet it seemed to me that Gerald appeared to be more Chinese than you in many ways.'

Again Chang considered the question. 'Yes, I can understand that. Perhaps it was because we were both of us, for different reasons, trying to change our . . . what is the word? . . . ah yes, our *ethnicity* to match the surroundings into which we had been placed. Me, you see, to be more English, to match my mother and father, and Gerald to be more Chinese to match his surroundings and the many Chinese friends he had made.'

'But did you notice that Gerald, perhaps, took this rather further than you? You have never, as far as I can see, become anti-Chinese – although, I hasten to add that I know you do not like the Boxers, and with good reason. But you have never expressed your dislike of the Chinese people in general. Gerald, on the other hand, seems to have become almost virulently anti-British.'

Another pause. Then: 'Yes, I think that is probably so. He has studied history, you see, and he has become very annoyed at the way the Foreign Powers have, in one way or another, colonised parts of China. And I think he has never forgiven the British in the way that they created the Opium Wars so that they could take their own share of our country and also continue to benefit by the trade in opium.'

'But you know these things too, Chang, and you seem to have less antagonism towards us than your brother.'

The old smile came back to Chang, lighting up his battered face. 'Ah, that is because I like you more, you see. And I think your culture is as great as ours – Shakespeare, Milton, Pope and so on. If you can't beat the jolly old British, I say, then you should jolly well join them.'

At this, everyone grinned. 'Blimey, Changy,' said Jenkins, 'you'll be playing cricket soon.'

Chang's face lightened again. 'Oh, but I do already, Mr Jenkins. I can bowl this new googly that everyone is talking about. Look, I can show you how you do it—'

Fonthill held up a hand. 'Not just now, cousin,' he said. 'Perhaps some other time.'

The advance continued, as did the hardship, particularly the heat and the lack of water. The Russians and the Japanese seemed to stand it best, despite the fact that the Japanese remained in the lead now and bore the brunt of what fighting was left. On 12th August, they blew up the South Gate of the City of Tungchow and the Chinese garrison streamed away without a fight. The Allies made camp, resting there and replenishing their supplies. The city was the site of a large American mission that had been brutally sacked by the Boxers with much loss of life in the early days of the uprising. One officer suggested that what was left of the mission should be burnt as an example to the local populace. Fonthill was with General Gaselee when the suggestion was made. But the old general demurred.

'My dear fellow,' he said, putting a paternal hand on the officer's shoulder, 'I do not agree. I intend, in fact, to establish a market here, right away, so that it is operating before we leave. A place where the local populace can come in and trade with us. Now don't you think that would be better than setting these ruins on fire again? After all, we do not wish to antagonise the three hundred and fifty million people of China, now, do we?'

He turned to Fonthill. 'Would you be so kind as to ask your Chinese chap – Chang, isn't it? – to write a suitable notice in the local dialect, asking the people to come in and bring their local produce to sell to us. We will put it up here. So much better, I think, than more burning. Don't you agree?'

'Oh, very much so, sir. I will ask him right away.' He turned away and smiled to himself. How refreshing to meet a military commander who considered the feelings of the civilian population!

Very tentatively, the Chinese who had fled their city began to drift back, bringing rice and other vegetables to trade with the column. Rumours also began to flood into the camped army as it rested at Tungchow. It was said that the general commanding the retreating Chinese forces, the xenophobic Li Ping-heng, had poisoned himself and that Yu Lu, the viceroy of the Chihli province, had blown out his brains – stories that later were found to be true. More concerning for Fonthill, however, was the rumour that the legations had fallen and that all of the foreigners within had been murdered. This was quickly quashed, however, when a cavalry patrol sent out from Tungchow to probe the state of the country between the city and the capital was able to ride virtually to the walls of Peking without meeting any organised resistance. The patrol reported, however, that it could hear heavy gunfire coming from within the city. So the siege continued!

Simon, of course, was vastly relieved but was also full of frustration once again at the seeming sanguineness of the Allied leaders who were resting their troops almost within sound of the Chinese cannon at Peking.

He expressed his concern to General Gaselee, whose own patience was beginning to show signs of fraying at the repeated demands of his fellow countryman.

'You know, my dear fellow,' he said, fixing Fonthill with his kindly eyes, 'we cannot trot up to Peking non-stop. This relief force has done remarkably well to get this far so quickly, with such success and sustaining so few casualties – particularly considering that we are more a not-so-mobile Tower of Babel than a military force. We have marched for some seventy miles in this burning heat and with very poor water supplies and we have defeated the Chinese whenever we have met them. To charge on to Peking without pause for breath or consideration of how we are going to get through those great walls would be the very negation of well-established, military, strategic thinking. And you, as a former soldier and a distinguished servant of the Empire over many campaigns, ought to know that.'

The general's tone softened and he leant over and put a hand on Fonthill's knee. 'I well understand your concern about your wife,' he went on, 'but we now know that the defenders are still holding out. In addition to the report of our own cavalry, one or two messages have filtered through from Chinese sources to say that the legations are still manning their barricades, although we understand that they are hard-pressed now.' He sighed. 'But the attack on Peking will be by far the most difficult thing we have undertaken. It is vital it succeeds.

'Now, the council is meeting tomorrow and – I may say to my great relief – we will then formulate a plan in detail to allocate roles and to decide on our tactics for the final attack. We have already decided to press on immediately afterwards and to regroup within three miles of Peking from where we shall spring forward to the attack. I promise that I will report back to you and inform you on those plans, because, as I have already said, I would wish to use your local knowledge. You have already explained that the only way to penetrate the outer walls, given that we have no siege artillery – nor time, for that matter – is to attack the great gates. We shall need you, once we are inside the Chinese City, to show the best way through to the legations. So, my dear Fonthill,' the eyes under the great bushy brows were twinkling again now, 'do rest content for the moment, I implore you.'

Simon responded with a slow smile. 'I accept all that you say, of course, General, and I really am most grateful to you for taking me into your confidence in this way. It goes without saying, of course, that my companions and I will do all that we can to assist in the attack. I look forward to hearing from you tomorrow.'

That night, Fonthill did not sleep well. He had to confess to himself that he had no real confidence in the ability of the generals leading the relief force to prepare an attack based on military principles rather than national considerations. Each would want to report back to their anxious governments and peoples back home that they and their own troops had performed gloriously in the relief of Peking. There would be honour and medals to be won. And, he reflected sadly, lives to be lost. He just hoped feverishly that one of them would not be Alice's.

The council took place the next day and lasted for some time.

True to his word, Gaselee, whom Simon suspected was beginning to grow in stature among his international colleagues, not only for his seniority in rank but because of his sagacity and experience, summoned Simon to his tent.

He explained that the Russian commander, General Lineivitch – a soldier of similar seniority to Gaselee – had reported that his men were too exhausted to carry out an assault immediately on completing the approach march and he had persuaded the generals that the attack should be carried out in two phases. The column would bivouac three miles from the walls and the army would put in a coordinated attack on the morning of 14th August.

'Coordinated?' enquired Fonthill with a lifted eyebrow.

'Oh yes. For once, we have agreed on the details. Each of the five nations will attack one of the four gates in the walls on the eastern side of the city, swinging round in a synchronised attack—'

Simon interrupted him. '*Five* nations, sir?'

Gaselee smiled. 'Yes, the tiny French contingent, which, you will remember, had to retreat to Tientsin, have burst their buttons to catch us up and are at this moment very, very proud of themselves.' His smile broadened. 'You know what the French are like. So . . . the plan is as follows: the Russians will attack the Tung Chih Men Gate in the north, on our right flank; and the Japanese will go for the Chi Hua Men, the next one down in the wall, so to speak. They will both attack on the north side of the Imperial Canal. We and the Americans will be on the south side of the canal. The Americans, with the . . . um . . . no doubt gallant assistance of the French, will attack the Tung Pien Men and we will go for the Hsia Kuo Men, the southernmost gate in the eastern wall, leading directly into the Chinese City.'

The general's virtually permanent half-smile lapsed now into a broad grin. 'You will be glad to hear, Fonthill, that our target is quite near to the Legation Quarter, which, my dear fellow, you will take us to with the utmost alacrity. So, with any luck, we just might be the first nation to free the defenders of the Legation. Not, of course, that being the first in is of any concern to any of us.'

Fonthill did not return the grin. 'I just hope that we shall be in time, General,' he said. 'Those poor folk in the Quarter must be down to eating tree bark and hurling bricks at the Chinese by now.'

Gaselee gave a sympathetic frown. 'Quite so. Quite so. But I have every confidence, Fonthill, that we shall break through and get there in time. Now, as usual, you will march with us.' He stood. 'Good luck, my dear fellow.'

They shook hands. 'And good luck to you, sir.'

That evening, Gaselee's ADC, a young man of boundless good humour and, even in China, elegant trousers, approached Fonthill. 'I say, sir,' he said. 'Have you seen this?' He held out a piece of paper covered in writing in a rough and ready hand.

'What is it?'

'Well, as you may have heard, the jolly old French have just marched in – all hundred and fifty or so of 'em. They're in pretty parlous condition, don't you know, but their commanding officer – he's a general, no less, called Frey; he's the chap who's marched the poor buggers up and down from Tientsin . . . but anyway,' he paused for breath, 'one of our chaps has caught sight of his orders to his men for the final attack on Peking, although the place is still bloody miles away and we ain't ready to attack yet anyway.'

'Yes?' enquired Fonthill coldly.

'Yes, well sir, our chap has translated it from the French and this is what it says. I think the little chap thinks he's Napoleon. Do have a read, sir.'

Simon did so and read:

'This evening the German, Austrian and Italian columns will lie alongside the French troops. Tomorrow, under the walls of Peking, when the foreign national anthems are played, a complete silence will be maintained; each anthem will be heard with respect. When the French national anthem is played, it will be sung as loudly as possible, in tune, by the whole of the French Expeditionary Corps. Our compatriots and the occupants of the foreign legations beleaguered on the other side of the walls of the Chinese capital will know, when they hear our noble war chant, that deliverance is at hand.'

The ADC regained his paper and chortled again. 'You see, sir, the French haven't fired a shot yet and the German, Austrians and Italians are miles away down the road to Tientsin and will never arrive in time. All a bit vainglorious, don't you think? Eh? What?'

Fonthill recalled the far-from-gallant part played in the defence of the Legation by the French minister, Monsieur Pichon, and couldn't stifle a smile. 'Well,' he said, 'at least the Frogs have arrived. Let's hope that their national anthem frightens the hell out of the Chinese. Eh? What?'

His smile had disappeared as soon as he turned away, however. The attack on Peking was not some point-scoring contest between the Great Powers, for God's sake! Lives were at stake here, not national glory. He just hoped that the various contingents would work together when it came to attacking the great walled city. The eyes of the world would be upon them.

CHAPTER FIFTEEN

Alice did not go to her bed on reaching the British Legation after leaving Gerald, for she realised that the man must have time to see his mother, with whom she shared a room, and explain to her why he would be leaving the Legation. Nor did she wake Sir Claude MacDonald, of course, for Gerald must be given his half an hour to pack his belongings and get out. Tomorrow would be time enough to see the minister.

In the end, she crept into the hospital and explained to the duty nurse that she was having trouble in sleeping in the same room as Mrs Griffith (she felt guilty at complaining about her snoring, for her aunt was a deep and silent sleeper) and begged permission to doze on a makeshift stretcher for the night. Comfortable it was not, but better than having to face Aunt Lizzie in these early hours.

She was forced to dissemble again when she met her aunt the next morning. The old lady looked withdrawn and grey and Alice wondered what excuse Gerald had given her. It did not matter, as long as it did not involve *her*. The young man, of course, was a skilled and compulsive liar.

In fact, Mrs Griffith seemed more concerned about the fact that her niece had not slept in her bed that night. 'Wherever have you been, my dear?' she asked.

'Oh, Aunt, I am sorry. I should have sent a message to you. I altered my shift at the hospital and did night nurse duty, together with Mrs de Courcy. I am sorry if you were worried.'

'Well, I was. The next time, do tell me, please?'

'Yes, it was remiss of me.' She had no intention of telling her aunt about her son's treachery. Mrs Griffith would have to learn some other way, but what had he told her about his intentions? She tried to be nonchalant. 'Have you seen Gerald?' she asked. 'He . . . er . . . wanted to borrow a book of mine.'

For the first time, the old lady looked uncomfortable. 'Oh, he has gone to stay with a friend in the American Legation, I think,' she said. 'He may stay some while, I understand . . . er . . . something to do with working together on a project.' She put up a stick-like hand to her head and pushed away a wispy, grey lock.

Alice felt a sudden surge of affection for her aunt. She was obviously worried about her son and Alice yearned to comfort her. But it was impossible. Better to stick to the lies and brazen it out.

Shortly after breakfast, however – an unappetising bowl of millet porridge – she made her way to Sir Claude's quarters and requested an interview. He saw her immediately and listened quietly and with surprisingly little emotion to her story.

At the end, he nodded. 'Thank you, Mrs Fonthill. I am grateful to you for telling me all of this. We have always known, of course, that information was somehow getting to the Chinese about our fortifications and so on.' He gave a sad smile. 'This place is rather like a colander, you know, in terms of leaking things. With so many Chinese within the legations it was impossible to keep everything tight, so to speak. But I have to say that I have long suspected that young man of being up to something. Lolling about all day and declining to take his part in the defence – it was all rather suspicious, you know. But I couldn't bring myself to consider him to be an out-and-out traitor. Does his mother know?'

'No – at least I am fairly certain he has made up some excuse to leave the British Legation.'

'Very well. I will, of course, keep this matter confidential, but if the young fellow turns up again in the Legation I will have no hesitation in putting him behind bars.'

'Thank you. But will you respond to the Chinese invitation?'

'Certainly not.' His winged, tightly waxed moustache twitched as he allowed himself a dismissive smile. 'I am quite aware that there are certain elements at the Chinese court – and particularly in the foreign service there – that have always quite genuinely disliked the Boxer Uprising and deprecate the attack on the Quarter, but I could not possibly advise the ministers to trust them to the point that we lay down our arms. Chinese politics are far too volatile and I sense that the hatred of Her Royal Highness the Dragon Lady,' his smile widened at his daring in using the colloquialism, 'for we foreigners is far too deep-seated for us to put ourselves completely at her mercy. No, Mrs Fonthill, we hang on here and continue to fight.'

Alice nodded. 'I am sure you are right. But I sense that conditions here are becoming much worse. Am I right?'

His face returned to its customary solemn mien. 'I am afraid so. We killed our last pony last night and therefore I am afraid that meat will shortly drop off our menu. I am concerned about the number of casualties that we continue to sustain, our ammunition is running low and I live in constant fear that the Chinese will, as you have mentioned, subject us to a sustained artillery bombardment. Nevertheless,' and his eyes brightened, 'our morale is high as is our spirit. For all their shouting and blaring of trumpets, the Chinese are clearly frightened of our firepower and no longer seem to threaten any direct attacks on the perimeter. I could not wish to have better people to man our barricades. No, Mrs Fonthill, we will endure and we will prevail. Yes, we will prevail, I am certain of that.'

Alice bowed her head for the moment, so that Sir Claude could not see the moisture in her eyes. Then she looked up. 'Of course, you would have told me if you had heard any news of my husband?'

'Indeed. But it has been my experience so far in this highly unusual situation that bad news will almost always find its way to me quickly. I would expect to have heard if he had been intercepted. I have heard nothing. But I do know that there has been heavy fighting in Tientsin. I remain confident that we will be relieved.'

'How long can we hold out, then?'

He rose to his feet. 'The answer to that question, my dear lady, depends upon too many imponderables, so forgive me if I do not attempt to answer it. And also forgive me if I ask you to excuse me now. There is much to do, I am afraid.'

'Oh, of course, Sir Claude. It is good of you to give me so much of your time.'

They shook hands. Then the minister held her hand for a moment or two longer. 'I would like you to know, madam,' he said in a low voice – one that seemed to contain a hint of embarrassment – 'that I admire your courage in following that young scoundrel out of the Quarter and appreciate all that you do in the defence: your hospital work and the other, more . . . ah . . . active roles you play. You set a splendid example, madam.'

Alice felt the colour rise to her cheeks. It was so unlike this withdrawn Scotsman to distribute compliments. She felt unable to speak, so she bowed, smiled and left him.

She was relieved and glad, however, that the minister had rejected out of hand the proposal that the defenders should lay down their arms and allow themselves to be escorted to the coast by the Imperial army. She recalled similar instances – in Afghanistan and India not so many years ago – when such trust had been broken and massacres had resulted. She shuddered.

Nevertheless, Alice did not need MacDonald to tell her that conditions were worsening within the Quarter. A rare batch of newly hatched eggs was offered for sale in the market on the lawn before the British Legation for five cents each. They were all snapped up within minutes. Dog meat, which had been the staple diet of the Chinese within the Quarter since the siege began, was now on offer to everyone. It was the many children, white, brown and yellow, within the compounds who were suffering the most and Alice became more and more depressed as she noticed how malnourished they were becoming. The Chinese converts, who crowded within the legations, were particularly hard hit. The men who worked on the barricades or who did other labouring work were granted extra rations but those who could not work were nearing a state of near-starvation. The trees in their corner of the Fu were stripped of leaves and bark to eke out their food. Marksmen contravened the order to conserve ammunition by firing at crows to help them.

Small incidents played their part in lifting spirits. The British contingent heard with glee that the fiercely unpopular Monsieur Pichon, the French minister, had protested to Sir Claude that the Union Jack, which had always flown proudly from the Legation lawn, was attracting Chinese fire and was therefore a danger. He demanded that it should be removed. The demand was rejected curtly and the dapper little Frenchman was sent on his way, to the rejoicing of the British.

Alice had struck up a friendship with Dr Morrison, the correspondent for *The Times,* and a faux rivalry had ensued between them, for both knew that the other was now keeping extensive notes of the siege, for publication at its end. Pichon, with his histrionic pessimism and complete inactivity, was a welcome source of amusement for them both, particularly when it was learnt that the Frenchman and his brave counterpart in the Russian Legation had both been seen burning their records.

'Huh,' said Morrison. 'I'd give fifty thousand dollars for a sight of the Russian papers.'

'How much for Pichon's?' asked Alice.

Morrison grinned. 'Possibly . . . maybe . . . perhaps, on a bad news day, I would run to five thousand.'

Alice was not at all sure, however, that Sir Claude's practice of publishing the list of killed and wounded was conducive to maintaining morale. The latest list showed that in the four weeks since the siege had begun, fifty-seven of the defenders had been killed and eighty-seven wounded. It was disconcerting to find that the British, with three killed and seventeen wounded, were among the highest casualties. The Japanese, who, as always, bore the brunt of the fighting at the Fu, the most vulnerable part of the defences, had suffered almost equally, with eight killed and thirteen wounded.

She tried to comfort herself with the thought that, if Simon and Jenkins had stayed within the Quarter, they might well have been included in the casualty figures, given their energy and bravery. But it was of little solace. Where, oh where were they?

Then, at last, a strange quiet fell over the Quarter once more. The defenders had been conserving their ammunition for some time now, only returning fire when it was absolutely necessary. But gradually the Chinese fire fell away, too, although there was no formal restoration of a truce. The Dowager Empress compounded the surrealism of the moment by sending Sir Claude a personal gift of melons and other fruits.

Alice met the British minister when he was distributing the fruit to Chinese children. 'What's it all about, Sir Claude?' she asked.

The tall man shrugged his shoulders. 'The unpredictability of the Chinese never fails to astound me,' he said. 'They must know that we are in a weakened state and yet they relax their attacks. My own feeling is that this must reflect the fact that our people in Tientsin have won some sort of victory. The old lady may have heard that a relief column is on its way and the pro-foreigners at the court have won a hearing at last. I don't think it's likely to last, but let's enjoy it while we can.'

And so they did. Spirits were sent soaring when it became known that a message had got through to Sir Claude to say that, in fact, the foreign settlements had been relieved, Tientsin had been taken by the Allied powers and that a relief column at last was on its way to Peking. So many false alarms had been sounded from various quarters but it was clear that this news was real. Alice clutched her hands together. Was Simon on his way, too?

To the besieged within the defensive ring, the decline in the intensity of gunfire was somehow intrusive, as though a vital element in daily life had been withdrawn. Once again birds could be heard singing in the Quarter and, almost inevitably, the British began playing cricket on what was left of their Legation lawn. Even more surreal were the reports of fraternal exchanges now taking place between the Chinese and the defenders across the barricades.

Alice had made friends with one of the student-interpreters in the consular service, Lance Giles, whom she met on his return from one such exchange.

'Strange business, Mrs Fonthill,' he said. 'I went to the German Legation, which is very much of a wreck in parts, you know?'

Alice nodded.

'Well, the German and the Chinese positions there are separated only by a wall, seven or eight feet high and about two feet wide. It is loopholed and so can be a bit of a death trap. It's probably the thinnest and most fragile of the interfaces between us and them in the whole of the perimeter. I took my camera to take advantage of the truce and climbed up the wall to take a picture.'

'Bit of a risk, Lance.'

The young man looked a little sheepish. 'I suppose so, but it all seemed so peaceful. Anyway, at the top I looked down on some Chinese soldiers on the other side. They shouted, in Chinese of course, "What do you want?" I replied, "*Yao chao hsiang*" – I want to photograph you. They shouted back, "*Yao k'ai ch'iang ma*" – Do you want to shoot us? I told 'em I didn't, of course, and showed them my camera, so the chaps stood there a bit sheepishly, posing for me. I would have had a good picture of them but suddenly one of their officers came out and shooed them away.' He grinned. 'It's all a bit mad, this war, isn't it?'

The madness took another strange turn when the guns crashed out again with a noise that seemed all the more frightening because of the greater intensity of the firing. It was as though the Chinese had suddenly become ashamed of their strange lethargy.

Alice had half hoped, half feared that Gerald would show up during the comparative quiet with some cock-and-bull story about the reason for his absence and hope that his cousin's affection for his mother might have prevented her from revealing his treachery. But there were no sightings of him, either in the legations or beyond the barriers. It was, then, partly with expectations of catching a glimpse of him, but also to see how Colonel Shiba and his gallant Japanese were resisting the renewed aggression, that Alice retrieved her Colt from under her bed and scrambled to the Fu hotspot. It was, of course, from there that she had caught sight of Gerald fighting with, or at least present among, the Chinese.

She found that Shiba was, as ever, glad to see her, welcoming her with a full ceremonial bow. Resourceful as ever, she also found that the little colonel had commandeered the old muzzle-loaded gun to repel an attack by loading it with scrap iron. He reported that many, if not all, of Tung Fu-hsiang's Kansu soldiers had left the Fu

– presumably, he said, to take part in the fighting at Tientsin or even to oppose the relief force. It seemed another confirmation that help was on its way – as was, surely, the intensity of the new firings. But if Tung Fu-hsiang had left for the south, who was now influencing the Dragon Lady?

While she was musing this, there was a cry of warning and Shibo rushed to the wall. The Japanese all began firing rapidly and it was clear that the Chinese had launched an attack. The wall of rubble was loosely loopholed and Alice suddenly realised that, in a far corner where the wall angled away, a rifle was being poked through from the Chinese side. She ducked away and ran towards it as fast as she could, drawing her revolver as she did. She arrived just as it fired and, from the corner of her eye, she saw one of the defenders twist around and fall.

Alice seized the muzzle of the rifle and, in the same movement, presented her Colt through the loophole. She fired as she felt the Chinese gun being pulled away from her and then the rifle went limp in her hands and she pulled it through, throwing it to the ground. Without exposing herself, she fired twice more through the aperture then jammed a brick into the hole.

She sat for a moment against the rubble, the perspiration running down her face, and realised that she was shaking. Ah, this would never do! She shook her head dismissively. She was in the middle of a war and this was not the first time she had killed a man, for goodness' sake! Why else did she carry a heavy .45 calibre Navy Colt? Certainly not as a fashion accessory. She looked up into the smiling face of Colonel Shiba, who held out a hand to help her to her feet.

'Very good, madam,' he said. 'Very quick. You have gained us a rifle and removed one of the enemy. I could not ask more. Now, please come away or they shoot you. That must not happen.'

'Thank you, Colonel. I am quite all right, thank you. Just the heat, you know. Made me want to sit for a moment. Now please get back to the wall.'

'Attack over, madam. But we must watch.'

'Indeed. Do go back to your post.'

Alice retreated to one of the many ruined buildings in the Fu and cautiously climbed up the shifting rubble until she could see over the top of the barricade towards the Chinese line. Shielding her eyes against the glare, she looked to where, out of rifle range, the enemy soldiers were moving. She was searching for a white-coloured suit, but nothing stood out amongst the dun-coloured uniforms and occasional green jackets that moved there. But then she frowned. Was that . . . ? Was it a man in a white – but now severely discoloured – jacket and trousers? She couldn't be sure. She scrambled down the half-destroyed wall, disregarding a cut to her ankle, and ran to Colonel Shiba.

'Colonel,' she panted, 'may I borrow your field glasses for a moment?'

'Of course, lady.'

Grabbing them less than courteously, Alice ran back to the ruin and clambered back up to the top of the wall. This time she rejected thoughts of safety and exposed herself, the better to get a view. She levelled the glasses and attempted to focus them. Yes, there he was. A man in a white suit! She adjusted the focus more delicately and Gerald's face came into view, partially concealed by— Hell! He was looking at her through a pair of binoculars. They were undoubtedly studying each other. She resisted the ridiculous instinct to wave. Was he armed? She moved the glasses just a touch downwards and there, leaning against his leg, was a rifle. She put away the glasses for a moment and wiped her eyes. She must be sure. Then she focused the glasses again and held them steady. Gerald – it was undoubtedly him – had put down the glasses and was looking directly at her before turning to move away. There was no doubt about it, it was her cousin: tall and thin, the rather sallow face, and the mandarin moustache.

And he had a rifle.

That settled it. Whatever doubts Alice had about her cousin's treachery – and very few remained – they were dispelled now by that fact. Carrying a rifle meant that he was actively taking part in the attacks on the Legation Quarter. He had now completely thrown in his lot with that of the Boxers and the Manchu court. The final count in his indictment had been proven.

Alice climbed down the rubble with care this time but deep in thought. She must inform Sir Claude, of course, for there could now be no chance of allowing Gerald back into the Quarter. The question was, should she now tell Aunt Lizzie about her son's treachery? She would have to know sooner or later. Better now than later? No. Alice shook her head. Leave it for the moment. Who knew what the future held? There might be some twist of fate in store that could affect the decision. She would let it lie – and she immediately felt better for having made the decision. But oh, Simon . . . !

The enemy now seemed to have new energy. From all around the perimeter the Chinese trumpets blared and the old cries of 'Sha! Sha!'

were heard from the other sides of the barricades. All day the fire poured down onto the defenders and, as dusk neared, a new sound was heard. It came from a two-inch, quick-firing Krupp, brought to an emplacement high up in the wall of the Imperial City – a site not used before. Immediately Sir Claude – the former subaltern now proving himself to be a skilled defensive soldier – ordered up his two machine guns, the American Colt and the Austrian Maxim, and had them trained on the gun. It was ten minutes before they could be set up to open fire and, in that time, the cannon had begun causing heavy damage – the worst of the siege. Once *in situ*, however, the two machine guns began firing over fixed lines, despite the fall of darkness, and, within minutes, the Krupp was silenced.

The other firing, however, continued. Alice joined her aunt and the rest of the ladies in doing double duties at the hospital as the casualties mounted. Rumours reached the hospital that the defenders were running out of ammunition and Alice retrieved her Colt and tucked it into her waistband as a precaution. Would the relief, now said to be so near, come too late, right at the end? Alice and her hard-working companions in the sweltering heat of the hospital carefully avoided eye contact and got on with their jobs. So, too, did the defenders on the walls and barricades and, although those at the flimsiest defences who were linguists could hear the Chinese officers urging their troops forward, no breaks were made at any point in the perimeter.

The fury continued for two days and, on the evening of the second, Alice was sitting on the ground taking a break outside the hospital, drinking a cup of brackish, lukewarm water, when a Chinese coolie approached her, bowed low and asked: 'Mrs Fonthill?' She nodded and he pressed an envelope into her hand, bowed and walked away quickly before she could question him.

She opened it and read:

Dear Alice,

I must speak to you. The so-called relief column is still far away and is meeting strong opposition. It will not get through. My mentor, General Jung Lu, has lost influence and, as you have seen, the decision has been taken now to overwhelm the defences. Once the breakthrough has been made the Boxers will be given their head and I fear for your safety and that of my mother. There will be wide-scale slaughter. But I can save you. I also have news of your husband. Meet me tonight at midnight (safest time) at the same tunnel as last time. It has been reopened. Come alone.
Gerald.

Alice put her hand to her head and sighed. Then she read it again. It was all almost certainly rubbish. And yet . . . Jung Lu, who seemed to have been a moderating influence, had obviously lost the ear of the Empress, if this new, fierce attack was any indication. And did Gerald really have news of Simon? She drew in her breath. She must know. So she would have to go. Tell Sir Claude? No. He would almost certainly try to stop her going or even try to arrest or perhaps even kill Gerald. And that would be disastrous for Aunt Lizzie. She would meet Gerald, for she had nothing to lose. He would not dare to try and restrain her.

She got up, tossed her head and returned to the hospital. Luckily, she was not on the night shift and so, at ten-thirty she returned to the room she shared with her aunt, who was now fast asleep after a hard day at the hospital. Alice lay sleeplessly on her bed for just over an hour and then rose, pulled on her long riding boots, pushed the Colt into her midriff sash and set off. After ten paces, she returned, retrieved the little French automatic pistol and slipped it into the top and at the back of a riding boot and continued on her way.

Gerald was waiting for her, peering from the low entrance to the tunnel. She paused by the pile of debris. 'I am not coming in there,' she hissed.

'You must. We can easily be overheard outside by the guards on the walls. Come on.'

He held out a hand to her from the blackness and, reluctantly, she climbed the pile of stone and bricks and, ignoring his hand, bent her head and stepped into the tunnel. Immediately, strong hands grabbed her, pulled her far inside and then pinned her arms to her side. She was aware of two men on either side, holding her firmly, and realised that Gerald was pulling bricks back into the entrance, leaving only a shaft of light to penetrate at the top.

'You little swine,' she said. 'So it was all a trick.'

'Not at all.' His voice was bland in her ear. 'Seeing how badly you behaved the last time we met, I felt I needed a little help. These two men are good friends and will do anything I ask, so please do not try and struggle. Now,' he reached down and withdrew the Colt from her cummerbund and threw it to the ground, 'you won't need that.'

'What do you want? Tell me about Simon.'

'What do I want? I want you, my sweet, and, one way or another, I will have you.' His face was close to hers and she could see, now that her eyes were accustomed to the dim light, that he was perspiring. She could smell tobacco and traces of something sweet – opium? – on his breath. The two men holding her were Chinese. Their faces were quite expressionless.

'As for Simon, I was telling the truth when I said that he is dead. If he was not, surely you would have heard from him by now, eh?'

'I don't believe you. Give me proof.'

'Alas, dear cousin, I can't do that. But I have it on good authority that he was blown up, together with that Welsh brute of his, at the gates of Tientsin as he tried to plant dynamite there. Proof will undoubtedly emerge when you come with me.'

Alice felt herself trembling. Was he lying? He was a born liar. Simon Fonthill, her brave, bold, fearless husband could not be dead, particularly not with Jenkins at his side. And yet something about the picture that Gerald had painted so briefly had the ring of truth to it. Planting dynamite at a fortress's door – that is exactly the sort of thing the two would attempt to do. They had undertaken such daring, hare-brained schemes so often in the past that eventually their luck was bound to run out. Had it happened now? She refused to believe it. She felt her eyes brim with tears. That would never do. She must never give this brute the satisfaction of seeing her crying.

But Gerald was continuing, now with a softened voice. 'I ask you again to come with me, Alice, to a new life. Here, in China. After this mess, the court and the Foreign Office will be reconstituted and I have been promised a most senior post here. You will be a widow – you *are* a widow – and will need support. With my mother we can live together well in one of the most cultivated countries in the East.'

'What? In a land where brutal young peasants butcher missionaries and their wives and children? No thank you.'

'Look, I am trying to be reasonable. The alternative is horrible to contemplate. These flimsy defences in the Quarter will be torn down, if not tomorrow, then the next day, and you, my dear, will be raped and then subjected to a terrible death. The executioners these days take a hell of a long time to behead someone. I know. I have seen it. I could not prevent that but I can if you come with me now to a safe house. Fetch my mother and we can all leave this horrible place.'

He paused and put his face close to hers. Once again she felt his breath on her cheek. With hardly a thought, Alice gathered a mouthful of saliva and spat in his face.

Her two guards hissed and Gerald staggered back, drew a handkerchief and wiped his face.

'You bitch,' he swore. 'You spoilt, Christian bitch. Very well, you can go back but not before I have finished with you.' He gave a command to the two men and Alice felt her feet forced apart so that she was spreadeagled against the curved wall. She heard the Chinamen laugh and realised with horror that Gerald was unbuttoning his trousers.

'I love older women,' he said, 'even as old as you.'

She felt a rough hand undo her cummerbund and then the belt beneath it. Then her riding breeches were forced down and fingers inserted between her legs. He pushed his cheek against hers and then inserted his tongue into her ear.

With sudden inspiration, Alice slumped completely, letting her head fall forwards, her legs bend and her forearms and hands flop, so that she suddenly became a rag doll and a weight upon the two Chinese and upon Gerald himself. It was as though she had fainted.

The guard to her right, anxious to assist in the rape, relaxed his grip on her arm to hold her upright around her waist and she reached forward, grasped his testicles through the loose cotton pantaloons and squeezed hard. With a cry, he pushed her away and Alice slumped down, lifted her right leg, grabbed the little automatic from the back of her boot and shot blindly downwards, to her left.

The shot boomed and echoed in the tunnel and it took the man on her left in his foot, so that, cursing, he staggered backwards and then fell over, clutching his foot. Alice stuck the muzzle of her revolver into Gerald's stomach.

'Get away from me, or I will blow a hole in you.'

He jumped away, bumping into the Chinaman who was bent over, both hands holding the ache in his loins. 'Don't shoot,' Gerald cried, holding up his hands. 'Don't shoot. It was a joke. Don't kill me.'

'Why not? No one would ever find you in here.' Alice put her left hand onto that which held the gun to stop it shaking and backed away slowly, breathing heavily, but covering both men. A dozen thoughts ran through her head, then she spoke in a low but steady voice. 'Tell your two partners in rape to get out of this tunnel, otherwise I will kill them and you. But you stay. I want to talk to you.'

Falteringly, Gerald spoke to the two men and jerked his head, his anxious eyes all the time on his cousin. The Chinamen hobbled away, one bent double, the other leaning on him, hopping on one foot and leaving a trail of blood behind him. They let in a shaft of light as they opened the door to the tunnel.

Alice watched them exit to ensure that no one entered and then she turned back to Gerald. 'Now listen to me. You are a coward and a traitor, cousin,' she said, her voice now trembling with emotion. 'You undoubtedly caused the death of your father and you were going to rape me. So you deserve to die. But as you are the son of my father's brother, I will give you a chance. Now,' she held up the pistol. 'I have five more cartridges left. I will let you turn and run towards the opening at that end, the one that leads into *your* world. I will count to six and then I will start shooting. That's the only chance I will give you. Go. Go on. Go. Now! One . . . Two . . .'

He turned and half-fell over the pipe that ran along the length of the tunnel, scrambled on his hands and knees for a moment and then continued slipping and sliding towards the far end of the tunnel. Alice let off one parting shot, aimed directly at the ground well behind him to hasten him on his way. Then, as she saw him disappear, she adjusted her breeches, picked up her Colt from the ground and trod carefully back the way she had come, scrambled through the hole and then replaced the bricks to cover the entrance.

Anxious not to draw the attention of the guards on the wall high above her, she walked quietly away, begging the god that she had followed trustingly all her life not to make her a widow.

Chapter Sixteen

Their plans laid for the attack on Peking, the troops of the strange, multinational army of the Foreign Powers marched on from the city of Tungchow, turned to the west and left the river behind them. They reached their agreed bivouac site, some three miles to the east of the capital and well within sound of the gunfire that sounded from within the walled city. The march had been difficult, although no attack had been launched on them. The humidity and heat had remained high and the Bengal Lancers in the British contingent looked bizarre as they rode with long maize fronds tucked under their helmets and hanging down their backs to avoid sunstroke. Then heavy rain fell, turning the main path and numerous rutted tracks that the troops followed into slippery channels.

On the eve of the planned attack, therefore, it was with relief that the men erected their tents under the heavy downpour and tried to snatch some sleep before the final approach to the city.

Fonthill, trudging along with his two companions, had considered leaving the column and walking across the fields of *kaoliang,* the sunken paths and the irrigation ditches and finding some way through the black walls of the city to satisfy himself that Alice was still alive. But then he realised that he must keep his promise to Gaselee to take the British troops into the Legation Quarter once they had fought their way through the outside walls.

And, as Jenkins had pointed out, ''Ow the 'ell would we get through them bloody great gates? We can't blow 'em down on our own.' So now Jenkins, Chang and Simon were huddled together in their small bivouac tent, surrounded by the Sikhs, Rajputs and Welshmen of the British contingent, listening to the rain and trying to sleep.

Fonthill's thoughts, as ever, concentrated on Alice. He knew her temperament and he was convinced that she would not be content to stay with the other women, tending to the sick in the hospital. She would want to be on the walls and the barricades, fighting with the defenders and consequently putting her life at risk. These thoughts did nothing to help him find sleep and his mind wandered to the events of the last few weeks and of how his life, perforce, had been plunged back into violence.

He speculated with a sinking heart that he had probably been involved with the killing of more men personally since his arrival in China than in all of his previous career as an infantry officer, member of the Corps of Guides in India and army scout in two continents and only God knew how many countries. Simon stirred under his blanket. This had to stop. He was becoming a butcher.

* * *

He must have dozed off because he was suddenly woken by a hand on his shoulder. He sat upright. 'Listen,' said Jenkins in his ear. 'Gunfire. Much nearer. Either we're bein' attacked or somebody's launched our attack too soon.'

Fonthill put his head outside the tent. The rain had slackened somewhat but it was still bouncing off the canvas. He saw bright flashes to the left, due east, at the base of the great black mass that was the walled city of Peking. 'That's just about where the Tung Pien Men Gate should be,' he mused. 'That's the Americans' objective. They must have jumped the gun.'

'No, cousin.' Chang materialised from out of the blackness. 'I couldn't sleep so I went to look. All the Americans' tents are still standing and their guards are posted.' He frowned. 'It is all frightfully strange, is it not?'

'Frightfully,' echoed Simon. 'Well, if anybody has stolen a march to be first into the legations, I want to be among them.' He ducked back into the tent and began pulling on his boots. 'You two needn't come with me. I will rejoin the British contingent as soon as I can.'

'You're not going without me,' grunted Jenkins, throwing aside his blankets.

'Nor me,' said Chang, ducking back into the tent and grabbing the tattered cloak that he used as a mackintosh.

'Very well. Keep the breech blocks and magazines of your rifles dry under your jackets. Come on.'

The three set off in the rain across the muddy fields, guided by the flashes of the cannon fire that stood out from the blackness of the city walls. They had not gone far when they met Gaselee's young ADC riding back towards the camp, his smart, upwards-brushed moustache now looking decidedly bedraggled.

He recognised Fonthill. 'It's the bloody Russians, old boy – oh, sorry, I mean sir,' he said reining in. 'What a capital mess! They're the very people who wanted us to rest here before attacking because their general said they were tired. Now they're going at that gate hammer and tongs. What's more, the bloody fools are attacking the wrong gate. They're supposed to go in the morning for the Tung Chih Men in the north, but they're attacking the Tung Pien Men in the south.'

'What, the whole Russian contingent?'

'In fairness, sir, no.' Steam rose from his horse's flanks as he curbed the bridle. 'It looks as though what happened is that their general sent a fairly strong force – a battalion and half an artillery battery – to reconnoitre the approach to their objective ready for the attack in the morning. But their leader – they've even got a bloody general in charge of that, a whole general, mind you – saw that the outer guardhouse was lightly defended and couldn't resist attacking. But the fool's got the wrong gate, don't y'know.'

'Has he broken through?'

'His artillery is pounding the gate now. Now you must excuse me, sir. I must report to General Gaselee. He'll be furious when he knows what's happened. Mind what you're doing . . . er, with respect, sir. The Chinks seem to be fighting back hard.'

'Thank you. We will.'

'I don't like the sound of all that, bach sir.' Jenkins's face looked lugubrious in the rain, with his black hair plastered over his forehead and his moustache – he had long ago given up trying to grow it Chinese fashion – looking like some feral excrescence under his nose. 'We know 'ow difficult them gates are to knock down an' these Russkies sound barmy to me. Shouldn't we wait until our lot comes up in the mornin', look you?'

Fonthill shook his head. 'No. If they break through I want to be among them. I've got to see if Alice is all right. You two go back if you want to.'

'No. We'll stay.'

The three pressed on, sometimes wading thigh-deep through the irrigation channels which, bone dry for the previous four months, were now running high in rainwater. As they neared the gate, they could see that the walls above the gate and on either side were manned by Chinese riflemen, who were pouring a steady stream of fire down onto the Russian infantry, who were desperately trying to find cover in the featureless landscape. Two Russian pieces of field artillery, their crews protected by their gun shields, were punching holes into the iron-clad gates and, as they watched, the doors were breached. With a cheer, the leading company of the infantry battalion ran towards the opening, pushed aside the wreckage and rushed through.

'Hell!' cried Fonthill. 'They should have tried to clear the walls first.'

Jenkins frowned. 'Why is that, then?'

'Because Chang tells me that there are always two gates in these big Peking walls. So they will rush into a courtyard only to find another door. And they will be fired down upon and caught like fish in a barrel. It's all very medieval-castle stuff, really.'

Simon had retained the wide-brimmed slouch hat given to him by the American in the attack on Yungtsun and, wearing it now in the rain and half-light, he looked at first sight as though he were a Yankee soldier. He caught the sleeve of a Russian officer. 'Do you speak English?'

'A leettle.'

'Why are you attacking this gate?' Fonthill demanded. 'This is the American target. Our objective.'

The Russian shrugged. 'Same city,' he grunted. And moved away.

From beyond the broken gate a fusillade of musketry could be heard, mingled with cries as the bullets found their targets. 'They'll be ages trying to get through there,' muttered Simon. He turned to Chang. 'Is there any other way we can get through these outer walls?'

The young man shrugged his shoulders. 'Afraid no, Simon. These are big walls and meant to be defended. Gates only way in.' He paused and then frowned thoughtfully. 'Except perhaps . . .'

'Yes, yes. What?'

'Well, when I was a boy, with other boys, we sometimes climbed the walls, you know?'

Jenkins scowled and ran his eye along the sheer, forty-foot-high brick face. 'You must 'ave been like monkeys then, Changy, that's all I can say.'

The Chinaman's face brightened. 'No. Not so very difficult. Because, you see, these walls are very old and are cracked in many places. Cracked vertically, you know. Gives spaces to put toes in. Almost like ladder.'

Fonthill looked dubious. 'Impossible to climb when riflemen are firing down on you, of course. Can you remember where these cracks are, Chang?'

'Ah yes. Think so. Let us go along here.'

'Wait a moment. You might be able to get up but neither Jenkins nor I could, with or without bullets coming down on our heads. We need a rope. We passed a couple of hauliers' carts back there, 352, behind the guns. See if you can filch something.'

Jenkins sniffed. 'I'll find a rope but you know what I'm like with heights, bach sir. You'll never get me climbin' up that bloody wall.'

'Just find a rope. That's all. If the top of the wall is manned, then there's no way any of us can get up. But it's worth investigating. Get us a blasted rope, there's a good chap. We'll walk on this way, right close to the wall, so, hopefully, we won't be seen.'

Mumbling to himself Jenkins departed and Simon and Chang walked away from the gate to the right, away from the shooting, until Fonthill could see no sign of life on top of the castellated wall. Then the two scrambled quickly to the base and huddled there for a moment.

Fonthill looked up, his rifle at the ready. There seemed to be no one on the top. 'It looks as though the Chinese have gathered their defenders around the gates,' he said. 'If there's one of your cracks along here, we might be able to get up. Though God knows how we're going to get old 352 up there. Best not be underneath him when he tries because he's bound to soil his breeches.'

Chang grinned. 'I think there is big crack along here, if I can remember right. I think by this old, stunted tree.'

Sure enough, the wall bulged outwards at this point and had cracked visibly where water had cascaded down, revealing a zigzag of broken bricks leading to the top. It glistened now in the rain. *Not an easy climb*, thought Simon. And what if troops appeared?

'Let us wait to see if the top is patrolled,' he whispered. 'If it isn't, do you think you could get up?'

'Oh yes, cousin. I think so, if no men on top with guns.'

They waited, scanning the battlements above them, for about five minutes before Jenkins materialised out of the gloom, predictably carrying a rope, coiled round his shoulder. 'Got it from a Russky,' he said, gloomily. ''Ad to tap 'im on the 'ead to get it, mind you. But it would never take my weight now, would it?'

Simon tested it. 'Of course it would,' he said. 'Strong as steel.' He turned to his cousin. 'Now, Chang. It looks as though this part of the wall is not even patrolled, thank goodness. We will watch down here, rifles at the ready, while you climb. Coil this rope around your head and shoulder. Yes, that's it. When you reach the top take a good look before you climb onto the walkway. Be very careful. If the coast is clear, climb over, tie the rope firmly around one of the battlements and throw the end down. Jenkins will come up—'

'Oh bloody 'ell.'

'. . . And then I will follow.'

'What do we do then, Simon?'

'We will make towards the gate and attack from the rear the riflemen firing down. We should be able to take them completely by surprise, coming from out of the darkness behind them.'

'If we can get up 'ere, that is,' added Jenkins.

Thankfully, the rain had now stopped but, looking up, the climb still looked daunting, with the bricks glisteningly wet. Even Chang, slim, young and fit, now looked a touch disconcerted. 'I think I take off my shoes,' he said. 'Easier to climb.'

'Don't worry about anybody appearing up above,' assured Simon. 'We will pick them off with our rifles.' But his fingers were crossed.

His shoes tied around his neck, the youth took a deep breath, hung his rifle by its sling over his back, reached up with his hands and began the climb. It soon became apparent why he needed to go barefooted. Some of the crevices between the broken bricks were too narrow to take a shod foot and he needed to insert his toes to gain a foothold. Slowly, however, he began to scale the wall, reaching high up with his fingers, pulling himself upwards and then finding, somehow, a precarious foothold with his toes.

'Oh bloody 'ell,' exclaimed Jenkins, 'I can't look at 'im.'

'Then don't,' said Fonthill testily. 'Keep your rifle trained on the top of the wall. If you see a face, make sure you put a bullet through it. With all the firing at the gate, no one will hear. But we mustn't let anyone get away to raise the alarm.'

It seemed an eternity to the two men standing below, their rifles at their shoulders and sighted on the embrasures above. But, eventually, Chang reached the top. Holding on to the stone battlement, he poked his head through the opening, looked to left and right and then hauled himself through. Within seconds, the rope was firmly fastened and its end thrown down.

'Right,' said Simon. 'Hold the rope tightly, put your feet on the wall, lean back and just walk up. It's easy.'

'Look, bach sir. You go first and sort out old Changy up there and I'll follow you up. That would be better.'

'No it wouldn't. You would just walk away and get yourself killed at the gate. We will need you up there on the walkway when we take on those riflemen. Now, don't be such a bloody coward. Go on. Up you go.'

His face pouring with sweat, the Welshman seized the rope, leant back and put his foot against the wall. Immediately, it slipped off and he fell backwards. 'There you are,' he said. 'I told you, see. It's just not possible, look you. I'm too bloody 'eavy, isn't it.'

At the back of his mind, Fonthill noted once again how Jenkins's Welshness increased exponentially to the danger of the situation. 'Nonsense, you're just not trying. Go on. We can't leave Chang on his own up there. He will be shot if we hang about much longer. Look, this is how to do it.'

Simon demonstrated and took about five steps up the wall, gritting his teeth at the pain shooting up his leg from the burnt ankle. 'There.' He slid down. 'If I can do it with a buggered-up leg, you can do it easily. Get up that bloody wall. Now!'

Jenkins closed his eyes, seized the rope and tried again. In fact, the strength in his arms and shoulders were such that he could have hauled himself easily up the rope without using his feet but, as it was, he made remarkably good progress – with his eyes firmly shut all the way. At the top, Chang seized his jacket and pulled the Welshman through the embrasure head first, where he lay on the walkway, panting. Then Chang waved for Simon to make the ascent, which he did but not without considerable difficulty, to Jenkins's evident joy.

'No trouble, then, bach sir, was it, eh?'

'Oh, do be quiet. Pull the rope up, Chang, we might need it again. That's it. Good. Right, now, a bullet up the spout in each rifle and off we go. We'd better fix bayonets but don't fire until I give the order. We are going to be severely outnumbered, so surprise is the thing. Stay quiet.'

Simon checked himself and looked at Chang. The youth was now so self-confident and competent in most things that it was easy to forget that he was only sixteen. Slim and fit, certainly, but not as strong nor as skilled in battle as a professional soldier. They could certainly do with his rifle in clearing the battlements above the gate, but it would be thoughtless and heartless to pitch him into a confrontation that would demand all the experience and guts of a seasoned warrior.

'I think, Chang,' he said, 'that it would be better perhaps if you stayed here, fixed the rope again and defended it in case we have to double back and make a quick exit.'

The young man stared at his cousin in consternation and tears came into his eyes. 'Oh no, Simon,' he cried. 'You do not leave me behind. I can fight. There will be plenty of enemy. You will need me. I don't stay here.'

Jenkins interrupted softly. 'He's right, bach sir,' he said. 'We're goin' to need 'im and I couldn't think of a better bloke to 'ave up there, look you.'

Chang shot him a glance of gratitude and Fonthill sighed. 'Very well,' he said, 'but stay close. If you get killed your mother will never forgive me.' He grinned. 'Good. Let's go.'

Rifles at the trail, the three set off trotting along the wide walkway that formed the parapet. Fonthill was surprised that they met no one and then he heard, from the north, firing and shouting. He realised that the Russians' *coup de main* had forced the rest of the column to bring forward their attacks and that the other gates were now under fire. The Chinese had obviously concentrated their forces at these entrances to the city, the most vulnerable points in the defences. To their eyes, the walls were unclimbable and the city's long perimeter therefore needed no defenders all the way round.

The tall tower above the gate loomed up out of the darkness and the steady rattle of rifle fire showed that the Russians were still pinned down in the courtyard in front of the second gate. A row of Chinamen were lined up, leaning over the parapet as it turned to overlook the courtyard, and were firing down upon the Russians.

Simon held up his hand and whispered: 'I've just about had enough of killing and I'll be damned if I'll shoot men in the back. There's not many and, given their record on the way here, I reckon we can frighten 'em off. Shoot to kill only if we have to. There's no cover up here, so line up across the walkway and kneel to present the smallest target. Then fire rapidly, *over their heads*, when I give the order.' Then to Chang, 'That means work the bolt in the breech as quickly as possible, reload and keep firing. Right?'

The boy nodded, wide-eyed.

'Good. Now kneel, just over their heads, aim, fire!'

Despite the noise from below, the resultant volley sounded startlingly loud on the narrow walkway and the Chinese riflemen turned, as one man, their eyes wide in fear. One brought his rifle to his shoulder to fire but Jenkins's second shot caught him in the chest and he fell. Simon and Chang worked their breech bolts and sent two further shots close over the heads of the remainder and they, seeing rifles flashing in the darkness from so close behind them, turned and fled through the open door of the tower – all except one.

Made of sterner stuff, this man jettisoned his rifle, drew a sword and hurled himself at Chang, the nearest of the three, who was reloading, as was Fonthill, and in no position to defend himself. It was now that Jenkins, a terrified coward on the wall face, revealed his colours as a warrior.

The Welshman caught the descending blade with the tip of his bayonet, which shattered. His assailant gave a jubilant yell and brought the sword around in a great sweep, catching Jenkins's rifle and sending it spinning away. Chang fired but missed. Fonthill worked the bolt of his rifle and found that the round had jammed within the breech. Cursing, he reversed his grip on the gun to attack with the bayonet but he was not needed. Jenkins, as light as a cat, had dodged the next sweep of the sword, bent low and hooked his leg around that of the Chinaman, pushed hard with his elbow and upended him. Chang quickly swept the sword away with his own bayonet and then, Jenkins, in a quick, seemingly effortless movement, picked up the man by the front of his tunic, swept away his legs, hoisted him on his shoulders, whirled around to gain momentum and tossed him over the edge of the parapet.

The Welshman regained his rifle, wiped the perspiration from his bow and nodded to Chang in appreciation. Then he grinned to Simon. 'They don't fight as well as the Zulus, now, do they?'

'Bloody well done, 352. Here, lend me your knife to get this damned cartridge out.' Fonthill took Jenkins's blade, inserted it into the breech and flicked out the offending round. The parapet before them was now unmanned, so he ran to the door in the tower. 'It looks as though this leads down to behind the inner gate,' he shouted. 'We'll go down, fire a volley at whoever is down below and then you, Chang, will open the gate while we keep off the Chinese to give you time. Get behind the bloody thing when it's open, otherwise those mad Russians will kill us all. Ready? Go.'

They thundered down the stone, circular steps and came out behind the great doors, which were now being assaulted by some sort of battering ram, fashioned by the Russians. Iron-bound, however, they were showing no signs of breaking. A handful of Chinese away to the right were hastily assembling a machine gun mounted on a tripod, preparing to mow down the attackers if they broke through. Others were trying to erect a barricade.

'Bring down the gunners,' ordered Fonthill. The resultant volley killed the men at the gun and, as one man, the others at the half-assembled barricade turned and fled, no doubt thinking that the attacking army had somehow scaled the walls. Simon and his comrades were now sole custodians of the gates, which were held in place by two sturdy pieces of timber slotted horizontally into brackets and a great, iron lock in which the gatekeeper had conveniently left the huge key. Two large iron bolts completed the security.

'Wait,' shouted Fonthill. He was conscious that, on the other side of the gates, the battlements were still manned by armed Chinese. He ran to the door leading to the top of that wall and the tower and found that it, too, had a key in its lock on the inside. He heard someone running down the steps, so he withdrew the key, slammed the door shut and turned the key in the lock.

'Now,' he called, '352, see if you can turn that damned great key. Then we'll lift off these cross-beams and pull back these gates. Stand well behind them as they open or we'll get shot.'

With great effort, the key was turned, the bolts pulled back, the beams lifted off and the three struggled to pull back the doors. There was no immediate result. It was as though the Russians were too dumfounded, after all their aggression, to find the gates suddenly opened for them – or perhaps they suspected a trap. Then, after some thirty seconds, there was a great roar and the troops rushed through, immediately spreading out to make their way up the network of streets that opened up before them and from which came the sound of gunfire, showing that the Chinese had by no means given up.

Fonthill and his comrades were still wearing their Welch Regiment khaki jackets and these, together with Simon's angry gesticulations, certainly saved them from being shot by the Russians, who had been denied entry for so long and who had lost so many men in the courtyard. The three made their way through the throng of attackers out beyond the walls, to find that the rain had stopped completely and that the dawn was now well established, colouring the sky to the east in shafts of orange and red.

'I thought you wanted to go straight to the British barracks, or whatever they're called,' said Jenkins.

Fonthill shook his head. 'I reckon that the Russians will have a bit of a fight on their hands to get through the streets of the Chinese City till they get to the Legation. I promised I would lead General Gaselee through the inner walls to the British Legation. Our men are supposed to be attacking the Hsia Kuo Men Gate further down the wall and I want to get there as quickly as I can. It's this way. We just follow the wall down. Come on.'

Fonthill seemed to be possessed by a surge of almost demonic energy and his two comrades now followed him doggedly, as the sound of rifle fire intensified from within the city as the Russians began their struggle to penetrate the narrow streets. Then, as they moved southwards the sound died away, making Simon wonder why it was not replaced by that of the British attacking further along.

The tower above the Hsia Kuo Men soon came into sight and, milling before it, Simon could see the troops of the British contingent in their recognisable khaki, the turbans of the Sikhs standing out in particular. Behind them, a battery of the 12th Regiment, Royal Field Artilley, were unlimbering.

'Good Lord,' cried Fonthill. 'There seems to be no firing.' They pushed their way through the troops to where they could see a knot of officers on horseback, prominent among them the portly figure of Lieutenant General Sir Alfred Gaselee.

'Where the hell have you been, Fonthill?' demanded the general. 'I thought you were anxious to get in. We're just about to attack and get these damned gates down.'

As briefly as he could, Simon explained what had happened and that the Russians had now broken through. He looked up at the seemingly undefended line of battlements before them.

'I think it's quite possible,' he said, 'that the Chinese are not defending these gates, suspecting that our attacks will be launched on the gates in the eastern walls, the direction from which we have approached the city.' He cast a glance at the light cannon now unlimbering. 'And, with respect, sir, it is going to take you some time to bring those gates down – they're iron-clad, you see – with those guns.'

'Well, is there any other way in?'

Fonthill looked at Chang. 'I think so.' He explained how they had climbed the walls on the eastern face. 'Let Chang here find a way up, while we make sure he's not fired on from up top, then he can let that line down and I suggest that your Sikhs could be up that wall in a flash – as long as they took their boots off.'

The general's white eyebrows descended in a frown and he turned to his staff. 'What d'yer think, eh?'

There was a general chorus of approval and Chang once again was despatched to find a convenient crack in the wall. No Chinese appeared on the ramparts, although rifle fire could now be heard more clearly from within the city. Within minutes, Chang was lowering his rope down and a whole group of bootless Sikhs, their dark faces split by great watermelon grins at the unusual nature of the task given them, were forming a line to climb up the wall. Some shots were exchanged as they disappeared from sight but it was not long before the great gates of the Hsia Kuo Men were being grindingly pulled back. The British contingent of the relief force had gained admission to the outer Chinese City of Peking with the exchange of only five shots and without sustaining a single casualty.

The strange tranquillity was broken, however, as soon as they began forming up, inside the gates.

'Which way, Fonthill?' cried Gaselee, astride his horse.

'To the right, sir. But I suggest that you and your staff dismount because you will present too obvious a target if we meet trouble within these narrow streets.'

Trouble, in fact, was not late in arriving. Uniformed troops of the Imperial army were to be seen running towards them down several streets and an irregular firing began. The alarm had obviously been given and soldiers from the Imperial City, only a few kilometres away, had been summoned.

The British contingent consisted of the Royal Welch Fusiliers, the Bengal Lancers, 1st Sikhs, 7th Rajputs and 24th Punjab Infantry, the Chinese-based Weihaiwei Regiment, the 12th Regiment Royal Field Artillery, the Hong Kong Artillery and a small detachment of Royal Engineers. But it was the Indian infantry now who led the way through the winding streets, firing from doorways, occasionally charging with the bayonets to clear specific knots of dedicated resistance, but all the time moving forward, towards the inner wall which marked the southern boundary of the British Legation.

Fonthill, Jenkins and Chang were with them, Chang pointing the way whenever there was doubt. This was urban fighting, street warfare, and among the most dangerous form of conflict in the world, for the range was short, the options for cover limited and the terrain narrow and constricted. But the Rajputs and the Sikhs, accustomed to putting down rebellious conflagrations in the towns of the British Raj, were good at it: light on their feet, flitting from doorway to doorway like cat burglars and as brave as lions.

Nevertheless, the Chinese gave ground reluctantly, firing steadily as they retreated and making Fonthill wonder why this kind of sturdy resistance had not been met on the march to Peking, where the countryside offered so many more opportunities for ambush and counter-attack.

The danger from Chinese rifle fire in the narrow streets was compounded by fragments of masonry and brickwork that flew from dwellings on both sides as bullets went astray. Fonthill was cut in the cheek by one such as a man in a white suit shot at him from an upper storey. He responded quickly with his own rifle but the man ducked away. Across Simon's brain flashed the thought that it was strange to see a Chinaman dressed in European clothing fighting with the Imperial troops, and then it disappeared as he strained to see ahead to catch a precious glimpse of a legation flag. In fact, this street alley fighting was so perilous that his mind had had little time to dwell on the agonising questions: were the legations holding out and, most of all, was Alice still alive?

The first question was answered when, at last, they broke out of the Chinese City to emerge facing the Tartar Wall, beyond which lay the Legation Quarter. And there, to everyone's blessed relief, the American Stars and Stripes was flying proudly from the top of the wall to show that the Foreign Powers at least still held this most southerly of the Quarter's defences. 'Thank God for that,' murmured Fonthill, as he looked up.

To their left stood the stunted tower of Chien Men, from which

Fonthill had toppled the Chinese cannon, and beneath it the firmly bolted gate leading to the inner city. 'Do we attack that gate?' demanded the perspiring captain commanding the leading company of Rajputs.

'No,' said Simon. 'There's an easier way through. Here to the right. Come on, but we must watch our backs, for we could be fired on from these houses.'

He ran across the road to the foot of the wall, moving to the right until he found the sluice gates through which he had led the sortie to attack the guns. They were closed, of course, but, as before, there remained enough space for men singly to slip through the space between the grill and curved wall of the opening, avoiding most, at least, of the putrid effluent underfoot by hugging the wall on either side.

Fonthill rolled up his cotton pantaloons and led the way, followed by Jenkins and Chang and then the first of the Rajputs, their boots slipping and sliding in the mud that banked the noxious stream. Above them, as they emerged from the archway, they heard cheering as the Americans on their sector of the wall welcomed their liberators now pouring into the streets below them.

For the Rajputs, it was a momentous victory to have beaten their great rivals the Sikhs to the sluice gates and therefore the Legation Quarter by a few yards. This would be recorded in their histories.

Once clear of the archway, Jenkins seized Simon's hand and shook it. 'My God, we've made it,' he gasped. 'Well done, bach sir.'

Chang joined in the celebrations. 'Splendid effort, my dear cousin,' he said, characteristically. 'Very fine indeed.'

But Fonthill showed no sign of elation. 'But are we in time?' he asked. 'Are we in time? Come on. Come on.'

CHAPTER SEVENTEEN

Alice had decided that she would not tell Sir Claude about seeing Gerald with the rifle, fighting for the Chinese at the Fu, nor about the attempted rape. Time enough to face up to that problem when the relief column arrived and she could confide in Simon. He would be with them. Of course he would.

Nevertheless, she could not but be depressed by the increase in the rifle fire that now rained down on the Quarter, not merely that which crashed along the wall and the barricades but also in the activities of the snipers, whose firing from the high points of buildings outside the perimeter made walking within the grounds of even the British Legation dangerous.

To this was added the fact that she knew that she had made a mortal enemy of Gerald Griffith. She had no doubt that her humiliation of him in the tunnel meant that he would have no hesitation in killing her, should he have the opportunity. And if the Chinese broke through . . . ! She took to wearing the long-barrelled Colt revolver everywhere, except when working in the hospital.

The Quarter had always been a hotbed of rumour but now the place seethed with story and counter-story. The relief force had been defeated right under the walls of the Chinese City and then, no, it had been forced to turn back again deep in the countryside. The distant rattle of machine gun fire that could be heard, it was stated authoritatively by *someone who knew*, undoubtedly came from the Chinese, who had recently bought fifty British Maxims. The rumours, it seemed, were always pessimistic.

Part of the problem for the civilians crowded in the British Legation was that, after nearly two months of the siege, everyone within its confines was now suffering from some form or another of claustrophobia. Unlike for the defenders of, say, Lucknow, during the Indian Mutiny, there were no high battlements from which to scan the surrounding countryside for a glimpse of the banners of the relieving force, no positions of advantage from which to listen for the sound of distant trumpets or bagpipes. Even from the part of the Tartar Wall held by the Americans and Germans, the view was only of hostile dwellings, almost, it seemed, only an arm's length away. And for everyone else, it was of ruined buildings and barricades of rubble and furniture, pressing in, always pressing in.

Those who suffered the most within the Quarter were the Chinese converts to Christianity, who far outnumbered the foreigners and who now lived in appalling poverty. At the bottom of the pecking order, they lacked decent food and, often, a roof over their heads. They suffered from the sudden downpours that were a feature of recent weeks and also from the appalling heat and humidity that were even worse than the rain. Pitiful Chinese mothers crouched against piles of masonry desperately seeking shade and shelter and constantly flicking the flies away from their babies.

The number of casualties recorded by Sir Claude had now risen to sixty-eight of the besieged foreigners killed and more than one hundred and fifty wounded. His figures, however, made no mention of Chinese deaths or casualties from within the Quarter. Alice had taken to gathering whatever scraps of food she could beg from the white families and doling them out to the Chinese Christians. She lost count of the number of pathetic little forms she saw, wrapped in fragments of cloth and lying near to their sobbing mothers, awaiting burial.

When she was not working in the hospital Alice took to spending much of her time with Colonel Shiba, still manning his barricades in the Fu. Her admiration for the Japanese soldiers had grown the more she saw of them. As far as she could see, they always remained cheerful, they never complained and they were completely resolute in their defence of this most attacked and vulnerable section of the Quarter's perimeter. She reflected this in the diary she kept every day and in the series of features that she was writing for eventual publication – she hoped and expected – in the *Morning Post*. In his spare moments, the colonel spoke to her of his home and of his yearning to return there and this had turned Alice to thinking of the future.

She had married Simon Fonthill in 1885 and their only child had died at birth. Her time with Fonthill and their beloved servant and comrade, Jenkins, had been a strange mixture of tranquillity in Norfolk and the excitement of travelling and campaigning abroad. She had followed Simon and Jenkins in their many adventures, not only from love and faithful duty, but also because of the access it provided her in reporting on these wars for the *Morning Post*. She knew that the attention of the great capitals of the world would be on the siege of Peking and she was determined to be the first to report on it and on its relief as soon as cabling facilities became available again. And this work had to be done despite the fact that at the back of her mind increasingly now was the cry 'Has Simon survived?'

Alice prayed night and morning that her husband would be spared and she resolved, as do all lovers in such circumstances, that, if he was, then she would be a better, more supportive, less harping wife, worthy of such a hero. If only . . . if only . . . ! Then she sharpened her pencil and returned to her despatch for the *Morning Post*.

So it was that, a little after midday, on 14th August, on the fifty-fifth day of the siege, Alice was scribbling away. Mrs Griffith had been on night duty at the hospital and was fast asleep, so, to avoid disturbing her, Alice had taken her writing pad and found a corner in a vastly overcrowded office of the British Legation. Although deep in concentration, she suddenly became aware of a deal of hustle and bustle around her. Sir Claude strode through, cutting a gangling, elegant figure in his cream-coloured cotton suit and wearing a startlingly white shirt topped by a polished, starched collar under his best wide-brimmed Manila hat. Outside, she glimpsed women she had hardly noticed before now wearing the most tightly waisted of dresses and smart garden-party hats. What was happening?

'They're coming, they're coming!' shouted a young clerk. 'Some have got through the sluice gate already.'

There was no need to ask who 'they' were. Alice felt the colour drain from her face. What if he . . . what if he was not among them? She banished the thought and looked down at herself. She was wearing patched jodhpurs without the riding boots, broken sandals and an unwashed cotton shirt. This would never do. No way to welcome back . . . Putting away her notepad, she hurried to the room she shared with her aunt, who was still sleeping peacefully. Quickly but quietly, Alice shook out the creases from her best dress and slipped smart and high-heeled sandals on her feet. She brushed her hair feverishly, applied a little rouge to lips and cheeks and stole a look at herself in the one mirror the two women shared. Ah, how she had lost weight! The dress positively drooped around her midriff. She found her red bandana and tied it round her waist as a cummerbund. A hat. She must wear a hat! She found her old straw boater and looped a scarf of matching colour to the bandana over its top and under her chin and then ran outside.

The lawn and tennis courts in front of the Residency were thronged with men wearing unfamiliar best suits and women dressed as though for Ascot. But no soldiers were to be seen. Alice saw Dr Morrison and seized his elbow. 'Is it true?' she cried.

'Absolutely, my dear Alice. They're on the way up now. Don't know who they are, though.'

Suddenly a shot rang out and a Belgian woman of Alice's acquaintance screamed and fell to the ground, blood streaming from her blouse.

'Take cover.' Sir Claude was waving his arms unhurriedly, as though quelling excited schoolchildren. 'Snipers are still active. You all know the lines of fire. Stay away from them, but there is no need to panic.'

Indeed, there *was* no panic. After weeks of being under fire, most of the occupants knew exactly where the danger points of the Legation were and no one was going to miss seeing the relieving troops arrive. The wounded lady was helped inside and given treatment. Alice, however, frowned, thought for a moment, and then retreated to her room, where

Aunt Lizzie was still sleeping, and retrieved the Colt from the box under her bed and slipped it into her cummerbund behind her back. Then, biting her lip with anxiety, she rushed out again onto the crowded lawn.

At last they came. Not the tanned British, or American or German soldiers they all expected – not even the little nut-brown men of Japan – but bashful Indian troops, wearing exotic turbans and with their boots and calves covered in black, foul-smelling mud. Someone had broken open several cases of champagne and these grinning men of the subcontinent were being offered and sheepishly declining the sparkling wine served from long-stemmed glasses. Thirsty as they were, alcohol was not for them.

In growing agony, Alice scanned the crowd. *He was not there.* And then she heard a shout. 'Alice!'

At first she did not recognise any of them: three men – a broken-nosed young Chinaman, a squat, broad man with an unkempt moustache and a slim, taller man. All wore strange cotton trousers, splashed with mud, and filthy khaki jackets. The slim man was beaming at her from underneath a peculiar hat at the base of which three acorns rested on its broad brim and his arms were spread wide.

'Oh, thank you, God!' she shouted and ran into her husband's arms, knocking his hat off and kissing him desperately. They stayed locked in each other's arms until Alice broke free and caused extreme embarrassment to Jenkins by kissing him on the lips and then embracing Chang.

'I have been *so* worried,' she said, tears coursing down her cheeks. Then she kissed Simon again. 'My God,' she exclaimed, trying to grin through the tears, 'you smell foul.'

'Ah well,' said Jenkins, 'that's because the captain would insist on comin' in 'ere up the back passage.' He then realised that he had delivered a scatological double entendre and added lamely, 'so to speak, that is.'

Everybody laughed. 'May I enquire how my mother is?' asked Chang with his customary gravity.

'Oh, she is well, Chang.' Alice smiled at him. 'I hope she approves of your new nose. I think it rather becomes you. Look, she is asleep but I will run and warn her. She will want to look her best when she sees you. So excuse me just for a moment.' She looked at them all in turn. 'Don't you dare run away again, any of you.'

She ran to the Residency and gently woke Mrs Griffith who smiled with relief and immediately knelt in prayer. 'I will be out in a moment,' she said. 'I must say thanks.'

Alice ran out into the heat and sunshine again and then her eye caught a movement to her right, a flash of white, where the rubble wall of the Legation met the old battlefield of the Mongol Market. She stopped, frozen. Along the top of the wall a man in a white suit was lying and about to level a rifle at the crowd on the lawn. She turned her head. Nearest to him on the edge of the crowd, and offering a perfect target, was the broad back of Simon, who was talking to Sir Claude. Away from them, Jenkins had found a lady with a silver tray of glasses filled with champagne and was offering one to Chang.

Focusing on the figure on the wall, Alice immediately recognised her cousin Gerald. She stood transfixed as she saw him slowly draw back the bolt on his rifle and aim at Simon.

'No, no!' Alice screamed. But there was still desultory rifle fire from outside the Legation and people were still cheering somewhere. Her voice was lost. Reflexively, she whipped out the Colt revolver from the cummerbund, held it with both hands in front of her, held her breath, took careful aim and then squeezed the trigger.

The sound of the shot, away from the crowd, was lost in the background noise but Simon and Sir Claude heard it and whirled round. They saw Gerald start, turn his head towards Alice, drop his jaw in surprise and then slump over his rifle, a red stain growing under his left armpit before he fell away, out of sight behind the wall.

Fonthill ran towards Alice, who was staring white-faced at him.

'Alice,' he shouted as he ran, 'what have you done?'

She could not answer for a moment, then she dropped the Colt onto the grass, stared at her husband and said, 'I think I've killed Gerald.'

'For God's sake, why?'

'Because he was trying to shoot you. I knew he would try to kill either you or me. But it was you he was aiming at.'

MacDonald had now joined them. 'Your wife is right, Fonthill,' he said. 'I suddenly became aware that I was staring right at his rifle when the bullet hit him. He could only have been aiming at either you or me.' He turned to Alice. 'Damn fine shooting, madam. Now, go inside and sit down. You are understandably shaken. I will get a couple of chaps and go and see if the man has been finished or merely wounded. Frankly, I hope it is the former, from what you have told me. Excuse me.'

Alice had now begun to shake. 'What can I tell Aunt Lizzie?' she asked, white-faced.

Simon put his arm around her and walked her away to a bench under the wrought iron balcony. 'Here. Sit down, darling. I think you had better tell me what has been going on.'

Slowly, and then with increasing urgency, Alice relayed the story of Gerald's treachery, his twice-repeated proposal and his attempted rape. Then, at the end, she put her hand to her mouth and asked, once again, 'What am I going to tell his mother? How am I going to explain that I've killed her son. She's lost her husband and now her son. Oh, Simon.' She buried her face in his tunic.

He patted her head. 'Look, we don't know yet that he is dead, my love. But if he is, I know exactly what we are going to say to her. Gerald died a hero's death, right at the moment of relief. He saw a sniper aiming into the crowd from a house beyond the Austrian ruins over there. There are still plenty of them about. He rushed to get his rifle but before he could fire, he was hit. He died well. That is what she must remember. Now, Sir Claude is coming back. If the man is dead, let me see if he will concur. I'm sure he will. It's a harmless subterfuge and solves all the problems. Just stay here a moment.'

He was back within minutes. Alice had dried her tears and was staring sightlessly at the ground. Simon took her hand. 'I'm afraid Gerald is dead, my dear. Shot through the heart. Sir Claude knew of the little swine's treachery and it was confirmed when he saw him aim at me. He agrees completely with the subterfuge. By far the best way out. It seems no one noticed the incident in all the excitement.' He released her hand. 'Now wipe your face, my love. Here comes Jenkins with a glass of champagne for you.' He grinned. 'Rescuing us all, once again.'

Jenkins handed her the glass. 'Cheer up, Miss Alice. I know we all smell a bit, but you shouldn't turn your nose up at us, you know. We're all you've got, see.'

Alice accepted the glass and a sad smile crept across her face. 'Oh yes, my dear 352,' she said. 'And I couldn't wish for better. I am very, very lucky.'

EPILOGUE

Mrs Griffith accepted the death of her son with the typical stoicism and faith of a missionary's wife. She always knew, she said, that he was engaged in dangerous work somewhere – 'intelligence work for Sir Claude, you know.' Too secret to be admitted even now, but it did explain his absences. She was sure that her husband would have been proud of him and so it was fitting that he should be buried next to him in the Legation's little cemetery.

Even so, Alice realised that she could not face her aunt on an everyday basis for long and she urged Simon to make haste to get them away. First, however, she had to complete her despatches and send them off as soon as cable facilities were re-established in the Quarter. This was done and accepted with enthusiastic alacrity by the *Morning Post* in London's Fleet Street. She had filed a separate story on Simon's adventures in getting to Tientsin and on his part in the attack on the city there, as well as the relief of Peking. This was, of course, her scoop on Dr Morrison's despatch for *The Times* and it made Fonthill a celebrity in the war-torn capital, much to his embarrassment.

The siege of Peking and its relief had made front-page news in all the great capitals of the world. Yet the atmosphere in the Legation Quarter, particularly in the impossibly troop-crowded British Legation, was now one of anticlimax. Free from the danger, the noise and the rumour-fed tension of the last fifty-five days, the inhabitants of the Legation were at a loss. The civilians wandered around, rather dreamily, inspecting the barricades and complaining now of the crowded living conditions. Monsieur Pichon, the despised French minister, made it known that he was already halfway through his account of the siege and that he had secured a publisher for it in Paris. The hard-pressed medical staff in the hospital were relieved of their duties by the army doctors and orderlies and, with more sophisticated care and supplies now available, the wounded began to make much quicker progress.

To Alice's relief, her aunt announced on the day of Gerald's burial that she intended to return immediately to her home and recommence her work in the mission there. Somewhat to everyone's surprise, however, Chang decided that he wished to take holy orders and help his mother in her work in the village.

'I think I am not really a soldier,' he confided to Simon and Jenkins. 'I find I get afraid too much, you know.'

'Blimey, Changy,' said Jenkins, 'don't we all?'

Chang gave a smile that wrinkled his battered nose. 'Oh no, Mr Jenkins,' he said. 'Not you two. No, not you two.'

So the five of them sadly retraced their steps to the house in the little village that they had left in such a hurry two months before. They found it still locked and untouched. The Fonthills and Jenkins stayed just long enough to ensure that Mrs Griffith and Chang were safely reinstalled before returning to Peking. There, Simon began to make arrangements for their passage home to Norfolk, England.

These were not completed when a cable arrived addressed to him. This was unusual because, although Alice was now in frequent touch with her editor in Fleet Street, Fonthill rarely received urgent mail.

'It's a knighthood, darling,' said Alice. 'No more than you deserve.'

'Don't be ridiculous. It's probably a bill.'

He tore it open, read the message, reread it and then silently handed it to his wife. She read:

WE NEVER MET IN SUDAN BUT WARMEST CONGRATS ON YOUR WORK CHINA STOP WAR WITH BOERS HERE FAR FROM OVER STOP DESPERATELY NEED YOU HERE FOR URGENT TASK STOP CAN YOU SHIP CAPE TOWN SOONEST STOP LETTER FOLLOWS STOP KITCHENER

Alice looked up, frowning. 'Kitchener. He was an intelligence major when we were in the Sudan, wasn't he?'

'Yes. Never met him. Of course, he became a general and beat the Sudanese finally at Omdurman two years ago and I understand that he has taken over from Roberts in command of the British army in South Africa. So the war there continues.'

'Seems like it.' Alice looked hard at him. 'You are getting famous, my love.'

'Umph. Don't know about that. I'm also getting old. I wonder what "urgent task" means?'

'Don't you think we ought to go home via the Cape and find out?'

'What? Do you mean it? Honestly?'

'Of course. I think Jenkins would get awfully bored in Norfolk again, don't you?'

He grinned and kissed her. 'You're marvellous,' he said. Then he called through the open door, '352, can you spare a minute?'

AUTHOR'S NOTE

The War of the Dragon Lady is a novel, of course, but I have tried to relate the main events of the Boxer Rebellion and the Siege of Peking as accurately as a study of respected accounts of the conflict allows. It is important, however, to distinguish between fact and fiction. Fonthill, Jenkins, Alice, Chang and the Griffiths sprang from my imagination, as did Gerald's mentor, Kuang Li. However, Sir Claude MacDonald very much existed, as did the Generals Jung Lu, Tung Fu-hsiang, Lineivitch, Frey and Gaselee, Admiral Seymour, Brigadier Dorward, Colonel Shiba, Dr Morrison, Monsieur Pichon – who published a best-selling memoir of the siege, portraying himself as a hero – and the Dragon Lady herself, of course, the Dowager Empress.

A way into the Chinese City of Peking *was* found by barefooted Sikhs, who climbed up cracks in the great outer wall; the Rajputs *did* enter the Legation Quarter via the sluice gate and were the first into the Quarter; the Russians *did* attack the wrong gate; and a Belgian lady *was* shot by a sniper as she stood on the Legation lawn to welcome the relieving troops. Other individual incidents I relate as occurring during the siege – such as the destroying of the Chinese guns on the Chien Men tower, the counter-attack at the destroyed Austrian Legation, and the 'friendly fire' falling on the Americans at Yangtsun – did take place. It is also true that spies frequently found easy methods of entry and exit into the Quarter throughout the siege.

I must confess, however, to diverting from the truth a touch here and there in recounting the detail of the siege. For instance, the gallant and popular Captain Strouts was not killed on the attack on the Krupps guns but during a defence of the French Legation. By the same token, I have taken liberties occasionally in the timing of the events of the Uprising, mainly so that I could involve Simon, Jenkins and Chang in them without stretching chronology and geography too far. I believe, however, that these indulgencies have not altered the overall veracity of my story of the rise of the Boxers and the Siege of Peking. This is a novel, after all. Nevertheless, I extend my apologies to scholars of the period who may be offended by these minor departures from fact.

The Boxer Rebellion shocked the world by the ferocity with which the Boxers attacked foreign missionaries throughout northern China in 1900. Stories emerged of elderly Europeans and their families being brought into village squares and beheaded, one by one. Wives of missionaries were forced to watch their husbands decapitated, as, holding the hands of their children, they waited their turn. On one such occasion, more than three hundred men, women and children were killed.

The Foreign Powers, of course, took their revenge after the relief of Peking. Punitive columns were sent out into the provinces to find the perpetrators and shoot or hang them. Some of the Chinese military leaders were executed and others, as related, committed suicide. Financial and other reparations were levied on the Chinese Government that ended the long reign of the Manchu dynasty, held back the growth of that country for generations and led to the eventual coming to power of the Communist Party.

And the Dragon Lady herself? With the relief column at the eastern wall, she hurriedly packed and escaped to the north before setting off on a seven-hundred-mile 'tour of inspection' to the south and west. She was not pursued and eventually returned to the capital two months later. As she stepped down from her ceremonial chair at the entrance to the city, the wall was lined by survivors of the siege. She looked up at them, gave a distant smile, clasped her hands together and bowed. Immediately, the survivors applauded her. It was a strange ending to an even stranger conflict.

ACKNOWLEDGEMENTS

As ever, I owe a debt to the staff of the London Library for helping with my research; to my agent, Jane Conway-Gordon, for her constant support; and to my wife, Betty, devoted proofreader, research assistant and lifelong mate.

The Siege of Peking provoked scores of books, not all of them consistent in their recording of events, nor in their Western spelling of Chinese names. I read many but, in the end, relied heavily on *The Siege at Peking*, by Peter Fleming, published by Rupert Hart-Davis (London 1959); *The Siege of the Peking Legations, a Diary,* by Lancelot Giles; and *Chinese Anti-Foreignism and the Boxer Uprising* by L.R. Marchant, both published by the University of Western Australia Press.